# THE PAN DICTIONARY OF FAMOUS QUOTATIONS

Robin Hyman, the son of a well-known antiquarian bookseller, went into publishing in 1955 after taking an honours degree in English. He was Managing Editor of Evans for several years and in 1977 he became Chairman of Bell & Hyman. When Bell & Hyman merged with Allen and Unwin in 1986, Robin Hyman became Managing Director and later Chairman of the combined business, Unwin Hyman. He is currently President of the Publishers Association.

Apart from compiling *The Pan Dictionary of Famous Quotations*, Robin Hyman is author or joint author of several books, including the very successful *Boys' and Girls' First Dictionary*. With his wife Inge, he has written the stories for fifteen children's picture books, including *Runaway James and the Night Owl* and *Peter's Magic Hide-and-Seek*.

He and his wife live with their two sons and a daughter in Hampstead Garden Suburb.

# THE PAN DICTIONARY OF FAMOUS QUOTATIONS

compiled by Robin Hyman

*revised edition*

**PAN BOOKS**
London, Sydney and Auckland

First published 1962 as *The Modern Dictionary of Quotations* by
Evans Brothers Ltd
This edition published 1989 by
Pan Books Ltd, Cavaye Place, London SW10 9PG
Revised 1973, 1983, 1989
9 8 7 6 5 4 3 2 1
© Robin Hyman 1962, 1973, 1983, 1989
ISBN 0 330 31200 6

Printed and bound in Great Britain by
Richard Clay Ltd, Bungay, Suffolk

# Introduction

*The Pan Dictionary of Famous Quotations* has been planned as a useful and comprehensive work of reference and also as a book which I hope will give pleasure to readers who use it as an anthology. The selection of entries, as well as the arrangement in single rather than double column, is intended to encourage the browser in addition to anyone looking up specific quotations. The number of quotations selected from an author is not, of course, any indication of the author's popularity or literary merit. Some authors, like Pope and Wilde, wrote in an epigrammatic form which lends itself well to quotation; by comparison few novelists, apart from Dickens, have this particular quality. The criterion in selection is what is likely to be familiar to the general reader whose mother tongue is English. A few quotations are included from French, German, Greek, Italian, Latin and Spanish sources which seem likely to be known to many readers and in all such cases a translation is given. As well as quotations over one thousand proverbs are included. Often one does not know whether a familiar phrase is proverbial or whether it has a specific literary origin. Because of this it seemed helpful to include the best-known proverbs.

It is often extremely difficult to assess the degree of familiarity of quotations and this is particularly true when considering what to include from writing and speech of recent years. Which of the following, for example, are likely to be remembered in the year 2000?

'*One small step for man, one giant leap for mankind.*'
Neil Armstrong, the first man on the moon, 21 July 1969

'*Five per cent? Five per cent? You must be out of your minds.*' Prince Philip on the birthrate in the Solomon Islands, 1982

'*As I look ahead, I am filled with foreboding. Like the Roman I seem to see "the river Tiber foaming with much blood".*' Enoch Powell, Speech on immigration, Birmingham, 20 April 1968

'*I have lived seventy-eight years without hearing of bloody places like Cambodia.*' Sir Winston Churchill, 28 April 1953, as quoted in Lord Moran's book on Churchill in 1966

'*From now, the pound is worth 14 per cent or so less in terms of other currencies. It does not mean, of course, that the pound here in Britain, in your pocket or purse or in your bank, has been devalued.*' Harold Wilson, Speech after devaluation of the pound, 20 Nov. 1967

'*In a hierarchy every employee tends to rise to his level of incompetence.*' Laurence J. Peter and Raymond Hull, *The Peter Principle*, 1969

'*Please accept my resignation. I don't want to belong to any club that will accept me as a member.*' Groucho Marx, attributed

'*There can be no whitewash at the White House.*' Richard Nixon on Watergate, April 1973

'*Every so often I lose weight and, to my horror and indignation, I find in the quiet of the night somebody has put it back on.*' Lord Goodman, 1973

'*More will mean worse.*' Kingsley Amis, *Encounter*, 1960

Many quotations from the twentieth century are included in this book but, as the test for selection is that a quotation is likely to remain well known for several years, I have, of course, excluded most current television and radio sayings, advertising slogans and political phrases. I hope in a future edition to have the opportunity of considering whether the ten quotations above and many others from literature and speech of the last few years show signs of standing the test of time.

The quotations in the book have been arranged alphabetically by author and, wherever possible, line references have been given in poems, and act and scene references in plays. The name of the speaker has been given in all quotations from plays, and this enables one to find out without reference to the original test that, for example, it was Marcellus, and not Hamlet or Horatio as one might have supposed, who said, 'Something is rotten in the state of Denmark'.

A comprehensive index with over 25,000 entries has been provided at the end of the dictionary and this contains the key words in each quotation. It gives not only the page reference, but the number of the quotation on the page. From this index it is easy to trace quickly a half-remembered quotation by looking up one of the key words and, also, should one refer to individual words in the index like *man* or *beauty*, to find quotations on these subjects. References in most cases are to the Oxford Editions of Standard Authors, but line references obviously vary from edition to edition with authors, like Shakespeare, who wrote partly in prose and partly in poetry.

ROBIN HYMAN

# Acknowledgements

Many friends gave encouragement and helpful advice during the five years of preparation of this book. Thanks are due in particular to the Rev. S. R. Cutt for his assistance in the selection of quotations from the Bible; Mrs. E. M. Hatt who undertook the immense task of compiling the index; and Miss Barbara Hall and Miss Pamela Jones for their careful checking of the proofs. Librarians in England and the United States have answered numerous enquiries with great courtesy, and the staff of the British Museum have been especially helpful. The verification of contemporary references has in many cases. been made easier by the ready co-operation of the writers and speakers themselves.

*To*

*MY MOTHER AND FATHER*
*who taught me to enjoy reading*

# A Dictionary of Famous Quotations

**ACTON, John Emerich Edward Dalberg, 1st Baron 1834–1902**

1 Power tends to corrupt, and absolute power corrupts absolutely. Great men are almost always bad men . . . There is no worse heresy than that the office sanctifies the holder of it.

*Historical Essays and Studies, Appendix,*
*Letter to Bishop Mandell Creighton*

**ADAMS, John Quincy, 1767–1848**

2 Think of your forefathers! Think of your posterity!  *Speech,*
*Plymouth, Massachusetts, 22 Dec. 1802*

**ADAMS, Sarah Flower, 1805–1848**

3 Nearer, my God to thee,
  Nearer to thee!
E'en though it be a cross
  That raiseth me.  *Nearer, my God, to Thee*

**ADDISON, Joseph, 1672–1719**

4 'Tis not in mortals to command success,
But we'll do more, Sempronius; we'll deserve it. PORTIUS
*Cato, Act 1, Scene 2*

5 The woman that deliberates is lost. MARCIA *Ib, Act 4, Scene 1*

6 Thus I live in the world rather as a Spectator of mankind, than as one of the species, by which means I have made myself a speculative statesman, soldier, merchant, and artisan, without ever meddling with any practical part of life.  *The Spectator,*
*No. 1, 1 March 1711*

7 Sunday clears away the rust of the whole week.  *Ib, No. 112*
*9 July 1711*

8 [*Sir Roger*] told them, with the air of a man who would not give his judgment rashly, that 'much might be said on both sides'.
*Ib, No. 122, 20 July 1711*

9 The spacious firmament on high,
With all the blue ethereal sky,
And spangled heavens, a shining frame,
Their great Original proclaim. *Ib, No. 465, 23 Aug. 1712, Ode*

10 A woman seldom asks advice until she has bought her wedding clothes.  *Ib, No. 475, 4 Sept. 1712*

11 We are always doing something for posterity, but I would fain
see posterity do something for us.   *The Spectator, No. 583,*
*20 Aug. 1714*

12 See in what peace a Christian can die.   *Last words*

**ADY, Thomas, c. 1655**

13 Matthew, Mark, Luke and John,
The bed be blest that I lie on.
Four angels to my bed,
Four angels round my head,
One to watch, and one to pray,
And two to bear my soul away.   *A Candle in the Dark*

**AKINS, Zoë, 1886–1958**

14 The Greeks Had a Word for It.   *Title of play, 1930*

**ALCUIN, 735–804**

15 *Vox populi, vox dei.* The voice of the people is the voice of God.
*Letter to Charlemagne*

**ALDRICH, Henry, 1647–1710**

16 If all be true that I do think,
There are five reasons we should drink:
Good wine – a friend – or being dry –
Or lest we should be by and by –
Or any other reason why.   *Reasons for Drinking*

**ALEXANDER, Cecil Frances, 1818–1895**

17 All things bright and beautiful,
All creatures great and small,
All things wise and wonderful,
The Lord God made them all
*All Things Bright and Beautiful*

18 The rich man in his castle,
The poor man at his gate,
God made them, high or lowly,
And order'd their estate.   *Ib*

19 Once in royal David's city
Stood a lowly cattle shed,
Where a Mother laid her Baby
In a manger for His bed:
Mary was that Mother mild,
Jesus Christ her little child.   *Once in Royal David's City*

20 There is a green hill far away,
       Without a city wall,
   Where the dear Lord was crucified,
       Who died to save us all.          *There is a Green Hill*

**ALLAINVAL, Abbé Léonor d', 1700–1753**
21 *L'embarras des richesses.* A superfluity of good things.
                                        *Title of play, 1726*

**ALLINGHAM, William, 1824–1889**
22 Up the airy mountain
   Down the rushy glen,
   We daren't go a-hunting,
   For fear of little men.                 *The Fairies*

**AMBROSE, St, 340?–397?**
23 *Si fueris Romae, Romano vivito more;*
   *Si fueris alibi, vivito sicut ibi.*
   When in Rome, live as the Romans do: when elsewhere, live as
   they live elsewhere.   *Advice to St Augustine, quoted by Jeremy*
                                                          *Taylor*

**ANDERSEN, Hans Christian, 1805–1875**
24 The Ugly Duckling.                    *Title of Story*

**ANONYMOUS**
**Advertisements**
25 Daddy, what did you do in the Great War?
                        *Recruiting Poster, 1914–1918 War*
26 Drinka pinta milka day.              *Milk Marketing Board*
27 Friday night is Amami night.
28 Guinness is good for you.
29 Is your journey really necessary? *Railway Poster, 1939–1945 War*
30 That schoolgirl complexion.             *Palmolive Soap*
31 Stop me and buy one.                   *Wall's Ice Cream*
32 They come as a boon and a blessing to men,
   The Pickwick, The Owl, and the Waverley pen.
33 Top People take *The Times.*
34 Worth a guinea a box.                  *Beecham's Pills*
35 You want the best seats; we have them   *Keith Prowse & Co.*
                                                          *Ltd*

**Ballads**

36 In Scarlet town, where I was born,
　　There was a fair maid dwellin',
　　Made every youth cry *Well-a-way*!
　　Her name was Barbara Allen.　　　　*Barbara Allen's Cruelty*
　　　　　　　　　　　　　　　　　　　　　*Stanza 1*

37 The King sits in Dunfermline town
　　Drinking the blude red wine.　　　　*Sir Patrick Spens, 1*

38 To Noroway, to Noroway,
　　To Noroway o'er the faem;
　　The King's daughter o' Noroway,
　　　'Tis thou must bring her hame.　　　*Ib, 13*

39 There were three ravens sat on a tree,
　　They were as black as they might be.
　　The one of them said to his make,
　　'Where shall we our breakfast take?'　　*The Three Ravens, 1*

40 As I was walking all alane
　　I heard twa corbies making a mane:
　　The tane unto the tither did say,
　　'Whar shall we gang and dine the day?'　　*The Twa Corbies*

**Epitaphs**

41 Here lie I and my four daughters,
　　Killed by drinking Cheltenham waters.
　　Had we but stick to Epsom salts,
　　We wouldn't have been in these here vaults.
　　　　　　　　　　　　　　　　　*Cheltenham Waters*

42 Here lies a man who was killed by lightning;
　　He died when his prospects seemed to be brightening.
　　He might have cut a flash in this world of trouble,
　　But the flash cut him, and he lies in the stubble.　　*At Great*
　　　　　　　　　　　　　　　　　　　　　　*Torrington, Devon*

43 Here lies a poor woman who was always tired,
　　She lived in a house where help wasn't hired:
　　Her last words on earth were: 'Dear friends, I am going
　　To where there's no cooking, or washing, or sewing,
　　For everything there is exact to my wishes,
　　For where they don't eat there's no washing of dishes.
　　I'll be where loud anthems will always be ringing,
　　But having no voice I'll be quit of the singing.
　　Don't mourn for me now, don't mourn for me never,
　　I am going to do nothing for ever and ever.'
　　　　　　　　　　　　　　　　　　　　*On a Tired Housewife*

44  Here lies my wife,
    Here lies she;
    Hallelujah!
    Hallelujee!                                   *At Leeds*

45  Here lies the body of Richard Hind,
    Who was neither ingenious, sober, nor kind.   *On Richard Hind*

46  Here lies the body of Mary Ann Lowder,
    She burst while drinking a seidlitz powder.
    Called from the world to her heavenly rest,
    She should have waited till it effervesced.   *On Mary Ann*
                                                  *Lowder*

47  Here lies Will Smith – and, what's something rarish,
    He was born, bred, and hanged, all in the same parish.
                                                  *On Will Smith*

48  Mary Ann has gone to rest,
    Safe at last on Abraham's breast,
    Which may be nuts for Mary Ann,
    But is certainly rough on Abraham.            *Mary Ann*

49  Stranger! Approach this spot with gravity!
    John Brown is filling his last cavity.        *A Dentist*

50  This is the grave of Mike O'Day
    Who died maintaining his right of way.
    His right was clear, his will was strong.
    But he's just as dead as if he'd been wrong.  *20th century*

## Limericks

51  There was a faith-healer of Deal,
    Who said, 'Although pain isn't real,
        If I sit on a pin
        And it punctures my skin,
    I dislike what I fancy I feel.'

52  There was a young lady of Riga,
    Who went for a ride on a tiger;
        They returned from the ride
        With the lady inside,
    And a smile on the face of the tiger.

53  There was a young man of Boulogne
    Who sang a most topical song.
        It wasn't the words
        That frightened the birds,
    But the horrible *double entendre*.

54  There was a young man of Japan
    Whose limericks never would scan;

When they said it was so,
He replied, 'Yes, I know,
But I always try to get as many words into the last line as ever I
possibly can.'

55 There was a young woman called Starkie,
Who had an affair with a darky.
    The result of her sins
    Was quadruplets, not twins –
One black, and one white, and two khaki.

56 There was an old man from Darjeeling,
Who boarded a bus bound for Ealing,
    He saw on the door:
    'Please don't spit on the floor',
So he stood up and spat on the ceiling.

57 There's a wonderful family called Stein,
There's Gert and there's Epp and there's Ein;
    Gert's poems are bunk,
    Epp's statues are junk,
And no one can understand Ein.

For other limericks, see Arnold Bennett (33 : 12), A. H. R. Buller
(76 : 52), A. H. Euwer (134 : 53), M. E. Hare (158 : 68), R. A. Knox
(191 : 20), Edward Lear (195 : 65 and 66), D. L. Merritt (209 : 38)
and W. C. Monkhouse (224 : 52).

## Play

58 Everyman, I will go with thee and be thy guide,
In thy most need to go by thy side.  KNOWLEDGE  *Everyman*
                                    *(15th century morality play)*

## Poems and Sayings

59 A beast, but a just beast.  *Of Dr Temple, Headmaster of Rugby*

60 From ghoulies and ghosties and long-leggety beasties
And things that go bump in the night,
Good Lord, deliver us!                     *Scottish prayer*

61 He that fights and runs away
May live to fight another day.      *Musarum Deliciae (17th*
                                          *century)*

62 'How different, how very different, from the home life of our own
dear Queen!'      *Irvin S. Cobb, A Laugh a Day. Remark of*
            *Victorian lady after a performance of Anthony and*
                                          *Cleopatra*

63 I always eat peas with honey
   I've done it all my life,
   They do taste kind of funny,
   But it keeps them on the knife.        *Peas*

64 I know two things about the horse,
   And one of them is rather coarse.    *The Horse (20th century)*

65 If all the world were paper,
   And all the sea were ink,
   And all the trees were bread and cheese,
   What should we do for drink?    *If All the World were Paper*
                                             *(17th century)*

66 King Charles the First walked and talked
   Half an hour after his head was cut off.    *Peter Puzzlewell,*
           *A Choice Collection of Riddles, Charades, and*
                              *Rebuses (18th century)*

67 Lizzie Borden took an axe
   And gave her mother forty whacks;
   When she saw what she had done,
   She gave her father forty-one.    *On an American Trial of the*
                                           *1890's*

68 Miss Buss and Miss Beale
   Cupid's darts do not feel.
   How different from us,
   Miss Beale and Miss Buss    *On Two Victorian Headmistresses*

69 Please to remember
   The Fifth of November,
   Gunpowder treason and plot.        *Guy Fawkes Day*

70 The rabbit has a charming face;
   Its private life is a disgrace.    *The Rabbit (20th century)*

71 Sumer is icumen in
   Lhude sing cucu!
   Groweth sed and bloweth med
   And springth the wude nu.    *Sumer is Icumen In (13th century)*

## Songs

72 Absence makes the heart grow fonder.    *Davison, Poetical*
                                        *Rhapsody, 1602*

73 The animals went in one by one,
   There's one more river to cross.      *One More River*

74 As I sat on a sunny bank,
   On Christmas Day in the morning,
   I spied three ships come sailing by.    *Carol, As I sat on a*
                                           *Sunny Bank*

75 Begone, dull care! I prithee begone from me!
   Begone, dull care, you and I shall never agree.       *Begone Dull*
                                                                *Care*

76 The bells of hell go ting-a-ling-a-ling
   For you but not for me.       *Song of 1914–1918 War*

77 The Campbells are comin', oho, oho.       *The Campbells are*
                                                    *Comin'*

78 Come landlord, fill the flowing bowl,
   Until it doth run over ...
      For tonight we'll merry, merry be,
      Tomorrow we'll be sober.       *Come, Landlord, Fill the*
                                              *Flowing Bowl*

79 Come lasses and lads, get leave of your dads,
   And away to the Maypole hie,
   For every he has got him a she,
   And the fiddler's standing by.       *Come Lasses and Lads*

80 Early one morning, just as the sun was rising,
   I heard a maid singing in the valley below:
   'Oh, don't deceive me; Oh, never leave me!
   How could you use a poor maiden so?'       *Early One Morning*

81 Frankie and Johnny were lovers, lordee, and how they could love,
   Swore to be true to each other, true as the stars above;
   He was her man, but he done her wrong.       *Frankie and Johnny*

82 God rest you merry, gentlemen,
   Let nothing you dismay.       *God Rest you Merry*

83 Greensleeves was all my joy,
      Greensleeves was my delight,
   Greensleeves was my heart of gold,
      And who but Lady Greensleeves.       *Greensleeves*

84 Ha, ha, ha, you and me,
   Little brown jug, don't I love thee!       *The Little Brown Jug*

85 Here's a health unto his Majesty, ....
   Confusion to his enemies, ...
   And he that will not drink his health,
   I wish him neither wit nor wealth,
   Nor yet a rope to hang himself.       *Here's a Health unto his*
                                                  *Majesty*

86 Here we come gathering nuts in May
            Nuts in May,
   On a cold and frosty morning.       *Children's Song*

87 The holly and the ivy,
   When they are both full grown,

Of all the trees that are in the wood,
The holly bears the crown.
The rising of the sun
And the running of the deer,
The playing of the merry organ,
Sweet singing in the choir.          *Carol, The Holly and the Ivy*

88 I feel no pain, dear mother, now
But oh, I am so dry!
O take me to a brewery
And leave me there to die.                          *Shanty*

89 In Dublin's fair city, where the girls are so pretty,
I first set my eyes on sweet Molly Malone,
As she wheeled her wheelbarrow, through streets broad and
   narrow,
Crying, Cockles and mussels! alive, alive, O!      *Cockles and
                                                      Mussels*

90 She was a fishmonger, but sure 'twas no wonder,
For so were her father and mother before.              *Ib*

91 In good King Charles's golden days,
When loyalty no harm meant,
A zealous High Churchman was I,
And so I got preferment.                      *The Vicar of Bray*

92 And this is law, that I'll maintain,
Unto my dying day, Sir,
That whatsoever King shall reign,
I'll be the Vicar of Bray, Sir.                       *Ib*

93 It is good to be merry and wise,
It is good to be honest and true,
It is best to be off with the old love,
Before you are on with the new.              *Songs of England and
                                                Scotland, 1835*

94 My Bonnie is over the ocean,
My Bonnie is over the sea,
My Bonnie is over the ocean,
Oh, bring back my Bonnie to me.                    *My Bonnie*

95 Now I am a bachelor, I live by myself and I work at the weaving
   trade,
And the only only thing that I ever did wrong
Was to woo a fair young maid.                   *Weaver's Song*

96 She sighed, she cried, she damned near died: she said 'What
   shall I do?'
So I took her into bed and covered up her head
Just to save her from the foggy, foggy dew.          *Ib*

97 Oh, I went down South for to see my Sal,
   Sing 'Polly-wolly-doodle' all the day!     *Polly-Wolly-Doodle*

98 Oh, 'tis my delight on a shining night, in the season of the year.
                                    *The Lincolnshire Poacher*

99 Old soldiers never die;
   They only fade away.               *War Song, 1914–1918*

 1 O, Shenandoah, I long to hear you
   Away, you rolling river.                    *Shenandoah*

 2 O ye'll tak' the high road, and I'll tak' the low road,
   And I'll be in Scotland afore ye,
   But me and my true love will never meet again,
   On the bonnie, bonnie banks o' Loch Lomon'.
                          *The Bonnie Banks o' Loch Lomon'*

 3 She was poor but she was honest
   Victim of a rich man's game.
   First he loved her, then he left her,
   And she lost her maiden name. *She was Poor but she was Honest*

 4 See her on the bridge at midnight,
   Saying 'Farewell, blighted love.'
   Then a scream, a splash and goodness,
   What is she a-doin' of?                            *Ib*

 5 It's the same the whole world over,
   It's the poor wot gets the blame,
   It's the rich wot gets the gravy.
   Ain't it all a bleedin' shame?                     *Ib*

 6 Some talk of Alexander, and some of Hercules,
   Of Hector and Lysander, and such great names as these;
   But of all the world's brave heroes there's none that can compare
   With a tow, row, row, row, row, row for the British Grenadier.
                                    *The British Grenadiers*

 7 The sons of the prophet were brave men and bold,
   And quite unaccustomed to fear,
   But the bravest by far in the ranks of the Shah
   Was Abdul the Bulbul Amir.        *Abdul the Bulbul Amir*

 8 Swing low sweet chariot,
   Comin' for to carry me home,
   I looked over Jordan an' what did I see?
   A band of Angels coming after me,
   Comin' for to carry me home.    *Swing Low, Sweet Chariot*

 9 There is a lady sweet and kind,
   Was never face so pleased my mind;
   I did but see her passing by,
   And yet I love her till I die.            *Passing By*

10 There is a tavern in the town,
   And there my dear love sits him down,
   And drinks his wine 'mid laughter free,
   And never, never thinks of me.   *There is a Tavern in the Town*

11 Fare thee well, for I must leave thee,
   Do not let this parting grieve thee,
   And remember that the best of friends must part.          *Ib*

12 Tom Pearse, Tom Pearse, lend me your grey mare,
   All along, down along out along Lee.
   For I want for to go to Widdicombe Fair,
   Wi' Bill Brewer, Jan Stewer, Peter Gurney, Peter Davey, Dan'l
      Whiddon, Harry Hawk, Old Uncle Tom Cobbleigh and all.
                                          *Widdicombe Fair*

13 We're here because we're here because we're here because we're
      here.                          *Army Song, 1914–1918*

14 What shall we do with the drunken sailor
   Early in the morning?
   Hoo-ray and up she rises
   Early in the morning.      *What shall we do with the Drunken
                                                      Sailor?*

**French**

15 *Liberté! Égalité! Fraternite!* Liberty! Equality! Fraternity!
                                          *French Revolution*

16 *Revenons à nos moutons.* Let us return to our sheep (i.e. to the
   subject).                          *Maistre Pierre Pathelin*

**Greek**

17 Nothing in excess                *In the temple at Delphi*

**Latin**

18 *Ad majorem Dei gloriam.* To the greater glory of God.
                                *Motto of the Society of Jesus*

19 *Et in Arcadia ego.* I too am in Arcadia.      *Inscription on tomb*

20 *Gaudeamus igitur,*
   *Iuvenes dum sumus*
   Let us be happy while we are young.      *Students' song (13th
                                                      century)*

21 *Tempora mutantur, et nos mutamur in illis.* Times change, and we
   change with them.   *Quoted in Harrison, Description of Britain,
                                                      1577*

## ARABIAN NIGHTS

22 Who will change old lamps for new ones?... new lamps for
old ones?       *The History of Aladdin*

23 Open Sesame!       *The History of Ali Baba*

## ARCHIMEDES, 287–212 B.C.

24 Give me a firm place to stand, and I will move the earth.
      *On the Lever*

25 I have found it! [Eureka!]       *On making a discovery*

## ARISTOTLE, 384–322 B.C.

26 Man is by nature a political animal.       *Politics, Book 1*

27 Inferiors revolt in order that they may be equal, and equals that
they may be superior. Such is the state of mind which creates
revolutions.       *Ib, Book 5*

28 Plato is dear to me, but dearer still is truth.       *Attributed*

## ARNOLD, George, 1834–1865

29 The living need charity more than the dead.       *The Jolly Old
Pedagogue*

## ARNOLD, Matthew, 1822–1888

30 The sea is calm to-night,
The tide is full, the moon lies fair
Upon the Straits.       *Dover Beach*

31 Is it so small a thing
To have enjoy'd the sun,
To have lived light in the spring,
To have loved, to have thought, to have done?
      *Empedocles on Etna*

32 Come, dear children, let us away;
Down and away below.       *The Forsaken Merman*

33 Children dear, was it yesterday
(Call yet once) that she went away?       *Ib*

34 She left lonely for ever
The kings of the sea.       *Ib*

35 Who saw life steadily, and saw it whole:
The mellow glory of the Attic stage.       *Sonnets, To a Friend*

36 Wandering between two worlds, one dead,
The other powerless to be born.       *The Grande Chartreuse*

37 Strew on her roses, roses,
  And never a spray of yew.
  In quiet she reposes:
  Ah! would that I did too. *Requiescat*

38 Tonight it doth inherit
  The vasty Hall of Death. *Ib*

39 Go, for they call you, Shepherd, from the hill. *The Scholar Gipsy, 1*

40 All the live murmur of a summer's day. *Ib, 20*

41 Tired of knocking at Preferment's door. *Ib, 35*

42 Before this strange disease of modern life,
  With its sick hurry, its divided aims. *Ib, 203*

43 Still nursing the unconquerable hope,
  Still clutching the inviolable shade. *Ib, 211*

44 Others abide our question. Thou art free.
  We ask and ask: Thou smilest and art still,
  Out-topping knowledge. *Shakespeare*

45 Truth sits upon the lips of dying men. *Sohrab and Rustum*

46 And that sweet City with her dreaming spires
  She needs not June for beauty's heightening. *[Of Oxford] Thyrsis, 19*

47 The pursuit of perfection, then, is the pursuit of sweetness and light. *Culture and Anarchy*

48 Thus we have got three distinct terms, Barbarians, Philistines, Populace, to denote roughly the three great classes into which our society is divided. *Ib*

49 Home of lost causes, and forsaken beliefs, and unpopular names, and impossible loyalties! *[Of Oxford] Essays in Criticism, First Series, Preface*

50 I am bound by my own definition of criticism: a disinterested endeavour to learn and propagate the best that is known and thought in the world. *Ib, Functions of Criticism at the Present Time*

51 In poetry, no less than in life, he is 'a beautiful and ineffectual angel, beating in the void his luminous wings in vain.' *[Of Shelley] Ib, Second Series*

52 Culture is the passion for sweetness and light, and (what is more) the passion for making them prevail. *Literature and Dogma, Preface*

53 Culture, the acquainting ourselves with the best that has been known and said in the world, and thus with the history of the human spirit. *Ib*

## ARNOLD, Thomas, 1795–1842

54 What we must look for here is, first, religious and moral principles; secondly, gentlemanly conduct; thirdly, intellectual
ability.                          *Address to his Scholars at Rugby*

55 My object will be, if possible to form Christian men, for
Christian boys I can scarcely hope to make.   *Letter on appoint-
ment as Headmaster of Rugby, 1828*

## ASAF, George (George H. Powell), 1880–1951

56 What's the use of worrying?
     It never was worth while,
So, pack up your troubles in your old kit-bag,
     And smile, smile, smile.
                    *Pack up your Troubles in your old Kit-Bag (1915)*

## ASQUITH, Herbert Henry, 1st Earl of Oxford and Asquith, 1852–1928

57 Wait and see.                          *Various Speeches, 1910*

## AUDEN, Wystan Hugh, 1907–1973

58 To save your world you asked this man to die:
Would this man, could he see you now, ask why?
                          *Epitaph for an Unknown Soldier*

59 When statesmen gravely say – 'We must be realistic –'
The chances are they're weak and therefore pacifistic:
But when they speak of Principles – look out – perhaps
Their generals are already poring over maps.        *Footnotes*

60 Lay your sleeping head, my love,
Human on my faithless arm.                          *Lullaby*

61 To the man-in-the-street, who, I'm sorry to say
Is a keen observer of life,
The word Intellectual suggests straight away
A man who's untrue to his wife.        *Note on Intellectuals*

62 Our researchers into Public Opinion are content
That he held the proper opinions for the time of year;
When there was peace, he was for peace; when there was war,
     he went.                          *The Unknown Citizen*

## AUGUSTINE, St, 354–430

63 Give me chastity and continence, but not yet.   *Confessions, 8*

**AUSTEN, Jane, 1775–1817**

64 The yeomanry are precisely the order of people with whom I feel
   I can have nothing to do. A degree or two lower, and . . . I might
   hope to be useful to their families in some way or other.  EMMA
                                                    *Emma, Ch. 4*

65 One half of the world cannot understand the pleasures of the
   other.  EMMA                                    *Ib, Ch. 9*

66 Nobody is healthy in London, nobody can be.  MR WOODHOUSE
                                                    *Ib, Ch. 12*

67 Human nature is so well disposed towards those who are in
   interesting situations, that a young person, who either marries or
   dies, is sure of being kindly spoken of.         *Ib, Ch. 22*

68 Business, you know, may bring money, but friendship hardly
   ever does.  JOHN KNIGHTLEY                       *Ib, Ch. 34*

69 It will, I believe, be everywhere found, that as the clergy are, or
   are not what they ought to be, so are the rest of the nation.
   EDMUND                                  *Mansfield Park, Ch. 9*

70 To sit in the shade on a fine day, and look upon verdure is the
   most perfect refreshment.  FANNY                 *Ib, Ch. 9*

71 Let other pens dwell on guilt and misery.        *Ib, Ch. 48*

72 But are they all horrid, are you sure they are all horrid?
   CATHERINE MORLAND              *Northanger Abbey, Ch. 6*

73 A woman, especially if she have the misfortune of knowing
   anything, should conceal it as well as she can.   *Ib, Ch. 14*

74 One does not love a place the less for having suffered in it,
   unless it has all been suffering, nothing but suffering.
                                           *Persuasion, Ch. 20*

75 It is a truth universally acknowledged, that a single man in
   possession of a good fortune must be in want of a wife.
                                      *Pride and Prejudice, Ch. 1*

76 Happiness in marriage is entirely a matter of chance.  *Ib, Ch. 6*

77 How can you contrive to write so even?  MISS BINGLEY  *Ib, Ch. 10*

78 It is happy for you that you possess the talent of flattering with
   delicacy. May I ask whether these pleasing attentions proceed
   from the impulse of the moment, or are the result of previous
   study?  MR BENNET                                *Ib, Ch. 14*

79 Nobody is on my side, nobody takes part with me: I am cruelly
   used, nobody feels for my poor nerves.  MRS BENNET  *Ib, Ch. 48*

80 'I am afraid' replied Elinor, 'that the pleasantness of an employment does not always evince its propriety.'          *Sense and
                                                    Sensibility, Ch. 13*

81 What dreadful hot weather we have! It keeps me in a continual
state of inelegance. *Letter, 18 Sept. 1796*

## AUSTIN, Alfred, 1835–1913

82 An earl by right, by courtesy a man. *The Season*

83 Across the wires the electric message came:
'He is no better, he is much the same.' *On the Illness of the
Prince of Wales, Attributed*

## BACON, Francis, 1st Baron Verulam, 1561–1626

84 My Essayes . . . come home, to Mens Businesse, and Bosomes.
*Essays. Dedication*

85 What is truth? said jesting Pilate, and would not stay for an
answer. *Essay 1. Of Truth*

86 Men fear death, as children fear to go in the dark; and as that
natural fear in children is increased with tales, so is the other.
*2. Of Death*

87 It is natural to die as to be born; and to a little infant, perhaps,
the one is as painful as the other. *Ib*

88 All colours will agree in the dark. *3. Of Unity in Religion*

89 Revenge is a kind of wild justice; which the more man's nature
runs to, the more ought law to weed it out. *4. Of Revenge*

90 Prosperity is the blessing of the Old Testament; adversity is the
blessing of the New. *5. Of Adversity*

91 Prosperity is not without many fears and distastes; and adversity
is not without comforts and hopes. *Ib*

92 Prosperity doth best discover vice; but adversity doth best
discover virtue. *Ib*

93 He that talketh what he knoweth, will also talk what he knoweth
not. *6. Of Simulation and Dissimulation*

94 The joys of parents are secret, and so are their griefs and fears.
*7. Of Parents and Children.*

95 Children sweeten labours, but they make misfortunes more
bitter. *Ib*

96 He that hath wife and children hath given hostages to fortune;
for they are impediments to great enterprises, either of virtue
or mischief. *8. Of Marriage and Single Life*

97 Wives are young men's mistresses; companions for middle age;
and old men's nurses. *Ib*

98 He was reputed one of the wise men, that made answer to the
   question, when a man should marry? A young man not yet, an
   elder man not at all.          *8. Of Marriage and Single Life*

99 Nuptial love maketh mankind; friendly love perfecteth it; but
   wanton love corrupteth and embaseth it.          *10. Of Love*

 1 Men in great places are thrice servants: servants of the sovereign
   or state; servants of fame; and servants of business.
                                         *11. Of Great Place*

 2 There is in human nature generally more of the fool than of the
   wise.                                   *12. Of Boldness*

 3 If the hill will not come to Mahomet, Mahomet will go to the
   hill.                                              *Ib*

 4 In charity there is no excess.   *13. Of Goodness, and Goodness
                                                      of Nature*

 5 If a man be gracious and courteous to strangers, it shews he is a
   citizen of the world.                              *Ib*

 6 New nobility is but the act of power; but ancient nobility is the
   act of time.                             *14. Of Nobility*

 7 So when any of the four pillars of government are mainly
   shaken or weakened (which are religion, justice, counsel, and
   treasure), men had need to pray for fair weather.
                                   *15. Of Seditions and Troubles*

 8 Money is like muck, not good except it be spread.          *Ib*

 9 The remedy is worse than the disease.                     *Ib*

10 A little philosophy inclineth man's mind to atheism; but depth
   in philosophy bringeth men's minds about to religion.
                                            *16. Of Atheism*

11 It were better to have no opinion of God at all, than such an
   opinion as is unworthy of him.          *17. Of Superstition*

12 Travel, in the younger sort, is a part of education; in the elder,
   a part of experience.                     *18. Of Travel*

13 It is a miserable state of mind to have few things to desire and
   many things to fear.                       *19. Of Empire*

14 Nothing destroyeth authority so much as the unequal and untimely interchange of power pressed too far, and relaxed too
   much.                                              *Ib*

15 There be that can pack the cards, and yet cannot play well.
                                            *22. Of Cunning*

16 Be so true to thyself, as thou be not false to others.
                                   *23. Of Wisdom for a Man's Self*

17 He that will not apply new remedies must expect new evils: for time is the greatest innovator. *24. Of Innovations*

18 To choose time is to save time. *25. Of Dispatch*

19 The French are wiser than they seem, and the Spaniards seem wiser than they are. *26. Of Seeming Wise*

20 Whosoever is delighted in solitude is either a wild beast or a god. *27. Of Friendship*

21 Riches are for spending. *28. Of Expense*

22 Age will not be defied. *30. Of Regiment of Health*

23 Suspicions amongst thoughts are like bats amongst birds, they ever fly by twilight. *31. Of Suspicion*

24 Of great riches there is no real use, except it be in the distribution. *34. Of Riches*

25 Nature is often hidden, sometimes overcome, seldom extinguished. *38. Of Nature in Men*

26 A man that is young in years may be old in hours, if he have lost no time. *42. Of Youth and Age*

27 Virtue is like a rich stone, best plain set. *43. Of Beauty*

28 Houses are built to live in, and not to look on. *45. Of Building*

29 God Almighty first planted a garden. And indeed it is the purest of human pleasures. *46. Of Gardens*

30 Studies serve for delight, for ornament, and for ability. *50. Of Studies*

31 To spend too much time in studies is sloth. *Ib*

32 Some books are to be tasted, others to be swallowed, and some few to be chewed and digested. *Ib*

33 Reading maketh a full man; conference a ready man; and writing an exact man. *Ib*

34 Histories make men wise; poets witty; the mathematics subtile; natural philosophy deep; moral grave; logic and rhetoric able to contend. *Ib*

35 Fame is like a river, that beareth up things light and swoln, and drowns things weighty and solid. *53. Of Praise*

36 The place of justice is an hallowed place. *56. Of Judicature*

37 If a man will begin with certainties, he shall end in doubts, but if he will be content to begin with doubts, he shall end in certainties. *The Advancement of Learning, 1, 5, 8*

38 Hope is a good breakfast, but it is a bad supper. *Apophthegms, 36*

39 I have taken all knowledge to be my province.      *Letter to*
                                                 *Lord Burleigh, 1592*

40 God's first creature, which was light.      *The New Atlantis*

41 There are four classes of Idols which beset men's minds. To
these for distinction sake I have assigned names – calling the
first class, Idols of the Tribe; the second, Idols of the Cave; the
third, Idols of the Market-place; the fourth, Idols of the Theatre.
                                                 *Novum Organum*

42 Nature, to be commanded, must be obeyed.                    *Ib*

### BAGEHOT, Walter, 1826–1877

43 *The Times* has made many ministries.    *The English Consitution,*
                                                          *Ch. 1*

44 Women – one half the human race at least – care fifty times more
for a marriage than a ministry.                    *Ib, Ch. 2*

45 Of all nations in the World, the English are perhaps the least a
nation of pure philosophers.                              *Ib*

46 Poverty is an anomaly to rich people. It is very difficult to make
out why people who want dinner do not ring the bell.
                                                 *Literary Studies, 2*

### BAIRNSFATHER, Charles Bruce, 1888–1959

47 Well, if you knows of a better 'ole, go to it.    *Fragments from*
                                                         *France, 1*

### BALFOUR, Arthur James, 1848–1930

48 The energies of our system will decay, the glory of the sun will be
dimmed, and the earth, tideless and inert, will no longer tolerate
the race which has for a moment disturbed its solitude. Man
will go down into the pit, and all his thoughts will perish.
                                  *The Foundations of Belief, Part 1, Ch. 1*

49 It is unfortunate, considering that enthusiasm moves the world,
that so few enthusiasts can be trusted to speak the truth.
                                            *Letter to Mrs Drew, 1918*

### BALL, John, ?–1381

50 When Adam delved and Eve span,
Who was then the gentleman?     *Text for sermon on Peasants'*
                                                       *Revolt*

### BARHAM, Richard Harris, 1788–1845

51 A servant's too often an impudent elf;
– If it's business of consequence, *do it yourself!   The Ingoldsby*
                              *Legends, The Ingoldsby Penance, Moral*

52 The Jackdaw sat on the Cardinal's chair!
Bishop and abbot, and prior were there.      *The Ingoldsby
Legends, The Jackdaw of Rheims*

53                     Never, I ween,
                   Was a prouder seen,
Read of in books, or dreamt of in dreams,
Than the Cardinal Lord Archbishop of Rheims!              *Ib*

54 He long lived the pride of that country side,
And at last in the odour of sancity died.                *Ib*

55 He smiled and said, 'Sir, does your mother know that you are
out?'                          *Ib, Misadventures at Margate*


**BARING-GOULD, Sabine, 1834–1924**

56 Now the day is over,
Night is drawing nigh,
Shadows of the evening
Steal across the sky.                    *Now the Day is over*

57 Onward Christian soldiers
Marching as to war,
With the Cross of Jesus
Going on before.                    *Onward Christian Soldiers*


**BARNUM, Phineas Taylor, 1810–1891**

58 There's a sucker born every minute.                *Attributed*


**BARRIE, Sir James Matthew, 1860–1937**

59 When the first baby laughed for the first time, the laugh broke
into a thousand pieces and they all went skipping about, and
that was the beginning of fairies.  PETER PAN  *Peter Pan, Act 1*

60 Every time a child says 'I don't believe in fairies' there is a little
fairy somewhere that falls down dead.  PETER PAN           *Ib*

61 To die will be an awfully big adventure.  PETER PAN  *Ib, Act 3*

62 Do you believe in fairies? Say quick that you believe. If you
believe, clap your hands!  PETER PAN             *Ib, Act 4*

63 One's religion is whatever he is most interested in, and yours is
Success.  KATE                    *The Twelve-Pound Look*

64 You've forgotten the grandest moral attribute of a Scotsman,
Maggie, that he'll do nothing which might damage his career.
JOHN SHAND                *What Every Woman Knows, Act 2*

**BARRINGTON, George, 1755–1810?**

65 True patriots we; for be it understood,
   We left our country for our country's good. *Prologue for*
   *opening of Playhouse, Sydney, 16 Jan. 1796 by company*
   *of convicts*

**BATEMAN, Edgar, 19th century**

66 Wiv a ladder and some glasses,
   You could see to 'Ackney Marshes,
   If it wasn't for the 'ouses in between. *If it wasn't for the*
   *'Ouses in between*

**BATES, Katherine Lee, 1859–1929**

67 America! America!
   God shed His grace on thee
   And crown thy good with brotherhood
   From sea to shining sea! *America the Beautiful*

**BAYLY, Thomas Haynes, 1797–1839**

68 Absence makes the heart grow fonder,
   Isle of Beauty, Fare thee well! *Isle of Beauty*

**BEATTY, David, 1st Earl Beatty, 1871–1936**

69 There's something wrong with our bloody ships today.
   *Remark during Battle of Jutland, 1916*

**BEAUMONT, Francis, 1584–1616**

70       What things we have seen,
   Done at the Mermaid! heard words that have been
   So nimble, and so full of subtle flame,
   As if that everyone from whence they came
   Had meant to put his whole wit in a jest,
   And had resolved to live a fool the rest
   Of his dull life. *Letter to Ben Jonson*

71 Mortality, behold and fear!
   What a change of flesh is here. *On the Tombs in Westminster*
   *Abbey*

**BEAUMONT, Francis, 1584–1616, and FLETCHER, John,
1579–1625**

72 But what is past my help is past my care. *The Double*
   *Marriage, Act 1, Scene 1*

73 There is no other purgatory but a woman. ELDER LOVELESS
   *The Scornful Lady, Act 3, Scene 1*

**BECKETT, Samuel, 1906–**

74 Nothing happens, nobody comes, nobody goes, it's awful!
ESTRAGON *Waiting for Godot, Act 1*

75 VLADIMIR: That passed the time.
ESTRAGON: It would have passed in any case.
VLADIMIR: Yes, but not so rapidly. *Ib, Act 1*

76 Habit is a great deadener. VLADIMIR *Ib, Act 3*

**BECKFORD, William, 1759–1844**

77 I am not over-fond of resisting temptation. *Vathek*

**BECON, Thomas, 1512–1567**

78 For when the wine is in, the wit is out. *Catechism, 375*

**BEE, Bernard Elliott, 1823–1861**

79 There is Jackson standing like a stone wall. *First Battle of Bull Run, 1861*

**BEECHING, Henry Charles, 1859–1919**

80 First come I; my name is Jowett.
There's no knowledge but I know it.
I am Master of this College:
What I don't know isn't knowledge. *The Masque of Balliol*

**BEERBOHM, Sir Max, 1872–1956**

81 Most women are not so young as they are painted.
*A Defence of Cosmetics*

82 Zuleika, on a desert island, would have spent most of her time
in looking for a man's footprint. *Zuleika Dobson, Ch. 2*

83 She was one of the people who say, 'I don't know anything
about music really, but I know what I like.' *Ib, Ch. 9*

**BEERS, Ethel Lynn, 1827–1879**

84 All quiet along the Potomac tonight,
No sound save the rush of the river,
While soft falls the dew on the face of the dead –
The picket's off duty forever. *All Quiet Along the Potomac*

**BEHN, Aphra, 1640–1689**

85 Love ceases to be a pleasure, when it ceases to be a secret.
*La Montre, or The Lover's Watch, Four o'clock*

86 Variety is the soul of pleasure. WILLMORE *The Rover, Part 2, Act 1*

87 Fine clothes, rich furniture, jewels and plate are more inviting
than beauty unadorn'd.  PETRONELLA  *The Rover, Part 4, Act 2*

**BELLOC, Hilaire, 1870–1953**

88 Child! do not throw this book about;
   Refrain from the unholy pleasure
Of cutting all the pictures out!
   Preserve it as your chiefest treasure.   *The Bad Child's Book
of Beasts, Dedication*

89 When people call this beast to mind,
They marvel more and more
At such a little tail behind,
So large a trunk before.   *Ib, The Elephant*

90 The Chief Defect of Henry King
Was chewing little bits of String.   *Cautionary Tales, Henry
King*

91 Physicians of the Utmost Fame
Were called at once; but when they came
They answered, as they took their Fees,
'There is no Cure for this Disease.'   *Ib*

92 'Oh, my Friends, be warned by me,
That Breakfast, Dinner, Lunch and Tea
Are all the Human Frame requires. . . .'
With that the Wretched Child expires.   *Ib*

93 When I am dead, I hope it may be said:
'His sins were scarlet, but his books were read.'   *Epigrams,
On His Books*

94 Lord Finchley tried to mend the Electric Light
Himself. It struck him dead: And serve him right!
It is the business of the wealthy man
To give employment to the artisan.   *Ib, Lord Finchley*

95 The accursèd power which stands on Privilege
(And goes with Women, and Champagne and Bridge)
Broke – and Democracy resumed her reign:
(Which goes with Bridge, and Women and Champagne).
   *Ib, On a General Election*

96 The Devil, having nothing else to do,
Went off to tempt My Lady Poltagrue.
My Lady, tempted by a private whim,
To his extreme annoyance, tempted him.   *Ib, On Lady
Poltagrue, A Public Peril*

97 I said to Heart, 'How goes it?' Heart replied:
'Right as a Ribstone Pippin!' But it lied.   *The False Heart*

98 I'm tired of Love: I'm still more tired of Rhyme.
   But Money gives me pleasure all the Time.                  *Fatigue*

99 Birds in their little nests agree
   With Chinamen, but not with me.                            *On Food*

1 Remote and ineffectual Don
  That dared attack my Chesterton.                        *Lines to a Don*

2 The Microbe is so very small
  You cannot make him out at all.            *More Beasts for Worse
                                              Children, The Microbe*

3 Lord Hippo suffered fearful loss
  By putting money on a horse
  Which he believed, if it were pressed,
  Would run far faster than the rest.     *More Peers, Lord Hippo*

4 Lord Lucky, by a curious fluke,
  Became a most important duke,
  From living in a vile Hotel
  A long way east of Camberwell
  He rose in less than half an hour
  To riches, dignity and power.            *More Peers, Lord Lucky*

5 When I am living in the Midlands
     That are sodden and unkind,
  I light my lamp in the evening:
     My work is left behind;
  And the great hills of the South Country
     Come back into my mind.                   *The South Country*

6 If I ever become a rich man,
     Or if ever I grow to be old,
  I will build a house with deep thatch
     To shelter me from the cold,
  And there shall the Sussex songs be sung
     And the story of Sussex told.                              *Ib*

7 I will hold my house in the high wood
     Within a walk of the sea,
  And the men that were boys when I was a boy
     Shall sit and drink with me.                               *Ib*

8 Do you remember an Inn,
  Miranda?                                              *Tarantella*


**BENNETT, Enoch Arnold, 1867–1931**

9 'Ye can call it influenza if ye like,' said Mrs Machin. 'There was
  no influenza in my young days. We called a cold a cold.'
                                               *The Card, Ch. 8*

10 'And yet,' demanded Councillor Barlow ... 'what great cause is
he identified with?'
'He is identified,' said the speaker, 'with the great cause of
cheering us all up.'                                  *The Card, Ch. 12*

11 Being a husband is a whole-time job. That is why so many
husbands fail. They cannot give their entire attention to it.
CULVER                                              *The Title, Act 1*

12 There was a young man of Montrose,
Who had pockets in none of his clothes,
　　When asked by his lass
　　Where he carried his brass,
He said, 'Darling, I pay through the nose.'            *Limerick*

## BENSON, Arthur Christopher, 1862–1925

13 Land of Hope and Glory, Mother of the Free,
How shall we extol thee, who are born of thee?
Wider still and wider shall thy bounds be set;
God who made thee mighty, make thee mightier yet.
　　　*Land of Hope and Glory (Music by Sir Edward Elgar)*

## BENTHAM, Jeremy, 1748–1832

14 The greatest happiness of the greatest number is the foundation
of morals and legislation.                   *The Commonplace Book*

## BENTLEY, Edmund Clerihew, 1875–1956

15 The Art of Biography
Is different from Geography.
Geography is about Maps,
But Biography is about Chaps.               *Biography for Beginners,*
　　　　　　　　　　　　　　　　　　　　　　　*Introductory Remarks*

16 Sir Christopher Wren
Said, 'I am going to dine with some men.
If anybody calls
Say I am designing St Paul's.'          *Ib, Sir Christopher Wren*

17 What I like about Clive
Is that he is no longer alive.
There is a great deal to be said
For being dead.                                        *Ib, Clive*

18 Sir Humphry Davy
Detested gravy.
He lived in the odium
Of having discovered Sodium.            *Ib, Sir Humphry Davy*

19 George the Third
Ought never to have occurred.

One can only wonder
At so grotesque a blunder.    *More Biography, George the Third*

20  When their lordships asked Bacon
How many bribes he had taken
He had at least the grace
To get very red in the face.    *Baseless Biography, Bacon*

**BENTLEY, Nicolas Clerihew, 1907–1978**
21  Cecil B. de Mille,
Rather against his will,
Was persuaded to leave Moses
Out of 'The Wars of the Roses'.    *Clerihew*

**BERLIN, Irving, 1888–1989**
22  Come on and hear, come on and hear, Alexander's Ragtime
Band.    *Alexander's Ragtime Band*

**BERNARD, William Bayle, 1807–1875**
23  A Storm in a Teacup.    *Title of Farce*

**BETJEMAN, Sir John, 1906–1984**
24  The Church's Restoration
In eighteen-eighty-three
Has left for contemplation
Not what there used to be.    *Hymn*

25  Miss J. Hunter Dunn, Miss J. Hunter Dunn,
Furnish'd and burnish'd by Aldershot sun.    *A Subaltern's
Love-song*

# THE BIBLE
(Quotations are from the Authorised Version, 1611, unless otherwise
stated)

## OLD TESTAMENT
**Genesis**
26  In the beginning God created the heaven and the earth.
And the earth was without form, and void.    *1, 1–2*

27  And God said, Let there be light: and there was light.    *1, 3*

28  So God created man in his own image, in the image of God
created he him; male and female created he them.    *1, 27*

29  Be fruitful, and multiply, and replenish the earth.    *1, 28*

30 And God saw everything that he had made, and, behold, it was
   very good.                                         *Genesis, 1, 31*

31 And the Lord God took the man, and put him into the garden of
   Eden to dress it and to keep it.                          *2, 15*

32 And the Lord God said, It is not good that the man should be
   alone; I will make him an help meet for him.              *2, 18*

33 And the rib, which the Lord God had taken from man, made he
   a woman.                                                  *2, 22*

34 This is now bone of my bones, and flesh of my flesh.        *2, 23*

35 And they were both naked, the man and his wife, and were not
   ashamed.                                                  *2, 25*

36 Ye shall be as gods, knowing good and evil.                  *3, 5*

37 And they sewed fig leaves together, and made themselves
   aprons.                                                    *3, 7*

38 In the sweat of thy face shalt thou eat bread.              *3, 19*

39 For dust thou art, and unto dust shalt thou return.         *3, 19*

40 The mother of all living.                                   *3, 20*

41 Am I my brother's keeper?                                    *4, 9*

42 And the Lord set a mark upon Cain.                          *4, 15*

43 And all the days of Methuselah were nine hundred sixty and
   nine years.                                               *5, 27*

44 There were giants in the earth in those days.               *6, 4*

45 There went in two and two unto Noah into the ark, the male
   and the female.                                            *7, 9*

46 And the ark rested in the seventh month, on the seventeenth day
   of the month, upon the mountains of Ararat.               *8, 4*

47 And the dove came in to him in the evening; and, lo, in her
   mouth was an olive leaf pluckt off.                       *8, 11*

48 While the earth remaineth, seedtime and harvest, and cold and
   heat, and summer and winter, and day and night shall not cease.
                                                             *8, 22*

49 Whoso sheddeth man's blood, by man shall his blood be shed.
                                                              *9, 6*

50 I do set my bow in the cloud.                              *9, 13*

51 Even as Nimrod the mighty hunter before the Lord.          *10, 9*

52 Therefore is the name of it called Babel; because the Lord did
   there confound the language of all the earth.            *11, 9*

53 His hand will be against every man, and every man's hand
   against him.                                             *16, 12*

54 Shall not the Judge of all the earth do right?            *18, 25*

55 If I find in Sodom fifty righteous within the city, then I will spare
all the place for their sakes.                                   *Genesis, 18, 26*

56 But his wife looked back from behind him, and she became a
pillar of salt.                                                              *19, 26*

57 In thy seed shall the nations of the earth be blessed.        *22, 18*

58 He sold his birthright unto Jacob.                                      *25, 33*

59 Esau my brother is a hairy man, and I am a smooth man.
                                                                                   *27, 11*

60 The voice is Jacob's voice, but the hands are the hands of Esau.
                                                                                   *27, 22*

61 A ladder set up on the earth, and the top of it reached to heaven.
                                                                                   *28, 12*

62 He made him a coat of many colours.                              *37, 3*

63 Behold, this dreamer cometh.                                          *37, 19*

64 Jacob saw that there was corn in Egypt.                          *42, 1*

65 Ye shall eat the fat of the land.                                        *45, 18*

66 Unstable as water, thou shalt not excel.                          *49, 4*


## Exodus

67 Now there arose up a new king over Egypt, which knew not
Joseph.                                                                             *1, 8*

68 I have been a stranger in a strange land.                          *2, 22*

69 Behold, the bush burned with fire, and the bush was not
consumed.                                                                          *3, 2*

70 A land flowing with milk and honey.                                *3, 8*

71 I AM THAT I AM.                                                              *3, 14*

72 Ye shall no more give the people straw to make brick.      *5, 7*

73 Let my people go, that they may serve me.                       *8, 1*

74 This is the finger of God.                                                  *8, 19*

75 Darkness which may be felt.                                            *10, 21*

76 But the Lord hardened Pharaoh's heart, and he would not let
them go.                                                                            *10, 27*

77 The Lord smote all the firstborn in the land of Egypt.      *12, 29*

78 And the children of Israel went into the midst of the sea upon
the dry ground.                                                                  *14, 22*

79 Would to God we had died by the hand of the Lord in the land
of Egypt, when we sat by the flesh pots, and when we did eat
bread to the full.                                                               *16, 3*

80 And when the children of Israel saw it, they said one to another,
It is manna: for they wist not what it was. And Moses said unto
them, This is the bread which the Lord hath given you to eat.
*Exodus, 16, 15*

81 I am the Lord thy God, which have brought thee out of the land
of Egypt, out of the house of bondage. *20, 2*

82 Thou shalt have no other gods before me. *20, 3*

83 Thou shalt not make unto thee any graven image. *20, 4*

84 For I the Lord thy God am a jealous God, visiting the iniquity
of the fathers upon the children unto the third and fourth
generation of them that hate me. *20, 5*

85 Thou shalt not take the name of the Lord thy God in vain.
*20, 7*

86 Remember the sabbath day, to keep it holy.
Six days shalt thou labour, and do all thy work:
But the seventh day is the sabbath of the Lord thy God.
*20, 8–10*

87 Honour thy father and thy mother: that thy days may be long
unto the land which the Lord thy God giveth thee. *20, 12*

88 Thou shalt not kill. *20, 13*

89 Thou shalt not commit adultery. *20, 14*

90 Thou shalt not steal. *20, 15*

91 Thou shalt not bear false witness against thy neighbour.
*20, 16*

92 Thou shalt not covet thy neighbour's house, thou shalt not
covet thy neighbour's wife, nor his manservant, nor his maid-
servant, nor his ox, nor his ass, nor any thing that is thy neighbour's. *20, 17*

93 Thou shalt give life for life,
Eye for eye, tooth for tooth, hand for hand, foot for foot.
*21, 23–24*

94 Thou shalt not suffer a witch to live. *22, 18*

95 Thou art a stiffnecked people. *33, 3*

**Leviticus**

96 Let him go for a scapegoat into the wilderness. *16, 10*

97 Ye shall be holy; for I the Lord your God am holy. *19, 2*

98 And thou shalt not glean thy vineyard, neither shalt thou gather
every grape of thy vineyard; thou shalt leave them for the poor
and stranger. *19, 10*

99 Thou shalt love thy neighbour as thyself. *19, 18*

1 Thou shalt rise up before the hoary head, and honour the face
of the old man. *Leviticus, 19, 32*

## Numbers

2 The Lord bless thee, and keep thee: The Lord make his face
shine upon thee, and be gracious unto thee: the Lord lift up
his countenance upon thee, and give thee peace. *6, 24–26*

3 We will go by the king's high way. *20, 17*

4 Let me die the death of the righteous, and let my last end be
like his! *23, 10*

## Deuteronomy

5 Hear, O Israel: The Lord our God is one Lord. *6, 4*

6 And thou shalt love the Lord thy God with all thine heart, and
with all thy soul, and with all thy might. *6, 5*

7 Man doth not live by bread only, but by every word that proceedeth out of the mouth of the Lord doth man live. *8, 3*

8 As a man chasteneth his son, so the Lord God chasteneth thee.
*8, 5*

9 And now, Israel, what doth the Lord thy God require of thee,
but to fear the Lord thy God, to walk in all his ways, and to love
him and to serve the Lord thy God with all thy heart and with all
thy soul. *10, 12*

10 Love ye therefore the stranger: for ye were strangers in the land
of Egypt. *10, 19*

11 For the poor shall never cease out of the land. *15, 11*

12 Thou shalt not muzzle the ox when he treadeth out the corn.
*25, 4*

13 I have set before you life and death, blessing and cursing: therefore choose life, that both thou and thy seed may live. *30, 19*

14 He kept him as the apple of his eye. *32, 10*

15 Jeshurun waxed fat, and kicked. *32, 15*

16 As thy days, so shall thy strength be. *33, 25*

17 The eternal God is thy refuge, and underneath are the everlasting
arms. *33, 27*

## Joshua

18 Be strong and of a good courage. *1, 6*

19 Hewers of wood and drawers of water. *9, 21*

20 Sun, stand thou still upon Gibeon; and thou, Moon, in the
valley of Ajalon. *10, 12*

## Judges

21 I arose a mother in Israel.      *5, 7*

22 The stars in their courses fought against Sisera.      *5, 20*

23 She brought forth butter in a lordly dish.      *5, 25*

24 Have they not divided the prey; to every man a damsel or two?
     *5, 30*

25 Faint, yet pursuing.      *8, 4*

26 Say now Shibboleth.      *12, 6*

27 Out of the eater came forth meat, and out of the strong came
forth sweetness.      *14, 14*

28 He smote them hip and thigh.      *15, 8*

29 If I be shaven, then my strength will go from me.      *16, 17*

30 He bowed himself with all his might; and the house fell upon the
lords, and upon all the people that were therein.      *16, 30*

31 From Dan even to Beer-sheba.      *20, 1*

32 Every man did that which was right in his own eyes.      *21, 25*

## Ruth

33 Whither thou goest, I will go; and where thou lodgest, I will
lodge: thy people shall be my people, and thy God my God.
     *1, 16*

34 The Lord do so to me, and more also, if ought but death part
thee and me.      *1, 17*

35 And she went, and came, and gleaned in the field after the
reapers.      *2, 3*

## 1 Samuel

36 Speak, Lord; for thy servant heareth.      *3, 9*

37 It is the Lord: let him do what seemeth him good.      *3, 18*

38 Quit yourselves like men.      *4, 9*

39 Is Saul also among the prophets?      *10, 11*

40 The Lord hath sought him a man after his own heart.      *13, 14*

41 Agag came unto him delicately.      *15, 32*

42 Man looketh on the outward appearance, but the Lord looketh
on the heart.      *16, 7*

43 David took an harp, and played with his hand.      *16, 23*

44 Saul hath slain his thousands, and David his ten thousands.
     *18, 7*

45 David therefore departed thence, and escaped to the cave
Adullam.      *22, 1*

## 2 Samuel

46 How are the mighty fallen!     *1, 19*

47 Tell it not in Gath, publish it not in the streets of Askelon; lest the daughters of the Philistines rejoice, lest the daughters of the uncircumcised triumph.     *1, 20*

48 Saul and Jonathan were lovely and pleasant in their lives, and in their death they were not divided: they were swifter than eagles, they were stronger than lions.     *1, 23*

49 Thy love to me was wonderful, passing the love of women.
    *1, 26*

50 Abner with the hinder end of the spear smote him under the fifth rib.     *2, 23*

51 Would God I had died for thee, O Absalom, my son, my son!
    *18, 33*

52 The sweet psalmist of Israel.     *23, 1*


## 1 Kings

53 Divide the living child in two.     *3, 25*

54 There came of all people to hear the wisdom of Solomon.
    *4, 34*

55 The barrel of meal shall not waste, neither shall the cruse of oil fail.     *17, 14*

56 How long halt ye between two opinions?     *18, 21*

57 There ariseth a little cloud out of the sea, like a man's hand.
    *18, 44*

58 A still small voice.     *19, 12*

59 Elijah passed by him, and cast his mantle upon him.     *19, 19*


## 2 Kings

60 Go up, thou bald head.     *2, 23*

61 There is death in the pot.     *4, 40*

62 The driving is like the driving of Jehu the son of Nimshi; for he driveth furiously.     *9, 20*


## Esther

63 Let it be written among the laws of the Persians and the Medes, that it be not altered.     *1, 19*

64 The king loved Esther above all the women.     *2, 17*

**Job**

65 Naked came I out of my mother's womb, and naked shall I return thither: the Lord gave, and the Lord hath taken away; blessed be the name of the Lord. *1, 21*

66 Shall mortal man be more just than God? shall a man be more pure than his maker? *4, 17*

67 Man is born unto trouble, as the sparks fly upward. *5, 7*

68 Though he slay me, yet will I trust in him. *13, 15*

69 Man that is born of a woman is of few days, and full of trouble. *14, 1*

70 Miserable comforters are ye all. *16, 2*

71 I am escaped with the skin of my teeth. *19, 20*

72 I know that my redeemer liveth. *19, 25*

73 The price of wisdom is above rubies. *28, 18*

74 I was eyes to the blind, and feet was I to the lame. *29, 15*

75 Great men are not always wise. *32, 9*

76 Who is this that darkeneth counsel by words without knowledge? *38, 2*

77 Hath the rain a father? *38, 28*

78 Canst thou draw out leviathan with an hook? *41, 1*

79 I have heard of thee by the hearing of the ear: but now mine eye seeth thee. *42, 5*

**Psalms**

80 Why do the heathen rage, and the people imagine a vain thing? *2, 1*

81 Out of the mouth of babes and sucklings hast thou ordained strength. *8, 2*

82 What is man, that thou art mindful of him? *8, 4*

83 Thou hast made him a little lower than the angels. *8, 5*

84 The fool hath said in his heart, There is no God. *14, 1*

85 Keep me as the apple of the eye, hide me under the shadow of thy wings. *17, 8*

86 The heavens declare the glory of God; and the firmament sheweth his handywork. *19, 1*

87 Day unto day uttereth speech, and night unto night sheweth knowledge. *19, 2*

88 More to be desired are they than gold, yea, than much fine gold: sweeter also than honey and the honeycomb. *19, 10*

89 Let the words of my mouth, and the meditation of my heart, be acceptable in thy sight, O Lord, my strength, and my redeemer.
*Psalms, 19, 14*

90 Some trust in chariots, and some in horses: but we will remember the name of the Lord our God.                    *20, 7*

91 The Lord is my shepherd; I shall not want.                    *23, 1*

92 He maketh me to lie down in green pastures: he leadeth me beside the still waters.                    *23, 2*

93 Yea, though I walk through the valley of the shadow of death, I will fear no evil: for thou art with me; thy rod and thy staff they comfort me.                    *23, 4*

94 The earth is the Lord's, and the fulness thereof; the world, and they that dwell therein.                    *24, 1*

95 Weeping may endure for a night, but joy cometh in the morning.
*30, 5*

96 Into thy hands I commend my spirit.   *31, 6, Book of Common Prayer version*

97 Praise the Lord with harp: sing unto him with the psaltery and an instrument of ten strings.                    *33, 2*

98 Sing unto him a new song, play skilfully with a loud noise.  *33, 3*

99 O taste and see that the Lord is good.                    *34, 8*

1 The Lord is nigh unto them that are of a broken heart. *34, 18*

2 But the meek shall inherit the earth.                    *37, 11*

3 I have been young, and now am old; yet have I not seen the righteous forsaken, nor his seed begging bread.   ·   *37, 25*

4 I myself have seen the ungodly in great power: and flourishing like a green bay-tree.   *37, 36, Book of Common Prayer version*

5 Lord, make me to know mine end, and the measure of my days.
*39, 4*

6 Blessed is he that considereth the poor.                    *41, 1*

7 God is our refuge and strength, a very present help in trouble.
*46, 1*

8 Purge me with hyssop, and I shall be clean, wash me, and I shall be whiter than snow.                    *51, 7*

9 The sacrifices of God are a broken spirit: a broken and a contrite heart, O God, thou wilt not despise.                    *51, 17*

10 Oh that I had wings like a dove!                    *55, 6*

11 They are like the deaf adder that stoppeth her ear.    *58, 4*

12 They grin like a dog, and run about through the city.
*59, 6, Book of Common Prayer version*

13 Make a joyful noise unto God.                 *Psalms, 66, 1*

14 They go from strength to strength.                      *84, 7*

15 I had rather be a doorkeeper in the house of my God, than to dwell in the tents of wickedness.                      *84, 10*

16 For a thousand years in thy sight are but as yesterday when it is past, and as a watch in the night.                      *90, 4*

17 The days of our years are threescore years and ten; and if by reason of strength they be fourscore years, yet is their strength labour and sorrow; for it is soon cut off, and we fly away. *90, 10*

18 So teach us to number our days, that we may apply our hearts unto wisdom.                      *90, 12*

19 He shall cover thee with his feathers, and under his wings shalt thou trust.                      *91, 4*

20 Thou shalt not be afraid for the terror by night; nor for the arrow that flieth by day.                      *91, 5*

21 Nor for the pestilence that walketh in darkness: nor for the destruction that wasteth at noonday.                      *91, 6*

22 Like as a father pitieth his children, so the Lord pitieth them that fear him.                      *103, 13*

23 As for man, his days are as grass: as a flower of the field, so he flourisheth.                      *103, 15*

24 Wine that maketh glad the heart of man.                      *104, 15*

25 The iron entered into his soul.      *105, 18, Book of Common Prayer version*

26 They that go down to the sea in ships, that do business in great waters.                      *107, 23*

27 They reel to and fro, and stagger like a drunken man, and are at their wits' end.                      *107, 27*

28 The fear of the Lord is the beginning of wisdom.      *111, 10*

29 The mountains skipped like rams, and the little hills like lambs.
                      *114, 4*

30 They have mouths, but they speak not: eyes have they, but they see not.                      *115, 5*

31 They have ears, but they hear not: noses have they, but they smell not.                      *115, 6*

32 I said in my haste, All men are liars.                      *116, 11*

33 Precious in the sight of the Lord is the death of his saints.
                      *116, 15*

34 It is better to trust in the Lord than to put confidence in man.
                      *118, 8*

35 The stone which the builders refused is become the head stone of the corner.      *Psalms, 118, 22*

36 I am for peace: but when I speak, they are for war.      *120, 7*

37 I will lift up mine eyes unto the hills, from whence cometh my help.      *121, 1*

38 The sun shall not smite thee by day, nor the moon by night.      *121, 6*

39 The Lord shall preserve thy going out and thy coming in from this time forth, and even for evermore.      *121, 8*

40 They that sow in tears shall reap in joy.      *126, 5*

41 Except the Lord build the house, they labour in vain that build it.      *127, 1*

42 It is vain for you to rise up early, to sit up late, to eat the bread of sorrows: for so he giveth his beloved sleep.      *127, 2*

43 Behold, how good and how pleasant it is for brethren to dwell together in unity!      *133, 1*

44 By the rivers of Babylon, there we sat down, yea, we wept, when we remembered Zion.      *137, 1*

45 We hanged our harps upon the willows in the midst thereof.      *137, 2*

46 Sing us one of the songs of Zion.      *137, 3*

47 How shall we sing the Lord's song in a strange land?      *137, 4*

48 If I forget thee, O Jerusalem, let my right hand forget her cunning.      *137, 5*

49 If I do not remember thee, let my tongue cleave to the roof of my mouth.      *137, 6*

50 I am fearfully and wonderfully made.      *139, 14*

51 Set a watch, O Lord, before my mouth; keep the door of my lips.      *141, 3*

52 The eyes of all wait upon thee; and thou givest them their meat in due season.      *145, 15*

53 Put not your trust in princes.      *146, 3*

**Proverbs**

54 The fear of the Lord is the beginning of knowledge.      *1, 7*

55 Whom the Lord loveth he correcteth.      *3, 12*

56 Her ways are ways of pleasantness, and all her paths are peace.      *3, 17*

57 Go to the ant, thou sluggard; consider her ways, and be wise.      *6, 6*

58 For wisdom is better than rubies.               *Proverbs, 8, 11*

59 Wisdom hath builded her house, she hath hewn out her seven
   pillars.                                                   *9, 1*

60 Stolen waters are sweet, and bread eaten in secret is pleasant.
                                                             *9, 17*

61 A wise son maketh a glad father: but a foolish son is the heaviness of his mother.                                       *10, 1*

62 The memory of the just is blessed.                        *10, 7*

63 In the multitude of counsellers there is safety.         *11, 14*

64 As a jewel of gold in a swine's snout, so is a fair woman which is
   without discretion.                                      *11, 22*

65 A virtuous woman is a crown to her husband: but she that
   maketh ashamed is as rottenness in his bones.            *12, 4*

66 Hope deferred maketh the heart sick.                     *13, 12*

67 He that spareth his rod hateth his son: but he that loveth him
   chasteneth him betimes.                                  *13, 24*

68 Righteousness exalteth a nation.                         *14, 34*

69 A soft answer turneth away wrath.                         *15, 1*

70 A merry heart maketh a cheerful countenance.             *15, 13*

71 Better is a dinner of herbs where love is, than a stalled ox and
   hatred therewith.                                        *15, 17*

72 Pride goeth before destruction, and an haughty spirit before a
   fall.                                                    *16, 18*

73 Even a fool, when he holdeth his peace, is counted wise. *17, 28*

74 Wealth maketh many friends.                               *19, 4*

75 Wine is a mocker, strong drink is raging: and whosoever is
   deceived thereby is not wise.                             *20, 1*

76 Even a child is known by his doings.                     *20, 11*

77 It is naught, it is naught, saith the buyer; but when he is gone
   his way, then he boasteth.                               *20, 14*

78 The glory of young men is their strength.                *20, 29*

79 A good name is rather to be chosen than great riches.    *22, 1*

80 Train up a child in the way he should go: and when he is old,
   he will not depart from it.                               *22, 6*

81 If thine enemy be hungry, give him bread to eat; and if he be
   thirsty, give him water to drink:
   For thou shalt heap coals of fire upon his head, and the Lord
   shall reward thee.                                     *25, 21–22*

82 As cold waters to a thirsty soul, so is good news from a far
   country.                                                *25, 25*

83 A whip for the horse, a bridle for the ass, and a rod for the fool's back. *Proverbs, 26, 3*

84 As a dog returneth to his vomit, so a fool returneth to his folly. *26, 11*

85 Whoso diggeth a pit shall fall therein. *26, 27*

86 Open rebuke is better than secret love. *27, 5*

87 Faithful are the wounds of a friend. *27, 6*

88 He that maketh haste to be rich shall not be innocent. *28, 20*

89 Where there is no vision, the people perish. *29, 18*

90 Give me neither poverty nor riches; feed me with food convenient for me. *30, 8*

91 There be three things which are too wonderful for me, yea, four which I know not: The way of an eagle in the air; the way of a serpent upon a rock; the way of a ship in the midst of the sea; and the way of a man with a maid. *30, 18–19*

92 Who can find a virtuous woman? for her price is far above rubies. *31, 10*

## Ecclesiastes

93 Vanity of vanities, saith the Preacher, vanity of vanities; all is vanity. *1, 2*

94 What profit hath a man of all his labour which he taketh under the sun? *1, 3*

95 One generation passeth away, and another generation cometh: but the earth abideth for ever. *1, 4*

96 There is no new thing under the sun. *1, 9*

97 For in much wisdom is much grief: and he that increaseth knowledge increaseth sorrow. *1, 18*

98 To every thing there is a season, and a time to every purpose under the heaven. *3, 1*

99 A threefold cord is not quickly broken. *4, 12*

 1 God is in heaven, and thou upon earth: therefore let thy words be few. *5, 2*

 2 The sleep of a labouring man is sweet. *5, 12*

 3 A good name is better than precious ointment; and the day of death than the day of one's birth. *7, 1*

 4 For as the crackling of thorns under a pot, so is the laughter of the fool. *7, 6*

 5 Say not thou, What is the cause that the former days were better than these? for thou dost not inquire wisely concerning this. *7, 10*

6 Be not righteous over much.                    *Ecclesiastes, 7, 16*

7 Whatsoever thy hand findeth to do, do it with thy might.
                                                        *9, 10*

8 The race is not to the swift, nor the battle to the strong, neither yet bread to the wise, nor yet riches to men of understanding, nor yet favour to men of skill; but time and chance happeneth to them all.                                       *9, 11*

9 Cast thy bread upon the waters: for thou shalt find it after many days.                                                *11, 1*

10 Rejoice, O young man, in thy youth.              *11, 9*

11 Remember now thy Creator in the days of thy youth, while the evil days come not, nor the years draw nigh, when thou shalt say, I have no pleasure in them.              *12, 1*

12 Man goeth to his long home.                      *12, 5*

13 Of making many books there is no end; and much study is a weariness of the flesh.                              *12, 12*

14 Let us hear the conclusion of the whole matter: Fear God, and keep his commandments: for this is the whole duty of man.
                                                        *12, 13*

## The Song of Solomon

15 Let him kiss me with the kisses of his mouth: for thy love is better than wine.                                *1, 2*

16 I am black, but comely, O ye daughters of Jerusalem.    *1, 5*

17 I am the rose of Sharon, and the lily of the valleys.    *2, 1*

18 His banner over me was love.                      *2, 4*

19 Stay me with flagons, comfort me with apples: for I am sick of love.                                            *2, 5*

20 Rise up, my love, my fair one, and come away.     *2, 10*

21 For, lo, the winter is past, the rain is over and gone.   *2, 11*

22 The flowers appear on the earth; the time of the singing of birds is come, and the voice of the turtle is heard in our land.  *2, 12*

23 Our vines have tender grapes.                      *2, 15*

24 Until the day break, and the shadows flee away.    *2, 17*

25 I sleep, but my heart waketh.                      *5, 2*

26 Terrible as an army with banners.                  *6, 4*

27 Love is strong as death; jealousy is cruel as the grave.   *8, 6*

28 Many waters cannot quench love.                    *8, 7*

Isaiah

29 The ox knoweth his owner, and the ass his master's crib. *1, 3*

30 Though your sins be as scarlet, they shall be as white as snow.
*1, 18*

31 They shall beat their swords into plowshares, and their spears into pruning-hooks: nation shall not lift up sword against nation, neither shall they learn war any more. *2, 4*

32 What mean ye that ye beat my people to pieces, and grind the faces of the poor? *3, 15*

33 Woe unto them that call evil good, and good evil. *5, 20*

34 A virgin shall conceive, and bear a son, and shall call his name Immanuel. *7, 14*

35 The people that walked in darkness have seen a great light. *9, 2*

36 For unto us a child is born, unto us a son is given: and the government shall be upon his shoulder: and his name shall be called Wonderful, Counseller, The mighty God, The everlasting Father, The Prince of Peace. *9, 6*

37 The wolf also shall dwell with the lamb, and the leopard shall lie down with the kid; and the calf and the young lion and the fatling together; and a little child shall lead them. *11, 6*

38 How art thou fallen from heaven, O Lucifer, son of the morning!
*14, 12*

39 Watchman, what of the night? *21, 11*

40 Let us eat and drink; for to-morrow we shall die. *22, 13*

41 Set thine house in order: for thou shalt die. *38, 1*

42 All flesh is grass. *40, 6*

43 Behold, the nations are as a drop of a bucket. *40, 15*

44 A bruised reed shall he not break, and the smoking flax shall he not quench. *42, 3*

45 There is no peace, saith the Lord, unto the wicked. *48, 22*

46 How beautiful upon the mountains are the feet of him that bringeth good tidings. *52, 7*

47 He is despised and rejected of men; a man of sorrows, and acquainted with grief. *53, 3*

48 All we like sheep have gone astray. *53, 6*

49 He is brought as a lamb to the slaughter. *53, 7*

50 Seek ye the Lord while he may be found, call ye upon him while he is near. *55, 6*

51 For my thoughts are not your thoughts, neither are your ways my ways, saith the Lord. *55, 8*

52 Is it such a fast that I have chosen? a day for a man to afflict his soul? *Isaiah, 58, 5*

53 To give unto them beauty for ashes, the oil of joy for mourning, the garment of praise for the spirit of heaviness. *61, 3*

## Jeremiah

54 They have healed also the hurt of the daughter of my people slightly, saying, Peace, peace; when there is no peace. *6, 14*

55 Is there no balm in Gilead; is there no physician there? *8, 22*

56 Can the Ethiopian change his skin, or the leopard his spots? *13, 23*

57 As the clay is in the potter's hand, so are ye in mine hand, O house of Israel. *18, 6*

58 The fathers have eaten a sour grape, and the children's teeth are set on edge. *31, 29*

## Lamentations

59 Is it nothing to you, all ye that pass by? behold, and see if there be any sorrow like unto my sorrow. *1, 12*

60 Remembering mine affliction and my misery, the wormwood and the gall. *3, 19*

61 His compassions fail not. They are new every morning. *3, 22–23*

62 It is good for a man that he bear the yoke in his youth. *3, 27*

## Ezekiel

63 They four had one likeness, as if a wheel had been in the midst of a wheel. *10, 10*

64 The king of Babylon stood at the parting of the way. *21, 21*

65 O ye dry bones, hear the word of the Lord. *37, 4*

66 Son of man, set thy face against Gog, the land of Magog. *38, 2*

## Daniel

67 And he commanded the most mighty men that were in his army to bind Shadrach, Meshach, and Abed-nego, and to cast them into the burning fiery furnace. *3, 20*

68 MENE, MENE, TEKEL, UPHARSIN. *5, 25*

69 Thou art weighed in the balances, and art found wanting. *5, 27*

70 Thy kingdom is divided, and given to the Medes and Persians. *5, 28*

71 The law of the Medes and Persians, which altereth not.
*Daniel, 6, 12*

72 They brought Daniel, and cast him into the den of lions. *6, 16*

73 The Ancient of days. *7, 13*

74 O Daniel, a man greatly beloved. *10, 11*

## Hosea
75 I desired mercy, and not sacrifice; and the knowledge of God more than burnt offerings. *6, 6*

76 They have sown the wind, and they shall reap the whirlwind. *8, 7*

77 I drew them with cords of a man, with bands of love. *11, 4*

## Joel
78 Rend your heart, and not your garments. *2, 13*

79 The years that the locust hath eaten. *2, 25*

80 Your old men shall dream dreams, your young men shall see visions. *2, 28*

81 Multitudes in the valley of decision. *3, 14*

## Amos
82 Can two walk together, except they be agreed? *3, 3*

83 Prepare to meet thy God. *4, 12*

84 Woe to them that are at ease in Zion. *6, 1*

## Jonah
85 So they cast lots, and the lot fell upon Jonah. *1, 7*

86 Jonah was in the belly of the fish three days and three nights. *1, 17*

87 And God said to Jonah, Doest thou well to be angry for the gourd? *4, 9*

88 And should not I spare Nineveh, that great city, wherein are more than sixscore thousand persons that cannot discern between their right hand and their left hand; and also much cattle? *4, 11*

## Micah
89 They shall sit every man under his vine and under his fig tree. *4, 4*

90 O my people, what have I done unto thee? and wherein have I wearied thee? *6, 3*

91 What doth the Lord require of thee, but to do justly, and to love mercy, and to walk humbly with thy God?     *Micah*, *6, 8*

**Habakkuk**

92 Thou art of purer eyes than to behold evil.      *1, 13*

93 Write the vision, and make it plain upon tables, that he may run that readeth it.      *2, 2*

**Haggai**

94 The glory of this latter house shall be greater than of the former.      *2, 9*

**Zechariah**

95 Is not this a brand plucked out of the fire?      *3, 2*

96 Who hath despised the day of small things?      *4, 10*

97 What are these wounds in thine hands? Then he shall answer, Those with which I was wounded in the house of my friends.      *13, 6*

**Malachi**

98 Have we not all one father? hath not one God created us?   *2, 10*

99 The Lord, whom ye seek, shall suddenly come to his temple.      *3, 1*

 1 Unto you that fear my name shall the Sun of righteousness arise with healing in his wings.      *4, 2*


## THE NEW TESTAMENT

**St Matthew**

 2 Where is he that is born King of the Jews? for we have seen his star in the east, and are come to worship him.      *2, 2*

 3 Rachel weeping for her children, and would not be comforted, because they are not.      *2, 18*

 4 Repent ye: for the kingdom of heaven is at hand.      *3, 2*

 5 The voice of one crying in the wilderness.      *3, 3*

 6 O generation of vipers, who hath warned you to flee from the wrath to come?      *3, 7*

 7 Man shall not live by bread alone, but by every word that proceedeth out of the mouth of God.      *4, 4*

 8 Follow me, and I will make you fishers of men.      *4, 19*

 9 Blessed are the meek: for they shall inherit the earth.      *5, 5*

10 Blessed are the pure in heart: for they shall see God.
*St Matthew, 5, 8*

11 Ye are the salt of the earth: but if the salt have lost his savour, wherewith shall it be salted? *5, 13*

12 An eye for an eye, and a tooth for a tooth. *5, 38*

13 Resist not evil: but whosoever shall smite thee on thy right cheek, turn to him the other also. *5, 39*

14 Love your enemies. *5, 44*

15 He maketh his sun to rise on the evil and on the good, and sendeth rain on the just and on the unjust. *5, 45*

16 Let not thy left hand know what thy right hand doeth. *6, 3*

17 Use not vain repetitions. *6, 7*

18 After this manner therefore pray ye: Our Father which art in heaven, Hallowed be thy name. Thy kingdom come. Thy will be done in earth, as it is in heaven. Give us this day our daily bread. And forgive us our debts, as we forgive our debtors. And lead us not into temptation, but deliver us from evil: For thine is the kingdom, and the power, and the glory, for ever. Amen. *6, 9–13*

19 No man can serve two masters. *6, 24*

20 Ye cannot serve God and mammon. *Ib*

21 Consider the lilies of the field, how they grow; they toil not, neither do they spin. *6, 28*

22 Sufficient unto the day is the evil thereof. *6, 34*

23 Judge not, that ye be not judged. *7, 1*

24 Neither cast ye your pearls before swine. *7, 6*

25 Therefore all things whatsoever ye would that men should do to you, do ye even so to them: for this is the law and the prophets. *7, 12*

26 Enter ye in at the strait gate. *7, 13*

27 Beware of false prophets, which come to you in sheep's clothing, but inwardly they are ravening wolves. *7, 15*

28 A man under authority. *8, 9*

29 What went ye out into the wilderness to see? A reed shaken with the wind? *11, 7*

30 He that is not with me is against me. *12, 30*

31 One pearl of great price. *13, 46*

32 A prophet is not without honour, save in his own country. *13, 57*

33 If the blind lead the blind, both shall fall into the ditch. *15, 14*

34 Thou art Peter, and upon this rock I will build my church; and the gates of hell shall not prevail against it. *St Matthew, 16, 18*

35 The keys of the kingdom of heaven.                    *16, 19*

36 Get thee behind me, Satan.                            *16, 23*

37 Except ye be converted, and become as little children, ye shall not enter into the kingdom of heaven.         *18, 3*

38 But whoso shall offend one of these little ones which believe in me, it were better for him that a millstone were hanged about his neck, and that he were drowned in the depth of the sea.
*18, 6*

39 If thine eye offend thee, pluck it out.               *18, 9*

40 Until seventy times seven.                            *18, 22*

41 It is easier for a camel to go through the eye of a needle, than for a rich man to enter into the kingdom of God.     *19, 24*

42 For many are called, but few are chosen.             *22, 14*

43 Render therefore unto Caesar the things which are Caesar's; and unto God the things that are God's.         *22, 21*

44 Ye blind guides, which strain at a gnat, and swallow a camel.
*23, 24*

45 Wars and rumours of wars.                            *24, 6*

46 For unto every one that hath shall be given, and he shall have abundance: but from him that hath not shall be taken away even that which he hath.                              *25, 29*

47 As a shepherd divideth his sheep from the goats.     *25, 32*

48 Inasmuch as ye have done it unto one of the least of these my brethren, ye have done it unto me.              *25, 40*

49 Ye have the poor always with you.                     *26, 11*

50 Watch and pray, that ye enter not into temptation: the spirit indeed is willing, but the flesh is weak.       *26, 41*

51 He took water, and washed his hands before the multitude, saying, I am innocent of the blood of this just person.   *27, 24*

52 I am with you alway, even unto the end of the world.  *28, 20*

**St Mark**

53 They that are whole have no need of the physician, but they that are sick.                                       *2, 17*

54 The sabbath was made for man, and not man for the sabbath.
*2, 27*

55 If a house be divided against itself, that house cannot stand.
*3, 25*

56 He that hath ears to hear, let him hear. *St Mark, 4, 9*

57 My name is Legion: for we are many. 5, 9

58 For what shall it profit a man, if he shall gain the whole world and lose his own soul? 8, 36

59 I believe: help thou mine unbelief. 9, 24

60 What therefore God hath joined together, let not man put asunder. 10, 9

61 Suffer the little children to come unto me, and forbid them not: for of such is the kingdom of God. 10, 14

62 Is it not written, My house shall be called of all nations the house of prayer? but ye have made it a den of thieves. 11, 17

63 And there came a certain poor widow, and she threw in two mites, which make a farthing. 12, 42

64 Take ye heed, watch and pray. 13, 33

65 Before the cock crow twice, thou shalt deny me thrice. 14, 30

66 Crucify him. 15, 13

## St Luke

67 There was no room for them in the inn. 2, 7

68 And there were in the same country shepherds abiding in the field, keeping watch over their flock by night. 2, 8

69 Ye shall find the babe wrapped in swaddling clothes, lying in a manger. 2, 12

70 Glory to God in the highest, and on earth peace, good will toward men. 2, 14

71 Be content with your wages. 3, 14

72 Physician, heal thyself. 4, 23

73 No man putteth new wine into old bottles. 5, 37

74 No man, having put his hand to the plough, and looking back, is fit for the kingdom of God. 9, 62

75 The labourer is worthy of his hire. 10, 7

76 Fell among thieves. 10, 30

77 He passed by on the other side. 10, 31

78 Friend, go up higher. 14, 10

79 The poor, and the maimed, and the halt, and the blind.
14, 21

80 Joy shall be in heaven over one sinner that repenteth, more than over ninety and nine just persons, which need no repentance.
15, 7

81 And he would fain have filled his belly with the husks that the swine did eat. *St Luke*, *15, 16*

82 Bring hither the fatted calf, and kill it. *15, 23*

83 I cannot dig; to beg I am ashamed. *16, 3*

84 The children of this world are in their generation wiser than the children of light. *16, 8*

85 Make to yourselves friends of the mammon of unrighteousness. *16, 9*

86 The crumbs which fell from the rich man's table. *16, 21*

87 Between us and you there is a great gulf fixed. *16, 26*

88 Remember Lot's wife. *17, 32*

89 I thank thee, that I am not as other men are. *18, 11*

90 Out of thine own mouth will I judge thee. *19, 22*

91 Father, forgive them; for they know not what they do. *23, 34*


## St John

92 In the beginning was the Word, and the Word was with God, and the Word was God. *1, 1*

93 The true Light, which lighteth every man that cometh into the world. *1, 9*

94 He came unto his own, and his own received him not. *1, 11*

95 The Word was made flesh, and dwelt among us. *1, 14*

96 Can there any good thing come out of Nazareth? *1, 46*

97 Ye must be born again. *3, 7*

98 The wind bloweth where it listeth. *3, 8*

99 For God so loved the world, that he gave his only begotten Son, that whosoever believeth in him should not perish, but have everlasting life. *3, 16*

1 Men loved darkness rather than light, because their deeds were evil. *3, 19*

2 Judge not according to the appearance, but judge righteous judgment. *7, 24*

3 He that is without sin among you, let him first cast a stone at her. *8, 7*

4 I am the light of the world. *8, 12*

5 The night cometh, when no man can work. *9, 4*

6 The good shepherd giveth his life for the sheep. *10, 11*

7 Jesus wept. *11, 35*

8 A new commandment I give unto you, That ye love one another.
*St John, 13, 34*

9 In my Father's house are many mansions.      *14, 2*

10 Greater love hath no man than this, that a man lay down his life for his friends.      *15, 13*

11 Whither goest thou?      *16, 5*

12 Pilate saith unto him, What is truth?      *18, 38*

13 What I have written I have written.      *19, 22*

14 Blessed are they that have not seen, and yet have believed.
*20, 29*

## Acts of the Apostles

15 Silver and gold have I none; but such as I have give I thee.
*3, 6*

16 Thy money perish with thee, because thou hast thought that the gift of God may be purchased with money.      *8, 20*

17 He went on his way rejoicing.      *8, 39*

18 It is hard for thee to kick against the pricks.      *9, 5*

19 God is no respecter of persons.      *10, 34*

20 In him we live, and move, and have our being.      *17, 28*

21 Great is Diana of the Ephesians.      *19, 34*

22 It is more blessed to give than to receive.      *20, 35*

23 A citizen of no mean city.      *21, 39*

24 Brought up in this city at the feet of Gamaliel.      *22, 3*

25 I appeal unto Caesar.      *25, 11*

26 Hast thou appealed unto Caesar? unto Caesar shalt thou go.
*25, 12*

27 I was not disobedient unto the heavenly vision.      *26, 19*

28 Almost thou persuadest me to be a Christian.      *26, 28*

## Romans

29 The just shall live by faith.      *1, 17*

30 These, having not the law, are a law unto themselves.      *2, 14*

31 Death hath no more dominion over him.      *6, 9*

32 The wages of sin is death.      *6, 23*

33 For the good that I would I do not: but the evil which I would not, that I do.      *7, 19*

34 And we know that all things work together for good to them that love God.      *8, 28*

35 If God be for us, who can be against us?      *Romans, 8, 31*

36 So we, being many, are one body in Christ, and every one members one of another.      *12, 5*

37 Let love be without dissimulation. Abhor that which is evil; cleave to that which is good.      *12, 9*

38 Rejoice with them that do rejoice, and weep with them that weep.      *12, 15*

39 Be not wise in your own conceits.      *12, 16*

40 Vengeance is mine; I will repay, saith the Lord.      *12, 19*

41 Be not overcome of evil, but overcome evil with good.      *12, 21*

42 The powers that be are ordained of God.      *13, 1*

43 Love worketh no ill to his neighbour: therefore love is the fulfilling of the law.      *13, 10*

44 None of us liveth to himself, and no man dieth to himself.      *14, 7*

45 We then that are strong ought to bear the infirmities of the weak.      *15, 1*

## 1 Corinthians

46 I have planted, Apollos watered; but God gave the increase.      *3, 6*

47 Absent in body, but present in spirit.      *5, 3*

48 Know ye not that a little leaven leaveneth the whole lump?      *5, 6*

49 All things are lawful unto me, but all things are not expedient.      *6, 12*

50 It is better to marry than to burn.      *7, 9*

51 All things to all men.      *9, 22*

52 If a woman have long hair, it is a glory to her.      *11, 15*

53 When I become a man, I put away childish things.      *13, 11*

54 Now we see through a glass, darkly; but then face to face.      *13, 12*

55 And now abideth faith, hope, charity, these three; but the greatest of these is charity.      *13, 13*

56 Let your women keep silence in the churches.      *14, 34*

57 Let all things be done decently and in order.      *14, 40*

58 One born out of due time.      *15, 8*

59 By the grace of God I am what I am.      *15, 10*

60 O death, where is thy sting? O grave, where is thy victory?      *15, 55*

## 2 Corinthians

61 The letter killeth, but the spirit giveth life. *3, 6*

62 We walk by faith, not by sight. *5, 7*

63 God loveth a cheerful giver. *9, 7*

64 For ye suffer fools gladly, seeing ye yourselves are wise.
*11, 19*

65 A thorn in the flesh. *12, 7*

66 My grace is sufficient for thee: for my strength is made perfect in weakness. *12, 9*

## Galatians

67 The right hands of fellowship. *2, 9*

68 Ye are fallen from grace. *5, 4*

69 Bear ye one another's burdens. *6, 2*

70 Be not deceived; God is not mocked: for whatsoever a man soweth, that shall he also reap. *6, 7*

## Ephesians

71 Be ye angry, and sin not; let not the sun go down upon your wrath. *4, 26*

72 For this cause shall a man leave his father and mother, and shall be joined unto his wife, and they two shall be one flesh. *5, 31*

73 Put on the whole armour of God. *6, 11*

74 For we wrestle not against flesh and blood, but against principalities, against powers, against the rulers of the darkness of this world, against spiritual wickedness in high places. *6, 12*

## Philippians

75 Work out your own salvation with fear and trembling. *2, 12*

76 Whose God is their belly, and whose glory is in their shame.
*2, 19*

77 Our conversation is in heaven. *3, 20*

78 The peace of God, which passeth all understanding. *4, 7*

79 Whatsoever things are true, whatsoever things are honest, whatsoever things are just, whatsoever things are pure, whatsoever things are lovely, whatsoever things are of good report; if there be any virtue, and if there be any praise, think on these things.
*4, 8*

80 I have learned, in whatsoever state I am, therewith to be content.
*4, 11*

**Colossians**

81 Touch not; taste not; handle not.                    *2, 21*

82 Set your affection on things above, not on things on the earth.
                                                         *3, 2*

**1 Thessalonians**

83 Remembering without ceasing your work of faith, and labour
   of love.                                              *1, 3*

84 Pray without ceasing.                                 *5, 17*

85 Prove all things: hold fast that which is good.       *5, 21*

**2 Thessalonians**

86 If any would not work, neither should he eat.         *3, 10*

**1 Timothy**

87 Not greedy of filthy lucre.                           *3, 3*

88 Refuse profane and old wives' fables.                 *4, 7*

89 Let no man despise thy youth.                         *4, 12*

90 Drink no longer water, but use a little wine for thy stomach's
   sake and thine often infirmities.                     *5, 23*

91 For we brought nothing into this world, and it is certain we can
   carry nothing out.                                    *6, 7*

92 The love of money is the root of all evil.            *6, 10*

93 Fight the good fight of faith.                        *6, 12*

**2 Timothy**

94 All scripture is given by inspiration of God.         *3, 16*

95 I have fought a good fight, I have finished my course, I have kept
   the faith.                                            *4, 7*

**Titus**

96 Unto the pure all things are pure.                    *1, 15*

**Hebrews**

97 It is appointed unto men once to die, but after this the judgment.
                                                         *9, 27*

98 It is a fearful thing to fall into the hands of the living God.
                                                         *10, 31*

99 Faith is the substance of things hoped for, the evidence of things
   not seen.                                             *11, 1*

1 Whom the Lord loveth he chasteneth.          *Hebrews, 12, 6*

2 Let brotherly love continue.                          *13, 1*

3 Jesus Christ the same yesterday, and today, and for ever.

*13, 8*

## James

4 Faith without works is dead.                          *2, 20*

5 The tongue can no man tame; it is an unruly evil.     *3, 8*

6 Resist the devil, and he will flee from you.          *4, 7*

7 Ye have heard of the patience of Job.                 *5, 11*

## 1 Peter

8 All flesh is as grass.                                *1, 24*

9 Honour all men. Love the brotherhood. Fear God. Honour the king.                                           *2, 17*

10 Giving honour unto the wife, as unto the weaker vessel.   *3, 7*

11 Charity shall cover the multitude of sins.           *4, 8*

12 Be sober, be vigilant; because your adversary the devil, as a roaring lion, walketh about, seeking whom he may devour.

*5, 8*

## 2 Peter

13 The dog is turned to his own vomit again; and the sow that was washed to her wallowing in the mire.           *2, 22*

14 One day is with the Lord as a thousand years, and a thousand years as one day.                                *3, 8*

## 1 John

15 Shutteth up his bowels of compassion.                *3, 17*

16 God is love.                                         *4, 8*

17 There is no fear in love; but perfect love casteth out fear.

*4, 18*

## 2 John

18 The elder unto the elect lady.                       *1, 1*

## Revelation

19 I am Alpha and Omega, the beginning and the ending.   *1, 8*

20 Be thou faithful unto death, and I will give thee a crown of life.

*2, 10*

21 He shall rule them with a rod of iron.               *2, 27*

22 I will not blot out his name out of the book of life. *Revelation, 3, 5*

23 Because thou art lukewarm, and neither cold nor hot, I will spue thee out of my mouth.                                                    *3, 16*

24 Behold, I stand at the door, and knock.                          *3, 20*

25 He went forth conquering, and to conquer.                   *6, 2*

26 Behold a pale horse: and his name that sat on him was Death, and Hell followed with him.                                    *6, 8*

27 And when he had opened the seventh seal, there was silence in heaven about the space of half an hour.          *8, 1*

28 The bottomless pit.                                                   *9, 1*

29 They had tails like unto scorpions, and there were stings in their tails.                                                               *9, 10*

30 Let him that hath understanding count the number of the beast: for it is the number of a man; and his number is Six hundred threescore and six.                                          *13, 18*

31 A place called in the Hebrew tongue Armageddon.     *16, 16*

32 And I saw a new heaven and a new earth: for the first heaven and the first earth were passed away; and there was no more sea.
                                                                              *21, 1*

33 The holy city, new Jerusalem, coming down from God out of heaven, prepared as a bride adorned for her husband.     *21, 2*

34 And God shall wipe away all tears from their eyes; and there shall be no more death, neither sorrow, nor crying, neither shall there be any more pain: for the former things are passed away.
                                                                              *21, 4*

35 If any man shall add unto these things, God shall add unto him the plagues that are written in this book.          *22, 18*


# APOCRYPHA

## 1 Esdras

36 The first wrote, Wine is the strongest.
   The second wrote, The King is strongest.
   The third wrote, Women are strongest: but above all things Truth beareth away the victory.                                      *3, 10*

37 Great is Truth, and mighty above all things.          *4, 41*

## 2 Esdras

38 I shall light a candle of understanding in thine heart, which shall not be put out.                                              *14, 25*

**Tobit**

39 If thou hast abundance, give alms accordingly: if thou have but a little, be not afraid to give according to that little.            *4, 8*

40 So they went forth both, and the young man's dog with them.
            *5, 16*


**Wisdom of Solomon**

41 Let us crown ourselves with rosebuds, before they be withered.
            *2, 8*

42 Through envy of the devil came death into the world.            *2, 24*

43 The souls of the righteous are in the hand of God, and there shall no torment touch them.            *3, 1*

44 The corruptible body presseth down the soul.            *9, 15*

45 O Lord, thou lover of souls.            *11, 26*


**Ecclesiasticus**

46 My son, if thou come to serve the Lord, prepare thy soul for temptation.            *2, 1*

47 A faithful friend is the medicine of life.            *6, 16*

48 Miss not the discourse of the elders.            *8, 9*

49 Open not thine heart to every man.            *8, 19*

50 Give not thy soul unto a woman.            *9, 2*

51 Forsake not an old friend.            *9, 10*

52 Judge none blessed before his death.            *11, 28*

53 He that toucheth pitch shall be defiled therewith.            *13, 1*

54 Be not made a beggar by banqueting upon borrowing.            *18, 33*

55 All wickedness is but little to the wickedness of a woman.
            *25, 19*

56 Let thy speech be short, comprehending much in few words.
            *32, 8*

57 Honour a physician with the honour due unto him.            *38, 1*

58 How can he get wisdom . . . whose talk is of bullocks?            *38, 25*

59 Let us now praise famous men, and our fathers that begat us.
            *44, 1*

60 Rich men furnished with ability, living peaceably in their habitations.            *44, 6*

61 And some there be, which have no memorial.            *44, 9*

62 Their bodies are buried in peace, but their name liveth for evermore.            *44, 14*

**1 Maccabees**

63 Consider ye throughout all ages, that none that put their trust
in him shall be overcome.                                    *2, 61*


**2 Maccabees**

64 When he was at the last gasp.                             *7, 9*

65 It was an holy and good thought.                          *12, 45*


## THE BOOK OF COMMON PRAYER

66 We have erred, and strayed from thy ways like lost sheep.
*Morning Prayer, General Confession*

67 We have left indone those things which we ought to have done;
And we have done those things which we ought not to have
done.                                                       *Ib, Ib*

68 As it was in the beginning, is now, and ever shall be: world
without end.                                                *Ib, Gloria*

69 The noble army of Martyrs.                               *Ib, Te Deum*

70 Give peace in our time, O Lord.                          *Ib, Versicles*

71 Whose service is perfect freedom. *Ib, Second Collect, for Peace*

72 In Quires and Places where they sing.   *Ib, Rubric after Third
Collect*

73 When two or three are gathered together in thy Name thou wilt
grant their requests.            *Ib, Prayer of St Chrysostom*

74 Lighten our darkness.   *Evening Prayer, Third Collect, for Aid
Against all Perils*

75 Defend us from all perils and dangers of this night.     *Ib, Ib*

76 Have mercy upon us miserable sinners.                    *Litany*

77 Envy, hatred, and malice, and all uncharitableness.      *Ib*

78 All the deceits of the world, the flesh, and the devil.  *Ib*

79 In the hour of death, and in the day of judgement.       *Ib*

80 Preserve to our use the kindly fruits of the earth.      *Ib*

81 All sorts and conditions of men.   *Prayer for all Conditions of
men*

82 All who profess and call themselves Christians.          *Ib*

83 Those who are any ways afflicted, or distressed, in mind, body,
or estate.                                                  *Ib*

84 Patience under their sufferings, and a happy issue out of all
their afflictions.                                          *Ib*

85 Our creation, preservation, and all the blessings of this life.
*A General Thanksgiving*

86 Read, mark, learn and inwardly digest.
*Collect, 2nd Sunday in Advent*

87 All our doings without charity are nothing worth.
*Ib Quinquagesima Sunday*

88 Jews, Turks, Infidels, and Hereticks.    *Ib, Third Collect for
Good Friday*

89 A right judgement in all things.     *Ib, Whit-Sunday*

90 The author and giver of all good things.
*Ib, 7th Sunday after Trinity*

91 Whom truly to know is everlasting life.    *Ib, St Philip and St
James's Day*

92 Constantly speak the truth, boldly rebuke vice, and patiently
suffer for the truth's sake.    *Ib, St John Baptist's Day*

93 An open and notorious evil liver.     *Holy Communion,
Introductory Rubric*

94 Grant that the old Adam in this Child may be so buried, that
the new man may be raised up in him.    *Publick Baptism of
Infants, Blessing*

95 Renounce the devil and all his works.      *Ib*

96 The pomps and vanity of this wicked world.    *Catechism*

97 To order myself lowly and reverently to all my betters.   *Ib*

98 To keep my hands from picking and stealing.     *Ib*

99 To do my duty in that state of life, unto which it shall please God
to call me.     *Ib*

1 An outward and visible sign of an inward and spiritual grace.
*Ib*

2 Being now come to the years of discretion.
*Order of Confirmation*

3 If any of you know cause, or just impediment. *Solemnization of
Matrimony*

4 Brute beasts that have no understanding.      *Ib*

5 Let him now speak, or else hereafter for ever hold his peace.
*Ib*

6 Wilt thou have this Woman to thy wedded wife?     *Ib*

7 To have and to hold from this day forward, for better for worse,
for richer for poorer, in sickness and in health, to love and to
cherish, till death us do part.     *Ib*

8 To love, cherish, and to obey.      *Ib*

9 With this ring I thee wed, with my body I thee worship, and with all my worldly goods I thee endow. *Solemnization of Matrimony*

10 Those whom God hath joined together let no man put asunder. *Ib*

11 I pronounce that they be Man and Wife together. *Ib*

12 The Office ensuing is not to be used for any that die unbaptized, or excommunicate, or have laid violent hands upon themselves. *Burial of the Dead, Introductory Rubric*

13 Man that is born of a woman hath but a short time to live, and is full of misery. *Ib*

14 In the midst of life we are in death. *Ib*

15 We therefore commit his body to the ground; earth to earth, ashes to ashes, dust to dust. *Ib*

**BICKERSTAFFE, Isaac, 1735?–1812?**

16 There was a jolly miller once
   Lived on the river Dee;
   He worked and sang from morn till night;
   No lark more blithe than he. *Love in a Village, Act, 1, Scene 5*

17 I care for nobody, not I,
   If no one cares for me. *Ib*

18 But if I'm content with a little
   Enough is as good as a feast. *Ib, Act 3, Scene 1*

**BICKERSTETH, Edward Henry, 1825–1906**

19 Peace, perfect peace, in this dark world of sin?
   The blood of Jesus whispers peace within. *Songs in the House of Pilgrimage*

**BINYON, Laurence Robert, 1869–1943**

20 They shall grow not old, as we that are left grow old:
   Age shall not weary them, nor the years condemn.
   At the going down of the sun and in the morning
   We will remember them. *For the Fallen (1914–1918)*

**BIRRELL, Augustine, 1850–1933**

21 That great dust-heap called 'history'. *Obiter Dicta, 1st series, Carlyle*

**BISMARCK, Otto von, 1815–1898**

22 *Nach Canossa gehen wir nicht.* We will not go to Canossa. *Speech, Reichstag, 14 May 1872*

23 *Blut und Eisen.* Blood and Iron.    *Speech, Prussian Chamber, 28 Jan. 1886*

**BLACKSTONE, Sir William, 1723–1780**

24 The king never dies.    *Commentaries on the Laws of England, Book 1, 7*

25 That the king can do no wrong, is a necessary and fundamental principle of the English constitution.    *Ib, Book 3, 17*

26 It is better that ten guilty persons escape than one innocent suffer.    *Ib, Book, 4, 27*

**BLAIR, Eric, see ORWELL, George**

**BLAKE, William, 1757–1827**

27 To see a World in a grain of sand,
And a Heaven in a wild flower,
Hold Infinity in the palm of your hand,
And Eternity in an hour.    *Auguries of Innocence, 1*

28 A robin redbreast in a cage
Puts all Heaven in a rage.    *Ib, 5*

29 A truth that's told with bad intent
Beats all the lies you can invent.    *Ib, 53*

30 Man was made for joy and woe;
And when this we rightly know,
Thro' the world we safely go.    *Ib, 56*

31 God appears, and God is Light,
To those poor souls who dwell in Night;
But does a Human Form display
To those who dwell in realms of Day.    *Ib, 129*

32 Does the Eagle know what is in the pit
Or wilt thou go ask the Mole?
Can Wisdom be put in a silver rod,
Or love in a golden bowl?    *The Book of Thel, Thel's Motto*

33 Mutual Forgiveness of each vice,
Such are the Gates of Paradise.    *The Gates of Paradise, Prologue*

34 He who bends himself a Joy,
Doth the wingèd life destroy;
But he who kisses the Joy as it flies
Lives in Eternity's sunrise.
    *Gnomic Verses, XVII, Several Questions Answered*

35 For a Tear is an Intellectual thing;
And a Sigh is the sword of an angel king;

And the bitter groan of a Martyr's woe
Is an arrow from the Almighty's bow.          *Jerusalem, f. 52*

36 He who would do good to another must do it in Minute
   Particulars.
   General Good is the plea of the scoundrel, hypocrite, and
   flatterer.                                    *Ib, f. 55*

37 I care not whether a man is Good or Evil; all that I care
   Is whether he is a Wise Man or a Fool. Go! put off Holiness,
   And put on Intellect.                         *Ib, f. 91*

38 And did those feet in ancient time
      Walk upon England's mountains green?
   And was the holy lamb of God
      On England's pleasant pastures seen?

   Bring me my bow of burning gold!
      Bring me my arrows of desire!
   Bring me my spear! O clouds, unfold!
      Bring me my chariot of fire!

   I will not cease from mental fight,
      Nor shall my sword sleep in my hand,
   Till we have built Jerusalem
      In England's green and pleasant land.    *Milton, Preface*

39 Mock on, mock on, Voltaire, Rousseau;
   Mock on, mock on; 'tis all in vain!
   You throw the sand against the wind,
   And the wind blows it back again.        *Mock on, mock on,*
                                             *Voltaire, Rousseau*

40 Never seek to tell thy love,
   Love that never told can be;
   For the gentle wind does move
   Silently, invisibly.              *Never seek to tell thy Love*

41 Soon as she was gone from me,
   A traveller came by,
   Silently, invisibly:
   He took her with a sigh.                          *Ib*

42 A petty sneaking knave I knew –
   O! Mr Cromek, how do ye do?                 *On Cromek*

43 Love seeketh not itself to please,
   Nor for itself hath any care,
   But for another gives its ease,
   And builds a Heaven in Hell's despair.
                *Songs of Experience, The Clod and the Pebble*

44 My mother groan'd, my father wept,
   Into the dangerous world I leapt;

Helpless, naked, piping loud,
Like a fiend hid in a cloud. *Songs of Experience, Infant Sorrow*

45 But if at the Church they would give us some ale,
And a pleasant fire our souls to regale,
We'd sing and we'd pray all the livelong day,
Nor ever once wish from the Church to stray.
*Ib, The Little Vagabond*

46 Tiger! Tiger! burning bright
In the forests of the night,
What immortal hand or eye
Could frame thy fearful symmetry? *Ib, The Tiger*

47 When the stars threw down their spears,
And water'd heaven with their tears,
Did he smile his work to see?
Did he who made the Lamb make thee? *Ib*

48 Piping down the valleys wild,
Piping songs of pleasant glee,
On a cloud I saw a child. *Songs of Innocence, Introduction*

49 'Pipe a song about a Lamb!'
So I piped with merry cheer. *Ib*

50 Little Lamb, who made thee?
Dost thou know who made thee? *Ib, The Lamb*

51 My mother bore me in the southern wild,
And I am black, but O! my soul is white. *Ib, The Little Black Boy*

52 When the voices of children are heard on the green,
And laughing is heard on the hill. *Ib, Nurse's Song*

53 Can I see another's woe,
And not be in sorrow too? *Ib, On Another's Sorrow*

54 Whether on Ida's shady brow,
Or in the chambers of the East,
The chambers of the sun, that now
From ancient melody have ceas'd. *To the Muses*

55 How have you left the ancient love
That bards of old enjoy'd in you!
The languid strings do scarcely move!
The sound is forc'd, the notes are few! *Ib*

56 Without Contraries is no progression. Attraction and Repulsion,
Reason and Energy, Love and Hate, are necessary to Human
existence. *The Marriage of Heaven and Hell, The Argument*

57 Energy is Eternal Delight. *Ib, The Voice of the Devil*

58 The road of excess leads to the palace of Wisdom.
> *The Marriage of Heaven and Hell, Proverbs of Hell*

59 He who desires but acts not, breeds pestilence.                    *Ib*

60 A fool sees not the same tree that a wise man sees.             *Ib*

61 Damn braces. Bless relaxes.                                            *Ib*

62 Exuberance is Beauty.                                                    *Ib*

63 Where man is not, nature is barren.                                *Ib*

64 If the doors of perception were cleansed everything would
   appear to man as it is, infinite.          *Ib, A Memorable Fancy*

## BORROW, George Henry, 1803–1881

65 There's night and day, brother, both sweet things; sun, moon,
   and stars, brother, all sweet things; there's likewise a wind on
   the heath. Life is very sweet, brother; who would wish to die?
   > *Lavengro, Ch. 25*

## BOSQUET, Marshal Pierre, 1810–1861

66 *C'est magnifique, mais ce n'est pas la guerre.* It is magnificent, but
   it is not war.          *Watching the Charge of the Light Brigade,*
   > *Balaclava, 1854*

## BOSSIDY, John Collins, 1860–1928

67 And this is good old Boston,
   The Home of the bean and the cod,
   Where the Lowells talk to the Cabots,
   And the Cabots talk only to God.          *On the Aristocracy of*
   > *Harvard*

## BOULTON, Sir Harold Edwin, 1859–1935

68 When Adam and Eve were dispossessed
   Of the garden hard by Heaven,
   They planted another one down in the West,
   'Twas Devon, glorious Devon!          *Glorious Devon*

69 Speed, bonny boat, like a bird on the wing;
   'Onward!' the sailors cry;
   Carry the lad that's born to be king
   Over the sea to Skye.          *Skye Boat Song*

## BOURDILLON, Francis William, 1852–1921

70 The night has a thousand eyes,
   And the day but one;
   Yet the light of the bright world dies
   With the dying sun.                                                  *Light*

**BOWEN, Charles, 1st Baron, 1835–1894**

71 The rain it raineth on the just
 And also on the unjust fella:
But chiefly on the just, because
 The unjust steals the just's umbrella.  *Sichel, Sands of Time*

**BOWEN, Edward Ernest, 1836–1901**

72 Forty years on, growing older and older,
 Shorter in wind, as in memory long,
Feeble of foot, and rheumatic of shoulder,
 What will it help you that once you were strong?
           *Forty Years on,*
          *Harrow School Song*

**BRADFORD, John, 1510?–1555**

73 There, but for the grace of God, goes John Bradford. *Remark*
     *on seeing some criminals led to execution*

**BRATHWAITE, Richard, 1588?–1673**

74 To Banbury came I, O profane one!
 Where I saw a Puritane-one
Hanging of his cat on Monday,
 For killing of a mouse on Sunday.  *Barnabee's Journal, 1*

**BRIDGES, Robert, 1844–1930**

75 Awake, my heart, to be loved, awake, awake!
 The darkness silvers away, the morn doth break,
 It leaps in the sky: unrisen lustres slake
The o'ertaken moon. Awake, O heart, awake!
        *Awake, My Heart, to be Loved*

76 I heard a linnet courting
 His lady in the spring.    *I heard a Linnet courting*

77 I never shall love the snow again
 Since Maurice died.  *I never shall love the Snow again*

78 Perfect little body, without fault or stain on thee,
With promise of strength and manhood full and fair!
           *On a Dead Child*

79 When Death to either shall come, –
 I pray it be first to me. *When Death to either shall come*

**BRIGHT, John, 1811–1889**

80 The Angel of Death has been abroad thoughout the land; you
may almost hear the beating of his wings. *Speech, House of*
        *Commons, 23 Feb. 1855*

81 England is the mother of parliaments.    *Speech, Birmingham,*
                                                        *18 Jan. 1865*

82 The right honourable gentleman... has retired into what may be
   called his political Cave of Adullam.        *Speech, House of*
                                            *Commons, 13 March 1866*

83 Force is not a remedy.    *Speech, Birmingham, 16 Nov. 1880*


## BRONTË, Emily, 1818–1848

84     No coward soul is mine,
   No trembler in the world's storm-troubled sphere:
       I see Heaven's glories shine,
   And faith shines equal, arming me from fear.        *Last Lines*

85       Vain are the thousand creeds
   That move men's hearts: unutterably vain;
       Worthless as wither'd weeds.                          *Ib*

86 Riches I hold in light esteem,
       And Love I laugh to scorn;
   And lust of fame was but a dream
       That vanish'd with the morn.            *The Old Stoic*

87 O! dreadful is the check – intense the agony –
   When the ear begins to hear, and the eye begins to see;
   When the pulse begins to throb – the brain to think again –
   The soul to feel the flesh, and the flesh to feel the chain.
                                                *The Prisoner*


## BROOKE, Rupert, 1887–1915

88 Blow out, you bugles, over the rich Dead.        *The Dead*

89 Just now the lilac is in bloom
   All before my little room.    *The Old Vicarage, Grantchester*

90 For England's the one land, I know,
   Where men with Splendid Hearts may go.                    *Ib*

91 Stands the Church clock at ten to three?
   And is there honey still for tea?                         *Ib*

92 If I should die, think only this of me:
   That there's some corner of a foreign field
   That is forever England.                       *The Soldier*

93 A dust whom England bore, shaped, made aware,
   Gave, once, her flowers to love, her ways to roam,
   A body of England's, breathing English air,
   Washed by the rivers, blest by suns of home.              *Ib*

94 And laughter, learnt of friends; and gentleness,
   In hearts at peace, under an English heaven.              *Ib*

**BROOKS, Phillips, 1835–1893**

95 O little town of Bethlehem,
   How still we see thee lie;
   Above thy deep and dreamless sleep
   The silent stars go by.        *O Little Town of Bethlehem*

**BROWN, Thomas, 1663–1704**

96 I do not love thee, Doctor Fell,
   The reason why I cannot tell;
   But this alone I know full well,
   I do not love thee, Doctor Fell.    *Translation of Martial*
                                       *Epigrams, 1, 32*

**BROWN, Thomas Edward, 1830–1897**

97 A garden is a lovesome thing, God wot!        *My Garden*

**BROWNE, Charles Farrar, see WARD, Artemus**

**BROWNE, Sir Thomas, 1605–1682**

98 He who discommendeth others obliquely commendeth himself.
                                       *Christian Morals*

99 I dare, without usurpation, assume the honourable style of
   Christian.                 *Religio Medici, Part, 1, 1*

1 All things are artificial, for nature is the art of God.    *Ib, 16*

2 I am of a constitution so general that it consorts and sympa-
   thizeth with all things. I have no antipathy, or rather idiosyncrasy,
   in diet, humour, air, any-thing.               *Ib, Part 2, 1*

3 It is the common wonder of all men, how among so many
   million of faces, there should be none alike.            *Ib, 2*

4 No man can justly censure or condemn another, because indeed
   no man truly knows another.                      *Ib, 4*

5 I could be content that we might procreate like trees, without
   conjunction, or that there were any way to perpetuate the world
   without this trivial and vulgar way of coition.    *Ib, Part 2, 9*

6 Lord, deliver me from myself.                    *Ib, 10*

7 Man is a noble animal, splendid in ashes, and pompous in the
   grave.                              *Urn Burial, Ch. 5*

**BROWNE, Sir William, 1692–1774**

8 The King to Oxford sent a troop of horse,
   For Tories own no argument but force:

With equal skill to Cambridge books he sent,
For Whigs admit no force but argument.      *Reply to Trapp's*
                                            *Epigram (see 393 : 54)*

**BROWNING, Elizabeth Barrett, 1806–1861**

9              Let no one till his death
Be called unhappy. Measure not the work
Until the day's out and the labour done.      *Aurora Leigh,*
                                              *Book 5*

10 Since when was genius found respectable?      *Ib, Book 6*

11 Do you hear the children weeping, O my brothers,
Ere the sorrow comes with years?      *The Cry of the Children*

12 I tell you hopeless grief is passionless.      *Grief*

13 What was he doing, the great god Pan,
Down in the reeds by the river?      *A Musical Instrument*

**BROWNING, Robert, 1812–1889**

14              Love, we are in God's hand.
How strange now, looks the life he makes us lead!
So free we seem, so fettered fast we are!      *Andrea del Sarto*

15 Ah, but a man's reach should exceed his grasp,
Or what's a heaven for?                              *Ib*

16 One who never turned his back but marched breast forward,
              Never doubted clouds would break,
Never dreamed, though right were worsted, wrong would
    triumph,
Held we fall to rise, are baffled to fight better,
              Sleep to wake.      *Asolando, Epilogue*

17 Just when we are safest, there's a sunset-touch,
A fancy from a flower-bell, some one's death,
A chorus-ending from Euripides, –
And that's enough for fifty hopes and fears
As old and new at once as Nature's self,
To rap and knock and enter in our soul.      *Bishop Blougram's*
                                              *Apology*

18 No, when the fight begins within himself,
A man's worth something.                              *Ib*

19 Oh, the little more, and how much it is!
              And the little less, and what worlds away!
                                              *By The Fire-side, 39*

20              We loved, sir – used to meet:
How sad and bad and mad it was –
              But then, how it was sweet!      *Confessions*

21 Oh, to be in England
   Now that April's there,
   And whoever wakes in England
   Sees, some morning, unaware,
   That the lowest boughs and the brushwood sheaf
   Round the elm-tree bole are in tiny leaf,
   While the chaffinch sings on the orchard bough
   In England – now!            *Home-Thoughts, from Abroad*

22 And after April, when May follows,
   And the whitethroat builds, and all the swallows!            *Ib*

23 That's the wise thrush; he sings each song twice over,
   Lest you should think he never could recapture
   The first fine careless rapture!            *Ib*

24 Nobly, nobly Cape Saint Vincent to the North-west died away;
   Sunset ran, one glorious blood-red, reeking into Cadiz Bay.
                              *Home-Thoughts, from the Sea*

25 Whoso turns, as I, this evening, turn to God to praise and pray,
   While Jove's planet rises yonder, silent over Africa.            *Ib*

26 I sprang to the stirrup, and Joris, and he;
   I galloped, Dirck galloped, we galloped all three.
              *How they brought the Good News from Ghent to Aix*

27          Escape me?
            Never –
            Beloved!
   While I am I, and you are you.            *Life in a Love*

28 Just for a handful of silver he left us,
       Just for a riband to stick in his coat. *The Lost Leader*

29 Never glad confident morning again!            *Ib*

30 Ah, did you once see Shelley plain,
       And did he stop and speak to you?
   And did you speak to him again,
       How strange it seems, and new!            *Memorabilia*

31 Never the time and the place
       And the loved one all together!   *Never the Time and
                                              the Place*

32 Dante, who loved well because he hated,
   Hated wickedness that hinders loving.   *One Word More, 5*

33 Where my heart lies, let my brain lie also!            *Ib, 14*

34 God be thanked, the meanest of his creatures
   Boasts two soul-sides, one to face the world with,
   One to show a woman when he loves her.            *Ib, 17*

35 It was roses, roses all the way.            *The Patriot*

36          Hamelin Town's in Brunswick,
By famous Hanover city;
      The river Weser, deep and wide,
      Washes its wall on the southern side.
*The Pied Piper of Hamelin*, *1*

37          Rats!
They fought the dogs and killed the cats,
      And bit the babies in the cradles.       *Ib, 2*

38          With shrieking and squeaking
In fifty different sharps and flats.       *Ib, 2*

39 'If I can rid your town of rats
Will you give me a thousand guilders?'
'One? fifty thousand!' – was the exclamation
Of the astonished Mayor and Corporation.       *Ib, 6*

40 And the muttering grew to a grumbling;
And the grumbling grew to a mighty rumbling;
And out of the houses the rats came tumbling.       *Ib, 7*

41 So, munch on, crunch on, take your nuncheon,
Breakfast, supper, dinner, luncheon!       *Ib*

42 'You threaten us, fellow? Do your worst,
Blow your pipe there till you burst!'       *Ib, 9*

43 All the little boys and girls,
With rosy cheeks and flaxen curls,
And sparkling eyes, and teeth like pearls,
Tripping and skipping, ran merrily after
The wonderful music with shouting and laughter.       *Ib, 12*

44 The year's at the spring,
And day's at the morn;
Morning's at seven;
The hill-side's dew-pearled;
The lark's on the wing;
The snail's on the thorn;
God's in His heaven –
All's right with the world.       *Pippa Passes, 1, Morning*

45 All service ranks the same with God –
With God, whose puppets, best and worst,
Are we: there is no last nor first.       *Ib, 4, Night*

46 Grow old along with me.
The best is yet to be,
The last of life, for which the first was made:
Our times are in His hand

Who saith 'A whole I planned,
Youth shows but half; trust God: see all nor be afraid!'
*Rabbi Ben Ezra*

47 Let age approve of youth, and death complete the same!   *Ib*

48 What of soul was left, I wonder, when the kissing had to stop?
*A Toccata of Galuppi's, 14*

**BUCHANAN, Robert Williams, 1841–1901**

49 The Fleshly School of Poetry.   *Title of article in the Contemporary Review, Oct. 1871*

50           She just wore
Enough for modesty – no more. *White Rose and Red, Part 1, 5*

**BUFFON, Georges Louis Leclerc, Comte de, 1707–1788**

51 *Le style est l'homme même.* Style is the man himself.
*Discours sur le style*

**BULLER, Arthur Henry Reginald, 1874–1944**

52 There was a young lady named Bright,
  Whose speed was far faster than light;
    She set out one day
    In a relative way,
And returned home the previous night.          *Limerick*

**BULWER-LYTTON, Edward, 1803–1873**

53 Here Stanley meets, – how Stanley scorns, the glance!
  The brilliant chief, irregularly great,
  Frank, haughty, rash, – the Rupert of Debate.
*The New Timon, 1, 6*

54 Beneath the rule of men entirely great,
  The pen is mightier than the sword.          *Richelieu, 2, 2*

**BUNN, Alfred, 1796?–1860**

55 I dreamt that I dwelt in marble halls,
  With vassals and serfs at my side.  ARLINE *The Bohemian Girl,
Act 2*

**BUNYAN, John, 1628–1688**

56 Some said, John, print it; others said, Not so;
  Some said, It might do good; others said, No.
*Pilgrim's Progress, Author's Apology*

57 As I walked through the wilderness of this world.   *Ib, Part 1*

58 The name of the slough was Despond. *Pilgrim's Progress, Part 1*

59 The gentleman's name that met him was Mr Worldly Wiseman.
                                                                *Ib*

60 It beareth the name of Vanity Fair, because the town where 'tis
   kept is lighter than vanity.                                 *Ib*

61 Mr Facing-both-ways.                                         *Ib*

62 A castle called Doubting Castle, the owner whereof was Giant
   Despair.                                                     *Ib*

63 So I awoke, and behold it was a dream.                       *Ib*

64 He who would valiant be
   'Gainst all disaster,
   Let him in constancy
           Follow the Master.
   There's no discouragement
   Shall make him once relent
   His first avowed intent
           To be a pilgrim.    *Ib, Part 2, English Hymnal Version*

65 I'll fear not what men say,
   I'll labour night and day
           To be a pilgrim.                                     *Ib*

66 He that is down needs fear no fall;
       He that is low, no pride.     *Ib, Shepherd Boy's Song*

67 So he passed over, and all the trumpets sounded for him on the
   other side.                                                  *Ib*

## BURGESS, Gelett, 1866–1951

68 I never saw a Purple Cow,
   I never hope to see one;
   But I can tell you, anyhow,
   I'd rather see than be one.                        *The Purple Cow*

69 Ah, yes, I wrote 'Purple Cow' –
   I'm sorry, now, I wrote it!
   But I can tell you anyhow,
   I'll kill you if you quote it.                              *Reply*

## BURGON, John William, 1813–1888

70 Match me such marvel save in Eastern clime,
   A rose-red city half as old as time.                  *Petra, 132*

## BURKE, Edmund, 1729–1797

71 The concessions of the weak are the concessions of fear.
          *Speech on Conciliation with America, 22 March 1775*

72 The use of force alone is but *temporary*. It may subdue for a
moment; but it does not remove the necessity of subduing again:
and a nation is not governed, which is perpetually to be conquered.   *Speech on Conciliation with America, 22 March 1775*

73 I do not know the method of drawing up an indictment against
an whole people.                                              *Ib*

74 All government, indeed every human benefit and enjoyment,
every virtue, and every prudent act, is founded on compromise
and barter.                                                  *Ib*

75 The people are the masters.      *Speech on the Economical
Reform, 11 Feb. 1780*

76 He was not merely a chip of the old block, but the old block
itself.                  *Of Pitt's first speech, 26 Feb. 1781*

77 There is, however, a limit at which forbearance ceases to be a
virtue.      *Observations on 'The Present State of the Nation',
1769*

78 But the age of chivalry is gone. That of sophisters, economists,
and calculators, has succeeded; and the glory of Europe is
extinguished for ever.      *Reflections on the Revolution in
France*

79 Man is by his constitution a religious animal.             *Ib*

80 Superstition is the religion of feeble minds.              *Ib*

81 Good order is the foundation of all good things.           *Ib*

82 Example is the school of mankind, and they will learn at no
other.           *Letters on a Regicide Peace, 1, 1796*

83 And having looked to government for bread, on the very first
scarcity they will turn and bite the hand that fed them.
*Thoughts and Details on Scarcity*

84 If any ask me what a free government is, I answer, that, for any
practical purpose, it is what the people think so.
*Letter to the Sheriffs of Bristol, 1777*

85 Liberty, too, must be limited in order to be possessed.    *Ib*

86 Among a people generally corrupt, liberty cannot long exist.  *Ib*

87 The greater the power, the more dangerous the abuse.
*Speech, House of Commons, 7 Feb. 1771*

88 I am convinced that we have a degree of delight, and that no
small one, in the real misfortunes and pains of others.
*On the Sublime and Beautiful, 1, 14*

89 Power gradually extirpates from the mind every humane and
gentle virtue.           *A Vindication of Natural Society*

**BURNET, Bishop Gilbert, 1643–1715**

90 There was a sure way to see it lost, and that was to die in the last
ditch. *History of his own Times, 1*

**BURNEY, Fanny (Mme D'Arblay), 1752–1840**

91 Dancing? Oh, dreadful! How it was ever adopted in a civilized
country I cannot find out; 'tis certainly a Barbarian exercise,
and of savage origin. MR MEADOWS *Cecilia, Book 3*

92 'True, very true ma'am,' said he, yawning, 'one really lives nowhere; one does but vegetate and wish it all at an end.' MR
MEADOWS *Ib, Book 4*

93 Indeed, the freedom with which Dr Johnson condemns whatever
he disapproves is astonishing. *Diary, 23 Aug. 1778*

**BURNS, John, 1858–1943**

94 Every drop of the Thames is liquid history.
*Attributed by Sir Frederick Whyte*

**BURNS, Robert, 1759–1796**

95 Ae fond kiss, and then we sever! *Ae Fond Kiss, 1*

96 But to see her was to love her,
Love but her, and love for ever. *Ib, 11*

97 Had we never lov'd sae kindly,
Had we never lov'd sae blindly,
Never met – or never parted,
We had ne'er been broken-hearted. *Ib, 13*

98 Flow gently, sweet Afton, among thy green braes,
Flow gently, I'll sing thee a song in thy praise. *Afton Water, 1*

99 Should auld acquaintance be forgot,
And never brought to min'? *Auld Lang Syne, 1*

1 We'll tak a cup o' kindness yet,
For auld lang syne. *Ib, 7*

2 Freedom and Whisky gang thegither! *The Author's Earnest
Cry and Prayer, 185*

3 Gin a body meet a body
Coming through the rye;
Gin a body kiss a body,
Need a body cry? *Coming through the Rye, 5*

4 I wasna fou, but just had plenty.
*Death and Doctor Hornbrook, 14*

5 On ev'ry hand it will allow'd be,
  He's just – nae better than he should be.
                        *A Dedication to Gavin Hamilton, 25*

6 A man's a man for a' that.       *For a' that and a' that, 12*

7 Green grow the rashes O,
    Green grow the rashes O;
  The sweetest hours that e'er I spent,
    Are spent amang the lasses O!   *Green Grow the Rashes, 1*

8 The wisest man the warl' saw,
    He dearly lov'd the lasses O.            *Ib, 19*

9 The golden hours on angel wings
    Flew o'er me and my dearie;
  For dear to me as light and life
    Was my sweet Highland Mary.    *Highland Mary, 13*

10 There's some are fou o' love divine,
    There's some are fou o' brandy.    *The Holy Fair, 239*

11 John Anderson my jo, John,
    When we were first acquent,
  Your locks were like the raven,
    Your bonnie brow was brent.   *John Anderson My Jo, 1*

12 True it is, she had one failing,
    Had a woman ever less?
           *Lines, written under picture of Miss Burns*

13              Nature's law,
  That man was made to mourn.   *Man was Made to Mourn, 31*

14 Man's inhumanity to man
    Makes countless thousands mourn!         *Ib, 55*

15 O Mary, at thy window be,
    It is the wish'd, the trysted hour!    *Mary Morison, 1*

16 Wee, sleekit, cow'rin', tim'rous beastie,
    O what a panic's in thy breastie!      *To a Mouse, 1*

17 I'm truly sorry man's dominion
    Has broken Nature's social union.        *Ib, 7*

18 The best laid schemes o' mice an' men
             Gang aft a-gley,
  An' lea'e us nought but grief an' pain
             For promis'd joy.          *Ib, 39*

19 Still thou art blest compar'd wi' me!
  The present only toucheth thee:
  But oh! I backward cast my e'e
            On prospects drear!

An' forward tho' I canna see,
I guess an' fear! *To a Mouse, 43*

20 My heart's in the Highlands, my heart is not here;
My heart's in the Highlands a-chasing the deer;
Chasing the wild deer, and following the roe,
My heart's in the Highlands, wherever I go.
*My Heart's in the Highlands, 1*

21 My love is like a red red rose
That's newly sprung in June:
My love is like the melodie
That's sweetly play'd in tune. *A Red, Red Rose*

22 Scots, wha hae wi' Wallace bled,
Scots, wham Bruce has aften led,
Welcome to your gory bed,
Or to victorie. *Scots, Wha Hae, 1*

23 Liberty's in every blow!
Let us do or die! *Ib, 23*

24 Some hae meat, and canna eat,
And some wad eat that want it;
But we hae meat and we can eat,
And sae the Lord be thankit. *The Selkirk Grace*

25 But pleasures are like poppies spread –
You seize the flow'r, its bloom is shed;
Or like the snow falls in the river –
A moment white, then melts for ever. *Tam o' Shanter, 59*

26 Ye banks and braes o' bonnie Doon,
How can ye bloom sae fresh and fair?
How can ye chant, ye little birds,
And I sae weary fu' o' care? *Ye Banks and Braes, 1*

27 Thou minds me o' departed joys,
Departed never to return. *Ib, 7*

28 And my fause lover stole my rose,
But ah! he left the thorn wi' me. *Ib, 15*


**BURTON, Robert, 1577–1640**

29 All my joys to this are folly,
Naught so sweet as Melancholy. *Anatomy of Melancholy,*
*Author's Abstract of Melancholy*

30 *Hinc quam sit calamus saevior ense patet.* From this it is clear
how much more cruel the pen is than the sword. *Ib, Part 1*

31 England is a paradise for women, and hell for horses: Italy a
paradise for horses, hell for women. *Ib, Part 3*

32 One religion is as true as another. *Anatomy of Melancholy, Part 3*

33 Be not solitary, be not idle. *Ib, Last words*

## BUSSY-RABUTIN, Comte de, 1618–1693

34 *L'absence est à l'amour ce qu'est au feu le vent; il éteint le petit, il allume le grand.* Absence is to love what wind is to fire; it extinguishes the small, it inflames the great.

*Histoire Amoureuse des Gaules*

## BUTLER, Samuel, 1612–1680

35 When civil fury first grew high,
And men fell out they knew not why. *Hudibras, 1, 1, 1*

36 For every why he had a wherefore. *Ib, 1, 1, 132*

37 Oaths are but words, and words but wind. *Ib, 2, 2, 107*

38 What makes all doctrines plain and clear?
About two hundred pounds a year.
And that which was prov'd true before
Prove false again? Two hundred more. *Ib, 3, 1, 1277*

39 He that complies against his will,
Is of his own opinion still. *Ib, 3, 3, 547*

40 The souls of women are so small,
That some believe they've none at all. *Miscellaneous Thoughts*

## BUTLER, Samuel, 1835–1902

41 It has been said that the love of money is the root of all evil.
The want of money is so quite as truly. *Erewhon, Ch. 20*

42 I keep my books at the British Museum and at Mudie's.
*The Humour of Homer, Ramblings in Cheapside*

43 Life is one long process of getting tired. *Note-books, Life, 7*

44 Life is the art of drawing sufficient conclusions from insufficient premises. *Ib, 9*

45 All progress is based upon a universal innate desire on the part of every organism to live beyond its income. *Ib, 16*

46 To live is like love, all reason is against it, and all healthy instinct for it. *Ib, Higgledy-Piggledy, Life and Love*

47 Stowed away in a Montreal lumber room
The Discobolus standeth and turneth his face to the wall;
Dusty, cobweb-covered, maimed and set at naught,
Beauty crieth in an attic and no man regardeth.
O God! O Montreal! *A Psalm of Montreal*

48 The advantage of doing one's praising for oneself is that one can
lay it on so thick and exactly in the right places.
*The Way of All Flesh, Ch. 34*

49 A man's friendships are, like his will, invalidated by marriage –
but they are also no less invalidated by the marriage of his
friends. *Ib, Ch. 75*

50 'Tis better to have loved and lost than never to have lost at all.
*Ib, Ch. 77 (see also 103 : 31 and 386 : 59)*

51 Brigands demand your money or your life; women require both.
*Attributed*

**BYROM, John, 1692–1763**

52 Christians awake, salute the happy morn,
Whereon the Saviour of the world was born.
*Hymn for Christmas Day*

53 God bless the King, I mean the Faith's Defender;
God bless – no harm in blessing – the Pretender;
But who Pretender is, or who is King,
God bless us all – that's quite another thing.
*To an Officer in the Army*

**BYRON, George Gordon, 6th Baron, 1788–1824**

54 In short, he was a perfect cavaliero,
And to his very valet seem'd a hero. *Beppo, 33*

55 I like the weather, when it is not rainy,
That is, I like two months of every year. *Ib, 48*

56 Maidens, like moths, are ever caught by glare,
And Mammon wins his way where Seraphs might despair.
*Childe Harold's Pilgrimage, Canto 1, 9*

57 Adieu, adieu! my native shore
Fades o'er the waters blue. *Ib, 1, 13*

58 My native Land – Good Night! *Ib*

59 There was a sound of revelry by night,
And Belgium's capital had gather'd then
Her Beauty and her Chivalry, and bright
The lamps shone o'er fair women and brave men.
*Ib, Canto 3, 21*

60 On with the dance! let joy be unconfined;
No sleep till morn, when Youth and Pleasure meet
To chase the glowing Hours with flying feet. *Ib, 3, 22*

61 I have not loved the world, nor the world me;
I have not flatter'd its rank breath, nor bow'd
To its idolatries a patient knee. *Ib, 3, 113*

62 I stood in Venice, on the Bridge of Sighs;
A palace and a prison on each hand. *Childe Harold's*
*Pilgrimage, Canto 4, 1*

63 Yet, Freedom! yet thy banner, torn, but flying,
Streams like the thunder-storm *against* the wind. *Ib, 4, 98*

64 While stands the Coliseum, Rome shall stand;
When falls the Coliseum, Rome shall fall;
And when Rome falls – the World. *Ib, 4, 145*

65 There is a pleasure in the pathless woods,
There is a rapture on the lonely shore,
There is society, where none intrudes,
By the deep Sea, and music in its roar:
I love not Man the less, but Nature more. *Ib, 4, 178*

66 What men call gallantry, and gods adultery,
Is much more common where the climate's sultry.
*Don Juan, Canto 1, 63*

67 A little still she strove, and much repented,
And whispering 'I will ne'er consent' – consented. *Ib, 1, 117*

68 Sweet is revenge – especially to women. *Ib, 1, 124*

69 Pleasure's a sin, and sometimes sin's a pleasure. *Ib, 1, 133*

70 Man's love is of man's life a thing apart,
'Tis woman's whole existence. *Ib, 1, 194*

71 Man, being reasonable, must get drunk;
The best of life is but intoxication. *Ib, Canto 2, 179*

72 Alas! the love of women! it is known
To be a lovely and a fearful thing. *Ib, 2, 199*

73 In her first passion woman loves her lover,
In all the others all she loves is love. *Ib, Canto 3, 3*

74 'Tis melancholy, and a fearful sign
Of human frailty, folly, also crime,
That love and marriage rarely can combine. *Ib, 3, 5*

75 All tragedies are finish'd by a death,
All comedies are ended by a marriage. *Ib, 3, 9*

76 Dreading that climax of all human ills
The inflammation of his weekly bills. *Ib, 3, 35*

77 The isles of Greece, the isles of Greece!
Where burning Sappho loved and sung,
Where grew the arts of war and peace,
Where Delos rose, and Phoebus sprung!
Eternal summer gilds them yet,
But all, except their sun, is set. *Ib, 3, 86, 1*

78 The mountains look on Marathon –
And Marathon looks on the sea;

And musing there an hour alone,
  I dream'd that Greece might still be free.        *Don Juan,*
                                                *Canto, 3, 86, 3*

79 And if I laugh at any mortal thing,
    'Tis that I may not weep.                     *Ib, Canto, 4, 4*

80 There is a tide in the affairs of women,
    Which, taken at the flood, leads – God knows where.
                                                *Ib, Canto 6, 2*

81 A lady of a 'certain age', which means
    Certainly aged.                               *Ib, 6, 69*

82 And, after all, what is a lie? 'Tis but
    The truth in masquerade.                     *Ib, Canto 11, 37*

83 'Tis strange the mind, that very fiery particle,
    Should let itself be snuff'd out by an article.   *[John Keats]*
                                                *Ib, 11, 60*

84 Now hatred is by far the longest pleasure;
    Men love in haste, but they detest at leisure.   *Ib, Canto 13, 6*

85 The English winter – ending in July,
    To recommence in August.                    *Ib, 13, 42*

86 Society is now one polish'd horde,
    Form'd of two mighty tribes, the *Bores* and *Bored.*
                                                *Ib, 13, 95*

87 'Tis strange – but true; for truth is always strange;
    Stranger than fiction: if it could be told,
    How much would novels gain by the exchange!
                                                *Ib, Canto 14, 101*

88                       I'll publish, right or wrong:
    Fools are my theme, let satire be my song.
                          *English Bards and Scotch Reviewers, 5*

89 'Tis pleasant, sure, to see one's name in print;
    A book's a book, although there's nothing in't.   *Ib, 51*

90 A man must serve his time to every trade
    Save censure – critics all are ready made.   *Ib, 63*

91                               As soon
    Seek roses in December – ice in June;
    Hope constancy in wind, or corn in chaff;
    Believe a woman or an epitaph,
    Or any other thing that's false, before
    You trust in critics, who themselves are sore.   *Ib, 75*

92 Better to err with Pope, than shine with Pye.   *Ib, 102*

93 Fare thee well! and if for ever,
    Still for ever, fare thee well.              *Fare Thee Well, 1*

94 Who kill'd John Keats?
   'I,' says the Quarterly,
So savage and Tartarly;
   ' 'Twas one of my feats.'         *John Keats*

95 Maid of Athens, ere we part,
   Give, oh give me back my heart!
               *Maid of Athens, ere we Part*

96 She walks in beauty, like the night
   Of cloudless climes and starry skies;
And all that's best of dark and bright
   Meet in her aspect and her eyes.    *She Walks in Beauty*

97 So, we'll go no more a roving
   So late into the night,
Though the heart be still as loving,
   And the moon be still as bright.
               *So, we'll go no more a roving*

98 Though the night was made for loving,
   And the day returns too soon,
Yet we'll go no more a roving
   By the light of the moon.               *Ib*

99 When we two parted
   In silence and tears,
Half broken-hearted
   To sever for years,
Pale grew thy cheek and cold,
   Colder thy kiss;
Truly that hour foretold
   Sorrow to this.              *When we two parted*

1 If I should meet thee
   After long years,
How should I greet thee? –
   With silence and tears.               *Ib*

2 I awoke one morning and found myself famous.    *Entry in*
    *Memoranda after publication of Childe Harold*

**BYRON, Henry James, 1834–1884**

3 Life's too short for chess.            *Our Boys, Act 1*

**CAESAR, Augustus, 63 B.C.–A.D. 14**

4 *Quintili Vare, legiones redde.* Quintilius Varus, give me back my
   legions.            *Suetonius, Divus Augustus, 23*

5 *Ad Kalendas Graecas soluturos.* To be paid at the Greek Kalends.
                        *Ib, 87*

**CAESAR, Julius, 102?–44 B.C.**

6 *Gallia est omnis divisa in partes tres.* All Gaul is divided into
  three parts.                                    *De Bello Gallico, 1, 1*

7 *Iacta alea est.* The die is cast.           *On Crossing the Rubicon,*
                                                            *49* B.C.

8 *Veni, vidi, vici.* I came, I saw, I conquered.      *After Victory at*
                                                      *Zela, 47* B.C.

9 *Et tu, Brute.* You too, Brutus?           *Last Words, attributed*

10 Caesar's wife must be above suspicion.              *Plutarch,*
                                                     *Life of Caesar*


**CALVERLEY, Charles Stuart, 1831–1884**

11 The auld wife sat at her ivied door
    (Butter and eggs and a pound of cheese)
    A thing she had frequently done before;
    And her spectacles lay on her aproned knees.          *Ballad*

12 The heart which grief hath cankered
    Hath one unfailing remedy – the Tankard.               *Beer*

13 For I've read in many a novel that, unless they've souls that
     grovel,
    Folks *prefer* in fact a hovel to your dreary marble halls.
                                                  *In the Gloaming*

14 How Eugene Aram, though a thief, a liar, and a murderer
    Yet, being intellectual, was amongst the noblest of mankind.
                                                      *Of Reading*

15 I have a liking old
    For thee, though manifold
    Stories, I know, are told,
       Not to thy credit.                            *Ode to Tobacco*


**CAMDEN, William, 1551–1623**

16 Betwixt the stirrup and the ground
    Mercy I asked, mercy I found.          *Epitaph for a Man killed*
                                            *by falling from his Horse*


**CAMPBELL, Roy, 1902–1957**

17 You praise the firm restraint with which they write,
    I'm with you there, of course:
    They use the snaffle and the curb all right,
    But where's the bloody horse?
                          *On Some South African Novelists*

## CAMPBELL, Thomas, 1777-1844

18  O leave this barren spot to me!
   Spare, woodman, spare the beechen tree.
                                    *The Beech-Tree's Petition*

19  A chieftain to the Highlands bound
   Cries 'Boatman, do not tarry!
   And I'll give thee a silver pound
   To row us o'er the ferry.'           *Lord Ullin's Daughter*

20  'Tis distance lends enchantment to the view,
   And robes the mountain in its azure hue.
                                    *Pleasures of Hope, 1, 7*

21  Ye mariners of England
   That guard our native seas,
   Whose flag has braved, a thousand years,
   The battle and the breeze.          *Ye Mariners of England*

22  Now Barabbas was a publisher.              *Attributed*

## CAMPION, Thomas, 1567-1620

23  Follow thy fair sun, unhappy shadow.     *Follow thy Fair Sun*

24  There is a garden in her face,
   Where roses and white lilies grow.
                                    *There is a Garden in her Face*

25  There cherries grow, which none may buy
   Till 'Cherry Ripe' themselves do cry.              *Ib*

## CANNING, George, 1770-1827

26  I called the New World into existence to redress the balance of
   the Old.                          *Speech, 12 Dec. 1826*

27  But of all plagues, good Heaven, thy wrath can send,
   Save me, oh, save me, from the candid friend.
                                    *New Morality, 209*

28  Pitt is to Addington
   As London is to Paddington.              *The Oracle*

## CAREY, Henry, 1693?-1743

29  God save our Gracious King,
   Long live our noble King,
   God save the King.
   Send him victorious,
   Happy and glorious.     *God Save the King. Origin is disputed.*
           *See Dr Percy A. Scholes, God Save the Queen, 1954*

30  Confound their politics
   Frustrate their knavish tricks                    *Ib*

31 Of all the girls that are so smart
There's none like pretty Sally;
She is the darling of my heart
And she lives in our alley.                    *Sally in our Alley*

### CARLYLE, Thomas, 1795–1881

32 A witty statesman said, you might prove anything by figures.
*Essay on Chartism*

33 Genius (which means transcendent capacity of taking trouble,
first of all).                    *Frederick the Great, Book 4, Ch. 3*

34 A whiff of grapeshot. *History of the French Revolution, 1, 5, 3*

35 The seagreen Incorruptible. (*Robespierre*)          *Ib, 2, 4, 4*

36 No great man lives in vain. The history of the world is but the
biography of great men.          *Heroes and Hero-Worship, 1,*
*The Hero as Divinity*

37 The true University of these days is a collection of books.
*Ib, 5, The Hero as Man of Letters*

38 History is the essence of innumerable biographies.
*Essay on History*

39 No man who has once heartily and wholly laughed can be
altogether irreclaimably bad. *Sartor Resartus, Book 1, Ch. 4*

### CARNEGIE, Dale, 1888–

40 How to Win Friends and Influence People.          *Title of Book*

### CARNEY, Julia A. Fletcher, 1823–1908

41 Little drops of water, little grains of sand,
Make the mighty ocean and the pleasant land.
So the little minutes, humble though they be,
Make the mighty ages of eternity                    *Little Things*

### CARROLL, Lewis (Charles Lutwidge Dodgson), 1832–1898

42 'What is the use of a book,' thought Alice, 'without pictures or
conversation?'          *Alice's Adventures in Wonderland, Ch. 1*

43 She found a little bottle on it, ('which certainly was not here
before,' said Alice,) and round its neck a paper label, with the
words 'DRINK ME' beautifully printed on it in large letters.
*Ib, Ch. 1*

44 'Curiouser and curiouser!' cried Alice.          *Ib, Ch. 2*

45 How doth the little crocodile
Improve his shining tail,

And pour the waters of the Nile
  On every golden scale!
How cheerfully he seems to grin,
  How neatly spread his claws,
And welcomes little fishes in
  With gently smiling jaws!   ALICE       *Alice's Adventures in*
                                          *Wonderland, Ch. 2*

46 'I'll be judge, I'll be jury,' said cunning old Fury: 'I'll try the
   whole cause, and condemn you to death.'          *Ib, Ch. 3*

47 The Duchess! The Duchess! Oh my dear paws! Oh my fur and
   whiskers!   THE WHITE RABBIT                      *Ib, Ch. 4*

48 'You are old, Father William,' the young man said,
     'And your hair has become very white;
   And yet you incessantly stand on your head –
     Do you think at your age, it is right?'
   'In my youth,' Father William replied to his son,
     'I feared it might injure the brain;
   But, now that I'm perfectly sure I have none,
     Why, I do it again and again.'   ALICE          *Ib, Ch. 5*

49 'I have answered three questions, and that is enough.'
     Said his father; 'don't give yourself airs!
   Do you think I can listen all day to such stuff?
     Be off or I'll kick you downstairs!'   ALICE     *Ib, Ch. 5*

50 'If everybody minded their own business,' the Duchess said in a
   hoarse growl, 'the world would go round a deal faster than it
   does.'                                             *Ib, Ch. 6*

51 Speak roughly to your little boy,
     And beat him when he sneezes:
   He only does it to annoy,
     Because he knows it teases.   THE DUCHESS        *Ib, Ch. 6*

52 I speak severely to my boy,
     I beat him when he sneezes;
   For he can thoroughly enjoy
     The pepper when he pleases!   THE DUCHESS        *Ib. Ch. 6*

53 Twinkle, twinkle, little bat!
   How I wonder what you're at!   THE HATTER          *Ib, Ch. 7*

54 Up above the world you fly,
   Like a tea-tray in the sky.   THE HATTER           *Ib, Ch. 7*

55 'Take some more tea,' the March Hare said to Alice, very
     earnestly.
   'I've had nothing yet,' Alice replied in an offended tone, 'so I
     can't take more.'
   'You mean you can't take *less*,' said the Hatter: 'it's very easy
     to take *more* than nothing.'                    *Ib, Ch. 7*

56 The Queen was in a furious passion, and went stamping about,
and shouting 'Off with his head!' or 'Off with her head!' about
once in a minute.     *Alice's Adventures in Wonderland, Ch. 8*

57 Everything's got a moral, if only you can find it.   THE DUCHESS
*Ib. Ch. 9*

58 Take care of the sense, and the sounds will take care of themselves.   THE DUCHESS                                    *Ib, Ch. 9*

59 'Why did you call him Tortoise, if he wasn't one?' Alice asked.
'We called him Tortoise because he taught us,' said the Mock
Turtle angrily: 'really you are very dull!'             *Ib, Ch. 9*

60 'Reeling and Writhing, of course, to begin with,' the Mock
Turtle replied; 'and then the different branches of Arithmetic
– Ambition, Distraction, Uglification, and Derision.'  *Ib, Ch. 9*

61 'That's the reason they're called lessons,' the Gryphon remarked: 'because they lessen from day to day.'        *Ib, Ch. 9*

62 'Will you walk a little faster?' said a whiting to a snail.
'There's a porpoise close behind us, and he's treading on my tail.'
THE MOCK TURTLE                                        *Ib, Ch. 10*

63 Will you, won't you, will you, won't you, will you join the
dance?   THE MOCK TURTLE                               *Ib, Ch. 10*

64 'Tis the voice of the Lobster; I heard him declare,
'You have baked me too brown, I must sugar my hair.'   ALICE
*Ib, Ch. 10*

65 Soup of the evening, beautiful Soup!   THE MOCK TURTLE
*Ib, Ch. 10*

66 'The Queen of Hearts, she made some tarts,
         All on a summer day:
The Knave of Hearts, he stole those tarts,
         And took them quite away!'   THE WHITE RABBIT (reading)
*Ib, Ch. 11*

67 They told me you have been to her,
         And mentioned me to him:
She gave me a good character,
         But said I could not swim.   THE WHITE RABBIT (reading)
*Ib, Ch. 12*

68 'No, no!' said the Queen. 'Sentence first – verdict afterwards.'
'Stuff and nonsense!' said Alice loudly.              *Ib, Ch. 12*

69 'Twas brillig, and the slithy toves
         Did gyre and gimble in the wabe;
All mimsy were the borogoves,
         And the mome raths outgrabe.   ALICE (reading)
*Through the Looking-Glass, Ch. 1*

70 One, two! One, two! And through and through
   The vorpal blade went snicker-snack!
   He left it dead, and with its head
   He went galumphing back.   ALICE (reading)     *Through the*
                                            *Looking Glass, Ch. 1*

71 'And hast thou slain the Jabberwock?
   Come to my arms, my beamish boy!
   O frabjous day! Callooh! Callay!'
   He chortled in his joy.   ALICE (reading)          *Ib, Ch. 1*

72 Now, *here*, you see, it takes all the running *you* can do, to keep
   in the same place. If you want to get somewhere else, you must
   run at least twice as fast as that!   THE QUEEN     *Ib, Ch. 2*

73 'If you think we're wax-works,' he said, 'you ought to pay, you
      know.
   Wax-works weren't made to be looked at for nothing. Nohow!'
   TWEEDLEDUM                                            *Ib, Ch. 4*

74 Tweedledum and Tweedledee
      Agreed to have a battle;
   For Tweedledum said Tweedledee
      Had spoiled his nice new rattle.   ALICE          *Ib, Ch. 4*

75 'Contrariwise,' continued Tweedledee, 'if it was so, it might be;
   and if it were so, it would be: but as it isn't, it ain't. That's logic.'
                                                         *Ib, Ch. 4*

76 The sun was shining on the sea,
      Shining with all his might:
   He did his very best to make
      The billows smooth and bright –
   And this was odd, because it was
      The middle of the night.   TWEEDLEDEE (reciting *The Walrus*
                                      *and The Carpenter) Ib, Ch. 4*

77 'It's very rude of him,' she said,
      'To come and spoil the fun!'   TWEEDLEDEE          *Ib, Ch. 4*

78 The Walrus and the Carpenter
      Were walking close at hand;
   They wept like anything to see
      Such quantities of sand:
   'If this were only cleared away,'
      They said, 'it *would* be grand!'   TWEEDLEDEE     *Ib, Ch. 4*

79 'If seven maids with seven mops
      Swept it for half a year,
   Do you suppose,' the Walrus said,
      'That they could get it clear?'
   'I doubt it,' said the Carpenter,
      And shed a bitter tear.   TWEEDLEDEE                *Ib, Ch. 4*

80 'The time has come,' the Walrus said,
    'To talk of many things:
 Of shoes – and ships – and sealing-wax –
    Of cabbages – and kings –
 And why the sea is boiling hot –
    And whether pigs have wings.' TWEEDLEDEE (reciting *The
 Walrus and the Carpenter*) *Through the Looking Glass, Ch. 4*

81 'I weep for you,' the Walrus said:
    'I deeply sympathize.'
 With sobs and tears he sorted out
    Those of the largest size,
 Holding his pocket-handkerchief
    Before his streaming eyes. TWEEDLEDEE         *Ib, Ch. 4*

82 'O Oysters,' said the Carpenter,
    'You've had a pleasant run!
 Shall we be trotting home again?'
    But answer came there none –
 And this was scarcely odd, because
    They'd eaten every one. TWEEDLEDEE           *Ib, Ch. 4*

83 The rule is, jam tomorrow and jam yesterday – but never jam
 today. THE QUEEN                                *Ib, Ch. 5*

84 Humpty Dumpty sat on a wall:
 Humpty Dumpty had a great fall.
 All the King's horses and all the King's men
 Couldn't put Humpty Dumpty in his place again. ALICE
                                                 *Ib, Ch. 6*

85 'They gave it me,' Humpty Dumpty continued thoughtfully,
 . . . 'for an un-birthday present.'             *Ib, Ch. 6*

86 'When *I* use a word,' Humpty Dumpty said in rather a scornful
 tone, 'it means just what I choose it to mean – neither more nor
 less.'                                          *Ib, Ch. 6*

87 In winter, when the fields are white,
 I sing this song for your delight – HUMPTY DUMPTY *Ib, Ch. 6*
88 In spring, when woods are getting green,
 I'll try and tell you what I mean. HUMPTY DUMPTY  *Ib, Ch. 6*
89 I sent a message to the fish:
 I told them 'This is what I wish.' HUMPTY DUMPTY  *Ib, Ch. 6*
90 The little fishes of the sea,
 They sent an answer back to me.
 The little fishes' answer was
 'We cannot do it, Sir, because – '. HUMPTY DUMPTY *Ib, Ch. 6*
91 I said it very loud and clear;
 I went and shouted in his ear. HUMPTY DUMPTY     *Ib, Ch. 6*

92 He's an Anglo-Saxon Messenger – and those are Anglo-Saxon attitudes.   THE KING        *Through the Looking Glass, Ch. 7*

93 It's as large as life, and twice as natural!   HAIGHA   *Ib, Ch. 7*

94 The Lion looked at Alice wearily. 'Are you animal – or vegetable – or mineral?' he said, yawning at every other word.
*Ib, Ch. 7*

95 I'll tell thee everything I can;
There's little to relate.
I saw an aged aged man,
A-sitting on a gate.   THE KNIGHT        *Ib, Ch. 8*

96 'Speak when you're spoken to!' the Red Queen sharply interrupted her.        *Ib, Ch. 9*

97 No admittance till the week after next!   CREATURE WITH A LONG BEAK        *Ib, Ch. 9*

98 'You look a little shy; let me introduce you to that leg of mutton,' said the Red Queen. 'Alice – Mutton; Mutton – Alice.'
*Ib, Ch. 9*

## CARY, Phoebe, 1824–1871

99 And though hard be the task,
'Keep a stiff upper lip.'        *Keep a Stiff Upper Lip*

## CASTLING, Harry, 19th century

1 Let's all go down the Strand.        *Title of Song*

## CATO, Marcus Porcius, 234–149 B.C.

2 *Delenda est Carthago.* Carthage must be destroyed.
*Plutarch, Life of Cato*

## CATULLUS, Gaius Valerius, 87–54? B.C.

3 *Vivamus, mea Lesbia, atque amemus*
*Rumoresque senum severiorum*
*Omnes unius aestimemus assis.*
Let us live, my Lesbie, and love, and pay no heed to all the talk of censorious old men.        *Carmina, 5*

4 *Da mi basia mille.*
Give me a thousand kisses.        *Ib*

5 *Odi et amo. Quare id faciam, fortasse requiris.*
*Nescio, sed fieri sentio et excrucior.*
I hate and love. Why I do so, perhaps you ask.
I do not know, but I feel it and am in torment.        *Ib, 85*

6 *Atque in perpetuum, frater, ave atque vale.*
And for ever, brother, hail and farewell!        *Ib, 101*

## CAVELL, Edith, 1865–1915

7 I realize that patriotism is not enough. I must have no hatred or bitterness towards anyone. *Last Words*

## CERVANTES, Miguel de, 1547–1616

8 The knight of the sorrowful countenance.
*Don Quixote, Part 1, Ch. 19*

9 Every man is as Heaven made him, and sometimes a great deal worse. *Ib, Part 2, Ch. 4*

10 There are only two families in the world, my old grandmother used to say, The *Haves* and the *Have-Nots*. *Ib, Ch. 20*

11 A private sin is not so prejudicial in the world as a public indecency. *Ib, Ch. 22*

12 Tell me what company thou keepest, and I'll tell thee what thou art. *Ib, Ch. 23*

## CHAMBERLAIN, Joseph, 1836–1914

13 Provided that the City of London remains as at present, the Clearing-house of the World
*Speech, Guildhall, London, 19 Jan. 1904*

14 The day of small nations has long passed away. The day of Empires has come. *Speech, Birmingham, 12 May 1904*

## CHAMBERLAIN, Neville, 1869–1940

15 In war, whichever side may call itself the victor, there are no winners, but all are losers. *Speech, Kettering, 3 July 1938*

16 I believe it is peace for our time . . . peace with honour.
*Broadcast after Munich Agreement, 1 Oct. 1938*

17 Hitler has missed the bus. *Speech, House of Commons, 4 April 1940*

## CHANDLER, John, 1806–1876

18 Conquering kings their titles take
From the foes they captive make:
Jesu, by a nobler deed
From the thousands He hath freed.
*Conquering Kings their Titles Take*

## CHARLES I of Great Britain, 1600–1649

19 Never make a defence or apology before you be accused.
*Letter to Lord Wentworth, 3 Sept. 1636*

## CHARLES II of Great Britain, 1630–1685

20 He had been, he said, a most unconscionable time dying; but
he hoped that they would excuse it.
*Macaulay, History of England, Vol. 1, Ch. 4*

21 Not a religion for gentlemen. [*Presbyterianism*]
*Burnet, History of My Own Time, Vol. 1, Book 2, Ch. 2*

22 Let not poor Nelly starve. [*Said on his death-bed*]
*Ib, Vol. 2, Book 3, Ch. 17*

23 Better than a play.
*On House of Lords Debate on Divorce Bill, 1670*

## CHARLES V, Holy Roman Emperor, 1500–1558

24 I speak Spanish to God, Italian to women, French to men, and
German to my horse.                              *Attributed*

## CHARLES, Hughie, see PARKER, Ross

## CHAUCER, Geoffrey, 1340?–1400

25 Whan that Aprille with his shoures sote
The droghte of Marche hath perced to the rote.
*The Canterbury Tales, Prologue, 1*

26 He was a verray parfit gentil knight.            *Ib, 72*

27 He was as fresh as is the month of May.    *Ib, 92 (Squire)*

28 And Frensh she spak ful faire and fetisly,
After the scole of Stratford atte Bowe,
For Frensh of Paris was to hir unknowe.    *Ib, 124 (Prioress)*

29 He yaf nat of that text a pulled hen,
That seith, that hunters been nat holy men.    *Ib, 177 (Monk)*

30 What sholde he studie, and make himselven wood,
Upon a book in cloistre alwey to poure,
Or swinken with his handes, and laboure,
As Austin bit? How shal the world be served?
Lat Austin have his swink to him reserved.    *Ib, 184 (Monk)*

31 A Clerk ther was of Oxenford also,
That un-to logik hadde longe y-go.              *Ib, 285*

32 As lene was his hors as is a rake.    *Ib, 287 (Clerk)*

33 For him was lever have at his beddes heed
Twenty bokes, clad in blak or reed,
Of Aristotle and his philosophye,
Than robes riche, or fithele, or gay sautrye.
But all be that he was a philosophre,
Yet hadde he but litel gold in cofre.    *Ib, 293 (Clerk)*

34 Souninge in moral vertu was his speche,
   And gladly wolde he lerne, and gladly teche.   *The Canterbury*
                                             *Tales, Prologue, 307 (Clerk)*

35 No-wher so bisy a man as he ther nas,
   And yet he semed bisier than he was.   *Ib, 321 (Man of Law)*

36 It snewed in his hous of mete and drinke.   *Ib, 345 (Franklin)*

37 His studie was but litel on the bible.   *Ib, 438 (Doctor)*

38 For gold in phisik is a cordial,
   Therfore he lovede gold in special.   *Ib, 443 (Doctor)*

39 She was a worthy womman al hir lyve,
   Housbondes at chirche-dore she hadde fyve,
   Withouten other companye in youthe.   *Ib, 459 (Wife of Bath)*

40 This noble ensample to his sheep he yaf,
   That first he wroghte, and afterward he taughte.
                                             *Ib, 496 (Parson)*

41 If gold ruste, what shal iren do?   *Ib, 500 (Parson)*

42 But Cristes lore, and his apostles twelve,
   He taughte, and first he folwed it himselve.   *Ib, 527 (Parson)*

43 His walet lay biforn him in his lappe,
   Bret-ful of pardoun come from Rome al hoot.
                                             *Ib, 686 (Pardoner)*

44 The smyler with the knyf under the cloke.
                                    *Ib, The Knight's Tale, 1141*

45 This world nis but a thurghfare ful of wo,
   And we ben pilgrimes, passinge to and fro;
   Deeth is an ende of every worldly sore.   *Ib, Ib, 1989*

46 So was hir joly whistle wel y-wet.   *Ib, The Reve's Tale, 235*

47 Tragedie is to seyn a certeyn storie,
   As olde bokes maken us memorie,
   Of him that stood in greet prosperitee
   And is y-fallen out of heigh degree
   Into miserie, and endeth wrecchedly.
                                    *Ib, The Monk's Prologue, 85*

48 Mordre wol out, that see we day by day.
                                    *Ib, The Nun's Priest's Tale, 232*

49 My sone, keep wel thy tongue and keep thy freend.
                                    *Ib, The Maunciple's Tale, 319*

50 The lyf so short, the craft so long to lerne,
   Th'assay so hard, so sharp the conquering.
                                    *The Parlement of Foules, 1*

51 For of fortunes sharp adversitee
   The worst kinde of infortune is this,

A man to have ben in prosperitee,
And it remembren, what it passed is.
                    *Troilus and Criseyde, 3, 1625*

52  Go, litel book, go litel myn tragedie.          *Ib, 5, 1786*

53  O moral Gower, this book I directe
To thee.                                           *Ib, 5, 1856*

**CHESTERFIELD, Philip Dormer Stanhope, 4th Earl of,
1694–1773**

54  Be wiser than other people if you can, but do not tell them so.
                    *Letter to his Son, 19 Nov. 1745*

55  Whatever is worth doing at all is worth doing well.
                    *Ib, 10 March 1746*

56  An injury is much sooner forgotten than an insult.
                    *Ib, 9 Oct. 1746*

57  Take the tone of the company you are in.        *Ib, 9 Oct. 1747*

58  Advice is seldom welcome; and those who want it the most
always like it the least.                          *Ib, 29 Jan. 1748*

59  In my mind, there is nothing so illiberal and so ill-bred, as
audible laughter.                                  *Ib, 9 March 1748*

60  A man of sense only trifles with them [*women*], plays with them,
humours and flatters them, as he does with a sprightly and
forward child; but he neither consults them about, nor trusts
them with, serious matters.                        *Ib, 5 Sept. 1748*

61  Idleness is only the refuge of weak minds.      *Ib, 20 July 1749*

62  Women are much more like each other than men: they have, in
truth, but two passions, vanity and love; these are their universal
characteristics.                                   *Ib, 19 Dec. 1749*

63  Every woman is infallibly to be gained by every sort of flattery,
and every man by one sort or other.    .           *Ib, 16 March 1752*

64  Unlike my subject will I frame my song,
It shall be witty and it shan't be long.
                    *Epigram on 'Long' Sir Thomas Robinson*

65  Give Dayrolles a chair.                         *Last words*

**CHESTERTON, Gilbert Keith, 1874–1936**

66  The strangest whim has seized me . . . After all
I think I will not hang myself today.      *A Ballade of Suicide*

67  When fishes flew and forests walked
And figs grew upon thorn,
Some moment when the moon was blood
Then surely I was born.                            *The Donkey*

68 The devil's walking parody
On all four-footed things *The Donkey*

69 Fools! For I also had my hour;
One far fierce hour and sweet;
There was a shout about my ears,
And palms before my feet. *Ib*

70 White founts falling in the Courts of the sun,
And the Soldan of Byzantium is smiling as they run. *Lepanto*

71 Strong gongs groaning as the guns boom far,
Don John of Austria is going to the war. *Ib*

72 Before the Roman came to Rye or out to Severn strode,
The rolling English drunkard made the rolling English road.
*The Rolling English Road*

73 The night we went to Birmingham by way of Beachy Head. *Ib*

74 For there is good news yet to hear and fine things to be seen,
Before we go to Paradise by way of Kensal Green. *Ib*

75 Smile at us, pay us, pass us, but do not quite forget,
For we are the people of England, that never have spoken yet.
*The Secret People*

76 God made the wicked Grocer
For a mystery and a sign,
That men might shun the awful shops
And go to inns to dine. *The Song Against Grocers*

77 And Noah he often said to his wife when he sat down to dine,
'I don't care where the water goes if it doesn't get into the wine'.
*Wine and Water*

78 The human race, to which so many of my readers belong.
*The Napoleon of Notting Hill, Book 1, Ch. 1, Opening Words*

## CHEVALIER, Albert, 1861–1923

79 'Wot cher!' all the neighbours cried,
'Who're yer goin' to meet Bill?
Have yer bought the street Bill?'
Laugh! I thought I should have died,
Knock'd 'em in the Old Kent Road.
*Knock'd 'em in the Old Kent Road*

80 We've been together now for forty years,
An' it don't seem a day too much;
There ain't a lady livin' in the land
As I'd 'swop' for my dear old Dutch! *My Old Dutch*

## CHEVALIER, Maurice, 1888–1972

81 I prefer old age to the alternative. *Remark, 1962*

## CHURCHILL, Charles, 1731–1764

82        Be England what she will,
With all her faults, she is my country still.    *The Farewell, 27*

83 The danger chiefly lies in acting well;
No crime's so great as daring to excel.
                      *Epistle to William Hogarth*

84 He for subscribers baits his hook,
And takes your cash, but where's the book?
No matter where; wise fear, you know,
Forbids the robbing of a foe;
But what, to serve our private ends,
Forbids the cheating of our friends?
        [*Dr Johnson and his Dictionary*] *The Ghost, 3, 801*

## CHURCHILL, Lord Randolph Spencer, 1849–1894

85 The old gang. [*Members of the Conservative Government*]
        *Speech, House of Commons, 7 March 1878*

86 An old man in a hurry. [*Gladstone*]    *Speech, June 1886*

87 I never could make out what those damned dots meant. [*The decimal point*]    *Quoted in Winston Churchill's Biography*

## CHURCHILL, Sir Winston Leonard Spencer, 1874–1965

88 It cannot in the opinion of His Majesty's Government be classified as slavery in the extreme acceptance of the word without some risk of terminological inexactitude.
        *Speech, House of Commons, 22 Feb. 1906*

89 The maxim of the British people is 'Business as usual'.
        *Speech, Guildhall, London, 9 Nov. 1914*

90 The German dictator, instead of snatching the victuals from the table, has been content to have them served to him course by course.    *Speech, House of Commons, 5 Oct. 1938*

91 I cannot forecast to you the action of Russia. It is a riddle wrapped in a mystery inside an enigma.
        *Broadcast, 1 Oct. 1939*

92 I would say to the House, as I said to those who have joined the Government: 'I have nothing to offer but blood, toil, tears and sweat.'    *Speech, House of Commons, 13 May 1940*

93 Victory at all costs, victory in spite of all terror, victory however long and hard the road may be; for without victory there is no survival.                           *Ib*

94 We shall not flag or fail. We shall fight in France, we shall fight on the seas and oceans, we shall fight with growing confidence

and growing strength in the air, we shall defend our island, whatever the cost may be, we shall fight on the beaches, we shall fight on the landing grounds, we shall fight in the fields and in the streets, we shall fight in the hills; we shall never surrender.
*Speech, House of Commons, 4 June 1940*

95 Let us therefore brace ourselves to our duties, and so bear ourselves that, if the British Empire and its Commonwealth last for a thousand years, men will still say, 'This was their finest hour'. *Speech, House of Commons, 18 June 1940*

96 Never in the field of human conflict was so much owed by so many to so few. *Speech, House of Commons, 20 Aug. 1940*
*on R.A.F. in Battle of Britain*

97 *Nous attendons l'invasion promise de longue date. Les poissons aussi.*
We are waiting for the long-promised invasion. So are the fishes.
*Broadcast to the French People, 21 Oct. 1940*

98 Here is the answer which I will give to President Roosevelt. . . . Give us the tools, and we will finish the job.
*Broadcast, 9 Feb. 1941*

99 What kind of a people do they [*the Japanese*] think we are?
*Speech, U.S. Congress, 26 Dec. 1941*

1 When I warned them [*the French Government*] that Britain would fight on alone whatever they did, their generals told their Prime Minister and his divided Cabinet: 'In three weeks England will have her neck wrung like a chicken.' Some chicken! Some neck!
*Speech, Canadian Parliament, 30 Dec. 1941*

2 This is not the end. It is not even the beginning of the end. But it is, perhaps, the end of the beginning.
*Speech, Mansion House, London, 10 Nov. 1942*

3 Let me, however, make this clear, in case there should be any mistake about it in any quarter. We mean to hold our own. I have not become the King's First Minister in order to preside over the liquidation of the British Empire. *Ib*

4 The soft under-belly of the Axis. *Speech, House of Commons,*
*11 Nov. 1942*

5 The problems of victory are more agreeable than those of defeat, but they are no less difficult. *Ib*

6 There is no finer investment for any community than putting milk into babies. Healthy citizens are the greatest asset any country can have.
*Broadcast: A Four Years' Plan, 21 March 1943*

7 I view with profound misgivings the retreat of the American
Army to our line of occupation in the central sector, thus bringing Soviet power into the heart of Western Europe and the
descent of an iron curtain between us and everything to the
eastward. *Cable to President Truman, 4 June 1945*
*Quoted in The Second World War, Vol. 6, Triumph and Tragedy,*
*1954, p. 523*

8 From Stettin in the Baltic to Trieste in the Adriatic, an iron
curtain has descended across the Continent.
*Speech, Westminster College, Fulton, U.S.A., 5 March 1946*

9 This is the sort of English up with which I will not put.
*Attributed. Marginal comment on document,*
*quoted by Sir Ernest Gowers in Plain Words, 1948, p. 74*

10 In War: Resolution. In Defeat: Defiance. In Victory: Magnanimity. In Peace: Goodwill. *The Second World War, Vol. 1,*
*The Gathering Storm, 1948, Moral of the Work*

11 I have never accepted what many people have kindly said,
namely that I inspired the nation. It was the nation and the race
dwelling all round the globe that had the lion heart. I had the
luck to be called upon to give the roar.
*Speech on 80th birthday, Westminster Hall, 30 Nov. 1954*

## CIBBER, Colley, 1671–1757

12 One had as good be out of the world, as out of the fashion.
*Love's Last Shift, Act 2*

13 Stolen sweets are best. *The Rival Fools, Act 1*

## CICERO, Marcus Tullius, 106–43 B.C.

14 *Nihil tam absurde dici potest, quod non dicatur, ab alique philoso-*
*phorum.* There is nothing so absurd but some philosopher has
said it. *De Divinatione, 2, 58*

15 *Salus populi suprema est lex.* The good of the people is the chief
law. *De Legibus, 3, 3, 8*

16 *Summum bonum.* The greatest good. *De Officiis, 1, 2*

17 *Cedant arma togae, concedant laurea laudi.* Let wars give way to
peace, laurels to paeans. *Ib, 1, 22*

18 *Mens cuiusque is est quisque.* The mind of each man is the man
himself. *De Republica, 6, 26*

19 *O tempora! O mores!* What times! What customs!
*In Catilinam, 1, 1*

20 *Civis Romanus sum.* I am a Roman citizen.
*In Verrem, 5, 57, 147*

21 *O fortunatam natam me consule Romam!* O happy Rome, born
   when I was consul.                    *Quoted in Juvenal, 10, 22*

**CLAY, Henry, 1777–1852**
22 I had rather be right than be President.          *Speech,   1850*

**CLEMENS, Samuel Langhorne, see TWAIN, Mark**

**CLEVELAND, Stephen Grover, 1837–1908**
23 However plenty silver dollars may become, they will not be
   distributed as gifts among the people.
                    *First Annual Message as President of U.S.A., 8 Dec. 1885*

**CLIVE, Lord Robert, 1725–1774**
24 By God, Mr Chairman, at this moment I stand astonished at
   my own moderation! *Reply during Parliamentary Inquiry, 1773*

**CLOUGH, Arthur Hugh, 1819–1861**
25 A world where nothing is had for nothing.
                        *The Bothie of Tober-na-Vuolich, 8, 5*
26 How pleasant it is to have money.  *Dipsychus, Part 1, Scene 4*
27 And almost every one when age,
       Disease, or sorrows strike him,
   Inclines to think there is a God,
       Or something very like Him.          *Ib, Part 1, Scene 5*
28 Thou shalt have one God only; who
   Would be at the expense of two?    *The Latest Decalogue, 1*
29 Thou shalt not kill; but needst not strive
   Officiously to keep alive.                       *Ib, 11*
30 Thou shalt not covet; but tradition
   Approves all forms of competition.               *Ib, 19*
31 'Tis better to have fought and lost,
   Than never to have fought at all.           *Peschiera*
32 Say not the struggle naught availeth,
       The labour and the wounds are vain.
   The enemy faints not, nor faileth,
       And as things have been, things remain.
                        *Say not the struggle naught availeth*
33 For while the tired waves, vainly breaking,
       Seem here no painful inch to gain,
   Far back through creeks and inlets making
       Comes silent, flooding in, the main.               *Ib*

34 And not by eastern windows only,
    When daylight comes, comes in the light,
  In front the sun climbs slow, how slowly,
    But westward, look, the land is bright.    *Say not the struggle*
                                                      *naught availeth*

COBBETT, William, 1762–1835

35 To be poor and independent is very nearly an impossibility.
                                              *Advice to Young Men*

36 But what is to be the fate of the great wen [*London*] of all?
                                                    *Rural Rides*

COBORN, Charles, 1852–1945

37 Two lovely black eyes,
  Oh, what a surprise!
  Only for telling a man he was wrong,
  Two lovely black eyes!        *Two Lovely Black Eyes*

COKE, Sir Edward, 1552–1634

38 How long soever it hath continued, if it be against reason, it is
  of no force in law.                          *First Institute*

39 A man's house is his castle.                *Third Institute*

40 Six hours in sleep, in law's grave study six,
  Four spend in prayer, the rest on Nature fix.    *Pandects*

COLERIDGE, Hartley, 1796–1849

41 She is not fair to outward view
    As many maidens be;
  Her loveliness I never knew
    Until she smiled on me.          *Song, She is not Fair*

COLERIDGE, Samuel Taylor, 1772–1834

42 It is an ancient Mariner,
  And he stoppeth one of three.
  'By thy long grey beard and glittering eye,
  Now wherefore stopp'st thou me?'
                *The Rime of the Ancient Mariner, Part 1, 1*

43 He holds him with his glittering eye.        *Ib, 1, 13*

44 The Sun came up upon the left,
  Out of the sea came he!
  And he shone bright, and on the right
  Went down into the sea.                        *Ib, 1, 25*

45 The bride hath paced into the hall,
  Red as a rose is she.                          *Ib, 1, 33*

46 The ice was here, the ice was there,
   The ice was all around:
   It cracked and growled, and roared and howled,
   Like noises in a swound!     *The Rime of the Ancient Mariner,*
                                                                *Part, 1, 59*

47 With my cross-bow
   I shot the albatross.                                        *Ib, 1, 81*

48 The fair breeze blew, the white foam flew,
   The furrow followed free;
   We were the first that ever burst
   Into that silent sea.                                        *Ib, Part 2, 103*

49 As idle as a painted ship
   Upon a painted ocean.                                        *Ib, 2, 117*

50 Water, water, every where,
   And all the boards did shrink;
   Water, water, every where,
   Nor any drop to drink.                                       *Ib, 2, 119*

51 I bit my arm, I sucked the blood,
   And cried, A sail! a sail!                                   *Ib, Part 3, 160*

52 Her lips were red, her looks were free,
   Her locks were yellow as gold:
   Her skin was as white as leprosy,
   The Night-mare Life-in-Death was she,
   Who thicks man's blood with cold.                            *Ib, 3, 190*

53 I fear thee, ancient Mariner!
   I fear thy skinny hand!                                      *Ib, Part 4, 224*

54 Alone, alone, all, all alone,
   Alone on a wide wide sea!
   And never a saint took pity on
   My soul in agony.                                            *Ib, 4, 232*

55 The many men, so beautiful!
   And they all dead did lie:
   And a thousand thousand slimy things
   Lived on; and so did I.                                      *Ib, 4, 236*

56 The moving Moon went up the sky,
   And no where did abide:
   Softly she was going up,
   And a star or two beside.                                    *Ib, 4, 263*

57 Oh sleep! it is gentle thing,
   Beloved from pole to pole!                                   *Ib, Part 5, 292*

58 We were a ghastly crew.                                      *Ib, 5, 340*

59 Quoth he, 'The man hath penance done,
   And penance more will do.'                                   *Ib, 5, 408*

60 Like one, that on a lonesome road
   Doth walk in fear and dread,
   And having once turned round walks on,
   And turns no more his head;
   Because he knows, a frightful fiend
   Doth close behind him tread.        *The Rime of the Ancient*
                                       *Mariner, Part 6, 446*

61 No voice; but oh! the silence sank
   Like music on my heart.                        *Ib, 6, 498*

62 O Wedding-Guest! this soul hath been
   Alone on a wide wide sea:
   So lonely 'twas, that God himself
   Scarce seemed there to be.                  *Ib, Part, 7, 597*

63 He prayeth well, who loveth well
   Both man and bird and beast.                  *Ib, 7, 612*

64 He prayeth best, who loveth best
   All things both great and small;
   For the dear God who loveth us,
   He made and loveth all.                       *Ib, 7, 614*

65 A sadder and a wiser man,
   He rose the morrow morn.                      *Ib, 7, 624*

66 A sight to dream of, not to tell!        *Christabel, 1, 253*

67 And constancy lives in realms above;
   And life is thorny; and youth is vain;
   And to be wroth with one we love
   Doth work like madness in the brain.         *Ib, 2, 410*

68 I see, not feel, how beautiful they are!  *Dejection: An Ode, 38*

69 I may not hope from outward forms to win
   The passion and the life, whose fountains are within.   *Ib, 45*

70 Swans sing before they die – 'twere no bad thing
   Should certain persons die before they sing.
                                  *Epigram on a Volunteer Singer*

71 In Xanadu did Kubla Khan
   A stately pleasure-dome decree:
   Where Alph, the sacred river, ran
   Through caverns measureless to man
       Down to a sunless sea.                   *Kubla Khan, 1*

72 A savage place! as holy and enchanted
   As e'er beneath a waning moon was haunted
   By woman wailing for her demon-lover!         *Ib, 14*

73 Through wood and dale the sacred river ran,
   Then reached the caverns measureless to man.  *Ib, 26*

74 And 'mid this tumult Kubla heard from far
   Ancestral voices prophesying war!       *Kubla Khan, 29*

75 It was a miracle of rare device,
   A sunny pleasure-dome with caves of ice!     *Ib, 35*

76 Weave a circle round him thrice,
   And close your eyes with holy dread,
   For he on honey-dew hath fed,
   And drunk the milk of Paradise.     *Ib, 51*

77 This Lime-tree Bower my Prison     *Title of Poem*

78 Tranquillity! thou better name
   Than all the family of Fame!     *Ode to Tranquillity*

79 That willing suspension of disbelief for the moment, which
   constitutes poetic faith.     *Biographia Literaria, Ch. 14*

80 Our myriad-minded Shakespeare.     *Ib, Ch. 15*

81 Summer has set in with its usual severity.
     *Remark quoted in C. Lamb's letter to V. Novello, 9 May 1826*

82 I wish our clever young poets would remember my homely
   definitions of prose and poetry; that is, prose = words in their
   best order;—poetry = the best words in the best order.
     *Table Talk, 12 July 1827*

83 No mind is thoroughly well organized that is deficient in a sense
   of humour.     *Table Talk*

84 What comes from the heart, goes to the heart.     *Ib*

**COLLINGS, Jesse, 1831–1921**

85 Three acres and a cow.     *Slogan for Land Reform, 1885*

**COLLINS, Mortimer, 1827–1876**

86 A man is as old as he's feeling,
   A woman as old as she looks.     *The Unknown Quantity*

**COLLINS, William, 1721–1759**

87 To fair Fidele's grassy tomb
   Soft maids, and village hinds shall bring
   Each op'ning sweet, of earliest bloom,
     And rifle all the breathing Spring.     *Dirge in Cymbeline, 1*

88 Hamlets brown, and dim-discover'd spires.   *Ode to Evening, 37*

89 How sleep the brave, who sink to rest,
   By all their country's wishes blest!
     *Ode written in the Year 1746, 1*

90 By fairy hands their knell is rung,
   By forms unseen their dirge is sung;

There Honour comes, a Pilgrim grey,
To bless the turf that wraps their clay,
And Freedom shall a-while repair,
To dwell a weeping hermit there!         *Ode written in the
                                            Year 1746, 7*

91 When Music, heavenly maid, was young.
                        *The Passions, An Ode for Music, 1*

92 With eyes up-rais'd, as one inspir'd,
   Pale Melancholy sate retir'd.                    *Ib, 57*

93 O Music, sphere-descended Maid,
   Friend of Pleasure, Wisdom's aid.                *Ib, 95*

## COLMAN, George, 1762–1836

94 Mum's the word.        *The Battle of Hexham, Act 2, Scene 1*

95 When taken
   To be well shaken.               *Newcastle Apothecary*

## COLTON, Charles Caleb, 1780?–1832

96 Men will wrangle for religion; write for it; fight for it; anything
   but – live for it.                        *Lacon, 1, No. 25*

97 When you have nothing to say, say nothing.      *Ib, No. 183*

98 Imitation is the sincerest form of flattery.    *Ib, No. 217*

99 Examinations are formidable even to the best prepared, for the
   greatest fool may ask more than the wisest man can answer.
                                              *Ib, No. 322*

 1 The debt which cancels all others.          *Ib, 2, No. 66*

## CONFUCIUS, 551–479 B.C.

 2 Men's natures are alike; it is their habits that carry them far
   apart.                                         *Analects*

 3 Study the past, if you would divine the future.        *Ib*

 4 Learning without thought is labour lost; thought without
   learning is perilous.                                 *Ib*

## CONGREVE, William, 1670–1729

 5 Music has charms to soothe a savage breast,
   To soften rocks, or bend a knotted oak.   ALMERIA
                              *The Mourning Bride, Act 1*

 6 Heaven has no rage like love to hatred turned,
   Nor hell a fury like a woman scorned.   ZARA     *Ib, Act 3*

 7 They come together like the coroner's inquest, to sit upon the
   murdered reputations of the week.   FAINALL
                        *The Way of the World, Act 1, Scene 1*

8 'Tis for the honour of England, that all Europe should know
that we have blockheads of all ages.  FAINALL
*The Way of the World, Act 1, Scene 5*

9 A wit should no more be sincere, than a woman constant; one
argues a decay of parts, as t'other of beauty.  WITWOUD
*Ib, Act 1, Scene 6*

10 Here she comes i' faith full sail, with her fan spread and
streamers out, and a shoal of fools for tenders.  MIRABELL
*Ib, Act 2, Scene 5*

11 I am persecuted with letters – I hate letters – nobody knows
how to write letters; and yet one has 'em, one does not know
why. – They serve one to pin up one's hair.  MRS MILLAMENT
*Ib*

12 MRS MILLAMENT: I believe I gave you some pain.
     MIRABEL: Does that please you?
   MRS MILLAMENT: Infinitely; I love to give pain.  *Ib*

13 Lord, what is a lover, that it can give? Why, one makes lovers
as fast as one pleases, and they live as long as one pleases, and
they die as soon as one pleases: and then if one pleases one
makes more.  MRS MILLAMENT  *Ib*

14 Love's but the frailty of the mind,
When 'tis not with ambition join'd.  SONG  *Ib, Act 3, Scene 12*

15 O, nothing is more alluring than a levee from a couch in some
confusion.  LADY WISHFORT  *Ib, Act 4, Scene 1*

16 I nauseate walking; 'tis a country diversion, I loathe the country
and everything that relates to it.  MRS MILLAMENT
*Ib, Act 4, Scene 4*

17 Let us never visit together, nor go to a play together, but let us
be very strange and wellbred: let us be as strange as if we had
been married a great while; and as wellbred as if we were not
married at all.  MRS MILLAMENT  *Ib, Act 4, Scene 5*

18 These articles subscribed, if I continue to endure you a little
longer, I may by degrees dwindle into a wife.
MRS MILLAMENT  *Ib*

19 I hope you do not think me prone to any iteration of
nuptials.  LADY WISHFORT  *Ib, Act 4, Scene 12*

20 O, she is the antidote to desire.  WAITWELL  *Ib, Act 4,
Scene 14*

## CONNELL, James, 1852–1929
21 Then raise the scarlet standard high!
Beneath its shade we'll live and die!

Though cowards flinch, and traitors jeer,
We'll keep the Red Flag flying here!            *The Red Flag*

## CONNOLLY, Cyril, 1903–1974

22 As repressed sadists are supposed to become policemen or
butchers so those with irrational fear of life become publishers.
*Enemies of Promise*

## CONNOR, T. W., 19th century

23 She was one of the early birds,
And I was one of the worms.
*She was a Dear Little Dickie-Bird*

## CONRAD, Joseph, 1857–1924

24 You shall judge of a man by his foes as well as by his friends.
*Lord Jim, Ch. 34*

25 A work that aspires, however humbly, to the condition of art
should carry its justification in every line.
*The Nigger of the Narcissus, Preface*

26 The sea never changes and its works, for all the talk of men, are
wrapped in mystery.            *Typhoon, Ch. 2*

27 The belief in a supernatural source of evil is not necessary;
men alone are quite capable of every wickedness.
*Under Western Eyes, Part 2*

## COOLIDGE, Calvin, 1872–1933

28 There is no right to strike against the public safety by anybody,
anywhere, any time.    *On the Boston police strike, 14 Sept. 1919*

29 He said he was against it.        *When asked what a clergyman
had said in a sermon on sin*

## COOPER, James Fenimore, 1789–1851

30 The Last of the Mohicans.            *Title of Novel*

## CORBUSIER, Le, 1887–1965

31 *Une maison est une machine-à-habiter.* A house is a machine for
living in.            *Vers une architecture, 1923*

## CORNEILLE, Pierre, 1606–1684

32 *À vaincre sans péril, on triomphe sans gloire.* We triumph without glory when we conquer without danger. DON GOMÈS
*Le Cid, Act 2, Scene 2*

33  *Faites votre devoir, et laissez faire aux dieux.* Do your duty and
    leave the rest to the Gods.     LE VIEIL HORACE
                                            *Horace, Act 2, Scene 8*

**CORNFORD, Frances Crofts, 1886–1960**

34  O why do you walk through the fields in gloves.
        Missing so much and so much?
    O fat white woman whom nobody loves
    Why do you walk through the fields in gloves
    When the grass is as soft as the breast of doves
        And shivering-sweet to the touch?
                                    *To a Fat Lady Seen from a Train*

**CORNUEL, Anne Bigot de, 1605–1694**

35  *Il n'y a pas de héros pour son valet de chambre.* No man is a hero
    to his valet.          *Lettres de Mlle. Aissé, 13 Aug. 1728*

**COUBERTIN, Baron Pierre de, 1863–1937**

36  *L'important dans ces olympiades, c'est moins d'y gagner que d'y
    prendre part. . . . L'important dans la vie ce n'est point le triomphe
    mais le combat.*
    The most important thing in the Olympic Games is not winning
    but taking part. . . . The essential thing in life is not conquering
    but fighting well.     *Speech at Banquet to Officials of Olympic
                                    Games, London, 24 July 1908*

**COUÉ, Émile, 1857–1926**

37  *Tous les jours, à tous points de vue, je vais de mieux en mieux.*
    Every day, in every way, I am getting better and better.
                            *Formula for his cures by auto-suggestion*

**COUSIN, Victor, 1792–1867**

38  *L'art pour l'art.* Art for art's sake.     *Lecture at Sorbonne, 1818*

**COWARD, Noel, 1899–1973**

39  The Stately Homes of England
        How beautiful they stand,
        To prove the upper classes
        Have still the upper hand.          *Operette, Act 1, Scene 7,
                                        The Stately Homes of England*

40  And tho' if the Van Dycks have to go
        And we pawn the Bechstein Grand,
        We'll stand by the Stately Homes of England.          *Ib*

41 A room with a view – and you
    And no one to worry us
No one to hurry us.
            *This Year of Grace, Act 1, A Room with a View*

42 At twelve noon the natives swoon
And no further work is done.
But mad dogs and Englishmen
Go out in the midday sun.
            *Words and Music, Mad Dogs and Englishmen*

43 Don't let's be Beastly to the Germans. *Title of Song*

44 Don't put your Daughter on the Stage, Mrs Worthington.
            *Title of song*

45 Poor Little Rich Girl. *Title of song*

## COWLEY, Abraham, 1618–1667

46 God the first garden made, and the first city Cain.
            *The Garden*

47 This only grant me, that my means may lie
Too low for envy, for contempt too high. *Of Myself*

## COWLEY, Hannah, 1743–1809

48 But what is woman? – only one of Nature's agreeable blunders.
            DOILEY  *Who's the Dupe? Act 2, Scene 2*

## COWPER, William, 1731–1800

49 Hark! the Gaul is at her gates! *Boadicea*

50 Regions Caesar never knew
        Thy posterity shall sway,
Where his eagles never flew,
        None invincible as they. *Ib*

51 He found it inconvenient to be poor. *Charity, 189*

52 A moral, sensible, and well-bred man
Will not affront me, and no other can. *Conversation, 193*

53 Pernicious weed! whose scent the fair annoys,
Unfriendly to society's chief joys,
Thy worst effect is banishing for hours
The sex whose presence civilizes ours. *Ib, 251*

54 John Gilpin was a citizen
Of credit and renown,
A train-band captain eke was he,
Of famous London town. *John Gilpin, 1*

55 Tomorrow is our wedding day
And we will then repair
Unto the Bell at Edmonton
All in a chaise and pair.                    *John Gilpin, 2*

56 O'erjoyed was he to find
That, though on pleasure she was bent,
She had a frugal mind.                                    *Ib, 8*

57 Away went Gilpin – who but he?
His fame soon spread around;
He carries weight! he rides a race,
'Tis for a thousand pound!                              *Ib, 29*

58 The dinner waits, and we are tired:
Said Gilpin, So am I!                                     *Ib, 37*

59 Said John, 'It is my wedding-day,
And all the world would stare,
If wife should dine at Edmonton,
And I should dine at Ware.'                             *Ib, 49*

60 'Twas for your pleasure you came here,
You shall go back for mine.                             *Ib, 50*

61 Now let us sing, Long live the King,
And Gilpin long live he;
And when he next doth ride abroad,
May I be there to see!                                   *Ib, 63*

62 What peaceful hours I once enjoyed!
How sweet their memory still!
But they have left an aching void,
The world can never fill.                        *Olney Hymns, 1*

63 God moves in a mysterious way,
His wonders to perform;
He plants His footsteps in the sea,
And rides upon the storm.                              *Ib, 35*

64 Toll for the brave,
The brave that are no more:
All sunk beneath the wave,
Fast by their native shore.     *On the Loss of the Royal George*

65 How much a dunce that has been sent to roam
Excels a dunce that has been kept at home.
                                    *Progress of Error, 415*

66 Thou god of our idolatry, the press.            *Ib, 461*

67 Absence of occupation is not rest,
A mind quite vacant is a mind distressed.      *Retirement, 623*

68 I sing the Sofa.                     *The Task, 1, The Sofa, 1*

69 God made the country, and man made the town. *The Task 1,*
*The Sofa, 749*

70 England, with all thy faults, I love thee still,
My country. *Ib, 2, The Timepiece, 206*

71 Variety's the very spice of life
That gives it all its flavour. *Ib, 2, 606*

72         Detested sport,
That owes its pleasure to another's pain. *Ib, 3, The Garden, 326*

73 Now stir the fire, and close the shutters fast,
Let fall the curtains, wheel the sofa round,
And, while the bubbling and loud-hissing urn
Throws up a steamy column, and the cups,
That cheer but not inebriate, wait on each,
So let us welcome peaceful evening in.
*Ib, 4, The Winter Evening, 36*

74 Nature is but a name for an effect
Whose cause is God. *Ib, 6, The Winter Walk at Noon, 223*

75 I would not enter on my list of friends
(Though graced with polished manners and fine sense,
Yet wanting sensibility) the man
Who needlessly sets foot upon a worm. *Ib, 6, 560*

76 The twentieth year is well-nigh past,
Since first our sky was overcast:
Ah, would that this might be the last
      My Mary! *To Mary*

77 I am monarch of all I survey
My right there is none to dispute.
*Verses supposed to be written by Alexander Selkirk*

78 O Solitude! Where are the charms
That sages have seen in thy face?
Better dwell in the midst of alarms
Than reign in this horrible place. *Ib*

## CRABBE, George, 1754–1832

79 Habit with him was all the test of truth,
'It must be right: I've done it from my youth.'
*The Borough, Letter 3, The Vicar, 138*

80 Books cannot always please, however good;
Minds are not ever craving for their food.
*Ib, Letter 24, Schools, 402*

81 A master-passion is the love of news. *The Newspaper, 279*

82 Secrets with girls, like loaded guns with boys,
Are never valued till they make a noise.
*Tales of the Hall, 11, The Maid's Story, 84*

**CRASHAW, Richard, 1612?–1649**

83 I would be married but I'd have no wife,
I would be married to a single life. *On Marriage*

84 Whoe'er she be,
That not impossible she
That shall command my heart and me.
*Wishes to his Supposed Mistress*

**CREIGHTON, Mandell, 1843–1901**

85 No people do so much harm as those who go about doing good.
*Life, 1904*

**CROKER, John Wilson, 1780–1857**

86 A game which a sharper once played with a dupe, entitled 'Heads
I win, tails you lose.' *Croker Papers*

87 We now are, as we always have been, decidedly and conscientiously attached to what is called the Tory, and which might with
more propriety be called the Conservative, party.
*Quarterly Review, Jan, 1830*

**CROMWELL, Oliver, 1599–1658**

88 I beseech you, in the bowels of Christ, think it possible you may
be mistaken. *Letter to the General Assembly of the Church
of Scotland, 3 Aug. 1650*

89 What shall we do with this bauble? There, take it away.
*Speech dismissing Parliament, 20 April 1653*

90 It is not fit that you should sit here any longer! . . . you shall
now give place to better men.
*Speech to the Rump Parliament, 22 Jan. 1654*

91 Mr Lely, I desire you would use all your skill to paint my
picture truly like me, and not flatter me at all; but remark all
these roughnesses, pimples, warts, and everything as you see me,
otherwise I will never pay a farthing for it.
*Horace Walpole's Anecdotes of Painting, Ch. 12*

**CUMBERLAND, Bishop Richard, 1631–1718**

92 It is better to wear out than to rust out.
*Quoted in G. Horne, The Duty of Contending for the Faith*

**CUMMINGS, Edward Estlin, 1894–1962**

93 a politician is an arse upon
which everyone has sat except a man. *a politician*

94 anyone lived in a pretty how town
   (with up so floating many bells down)
   spring summer autumn winter
   he sang his didn't he danced his did.
                    *anyone lived in a pretty how town*

95 Humanity i love you because
   when you're hard up you pawn your
   intelligence to buy a drink.          *humanity i love you*

## CUNNINGHAM, Allan, 1784–1842

96 A wet sheet and a flowing sea,
   A wind that follows fast,
   And fills the white and rustling sail,
   And bends the gallant mast.     *A Wet Sheet and a Flowing Sea*

97 It's hame and it's hame, hame fain wad I be,
   Oh, hame, hame, hame to my ain countree!
                         *It's Hame and It's Hame*

## CURRAN, John Philpot, 1750–1817

98 The condition upon which God hath given liberty to man is
   eternal vigilance.          *Speech on the Right of Election of
                              Lord Mayor of Dublin, 10 July 1790*

## DACRE, Harry, 19th century

99 Daisy, Daisy, give me your answer, do!
   I'm half crazy, all for the love of you!
      It won't be a stylish marriage,
      I can't afford a carriage,
   But you'll look sweet upon the seat
   Of a bicycle made for two!                    *Daisy Bell*

## DANA, Charles Anderson, 1819–1897

1 When a dog bites a man that is not news, but when a man bites
   a dog, that is news.   *What is News? The New York Sun, 1882*

## DANTE, Alighieri, 1265–1321

2 *Lasciate ogni speranza voi ch'entrate.* Abandon hope, all ye who
   enter here.                *Divine Comedy, Inferno, 3, 9*

3          *Nessun maggior dolore,*
   *Che ricordarsi del tempo felice*
   *Nella miseria.*
   There is no greater sorrow than to recall a time of happiness
   when in misery.                          *Ib, 5, 121*

4 *L'amor che muove il sole e l'altre stelle.* The love that moves the
sun and the other stars.         *Divine Comedy, Paradiso, 33, 145*

## DANTON, Georges Jaques, 1759–1794

5 *De l'audace, encore de l'audace, et toujours de l'audace!* Boldness,
and again boldness, and always boldness!
                    *Speech, French Legislative Committee, 2 Sept. 1792*

## DARWIN, Charles Robert, 1809–1882

6 Man with all his noble qualities . . . still bears in his bodily
frame the indelible stamp of his lowly origin.
                              *The Descent of Man, Last Words*

7 I have called this principle, by which each slight variation, if
useful, is preserved, by the term of Natural Selection.
                              *The Origin of Species, Ch. 3*

8 The expression often used by Mr Herbert Spencer of the Survival
of the Fittest is more accurate, and is sometimes equally convenient.                                        *Ib, Ch. 3*

## DAVENANT, Sir William, 1606–1668

9 I shall sleep like a top.   CELANIA          *The Rivals, Act 3*

10 Awake, awake! the morn will never rise,
Till she can dress her beauty at your eyes.                *Song*

## DAVIES, William Henry, 1871–1940

11 What is this life if, full of care,
We have no time to stand and stare?              *Leisure*

12 Sweet Stay-at-Home, sweet Well-content.   *Sweet Stay-at-Home*

## DAVIS, Jefferson, 1808–1889

13 All we ask is to be let alone.   *Attributed remark, Inaugural
Address as President of Confederated States of America, 1861*

## DAY LEWIS, Cecil, 1904–1972

14 Nothing so sharply reminds a man he is mortal
As leaving a place
In a winter morning's dark, the air on his face
Unkind as the touch of sweating metal.
                              *Departure in the Dark*

15 Tempt me no more; for I
Have known the lightning's hour,
The poet's inward pride,
The certainty of power.                   *Tempt me no more*

# DECATUR, Stephen, 1779–1820

16  Our country! In her intercourse with foreign nations, may she
always be in the right; but our country, right or wrong.
*Speech, Norfolk, Virginia, April 1816*

# DEFOE, Daniel, 1660?–1731

17  I takes my man Friday with me.        *Robinson Crusoe, Part 1*

18  Wherever God erects a house of prayer,
The Devil always builds a chapel there;
And 'twill be found, upon examination,
The latter has the largest congregation.
*The True-Born Englishman, Part 1, 1*

19  And of all plagues with which mankind are curst,
Ecclesiastic tyranny's the worst.        *Ib, Part 2, 299*

# DEKKER, Thomas, 1570?–1641?

20  Golden slumbers kiss your eyes,
Smiles awake you when you rise.
*Patient Grissil, Act 4, Scene 2*

21  Brave shoemakers, all gentlemen of the gentle craft.
*The Shoemaker's Holiday, Act 3, Scene 1*

# DE LA MARE, Walter, 1873–1956

22  Look thy last on all things lovely,
Every hour.        *Farewell*

23  'Is there anybody there?' said the Traveller,
Knocking on the moonlit door.        *The Listeners*

24  'Tell them I came, and no one answered,
That I kept my word,' he said.        *Ib*

25  Softly along the road of evening,
In a twilight dim with rose,
Wrinkled with age, and drenched with dew,
Old Nod, the shepherd, goes.        *Nod*

26  Three jolly Farmers
Once bet a pound
Each dance the others would
Off the ground.        *Off the Ground*

27  Slowly, silently, now the moon
Walks the night in her silver shoon.        *Silver*

**DENMAN, Thomas, 1st Baron, 1779–1854**.

28 Trial by jury itself, instead of being a security to persons who
   are accused, will be a delusion, a mockery, and a snare.
                     *Judgment in O'Connell v. The Queen, 4 Sept. 1844*


**DENNIS, John, 1657–1734**

29 A man who could make so vile a pun would not scruple to pick
   a pocket.                    *The Gentleman's Magazine, 1781*

**DE QUINCEY, Thomas, 1785–1859**

30 Murder considered as one of the Fine Arts.     *Title of Essay*

**DESCARTES, René, 1596–1650**

31 *Cogito, ergo sum.* I think, therefore I am.     *Le Discours de la
                                                         Méthode*


**DICKENS, Charles, 1812–1870**

32 'There are strings', said Mr Tappertit, 'in the human heart that
   had better not be wibrated.'        *Barnaby Rudge, Ch. 22*

33 This is a London particular . . . A fog, miss.   *Bleak House,
                                                          Ch. 3*

34 I expect a judgment. Shortly.   MISS FLITE                *Ib*

35 It is a melancholy truth that even great men have their poor
   relations.                             *Ib, Ch. 28*

36 'God bless us every one!' said Tiny Tim, the last of all.
                          *A Christmas Carol, Stave 3*

37 'I am a lone lorn creetur',' were Mrs Gummidge's words . . .
   'and everythink goes contrary with me.'    *David Copperfield,
                                                          Ch. 3*

38 Barkis is willin'.   BARKIS                    *Ib, Ch. 5*

39 I have known him [*Mr Micawber*] come home to supper with a
   flood of tears, and a declaration that nothing was now left but
   a jail; and go to bed making a calculation of the expense of
   putting bow-windows to the house, 'in case anything turned
   up,' which was his favourite expression.      *Ib, Ch. 11*

40 Annual income twenty pounds, annual expenditure nineteen
   nineteen six, result happiness. Annual income twenty pounds,
   annual expenditure twenty pounds ought and six, result misery.
   MR MICAWBER                              *Ib, Ch. 12*

41 We are so very 'umble.   URIAH HEEP            *Ib, Ch. 17*

42 I only ask for information.   ROSA DARTLE       *Ib, Ch. 20*

43 'It was as true', said Mr Barkis, 'as taxes is. And nothing's truer than them.' *David Copperfield, Ch. 21*

44 Accidents will occur in the best-regulated families.
MR MICAWBER *Ib, Ch. 28*

45 I'm Gormed – and I can't say no fairer than that.
MR PEGGOTTY *Ib, Ch. 63*

46 When found, make a note of. CAPTAIN CUTTLE
*Dombey and Son, Ch. 15*

47 Whatever was required to be done, the Circumlocution Office was beforehand with all the public departments in the art of perceiving – HOW NOT TO DO IT. *Little Dorrit, Book 1, Ch. 10*

48 Let us be moral. Let us contemplate existence. MR PECKSNIFF
*Martin Chuzzlewit, Ch. 10*

49 Here's the rule for bargains: 'Do other men, for they would do you.' That's the true business precept. JONAS CHUZZLEWIT
*Ib, Ch. 11*

50 He'd make a lovely corpse. MRS GAMP *Ib, Ch. 25*

51 Oh Sairey, Sairey, little do we know what lays afore us!
MRS GAMP *Ib, Ch. 40*

52 At Mr Wackford Squeers' Academy, Dotheboys Hall ... Youth are boarded, clothed, booked, furnished with pocket-money, provided with all necessaries, instructed in all languages living and dead ... No extras, no vacations, and diet unparalleled. *Nicholas Nickleby, Ch. 3*

53 Every baby born into the world is a finer one than the last.
*Ib, Ch. 36*

54 My life is one demd horrid grind! MR MANTALINI *Ib, Ch. 64*

55 Oliver Twist has asked for more. BUMBLE *Oliver Twist, Ch. 2*

56 Known by the *sobriquet* of 'The artful Dodger.' *Ib, Ch. 8*

57 I only know two sorts of boys. Mealy boys, and beef-faced boys.
MR GRIMWIG *Ib, Ch. 14*

58 'If the law supposes that,' said Mr Bumble ..., 'the law is a ass – a idiot.' *Ib, Ch. 51*

59 The question about everything was, would it bring a blush to the cheek of a young person? *Our Mutual Friend, 1, II*

60 Not presume to dictate, but broiled fowl and mushrooms – capital thing! JINGLE *Pickwick Papers, Ch. 2*

61 Kent, sir – everybody knows Kent – apples, cherries, hops and women. JINGLE *Ib*

62 I wants to make your flesh creep. JOE, THE FAT BOY *Ib, Ch. 8*

63 'It's always best on these occasions to do what the mob do.'
'But suppose there are two mobs?' suggested Mr Snodgrass.
'Shout with the largest,' replied Mr Pickwick.
*Pickwick Papers, Ch. 13*

64 Can I unmoved see thee dying
On a log,
Expiring frog! MRS LEO HUNTER                    *Ib, Ch. 15*

65. 'Sir,' said Mr Tupman, 'you're a fellow.' 'Sir,' said Mr Pickwick,
'you're another!' *Ib*

66 Mr Weller's knowledge of London was extensive and peculiar.
*Ib, Ch. 20*

67 Take example by your father, my boy, and be very careful o'
vidders all your life, specially if they've kept a public house,
Sammy. MR WELLER *Ib*

68 Poverty and oysters always seem to go together. SAM WELLER
*Ib, Ch. 22*

69 Wery glad to see you indeed, and hope our acquaintance may
be a long 'un, as the gen'l'm'n said to the fi' pun' note.
SAM WELLER *Ib, Ch. 25*

70 Wen you're a married man, Samivel, you'll understand a good
many things as you don't understand now; but vether it's worth
goin' through so much, to learn so little, as the charity-boy said
ven he got to the end of the alphabet, is a matter o' taste.
MR WELLER *Ib, Ch. 27*

71 A double glass o' the inwariable. MR WELLER *Ib, Ch. 33*

72 Poetry's unnat'ral; no man ever talked poetry 'cept a beadle on
boxin' day. MR WELLER *Ib*

73 It's my opinion, sir, that this meeting is drunk. STIGGINS *Ib*

74 Chops and Tomata sauce. Yours, Pickwick. *Ib, Ch. 34*

75 Put it down a we, my lord, put it down a we! MR WELLER *Ib*

76 Oh Sammy, Sammy vy worn't there a alleybi! MR WELLER *Ib*

77 Anythin' for a quiet life, as the man said wen he took the sitivation at the lighthouse. SAM WELLER *Ib, Ch. 43*

78 A smattering of everything, and a knowledge of nothing.
*Sketches by Boz, Tales, Ch. 3, Sentiment, Minerva House*

79 It is a far, far, better thing that I do, than I have ever done; it
is a far, far, better rest that I go to, than I have ever known.
SIDNEY CARTON *A Tale of Two Cities, Ch. 15*

**DICKINSON, Emily, 1830–1886**
80 Success is counted sweetest
By those who ne'er succeed. *Poems, Part 1, Life*

81 How dreary to be somebody!
How public, like a frog
To tell your name the livelong day
To an admiring bog! *Poems, Part 1, Life*

82 Parting is all we know of heaven,
And all we need of hell. *Ib*

83 There's a certain slant of light,
On winter afternoons,
That oppresses, like the weight
Of Cathedral tunes. *Ib, Part 2, Nature*

84 Because I could not stop for Death,
He kindly stopped for me;
The carriage held but just ourselves
And Immortality. *Ib, Part 4, Time and Eternity*

85 If I shouldn't be alive
When the robins come,
Give the one in red cravat
A memorial crumb. *Ib*

**DIOGENES, 412?–323? B.C.**

86 Stand a little less between me and the sun. *Plutarch, Life of Alexander, 14*

**DIONYSIUS of Halicarnassus, 40?–8 B.C.**

87 History is philosophy teaching by examples. *Ars rhetorica, 11, 2*

**DISRAELI, Benjamin, 1st Earl of Beaconsfield, 1804–1881**

88 I will sit down now, but the time will come when you will hear me. *Maiden Speech, House of Commons, 7 Dec. 1837*

89 The right honourable gentleman [*Sir Robert Peel*] caught the Whigs bathing, and walked away with their clothes. *Speech, House of Commons, 28 Feb. 1845*

90 A Conservative government is an organized hypocrisy. *Ib, 17 March 1845*

91 The question is this: Is man an ape or an angel? I, my lord, am on the side of the angels. *Speech, 25 Nov. 1864*

92 An author who speaks about his own books is almost as bad as a mother who talks about her own children. *Speech, Glasgow, 19 Nov. 1873*

93 Lord Salisbury and myself have brought you back peace – but a peace I hope with honour. *Speech, House of Commons, 16 July 1878*

94 A sophistical rhetorician [*Gladstone*] inebriated with the exuberance of his own verbosity.                    *Speech, 27 July, 1878*

95 Youth is a blunder; manhood a struggle; old age a regret.
SIDONIA                           *Coningsby, Book 3, Ch. 1*

96 Every woman should marry – and no man.   HUGO BOHUN
                                              *Lothair, Ch. 30*

97 To be conscious that you are ignorant is a great step to knowledge.                                  *Sybil, Book 1, Ch. 5*

98 I was told that the Privileged and the People formed Two
Nations.                              *Ib, Book 4, Ch. 8*

99 Variety is the mother of enjoyment.    *Vivian Grey, Book 5,*
                                                        *Ch. 4*

1 She is an excellent creature, but she never can remember which
came first, the Greeks or the Romans.   [*Of his wife*]
                                              *Attributed*

2 When I want to read a novel I write one.        *Attributed*

**DODGSON, Charles Lutwidge, see CARROLL, Lewis**

**DONNE, John, 1573–1631**

3 And new Philosophy calls all in doubt,
The Element of fire is quite put out;
The Sun is lost, and th' earth, and no man's wit
Can well direct him where to look for it.   *An Anatomy of the*
                                                 *World, 205*

4 Come live with me, and be my love,
And we will some new pleasures prove
Of golden sands, and crystal brooks,
With silken lines, and silver hooks.              *The Bait*

5 Reason is our Soul's left hand, Faith her right,
By these we reach divinity.      *To the Countess of Bedford, 1*

6 Love built on beauty, soon as beauty, dies.
                              *Elegies, No. 2, The Anagram, 27*

7 No Spring, nor Summer beauty hath such grace,
As I have seen in one Autumnal face.              *Ib, No. 9,*
                                              *The Autumnal, 1*

8 Whoever loves, if he do not propose
The right true end of love, he's one that goes
To sea for nothing but to make him sick.
                              *Ib, No. 18, Love's Progress, 1*

9 Licence my roving hands, and let them go,
Before, behind, between, above, below.

O my America! my new-found-land,
My Kingdom, safeliest when with one man man'd.
*Elegies, No. 19, Going To Bed, 25*

10 Death be not proud, though some have called thee
Mighty and dreadful, for, thou art not so,
For, those, whom thou think'st, thou dost overthrow,
Die not, poor death. *Holy Sonnets, 10*

11 Go, and catch a falling star,
Get with child a mandrake root,
Tell me, where all past years are,
Or who cleft the Devil's foot. *Song, Go and Catch a Falling Star*

12 But I do nothing upon myself, and yet I am mine own Executioner. *Devotions, 12*

13 No man is an Island, entire of itself; every man is a piece of the Continent, a part of the main. *Ib, 17*

14 Any man's death diminishes me, because I am involved in Mankind; And therefore never send to know for whom the bell tolls; it tolls for thee. *Ib, 17*

## DONNELLY, Ignatius, 1831–1901

15 The Democratic Party is like a mule – without pride of ancestry or hope of posterity. *Speech, Minnesota Legislature*

## DOUGLAS, William, 1672–1748

16 And for bonnie Annie Laurie
I'll lay me down and dee. *Annie Laurie*

## DOWSON, Ernest Christopher, 1867–1900

17 I have been faithful to thee, Cynara! in my fashion. *Non Sum Qualis Eram*

## DOYLE, Sir Arthur Conan, 1859–1930

18 It has long been an axiom of mine that the little things are infinitely the most important.
*The Adventures of Sherlock Holmes, A Case of Identity*

19 It is quite a three-pipe problem. *Ib, The Red-Headed League*

20 You know my methods, Watson.
*The Memoirs of Sherlock Holmes, The Crooked Man*

21 'Excellent!' [*Dr Watson*] cried. 'Elementary,' said he [*Holmes*].
*Ib*

22 He [*Professor Moriarty*] is the Napoleon of crime.
>> *The Memoirs of Sherlock Holmes, The Final Problem*

23 'Is there any point to which you would wish to draw my atten-
tion?'
'To the curious incident of the dog in the night-time.'
'The dog did nothing in the night-time.'
'That was the curious incident,' remarked Sherlock Holmes.
>> *Ib, Silver Blaze*

24 An experience of women which extends over many nations and
three continents. *The Sign of Four*

25 When you have eliminated the impossible, whatever remains,
however improbable, must be the truth. *Ib*

26 The Baker Street irregulars. *Ib*

27 London, that great cesspool into which all the loungers of the
Empire are irresistibly drained. *A Study in Scarlet*

28 The vocabulary of 'Bradshaw' is nervous and terse, but limited.
>> *Ib*


**DRAKE, Sir Francis, 1540?–1596**

29 I have singed the Spanish king's beard. *After destroying on
19 April 1587, a vast amount of shipping in the Harbour
of Cadiz*

30 There is plenty of time to win this game, and to thrash the
Spaniards too. *20 July 1588, while playing bowls, when the
Armada was sighted*


**DRAYTON, Michael, 1563–1631**

31 Fair stood the wind for France
When we our sails advance. *Agincourt*

32 Ill news hath wings, and with the wind doth go,
Comfort's a cripple and comes ever slow.
>> *The Barrons' Wars, 2*

33 Neat Marlowe, bathed in the Thespian springs,
Had in him those brave translunary things
That the first poets had. *Of Poets and Poesy*

34 Since there's no help, come let us kiss and part –
Nay, I have done, you get no more of me;
And I am glad, yea glad with all my heart
That thus so cleanly I myself can free.
>> *Sonnets, 61, The Parting*

**DRUMMOND, Thomas, 1797–1840**

35 Property has its duties as well as its rights.  *Letter to the Earl of Donoughmore, 22 May 1838*

**DRYDEN, John, 1631–1700**

36 In pious times, e'r Priest-craft did begin,
Before Polygamy was made a Sin.  *Absalom and Achitophel, Part, 1, 1*

37 What e'r he did was done with so much ease,
In him alone, 'twas Natural to please.  *Ib, 1, 27*

38 Of these the false Achitophel was first,
A Name to all succeeding Ages curst.
For close Designs and crooked Counsels fit,
Sagacious, Bold, and Turbulent of wit.  *Ib, 1, 150*

39 A fiery Soul, which working out its way,
Fretted the Pigmy Body to decay:
And o'r informed the Tenement of Clay.
A daring Pilot in extremity;
Pleas'd with the Danger, when the Waves went high
He sought the Storms; but, for a Calm unfit,
Would Steer too nigh the Sands to boast his Wit.
Great Wits are sure to Madness near alli'd
And thin Partitions do their Bounds divide.  *Ib, 1, 156*

40 Bankrupt of Life, yet Prodigal of Ease.  *Ib, 1, 168*

41 For Politicians neither love nor hate.  *Ib, 1, 223*

42 But far more numerous was the Herd of such,
Who think too little, and who talk too much.  *Ib, 1, 533*

43 A man so various, that he seem'd to be
Not one, but all Mankind's Epitome.
Stiff in Opinions, always in the wrong;
Was Everything by starts, and Nothing long:
But, in the course of one revolving Moon,
Was Chymist, Fidler, States-man, and Buffoon.  *Ib, 1, 545*

44 So over Violent, or over Civil,
That every Man, with him, was God or Devil.
In squandring Wealth was his peculiar Art:
Nothing went unrewarded, but Desert.  *Ib, 1, 557*

45 Did wisely from Expensive Sins refrain,
And never broke the Sabbath, but for Gain.  *Ib, 1, 587*

46 During his Office, Treason was no Crime.
The Sons of Belial had a Glorious Time:
For Shimei, though not prodigal of pelf,
Yet lov'd his wicked Neighbour as himself.  *Ib, 1, 597*

47 Nor is the Peoples Judgment always true:
The Most may err as grosly as the Few.          *Absalom and
Achitophel, Part 1, 781*

48 Beware the Fury of a Patient Man.                    *Ib, 1, 1005*

49 The Midwife laid her hand on his Thick Skull,
With this Prophetick blessing – Be thou Dull.   *Ib, Part 2, 476*

50 The lovely Thais by his side,
Sate like a blooming Eastern Bride.          *Alexander's Feast, 9*

51 None but the Brave deserves the Fair.              *Ib, 15*

52 Sound the Trumpets; beat the Drums.            *Ib, 50*

53 Bacchus Blessings are a Treasure;
Drinking is the Soldiers Pleasure;
     Rich the Treasure;
     Sweet the Pleasure;
Sweet is Pleasure after Pain.                         *Ib, 56*

54 Let old Timotheus yield the Prize,
     Or both divide the Crown:
He rais'd a Mortal to the Skies;
     She drew an Angel down.                         *Ib, 167*

55 Errors, like Straws, upon the surface flow;
He who would search for Pearls must dive below.
                                        *All for Love, Prologue*

56 Men are but children of a larger growth.   DOLABELLA
                                        *Ib, Act 4, Scene 1*

57 Her Poverty was glad; her Heart content,
Nor knew she what the Spleen or Vapors meant.
                                        *The Cock and the Fox, 29*

58 He [*Shakespeare*] was the man who of all modern, and perhaps
ancient poets, had the largest and most comprehensive soul.
                                        *Essay of Dramatic Poesy*

59 He was naturally learned; he needed not the spectacles of books
to read nature; he looked inwards, and found her there.   *Ib*

60 Here lies my wife: here let her lie!
Now she's at rest, and so am I.          *Epitaph intended for
Dryden's Wife*

61 For truth has such a face and such a meen
As to be lov'd needs only to be seen.          *The Hind and the
Panther, 1, 33*

62 Of all the Tyrannies on humane kind
The worst is that which Persecutes the mind.
Let us but weigh at what offence we strike,
'Tis but because we cannot think alike.          *Ib, 1, 239*

63 And love's the noblest frailty of the mind. CORTEZ
*The Indian Emperor, Act 2, Scene 2*

64 For all the happiness mankind can gain
Is not in pleasure, but in rest from pain. CORTEZ
*Ib, Act 4, Scene 1*

65 All heiresses are beautiful. ALBANACT    *King Arthur, Act 1,*
*Scene 2*

66 Three Poets, in three distant Ages born,
Greece, Italy, and England did adorn.
The first in Loftiness of Thought surpass'd,
The next in Majesty, in both the last:
The Force of Nature could no farther go;
To make a third she join'd the former two.    *Lines under*
*Portrait of Milton*

67 Cousin Swift, you will never be a poet.    *Quoted in Johnson's*
*Lives of the Poets, Swift*

68 All humane things are subject to decay,
And, when Fate summons, Monarchs must obey:
This Fleckno found, who, like Augustus, young
Was call'd to Empire and had govern'd long:
In Prose and Verse was own'd, without dispute
Through all the realms of Non-sense, absolute.
*Mac Flecknoe, 1*

69 Shadwell alone my perfect image bears,
Mature in dullness from his tender years;
Shadwell alone of all my Sons is he
Who stands confirm'd in full stupidity.
The rest to some faint meaning make pretence,
But Shadwell never deviates into sense.    *Ib, 15*

70 For I am young, a Novice in the Trade,
The Fool of Love, unpractis'd to persuade.
*Palamon and Arcite, 3, 325*

71 Happy the Man, and happy he alone,
He who can call to-day his own:
He who, secure within, can say,
Tomorrow do thy worst, for I have liv'd today.
*Translation of Horace, 3, 65*

72 Arms, and the man I sing, who, forced by fate,
And haughty Juno's unrelenting hate.    *Translation of Virgil*
*Aeneid, 1, 1*


**DUFFIELD, George, 1818–1888**
73 Stand up! Stand up for Jesus!    *Hymn*

**DUMAS, Alexandre, 1803–1870**

74 *Tous pour un, un pour tous.* All for one, and one for all.
*The Three Musketeers*

**DUNBAR, William, 1460?–1520?**

75 London, thou art the flower of Cities all!    *In honour of the City of London*

76 *Timor mortis conturbat me.*    *Lament for the Makaris*

**DYER, Sir Edward, 1540–1607**

77 My mind to me a kingdom is.    *Title of poem*

**DYER, John, 18th century**

78 And he that will this health deny,
Down among the dead men let him lie!    *Here's a Health to the King*

**EDISON, Thomas Alva, 1847–1931**

79 Genius is one per cent inspiration and ninety-nine per cent perspiration.    *Newspaper interview*

**EDWARD III of England, 1312–1377**

80 Let the boy win his spurs.    *Of the Black Prince at Crécy, 1345*

**EDWARD VIII of Great Britain (Duke of Windsor) 1894–1972**

81 I have found it impossible to carry the heavy burden of responsibility and to discharge my duties as King as I would wish to do without the help and support of the woman I love.
*Broadcast, 11 Dec. 1936*

**EDWARDS, Oliver, 1711–1791**

82 I have tried too in my time to be a philosopher; but, I don't know how, cheerfulness was always breaking in.
*Boswell's Johnson, 17 April 1778*

**EINSTEIN, Albert, 1879–1955**

83 I never think of the future. It comes soon enough.
*Interview, 1930*

**ELIOT, George (Mary Ann Evans), 1819–1880**

84 A prophetess? Yea, I say unto you, and more than a prophetess – a uncommon pretty young woman.    *Adam Bede, Ch. 1*

85 It's but little good you'll do a-watering the last year's crop.
*Adam Bede, Ch. 18*

86 The happiest women, like the happiest nations, have no history.
*The Mill on the Floss, Book 6, Ch. 3*

87 Animals are such agreeable friends – they ask no questions, they
pass no criticisms. *Scenes of Clerical Life, Mr Gilfil's
Love Story, Ch. 7*


**ELIOT, Thomas Stearns, 1888–1965**

88 Because I do not hope to turn again
Because I do not hope
Because I do not hope to turn. *Ash-Wednesday*

89 The readers of the Boston Evening Transcript
Sway in the wind like a field of ripe corn. *The Boston
Evening Transcript*

90 Time present and time past
Are both perhaps present in time future,
And time future contained in time past. *Burnt Norton*

91 Human kind
Cannot bear very much reality. *Ib*

92 Here I am, an old man in a dry month,
Being read to by a boy, waiting for rain. *Gerontion*

93 Thoughts of a dry brain in a dry season. *Ib*

94 We are the hollow men
We are the stuffed men
Leaning together
Headpiece filled with straw. *The Hollow Men*

95 Between the idea
And the reality
Between the motion
And the act
Falls the Shadow. *Ib*

96 This is the way the world ends
Not with a bang but a whimper. *Ib*

97 Ash on an old man's sleeve
Is all the ash the burnt roses leave.
Dust in the air suspended
Marks the place where a story ended. *Little Gidding*

98 Let us go then, you and I,
When the evening is spread out against the sky
Like a patient etherized upon a table. *The Love Song of
J. Alfred Prufrock*

99 In the room the women come and go
   Talking of Michelangelo. *The Love Song of J. Alfred Prufrock*

1 The yellow fog that rubs its back upon the window panes.   *Ib*

2 I have measured out my life with coffee spoons.      *Ib*

3 I grow old ... I grow old ...
   I shall wear the bottoms of my trousers rolled.      *Ib*

4 Shall I part my hair behind? Do I dare to eat a peach?
   I shall wear white flannel trousers, and walk upon the beach.
   I have heard the mermaids singing, each to each.      *Ib*

5 I do not think that they will sing to me.      *Ib*

6 Macavity, Macavity, there's no one like Macavity.
                    *Macavity: The Mystery Cat*

7 The winter evening settles down
   With smell of steaks in passageways.      *Preludes, 1*

8 And the wind shall say 'Here were decent godless people;
   Their only monument the asphalt road
   And a thousand lost golf balls.'      *The Rock*

9 Birth, and copulation, and death.
   That's all the facts when you come to brass tacks.
         *Sweeney Agonistes, Fragment of an Agon*

10 April is the cruellest month, breeding
    Lilacs out of the dead land, mixing
    Memory and desire, stirring
    Dull roots with spring rain.    *The Waste Land, The Burial*
                          *of the Dead, 1*

11 I read, much of the night, and go south in the winter.   *Ib, 18*

12 When lovely woman stoops to folly and
    Paces about her room again, alone,
    She smoothes her hair with automatic hand,
    And puts a record on the gramophone.    *Ib, The Fire Sermon,*
                              *253*

13 Webster was much possessed by death
    And saw the skull beneath the skin.   *Whispers of Immortality*

14 You've missed the point completely, Julia:
    There were no tigers. That was the point.   ALEX
                *The Cocktail Party, Act 1, Scene 1*

15 You shouldn't interrupt my interruptions:
    That's really worse than interrupting.   JULIA      *Ib, Act 3*

16 Yet we have gone on living,
    Living and partly living.   CHORUS     *Murder in the Cathedral,*
                              *Act 1*

17 The last temptation is the greatest treason:
To do the right deed for the wrong reason. THOMAS *Murder*
*in the Cathedral, Act 1*

18 However certain our expectation
The moment foreseeen may be unexpected
When it arrives. THOMAS *Ib, Act 2*

## ELIZABETH I of England, 1533–1603

19 I will make you shorter by a head. *Chamberlin, Sayings of*
*Queen Elizabeth*

20 I know I have the body of a weak and feeble woman, but I
have the heart and stomach of a King, and of a King of England
too. *Speech at Tilbury on the Approach of the Spanish Armada*

21 Though God hath raised me high, yet this I count the glory of
my crown: that I have reigned with your loves.
*The Golden Speech, 1601*

22 All my possessions for a moment of time. *Last words*

## ELLERTON, John, 1826–1893

23 Now the labourer's task is o'er;
Now the battle day is past;
Now upon the farther shore
Lands the voyager at last. *Now the Labourer's Task*

24 The day thou gavest, Lord, is ended,
The darkness falls at thy behest. *The Day Thou Gavest*

## ELLIOTT, Ebenezer, 1781–1849

25 What is a communist? One who has yearnings
For equal division of unequal earnings. *Epigram*

## EMERSON, Ralph Waldo, 1803–1882

26 Art is a jealous mistress. *Conduct of Life, Wealth*

27 The louder he talked of his honour, the faster we counted our
spoons. *Ib, Worship*

28 Nothing great was ever achieved without enthusiasm.
*Essays, Circles*

29 A Friend may well be reckoned the masterpiece of Nature.
*Ib, Friendship*

30 The only reward of virtue is virtue; the only way to have a friend
is to be one. *Ib*

31 There is properly no history; only biography. *Ib, History*

32 All mankind love a lover. *Ib, Love*

33 The reward of a thing well done is to have done it.
*Essays, New England Reformers*

34 Every man is wanted, and no man is wanted much.
*Ib, Nominalist and Realist*

35 In skating over thin ice, our safety is in our speed.
*Ib, Prudence*

36 Whoso would be a man must be a nonconformist.
*Ib, Self-Reliance*

37 To be great is to be misunderstood. *Ib*

38 Nothing can bring you peace but yourself. *Ib*

39 Next to the originator of a good sentence is the first quoter of it.
*Letters and Social Arms, Quotation and Originality*

40 By necessity, by proclivity, and by delight, we all quote. *Ib*

41 Every hero becomes a bore at last. *Representative Men,
Uses of Great Men*

42 Never read any book that is not a year old.
*Society and Solitude, Books*

43 Hitch your wagon to a star. *Ib, Civilization*

44 Poverty consists in feeling poor. *Ib, Domestic Life*

45 We boil at different degrees. *Ib, Eloquence*

46 America is a country of young men. *Ib, Old Age*

47 Can anybody remember when the times were not hard, and
money not scarce? *Ib, Works and Days*

48 If a man write a better book, preach a better sermon, or make
a better mouse-trap than his neighbour, though he build his
house in the woods, the world will make a beaten path to his
door. *Attributed*


**EMPSON, William, 1906–1984**

49 Seven Types of Ambiguity. *Title of book*


**ESTIENNE, Henri, 1531–1598**

50 *Si jeunesse savait; si vieillesse pouvait.* If only youth knew, if
only age could. *Les Prémices*


**EUCLID, c. 300 B.C.**

51 *Quod erat demonstrandum.* Which was to be proved.
*Translated from the Greek*

52 There is no royal road to geometry. *Said to Ptolemy 1*

**EUWER, Anthony Henderson, 1877–**

53 As a beauty I'm not a great star,
    There are others more handsome by far;
        But my face – I don't mind it
        Because I'm behind it;
    It's the folks out in front that I jar.           *Limerick*

**EVELYN, John, 1620–1706**

54 I saw Hamlet Prince of Denmark played, but now the old plays
   begin to disgust this refined age.           *Diary, 26 Nov. 1661*

**FARQUHAR, George, 1678–1707**

55 There's no scandal like rags, nor any crime so shameful as
   poverty.  ARCHER           *The Beaux' Strategem, Act 1, Scene 1*

56 How a little love and good company improves a woman.
   MRS SULLEN                           *Ib, Act 4, Scene 1*

57 Spare all I have, and take my life.  SCRUB    *Ib, Act 5, Scene 2*

**FERDINAND I, Holy Roman Emperor, 1503–1568**

58 *Fiat justitia, et pereat mundus.* Let justice be done, though the
   world perish.                                   *Attributed*

**FIELDING, Henry, 1707–1754**

59 When widows exclaim loudly against second marriage, I would
   always lay a wager that the man, if not the wedding-day, is
   absolutely fixed on.           *Amelia, Book 6, Ch. 10*

60 I am as sober as a Judge.    *Don Quixote in England, 3, 14*

61 Oh! the roast beef of England,
   And old England's roast beef.    *The Grub Street Opera, 3, 3*

62 Public schools are the nurseries of all vice and immorality.
                                   *Joseph Andrews, Book 3, Ch. 5*

63 Thwackum was for doing justice, and leaving mercy to heaven.
                                   *Tom Jones, Book 3, Ch. 10*

**FISHER, John Arbuthnot, 1st Baron, 1841–1920**

64 Sack the lot!           *Letter to the Times, 2 Sept. 1919*

**FITZGERALD, Edward, 1809–1883**

65 Awake! for Morning in the Bowl of Night
   Has flung the Stone that puts the Stars to Flight:
       And Lo! the Hunter of the East has caught
   The Sultan's Turret in a Noose of Light.
                       *Rubáiyát of Omar Khayyám (1st ed.) Verse 1*

66 Come, fill the Cup, and in the Fire of Spring
The Winter Garment of Repentance fling:
    The Bird of Time has but a little way
To fly – and Lo! the Bird is on the Wing.   *Rubáiyát of Omar*
                                   *Khayyám (1st ed.) Verse 7*

67 Here with a Loaf of Bread beneath the Bough,
A Flask of Wine, a Book of Verse – and Thou
    Beside me singing in the Wilderness –
And Wilderness is Paradise enow.                     *Ib, 11*

68 The Worldly Hope men set their Hearts upon
Turns Ashes – or it prospers; and anon,
    Like snow upon the Desert's dusty Face
Lighting a little Hour or two – is gone.               *Ib, 14*

69 Ah, my Belovèd, fill the Cup that clears
TODAY of past Regrets and future Fears:
    *Tomorrow!* – Why, Tomorrow I may be
Myself with Yesterday's Sev'n Thousand Years.     *Ib, 20*

70 Ah, make the most of what we yet may spend,
Before we too into the Dust descend;
    Dust into Dust, and under Dust, to lie,
Sans Wine, sans Song, sans Singer, and – sans End!   *Ib, 23*

71       One thing is certain, that Life flies;
    One thing is certain, and the Rest is Lies;
The Flower that once has blown for ever dies.       *Ib, 26*

72 I came like Water, and like Wind I go.             *Ib, 28*

73 There was a Door to which I found no key:
There was a Veil past which I could not see.       *Ib, 32*

74 Ah, fill the Cup: – what boots it to repeat
How Time is slipping underneath our Feet:
    Unborn TOMORROW, and dead YESTERDAY,
Why fret about them if TODAY be sweet!           *Ib, 37*

75       Better be merry with the fruitful Grape      *Ib, 39*
Than sadden after none, or bitter, Fruit.

76 You know, my Friends, how long since in my House
For a new Marriage I did make Carouse:
    Divorced old barren Reason from my Bed,
And took the Daughter of the Vine to Spouse.      *Ib, 40*

77 The Grape that can with Logic absolute
The Two-and-Seventy jarring Sects confute.       *Ib, 43*

78 'Tis all a Chequer-board of Nights and Days
Where Destiny with Men for Pieces plays:
    Hither and thither moves, and mates, and slays,
And one by one back in the Closet lays.         *Ib, 49*

79 The Moving Finger writes; and, having writ,
Moves on: nor all thy Piety nor Wit
    Shall lure it back to cancel half a Line,
Nor all thy Tears wash out a Word of it.    *Rubáiyát of Omar*
                                               *Khayyám (1st ed.) Verse 51*

80 And that inverted Bowl we call The Sky,
Whereunder crawling coop't we live and die,
    Lift not thy hands to *It* for help – for It
Rolls impotently on as Thou or I.                *Ib, 52*

81 Who *is* the Potter, pray, and who the Pot?      *Ib, 60*

82 Indeed the Idols I have loved so long
Have done my Credit in Men's Eye much wrong:
    Have drown'd my Honour in a shallow Cup,
And sold my Reputation for a Song.            *Ib, 69*

83 And when Thyself with shining Foot shall pass
Among the Guests Star-scattered on the Grass,
    And in thy joyous Errand reach the Spot
Where I made one – turn down an empty Glass!    *Ib, 75*

**FLECKER, James Elroy, 1884–1915**

84 For lust of knowing what should not be known,
We take the Golden Road to Samarkand.     *Hassan, 5, 2*

85 I have seen old ships sail like swans asleep,
Beyond the village which men still call Tyre.    *The Old Ships*

**FLETCHER, John, see BEAUMONT, Francis**

**FLORIO, John, 1553?–1625**

86 England is the paradise of women, the purgatory of men, and
the hell of horses.                        *Second Fruits*

**FOCH, Ferdinand, Marshal, 1851–1929**

87 *Mon centre cède, ma droite recule, situation excellente. J'attaque.*
My centre is giving way, my right is retreating. Situation excellent. I shall attack.
                                 *Message to Joffre, Sept. 1914*

**FONTAINE, Jean de la, 1621–1695**

88 *Elle alla crier famine*
*Chez la fourmi sa voisine.*
She went to cry famine at her neighbour's the ant's.
                *Fables, 1, 1, La Cigale et la Fourmi*

89 *Aide-toi, le ciel t'aidera.*
Help yourself and heaven will help you.   *Ib, 6, 18, Le Chartier*
                                              *Embourbé*

**FOOTE, Samuel, 1720–1777**

90  He is not only dull in himself, but the cause of dullness in others.
*Remark quoted in Boswell's Life of Johnson*

**FORD, Henry, 1863–1947**

91  History is bunk.  *In court, during libel action against Chicago
Tribune, 1919*

**FORD, John, 1586–1639?**

92  He hath shook hands with time.  BASSANES        *The Broken
Heart, Act 5, Scene 2*

93  'Tis Pity She's a Whore.                         *Title of Play*

**FORD, Lena Guilbert, ?–1916?**

94  Keep the home fires burning, while your hearts are yearning,
 Though your lads are far away they dream of home;
There's a silver lining through the dark cloud shining,
 Turn the dark cloud inside out, till the boys come home.
*Keep the Home Fires Burning*

**FORGY, Howell Maurice, 1908–**

95  Praise the Lord and pass the ammunition.        *Said at Pearl
Harbour, 7 Dec. 1941*

**FORSTER, Edward Morgan, 1879–1970**

96  Only connect.                               *Howard's End
Motto on title-page*

97  It will be generally admitted that Beethoven's Fifth Symphony
is the most sublime noise that has ever penetrated into the ear of
man.                                            *Ib, Ch. 5*

98  Two Cheers for Democracy.                    *Title of Book*

**FOSTER, Sir George Eulas, 1847–1931**

99  In these somewhat troublesome days when the great Mother
Empire stands splendidly isolated in Europe.
*Speech, Canadian House of Commons, 16 Jan. 1896*

**FOSTER, Stephen Collins, 1826–1864**

 1  Gwine to run all night!
Gwine to run all day!
I bet my money on de bob-tail nag,
Somebody bet on de bay.                          *Camptown Races*

2 I dream of Jeanie with the light brown hair.
*Jeanie with the Light Brown Hair*

3 Down in de cornfield
Hear dat mournful sound!
All de darkies am a weeping
Massa's in de cold, cold ground.     *Massa's in de Cold, Cold*
*Ground*

4   Weep no more, my lady,
Oh! weep no more today!
We will sing one song for the old Kentucky Home,
For the old Kentucky Home far away.
*My Old Kentucky Home*

5 'Way down upon de Swanee Ribber.     *Old Folks at Home*

6 All de world am sad and dreary,
Ev'ry-where I roam.
O darkies, how my heart grows weary,
Far from de old folks at home.     *Ib*

7 Gone are the days when my heart was young and gay,
Gone are my friends from the cotton fields away,
Gone from the earth to a better land I know.     *Poor old Joe*

8 I'm coming, I'm coming,
For my head is bending low,
I hear the gentle voices calling
'Poor old Joe.'     *Ib*

9 Dere's no more hard work for poor old Ned,
He's gone whar de good niggers go.     *Uncle Ned*


**FRANKLIN, Benjamin, 1706–1790**

10 Remember that time is money.     *Advice to a Young Tradesman*

11 No nation was ever ruined by trade.     *Essays, Thoughts on*
*Commercial Subjects*

12 Be in general virtuous, and you will be happy.
*Ib, On Early Marriages*

13 Here Skugg lies snug
As a bug in a rug.     *Letter to Miss G. Shipley, 26 Sept. 1772*

14 We must indeed all hang together, or most assuredly, we shall
all hang separately.     *Remark at signing of Declaration of*
*Independence, 4 July 1776*

15 There never was a good war or a bad peace.     *Letter to Josiah*
*Quincy, 11 Sept. 1783*

16 Our Constitution is in actual operation; everything appears to
promise that it will last; but in this world nothing is certain but
death and taxes.      *Letter to Jean-Baptiste Leroy, 13 Nov. 1789*

17 Man is a tool-making animal.    *Boswell's Life of Johnson, 1778*


### FREDERICK THE GREAT of Prussia, 1712–1786

18 You rogues, do you want to live for ever?     *When the Guards*
*hesitated at Kolin, 1757*

19 My people and I have come to an agreement which satisfies us
both. They are to say what they please, and I am to do what
I please.                                            *Attributed*


### FROHMAN, Charles, 1860–1915

20 Why fear death? It is the most beautiful adventure in life.
*Last words before going down in the Lusitania*


### FROST, Robert, 1875–1963

21         Earth's the right place for love:
I don't know where it's likely to go better.        *Birches*

22 Most of the change we think we see in life
Is due to truths being in and out of favour.  *The Black Cottage*

23 And nothing to look backward to with pride,
And nothing to look forward to with hope.
*The Death of the Hired Man*

24 Home is the place where, when you have to go there,
They have to take you in.                              *Ib*

25 Some say the world will end in fire,
Some say in ice,
From what I've tasted of desire
I hold with those who favour fire.        *Fire and Ice*

26 My apple trees will never get across
And eat the cones under his pines, I tell him.
He only says, 'Good fences make good neighbours.'
*Mending Wall*

27 Something there is that doesn't love a wall,
That wants it down.                                     *Ib*

28 Happiness makes up in Height for what it Lacks in Length.
*Title of poem*

29 Like a piece of ice on a hot stove, a poem must ride on its own
melting. A poem may be worked over once it is in being but
may not be worried into being.    *Preface, Collected Poems*

**FRY, Christopher, 1907–**

30 Why so shy, my pretty Thomasina?
Thomasin, O Thomasin,
Once you were so promising. 1ST GUARD, singing.
*The Dark is Light Enough, Act 2*

31          I travel light; as light
That is, as a man can travel who will
Still carry his body around because
Of its sentimental value. THOMAS      *The Lady's Not for*
*Burning, Act 1*

32          What after all
Is a halo? It's only one more thing to keep clean. THOMAS
*Ib*

33          What is official
Is incontestable. It undercuts
The problematical world and sells us life
At a discount. HUMPHREY      *Ib*

34 Where in this small-talking world can I find
A longitude with no platitude? THOMAS      *Ib, Act 3*

35          The best
Thing we can do is to make wherever we're lost in
Look as much like home as we can. NICHOLAS      *Ib*

36 Try thinking of love, or something.
Amor vincit insomnia. PRIVATE PETER ABLE
*A Sleep of Prisoners*

**FULLER, Thomas, 1608–1661**

37 There is a great difference between painting a face and not washing it.      *Church History, Book 7*

38 A proverb is much matter decorated into few words.
*The History of the Worthies of England, Ch. 2*

39 He knows little who will tell his wife all he knows.      *The Holy*
*and the Profane State, The Good Husband*

40 Learning hath gained most by those books by which the printers
have lost.      *Ib, Of Books*

**FYLEMAN, Rose, 1877–1957**

41 There are fairies at the bottom of our garden.      *Fairies*

**GALBRAITH, John Kenneth, 1908–**

42 The Affluent Society.      *Title of Book*

43 Wealth is not without its advantages and the case to the contrary, although it has often been made, has never proved widely persuasive.                                          *The Affluent Society, Ch. 1*

**GALILEO, 1564–1643**
44 *Eppur si muove.* But it does move.                          *Attributed*

**GARBO, Greta, 1905–**
45 I want to be alone.                                          *Attributed*

**GARDNER, Augustus P., 1865–1918**
46 Wake up, America.                                    *Speech, 16 Oct. 1916*

**GARRICK, David, 1717–1779**
47 For physic and farces
   His equal there scarce is;
   His farces are physic,
   His physic a farce is.    *Epigram, Written soon after Dr Hill's farce called 'The Rout' was acted*

48 Come, cheer up, my lads, 'tis to glory we steer,
   To add something more to this wonderful year;
   To honour we call you, as free-men, not slaves,
   For who are so free as the sons of the waves?
        Heart of oak are our ships,
        Jolly tars are our men.
        We always are ready,
        Steady, boys, steady;
   We'll fight and we'll conquer again and again.    *Heart of Oak*

49 Here lies Nolly Goldsmith, for shortness called Noll,
   Who wrote like an angel, but talked like poor Poll.
                              *Impromptu Epitaph on Goldsmith*

**GAVARNI, Paul, 1801–1866**
50 *Les enfants terribles.* The embarrassing young.    *Title of series of prints*

**GAY, John, 1685–1732**
51 O ruddier than the cherry
   O sweeter than the berry.                         *Acis and Galatea, 2*

52 Do you think your mother and I should have liv'd comfortably so long together, if ever we had been married?  PEACHUM
                              *The Beggar's Opera, Act 1, Scene 8*

53 MACHEATH: If with me you'd fondly stray
POLLY PEACHUM: Over the hills and far away. *The Beggar's
Opera, Act 1, Scene 13*

54 How happy could I be with either,
Were t'other dear charmer away! MACHEATH *Ib, Act 2,
Scene 13*

55 She who has never loved has never lived. ASTARBE *The
Captives, 2, 2*

56 Whence is thy learning? Hath thy toil
O'er books consumed the midnight oil? *Fables, Introduction*

57 Where yet was ever found a mother,
Who'd give her booby for another? *Ib, Part 1, No. 3*

58 Those who in quarrels interpose,
Must often wipe a bloody nose. *Ib, No. 34*

59 'Tis a gross error held in schools,
That fortune always favours fools. *Ib, Part 2, No. 12*

60 Life is a jest; and all things show it.
I thought so once; but now I know it. *My Own Epitaph*

## GEORGE II of Great Britain, 1683–1760

61 Oh! he is mad, is he? Then I wish he would *bite* some other of
my generals. *Of General Wolfe*

## GEORGE V of Great Britain, 1865–1936

62 Wake up, England. *Title of reprinted speech*
63 How is the Empire? *Last Words*

## GIBBON, Edward, 1737–1794

64 To the University of Oxford I acknowledge no obligation; and
she will as willingly renounce me for a son, as I am willing to
disclaim her for a mother. I spent fourteen months at Magdalen
College; they proved the fourteen months the most idle and
unprofitable of my whole life. *Autobiography*

65 Crowds without company, and dissipation without pleasure.
[*London*] *Ib*

66 History, which is, indeed, little more than the register of the
crimes, follies, and misfortunes of mankind. *Decline and Fall
of the Roman Empire, Ch. 3*

67 All that is human must retrograde if it does not advance. *Ib,
Ch. 71*

## GIBBONS, Stella, 1902–

68 Something nasty in the woodshed. *Cold Comfort Farm*

**GILBERT, Sir William Schwenk, 1836–1911**

69  In enterprise of martial kind,
    When there was any fighting,
He led his regiment from behind –
    He found it less exciting.    DUKE OF PLAZA-TORO
*The Gondoliers, Act 1*

70      That celebrated,
       Cultivated,
       Underrated,
         Nobleman,
The Duke of Plaza-Toro!  DUKE OF PLAZA-TORO        *Ib*

71  I stole the Prince, and I brought him here,
    And left him gaily prattling
With a highly respectable gondolier.  DON ALHAMBRA etc.  *Ib*

72  Of that there is no manner of doubt –
No probable, possible shadow of doubt –
    No possible doubt whatever.  DON ALHAMBRA etc.  *Ib*

73  A taste for drink, combined with gout,
    Had doubled him up for ever.  DON ALHAMBRA etc.  *Ib*

74  When a merry maiden marries,
Sorrow goes and pleasure tarries.  TESSA        *Ib*

75  Rising early in the morning,
    We proceed to light the fire,
Then our Majesty adorning
    In its workaday attire,
        We embark without delay
          On the duties of the day.  GIUSEPPE    *Ib. Act 2*

76      But the privilege and pleasure
    That we treasure beyond measure
Is to run on little errands for the Ministers of State.  GIUSEPPE
*Ib*

77  Take a pair of sparkling eyes.  MARCO        *Ib*

78  When every one is somebodee,
    Then no one's anybody!  DON ALHAMBRA    *Ib*

79  Tripping hither, tripping thither,
Nobody knows why or whither.  CHORUS OF FAIRIES  *Iolanthe,*
*Act 1*

80  Bow, bow, ye lower middle classes!
Bow, bow, ye tradesmen, bow, ye masses!  CHORUS OF PEERS
*Ib, Act 1*

81  The Law is the true embodiment
Of everything that's excellent.

It has no kind of fault or flaw,
And I, my lords, embody the Law.  LORD CHANCELLOR
*Iolanthe, Act 1*

82 A pleasant occupation for
A rather susceptible Chancellor!  LORD CHANCELLOR        *Ib*

83 When I went to the Bar as a very young man,
(Said I to myself – said I).  LORD CHANCELLOR        *Ib*

84 My learned profession I'll never disgrace
By taking a fee with a grin on my face,
When I haven't been there to attend to the case.
LORD CHANCELLOR   *Ib*

85 When all night long a chap remains
On sentry-go, to chase monotony
He exercises of his brains,
That is, assuming that he's got any.  PRIVATE WILLIS
*Ib, Act 2*

86 I am an intellectual chap,
And think of things that would astonish you.  PRIVATE WILLIS
*Ib*

87 I often think it's comical
How Nature always does contrive
That every boy and every gal
That's born into the world alive
Is either a little Liberal
Or else a little Conservative!  PRIVATE WILLIS        *Ib*

88 When in that House M.P.'s divide,
If they've a brain and cerebellum, too,
They've got to leave that brain outside,
And vote just as their leaders tell 'em to.  PRIVATE WILLIS   *Ib*

89 Yet Britain won her proudest bays
In good Queen Bess's glorious days!  LORD MOUNTARARAT   *Ib*

90 The House of Peers, throughout the war,
Did nothing in particular,
And did it very well.  LORD MOUNTARARAT        *Ib*

91 When you're lying awake with a dismal headache, and repose is
taboo'd by anxiety,
I conceive you may use any language you choose to indulge in,
without impropriety.  LORD CHANCELLOR        *Ib*

92 For you dream you are crossing the Channel, and tossing about
in a steamer from Harwich –
Which is something between a large bathing machine and a very
small second-class carriage.  LORD CHANCELLOR        *Ib*

93 Pooh-Bah (Lord High Everything Else)  *The Mikado, Dramatis
Personae*

94 If you want to know who we are,
    We are gentlemen of Japan.   CHORUS OF NOBLES
                                    *The Mikado, Act 1*

95 A wandering minstrel I –
    A thing of shreds and patches,
    Of ballads, songs and snatches,
    And dreamy lullaby!          NANKI-POO          *Ib*

96 But if patriotic sentiment is wanted,
    I've patriotic ballads cut and dried.   NANKI-POO   *Ib, Act 1*

97 I can trace my ancestry back to a protoplasmal primordial
   atomic globule.   POOH-BAH                            *Ib*

98 Taken from the county jail
    By a set of curious chances.   KO-KO                 *Ib*

99 As some day it may happen that a victim must be found,
    I've got a little list – I've got a little list
   Of society offenders who might well be underground,
       And who never would be missed – who never would be
       missed!
   There's the pestilential nuisances who write for autographs –
   All people who have flabby hands and irritating laughs.   KO-KO
                                                             *Ib*

 1 The idiot who praises, with enthusiastic tone,
    All centuries but this, and every country but his own.   KO-KO
                                                             *Ib*

 2 Three little maids from school are we,
    Pert as a school-girl well can be,
    Filled to the brim with girlish glee.      YUM-YUM, PEEP-BO AND
                                                  PITTI-SING   *Ib*

 3 To sit in solemn silence in a dull, dark dock,
    In a pestilential prison, with a life-long lock,
    Awaiting the sensation of a short sharp shock,
    From a cheap and chippy chopper on a big black block!
                              KO-KO, POOH-BAH AND PISH-TUSH   *Ib*

 4 Brightly dawns our wedding day;
     Joyous hour, we give thee greeting!   YUM-YUM, PITTI-SING,
                               NANKI-POO AND PISH-TUSH   *Ib, Act 2*

 5    Here's a how-de-do!
        If I marry you,
    When your time has come to perish,
    Then the maiden whom you cherish
          Must be slaughtered, too!
        Here's a how-de-do!   YUM-YUM
                                                             *Ib*

6   My object all sublime
    I shall achieve in time –
To let the punishment fit the crime –
    The punishment fit the crime.  MIKADO *The Mikado, Act 2*

7  A source of innocent merriment!  MIKADO         *Ib*

8  On a cloth untrue,
    With a twisted cue
And elliptical billiard balls!  MIKADO         *Ib*

9  I have a left shoulder-blade that is a miracle of loveliness.
People come miles to see it. My right elbow has a fascination
that few can resist.  KATISHA         *Ib*

10 Something lingering, with boiling oil in it, I fancy.  MIKADO  *Ib*

11 The flowers that bloom in the spring,
        Tra la,
    Have nothing to do with the case.
I've got to take under my wing,
        Tra la,
A most unattractive old thing,
        Tra la,
    With a caricature of a face.  KO-KO      *Ib, Act 2*

12 On a tree by a river a little tom-tit
    Sang 'Willow, titwillow, titwillow!'  KO-KO     *Ib*

13 Twenty love-sick maidens we,
    Love-sick all against our will.  CHORUS    *Patience, Act 1*

14 Now is not this ridiculous – and is not this preposterous?
    A thorough-paced absurdity – explain it if you can.
                  CHORUS OF DRAGOONS  *Ib*

15 If this young man expresses himself in terms too deep for *me*,
Why, what a very singularly deep young man this deep young
man must be!  BUNTHORNE         *Ib*

16 An attachment *à la* Plato for a bashful young potato, or a not-
too-French French bean!  BUNTHORNE         *Ib*

17 Prithee, pretty maiden, will you marry me?
    (Hey, but I'm hopeful, willow willow waly!)  GROSVENOR  *Ib*

18 A greenery-yallery, Grosvenor Gallery,
    Foot-in-the-grave young man!  BUNTHORNE    *Ib, Act 2*

19 We sail the ocean blue,
    And our saucy ship's a beauty.  CHORUS    *HMS Pinafore,*
                                       *Act 1*

20 For I'm called Little Buttercup – dear Little Buttercup,
    Though I could never tell why,

But still I'm called Buttercup – poor Little Buttercup,
Sweet Little Buttercup I!  LITTLE BUTTERCUP
*HMS Pinafore*, Act 1

21 CAPTAIN CORCORAN: I am the Captain of the *Pinafore*;
    ALL: And a right good captain, too!    *Ib*

22 CAPTAIN: I'm never, never sick at sea!
    ALL: What, never?
CAPTAIN: No, never!
    ALL: What, *never*?
CAPTAIN: Hardly ever!    *Ib*

23 Though 'Bother it' I may
    Occasionally say,
I never use a big, big D.  CAPTAIN CORCORAN  *Ib*

24 Then give three cheers, and one cheer more,
For the well-bred Captain of the *Pinafore*!  CREW  *Ib*

25 And so do his sisters, and his cousins, and his aunts!  CHORUS
    *Ib*

26 When I was a lad I served a term
As office boy to an Attorney's firm.
I cleaned the windows and I swept the floor,
And I polished up the handle of the big front door.
    I polished up that handle so carefullee
    That now I am the Ruler of the Queen's Navee!
      SIR JOSEPH PORTER  *Ib*

27 I grew so rich that I was sent
By a pocket borough into Parliament.
I always voted at my party's call,
And I never thought of thinking for myself at all.
    I thought so little, they rewarded me
    By making me the Ruler of the Queen's Navee!
      SIR JOSEPH PORTER  *Ib*

28 Never mind the why and wherefore.  CAPTAIN CORCORAN
    *Ib, Act 2*

29 For he himself has said it,
    And it's greatly to his credit,
That he is an Englishman!  BOATSWAIN  *Ib*

30 For he might have been a Roosian,
A French, or Turk, or Proosian,
Or perhaps Itali-an!  BOATSWAIN  *Ib*

31 I am the very model of a modern Major-General,
I've information vegetable, animal and mineral,
I know the kings of England, and I quote the fights historical,
From Marathon to Waterloo, in order categorical.
    MAJOR-GENERAL STANLEY  *The Pirates of Penzance*, Act 1

32 When the foeman bares his steel,
    Tarantara! tarantara!
We uncomfortable feel.   SERGEANT   *Pirates of Penzance*, Act 2

33 When constabulary duty's to be done –
    A policeman's lot is not a happy one.   SERGEANT   *Ib*

34 When the enterprising burglar's not a-burgling –
    When the cut-throat isn't occupied in crime –
    He loves to hear the little brook a-gurgling –
    And listen to the merry village chime.   SERGEANT   *Ib*

35 Politics we bar,
    They are not our bent;
On the whole we are
    Not intelligent.   ARAC   *Princess Ida*, Act 1

36 We will hang you, never fear,
    Most politely, most politely!   HILDEBRAND   *Ib*

37 Man's a ribald – Man's a rake,
    Man is Nature's sole mistake!   LADY PSYCHE   *Ib*, Act 2

38 While Darwinian Man, though well-behaved,
    At best is only a monkey shaved!   LADY PSYCHE   *Ib*

39 Hunger, I beg to state,
    Is highly indelicate.   LADY BLANCHE   *Ib*

40 Oh, don't the days seem lank and long
    When all goes right and nothing goes wrong,
    And isn't your life extremely flat
    With nothing whatever to grumble at!   GAMA   *Ib*, Act 3

41 Some word that teems with hidden meaning—like 'Basingstoke'.
                MAD MARGARET   *Ruddigore*, Act 2

42 She may very well pass for forty-three
    In the dusk, with a light behind her!   JUDGE   *Trial by Jury*

43 The screw may twist and the rack may turn,
    And men may bleed and men may burn.   DAME CARRUTHERS
                *The Yeomen of the Guard*, Act 1

44 Is life a boon?
        If so, it must befall
        That Death, whene'er he call,
Must call too soon.   FAIRFAX   *Ib*

45 POINT: I have a song to sing, O!
    ELSIE: Sing me your song, O!
    POINT: It is sung to the moon
        By a love-lorn loon.   *Ib*, Act 1

46 It's a song of a merryman, moping mum,
    Whose soul was sad, and whose glance was glum,

Who sipped no sup, and who craved no crumb,
As he sighed for the love of a ladye.  POINT   *The Yeomen of
the Guard, Act 1*

47 For he who'd make his fellow-creatures wise
Should always gild the philosophic pill!  POINT            *Ib*

48        Were I thy bride,
Then all the world beside
        Were not too wide
              To hold my wealth of love—
        Were I thy bride!  PHOEBE                          *Ib*

49 Oh! a private buffoon is a light-hearted loon,
If you listen to popular rumour.  POINT           *Ib, Act 2*

50 It is purely a matter of skill,
Which all may attain if they will:
        But every Jack,
        He must study the knack
If he wants to make sure of his Jill!

              ELSIE, PHOEBE AND FAIRFAX   *Ib*

**GLADSTONE, William Ewart, 1809–1898**
51 You cannot fight against the future. Time is on our side.
*Speech on Reform Bill, 1866*

52 [*The Turks*] one and all, bag and baggage, shall, I hope, clear
out from the province they have desolated and profaned.
*Speech, House of Commons, 7 May 1877*

53 All the world over, I will back the masses against the classes.
*Speech, Liverpool, 28 June 1886*

54 We are part of the community of Europe, and we must do our
duty as such.      *Speech, Caernarvon, 10 April 1888*

**GLASSE, Hannah, 18th century**
55 Take your hare when it is cased.  *Art of Cookery (Often mis-
quoted as 'First catch your hare' and wrongly attributed to
Mrs Beeton)*

**GLOUCESTER, William Henry, Duke of, 1743–1805**
56 Another damned, thick, square book! Always scribble, scribble,
scribble! Eh! Mr Gibbon?            *Attributed*

**GLOVER-KIND, John A., ?–1918**
57 I do Like to be Beside the Seaside.         *Title of Song*

**GOERING, Hermann, 1893–1946**
58 Guns will make us powerful; butter will only make us fat.
*Broadcast, 1936*

**GOETHE, Johann Wolfgang von, 1749–1832**

59 *Ein unnütz Leben ist ein früher Tod.* A useless life is an early
death.
*Iphigenie, 1, 2*

60 *Mehr Licht!* More light! *Last words, attributed*

**GOLDSMITH, Oliver, 1728?–1774**

61 Sweet Auburn! loveliest village of the plain.
*The Deserted Village, 1*

62 Ill fares the land, to hastening ills a prey
Where wealth accumulates, and men decay. *Ib, 51*

63 A time there was, ere England's griefs began
When every rood of ground maintained its man. *Ib, 57*

64 How happy he who crowns in shades like these,
A youth of labour with an age of ease. *Ib, 99*

65 The watchdog's voice that bayed the whispering wind,
And the loud laugh that spoke the vacant mind. *Ib, 121*

66 A man he was to all the country dear,
And passing rich with forty pounds a year. *Ib, 141*

67 Truth from his lips prevailed with double sway,
And fools, who came to scoff, remained to pray. *Ib, 179*

68 The village master taught his little school;
A man severe he was, and stern to view;
I knew him well, and every truant knew;
Well had the boding tremblers learned to trace
The day's disasters in his morning face. *Ib, 196*

69 And still they gazed, and still the wonder grew,
That one small head could carry all he knew. *Ib, 215*

70 The chest contrived a double debt to pay,
A bed by night, a chest of drawers by day. *Ib, 229*

71 In all the silent manliness of grief. *Ib, 384*

72 Man wants but little here below,
Nor wants that little long. *Edwin and Angelina, 31*

73 The King himself has followed her, –
When she has walked before. *Elegy on Mrs Mary Blaize, 19*

74 The doctors found, when she was dead, –
Her last disorder mortal. *Ib, 23*

75 Good people all, of every sort,
Give ear unto my song;
And if you find it wond'rous short,
It cannot hold you long.
*Elegy on the Death of a Mad Dog, 1*

76 The dog, to gain some private ends,
   Went mad and bit the man.                    *Elegy on the Death
                                                   of a Mad Dog, 19*

77 The man recovered of the bite,
   The dog it was that died.                                    *Ib, 31*

78 Here lies our good Edmund, whose genius was such,
   We scarcely can praise it, or blame it too much;
   Who, born for the Universe, narrowed his mind,
   And to party gave up what was meant for mankind.
                                        *[Edmund Burke] Retaliation, 29*

79 Too nice for a statesman, too proud for a wit:
   For a patriot, too cool; for a drudge, disobedient;
   And too fond of the *right* to pursue the *expedient*.
                                              *[Edmund Burke] Ib, 38*

80 Here lies David Garrick, describe me, who can,
   An abridgement of all that was pleasant in man.             *Ib, 93*

81 As a wit, if not first, in the very first line.      *[Garrick] Ib, 96*

82 On the stage he was natural, simple, affecting;
   'Twas only that when he was off he was acting.
                                                    *[Garrick] Ib, 101*

83 I love everything that's old: old friends, old times, old manners,
   old books, old wine.    HARDCASTLE         *She Stoops to Conquer,
                                                         Act 1, Scene 2*

84 It's a damned long, dark, boggy, dirty, dangerous way.
                        TONY LUMPKIN    *Ib, Act 1, Scene 2*

85 This is Liberty Hall, gentlemen.    HARDCASTLE          *Ib, Act 2*

86 We are the boys
   That fear no noise
   Where the thundering cannons roar.    TONY LUMPKIN         *Ib*

87 Ask me no questions, and I'll tell you no fibs.    TONY LUMPKIN
                                                            *Ib, Act 3*

88 Women and music should never be dated.        MISS HARDCASTLE
                                                                  *Ib*

89 Remote, unfriended, melancholy, slow.        *The Traveller, 1*

90 Where'er I roam, whatever realms to see,
   My heart untravelled fondly turns to thee.                   *Ib, 7*

91 Such is the patriot's boast, where'er we roam,
   His first, best country ever is, at home.                   *Ib, 73*

92 Where wealth and freedom reign, contentment fails,
   And honour sinks where commerce long prevails.             *Ib, 91*

93 Laws grind the poor, and rich men rule the law.           *Ib, 386*

94 Still to ourselves in every place consigned,
Our own felicity we make or find.          *The Traveller, 431*

95 A book may be amusing with numerous errors, or it may be
very dull without a single absurdity.
                              *The Vicar of Wakefield, Preface*

96 I was ever of opinion that the honest man who married and
brought up a large family, did more service than he who continued single and only talked of population.          *Ib, Ch. 1*

97 I . . . chose my wife, as she did her wedding gown, not for a
fine glossy surface, but such qualities as would wear well.
                                                    *Ib, Ch. 1*

98 Let us draw upon content for the deficiencies of fortune.
                                                    *Ib, Ch. 3*

99 I find you want me to furnish you with argument and intellects,
too.                                                *Ib, Ch. 7*

 1 They would talk of nothing but high life, and high-lived company, with other fashionable topics, such as pictures, taste,
Shakespeare, and the musical glasses.          *Ib, Ch. 9*

 2 When lovely woman stoops to folly,
              And finds too late that men betray,
What charm can soothe her melancholy,
              What art can wash her guilt away?     *Ib, Song, Ch. 9*

 3 There is no arguing with Johnson: for if his pistol misses fire,
he knocks you down with the butt end of it.
                              *1769, Boswell's Life of Johnson*

 4 [*To Dr Johnson*] If you were to make little fishes talk, they would
talk like whales.                                *1773, Ib*


**GOLDWYN, Samuel, 1882–1975**
 5 In two words: im - possible.          *Quoted in Alva Johnson,*
                                         *The Great Goldwyn*

 6 Include me out.                              *Attributed*


**GORDON, Adam Lindsay, 1833–1870**
 7 Life is mostly froth and bubble,
      Two things stand like stone,
Kindness in another's trouble,
      Courage in your own.          *Ye Wearie Wayfarer*


**GOSCHEN, George Joachim, 1st Viscount, 1831–1907**
 8 We have stood alone in what is called isolation – our splendid

isolation, as one of our Colonial friends was good enough to
call it.                                    *Speech, Lewes, 26 Feb. 1896*
                                           *(see Sir George Foster)*

## GRAHAM, Harry, 1874–1936

9  'There's been an accident,' they said,
   'Your servant's cut in half; he's dead!'
   ' Indeed!' said Mr Jones, 'and please,
   Send me the half that's got my keys.'
                                           *Ruthless Rhymes, Mr Jones*

10  I had written to Aunt Maud,
    Who was on a trip abroad,
    When I heard she'd died of cramp
    Just too late to save the stamp.                *Ib, Waste*

11  Billy, in one of his nice new sashes,
    Fell in the fire and was burned to ashes;
    Now, although the room grows chilly,
    I haven't the heart to poke poor Billy.        *Ib, Billy*

12  Weep not for little Leonie,
    Abducted by a French *Marquis*!
    Though loss of honour was a wrench,
    Just think how it's improved her French.    *Compensation*

## GRAHAME, Kenneth, 1859–1932

13  There is nothing – absolutely nothing – half so much worth
    doing as simply messing about in boats.  WATER RAT
                                           *The Wind in the Willows, Ch. 1*

14  The clever men at Oxford
      Know all that there is to be knowed.
    But they none of them know one half as much
      As intelligent Mr Toad.  TOAD               *Ib, Ch. 10*

## GRANT, Ulysses Simpson, 1822–1885

15  No terms except an unconditional and immediate surrender can
    be accepted.               *To General Buckner, 16 Feb. 1862*

16  I know no method to secure the repeal of bad or obnoxious laws
    so effective as their stringent execution.
                                           *Inaugural Address, 4 March 1869*

## GRANVILLE, George, 1st Baron Lansdowne, 1667–1735

17  Of all the plagues with which the world is curst,
    Of every ill, a woman is the worst.  AMADIS
                                           *The British Enchanters, Act 2*

## GRAVES, Alfred Perceval, 1846–1931

18 Of priests we can offer a charmin' variety,
   Far renowned for larnin' and piety.      *Father O'Flynn*

19 Checkin' the crazy ones, coaxin' unaisy ones,
   Liftin' the lazy ones on wid the stick.      *Ib*

## GRAVES, John Woodcock, 1795–1886

20 D'ye ken John Peel with his coat so gay,
   D'ye ken John Peel at the break of the day
   D'ye ken John Peel when he's far, far away
   With his hounds and his horn in the morning?

   For the sound of his horn brought me from my bed,
   And the cry of his hounds which he oft-times led;
   Peel's view halloo would a-waken the dead,
   Or a fox from his lair in the morning.      *John Peel*

## GRAVES, Robert, 1895–1985

21 Goodbye to All That.      *Title of Book*

22 As you are woman, so be lovely:
   As you are lovely, so be various,
   Merciful as constant, constant as various,
   So be mine, as I yours for ever.      *Pygmalion to Galatea*

## GRAY, Thomas, 1716–1771

23 'Twas on a lofty vase's side,
   Where China's gayest art had dy'd
     The azure flowers, that blow.
                   *Ode on the Death of a Favourite Cat, 1*

24 What female heart can gold despise?
   What Cat's averse to fish?      *Ib, 23*

25 A Fav'rite has no friend!      *Ib, 36*

26 Not all that tempts your wand'ring eyes
   And heedless hearts, is lawful prize;
     Nor all, that glisters, gold.      *Ib, 40*

27 Where once my careless childhood stray'd,
   A stranger yet to pain!      *Ode on a Distant Prospect of*
                              *Eton College, 13*

28 They hear a voice in every wind,
   And snatch a fearful joy.      *Ib, 39*

29         Where ignorance is bliss,
   'Tis folly to be wise.      *Ib, 99*

30 The Curfew tolls the knell of parting day,
   The lowing herd winds slowly o'er the lea,
   The plowman homeward plods his weary way,
   And leaves the world to darkness and to me.
               *Elegy written in a Country Church-Yard, 1*

31 Now fades the glimmering landscape on the sight,
   And all the air a solemn stillness holds,
   Save where the beetle wheels his droning flight,
   And drowsy tinklings lull the distant folds.     *Ib. 5*

32 Save that from yonder ivy-mantled tow'r
   The moping owl does to the moon complain.     *Ib, 9*

33 The rude Forefathers of the hamlet sleep.     *Ib, 16*

34 Let not Ambition mock their useful toil,
   Their homely joys, and destiny obscure;
   Nor Grandeur hear with a disdainful smile,
   The short and simple annals of the poor.     *Ib, 29*

35 The boast of heraldry, the pomp of pow'r.     *Ib, 33*

36 The paths of glory lead but to the grave.     *Ib, 36*

37 Full many a gem of purest ray serene,
   The dark unfathom'd caves of ocean bear:
   Full many a flower is born to blush unseen,
   And waste its sweetness on the desert air.     *Ib, 53*

38 Some village-Hampden, that with dauntless breast
   The little Tyrant of his fields withstood;
   Some mute inglorious Milton here may rest,
   Some Cromwell guiltless of his country's blood.     *Ib 57*

39 Far from the madding crowd's ignoble strife.     *Ib, 73*

40 Here rests his head upon the lap of Earth
   A Youth to Fortune and to Fame unknown.
   Fair Science frown'd not on his humble birth,
   And Melancholy mark'd him for her own.
               *Ib, The Epitaph, 117*

41 Large was his bounty, and his soul sincere,
   Heav'n did a recompense as largely send:
   He gave to Mis'ry all he had, a tear,
   He gain'd from Heav'n ('twas all he wish'd) a friend.     *Ib, 121*

42 No farther seek his merits to disclose,
   Or draw his frailties from their dread abode,
   (There they alike in trembling hope repose,)
   The bosom of his Father and his God.     *Ib, 125*

43 Daughter of Jove, relentless Power,
   Thou Tamer of the human breast,

Whose iron scourge and tort'ring hour,
The Bad affright, afflict the Best!         *Hymn to Adversity, 1*

44    Far from the sun and summer-gale,
In thy green lap was Nature's Darling laid.        [*Shakespeare*]
*The Progress of Poesy, 83*

45 Yet shall he mount, and keep his distant way
Beyond the limits of a vulgar fate,
Beneath the Good how far – but far above the Great.
[*Milton*]  *Ib, 121*

46 Too poor for a bribe, and too proud to importune,
He had not the method of making a fortune.
*Sketch of his own Character*

## GREELEY, Horace, 1811–1872

47 Go West, young man, and grow up with the country.
*Hints toward Reform*

## GREENE, Robert, 1560?–1592

48 Weep not, my wanton, smile upon my knee;
When thou art old there's grief enough for thee.
*Sephestia's Song*

49 For there is an upstart crow, beautified with our feathers, that
with his tiger's heart wrapped in a player's hide, supposes he is
as well able to bumbast out a blank verse as the best of you;
and being an absolute *Iohannes fac totum* is in his own conceit
the only shake-scene in a country.    [*Reference probably to
Shakespeare*]  *A Groatsworth of Wit*

## GREGORY 1, Pope, 540–604

50 *Non Angli, sed Angeli*. Not Angles, but angels.    *Attributed*
(*on seeing a group of English captives on sale at Rome*)

## GREY OF FALLODON, Edward, 1st Viscount, 1862–1933

51 The lamps are going out all over Europe; we shall not see them
lit again in our lifetime.    *On the eve of war, 3 Aug. 1914*

## GROSSMITH, George, 1847–1912, and GROSSMITH, Walter Weedon, 1854–1919

52 What's the good of a home, if you are never in it?
*The Diary of a Nobody, Ch. 1*

## GUINAN, Texas, 1884–1933

53 Fifty million Frenchmen can't be wrong.    *Attributed*

**GULBENKIAN, Nubar Sarkis, 1896–1972**

54 The best number for a dinner party is two – myself and a dam' good head waiter.                    *Interviewed in Daily Telegraph,*
*14 Jan. 1965*

**HALE, Sarah Josepha, 1788–1879**

55 Mary had a little lamb,
  Its fleece was white as snow;
And everywhere that Mary went
  The lamb was sure to go.                    *Mary's Little Lamb*

**HALIFAX, George Savile, 1st Marquis of, 1633–1695**

56 Men are not hanged for stealing horses, but that horses may not be stolen.    *Political Thoughts and Reflections of Punishment*

**HALL, Charles Sprague, 19th century**

57 John Brown's body lies a mould'ring in the grave,
  His soul is marching on!                    *John Brown's Body*

**HAMMERSTEIN, Oscar, 1895–1960**

58 The last time I saw Paris, her heart was young and gay,
I heard the laughter of her heart in every street café.
*The Last Time I saw Paris*

59 Ol' man river, dat ol' man river,
  He must know sumpin', but don't say nothin',
  He just keeps rollin', he keeps on rollin' along.
*Ol' Man River*

**HANDLEY, Thomas Reginald (Tommy), see KAVANAGH, Ted**

**HANFF, Minny Maud, c. 1900**

60 Since then they called him Sunny Jim.    *Advertisement for*
*Force, a breakfast food*

**HANKEY, Katherine, 1834–1911**

61 Tell me the old, old story,
  Of unseen things above.                    *Hymn*

**HARCOURT, Sir William, 1827–1904**

62 We are all Socialists now.                    *Speech*

**HARDY, E. J., 1849–1910**

63 How to be Happy though Married.    *Title of book, 1910*

**HARDY, Thomas, 1840–1928**

64 My argument is that War makes rattling good history; but Peace
is poor reading. *The Dynasts, Part 1*

65 A lover without indiscretion is no lover at all.
*The Hand of Ethelberta, Ch. 20*

66 Good, but not religious-good. *Under the Greenwood Tree,
Ch. 2*

67 This is the weather the cuckoo likes,
And so do I. *Weathers*

**HARE, Maurice Evan, 1886–**

68 There once was a man who said, 'Damn!
It is borne in upon me I am
An engine that moves
In determinate grooves,
I'm not even a bus but a tram.' *Limerick*

**HARGREAVES, William, 1846–1919**

69 I'm Burlington Bertie:
I rise at ten-thirty. *Burlington Bertie*

**HARINGTON, Sir John, 1561–1612**

70 Treason doth never prosper: what's the reason?
For if it prosper, none dare call it treason.
*Epigrams, Of Treason*

**HARRIS, Charles K., 1865–1930**

71 Many a heart is aching, if you could read them all,
Many the hopes that have vanished, after the ball.
*After the Ball*

**HARTE, Francis Bret, 1836–1902**

72 And on that grave where English oak and holly
And laurel wreaths entwine
Deem it not all a too presumptuous folly, –
This spray of Western pine! *Dickens in Camp*

73 He smiled a kind of sickly smile, and curled up on the floor,
And the subsequent proceedings interested him no more.
*The Society upon the Stanislaus*

**HAWKER, Robert Stephen, 1803–1875**

74 And have they fixed the where and when?
And shall Trelawny die?

Here's twenty thousand Cornish men
   Will know the reason why!   *Song of the Western Men*

## HAY, Ian (John Hay Beith), 1876–1952

75 Funny peculiar, or funny ha-ha?  "BUTTON' FARINGDON
                                             *Housemaster, Act 3*

## HAYES, J. Milton, 1884–1940

76 There's a one-eyed yellow idol to the north of Khatmandu,
   There's a little marble cross below the town,
   There's a broken-hearted woman tends the grave of Mad Carew,
   And the Yellow God forever gazes down.
               *The Green Eye of the Yellow God*

## HAZLITT, William, 1778–1830

77 His sayings are generally like women's letters; all the pith is in
   the postscript. [*Charles Lamb*]
         *Conversations of Northcote, Boswell Redivivus*

78 He [*Coleridge*] talked on for ever; and you wished him to talk
   on for ever.          *Lectures on the English Poets, 8*

79 The English (it must be owned) are rather a foul-mouthed
   nation.                   *On Criticism*

80 No young man believes he shall ever die.
        *On the Feeling of Immortality in Youth, 1*

81 One of the pleasantest things in the world is going a journey;
   but I like to go by myself.      *On Going a Journey*

82 There is not a more mean, stupid, dastardly, pitiful, selfish,
   spiteful, envious, ungrateful animal than the public. It is the
   greatest of cowards, for it is afraid of itself.
                    *On Living to Oneself*

83 The art of pleasing consists in being pleased.   *On Manner*

84 A nickname is the heaviest stone that the devil can throw at a
   man.                   *On Nicknames*

85 We never do anything well till we cease to think about the
   manner of doing it.          *On Prejudice*

## HEBER, Bishop Reginald, 1783–1826

86 From Greenland's icy mountains,
    From India's coral strand,
  Where Afric's sunny fountains,
    Roll down their golden sand.
            *From Greenland's Icy Mountains*

87 Though every prospect pleases,
   And only man is vile.     *From Greenland's Icy Mountains*

88 Holy, Holy, Holy! all the Saints adore Thee.   *Holy, Holy, Holy!*

## HEMANS, Felicia Dorothea, 1793–1835

89 The boy stood on the burning deck,
   Whence all but he had fled.     *Casabianca*

90 The stately homes of England!
   How beautiful they stand,
   Amidst their tall ancestral trees,
   O'er all the pleasant land.     *The Homes of England*

## HEMINGWAY, Ernest, 1898–1961

91 A Farewell to Arms     *Title of novel*

92 Bullfighting is the only art in which the artist is in danger of
   death and in which the degree of brilliance in the performance
   is left to the fighter's honour.   *Death in the Afternoon, Ch. 9*

## HENLEY, William Ernest, 1849–1903

93 Out of the night that covers me,
   Black as the pit from pole to pole,
   I thank whatever gods may be
   For my unconquerable soul.     *Invictus*

94 Under the bludgeonings of chance
   My head is bloody, but unbowed.     *Ib*

95 I am the master of my fate:
   I am the captain of my soul.     *Ib*

96 What have I done for you,
   England, my England?
   What is there I would not do,
   England, my own?
                    *Rhymes and Rhythms, 25, For England's Sake*

## HENRI IV of France, 1553–1610

97 *Paris vaut bien une messe.* Paris is well worth a mass.
                                                    *Attributed*

98 The wisest fool in Christendom. [*James I*]     *Attributed*

## HENRY II of England, 1133–1189

99 Will no one free me of this turbulent priest? [*Becket*]
                                                    *Attributed*

**HENRY, Matthew, 1662–1714**

1 They that die by famine die by inches.
*Commentaries, Psalms, 59, 15*

2 All this and heaven too.          *Life of Philip Henry*


**HENRY, O. (William Sydney Porter), 1862–1910**

3 Life is made up of sobs, sniffles, and smiles, with sniffles predominating.                               *Gift of the Magi*

4 If men knew how women pass the time when they are alone,
they'd never marry.          *Memoirs of a Yellow Dog*

5 Turn up the lights; I don't want to go home in the dark.
*Last words*


**HENRY, Patrick, 1736–1799**

6 I know not what course others may take; but as for me, give
me liberty or give me death.
*Speech in the Virginia Convention, 23 March 1775*


**HERBERT, Sir Alan Patrick, 1890–1971**

7 Not huffy or stuffy, nor tiny or tall,
But fluffy, just fluffy, with no brains at all.   *I Like them Fluffy*

8 This high official, all allow,
Is grossly overpaid,
There wasn't any board; and now
There isn't any trade.   *On the President of the Board of Trade*

9 The Englishman never enjoys himself except for a noble purpose.
*Uncommon Law*

10 Holy Deadlock.                          *Title of novel*


**HERBERT, George, 1593–1633**

11 Dare to be true: nothing can need a lie;
A fault, which needs it most, grows two thereby.
*The Temple, The Church Porch*

12 Love bade me welcome; yet my soul drew back,
Guilty of dust and sin.                   *Ib, Love*

13 'You must sit down,' says Love, 'and taste My meat,'
So I did sit and eat.                           *Ib*

14 Sweet day, so cool, so calm, so bright,
The bridal of the earth and sky.          *Ib, Virtue*

HERRICK, Robert, 1591–1674

15 Cherry ripe, ripe, ripe, I cry,
  Full and fair ones; come and buy:
  If so be, you ask me where
  They do grow? I answer, there
  Where my Julia's lips do smile;
  There's the land, or cherry-isle.  *Hesperides, Cherry Ripe*

16 A sweet disorder in the dress
  Kindles in clothes a wantonness.  *Ib, Delight in Disorder, 2*

17 A careless shoe-string, in whose tie
  I see a wild civility:
  Do more bewitch me, than when art
  Is too precise in every part.  *Ib*

18 Fair daffodils, we weep to see
    You haste away so soon:
  As yet the early-rising sun
    Has not attain'd his noon.  *Ib, To Daffodils*

19 I dare not ask a kiss;
    I dare not beg a smile;
  Lest having that, or this,
    I might grow proud the while.  *Ib, To Electra*

20 You say, to me-wards your affection's strong;
  Pray love me little so you love me long.
          *Ib, Love me little, love me long*

21 Night makes no difference 'twixt the Priest and Clerk;
  Joan as my Lady is as good i' th' dark.
          *Ib, No difference i' th' dark*

22 Attempt the end, and never stand to doubt;
  Nothing's so hard, but search will find it out.  *Ib, Seek and find*

23 Whenas in silks my Julia goes,
  Then, then (methinks) how sweetly flows
  That liquefaction of her clothes.  *Ib, Upon Julia's Clothes*

24 Gather ye rosebuds while ye may,
    Old time is still a-flying:
  And this same flower that smiles today
    Tomorrow will be dying.
          *Ib, To the Virgins, to make much of Time*

25 Then be not coy, but use your time;
    And while ye may, go marry:
  For having lost but once your prime,
    You may for ever tarry.  *Ib*

**HEYWOOD, Thomas, 1574?-1641**

26 Seven cities warred for Homer, being dead,
Who, living, had no roof to shroud his head.
*Hierarchy of the Blessed Angels*

27 A Woman Killed with Kindness.          *Title of play*

**HICKSON, William Edward, 1803-1870**

28 If at first you don't succeed,
Try, try again.                           *Try and Try Again*

**HILL, Rowland, 1744-1833**

29 He did not see any good reasons why the devil should have all
the good tunes.           *E. W. Broome, Rev. Rowland Hill*

**HIPPOCRATES, 460?-377? B.C.**

30 *Ars longa, vita brevis.* Art is long, but life is short.
*The Latin version of the Greek original*

**HITLER, Adolf, 1889-1945**

31 The Sudetenland is the last territorial claim I have to make in
Europe.                              *Speech, 26 Sept. 1938*

32 Germany will be either a world power or will not be at all.
*Mein Kampf*

**HOBBES, Thomas, 1588-1679**

33 The condition of man . . . is a condition of war of everyone
against everyone.                *Leviathan, Part 1, Ch. 4*

34 No arts; no letters; no society; and which is worst of all, continual fear and danger of violent death; and the life of man,
solitary, poor, nasty, brutish, and short.          *Ib, Ch. 13*

35 I am about to take my last voyage, a great leap in the dark.
*Last words*

**HOCH, Edward Wallis, 1849-1925**

36 There is so much good in the worst of us,
And so much bad in the best of us,
That it hardly becomes any of us
To talk about the rest of us.               *Good and Bad*

**HODGSON, Ralph, 1871-1962**

37 Time, you old gypsy man,
Will you not stay,
Put up your caravan
Just for one day?          *Time, you old Gypsy Man*

**HOFFMANN, August Heinrich, von Fallersleben, 1798–1874**

38 *Deutschland, Deutschland, uber alles.* Germany, Germany above
   all. *Song*

**HOFFMANN, Heinrich, 1809–1874**

39 But one day, one cold winter's day,
   He screamed out, 'Take the soup away!'
   *Struwwelpeter, Augustus*

40 Here is cruel Frederick, see!
   A horrid wicked boy was he. *Ib, Cruel Frederick*

41 Look at little Johnny there,
   Little Johnny Head-in-Air. *Ib, Johnny Head-In-Air*

42 Anything to me is sweeter
   Than to see Shock-headed Peter. *Ib, Shock-headed Peter*

**HOLMES, Oliver Wendell, 1809–1894**

43 When the last reader reads no more. *The Last Reader*

44 And silence, like a poultice, comes
   To heal the blows of sound. *The Music Grinders*

45 Wisdom has taught us to be calm and meek,
   To take one blow, and turn the other cheek;
   It is not written what a man shall do
   If the rude caitiff smite the other too. *Non-Resistance*

46 Ay, tear her tattered ensign down!
   Long has it waved on high,
   And many an eye has danced to see
   That banner in the sky. *Old Ironsides*

47 Man wants but little drink below,
   But wants that little strong. *A Song of other Days*
   *(Parody on Goldsmith, see 150:72)*

48 Man has his will, – but woman has her way.
   *The Autocrat of the Breakfast Table, Prologue*

49 A thought is often original, though you have uttered it a hundred times. *Ib, Ch. 1*

50 Build thee more stately mansions, O my soul,
   As the swift seasons roll!
   Leave thy low-vaulted past! *Ib, Ch. 4,*
   *The Chambered Nautilus*

51 The world's great men have not commonly been great scholars,
   nor great scholars great men. *Ib, Ch. 6*

52 To be seventy years young is sometimes far more cheerful and
   hopeful than to be forty years old.
   *On the Seventieth Birthday of Julia Ward Howe*

**HOME, Sir Alexander Frederick Douglas- (formerly 14th Earl of Home), 1903–**

53 I suppose Mr Wilson, when you come to think of it, is the 14th Mr Wilson. *Television, 21 Oct. 1963*

**HOMER, c. 900 B.C.**

54 As the generation of leaves, so also is that of men.
*Iliad, 6, 146*

55 Always to be best and distinguished above others. *Ib, 6, 208*

**HOOD, Thomas, 1799–1845**

56 One more Unfortunate,
Weary of breath,
Rashly importunate,
Gone to her death!

Take her up tenderly,
Lift her with care;
Fashion'd so slenderly,
Young, and so fair! *The Bridge of Sighs*

57 Ben Battle was a soldier bold,
And used to war's alarms;
But a cannon-ball took off his legs,
So he laid down his arms! *Faithless Nelly Gray*

58 For here I leave my second leg,
And the Forty-second Foot! *Ib*

59 His death, which happen'd in his berth,
At forty-odd befell:
They went and told the sexton, and
The sexton toll'd the bell. *Faithless Sally Brown*

60 I remember, I remember,
The house where I was born,
The little window where the sun
Came peeping in at morn. *I Remember, I Remember*

61 I remember, I remember,
The fir trees dark and high;
I used to think their slender tops
Were close against the sky. *Ib*

62 But evil is wrought by want of Thought,
As well as want of Heart! *The Lady's Dream*

63 When Eve upon the first of Men
The apple press'd with specious cant
Oh! what a thousand pities then
That Adam was not Adamant! *A Reflection*

64 With fingers weary and worn,
    With eyelids heavy and red,
A woman sat, in unwomanly rags,
    Plying her needle and thread –
        Stitch! stitch! stitch!
In poverty, hunger, and dirt.         *The Song of the Shirt*

65 Oh! God! that bread should be so dear,
    And flesh and blood so cheap.         *Ib*

**HOOVER, Herbert Clark, 1874–1964**
66 The American system of rugged individualism.
        *Speech, New York, 22 Oct. 1928*

**HOPKINS, Gerard Manley, 1844–1889**
67 The world is charged with the grandeur of God.
        *God's Grandeur*

68 Glory be to God for dappled things –
    For skies of couple-colour as a brinded cow;
    For rose-moles all in stipple upon trout that swim.
        *Pied Beauty*

**HORACE, Quintus Horatius Flaccus, 65–8 B.C.**
69                 *Brevis esse laboro,*
  *Obscurus fio.*
  I struggle to be brief, and become obscure.   *Ars Poetica, 25*

70 *Grammatici certant et adhuc sub iudice lis est.*
  Scholars dispute, and the case is still before the courts.  *Ib, 78*

71 *Indignor, quandoque bonus dormitat Homerus.*
  I think it shame when the worthy Homer nods.     *Ib, 359*

72 *Si possis recte, si non, quocumque modo rem.*
  By honest means, if you can, but by any means make money.
        *Epistles, 1, 1, 66*

73 *Pallida Mors aequo pulsat pede pauperum tabernas Regumque*
  *turris.*
  Pale Death with impartial foot knocks at the doors of poor
  men's hovels and of King's palaces.     *Odes 1, 4, 13*

74 *Carpe diem, quam minimum credula postero.*
  Seize the present day, trusting the morrow as little as you can.
        *Ib, 1, 11, 8*

75 *Integer vitae scelerisque purus.*
  The man of upright life unstained by guilt.     *Ib, 1, 22, 1*

76 *Eheu fugaces, Postume, Postume,*
   *Labuntur anni.*
   Alas, Postumus, Postumus, the fleeting years are slipping by.
                                                      *Odes, 2, 14, 1*

77 *Dulce et decorum est pro patria mori.*
   It is a sweet and seemly thing to die for one's country.
                                                      *Ib, 3, 2, 13*


**HORNE, Kenneth, see MURDOCH, Richard**


**HOUSMAN, Alfred Edward, 1859–1936**

78 The Grizzly Bear is huge and wild;
   He has devoured the infant child.
   The infant child is not aware
   He has been eaten by the bear.                    *Infant Innocence*

79 We'll to the woods no more,
   The laurels all are cut.                           *Last Poems*

80 And naked to the hangman's noose
      The morning clocks will ring
   A neck God made for other use
      Than strangling in a string.                    *A Shropshire Lad, 9*

81 When I was one-and-twenty
      I heard a wise man say,
   'Give crowns and pounds and guineas
      But not your heart away.'                        *Ib, 13*

82 Here of a Sunday morning
      My love and I would lie,
   And see the coloured counties,
      And hear the larks so high
      About us in the sky.                             *Ib, 21*

83 From far, from eve and morning
      And yon twelve-winded sky,
   The stuff of life to knit me
      Blew hither: here am I.                          *Ib, 32*

84 With rue my heart is laden
      For golden friends I had,
   For many a rose-lipt maiden
      And many a lightfoot lad.                        *Ib, 54*

85    Malt does more than Milton can
   To justify God's ways to man.                       *Ib, 62*

**HOWITT, Mary, 1799–1888**

86 'Will you walk into my parlour?' said a spider to a fly;
' 'Tis the prettiest little parlour that ever you did spy.'
*The Spider and the Fly*

**HOYLE, Edmond, 1672–1769**

87 When in doubt, win the trick. *Hoyle's Games, Whist,*
*Twenty-four Short Rules for Learners*

**HUBBARD, Elbert, 1856–1915**

88 Life is just one damned thing after another.
*A Thousand and One Epigrams*

**HUGHES, Thomas, 1822–1896**

89 Life isn't all beer and skittles. *Tom Brown's Schooldays,*
*Part 1, Ch. 2*

**HUME, David, 1711–1776**

90 Avarice, the spur of industry. *Essays, Of Civil Liberty*
91 Custom, then, is the great guide of human life.
*Inquiry Concerning Human Understanding, 5, 1*

**HUNGERFORD, Margaret, 1855?–1897**

92 Beauty is altogether in the eye of the beholder. *Molly Bawn*

**HUNT, George William, 1825–1904**

93 We don't want to fight, but by jingo if we do,
We've got the ships, we've got the men, we've got the money too.
*Music-Hall Song, 1878*

**HUNT, James Henry Leigh, 1784–1859**

94 Abou Ben Adhem (may his tribe increase!)
Awoke one night from a deep dream of peace.
*Abou Ben Adhem and the Angel*

95 Write me as one that loves his fellow-men. *Ib*

96 Jenny kissed me when we met,
Jumping from the chair she sat in. *Rondeau*

**HUXLEY, Aldous Leonard, 1894–1963**

97 The time of our Ford. *Brave New World, Ch. 3*
98 Ending is better than mending. *Ib*
99 The Ideal man is the non-attached man.
*Ends and Means, Ch. 1*

1 I can sympathize with people's pains, but not with their pleasures. There is something curiously boring about somebody
else's happiness.                              *Limbo, Cynthia*

2 There are not enough *bons mots* in existence to provide any
industrious conversationalist with a new stock for every social
occasion.                           *Point Counter Point, Ch. 7*

3 A bad book is as much a labour to write as a good one; it comes
as sincerely from the author's soul.                *Ib, Ch. 13*

4 A million million spermatozoa,
All of them alive:
Out of their cataclysm but one poor Noah
Dare hope to survive,
And among that billion minus one
Might have chanced to be
Shakespeare, another Newton, a new Donne –
But the One was Me.              *The Fifth Philosopher's Song*

5    But when the wearied Band
Swoons to a waltz, I take her hand,
And there we sit in peaceful calm,
Quietly sweating palm to palm.                       *Frascati's*


**HUXLEY, Thomas Henry, 1825–1895**

6 It is the customary fate of new truths to begin as heresies and
to end as superstitions.
            *The Coming of Age of the Origin of Species*


**IBSEN, Henrik, 1828–1906**

7 In that moment it burst upon me that I had been living here
these eight years with a strange man, and had borne him three
children. NORA HELMER                 *A Doll's House, Act 3*

8 The majority never has right on its side. Never I say! That is one
of the social lies that a free, thinking man is bound to rebel
against. Who makes up the majority in any given country?
Is it the wise men or the fools? I think we must agree that the
fools are in a terrible, overwhelming majority, all the wide
world over. DR STOCKMANN       *An Enemy of the People, Act 4*

9 A man should never put on his best trousers when he goes out
to battle for freedom and truth. DR STOCKMANN      *Ib, Act 5*

10 Mother, give me the sun. OSWALD ALVING       *Ghosts, Act 3*

11 What's a man's first duty? The answer's brief: To be himself.
            PEER GYNT   *Peer Gynt, Act 4, Scene 1*

### INGE, William Ralph, 1860–1954

12 Literature flourishes best when it is half a trade and half an art.
*The Victorian Age*

13 The nations which have put mankind and posterity most in their debt have been small states – Israel, Athens, Florence, Elizabethan England. *Marchant, Wit and Wisdom of Dean Inge*

### INGERSOLL, Robert Green, 1833–1899

14 An honest God is the noblest work of man.
*Gods, Part 1 (see also 250:16)*

### IRVING, Washington, 1783–1859

15 Whenever a man's friends begin to compliment him about looking young, he may be sure that they think he is growing old.
*Bracebridge Hall, Bachelors*

16 A woman's whole history is a history of the affections.
*The Sketch Book, The Broken Heart*

17 A sharp tongue is the only edged tool that grows keener with constant use. *Ib, Rip Van Winkle*

18 The almighty dollar, that great object of universal devotion throughout our land, seems to have no genuine devotees in these peculiar villages. *Wolfert's Roost, The Creole Village*

### JAMES I of England, 1566–1625

19 A custom loathsome to the eye, hateful to the nose, harmful to the brain, dangerous to the lungs, and in the black, stinking fume thereof nearest resembling the horrible Stygian smoke of the pit that is bottomless. *A Counterblast to Tobacco*

20 Dr Donne's verses are like the peace of God: they pass all understanding. *Attributed*

21 No bishop, no King. *Attributed*

### JAMES, Henry, 1843–1916

22 The deep well of unconscious cerebration.
*The American, Preface*

23 The only obligation to which in advance we may hold a novel without incurring the accusation of being arbitrary, is that it be interesting. *The Art of Fiction, Partial Portraits*

24 It takes a great deal of history to produce a little literature.
*Life of Nathaniel Hawthorne, Ch. 1*

25 He [*Thoreau*] was unperfect, unfinished, inartistic; he was worse than provincial – he was parochial. *Ib, Ch. 4*

## JEFFERSON, Thomas, 1743–1826

26 We hold these truths to be self-evident: that all men are created equal; that they are endowed by their Creator with certain unalienable rights; that among these are life, liberty, and the pursuit of happiness.
*Declaration of American Independence, 4 July 1776*

27 We mutually pledge to each other our lives, our fortunes, and our sacred honour. *Ib*

28 Error of opinion may be tolerated when reason is left free to combat it. *First Inaugural Address, 4 March 1801*

29 Peace, commerce, and honest friendship with all nations, entangling alliances with none. *Ib*

30 The care of human life and happiness, and not their destruction, is the first and only legitimate object of good government.
*To the Republican citizens of Washington County, Maryland, 1809*

31 Resistance to tyrants is obedience to God. *Epigrams*

32 Ignorance is preferable to error; and he is less remote from the truth who believes nothing, than he who believes what is wrong.
*Notes on the state of Virginia*

33 I tremble for my country when I reflect that God is just. *Ib*

## JEROME, Jerome Klapka, 1859–1927

34 Love is like the measles; we all have to go through with it.
*Idle Thoughts of an Idle Fellow, On Being in Love*

35 It always does seem to me that I am doing more work than I should do. It is not that I object to the work, mind you; I like work; it fascinates me. I can sit and look at it for hours. I love to keep it by me; the idea of getting rid of it nearly breaks my heart. *Three Men in a Boat, Ch. 15*

36 The Passing of the Third Floor Back. *Title of Play*

## JERROLD, Douglas William, 1803–1857

37 Religion's in the heart, not in the knees. *The Devil's Ducat, 1*

38 The best thing I know between France and England is the sea.
*Wit and opinions of Douglas Jerrold*

## JOAD, Cyril Edwin Mitchinson, 1891–1953

39 It all depends what you mean by . . .
*BBC Brains Trust, 1942–1948*

JOHNSON, Samuel, 1709–1784

40 When I took the first survey of my undertaking, I found our speech copious without order, and energetic without rules.
*Dictionary of the English Language, Preface*

41 I am not yet so lost in lexicography, as to forget that words are the daughters of earth, and that things are the sons of heaven.
*Ib*

42 Every quotation contributes something to the stability or enlargement of the language.
*Ib*

43 I have protracted my work till most of those whom I wished to please have sunk into the grave, and success and miscarriage are empty sounds; I therefore dismiss it with frigid tranquillity, having little to fear or hope from censure or from praise.
*Ib*

44 *Cricket.* – A sport, at which the contenders drive a ball with sticks in opposition to each other.
*Ib, Definitions*

45 *Grubstreet.* – Originally the name of a street near Moorfields in London much inhabited by writers of small histories, dictionaries, and temporary poems.
*Ib*

46 *Lexicographer.* – A harmless drudge.
*Ib*

47 *Network.* – Any thing reticulated or decussated, at equal distances, with interstices between the intersections.
*Ib*

48 *Oats.* – A grain, which in England is generally given to horses, but in Scotland supports the people.
*Ib*

49 *Patron.* – Commonly a wretch who supports with insolence, and is paid with flattery.
*Ib*

50 *Pension.* – An allowance made to any one without an equivalent. In England it is generally understood to mean pay given to a state hireling for treason to his country.
*Ib*

51 When two Englishmen meet, their first talk is of the weather.
*The Idler, 11*

52 Condemned to hope's delusive mine. *On the Death of Mr Levet*

53 Officious, innocent, sincere,
Of every friendless name the friend.
*Ib*

54 Of all the griefs that harass the distressed,
Sure the most bitter is a scornful jest.
*London*

55 This mournful truth is ev'rywhere confessed
Slow rises worth, by poverty depressed.
*Ib*

56 If the man who turnips cries,
Cry not when his father dies,
'Tis a proof that he had rather
Have a turnip than his father.
*Burlesque of lines by Lope De Vega*

57  Long expected, one-and-twenty,
    Lingering year, at length is flown.                    *One-and-twenty*

58  When learning's triumph o'er her barb'rous foes
    First rear'd the stage, immortal Shakspeare rose;
    Each change of many-colour'd life he drew,
    Exhausted worlds, and then imagin'd new:
    Existence saw him spurn her bounded reign,
    And panting time toil'd after him in vain.        *Prologue at the*
                          *Opening of the Theatre in Drury Lane, 1747*

59  For we that live to please, must please to live.                *Ib*

60  No place affords a more striking conviction of the vanity of
    human hopes, than a public library.
                                        *The Rambler, 23 March 1751*

61  Ye who listen with credulity to the whispers of fancy, and pursue
    with eagerness the phantoms of hope; who expect that age will
    perform the promises of youth, and that the deficiencies of the
    present day will be supplied by the morrow; attend to the
    history of Rasselas, prince of Abyssinia.        *Rasselas, Ch. 1*

62  Some desire is necessary to keep life in motion, and he whose
    real wants are supplied, must admit those of fancy.     *Ib, Ch. 8*

63  The business of a poet, said Imlac, is to examine, not the indi-
    vidual, but the species; to remark general properties and large
    appearances: he does not number the streaks of the tulip, or
    describe the different shades in the verdure of the forest.
                                                            *Ib, Ch. 10*

64  Human life is every where a state in which much is to be en-
    dured, and little to be enjoyed.                       *Ib, Ch. 11*

65  The life of a solitary man will be certainly miserable, but not
    certainly devout.                                      *Ib. Ch. 21*

66  To live without feeling or exciting sympathy, to be fortunate
    without adding to the felicity of others, or afflicted without
    tasting the balm of pity, is a state more gloomy than solitude:
    it is not retreat but exclusion from mankind. Marriage has many
    pains, but celibacy has no pleasures.                  *Ib, Ch. 26*

67  Let observation with extensive view,
    Survey mankind from China to Peru;
    Remark each anxious toil, each eager strife,
    And watch the busy scenes of crowded life.
                                      *The Vanity of Human Wishes*

68  There mark what ills the scholar's life assail,
    Toil, envy, want, the patron, and the jail.                    *Ib*

69 He left the name, at which the world grew pale,
To point a moral, or adorn a tale. *The Vanity of Human Wishes*

70 Hides from himself his state, and shuns to know
That life protracted is protracted woe. *Ib*

71 Still raise for good the supplicating voice,
But leave to Heaven the measure and the choice. *Ib*

72 JOHNSON: I have no notion that I was wrong or irreverent to my
tutor.
BOSWELL: That, Sir, was great fortitude of mind.
JOHNSON: No, Sir, stark insensibility.
*Boswell's Life of Johnson, 1728*

73 If you call a dog Hervey, I shall love him. *Ib, 1737*

74 When asked how he felt upon the ill success of his tragedy
[*Irene*], he replied, 'Like the Monument'. *Ib, 1750*

75 Johnson scolded him [*Langton*] for 'leaving his social friends to
go and sit with a set of wretched un-idea'd girls'. *Ib, 1752*

76 This man [*Lord Chesterfield*] I thought had been a Lord among
wits; but, I find, he is only a wit among Lords! *Ib, 1754*

77 They teach the morals of a whore, and the manners of a dancing-
master. [*Lord Chesterfield's Letters*] *Ib*

78 Is not a Patron, my Lord, one who looks with unconcern on a
man struggling for life in the water, and, when he has reached
ground, encumbers him with help? The notice which you have
been pleased to take of my labours, had it been early, had been
kind; but it has been delayed till I am indifferent, and cannot
enjoy it; till I am solitary, and cannot impart it; till I am known,
and do not want it. *Ib, Letter to Lord Chesterfield, 7 Feb. 1755*

79 When the messenger who carried the last sheet [*of Johnson's
Dictionary*] to Millar returned, Johnson asked him, 'Well, what
did he say?' – 'Sir, (answered the messenger) he said, thank
God I have done with him.' 'I am glad (replied Johnson, with a
smile,) that he thanks God for any thing.' *Ib, 1755*

80 I respect Millar, Sir; he has raised the price of literature. *Ib*

81 Ignorance, Madam, pure ignorance. [*When asked why, in his
Dictionary, he defined 'Pastern' as the 'knee of a horse'*] *Ib*

82 If a man does not make new acquaintances as he advances
through life, he will soon find himself left alone. A man, Sir,
should keep his friendship in constant repair. *Ib*

83 BOSWELL: I do indeed come from Scotland, but I cannot help
it . . .
JOHNSON: That, Sir, I find, is what a very great many of your
countrymen cannot help. *Ib, 1763*

84 The morality of an action depends on the motive from which we act. If I fling half a crown to a beggar with intention to break his head, and he picks it up and buys victuals with it, the physical effect is good; but, with respect to me, the action is very wrong.
*Boswell's Life of Johnson, 1763*

85 The noblest prospect which a Scotchman ever sees, is the high road that leads him to England. *Ib*

86 A man ought to read just as inclination leads him; for what he reads as a task will do him little good. *Ib*

87 In civilized society, personal merit will not serve you so much as money will. Sir, you may make the experiment. Go into the street, and give one man a lecture on morality, and another a shilling, and see which will respect you most. *Ib*

88 It is a sad reflection but a true one, that I knew almost as much at eighteen as I do now. *Ib*

89 Your levellers wish to level down as far as themselves; but they cannot bear levelling up to themselves. They would all have some people under them; why not then have some people above them? *Ib*

90 A woman's preaching is like a dog's walking on his hind legs. It is not done well, but you are surprised to find it done at all.
*Ib*

91 I mind my belly very studiously, and very carefully; for I look upon it, that he who does not mind his belly, will hardly mind any thing else. *Ib*

92 This was a good dinner enough, to be sure; but it was not a dinner to ask a man to. *Ib*

93 A very unclubbable man. [*Sir John Hawkins*] *Ib, 1764*

94 The longer we live, and the more we think, the higher value we learn to put on the friendship and tenderness of parents and of friends. Parents we can have but once; and he promises himself too much, who enters life with the expectation of finding many friends. *Ib, 1766*

95 I cannot see that lectures can do so much good as reading the books from which the lectures are taken. *Ib*

96 So far is it from being true that men are naturally equal, that no two people can be half an hour together, but one shall acquire an evident superiority over the other. *Ib*

97 JOHNSON: Well, we had good talk.
BOSWELL: Yes, Sir, you tossed and gored several persons.
*Ib, 1768*

98 It matters not how a man dies, but how he lives. *Ib, 1769*

99 Now that you are going to marry, do not expect more from life, than life will afford. *Boswell's Life of Johnson, 1769*

1 A gentleman who had been very unhappy in marriage, married immediately after his wife died: Johnson said, it was the triumph of hope over experience. *Ib, 1770*

2 I would not give half a guinea to live under one form of Government rather than another. It is of no moment to the happiness of an individual. *Ib, 1772*

3 The mass of every people must be barbarous where there is no printing. *Ib*

4 Much may be made of a Scotchman, if he be caught young. *Ib*

5 People seldom read a book which is given to them; and few are given. The way to spread a work is to sell it at a low price. No man will send to buy a thing that costs even sixpence, without an intention to read it. *Ib, 1773*

6 The Irish are not in a conspiracy to cheat the world by false representations of the merits of their countrymen. No, Sir; the Irish are a fair people; – they never speak well of one another. *Ib, 1775*

7 They [*the Americans*] are a race of convicts, and ought to be thankful for any thing we allow them short of hanging. *Ib*

8 There are few ways in which a man can be more innocently employed than in getting money. *Ib*

9 Fleet-street has a very animated appearance; but I think the full tide of human existence is at Charing-Cross. *Ib*

10 There may be other reasons for a man's not speaking in publick than want of resolution: he may have nothing to say. *Ib*

11 The greatest part of a writer's time is spent in reading, in order to write; a man will turn over half a library to make one book. *Ib*

12 Patriotism is the last refuge of a scoundrel. *Ib*

13 Being pressed upon this subject, and asked if he really was of opinion, that though, in general, happiness was very rare in human life, a man was not sometimes happy in the moment that was present, he answered, 'Never, but when he is drunk.' *Ib*

14 Knowledge is of two kinds. We know a subject ourselves, or we know where we can find information upon it. *Ib*

15 There is now less flogging in our great schools than formerly, but then less is learned there; so that what the boys get at one end they lose at the other. *Ib*

16 A ship is worse than a gaol. There is, in gaol, better air, better company, better conveniency of every kind; and a ship has the additional disadvantage of being in danger. When men come to like a sea-life, they are not fit to live on land.

> *Boswell's Life of Johnson, 1776*

17 There is no private house, (said he) in which people can enjoy themselves so well, as at a capital tavern.                                    *Ib*

18 Marriage is the best state for a man in general; and every man is a worse man, in proportion as he is unfit for the married state.                                    *Ib*

19 It is commonly a weak man, who marries for love.                                    *Ib*

20 Melancholy, indeed, should be diverted by every means but drinking.                                    *Ib*

21 No man but a blockhead ever wrote, except for money.                                    *Ib*

22 A man who has not been in Italy, is always conscious of an inferiority.                                    *Ib*

23 If I had no duties, and no reference to futurity, I would spend my life in driving briskly in a post-chaise with a pretty woman.
                                    *Ib, 1777*

24 Depend upon it, Sir, when a man knows he is to be hanged in a fortnight, it concentrates his mind wonderfully.                                    *Ib*

25 You find no man, at all intellectual, who is willing to leave London. No, Sir, when a man is tired of London, he is tired of life; for there is in London all that life can afford.                                    *Ib*

26 I am willing to love all mankind, except an American.   *Ib, 1778*

27 It is better to live rich than to die rich.                                    *Ib*

28 I have always said, the first Whig was the Devil.                                    *Ib*

29 Wine gives great pleasure; and every pleasure is of itself a good. It is a good, unless counterbalanced by evil.                                    *Ib*

30 What I gained by being in France was, learning to be better satisfied with my own country.                                    *Ib*

31 Claret is the liquor for boys; port for men; but he who aspires to be a hero must drink brandy.                                    *Ib, 1779*

32 BOSWELL: Is not the Giant's-Causeway worth seeing?
   JOHNSON: Worth seeing? Yes; but not worth going to see.   *Ib*

33 Sir, I have two very cogent reasons for not printing any list of subscribers; – one, that I have lost all the names, – the other, that I have spent all the money.                                    *Ib, 1781*

34 Clear your mind of cant. You may talk as other people do: you may say to a man, 'Sir, I am your most humble servant.' You are *not* his most humble servant.                                    *Ib, 1783*

35 Let your imports be more than your exports, and you'll never
go far wrong. *Boswell's Life of Johnson, 1783*

36 No man is a hypocrite in his pleasures. *Ib, 1784*

37 I look upon every day to be lost, in which I do not make a new
acquaintance. *Ib*

38 *Nullum quod tetigit non ornavit* – He touched nothing that he
did not adorn. *Epitaph on Goldsmith*

39 There is no tracing the connection of ancient nations, but by
language; and therefore I am always sorry when any language
is lost, because languages are the pedigree of nations.
*Boswell's Journal of a Tour to the Hebrides.*

40 Difficult do you call it, Sir? I wish it were impossible. [*Of a
violinist's performance*] *Anecdotes by William Seward*

41 What is written without effort is in general read without pleasure.
*Ib*

42 The great source of pleasure is variety.
*Lives of the English Poets, Butler*

43 But what are the hopes of man! I am disappointed by that stroke
of death, which has eclipsed the gaiety of nations and im-
poverished the public stock of harmless pleasure. [*Garrick's
death*] *Ib, Edmund Smith*

44 I have heard him assert, that a tavern chair was the throne of
human felicity. *Hawkin's Life of Johnson*

45 A man is in general better pleased when he has a good dinner
upon his table, than when his wife talks Greek.
*Johnsonian Miscellanies*

46 You could not stand five minutes with that man [*Edmund Burke*]
beneath a shed, while it rained, but you must be convinced you
had been standing with the greatest man you had ever yet seen.
*Attributed by Mrs Piozzi*

## JONSON, Ben, 1573–1637

47 Our scene is London, 'cause we would make known,
No country's mirth is better than our own.
*The Alchemist, Prologue*

48 Zeal-of-the-Land Busy. *Bartholomew Fair, name of character*

49 Drink to me only with thine eyes
And I will pledge with mine;
Or leave a kiss but in the cup
And I'll not look for wine. *To Celia*

50 Queen and Huntress, chaste and fair,
Now the sun is laid to sleep,

Seated in thy silver chair,
State in wonted manner keep:
    Hesperus entreats thy light,
    Goddess, excellently bright.  HESPERUS.
                            *Cynthia's Revels, Act 5, Scene 3*

51 Still to be neat, still to be drest,
   As you were going to a feast.  SONG  *Epicoene, Act 1, Scene 1*

52 Such sweet neglect more taketh me,
   Than all the adulteries of art;
   They strike mine eyes, but not my heart.  SONG          *Ib*

53                          Soul of the Age!
   The applause! delight! the wonder of our Stage.
                      *To the Memory of William Shakespeare*

54 Thou art a monument, without a tomb.                     *Ib*

55      How far thou didst our Lyly out-shine
   Or sporting Kyd, or Marlowe's mighty line.              *Ib*

56 Thou hadst small Latin, and less Greek.                  *Ib*

57 He was not of an age, but for all time!                  *Ib*

58 Sweet Swan of Avon!                                      *Ib*

59 Good morning to the day: and, next, my gold! –
   Open the shrine, that I may see my saint.  VOLPONE
                                    *Volpone, Act 1, Scene 1*

60 O, health! health! the blessing of the rich! the riches of the poor!
   who can buy thee at too dear a rate, since there is no enjoying
   the world without thee?  VOLPONE          *Ib, Act 2, Scene 1*

61 Come, my Celia, let us prove,
   While we can, the sports of love,
   Time will not be ours for ever,
   He, at length, our good will sever.  VOLPONE
                                          *Ib, Act 3, Scene 6*

62 O rare Ben Jonson.          *Epitaph in Westminster Abbey*


**JORDAN, Dorothea, 1762–1816**

63 'Oh! where, and Oh! where is your Highland Laddie gone?'
   'He's gone to fight the French, for King George upon the throne,
   And it's Oh! in my heart, how I wish him safe at home!'
                                   *The Blue Bells of Scotland*


**JOYCE, James, 1882–1941**
64 A Portrait of the Artist as a Young Man.      *Title of Book*

**JUDGE, Jack, see WILLIAMS, Harry**

## JUNIUS, 18th century

65 The Liberty of the press is the *Palladium* of all the civil, political and religious rights of an Englishman.　　*Letters, Dedication*

66 To be acquainted with the merit of a ministry, we need only observe the condition of the people.　　*Letter 1, 21 Jan. 1769*

67 There is a holy, mistaken zeal in politics, as well as religion. By persuading others we convince ourselves.
　　　　　　　　　　　　　　　　*Letter 35, 19 Dec. 1769*


## JUVENAL, 60–130? A.D.

68 *Nemo repente fuit turpissimus.* No one ever became thoroughly bad in one step.　　*Satires, 2, 83*

69 　　　　　　　*Quis custodiet ipsos*
*Custodes?*
Who is to guard the guards themselves?　　*Ib, 6, 347*

70 　　　　　　*Tenet insanabile multos*
*Scribendi cacoethes et aegro in corde senescit.*
An inveterate and incurable itch for writing besets many and grows old with their sick hearts.　　*Ib, 7, 51*

71 *Orandum est ut sit mens sana in corpore sano.*
Your prayer must be for a sound mind in a sound body.
　　　　　　　　　　　　　　　　*Ib, 10, 356*


## KARR, Alphonse, 1808–1890

72 *Plus ça change, plus c'est la même chose.* The more things change, the more they are the same.　　*Les Guêpes, Jan. 1849*


## KAVANAGH, Ted, 1892–1958

73 Can I do you now, sir? MRS MOP　　*Itma, BBC Radio Programme, 1939–1949, with Tommy Handley (1892–1949)*

74 Don't forget the diver.　　*Ib*

75 I don't mind if I do. COLONEL CHINSTRAP　　*Ib*

76 It's That Man Again.　　*Ib*

77 Wot, me? In my state of health? ATLAS　　*Ib*


## KEATS, John, 1795–1821

78 Season of mists and mellow fruitfulness,
　　Close bosom-friend of the maturing sun;
Conspiring with him how to load and bless
　　With fruit the vines that round the thatch-eves run.
　　　　　　　　　　　　　　　　*To Autumn*

79            To set budding more,
And still more, later flowers for the bees,
Until they think warm days will never cease,
    For Summer has o'er-brimm'd their clammy cells.
                                        *To Autumn*

80 Who hath not seen thee oft amid thy store?
    Sometimes whoever seeks abroad may find
    Thee sitting careless on a granary floor.               *Ib*

81 Where are the songs of Spring? Ay, where are they?
    Think not of them, thou hast thy music too.             *Ib*

82 The red-breast whistles from a garden-croft;
    And gathering swallows twitter in the skies.            *Ib*

83 Bards of Passion and of Mirth,
    Ye have left your souls on earth!
    Have ye souls in heaven too,
    Double lived in regions new?
                    *Ode, Written on the blank page before
            Beaumont and Fletcher's 'The Fair Maid of the Inn'*

84 The imagination of a boy is healthy, and the mature imagination
    of a man is healthy; but there is a space of life between, in
    which the soul is in a ferment, the character undecided, the way
    of life uncertain, the ambition thick-sighted: thence proceeds
    mawkishness.                            *Endymion, Preface*

85 A thing of beauty is a joy for ever:
    Its loveliness increases; it will never
    Pass into nothingness.                          *Ib, Book 1, 1*

86 Pleasure is oft a visitant; but pain
    Clings cruelly to us.                                *Ib, 906*

87            O Sorrow,
        Why dost borrow
    Heart's lightness from the merriment of May? *Ib, Book 4, 164*

88            It is a flaw
    In happiness, to see beyond our bourn, --
    It forces us in summer skies to mourn,
    It spoils the singing of the Nightingale.
                        *Epistle to John Hamilton Reynolds, 82*

89 St Agnes' Eve -- Ah, bitter chill it was!
    The owl, for all his feathers, was a-cold;
    The hare limp'd trembling through the frozen grass,
    And silent was the flock in woolly fold.  *The Eve of St Agnes, 1*

90 Upon the honey'd middle of the night.                    *Ib, 6*

91 And they are gone: aye, ages long ago
    These lovers fled away into the storm.               *Ib, 42*

92    The Beadsman, after thousand aves told,
For aye unsought for slept among his ashes cold.
*The Eve of St Agnes, 42*

93  Fanatics have their dreams, wherewith they weave
A paradise for a sect.    *The Fall of Hyperion, Book 1, 1*

94  The poet and the dreamer are distinct,
Diverse, sheer opposite, antipodes.
The one pours out a balm upon the World,
The other vexes it.    *Ib, 199*

95  Ever let the fancy roam,
Pleasure never is at home.    *Fancy, 1*

96  Deep in the shady sadness of a vale
Far sunken from the healthy breath of morn,
Far from the fiery noon, and eve's one star,
Sat gray-hair'd Saturn, quiet as a stone.  *Hyperion, Book 1, 1*

97         No stir of air was there,
Not so much life as on a summer's day
Robs not one light seed from the feather'd grass,
But where the dead leaf fell, there did it rest.    *Ib, 7*

98    As when, upon a tranced summer-night,
Those green-rob'd senators of mighty woods,
Tall oaks, branch-charmed by the earnest stars,
Dream, and so dream all night without a stir.    *Ib, 72*

99  For as in theatres of crowded men
Hubbub increases more they call out 'Hush!'    *Ib, 253*

1         For 'tis the eternal law
That first in beauty should be first in might.  *Ib, Book 2, 228*

2  Knowledge enormous makes a God of me.  *Ib, Book 3, 113*

3  Parting they seem'd to tread upon the air,
    Twin roses by the zephyr blown apart
Only to meet again more close, and share
    The inward fragrance of each other's heart.  *Isabella, 10*

4  But, for the general award of love,
    The little sweet doth kill much bitterness.    *Ib, 13*

5  So the two brothers and their murder'd man
    Rode past fair Florence.    *Ib, 27*

6         O cruelty,
To steal my Basil-pot away from me!    *Ib, 63*

7  Ah, what can ail thee, wretched wight,
    Alone and palely loitering;
The sedge is wither'd from the lake,
    And no birds sing.    *La Belle Dame Sans Merci, 1*

8  I met a lady in the meads
   Full beautiful, a faery's child;
   Her hair was long, her foot was light,
   And her eyes were wild.        *La Belle Dame Sans Merci, 4*

9  She look'd at me as she did love,
   And made sweet moan.                              *Ib, 6*

10 And sure in language strange she said,
   I love thee true.                                 *Ib, 7*

11 Love in a hut, with water and a crust,
   Is – Love, forgive us! – cinders, ashes, dust;
   Love in a palace is perhaps at last
   More grievous torment than a hermit's fast.    *Lamia, Part 2, 1*

12                    Do not all charms fly
    At the mere touch of cold philosophy?           *Ib, 229*

13 Philosophy will clip an Angel's wings.           *Ib, 234*

14 Souls of Poets dead and gone,
   What Elysium have ye known,
   Happy field or mossy cavern,
   Choicer than the Mermaid Tavern?
   Have ye tippled drink more fine
   Than mine host's Canary wine?
                          *Lines on the Mermaid Tavern, 1*

15 Ah! dearest love, sweet home of all my fears,
   And hopes, and joys, and panting miseries.  *Ode to Fanny, 2*

16 Thou still unravish'd bride of quietness,
   Thou foster-child of silence and slow time.
                               *Ode on a Grecian Urn, 1*

17 Heard melodies are sweet, but those unheard
   Are sweeter; therefore, ye soft pipes, play on;
   Not to the sensual ear, but, more endear'd,
   Pipe to the spirit ditties of no tone.          *Ib, 2*

18 She cannot fade, though thou hast not thy bliss,
   For ever wilt thou love, and she be fair!        *Ib*

19 For ever piping songs for ever new.              *Ib, 3*

20 'Beauty is truth, truth beauty,' – that is all
   Ye know on earth, and all ye need to know.       *Ib, 5*

21 No, no, go not to Lethe, neither twist
   Wolf's-bane, tight-rooted, for its poisonous wine.
                               *Ode on Melancholy, 1*

22 She dwells with Beauty – Beauty that must die;
   And Joy, whose hand is ever at his lips
   Bidding adieu.                                   *Ib, 3*

23 My heart aches, and a drowsy numbness pains
    My sense, as though of hemlock I had drunk.
                            *Ode to a Nightingale, 1*

24 O for a beaker full of the warm South,
    Full of the true, the blushful Hippocrene,
      With beaded bubbles winking at the brim,
      And purple-stained mouth;
  That I might drink, and leave the world unseen,
    And with thee fade away into the forest dim.     *Ib, 2*

25 Where youth grows pale, and spectre-thin, and dies
    Where but to think is to be full of sorrow
      And leaden-eyed despairs.     *Ib, 3*

26 Away! away! for I will fly to thee,
    Not charioted by Bacchus and his pards,
  But on the viewless wings of Poesy,
    Though the dull brain perplexes and retards:
  Already with thee! tender is the night,
    And haply the Queen-Moon is on her throne.     *Ib, 4*

27 I cannot see what flowers are at my feet,
    Nor what soft incense hangs upon the boughs.     *Ib, 5*

28 The murmurous haunt of flies on summer eves.     *Ib*

29 Darkling I listen; and, for many a time
    I have been half in love with easeful Death,
  Call'd him soft names in many a mused rhyme,
    To take into the air my quiet breath;
  Now more than ever seems it rich to die,
    To cease upon the midnight with no pain,
    While thou art pouring forth thy soul abroad
      In such an ecstasy!     *Ib, 6*

30 Thou wast not born for death, immortal Bird!
    No hungry generations tread thee down;
  The voice I hear this passing night was heard
    In ancient days by emperor and clown:
  Perhaps the self-same song that found a path
    Through the sad heart of Ruth, when, sick for home,
      She stood in tears amid the alien corn;
        The same that oft-times hath
      Charm'd magic casements, opening on the foam
      Of perilous seas, in faery lands forlorn.     *Ib, 7*

31 Forlorn! the very word is like a bell
    To toll me back from thee to my sole self!     *Ib, 8*

32 Was it a vision, or a waking dream?
    Fled is that music: — Do I wake or sleep?     *Ib*

33 A bright torch, and a casement ope at night,
   To let the warm Love in!                *Ode to Psyche, 66*

34 What is more gentle than a wind in summer?
                                          *Sleep and Poetry, 1*

35 Stop and consider! life is but a day;
   A fragile dew-drop on its perilous way
   From a tree's summit.                         *Ib, 85*

36 O for ten years, that I may overwhelm
   Myself in poesy; so I may do the deed
   That my own soul has to itself decreed.       *Ib, 96*

37 And can I ever bid these joys farewell?
   Yes, I must pass them for a nobler life,
   Where I may find the agonies, the strife
   Of human hearts.                             *Ib, 122*

38                        A drainless shower
   Of light is poesy; 'tis the supreme of power;
   'Tis might half slumb'ring on its own right arm.  *Ib, 235*

39                        The great end
   Of poesy, that it should be a friend
   To sooth the cares, and lift the thoughts of man.  *Ib, 245*

40 Much have I travell'd in the realms of gold,
   And many goodly states and kingdoms seen.
            *Sonnet, On First Looking into Chapman's Homer*

41 Then felt I like some watcher of the skies
   When a new planet swims into his ken;
   Or like stout Cortez when with eagle eyes
   He star'd at the Pacific – and all his men
   Look'd at each other with a wild surmise –
   Silent, upon a peak in Darien.                  *Ib*

42 The poetry of earth is never dead:
   When all the birds are faint with the hot sun,
   And hide in cooling trees, a voice will run
   From hedge to hedge about the new-mown mead.
            *Sonnet, On the Grasshopper and Cricket*

43 Happy is England! I could be content
   To see no other verdure than its own.
                      *Sonnet, Happy is England*

44 Happy is England, sweet her artless daughters;
   Enough their simple loveliness for me.          *Ib*

45 Four seasons fill the measure of the year;
   There are four seasons in the mind of man.
                      *Sonnet, The Human Seasons*

46 Glory and loveliness have pass'd away.  *Sonnet, To Leigh Hunt*

47 To one who has been long in city pent,
   'Tis very sweet to look into the fair
   And open face of heaven.  *Sonnet, To one who has been
                                       long in City pent*

48 When I have fears that I may cease to be
   Before my pen has glean'd my teeming brain.
                                *Sonnet, When I have fears*

49                      Then on the shore
   Of the wide world I stand alone, and think
   Till love and fame to nothingness do sink.  *Ib*

50 I am certain of nothing but of the holiness of the Heart's affections and the truth of Imagination – What the imagination
   seizes as Beauty must be truth – whether it existed before or not.
                      *Letter to Benjamin Bailey, 22 Nov. 1817*

51 O for a Life of Sensations rather than of Thoughts!  *Ib*

52 Negative Capability, that is, when a man is capable of being in
   uncertainties, mysteries, doubts, without any irritable reaching
   after fact and reason.
              *Letter to George and Thomas Keats, 28 Dec. 1817*

53 I am quite perplexed in a world of doubts and fancies – there
   is nothing stable in the world; uproar's your only music.
              *Letter to George and Thomas Keats, 13 Jan. 1818*

54 Poetry should be great and unobtrusive, a thing which enters
   into one's soul, and does not startle it or amaze it with itself,
   but with its subject.  *Letter to J. H. Reynolds, 3 Feb. 1818*

55 Poetry should surprise by a fine excess and not by Singularity –
   it should strike the Reader as a wording of his own highest
   thoughts, and appear almost a Remembrance.
                          *Letter to John Taylor, 27 Feb. 1818*

56 If Poetry comes not as naturally as the Leaves to a tree it had
   better not come at all.  *Ib*

57 Scenery is fine – but human nature is finer.
                      *Letter to Benjamin Bailey, 13 March 1818*

58 I have not the slightest feel of humility towards the Public – or
   to anything in existence, – but the eternal Being, the Principle
   of Beauty, and the Memory of great Men.
                      *Letter to J. H. Reynolds, 9 April 1818*

59 I find that I can have no enjoyment in the World but continual
   drinking of Knowledge.  *Letter to John Taylor, 24 April 1818*

60 I compare human life to a large Mansion of Many Apartments,
two of which I can only describe, the doors of the rest being as
yet shut upon me.            *Letter to J. H. Reynolds, 3 May 1818*

61 I would sooner fail than not be among the greatest.
                            *Letter to J. A. Hessey, 9 Oct. 1818*

62 I think I shall be among the English Poets after my death.
                 *Letter to George and Georgiana Keats, Oct. 1818*

63 Though the most beautiful Creature were waiting for me at the
end of a Journey or a Walk . . . my Happiness would not be so
fine, as my Solitude is sublime. Then instead of what I have
described, there is a Sublimity to welcome me home. The roaring of the wind is my wife and the Stars through the window
pane are my children. The mighty abstract Idea I have of
Beauty in all things stifles the more divided and minute domestic
happiness.                                                    *Ib*

64 A Man's life of any worth is a continual allegory, and very few
eyes can see the Mystery of his life – a life like the scriptures,
figurative – which such people can no more make out than they
can the hebrew Bible. Lord Byron cuts a figure – but he is not
figurative – Shakespeare led a life of Allegory: his works are
the comments on it.        *Letter to George and Georgiana Keats,
                                                      14 Feb. 1819*

65 I have two luxuries to brood over in my walks, your Loveliness
and the hour of my death. O that I could have possession of
them both in the same minute.
                            *Letter to Fanny Brawne, 25 July 1819*

66 I equally dislike the favour of the public with the love of a
woman – they are both a cloying treacle to the wings of independence.                    *Letter to John Taylor, 24 Aug. 1819*

67 Love is my religion – I could die for that.
                            *Letter to Fanny Brawne, 13 Oct. 1819*

68 'If I should die,' said I to myself, 'I have left no immortal work
behind me – nothing to make my friends proud of my memory –
but I have lov'd the principle of beauty in all things, and if I
had had time I would have made myself remember'd.'
                              *Letter to Fanny Brawne, Feb. 1820*

69 You, I am sure, will forgive me for sincerely remarking that you
might curb your magnanimity, and be more of an artist, and
load every rift of your subject with ore.
                            *Letter to P. B. Shelley, Aug. 1820*

70 Here lies one whose name was writ in water.            *Epitaph*

### KEMPIS, Thomas À, 1380–1471

71 Man proposes but God disposes.   *The Imitation of Christ, 1, 19*

72 *Sic transit gloria mundi.* Thus the glory of the world passes away.
*Ib, 3, 6*

73 It is much safer to obey than to rule.   *Ib, 9, 1*

### KENNEDY, John Fitzgerald, 1917–1963

74 Let the word go forth from this time and place, to friend and
foe alike, that the torch has been passed to a new generation of
Americans – born in this century, tempered by war, disciplined
by a hard and bitter peace, proud of our ancient heritage.
*Inaugural address, 20 Jan. 1961*

75 My fellow Americans: ask not what your country can do for
you, ask what you can do for your country. My fellow citizens
of the world: ask not what America will do for you, but what
together we can do for the freedom of man.   *Ib*

### KESSELRING, Joseph, 1902–1967

76 Arsenic and Old Lace.   *Title of play*

### KETHE, William, ?–1608

77 All people that on earth do dwell
Sing to the Lord with cheerful voice.
*All People that on Earth do Dwell*

78 For why, the Lord our God is good:
His mercy is for ever sure;
His truth at all times firmly stood,
And shall from age to age endure.   *Ib*

### KEY, Francis Scott, 1780–1843

79 O! say can you see, by the dawn's early light,
What so proudly we hailed at the twilight's last gleaming,
Whose broad stripes and bright stars, through the perilous fight,
O'er the ramparts we watched, were so gallantly streaming.
*The Star-Spangled Banner*

80 'Tis the star-spangled banner! O long may it wave,
O'er the land of the free, and the home of the brave.   *Ib*

### KHAYYÁM, Omar, see FITZGERALD, Edward

### KILMER, Joyce, 1886–1918

81 I think that I shall never see
A poem lovely as a tree.

A tree whose hungry mouth is pressed
Against the earth's sweet flowing breast.                    *Trees*

82 Poems are made by fools like me
But only God can make a tree.                                *Ib*

**KING, Benjamin Franklin, 1857–1894**

83 Nothing to do but work,
Nothing to eat but food,
Nothing to wear but clothes,
To keep one from going nude.                        *The Pessimist*

**KING, Stoddard, 1889–1933**

84 There's a long, long trail a-winding
Into the land of my dreams.                     *The Long, Long Trail*

**KINGSLEY, Charles, 1819–1875**

85 Airly Beacon, Airly Beacon;
    Oh the pleasant sight to see
Shires and towns from Airly Beacon,
    While my love climbed up to me.                    *Airly Beacon*

86 Be good, sweet maid, and let who will be clever;
    Do noble things, not dream them, all day long:
And so make life, death, and that vast for-ever
    One grand, sweet song.                      *A Farewell, to C.E.G.*

87 For men must work, and women must weep,
And the sooner it's over, the sooner to sleep.   *The Three Fishers*

88 When all the world is young, lad,
    And all the trees are green.
                        *Songs from the Water Babies, Young and Old*

89 Young blood must have its course, lad,
    And every dog its day.                                  *Ib*

90 He did not know that a keeper is only a poacher turned outside
in, and a poacher is a keeper turned inside out.
                                        *The Water Babies, Ch. 1*

91 More ways of killing a cat than choking her with cream.
                                        *Westward Ho! Ch. 20*

**KIPLING, Rudyard, 1865–1936**

92 Oh, East is East, and West is West, and never the twain shall
meet.                          *The Ballad of East and West*

93 Four things greater than all things are, –
Women and Horses and Power and War.
                                    *Ballad of the King's Jest*

94 And a woman is only a woman, but a good cigar is a smoke.
*The Betrothed*

95 Boots – boots – boots – boots – movin' up an' down again!
*Boots*

96 But the Devil whoops, as he whooped of old:
'It's clever, but is it art?' *The Conundrum of the Workshops*

97 And what should they know of England who only England
know? *The English Flag*

98 For the female of the species is more deadly than the male.
*The Female of the Species*

99 Gentlemen-rankers out on the spree,
Damned from here to Eternity. *Gentlemen Rankers*

1 You're a better man than I am, Gunga Din. *Gunga Din*

2 If you can keep your head when all about you
Are losing theirs and blaming it on you. *If*

3 If you can dream – and not make dreams your master. *Ib*

4 If you can meet with Triumph and Disaster
And treat those two impostors just the same. *Ib*

5 If you can fill the unforgiving minute
With sixty seconds' worth of distance run,
Yours is the Earth and everything that's in it,
And – which is more – you'll be a Man, my son! *Ib*

6 Now this is the Law of the Jungle – as old and true as the sky.
*The Law of the Jungle*

7 On the road to Mandalay
Where the flyin'-fishes play. *Mandalay*

8 Ship me somewhere East of Suez, where the best is like the worst,
Where there aren't no Ten Commandments, an' a man can raise
a thirst. *Ib*

9 The tumult and the shouting dies –
The captains and the kings depart. *Recessional*

10 Lest we forget, lest we forget! *Ib*

11 Oh, it's Tommy this, an' Tommy that, an' 'Tommy, go away';
But it's 'Thank you, Mister Atkins,' when the band begins to
play. *Tommy*

12 Take up the White Man's Burden. *The White Man's Burden*

13 This is too butch for be. *Just-so Stories, The Elephant's Child*

14 Led go! You are hurtig be! *Ib*

15 The camel's hump is an ugly lump
Which well you may see at the Zoo;

But uglier yet is the hump we get
From having too little to do.   *Ib, How the Camel got his Hump*

16 A man of infinite – resource – and – sagacity.
*Ib, How the Whale got his Throat*

17 The Light that Failed.                         *Title of novel*


**KLINGER, Friedrich von, 1752–1831**

18 *Sturm und Drang*. Storm and stress.            *Title of play*


**KNOX, John, 1505–1572**

19 The First Blast of the Trumpet Against the Monstrous Regiment
of Women.                         *Title of Pamphlet, 1558*


**KNOX, Ronald Arbuthnot, 1888–1957**

20 There once was a man who said, 'God
Must think it exceedingly odd
    If he finds that this tree
    Continues to be
When there's no one about in the Quad.'          *Limerick*

21 A loud noise at one end and no sense of responsibility at the
other.                         *Definition of a Baby*


**KYD, Thomas, 1558?–1594?**

22 In time the savage bull sustains the yoke,
In time all haggard hawks will stoop to lure,
In time small wedges cleave the hardest oak,
In time the flint is pierced with softest shower.   LORENZO
*The Spanish Tragedy, Act 2, Scene 1*


**LABOUCHERE, Henry, 1831–1912**

23 He [*Labouchère*] did not object, he once said, to Gladstone's
always having the ace of trumps up his sleeve, but only to his
pretence that God had put it there.
*Quoted in Dictionary of National Biography, 1912–1921*


**LAMB, Lady Caroline, 1785–1828**

24 Mad, bad, and dangerous to know. [*Byron*]          *Journal*


**LAMB, Charles, 1775–1834**

25 The human species, according to the best theory I can form of
it, is composed of two distinct races, the men who borrow, and
the men who lend.   *Essays of Elia, The Two Races of Men*

26 Borrowers of books – those mutilators of collections, spoilers
of the symmetry of shelves, and creators of odd volumes.
*Essays of Elia, The Two Races of Men*

27 'A clear fire, a clean hearth, and the rigour of the game.' This
was the celebrated wish of old Sarah Battle (now with God)
who, next to her devotions, loved a good game of whist.
*Ib, Mrs Battle's Opinions on Whist*

28 'Presents,' I often say, 'endear Absents.'
*Ib, A Dissertation upon Roast Pig*

29 I love to lose myself in other men's minds. When I am not
walking, I am reading; I cannot sit and think. Books think
for me.                                     *Last Essays of Elia,*
*Detached Thoughts on Books and Reading*

30 To be strong-backed and neat-bound is the desideratum of a
volume. Magnificence comes after.                          *Ib*

31 Newspapers always excite curiosity. No one ever lays one down
without a feeling of disappointment.                       *Ib*

32 I have had playmates, I have had companions,
In my days of childhood, in my joyful schooldays –
All, all are gone, the old familiar faces. *The Old Familiar Faces*


**LANDOR, Walter Savage, 1775–1864**

33 George the First was always reckoned
Vile, but viler George the Second;
And what mortal ever heard
Any good of George the Third?
When from earth the Fourth descended
God be praised, the Georges ended.                  *Epigram*

34 I strove with none; for none was worth my strife;
Nature I loved and, next to Nature, Art:
I warmed both hands before the fire of life;
It sinks, and I am ready to depart.                     *Finis*

35 I loved him not; and yet now he is gone,
I feel I am alone.
I check'd him while he spoke: yet, could he speak,
Alas! I would not check.            *The Maid's Lament*

36 Ah, what avails the sceptred race!
Ah, what the form divine!                     *Rose Aylmer*


**LANE, George Martin, 1823–1897**

37 The waiter roars it through the hall:
'We don't give bread with one fish-ball!'     *One Fish-ball*

## LANGBRIDGE, Frederick, 1849–1923

38 Two men look out through the same bars:
One sees the mud, and one the stars.
*A Cluster of Quiet Thoughts*

## LANGLAND, William, 1330?–1400?

39 In a somer seson, when soft was the sonne.
*A Vision of William concerning Piers the Plowman,*
*B Text, Prologue, 1*

## LATIMER, Bishop Hugh, 1485?–1555

40 Be of good comfort, Master Ridley, and play the man; we shall
this day light such a candle by God's grace in England, as I
trust shall never be put out.        *16 Oct. 1555, while Latimer*
*and Ridley were being burned at the stake for heresy*

## LAUDER, Sir Harry, 1870–1950

41 I love a lassie.                                           *Song*

42 Just a wee doch-an'-dorris
Before we gang awa' . . .
If you can say, 'It's a braw, bricht, moonlicht nicht'
Ye're a' richt.                                              *Song*

43 Keep right on to the end of the road,
Keep right on to the end.
'Though you're tired and weary still journey on.             *Song*

44 O! it's nice to get up in the mornin'
But it's nicer to lie in bed.                                *Song*

45 Roamin' in the gloamin'.                                   *Song*

## LAWRENCE, David Herbert, 1885–1930

46 How beastly the bourgeois is
especially the male of the species. *How beastly the Bourgeois is*

47 Nicely groomed, like a mushroom
Standing there so sleek and erect and eyeable –
and like a fungus, living on the remains of bygone life
sucking his life out of the dead leaves of greater life than his
own.                                                           *Ib*

48 My love lies underground
With her face upturned to mine,
And her mouth unclosed in a last long kiss
That ended her life and mine.                    *Hymn to Priapus*

49 When I read Shakespeare I am struck with wonder
That such trivial people should muse and thunder
In such lovely language. *When I Read Shakespeare, 1*


## LEACOCK, Stephen Butler, 1869–1944

50 If every day in the life of a school could be the last day but one,
there would be little fault to find with it.
*College Days, Memories and Miseries of a Schoolmaster*

51 Lord Ronald said nothing; he flung himself from the room,
flung himself upon his horse and rode madly off in all directions.
*Nonsense Novels, Gertrude the Governess*

52 Golf may be played on Sunday, not being a game within the
view of the law, but being a form of moral effort.
*Other Fancies, Why I refuse to play Golf*

53 The general idea, of course, in any first-class laundry is to see
that no shirt or collar ever comes back twice.
*Winnowed Wisdom, Ch. 6*


## LEAR, Edward, 1812–1888

54 Who, or why, or which, or *what*, is the Akond of Swat?
*The Akond of Swat*

55 On the Coast of Coromandel
Where the early pumpkins blow,
In the middle of the woods
Lived the Yonghy-Bonghy-Bò.
*The Courtship of the Yonghy-Bonghy-Bò*

56 The Dong! – the Dong!
The wandering Dong through the forest goes!
The Dong! – the Dong!
The Dong with a luminous Nose!
*The Dong with a Luminous Nose*

57 They went to sea in a sieve, they did
In a sieve they went to sea. *The Jumblies*

58 Far and few, far and few,
Are the lands where the Jumblies live;
Their heads are green, and their hands are blue,
And they went to sea in a sieve. *Ib*

59 'How pleasant to know Mr Lear!'
Who has written such volumes of stuff!
Some think him ill-tempered and queer,
But a few think him pleasant enough.
*Nonsense Songs, Preface*

60  The Owl and the Pussy-Cat went to sea
        In a beautiful pea-green boat,
    They took some honey, and plenty of money,
        Wrapped up in a five-pound note.
                                      *The Owl and the Pussy-Cat*

61  They sailed away for a year and a day,
        To the land where the Bong-tree grows,
    nd there in a wood a Piggy-wig stood,
        With a ring at the end of his nose.                    *Ib*

62  They dined on mince and slices of quince,
        Which they ate with a runcible spoon;
    And hand in hand, on the edge of the sand
        They danced by the light of the moon.                 *Ib*

63  He has gone to fish, for his Aunt Jobiska's
    Runcible Cat with crimson whiskers.
                                      *The Pobble who has no Toes*

64  Two old Bachelors were living in one house;
    One caught a Muffin, the other caught a Mouse.
                                           *The Two Old Bachelors*

65  There was an Old Man who said, 'Hush!
    I perceive a young bird in this bush!'
            When they said, 'Is it small?'
            He replied, 'Not at all!
    It is four times as big as the bush!'
                                      *The Old Man Who said 'Hush!'*

66  There was an Old Man with a beard,
    Who said, 'It is just as I feared! –
            Two Owls and a Hen,
            Four Larks and a Wren,
    Have all built their nests in my beard!'
                                           *The Old Man With a Beard*


**LEE, Nathaniel, 1655?–1692**

67  When Greeks joined Greeks, then was the tug of war.   CLYTUS
                                      *The Rival Queens, Act 4, Scene 2*


**LELAND, Charles Godfrey, 1824–1903**

68  Hans Breitmann gife a barty –
    Where ish dat barty now?            *Hans Breitmann's Barty*


**LENIN, Nikolai, 1870–1924**

69  It is true that liberty is precious – so precious that it must be
    rationed.                                      *Attributed*

## LÉVIS, Duc de, 1764–1830

70 *Noblesse oblige.* Nobility imposes its own obligations. *Maximes et Réflexions*

## LEYBOURNE, George, ?–1884

71 O, he flies through the air with the greatest of ease,
This daring young man on the flying trapeze.
*The Man on the Flying Trapeze*

## LINCOLN, Abraham, 1809–1865

72 If the good people in their wisdom shall see fit to keep me in the background, I have been too familiar with disappointments to be very much chagrined.      *Speech, 9 March 1832*

73 No man is good enough to govern another man without that other's consent.      *Speech, 1854*

74 The ballot is stronger than the bullet.      *Speech, 19 May, 1856*

75 We cannot be free men if this is, by our national choice, to be a land of slavery. Those who deny freedom to others, deserve it not for themselves.      *Ib*

76 That is the issue that will continue in this country when these poor tongues of Judge Douglas and myself shall be silent. It is the eternal struggle between these two principles – right and wrong – throughout the world. They are the two principles that have stood face to face from the beginning of time, and will ever continue to struggle.      *Speech, 15 Oct. 1858*

77 What is conservatism? Is it not adherence to the old and tried, against the new and untried?      *Speech, 27 Feb. 1860*

78 I intend no modification of my oft-expressed personal wish that all men everywhere could be free.
*Letter to Horace Greeley, 22 Aug. 1862*

79 That this nation, under God, shall have a new birth of freedom; and that government of the people, by the people, and for the people, shall not perish from the earth.      *Address at Dedication of National Cemetery, Gettysburg, 19 Nov. 1863*

80 An old Dutch farmer, who remarked to a companion once that it was not best to swap horses in mid-stream.
*Speech, 9 June 1864*

81 With malice toward none; with charity for all; with firmness in the right, as God gives us to see the right, – let us strive on to finish the work we are in: to bind up the nation's wounds; to care for him who shall have borne the battle, and for his widow

and his orphan; to do all which may achieve and cherish a just and lasting peace among ourselves, and with all nations.
*Second Inaugural Address, 1865*

82 You can fool some of the people all the time and all the people some of the time; but you can't fool all the people all the time.
*Attributed*

83 People who like this sort of thing will find this is the sort of thing they like.                              *Criticism of book*

**LITVINOV, Maxim, 1876–1951**

84 Peace is indivisible.                    *Speech, Geneva, 1 July 1936*

**LIVY, 59 B.C.–A.D. 17**

85 *Vae victis.* Woe to the vanquished.                   *History, 5, 48*

**LLOYD, Marie, 1870–1922**

86 A little of what you fancy does you good.                        *Song*

87 I'm one of the ruins that Cromwell knocked about a bit.   *Song*

88 Oh, mister porter, what shall I do?
I wanted to go to Birmingham, but they've carried me on to Crewe.                          *Song, words by Thomas Le Brunn*

**LLOYD, Robert, 1733–1764**

89 Slow and steady wins the race.          *The Hare and the Tortoise*

**LLOYD GEORGE, David, 1st Earl, 1863–1945**

90 What is our task? To make Britain a fit country for heroes to live in.                                   *Speech, 24 Nov. 1918*

**LONGFELLOW, Henry Wadsworth, 1807–1882**

91 I shot an arrow into the air,
It fell to earth I knew not where.        *The Arrow and the Song*

92 Thou, too, sail on, O Ship of State!
Sail on, O Union, strong and great!
Humanity with all its fears,
With all the hopes of future years
Is hanging breathless on thy fate!      *The Building of the Ship*

93 The shades of night were falling fast,
As through an Alpine village passed
A youth, who bore, 'mid snow and ice,
A banner with the strange device,
         Excelsior!                                   *Excelsior*

94 A traveller, by the faithful hound,
   Half-buried in the snow was found.                    *Excelsior*

95 Tell me not, in mournful numbers,
    Life is but an empty dream!
  For the soul is dead that slumbers,
    And things are not what they seem.

  Life is real! Life earnest!
    And the grave is not its goal;
  Dust thou art, to dust returnest,
    Was not spoken of the soul.                       *A Psalm of Life*

96 Art is long, and Time is fleeting,
    And our hearts, though stout and brave,
  Still, like muffled drums, are beating
    Funeral marches to the grave.                            *Ib*

97 Lives of great men all remind us
    We can make our lives sublime,
  And, departing, leave behind us
    Footprints on the sands of time.                         *Ib*

98 Let us, then, be up and doing,
    With a heart for any fate,
  Still achieving, still pursuing,
    Learn to labour and to wait.                             *Ib*

99 Though the mills of God grind slowly,
      yet they grind exceeding small;
  Though with patience He stands waiting,
      with exactness grinds He all.

              *Retribution (translation from von Logau)*

1 'Wouldst thou' – so the helmsman answered, –
  'Learn the secret of the sea?
  Only those who brave its dangers
    Comprehend its mystery.'                      *The Secret of the Sea*

2 From the waterfall he named her,
  Minnehaha, Laughing Water.               *The Song of Hiawatha, 4*

3 As unto the bow the cord is,
  So unto the man is woman,
  Though she bends him, she obeys him,
  Though she draws him, yet she follows,
  Useless each without the other!                          *Ib, 10*

4 Ships that pass in the night, and speak each other in passing,
  Only a signal shown and a distant voice in the darkness;
  So on the ocean of life we pass and speak one another,
  Only a look and a voice, then darkness again and a silence.
      *Tales of a Wayside Inn, 3, The Theologian's Tale*

5  There was a little girl
   Who had a little curl
   Right in the middle of her forehead,
   And when she was good,
   She was very, very good,
   But when she was bad she was horrid.    *There was a Little Girl*

6  Under a spreading chestnut-tree
       The village smithy stands;
   The smith, a mighty man is he,
       With large and sinewy hands.    *The Village Blacksmith*

7      He earns whate'er he can,
   And looks the whole world in the face,
       For he owes not any man.                              *Ib*

8  Something attempted, something done
       Has earned a night's repose.                          *Ib*

9  It was the schooner Hesperus,
       That sailed the wintry sea;
   And the skipper had taken his little daughter,
       To bear him company.    *The Wreck of the Hesperus*

**LOOS, Anita, 1893–1981**
10  Gentlemen Prefer Blondes.                    *Title of Book*
11  Kissing your hand may make you feel very very good but a
    diamond and safire bracelet lasts forever.    *Gentlemen Prefer
                                                    Blondes, Ch. 4*

**LOUIS XIV of France, 1638–1715**
12  *L'État c'est moi.* I am the State.                *Attributed*
13  *Il n'y a plus de Pyrénées.* The Pyrenees no longer exist.
                                                       *Attributed*

**LOUIS XVIII of France, 1755–1824**
14  *L'exactitude est la politesse des rois.* Punctuality is the politeness
    of kings.                                          *Attributed*

**LOVELACE, Richard, 1618–1658**
15  Stone walls do not a prison make,
        Nor iron bars a cage.        *To Althea, from Prison*
16  Tell me not, sweet, I am unkind,
        That from the nunnery
    Of thy chaste breast, and quiet mind,
        To war and arms I fly.    *To Lucasta, Going to the Wars*

17 I could not love thee, Dear, so much,
    Loved I not Honour more.    *To Lucasta, Going to the Wars*

**LOVELL, Maria Anne, 1803–1877**

18 Two souls with but a single thought,
    Two hearts that beat as one.    *Ingomar the Barbarian*
        *(translated from German)*

**LOVER, Samuel, 1797–1868**

19 When once the itch of literature comes over a man, nothing can
cure it but the scratching of a pen.    *Handy Andy, Ch. 36*

**LOWELL, James Russell, 1819–1891**

20 An' you've got to get up airly
    Ef you want to take in God.    *The Biglow Papers, 1st*
        *series, No. 1*

21 I *don't* believe in princerple,
    But O, I *du* in interest.    *Ib, No. 6*

22 No man is born into the world, whose work
Is not born with him; there is always work,
And tools to work withal, for those who will:
And blessed are the horny hands of toil!    *A Glance Behind*
        *the Curtain, 201*

23 The birch, most shy and ladylike of trees.    *An Indian Summer*
        *Reverie*

24 Once to every man and nation comes the moment to decide,
In the strife of Truth with Falsehood, for the good or evil side.
        *The Present Crisis*

25 And what is so rare as a day in June?
    Then, if ever, come perfect days;
    Then Heaven tries earth if it be in tune,
    And over it softly her warm ear lays.    *The Vision of Sir*
        *Launfal, Part 1, Prelude*

26 A wise scepticism is the first attribute of a good critic.
        *Among My Books, Shakespeare Once More*

27 There is no good in arguing with the inevitable. The only argument available with an east wind is to put on your overcoat.
        *Democracy and Addresses*

**LUTHER, Martin, 1483–1546**

28 *Wer nicht liebt Wein, Weib und Gesang,*
    *Der bleibt ein Narr sein Lebelang.*
    Who loves not wine, woman and song,
    Remains a fool his whole life long.    *Attributed*

## LYLY, John, 1554?–1606

29 Cupid and my Campaspe play'd
   At cards for kisses – Cupid paid.       *Campaspe, 3, 5*

30 O Love! has she done this to thee?
   What shall, alas! become of me?       *Ib*

## LYTE, Henry Francis, 1793–1847

31 Abide with me; fast falls the eventide;
   The darkness deepens; Lord, with me abide!
   When other helpers fail, and comforts flee,
   Help of the helpless, O abide with me.     *Abide with Me*

32 Change and decay in all around I see;
   O thou who changest not, abide with me.     *Ib*

33 I fear no foe with thee at hand to bless;
   Ills have no weight, and tears no bitterness.
   Where is death's sting? where, grave, thy victory?
   I triumph still, if thou abide with me.     *Ib*

34 Praise my soul, the King of Heaven;
     To his feet thy tribute bring.   *Praise, my soul, the King of*
                                  *Heaven*

## LYTTON, 1st Earl of, see MEREDITH, Owen

## MACAULAY, Thomas Babington, 1st Baron, 1800–1859

35 Lars Porsena of Clusium
   By the Nine Gods he swore
   That the great house of Tarquin
   Would suffer wrong no more.     *Lays of Ancient Rome,*
                                          *Horatius, 1*

36 And how can man die better
   Than facing fearful odds,
   For the ashes of his fathers,
   And the temples of his Gods?     *Ib, 27*

37 Now who will stand on either hand,
   And keep the bridge with me?     *Ib, 29*

38 Then none was for a party;
   Then all were for the state.     *Ib, 32*

39 But those behind cried 'Forward!'
   And those before cried 'Back!'     *Ib, 50*

40 Oh, Tiber! father Tiber!
   To whom the Romans pray,
   A Roman's life, a Roman's arms,
   Take thou in charge this day!     *Ib, 59*

41 And even the ranks of Tuscany
   Could scarce forbear to cheer.      *Lays of Ancient Rome,*
                                        *Horatius, 60*

42 Every schoolboy knows who imprisoned Montezuma, and who
   strangled Atahualpa.      *Essay in Edinburgh Review, Lord Clive*

43 The English Bible, a book which, if everything else in our
   language should perish, would alone suffice to show the whole
   extent of its beauty and power.         *Ib, On John Dryden*

44 The gallery in which the reporters sit has become a fourth estate
   of the realm.         *Ib, Hallam's Constitutional History*

45 The history of England is emphatically the history of progress.
   *Ib, Sir J. Mackintosh's History of the Revolution*

46 We know of no spectacle so ridiculous as the British public in
   one of its periodical fits of morality.   *Ib, Moore's Life of Lord*
                                               *Byron*

47 The Puritan hated bear-baiting, not because it gave pain to the
   bear, but because it gave pleasure to the spectators.
                                  *History of England, Ch. 2*

## McCRAE, John, 1872–1918

48 In Flanders fields the poppies blow
   Between the crosses, row on row.      *In Flanders Fields*

49 If ye break faith with us who die
   We shall not sleep, though poppies grow
   In Flanders fields.                                     *Ib*

## MACDONALD, George, 1824–1905

50 Here lie I, Martin Elginbrodde:
   Hae mercy o' my soul, Lord God;
   As I wad do, were I Lord God,
   And ye were Martin Elginbrodde.      *David Elginbrod, Book 1,*
                                         *Ch. 13*

## MACMAHON, Maurice de, 1808–1893

51 *J'y suis, j'y reste.* Here I am, and here I stay.      *Attributed at*
                                        *taking of Malakoff, 1855*

## MACMILLAN, Harold, 1894–1986

52 Most of our people have never had it so good. Go around the
   country – go to the industrial towns, go to the farms – and you
   will see a state of prosperity such as we have never had in my
   lifetime, or indeed ever in the history of this country.
                      *Speech, Bedford Football Ground, 20 July 1957*

53 The wind of change is blowing through the continent. Whether
we like it or not, this growth of national consciousness is a
political fact.                                 *Speech, South African*
                                   *Parliament, Cape Town, 3 Feb. 1960*

## MACNEICE, Louis, 1907–1963

54 It's no go the merrygoround, it's no go the rickshaw,
All we want is a limousine and a ticket for the peepshow.
                                                   *Bagpipe Music*

55 It's no go my honey love, it's no go my poppet;
Work your hands from day to day, the winds will blow the
    profit.
The glass is falling hour by hour, the glass will fall for ever,
But if you break the bloody glass you won't hold up the weather.
                                                              *Ib*

56 Between the enormous fluted Ionic columns
There seeps from heavily jowled or hawk-like foreign faces
The guttural sorrow of the refugees.      *The British Museum*
                                              *Reading Room*

57 Time was away and somewhere else,
There were two glasses and two chairs
And two people with one pulse
(Somebody stopped the moving stairs):
Time was away and somewhere else.          *Meeting Point*

## MAISTRE, Joseph de, 1754–1821

58 *Toute nation a le gouvernement qu'elle mérite.* Every nation has
the government it deserves.          *Letter about Russia, 1811*

## MALLET, David, 1705?–1765

59 O grant me, Heaven, a middle state,
Neither too humble nor too great;
More than enough, for nature's ends,
With something left to treat my friends.   *Imitation of Horace*

## MANDALE, W. R., 19th century

60 Up and down the City Road,
In and out the Eagle,
That's the way the money goes –
Pop goes the weasel!                      *Pop Goes the Weasel*

## MANNERS, Lord John, see RUTLAND, 7th Duke of

**MARIE-ANTOINETTE, Queen of France, 1755–1793**

61 *Qu'ils mangent de la brioche*. Let them eat cake.     *Attributed*
    (*Similar phrases date back to thirteenth century*)

**MARLOWE, Christopher, 1564–1593**

62 What doctrine call you this, *Che sera, sera,*
What will be, shall be? FAUSTUS     *Doctor Faustus*

63 Was this the face that launch'd a thousand ships
And burnt the topless towers of Ilium?
Sweet Helen, make me immortal with a kiss.
Her lips suck forth my soul: see, where it flies!
Come, Helen, come, give me my soul again.
Here will I dwell, for heaven is in these lips,
And all is dross that is not Helena. FAUSTUS     *Ib*

64 O, thou art fairer than the evening air
Clad in the beauty of a thousand stars. FAUSTUS     *Ib*

65 Now hast thou but one bare hour to live,
And then thou must be damn'd perpetually!
Stand still, you ever-moving spheres of heaven,
That time may cease, and midnight never come. FAUSTUS   *Ib*

66 Ugly hell, gape not! come not, Lucifer!
I'll burn my books! FAUSTUS     *Ib*

67 Cut is the branch that might have grown full straight,
And burned is Apollo's laurel-bough,
That sometime grew within this learned man. CHORUS   *Ib*

68 My men, like satyrs grazing on the lawns,
Shall with their goat-feet dance an antic hay. GAVESTON
    *Edward the Second*

69 I count religion but a childish toy,
And hold there is no sin but ignorance. MACHIAVEL   *The Jew
of Malta, Prologue*

70 And, as their wealth increaseth, so inclose
Infinite riches in a little room. BARABAS     *Ib, Act 1*

71 FRIAR BARNARDINE: Thou hast committed –
BARABAS:         Fornication: but that was in another
              country;
              And beside the wench is dead.   *Ib, Act 4*

72 Jigging veins of rhyming mother-wits. *Tamburlaine the Great,
Part 1, Prologue*

73 Zenocrate, lovelier than the love of Jove,
Brighter than is the silver Rhodope,
Fairer than whitest snow on Scythian hills. TAMBURLAINE
    *Ib, Act 1, Scene 2*

74 Accurs'd be he that first invented war.   MYCETES
                     *Tamburlaine the Great, Act 2, Scene 4*

75 Is it not passing brave to be a king,
   And ride in triumph through Persepolis?   TAMBURLAINE
                                   *Ib, Act 2, Scene 5*

76 Nature, that fram'd us of four elements
   Warring within our breasts for regiment,
   Doth teach us all to have aspiring minds:
   Our souls, whose faculties can comprehend
   The wondrous architecture of the world,
   And measure every wandering planet's course,
   Still climbing after knowledge infinite,
   And always moving as the restless spheres,
   Will us to wear ourselves, and never rest,
   Until we reach the ripest fruit of all,
   That perfect bliss and sole felicity,
   The sweet fruition of an earthly crown.   TAMBURLAINE
                                   *Ib, Act 2, Scene 7*

77 Ah, fair Zenocrate! – divine Zenocrate!
   Fair is too foul an epithet for thee.   TAMBURLAINE   *Ib, Act 5,*
                                                          *Scene 1*

78 Holla, ye pamper'd jades of Asia!
   What, can ye draw but twenty miles a-day?   TAMBURLAINE
                                   *Ib, Part 2, Act 4, Scene 3*

79 Tamburlaine, the scourge of God, must die.   TAMBURLAINE
                                   *Ib, Act 5, Scene 3*

80 It lies not in our power to love or hate,
   For will in us is over-rul'd by fate.        *Hero and Leander*

81 Where both deliberate, the love is slight:
   Who ever lov'd, that lov'd not at first sight?            *Ib*

82 Come live with me, and be my love;
   And we will all the pleasures prove
   That hills and valleys, dales and fields,
   Woods or steepy mountain yields.        *The Passionate Shepherd*
                                                     *to his Love*

**MARQUIS, Donald Robert, 1878–1937**

83 its cheerio
   my deario that
   pulls a lady through   *archy and mehitabel, cheerio my deario*

84 toujours gai archy
   toujours gai                                              *Ib*

85     so unlucky
that he runs into accidents
which started out to happen
to somebody else        *archy's life of mehitabel, archy says*

## MARRYAT, Frederick, 1792–1848

86 If you please, ma'am, it was a very little one. [*The Nurse: Of her
illegitimate baby*]               *Midshipman Easy, Ch. 3*

87 I never knows the children. It's just six of one and half-a-dozen
of the other.                        *The Pirate, Ch. 4*

88 Every man paddle his own canoe.     *Settlers in Canada, Ch. 8*

## MARVELL, Andrew, 1621–1678

89 Where the remote Bermudas ride,
In the ocean's bosom unespied.          *Bermudas, 1*

90 Echo beyond the Mexique Bay.            *Ib, 36*

91 And all the way, to guide their chime,
With falling oars they kept the time.      *Ib, 39*

92 Had we but world enough, and time,
This coyness, lady, were no crime.   *To his Coy Mistress, 1*

93 My vegetable love should grow
Vaster than empires and more slow.        *Ib, 11*

94 But at my back I always hear
Time's winged chariot hurrying near;
And yonder all before us lie
Deserts of vast eternity.                 *Ib, 21*

95 The grave's a fine and private place,
But none, I think, do there embrace.       *Ib, 31*

96 Thus, though we cannot make our sun
Stand still, yet we will make him run.      *Ib, 45*

97 My love is of a birth as rare
As 'tis, for object, strange and high;
It was begotten by Despair
Upon Impossibility.         *The Definition of Love, 1*

98 Therefore the love which us doth bind,
But fate so enviously debars,
Is the conjunction of the mind,
And opposition of the stars.              *Ib, 29*

99 Annihilating all that's made
To a green thought in a green shade.    *The Garden, 47*

 1 Casting the body's vest aside,
My soul into the boughs does glide.        *Ib, 51*

2 So restless Cromwell could not cease
  In the inglorious arts of peace.          *An Horatian Ode upon*
                                        *Cromwell's Return from Ireland, 9*

3 He nothing common did or mean,
  Upon that memorable scene.
    But with his keener eye
    The axe's edge did try.   [*Charles I*]              *Ib, 57*

4 Who can foretell for what high cause
  This darling of the Gods was born?        *The Picture of Little*
                                       *T.C. in a Prospect of Flowers, 9*

5 Gather the flowers, but spare the buds.                 *Ib, 35*

**MARX, Karl, 1818–1883**

6 From each according to his abilities, to each according to his
  needs.                        *Criticism of the Gotha Programme*

7 Religion . . . is the opium of the people.      *Criticism of the*
                             *Hegelian Philosophy of Right, Introduction*

8 The ruling ideas of each age have ever been the ideas of its
  ruling class.               *Manifesto of the Communist Party, 2*

9 The workers have nothing to lose but their chains. They have a
  world to gain. Workers of the world, unite.             *Ib, 4*

**MARY TUDOR, Queen of England, 1516–1558**

10 When I am dead and opened, you shall find 'Calais' lying in my
   heart.                       *Holinshed's Chronicles, 3, 1160*

**MASEFIELD, John, 1878–1967**

11 But the loveliest things of beauty God ever has showed to me,
   Are her voice, and her hair, and eyes, and the dear red curve of
   her lips.                                              *Beauty*

12 Quinquireme of Nineveh from distant Ophir
   Rowing home to haven in sunny Palestine,
   With a cargo of ivory,
   And apes and peacocks,
   Sandalwood, cedarwood, and sweet white wine.          *Cargoes*

13 Dirty British coaster with a salt-caked smoke-stack
   Butting through the Channel in the mad March days.       *Ib*

14 I must down to the seas again, to the lonely sea and the sky,
   And all I ask is a tall ship and a star to steer her by.
                                                       *Sea Fever*

15 I must down to the seas again, for the call of the running tide
   Is a wild call and a clear call that may not be denied.   *Ib*

16 I must down to the seas again, to the vagrant gypsy life,
   To the gull's way and the whale's way where the wind's like a
       whetted knife;
   And all I ask is a merry yarn from a laughing fellow-rover,
   And quiet sleep and a sweet dream when the long trick's over.
                                                      *Sea Fever*

17 It is good to be out on the road, and going one knows not
       where,
   Going through meadow and village, one knows not whither nor
       why.                                      *Tewkesbury Road*

## MASSINGER, Philip, 1583–1640

18 He that would govern others, first should be
   The master of himself.        *The Bondman, Act 1, Scene 3*
19 A New Way to Pay Old Debts.              *Title of Play*

## MAUGHAM, William Somerset, 1874–1965

20 People ask you for criticism, but they only want praise.
                                       *Of Human Bondage, Ch. 50*
21 Impropriety is the soul of wit.   *The Moon and Sixpence, Ch. 4*
22 I would sooner read a time-table or a catalogue than nothing at
   all. They are much more entertaining than half the novels that
   are written.                              *The Summing Up*
23 Life is too short to do anything for oneself that one can pay
   others to do for one.                                *Ib*

## MEARNS, Hughes, 1875–1965

24 As I was going up the stair
   I met a man who wasn't there.
   He wasn't there again today.
   I wish, I wish he'd stay away.              *The Psychoed*

## MELBOURNE, William Lamb, 2nd Viscount, 1779–1848

25 I like the Garter; there is no damned merit in it.
                                       *On the Order of the Garter*
26 Things have come to a pretty pass when religion is allowed to
   invade the sphere of private life.              *Attributed*
27 I wish that I was as cocksure of anything as Tom Macaulay is of
   everything.                                    *Attributed*

## MENCKEN, Henry Louis, 1880–1956

28 All successful newspapers are ceaselessly querulous and bellicose.
   They never defend anyone or anything if they can help it; if the

job is forced upon them, they tackle it by denouncing someone
or something else.                        *Prejudices, First Series*

29 The average schoolmaster is and always must be essentially an
ass, for how can one imagine an intelligent man engaging in so
puerile an avocation?                              *Ib, Third Series*

30 I've made it a rule never to drink by daylight and never to
refuse a drink after dark.                   *Quoted in New York Post,
                                                    18 Sept. 1945*

## MEREDITH, George, 1828–1909

31 Cynicism is intellectual dandyism.              *The Egoist, Ch. 7*

32 The actors are, it seems, the usual three:
Husband, and wife, and lover.             *Modern Love, Stanza 25*

33          We'll sit contentedly
And eat our pot of honey on the grave.            *Ib, Stanza 29*

34 Ah, what a dusty answer gets the soul
When hot for certainties in this our life!        *Ib, Stanza 50*

35 I expect that Woman will be the last thing civilized by Man.
                          *The Ordeal of Richard Feverel, Ch. 1*

36 Kissing don't last: cookery do!                     *Ib, Ch. 28*

## MEREDITH, Owen (Earl of Lytton), 1831–1891

37 Genius does what it must, and Talent does what it can.
                       *Last Words of a Sensitive Second-rate Poet*

## MERRITT, Dixon Lanier, 1879–1954

38 A wonderful bird is the pelican,
His beak holds more than his belican.
     He can take in his beak
     Enough food for a week,
But I'm damned if I know how the helican!           *The Pelican*

## MIKES, George, 1912–1987

39 On the Continent people have good food; in England people
have good table manners.                      *How to be an Alien*

40 Continental people have sex life; the English have hot-water
bottles.                                                      *Ib*

41 An Englishman, even if he is alone, forms an orderly queue of
one.                                                          *Ib*

## MILL, John Stuart, 1806–1873

42 All good things which exist are the fruits of originality.
                                               *On Liberty, Ch. 3*

43 The worth of a State in the long run is the worth of the individuals composing it. *On Liberty, Ch. 3*

44 That so few now dare to be eccentric marks the chief danger of the time. *Ib*


**MILLAY, Edna St Vincent, 1892–1950**

45 My candle burns at both ends;
    It will not last the night;
But, oh, my foes, and oh, my friends –
    It gives a lovely light. *Figs from Thistles, First Fig*

46 What lips my lips have kissed, and where, and why,
I have forgotten, and what arms have lain
Under my head till morning; but the rain
Is full of ghosts tonight, that tap and sigh
Upon the glass and listen for reply. *Sonnet, What Lips My Lips Have Kissed*

47 I only know that summer sang in me
A little while, that in me sings no more. *Ib*


**MILLIGAN, Spike, 1918–**

48 'Do you come here often?'
    'Only in the mating season.' *BBC programme, The Goon Show, with Spike Milligan, Harry Secombe and Peter Sellers*


**MILNE, Alan Alexander, 1882–1956**

49 The more it snows
        (Tiddely pom),
    The more it goes
        (Tiddely pom),
    The more it goes
        (Tiddely pom),
      On snowing.
    And nobody knows
        (Tiddely pom),
    How cold my toes
        (Tiddely pom),
    How cold my toes
        (Tiddely pom),
      Are growing. POOH *The House at Pooh Corner, Ch. 1*

50 Tiggers don't like honey. TIGGER *Ib, Ch. 2*

51 'Climbing trees is what they do best,' said Tigger. 'Much better than Poohs.' *Ib, Ch. 4*

52 King John was not a good man –
    He had his little ways.    *Now We are Six, King John's*
                                               *Christmas*

53 No one can tell me,
    Nobody knows,
Where the wind comes from,
    Where the wind goes.    *Ib, Wind on the Hill*

54 They're changing guard at Buckingham Palace –
Christopher Robin went down with Alice.
Alice is marrying one of the guard.
'A soldier's life is terrible hard,'
        Says Alice.    *When We Were Very*
                   *Young, Buckingham Palace*

55 'Do you think the King knows all about me?'
'Sure to, dear, but it's time for tea,'
        Says Alice.    *Ib*

56 James James
Morrison Morrison
Weatherby George Dupree
Took great
Care of his Mother,
Though he was only three.    *Ib, Disobedience*

57 You must never go down to the end of the town, if you don't go
down with me.    *Ib*

58 *What* is the matter with Mary Jane?
I've promised her sweets and a ride in the train,
And I've begged her to stop for a bit and explain –
What *is* the matter with Mary Jane?    *Ib, Rice Pudding*

59 The King asked
The Queen, and
The Queen asked
The Dairymaid:
'Could we have some butter for
The Royal slice of bread?'    *Ib, The King's Breakfast*

60 I do like a little bit of butter to my bread!    *Ib*

61 Little Boy kneels at the foot of the bed,
Droops on the little hands little gold head.
Hush! Hush! Whisper who dares!
Christopher Robin is saying his prayers,    *Ib, Vespers*

62 Isn't it funny
How a bear likes honey?

Buzz! Buzz! Buzz!
I wonder why he does?                    *Winnie-the-Pooh, Ch. 1*

63 'Well', said Owl, 'the customary procedure in such cases is as
   follows.'
   'What does Crustimoney Proseedcake mean?' said Pooh. 'For I
   am a Bear of Very Little Brain, and long words Bother me.'
                                              *Ib, Ch. 4*

64 Eeyore, the old grey Donkey, stood by the side of the stream, and
   looked at himself in the water.
   'Pathetic,' he said. 'That's what it is, Pathetic.'    *Ib, Ch.6*

65 Cottleston, Cottleston, Cottleston Pie.
   A fly can't bird, but a bird can fly.
   Ask me a riddle and I reply:
   '*Cottleston, Cottleston, Cottleston Pie.*'  POOH           *Ib*

66 Time for a little something.  POOH                           *Ib*

67 My spelling is Wobbly. It's good spelling but it Wobbles, and
   letters get in the wrong places.  POOH                     *Ib*

68 A Useful Pot to put things in.  POOH                        *Ib*

69 Sing Ho! for the life of a Bear.  POOH             *Ib, Ch. 8*

70 3 Cheers for Pooh!
   (For Who?)
   For Pooh –
   (Why What did he do?)
   I thought you knew;
   He saved his friend from a wetting.  ANXIOUS POOH SONG
                                              *Ib, Ch. 10*


**MILTON, John, 1608–1674**

71 Blest pair of Sirens, pledges of Heaven's joy,
   Sphere-born harmonious sisters, Voice and Verse.
                                        *At a Solemn Music, 1*

72 Before the starry threshold of Jove's court
   My mansion is.  ATTENDANT SPIRIT.        *Comus: A Mask, 1*

73 Above the smoke and stir of this dim spot
   Which men call Earth.  ATTENDANT SPIRIT            *Ib, 5*

74 What hath night to do with sleep?  COMUS         *Ib, 122*

75 Come, knit hands, and beat the ground
   In a light fantastic round.  COMUS               *Ib, 143*

76 'Tis chastity, my brother, chastity:
   She that has that, is clad in complete steel.  ELDER BROTHER
                                              *Ib, 420*

77  How charming is divine Philosophy!
    Not harsh and crabbed, as dull fools suppose.
    But musical as is Apollo's lute,
    And a perpetual feast of nectared sweets,
    Where no crude surfeit reigns.  SECOND BROTHER

                                    *Comus: A Mask, 476*

78              That power
    Which erring men call Chance.  ELDER BROTHER      *Ib, 587*

79  Beauty is Nature's coin; must not be hoarded,
    But must be current.  COMUS                       *Ib, 739*

80  Sabrina fair,
        Listen where thou art sitting
    Under the glassy, cool, translucent wave,
        In twisted braids of lilies knitting
    The loose train of thy amber-dropping hair.
                        ATTENDANT SPIRIT   *Ib, 859*

81      Mortals, that would follow me,
    Love Virtue, she alone is free.
    She can teach ye how to climb
    Higher than the sphery chime;
    Or, if Virtue feeble were,
    Heaven itself would stoop to her.  ATTENDANT SPIRIT  *Ib, 1018*

82  Hence, vain deluding Joys,
        The brood of Folly without father bred!   *Il Penseroso, 1*

83  But, hail! thou Goddess sage and holy
    Hail, divinest Melancholy!                        *Ib, 11*

84  Thy rapt soul sitting in thine eyes.             *Ib, 40*

85  Sweet bird, that shunn'st the noise of folly,
    Most musical, most melancholy!                    *Ib, 61*

86  Where glowing embers through the room
    Teach light to counterfeit a gloom,
    Far from all resort of mirth,
    Save the cricket on the hearth.                   *Ib, 79*

87  Where more is meant than meets the ear.          *Ib, 120*

88  And storied windows richly dight,
        Casting a dim religious light.                *Ib, 159*

89  Till old experience do attain
    To something like prophetic strain.               *Ib, 173*

90  These pleasures, Melancholy, give;
    And I with thee will choose to live.              *Ib, 175*

91  Hence, loathed Melancholy,
        Of Cerberus and blackest Midnight born

In Stygian cave forlorn
   'Mongst horrid shapes, and shrieks, and sights unholy!
                               *L'Allegro, 1*

92 So buxom, blithe, and debonair.             *Ib, 24*

93 Haste thee, Nymph, and bring with thee
   Jest, and youthful Jollity,
   Quips and Cranks and wanton Wiles,
   Nods and Becks and wreathed Smiles.      *Ib, 25*

94 Sport that wrinkled Care derides,
   And Laughter holding both his sides.
   Come, and trip it as you go
   On the light fantastic toe.            *Ib, 31*

95 The mountain-nymph, sweet Liberty.      *Ib, 36*

96 And, if I give thee honour due,
   Mirth, admit me of thy crew,
   To live with her, and live with thee,
   In unreproved pleasures free.          *Ib, 37*

97 To hear the lark begin his flight,
   And, singing, startle the dull night,
   From his watch-tower in the skies,
   Till the dappled dawn doth rise;
   Then to come, in spite of sorrow,
   And at my window bid good morrow
   Through the sweet-briar or the vine,
   Or the twisted eglantine.            *Ib, 41*

98 While the ploughman, near at hand,
   Whistles o'er the furrowed land,
   And the milkmaid singeth blithe,
   And the mower whets his scythe,
   And every shepherd tells his tale
   Under the hawthorn in the dale.       *Ib, 63*

99 Then to the spicy nut-brown ale.      *Ib, 100*

1 Towered cities please us then,
   And the busy hum of men.          *Ib, 117*

2     Store of ladies, whose bright eyes
   Rain influence, and judge the prize
   Of wit or arms.               *Ib, 121*

3 Such sights as youthful poets dream
   On summer eves by haunted stream.   *Ib, 129*

4 Or sweetest Shakespeare, Fancy's child,
   Warble his native wood-notes wild.   *Ib, 133*

5 Untwisting all the chains that tie
  The hidden soul of harmony.                          *L'Allegro, 143*

6 Such strains as would have won the ear
  Of Pluto, to have quite set free
  His half-regained Eurydice.                           *Ib, 148*

7   These delights if thou canst give,
  Mirth, with thee I mean to live.                      *Ib, 151*

8 Yet once more, O ye laurels, and once more,
  Ye myrtles brown, with ivy never sere,
  I come to pluck your berries harsh and crude,
  And with forced fingers rude
  Shatter your leaves before the mellowing year.        *Lycidas, 1*

9              He knew
  Himself to sing, and build the lofty rhyme.           *Ib, 10*

10   But, oh! the heavy change, now thou art gone,
  Now thou art gone, and never must return!             *Ib, 37*

11   Alas! what boots it with incessant care
  To tend the homely, slighted, shepherd's trade,
  And strictly meditate the thankless Muse?             *Ib, 64*

12 To sport with Amaryllis in the shade,
  Or with the tangles of Neaera's hair?                 *Ib, 68*

13 Fame is the spur that the clear spirit doth raise
  (That last infirmity of noble mind)
  To scorn delights, and live laborious days.           *Ib, 70*

14 Fame is no plant that grows on mortal soil.           *Ib, 78*

15 Blind mouths! that scarce themselves know how to hold
  A sheep-hook.                                         *Ib, 119*

16 And, when they list, their lean and flashy songs
  Grate on their scrannel pipes of wretched straw;
  The hungry sheep look up, and are not fed,
  But, swoln with wind and the rank mist they draw,
  Rot inwardly, and foul contagion spread.              *Ib, 123*

17 Bring the rathe primrose that forsaken dies.          *Ib, 142*

18 At last he rose, and twitched his mantle blue:
  To-morrow to fresh woods, and pastures new.           *Ib, 192*

19 This is the month, and this the happy morn.   *On the Morning*
                                             *of Christ's Nativity, 1*

20 It was the winter wild,
  While the Heaven-born Child
    All meanly wrapt in the rude manger lies.           *Ib, 29*

21 Time will run back and fetch the age of gold.         *Ib, 135*

22 So when the sun in bed,
   Curtained with cloudy red,
      Pillows his chin upon an orient wave.
                    *On the Morning of Christ's Nativity*, 229

23 What needs my Shakespeare for his honoured bones,
   The labour of an age in piled stones?    *On Shakespeare, 1*

24 Dear son of memory, great heir of fame,
   What need'st thou such weak witness of thy name?    *Ib, 5*

25 Kings for such a tomb would wish to die.    *Ib, 16*

26 Rhyme being no necessary adjunct or true ornament of poems
   or good verse, in longer works especially, but the invention of a
   barbarous age, to set off wretched matter and lame metre.
                    *Paradise Lost, Preface, The Verse*

27 Of Man's first disobedience, and the fruit
   Of that forbidden tree, whose mortal taste
   Brought death into the World, and all our woe,
   With loss of Eden, till one greater Man
   Restore us, and regain the blissful seat,
   Sing, Heavenly Muse.    *Ib, Book 1, 1*

28 Things unattempted yet in prose or rhyme.    *Ib, 1, 16*

29              What in me is dark
   Illumine, what is low raise and support;
   That, to the height of this great argument,
   I may assert Eternal Providence,
   And justify the ways of God to men.    *Ib, 1, 22*

30              What though the field be lost?
   All is not lost – the unconquerable will,
   And study of revenge, immortal hate,
   And courage never to submit or yield:
   And what is else not to be overcome?    *Ib, 1, 105*

31              To be weak is miserable,
   Doing or suffering.    *Ib, 1, 157*

32 And out of good still to find means of evil.    *Ib, 1, 165*

33 What reinforcement we may gain from hope,
   If not, what resolution from despair.    *Ib, 1, 190*

34              Farewell, happy fields,
   Where joy for ever dwells! Hail, horrors! hail.    *Ib, 1, 249*

35 A mind not to be changed by place or time.
   The mind is its own place, and in itself
   Can make a Heaven of Hell, a Hell of Heaven.    *Ib, 1, 253*

36 To reign is worth ambition, though in Hell:
   Better to reign in Hell than serve in Heaven.    *Ib, 1, 262*

37 Awake, arise, or be for ever fallen!    *Ib, 1, 330*

38              And when night
Darkens the streets, then wander forth the sons
Of Belial, flown with insolence and wine.     *Paradise Lost,*
                                                                        *Book 1, 500*

39 Th' imperial ensign; which, full high advanced,
Shone like a meteor streaming to the wind.         *Ib, 1, 536*

40 A shout that tore Hell's concave, and beyond
Frighted the reign of Chaos and old Night.         *Ib, 1, 542*

41            His form had yet not lost
All her original brightness, nor appeared
Less than Archangel ruined, and the excess
Of glory obscured.                           *Ib, I, 591*

42 Tears, such as Angels weep, burst forth.       *Ib, 1, 620*

43               Who overcomes
By force hath overcome but half his foe.         *Ib, 1, 648*

44               From morn
To noon he fell, from noon to dewy eve,
A summer's day, and with the setting sun
Dropped from the zenith, like a falling star.     *Ib, 1, 742*

45 High on a throne of royal state, which far
Outshone the wealth of Ormus and of Ind,
Or where the gorgeous East with richest hand
Showers on her kings barbaric pearl and gold,
Satan exalted sat, by merit raised
To that bad eminence.                   *Ib, Book 2, 1*

46 My sentence is for open war. Of wiles,
More unexpert, I boast not.             *Ib, 2, 51*

47         In our proper motion we ascend
Up to our native seat; descent and fall
To us is adverse.                        *Ib, 2, 75*

48            Though his tongue
Dropped manna, and could make the worse appear
The better reason.                     *Ib, 2, 112*

49            For who would lose,
Though full of pain, this intellectual being,
Those thoughts that wander through eternity,
To perish rather, swallowed up and lost
In the wide womb of uncreated Night,
Devoid of sense and motion?           *Ib, 2, 146*

50 Unrespited, unpitied, unreprieved,
Ages of hopeless end.                *Ib, 2, 185*

51 Our torments also may, in length of time,
Become our elements.                *Ib, 2, 274*

52                   With grave
Aspect he rose, and in his rising seemed
A pillar of state; deep on his front engraven
Deliberation sat, and public care;
And princely counsel in his face yet shone,
Majestic, though in ruin.     *Paradise Lost, Book 2, 300*

53         Another World, the happy seat
Of some new race, called Man, about this time
To be created like to us, though less
In power and excellence.     *Ib, 2, 347*

54                Long is the way
And hard that out of Hell leads up to light.     *Ib, 2, 432*

55 Others apart sat on a hill retired,
In thoughts more elevate, and reasoned high
Of Providence, Foreknowledge, Will, and Fate –
Fixed fate, free will, foreknowledge absolute –
And found no end, in wandering mazes lost.     *Ib, 2, 557*

56               The other Shape –
If shape it might be called that shape had none.     *Ib, 2, 666*

57 For Hot, Cold, Moist, and Dry, four champions fierce,
Strive here for mastery.     *Ib, 2, 898*

58 Hail, holy Light, Offspring of Heaven first-born!  *Ib, Book 3, 1*

59             Thus with the year
Seasons return; but not to me returns
Day, or the sweet approach of even or morn,
Or sight of vernal bloom, or summer's rose,
Or flocks, or herds, or human face divine;
But clouds instead and ever-during dark
Surrounds me.     *Ib, 3, 40*

60 Into a Limbo large and broad, since called
The Paradise of Fools; to few unknown.     *Ib, 3, 495*

61        At whose sight all the stars
Hide their diminished heads.     *Ib, Book 4, 34*

62 Me miserable! which way shall I fly
Infinite wrath and infinite despair?
Which way I fly is Hell; myself am Hell;
And, in the lowest deep, a lower deep
Still threat'ning to devour me opens wide,
To which the Hell I suffer seems a Heaven.     *Ib, 4, 73*

63 So farewell hope, and, with hope, farewell fear,
Farewell remorse! All good to me is lost;
Evil, be thou my Good.     *Ib, 4, 180*

64 Thence up he flew, and on the Tree of Life
The middle tree and highest there that grew,
Sat like a cormorant. *Paradise Lost, Book 4, 194*

65 A Heaven on Earth. *Ib, 4, 208*

66 For contemplation he and valour formed,
For softness she and sweet attractive grace;
He for God only, she for God in him. *Ib, 4, 297*

67 Adam, the goodliest man of men since born
His sons; the fairest of her daughters Eve. *Ib, 4, 323*

68 Imparadised in one another's arms. *Ib, 4, 506*

69 Now came still Evening on, and Twilight grey
Had in her sober livery all things clad. *Ib, 4, 598*

70 God is thy law, thou mine: to know no more
Is woman's happiest knowledge, and her praise.
With thee conversing, I forget all time. *Ib, 4, 637*

71 Hail, wedded Love, mysterious law, true source
Of human offspring. *Ib, 4, 750*

72 Not to know me argues yourselves unknown. *Ib, 4, 830*

73      Abashed the Devil stood,
And felt how awful goodness is, and saw
Virtue in her shape how lovely. *Ib, 4, 846*

74 But wherefore thou alone? Wherefore with thee
Came not all Hell broke loose? *Ib, 4, 917*

75 Now Morn, her rosy steps in th' eastern clime
Advancing, sowed the earth with orient pearl. *Ib, Book 5, 1*

76      Good, the more
Communicated, more abundant grows. *Ib, 5, 71*

77 Best image of myself, and dearer half. *Ib, 5, 95*

78 Him first, him last, him midst, and without end. *Ib, 5, 165*

79      Nor jealousy
Was understood, the injured lover's hell. *Ib, 5, 449*

80    Midnight brought on the dusky hour
Friendliest to sleep and silence. *Ib, 5, 667*

81 Among the faithless, faithful only he. *Ib, 5, 897*

82 Servant of God, well done! Well hast thou fought
The better fight, who single hast maintained
Against revolted multitudes the cause
Of truth, in word mightier than they in arms. *Ib, Book 6, 29*

83 More safe I sing with mortal voice, unchanged
To hoarse or mute, though fallen on evil days,

On evil days though fallen, and evil tongues;
In darkness, and with dangers compassed round,
And solitude.                    *Paradise Lost, Book 7, 24*

84                    God saw the light was good;
And light from darkness by the hemisphere
Divided: light the Day, and darkness Night,
He named.                                    *Ib, 7, 249*

85 The Angel ended, and in Adam's ear
So charming left his voice that he a while
Thought him still speaking, still stood fixed to hear. *Ib, Book 8, 1*

86                    To know
That which before us lies in daily life,
Is the prime wisdom.                         *Ib, 8, 192*

87                In solitude
What happiness? who can enjoy alone,
Or, all enjoying, what contentment find?     *Ib, 8, 364*

88 Accuse not Nature! she hath done her part;
Do thou but thine.                           *Ib, 8, 561*

89 My unpremeditated verse.            *Ib, Book 9, 24*

90 Since first this subject for heroic song
Pleased me, long choosing and beginning late.    *Ib, 9, 25*

91                Revenge, at first though sweet,
Bitter ere long back on itself recoils.      *Ib, 9, 171*

92 For solitude sometimes is best society,
And short retirement urges sweet return.     *Ib, 9, 249*

93 As one who, long in populous city pent,
Where houses thick and sewers annoy the air. *Ib, 9, 445*

94 O fairest of creation, last and best
Of all God's works, creature in whom excelled
Whatever can to sight or thought be formed,
Holy, divine, good, amiable, or sweet!
How art thou lost! how on a sudden lost,
Defaced, deflowered, and now to death devote! *Ib, 9, 896*

95                Yet I shall temper so
Justice with mercy as may illustrate most
Them fully satisfied, and thee appease.    *Ib, Book 10, 77*

96 A dismal universal hiss, the sound
Of public scorn.                          *Ib, 10, 508*

97 Demoniac frenzy, moping melancholy,
And moon-struck madness.             *Ib, Book 11, 485*

98 Nor love thy life, nor hate; but what thou liv'st
Live well; how long or short permit to Heaven.   *Ib, 11, 553*

99 A bevy of fair women, richly gay
In gems and wanton dress. *Paradise Lost, Book 11, 582*

1 An olive-leaf he brings, pacific sign. *Ib, 11, 860*

2 In me is no delay; with thee to go
Is to stay here; without thee here to stay
Is to go hence unwilling; thou to me
Art all things under Heaven, all places thou,
Who for my wilful crime art banished hence. *Ib, Book 12, 615*

3 The world was all before them, where to choose
Their place of rest, and Providence their guide:
They, hand in hand, with wandering steps and slow,
Through Eden took their solitary way. *Ib, 12, 646*

4            Most men admire
Virtue who follow not her lore. *Paradise Regained, Book 1*
                                                      *482*

5            Beauty stands
In the admiration only of weak minds
Led captive. *Ib, Book 2, 220*

6            The childhood shows the man,
As morning shows the day. *Ib, Book 4, 220*

7 The first and wisest of them all professed
To know this only, that he nothing knew. *Ib, 4, 293*

8 Deep-versed in books and shallow in himself. *Ib, 4, 327*

9            He, unobserved,
Home to his mother's house private returned. *Ib, 4, 638*

10 Let us with a gladsome mind,
Praise the Lord, for He is kind,
   For His mercies ay endure,
   Ever faithful, ever sure. *Paslm 136*

11 A little onward lend thy guiding hand
To these dark steps, a little further on. SAMSON
                                  *Samson Agonistes, 1*

12 Ask for this great deliverer now, and find him
Eyeless in Gaza at the mill with slaves. SAMSON *Ib, 40*

13 O dark, dark, dark, amid the blaze of noon,
Irrecoverably dark, total eclipse,
Without all hope of day! SAMSON *Ib, 80*

14 The Sun to me is dark
And silent as the Moon,
When she deserts the night,
Hid in her vacant interlunar cave. SAMSON *Ib, 86*

15
                        Wisest men
Have erred, and by bad women been deceived.  CHORUS
*Samson Agonistes, 210*

16 Just are the ways of God,
  And justifiable to men,
  Unless there be who think not God at all.  CHORUS    *Ib, 293*

17                   Let me here,
  As I deserve, pay on my punishment,
  And expiate, if possible, my crime,
  Shameful garrulity.  SAMSON             *Ib, 488*

18    But who is this, what thing of sea or land?
  Female of sex it seems,
  That, so bedecked, ornate, and gay,
  Comes this way sailing,
  Like a stately ship
  Of Tarsus, bound for th' isles
  Of Javan or Gadire,
  With all her bravery on, and tackle trim,
  Sails filled, and streamers waving,
  Courted by all the winds that hold them play.  CHORUS *Ib, 710*

19 Out, out, hyaena! These are thy wonted arts,
  And arts of every woman false like thee.  SAMSON   *Ib, 748*

20                Weakness is thy excuse,
  And I believe it; weakness to resist
  Philistian gold.  SAMSON              *Ib, 829*

21         At length, that grounded maxim,
  So rife and celebrated in the mouths
  Of wisest men, that to the public good
  Private respects must yield, with grave authority
  Took full possession of me, and prevailed.  DALILA   *Ib, 865*

22 In argument with men a woman ever
  Goes by the worse, whatever be her cause.  DALILA   *Ib, 903*

23 Fame, if not double-faced, is double-mouthed,
  And with contrary blast proclaims most deeds.  DALILA
                                           *Ib, 971*

24 Yet beauty, though injurious, hath strange power,
  After offence returning, to regain
  Love once possessed.  CHORUS           *Ib, 1003*

25 He's gone, and who knows how he may report
  Thy words by adding fuel to the flame?  CHORUS   *Ib, 1350*

26 All is best, though we oft doubt
  What th' unsearchable dispose
  Of Highest Wisdom brings about.  CHORUS     *Ib, 1745*

27 His servants he, with new acquist
   Of true experience from this great event,
   With peace and consolation hath dismissed,
   And calm of mind, all passion spent.   CHORUS
                                    *Samson Agonistes, 1755*

28 How soon hath Time, the subtle thief of youth,
       Stolen on his wing my three-and-twentieth year!   *Sonnet, On*
                           *being arrived at the age of twenty-three*

29 When I consider how my light is spent
   Ere half my days in this dark world and wide,
   And that one talent which is death to hide
   Lodged with me useless.           *Sonnet, On his Blindness*

30                 God doth not need
   Either man's work or his own gifts. Who best
   Bear his mild yoke, they serve him best: his state
   Is kingly: thousands at his bidding speed,
   And post o'er land and ocean without rest;
   They also serve who only stand and wait.              *Ib*

31 New Presbyter is but old Priest writ large.   *Sonnet, On the new*
                   *Forcers of Conscience under the Long Parliament*

32                 Peace hath her victories
   No less renowned than War.         *Sonnet, To the Lord General*
                                    *Cromwell, May 1652*

33 For what can war but endless war still breed?   *Sonnet, On the*
                                    *Lord General Fairfax*

34 Fly envious Time, till thou run out thy race,
   Call on the lazy, leaden-stepping hours.       *Sonnet, On Time*

35 Methought I saw my late espoused saint.        *Sonnet, On his*
                                    *deceased wife*

36 He who would not be frustrate of his hope to write well hereafter in laudable things ought himself to be a true poem.
                                    *Apology for Smectymnuus*

37 Who kills a man kills a reasonable creature, God's image; but he
   who destroys a good book, kills reason itself, kills the image of
   God, as it were in the eye.                   *Areopagitica*

38 A good book is the precious life-blood of a master spirit,
   embalmed and treasured up on purpose to a life beyond life.  *Ib*

39 I cannot praise a fugitive and cloistered virtue, unexercised and
   unbreathed, that never sallies out and sees her adversary, but
   slinks out of the race, where that immortal garland is to be run
   for, not without dust and heat.                           *Ib*

40 Our sage and serious poet Spenser, whom I dare be known to
   think a better teacher than Scotus or Aquinas.            *Ib*

41 God sure esteems the growth and completing of one virtuous person more than the restraint of ten vicious. *Areopagitica*

42 God is decreeing to begin some new and great period in His Church, even to the reforming of Reformation itself: what does He then but reveal Himself to His servants, and as His manner is, first to His Englishmen? *Ib*

43 Methinks I see in my mind a noble and puissant nation rousing herself like a strong man after sleep, and shaking her invincible locks. Methinks I see her as an eagle mewing her mighty youth, and kindling her undazzled eyes at the full midday beam. *Ib*

44 Give me the liberty to know, to utter, and to argue freely according to conscience, above all liberties. *Ib*

45 Let her and Falsehood grapple; who ever knew Truth put to the worse, in a free and open encounter? *Ib*

46 None can love freedom heartily, but good men; the rest love not freedom, but licence. *Tenure of Kings and Magistrates*

## MIRABEAU, Comte de, 1749–1791

47 *La guerre est l'industrie nationale de la Prusse.* War is the national industry of Prussia. *Attributed*

## MOLIÈRE (Jean Baptiste Poquelin), 1622–1673.

48 *Par ma foi! il y a plus de quarante ans que je dis de la prose sans que j'en susse rien.* M. JOURDAIN
Good heavens! I have been talking prose for over forty years without realizing it. *Le Bourgeois Gentilhomme, Act 2, Scene 4*

49 *C'est une folie à nulle autre seconde,*
*De vouloir se mêler à corriger le monde.* PHILINTE
It is a stupidity second to none, to want to busy oneself with the correction of the world. *Le Misanthrope, Act 1, Scene 1*

50 *Ah! pour être dévot, je n'en suis pas moins homme!* TARTUFFE
Oh, I may be devout, but I am human all the same. *Tartuffe, Act 3, Scene 3*

51 *La scandale du monde est ce qui fait l'offense,*
*Et ce n'est pas pécher que pécher en silence.* TARTUFFE
It is a public scandal that gives offence, and it is no sin to sin in secret. *Ib, Act 4, Scene 5*

## MONKHOUSE, William Cosmo, 1840–1901

52 There was an old party of Lyme,
Who married three wives at one time.

When asked, 'Why the third?'
He replied, 'One's absurd,
And bigamy, sir, is a crime!'                    *Limerick*


**MONSELL, John Samuel Bewley, 1811–1875**

53 Fight the good fight with all thy might,
Christ is thy strength, and Christ thy right;
Lay hold on life, and it shall be
Thy joy and crown eternally.          *Fight the Good Fight*


**MONTAIGNE, Michel de, 1533–1592**

54 The greatest thing in the world is to know how to be self-
sufficient.                                        *Essays, 1, 39*

55 When I play with my cat, who knows whether she is not amusing
herself with me more than I with her?              *Ib, 2, 12*

56 Marriage is like a cage; one sees the birds outside desperate to
get in, and those inside equally desperate to get out.   *Ib, 3, 5*

57 It might well be said of me that here I have merely made up a
bunch of other men's flowers, and provided nothing of my own
but the string to tie them together.               *Ib, 3, 12*


**MONTGOMERY OF ALAMEIN, Bernard Law, 1st Viscount, 1887–1976**

58 Anyone who votes Labour ought to be locked up.      *Speech,
Woodford, Essex, 1959*


**MONTROSE, Percy, 19th century**

59 In a cavern, in a canyon,
Excavating for a mine,
Dwelt a miner, Forty-niner,
And his daughter Clementine.
Oh my darling, oh my darling, oh my darling Clementine!
Thou art lost and gone for ever, dreadful sorry, Clementine.
                                                   *Clementine*

60 Light she was and like a fairy,
And her shoes were number nine;
Herring boxes, without topses,
Sandals were for Clementine.                       *Ib*

61 How I missed her, how I missed her.
How I missed my Clementine!
But I kissed her little sister,
And forgot my Clementine.                          *Ib*

**MOORE, Thomas, 1779–1852**

62 The harp that once through Tara's halls
    The soul of music shed,
Now hangs as mute on Tara's walls,
    As if that soul were fled.    *Irish Melodies, The Harp that*
                                *once through Tara's Halls*

63 'Tis the last rose of summer
    Left blooming alone;
All her lovely companions
    Are faded and gone.        *Ib, The Last Rose of Summer*

64 The Minstrel Boy to the war is gone,
    In the ranks of death you'll find him;
His father's sword he has girded on,
    And his wild harp slung behind him. *Ib, The Minstrel Boy*

65 'Come, Come,' said Tom's father, 'at your time of life,
    There's no longer excuse for thus playing the rake –
It is time you should think, boy, of taking a wife' –
    'Why, so it is, father – whose wife shall I take?'
                                  *A Joke Versified*

**MORE, Sir Thomas, 1478–1535**

66 I pray you, Master Lieutenant, see me safe up, and for coming
down let me shift for myself. [*On mounting the scaffold*]    *Roper,*
                                  *Life of Sir Thomas More*

67 Pluck up thy spirits, man, and be not afraid to do thine office;
my neck is very short; take heed therefore thou strike not awry,
for saving of thine honesty. [*To the executioner*]            *Ib*

**MORELL, Thomas, 1703–1784**

68 See, the conquering hero comes!
    Sound the trumpets, beat the drums!        *Joshua, Part 3*

**MORGAN, Augustus de, 1806–1871**

69 Great fleas have little fleas upon their backs to bite 'em,
And little fleas have lesser fleas, and so *ad infinitum.*
                                *A Budget of Paradoxes*

**MORLEY, Christopher Darlington, 1890–1957**

70 The man who never in his life
Has washed the dishes with his wife
Or polished up the silver plate –
He still is largely celibate.          *Washing the Dishes*

**MORRIS, William, 1834–1896**

71 Dreamer of dreams, born out of my due time,
  Why should I strive to set the crooked straight?
                             *The Earthly Paradise, An Apology*

72 Love is enough: though the world be a-waning,
  And the woods have no voice but the voice of complaining.
                                        *Love is Enough, 1*

**MOTLEY, John Lothrop, 1814–1877**

73 Give us the luxuries of life, and we will dispense with its necessities.    *O. W. Holmes, The Autocrat of the Breakfast Table,*
                                                    *Ch. 6*

**MOTTEUX, Peter Anthony, 1660–1718**

74 The devil was sick, the devil a monk wou'd be;
  The devil was well, and the devil a monk he'd be.    *Translation*
                 *of Rabelais, Gargantua and Pantagruel, Book 4,*
                                                    *Ch. 24*

**MUNRO, Hector Hugh, see 'SAKI'**

**MUNSTER, Ernst Friedrich Herbert, 1766–1839**

75 Absolutism tempered by assassination.
                        *[The Russian Constitution] Letter*

**MURDOCH, Richard, 1907– , and HORNE, Kenneth, 1900–1969**

76 Have you read any good books lately?    *Much Binding in the*
              *Marsh, BBC Radio Programme, 1945 to 1954*

**MURPHY, C. W., 19th century**

77 Has anybody here seen Kelly?
  Kelly from the Isle of Man?    *Has Anybody Here seen Kelly?*

**MUSSET, Alfred de, 1810–1857**

78 *Il faut qu'une porte soit ouverte ou fermée.* A door must be either
  open or shut.                              *Title of Play*

79 *On ne badine pas avec l'amour.* One must not trifle with love.
                                           *Title of Play*

**NAIRNE, Lady Caroline, 1766–1845**

80 Charlie is my darling, my darling, my darling,
  Charlie is my darling, the young Chevalier.    *Charlie is my*
                                                    *Darling*

81 Better lo'ed ye canna be,
Will ye no come back again? *Will ye no come back again?*

**NAPIER, Sir Charles James, 1782–1853**

82 *Peccavi.* [I have Sind]. *Despatch after victory of Hyderabad*
*in Sind, 1843*

**NAPOLEON, Bonaparte, 1769–1821**

83 *Soldats, songez que, du haut de ces pyramides, quarante siècles vous*
*contemplent.* – Think of it, soldiers, from the summit of these
pyramids, forty centuries look down upon you. *Speech before*
*Battle of the Pyramids, 1798*

84 *Du sublime au ridicule il n'y a qu'un pas.* – It is only a step from
the sublime to the ridiculous. *After the retreat from Moscow,*
*1812*

85 *L'Angleter re est nation de boutiquiers.* – England is a nation
of shopkeepers. *Attributed, See Adam Smith (374:98)*

86 *Tout soldat français porte dans sa giberne le bâton de maréchal*
*de France.* – Every French soldier carries in his cartridge-
pouch the baton of a marshal of France. *Attributed*

87 An army marches on its stomach. *Attributed*

**NASH, Ogden, 1902–1971**

88 A girl whose cheeks are covered with paint
Has an advantage with me over one whose ain't.
*Biological Reflection*

89 One would be in less danger
From the wiles of the stranger
If one's own kin and kith
Were more fun to be with. *Family Court*

90 Home is heaven and orgies are vile
But you need an orgy, once in a while. *Home, 99·44/100%*
*Sweet Home*

91 Beneath this slab
John Brown is stowed.
He watched the ads
And not the road. *Lather as You Go*

92 I have a bone to pick with fate,
Come here and tell me, girlie,
Do you think my mind is maturing late,
Or simply rotted early? *Lines on Facing Forty*

93 Children aren't happy with nothing to ignore,
And that's what parents were created for. *The Parent*

94 A bit of talcum
   Is always walcum.                    *Reflection on Babies*

95 Candy
   is dandy
   But liquor
   is quicker.                          *Reflection on Ice-breaking*

96 I test my bath before I sit,
   And I'm always moved to wonderment
   That what chills the finger not a bit
   Is so frigid upon the fundament.     *Samson Agonistes*

97 I think that I shall never see
   A billboard lovely as a tree.
   Perhaps unless the billboards fall,
   I'll never see a tree at all.        *Song of the Open Road*

98 The turtle lives 'twixt plated decks
   Which practically conceal its sex.
   I think it clever of the turtle
   In such a fix to be so fertile.      *The Turtle*

### NASHE, Thomas, 1567–1601

99 Brightness falls from the air;
   Queens have died young and fair;
   Dust hath closed Helen's eye.        *In Times of Pestilence*

### NEALE, John Mason, 1818–1866

 1 Brief Life is here our portion;
   Brief sorrow, short-lived care.      *Brief Life is Here*

 2 Good Christian men, rejoice
   With heart, and soul, and voice.     *Good Christian Men*

 3 Good King Wenceslas looked out
     On the Feast of Stephen;
   When the snow lay round about,
     Deep and crisp and even.           *Good King Wenceslas*

 4 Bring me flesh and bring me wine,
     Bring me pine logs hither.                      *Ib*

 5 In his master's steps he trod
     Where the snow lay dinted.                      *Ib*

### NELSON, Horatio, 1st Viscount, 1758–1805

 6 Westminster Abbey or victory.    *Remark at Battle of Cape St*
                                                    *Vincent*

 7 England expects every man will do his duty.
                                    *Battle of Trafalgar*

8 Thank God, I have done my duty. *Battle of Trafalgar*
9 Kiss me, Hardy. *Ib*

**NERO (Nero Claudius Caesar), A.D. 37–68**

10 *Qualis artifex pereo!* What an artist dies with me! *Last words, attributed*

**NEWBOLT, Sir Henry John, 1862–1938**

11 Drake he's in his hammock till the great Armadas come.
  (Capten, art tha sleepin' there below?)
  Slung atween the round shot, listenin' for the drum,
   An' dreamin' arl the time o' Plymouth Hoe. *Drake's Drum*

12 Where the old trade's plying an' the old flag flyin'
   They shall find him ware an' wakin', as they found him long
  ago! *Ib*

13 There's a breathless hush in the Close tonight –
   Ten to make and the match to win –
  A bumping pitch and a blinding light,
   An hour to play and the last man in. *Vitai Lampada*

14 But his captain's hand on his shoulder smote –
   'Play up! play up! and play the game!' *Ib*

**NEWMAN, John Henry, Cardinal, 1801–1890**

15 It is almost a definition of a gentleman to say that he is one who
  never inflicts pain. *The Idea of a University, Knowledge and Religious Duty*

16 Lead, Kindly Light, amid the encircling gloom,
   Lead thou me on;
  The night is dark, and I am far from home,
   Lead thou me on. *Lead Kindly Light*

**NICHOLAS I of Russia, 1796–1855**

17 Russia has two generals in whom she can confide – Generals
  Janvier and Février. *Punch, 10 March 1853*

**NORTH, Christopher (John Wilson), 1785–1854**

18 His Majesty's dominions, on which the sun never sets.
  *Noctes Ambrosianae, No. 20, April 1829*
19 Laws were made to be broken. *Ib, No. 24, May 1830*

**NOYES, Alfred, 1880–1958**

20 Go down to Kew in lilac-time, in lilac-time, in lilac-time,
   Go down to Kew in lilac-time (it isn't far from London!)

And you shall wander hand in hand with love in summer's
   wonderland;
  Go down to Kew in lilac-time (it isn't far from London!)
*The Barrel Organ*

21       Look for me by moonlight;
        Watch for me by moonlight;
I'll come to thee by moonlight, though hell should bar the way!
*The Highwayman*

## NURSERY RHYMES

*The Oxford Dictionary of Nursery Rhymes*, edited by Iona and Peter
Opie, gives the sources of over 500 nursery rhymes.
In many cases nursery rhymes have changed considerably since they
first appeared in print. It seemed most useful in the selection of
familiar nursery rhymes below, to give the version most commonly
in use today, together with title and date of the first known publication.

22 As I was going to St Ives,
  I met a man with seven wives.      *Mother Goose's Quarto,*
*c. 1825*

23 Baa, baa, black sheep,
   Have you any wool?
Yes, sir, yes, sir,
   Three bags full;
One for the master,
   And one for the dame,
And one for the little boy
   Who lives down the lane.     *Tommy Thumb's Pretty Song*
*Book, c. 1744*

24 Bobby Shafto's gone to sea,
   Silver buckles at his knee;
He'll come back and marry me,
   Bonny Bobby Shafto!     *Songs for the Nursery, 1805*

25 Boys and girls come out to play,
  The moon doth shine as bright as day.    *Useful Transactions*
*in Philosophy, William King, 1708–1709*

26 Cock a doodle doo!
  My dame has lost her shoe,
  My master's lost his fiddlestick,
  And knows not what to do.    *The Most Cruel and Bloody*
*Murder, 1606*

27 Curly locks, Curly locks,
   Wilt thou be mine?

Thou shalt not wash dishes
  Nor yet feed the swine,
But sit on a cushion
  And sew a fine seam,
And feed upon strawberries,
  Sugar and cream.         *Infant Institutes, 1797*

28 Ding dong, bell,
Pussy's in the well.
Who put her in?
Little Johnny Green.
Who pulled her out?
Little Tommy Stout.     *Mother Goose's Melody, c. 1765*

29 Eena, meena, mina, mo,
Catch a nigger by his toe;
If he squeals, let him go,
Eena, meena, mina, mo.     *Games and Songs of American*
                          *Children, Newell, 1883*

30 A frog he would a-wooing go,
  Heigh ho! says Rowley,
A frog he would a-wooing go,
Whether his mother would let him or no.
  With a rowley, powley, gammon and spinach,
  Heigh ho! says Anthony Rowley.     *Melismata,*
                        *Thomas Ravenscroft, 1611*

31 Georgie Porgie, pudding and pie,
Kissed the girls and made them cry;
When the boys came out to play,
Georgie Porgie ran away.     *Nursery Rhymes, J. O. Halliwell,*
                                      *1844*

32 Goosey, goosey gander,
  Whither shall I wander?
Upstairs and downstairs
  And in my lady's chamber.     *Gammer Gurton's Garland,*
                                  *1784*

33 Hey diddle diddle,
The cat and the fiddle,
The cow jumped over the moon;
The little dog laughed
To see such sport,
And the dish ran away with the spoon.     *Mother Goose's*
                                *Melody, c. 1765*

34 Hickory, dickory, dock,
  The mouse ran up the clock.

The clock struck one,
The mouse ran down,
Hickory, dickory, dock.        *Tommy Thumb's Pretty Song Book,*
                                                           *c. 1744*

35 Hot cross buns!
Hot cross buns!
One a penny, two a penny,
Hot cross buns!                     *Christmas Box, 1797*

36 How many miles to Babylon?
Three score miles and ten.
Can I get there by candle-light?
Yes, and back again.
If your heels are nimble and light,
You may get there by candle-light.     *Songs for the Nursery,*
                                                          *1805*

37 Humpty Dumpty sat on a wall,
Humpty Dumpty had a great fall.
  All the king's horses,
  And all the king's men,
Couldn't put Humpty together again.     *Gammer Gurton's*
                                                    *Garland, 1810*

38 Hush-a-bye, baby, on the tree top,
When the wind blows the cradle will rock;
When the bough breaks the cradle will fall,
Down will come baby, cradle, and all.        *Mother Goose's*
                                                      *Melody, c. 1765*

39 I had a little nut tree,
    Nothing would it bear
But a silver nutmeg
    And a golden pear;
The King of Spain's daughter
    Came to visit me,
And all for the sake
    Of my little nut tree.      *Newest Christmas Box, c. 1797*

40 I love sixpence, jolly little sixpence,
I love sixpence better than my life;
I spent a penny of it, I lent a penny of it,
  And I took fourpence home to my wife.     *Gammer Gurton's*
                                                      *Garland, 1810*

41 I'm the king of the castle,
  Get down you dirty rascal.     *Brand's Popular Antiquities, 1870*

42 I saw three ships come sailing by,
  Come sailing by, come sailing by,

I saw three ships come sailing by,
   On Christmas day in the morning.    *Bishoprick Garland,*
                                  *Sir Cuthbert Sharp, 1834*

43 I see the moon,
   And the moon sees me;
God bless the moon,
   And God bless me.    *Gammer Gurton's Garland, 1784*

44 Jack and Jill went up the hill
   To fetch a pail of water;
Jack fell down and broke his crown,
   And Jill came tumbling after.    *Mother Goose's Melody,*
                                       *c. 1765*

45 Jack Sprat could eat no fat,
   His wife could eat no lean,
And so between them both you see,
   They licked the platter clean.    *Paroemiologia Anglo-Latina,*
                                    *John Clark, 1639*

46 Ladybird, ladybird,
   Fly away home,
Your house is on fire
   And your children all gone.    *Tommy Thumb's Pretty Song*
                                    *Book, c. 1744*

47 The lion and the unicorn
   Were fighting for the crown;
The lion beat the unicorn
   All round about the town.

Some gave them white bread,
   And some gave them brown;
Some gave them plum cake
   And drummed them out of town.    *Useful Transactions in*
                 *Philosophy, William King, 1708–1709*

48 Little Bo-peep has lost her sheep,
   And can't tell where to find them;
Leave them alone, and they'll come home,
   And bring their tails behind them.    *Gammer Gurton's*
                                      *Garland, 1810*

49 Little Boy Blue,
   Come blow your horn,
The sheep's in the meadow,
   The cow's in the corn.    *Famous Tommy Thumb's Little*
                                 *Story Book, c. 1760*

50 Little Jack Horner
   Sat in the corner,
   Eating a Christmas pie;
   He put in his thumb,
   And pulled out a plum,
   And said, What a good boy am I!          *Namby Pamby,*
                                           *Henry Carey, 1725*

51 Little Miss Muffet
   Sat on a tuffet,
   Eating her curds and whey;
   There came a big spider,
   Who sat down beside her
   And frightened Miss Muffet away.        *Songs for the Nursery,*
                                                         *1805*

52 Little Tommy Tucker,
      Sings for his supper:
   What shall we give him?
      White bread and butter.
   How shall he cut it
      Without a knife?
   How will he be married
      Without a wife?          *Tommy Thumb's Pretty Song Book,*
                                                    *c. 1744*

53 London Bridge is broken down,
      My fair lady.            *Namby Pamby, Henry Carey,*
                                                   *1725*

54    The man in the moon
         Came down too soon,
   And asked his way to Norwich;
      He went by the south,
      And burnt his mouth
   With supping cold plum porridge.        *Gammer Gurton's*
                                           *Garland, 1784*

55 Mary, Mary, quite contrary,
      How does your garden grow?
   With silver bells and cockle shells,
      And pretty maids all in a row.      *Tommy Thumb's Pretty*
                                          *Song Book, c. 1744*

56 Monday's child is fair of face,
   Tuesday's child is full of grace,
   Wednesday's child is full of woe,
   Thursday's child has far to go,
   Friday's child is loving and giving,

Saturday's child works hard for his living,
And the child that is born on the Sabbath day
Is bonny and blithe, and good and gay.     *Traditions of Devon-
shire, A. E. Bray, 1838*

57 My mother said that I never should
Play with the gypsies in the wood;
If I did, she would say,
Naughty girl to disobey.     *Come Hither, Walter de la Mare,
1922*

58     Old King Cole
Was a merry old soul,
And a merry old soul was he;
He called for his pipe,
And he called for his bowl,
And he called for his fiddlers three.     *Useful Transactions in
Philosophy, William King, 1708–1709*

59     Old Mother Hubbard
Went to the cupboard,
To fetch her poor dog a bone;
But when she got there
The cupboard was bare
And so the poor dog had none.     *The Comic Adventures of
Old Mother Hubbard and Her Dog, 1805*

60 One, two,
Buckle my shoe;
Three, four,
Knock at the door.     *Songs for the Nursery, 1805*

61     Oranges and lemons,
Say the bells of St Clement's.

You owe me five farthings,
Say the bells of St Martin's.

When will you pay me?
Say the bells of Old Bailey.

When I grow rich,
Say the bells of Shoreditch.

When will that be?
Say the bells of Stepney.

I'm sure I don't know,
Says the great bell at Bow.

Here comes a candle to light you to bed,
Here comes a chopper to chop off your head.
     *Tommy Thumb's Pretty Song Book, c. 1744*

62 Pat-a-cake, pat-a-cake, baker's man,
   Bake me a cake as fast as you can;
   Pat it and prick it, and mark it with B,
   Put it in the oven for baby and me.        *The Campaigners,*
                                               *Tom D'Urfey, 1698*

63 Peter Piper picked a peck of pickled pepper;
   A peck of pickled pepper Peter Piper picked;
   If Peter Piper picked a peck of pickled pepper,
   Where's the peck of pickled pepper Peter Piper picked?
         *Peter Piper's Practical Principles of Plain and Perfect*
                                               *Pronunciation, 1819*

64 Pussy cat, pussy cat, where have you been?
   I've been to London to look at the queen.
   Pussy cat, pussy cat, what did you there?
   I frightened a little mouse under her chair.      *Songs for the*
                                                      *Nursery, 1805*

65 The Queen of Hearts
      She made some tarts,
   All on a summer's day;
      The Knave of Hearts
      He stole the tarts,
   And took them clean away.
                        *The European Magazine, April 1782*

66 Ride a cock-horse to Banbury Cross,
   To see a fine lady upon a white horse;
   Rings on her fingers and bells on her toes,
   And she shall have music wherever she goes.
                        *Gammer Gurton's Garland, 1784*

67 Ring-a-ring o' roses,
   A pocket full of posies,
      A-tishoo! A-tishoo!
   We all fall down.        *Mother Goose, Kate Greenway, 1881*

68 See-saw, Margery Daw,
   Jacky shall have a new master;
   Jacky shall have but a penny a day,
   Because he can't work any faster.
                        *Mother Goose's Melody, c. 1765*

69 Simple Simon met a pieman,
      Going to the fair;
   Says Simple Simon to the pieman,
      Let me taste your ware.
   Says the pieman to Simple Simon,
      Show me first your penny;

Says Simple Simon to the pieman,
Indeed I have not any.

*Simple Simon (Chapbook Advertisement), 1764*

70 Sing a song of sixpence,
 A pocket full of rye;
Four and twenty blackbirds,
 Baked in a pie.

When the pie was opened,
 The birds began to sing;
Was not that a dainty dish,
 To set before the king?

The king was in his counting-house,
 Counting out his money;
The queen was in the parlour,
 Eating bread and honey.

The maid was in the garden,
 Hanging out the clothes,
There came a little blackbird,
 And snapped off her nose.

*Tommy Thumb's Pretty Song Book, c. 1744*

71 Solomon Grundy,
Born on a Monday,
Christened on Tuesday,
Married on Wednesday,
Took ill on Thursday,
Worse on Friday,
Died on Saturday,
Buried on Sunday.
This is the end
Of Solomon Grundy.   *Nursery Rhymes, J. O. Halliwell, 1842*

72 The first day of Christmas,
My true love sent to me
A partridge in a pear tree.   *Mirth without Mischief, c. 1780*

73 The twelfth day of Christmas,
My true love sent to me
Twelve lords a-leaping,
Eleven ladies dancing,
Ten pipers piping,
Nine drummers drumming,
Eight maids a-milking,
Seven swans a-swimming,
Six geese a-laying,
Five gold rings,

Four colly birds,
Three French hens,
Two turtle doves, and
A partridge in a pear tree.          *Mirth without Mischief, c. 1780*

74 There was a crooked man, and he walked a crooked mile,
He found a crooked sixpence against a crooked stile:
He bought a crooked cat, which caught a crooked mouse,
And they all lived together in a little crooked house.
                    *Nursery Rhymes, J. O. Halliwell, 1842*

75 There was an old woman
    Lived under a hill,

And if she's not gone
    She lives there still.          *Academy of Complements, 1714*

76 There was an old woman who lived in a shoe,
She had so many children she didn't know what to do;
She gave them some broth without any bread;
She whipped them all soundly and put them to bed.
                    *Gammer Gurton's Garland, 1784*

77 Thirty days hath September,
April, June, and November;
All the rest have thirty-one,
Excepting February alone
And that has twenty-eight days clear
And twenty-nine in each leap year.          *Abridgement of the*
                    *Chronicles of England, Richard Grafton, 1570*

78 This little pig went to market,
This little pig stayed at home,
This little pig had roast beef,
This little pig had none,
And this little pig cried, Wee-wee-wee-wee-wee,
    I can't find my way home.          *The Famous Tommy Thumb's*
                    *Little Story Book, c. 1760*

79 This is the farmer sowing his corn,
That kept the cock that crowed in the morn,
That waked the priest all shaven and shorn,
That married the man all tattered and torn,
That kissed the maiden all forlorn,
That milked the cow with the crumpled horn,
That tossed the dog,
That worried the cat,
That killed the rat,
That ate the malt,
That lay in the house that Jack built.
                    *Nurse Truelove's New-Year-Gift, 1755*

80 Three blind mice, see how they run!
   They all run after the farmer's wife,
   Who cut off their tails with a carving knife,
   Did you ever see such a thing in your life,
      As three blind mice?
                    *Deuteromelia, Thomas Ravenscroft, 1609*

81 Tinker,
      Tailor,
   Soldier,
      Sailor,
   Rich man,
      Poor man,
   Beggarman,
      Thief.                *Popular Rhymes and Nursery Tales,*
                                      *J. O. Halliwell, 1849*

82 Tom, he was a piper's son,
   He learnt to play when he was young,
   And all the tune that he could play
   Was 'Over the hills and far away'.
                          *Tom, The Piper's Son, c. 1795*

83 Tom, Tom, the piper's son,
   Stole a pig and away he run;
      The pig was eat
      And Tom was beat,
   And Tom went howling down the street.          *Ib*

84 Two little dicky birds,
   Sitting on a wall;
   One named Peter,
   The other named Paul.
   Fly away, Peter!
   Fly away, Paul!
   Come back, Peter!
   Come back, Paul!          *Mother Goose's Melody, c. 1765*

85 What are little boys made of?
   What are little boys made of?
      Frogs and snails
      And puppy-dogs' tails,
   That's what little boys are made of.
   What are little girls made of?
   What are little girls made of?
      Sugar and spice
      And all that's nice,
   That's what little girls are made of.      *Nursery Rhymes,*
                                      *J. O. Halliwell, 1844*

86 Where are you going to, my pretty maid?
   I'm going a-milking, sir, she said.     *Archaeologia Cornu-*
                                           *Britannica, William Pryce, 1790*

87 What is your fortune, my pretty maid?
   My face is my fortune, sir, she said.

   Then I can't marry you, my pretty maid.
   Nobody asked you, sir, she said.                              *Ib*

88 Who killed Cock Robin?
   I, said the Sparrow,
   With my bow and arrow,
   I killed Cock Robin.

   Who saw him die?
   I, said the Fly,
   With my little eye,
   I saw him die.     *Tommy Thumb's Pretty Song Book, c. 1744*

89 All the birds of the air
   Fell a-sighing and a-sobbing,
   When they heard the bell toll
   For poor Cock Robin.                                          *Ib*

90 Yankee Doodle came to town,
      Riding on a pony;
   He stuck a feather in his cap
      And called it macaroni.     *Gammer Gurton's Garland, 1810*

   For other nursery rhymes, see Thomas Ady (10 : 13), S. J. Hale
   (157 : 55) and Jane Taylor (384 : 36)

**OAKELEY, Frederick, 1802–1880**

91 O come, all ye faithful,
   Joyful and triumphant,
   O come ye, O come ye to Bethlehem.     *Hymn translated from*
                                          *Latin, Adeste Fideles*

92 Sing, choirs of Angels,
   Sing in exultation,
   Sing, all ye citizens of heaven above.                        *Ib*

**OATES, Lawrence Edward Grace, 1880–1912**

93 I am just going outside, and may be some time.     *Last words.*
              *Recorded in Captain R. F. Scott's Antarctic Diary,*
                                                *16 March 1912*

**O'CASEY, Sean, 1884–1964**
94 The whole worl's in a state o' chassis.   BOYLE
                                        *Juno and the Paycock, Act 1*

**OCHS, Adolph S., 1858–1935**

95 All the news that's fit to print. *Motto of New York Times*

**O'KEEFE, Patrick, 1872–1934**

96 Say it with flowers. *Slogan for Society of American Florists*

**OPIE, John, 1761–1807**

97 I mix them with my brains, sir. *When asked with what he mixed his colours. Quoted in Samuel Smiles, Self Help, Ch. 4*

**ORWELL, George, (Eric Blair) 1903–1950**

98 All animals are equal but some animals are more equal than others. *Animal Farm, Ch. 10*

99 It was a bright cold day in April, and the clocks were striking thirteen. *Nineteen Eighty-Four, Part 1, Ch. 1*

1 Big Brother is watching you *Ib*

2 War is Peace, Freedom is Slavery, Ignorance is Strength. *Ib*

3 Down with Big Brother. *Ib*

4 Doublethink means the power of holding two contradictory beliefs in one's mind simultaneously, and accepting both of them. *Ib, Part 2, Ch. 9*

**OSBORNE, John, 1929–**

5 But I have a go, lady, don't I? I 'ave a go. ARCHIE RICE
*The Entertainer, No. 7*

6 Don't clap too hard – it's a very old building. ARCHIE RICE
*Ib*

7 Yes, thank God we're normal,
Yes, this was our finest shower! ARCHIE RICE *Ib*

8 How I long for a little ordinary human enthusiasm. Just enthusiasm – that's all. I want to hear a warm, thrilling voice cry out Hallelujah! Hallelujah! I'm alive! JIMMY PORTER
*Look Back in Anger, Act 1*

9 His knowledge of life and ordinary human beings is so hazy, he really deserves some sort of decoration for it – a medal inscribed 'For Vaguery in the Field'. JIMMY PORTER *Ib*

10 I don't think one 'comes down' from Jimmy's university. According to him, it's not even red brick, but white tile.
ALISON PORTER *Ib, Act 2, Scene 1*

**OTIS, James, 1725–1783**

11 Taxation without representation is tyranny.
*Watchword of the American Revolution*

**OVID (Publius Ovidius Naso), 43 B.C.–17 A.D.**

12 *Quae dant, quaeque negant, gaudent tamen esse rogatae.* Whether
they give or refuse, women are glad to have been asked.
*Ars Amatoria, 1*

13 *Inopem me copia fecit.* Plenty makes me poor.
*Metamorphoses, 3*

14 *Tempus edax rerum.* Time, the devourer of things.      *Ib, 15*

**OWEN, Robert, 1771–1858**

15 All the world is queer save thee and me, and even thou art a
little queer.      *Of his business partner, William Allen, 1828*

**OWEN, Wilfred, 1893–1918**

16 What passing-bells for those who die as cattle?
Only the monstrous anger of the guns.
*Anthem for Doomed Youth*

17 Move him into the sun –
Gently its touch awoke him once,
At home, whispering of fields unsown.      *Futility*

18 Above all I am not concerned with Poetry.
My subject is War, and the pity of War.
The Poetry is in the pity.      *Preface to Poems*

**PAINE, Thomas, 1737–1809**

19 The sublime and the ridiculous are often so nearly related that
it is difficult to class them separately. One step above the sublime makes the ridiculous; and one step above the ridiculous
makes the sublime again.      *The Age of Reason, Part 2*

20 Government, even in its best state, is but a necessary evil; in
its worst state, an intolerable one.      *Common Sense, Ch. 1*

**PALMERSTON, Henry John Temple, 3rd Viscount, 1784–1865**

21 Die, my dear Doctor, that's the last thing I shall do!
*Last words, attributed*

**PARKER, Dorothy, 1893–1967**

22 Men seldom make passes
At girls who wear glasses.      *News Item*

23 Guns aren't lawful;
Nooses give;

Gas smells awful;
You might as well live. *Résumé*

### PARKER, Ross, 1914–, and CHARLES, Hughie, 1907–

24 There'll always be an England
   While there's a country lane,
   Wherever there's a cottage small
      Beside a field of grain. *There'll Always be an England*

### PARKINSON, Cyril Northcote, 1909–

25 Work expands so as to fill the time available for its completion.
   General recognition of this fact is shown in the proverbial
   phrase 'It is the busiest man who has time to spare.'
                                                   *Parkinson's Law*

26 The Law of Triviality. Briefly stated, it means that the time spent
   on any item of the agenda will be in inverse proportion to the
   sum involved.
             *Ib, High Finance or the Point of Vanishing Interest*

### PASCAL, Blaise, 1623–1662

27 *Le nez de Cléopâtre: s'il eût été plus court, toute la face de la
   terre aurait changé.* – Had Cleopatra's nose been shorter, the
   whole history of the world would have been different.
                                                   *Pensées, 2, 162*

28 *Le cœur a ses raisons que la raison ne connaît point.* – The heart
   has its reasons which reason does not know. *Ib, 4, 277*

### PATER, Walter Horatio, 1839–1894

29 To burn always with this hard, gem-like flame, to maintain this
   ecstasy, is success in life. *The Renaissance, Conclusion*

### PATERSON, Andrew, 1864–1941

30 Once a jolly swagman camped by a billabong,
      Under the shade of a coolibah tree,
   And he sang as he sat and waited till his billy boiled,
      'You'll come a-waltzing, Matilda, with me.'
                                                   *Waltzing Matilda*

### PATMORE, Coventry Kersey Dighton, 1823–1896

31 'I saw you take his kiss!' 'Tis true,'
   'O, modesty!' 'Twas strictly kept:
   He thought me asleep; at least, I knew
   He thought I thought he thought I slept.'
                                    *The Angel in the House, Book 2, 8*

32 A woman is a foreign land,
Of which, though there he settle young,
A man will ne'er quite understand
The customs, politics, and tongue. *The Angel in the House,*
*Book 2, 9*

**PAUL, Leslie Allen, 1905–**

33 Angry Young Man. *Title of Book, 1951*

**PAYNE, John Howard, 1791–1852**

34 Mid pleasures and palaces though we may roam,
Be it ever so humble, there's no place like home.
*Clari, The Maid of Milan, Home, Sweet Home*

**PEACOCK, Thomas Love, 1785–1866**

35 Respectable means rich, and decent means poor. I should die if
I heard my family called decent. LADY CLARINDA
*Crotchet Castle, Ch. 3*

36 A book that furnishes no quotations is, *me judice,* no book – it
is a plaything. *Ib, Ch. 9*

37 There are two reasons for drinking: one is, when you are thirsty,
to cure it; the other, when you are not thirsty, to prevent it . . .
Prevention is better than cure. MR PORTPIPE
*Melincourt. Ch. 16*

38 The mountain sheep are sweeter,
But the valley sheep are fatter;
We therefore deemed it meeter
To carry off the latter. *The Misfortunes of Elphin, Ch. 11,*
*The War Song of Dinas Vawr*

**PENN, William, 1644–1718**

39 Men are generally more careful of the breed of their horses and
dogs than of their children.
*Reflexions and Maxims, Part 1, 85*

**PEPYS, Samuel, 1633–1703**

40 And so to bed. *Diary, 6 May 1660 and passim*

41 A silk suit, which cost me much money, and I pray God to make
me able to pay for it. *Ib, 1 July 1660*

42 Strange to say what delight we married people have to see these
poor fools decoyed into our condition. *Ib, 25 Dec. 1665*

43 Music and women I cannot but give way to, whatever my
business is. *Ib, 9 March 1666*

44 To church; and with my mourning, very handsome, and new
periwig, make a great show.·          *Diary, 31 March 1667*

45 And so I betake myself to that course, which is almost as much
as to see myself go into my grave; for which, and all the discomforts that will accompany my being blind, the good God prepare me!          *Ib, 31 May 1669 (final entry)*

## PERRAULT, Charles, 1628–1703

46 She [*Cinderella*] was as good as she was beautiful.   *Histoires ou
Contes du Temps Passé, 1697, First English Translation by
Robert Samber*

47 Sister Anne, sister Anne, do you see anyone coming?   BLUE
BEARD                                                     *Ib*

## PÉTAIN, Marshal Henri Phillipe, 1856–1951

48 *Ils ne passeront pas.* They shall not pass.   *Verdun, Feb. 1916*

## PETRONIUS, ?–66? A.D.

49 *Cave canem.* – Beware of the dog.          *Satyricon, 29, 1*

## PHELPS, Edward John, 1822–1900

50 The man who makes no mistakes does not usually make anything.          *Speech, Mansion House, London, 24 Jan. 1899*

## PHILLIPS, Wendell, 1811–1884

51 One on God's side is a majority.
          *Speech, Brooklyn, 1 Nov. 1859*

52 Every man meets his Waterloo at last.          *Ib*

## PINDAR, 522?–442? B.C.

53 Water is best.          *Olympian Odes, 1*

## PITT, William, 1st Earl of Chatham, 1708–1778

54 The atrocious crime of being a young man ... I shall neither
attempt to palliate nor deny.   *Speech, House of Commons,
27 Jan. 1741*

55 Unlimited power is apt to corrupt the minds of those who
possess it.          *Speech, House of Lords, 9 Jan. 1770*

## PITT, William, 1759–1806

56 Necessity is the plea for every infringement of human freedom.
It is the argument of tyrants; it is the creed of slaves.
          *Speech, House of Commons, 18 Nov. 1783*

57 England has saved herself by her exertions, and will, as I trust, save Europe by her example.          *Speech, Guildhall, 1805*

58 Roll up that map: it will not be wanted these ten years.
   *On hearing of Napoleon's victory at the Battle of Austerlitz*

59 I think I could eat one of Bellamy's veal pies.
                                          *Last words, attributed*

60 Oh, my country! How I leave my country! [Or 'love' for 'leave']
                                          *Last words, attributed*


## PLATO, 429?–347? B.C.

61 The good is the beautiful.                              *Lysis*

62 Our object in the construction of the state is the greatest happiness of the whole, and not that of any one class.     *Republic, 4*


## PLAUTUS, 254–184 B.C.

63 *Miles gloriosus.* – The Boastful Soldier.          *Title of Play*


## PLINY, The Elder, 23–79

64 *Ex Africa semper aliquid novi.* There is always something new out of Africa.               *Natural History, 2, 8, 42*

65 *In vino veritas.* Truth comes out in wine.         *Ib, 14, 141*


## POE, Edgar Allan, 1809–1849

66      The glory that was Greece
   And the grandeur that was Rome.                      *To Helen*

67 Take thy beak from out my heart, and take thy form from off my door!
   Quoth the Raven, 'Nevermore.'                      *The Raven*


## POMPADOUR, Madame de, 1721–1764

68 *Après nous le déluge.* After us the deluge.
                                   *After Battle of Rossbach, 1757*


## POPE, Alexander, 1688–1744

69 A wit with dunces, and a dunce with wits.
                                          *The Dunciad, 4, 90*

70 The right divine of kings to govern wrong.         *Ib, 4, 188*

71 O Grave! where is thy Victory?
   O Death! where is thy Sting?
                            *The Dying Christian to his Soul*

72 What beckoning ghost along the moonlight shade
Invites my steps, and points to yonder glade. *Elegy to the*
*Memory of an Unfortunate Lady, 1*

73 Is it, in heav'n, a crime to love too well? *Ib, 6*

74 Ambition first sprung from your blest abodes,
The glorious fault of angels and of gods. *Ib, 13*

75 Love, free as air, at sight of human ties,
Spreads his light wings, and in a moment flies.
*Eloisa to Abelard, 75*

76 How happy is the blameless vestal's lot!
The world forgetting, by the world forgot. *Ib, 207*

77 Shut, shut the door, good John! fatigued, I said;
Tie up the knocker, say I'm sick, I'm dead.
*Epistle to Dr Arbuthnot, 1*

78 Is there a parson much bemused in beer,
A maudlin poetess, a rhyming peer,
A clerk, foredoom'd his father's soul to cross,
Who pens a stanza, when he should engross? *Ib, 15*

79 No creature smarts so little as a fool. *Ib, 84*

80 Why did I write? whose sin to me unknown
Dipt me in ink, my parents', or my own?
As yet a child, nor yet a fool to fame,
I lisp'd in numbers, for the numbers came. *Ib, 125*

81 The Muse but serv'd to ease some friend, not Wife,
To help me through this long disease, my Life. *Ib, 131*

82 And He, whose fustian's so sublimely bad,
It is not Poetry, but prose run mad. *Ib, 187*

83 Damn with faint praise, assent with civil leer,
And, without sneering, teach the rest to sneer. *Ib, 201*

84 Who but must laugh, if such a man there be?
Who would not weep, if Atticus were he? *Ib, 213*

85 Curst be the verse, how well so'er it flow,
That tends to make one worthy man my foe. *Ib, 283*

86 Wit that can creep, and pride that licks the dust. *Ib, 333*

87 Unlearn'd, he knew no schoolman's subtle art,
No language but the language of the heart. *Ib, 398*

88 Nature and Nature's Laws lay hid in Night:
God said, Let Newton be! and all was Light.
*Epitaph, intended for Sir Isaac Newton*

89 In wit a man: simplicity a child. *Epitaph on Mr Gay*

90 'Tis hard to say, if greater want of skill
 Appear in writing or in judging ill.    *An Essay on Criticism, 1*

91 'Tis with our judgments as our watches, none
 Go just alike, yet each believes his own.    *Ib, 9*

92 First follow Nature, and your judgment frame
 By her just standard, which is still the same:
 Unerring Nature, still divinely bright,
 One clear, unchang'd, and universal light,
 Life, force, and beauty, must to all impart,
 At once the source, and end, and test of Art.    *Ib, 58*

93 Of all the causes which conspire to blind
 Man's erring judgment, and misguide the mind,
 What the weak head with strongest bias rules,
 Is Pride, the never-failing vice of fools.    *Ib, 201*

94 A little learning is a dangerous thing;
 Drink deep, or taste not the Pierian spring:
 There shallow draughts intoxicate the brain,
 And drinking largely sobers us again.    *Ib, 215*

95 A perfect judge will read each work of Wit
 With the same spirit that its author writ.    *Ib, 233*

96 Whoever thinks a faultless piece to see,
 Thinks what ne'er was, nor is, nor e'er shall be.    *Ib, 253*

97 True wit is nature to advantage dress'd;
 What oft was thought, but ne'er so well express'd.    *Ib, 297*

98             As some to church repair,
 Not for the doctrine, but the music there.    *Ib, 342*

99 True ease in writing comes from art, not chance,
 As those move easiest who have learn'd to dance.
 'Tis not enough no harshness gives offence,
 The sound must seem an echo to the sense.    *Ib, 362*

1 Yet let not each gay turn thy rapture move,
 For fools admire, but men of sense approve.    *Ib, 390*

2 Some praise at morning what they blame at night,
 But always think the last opinion right.    *Ib, 430*

3 Fondly we think we honour merit then,
 When we but praise ourselves in other men.    *Ib, 454*

4 To err is human, to forgive, divine.    *Ib, 525*

5 The bookful blockhead, ignorantly read,
 With loads of learned lumber in his head.    *Ib, 612*

6 For fools rush in where angels fear to tread.    *Ib, 625*

7 Awake, my St John! leave all meaner things
To low ambition, and the pride of kings.
Let us (since life can little more supply
Than just to look about us and to die)
Expatiate free o'er all this scene of man;
A mighty maze! but not without a plan.

*An Essay on Man, Epistle 1, 1*

8 Laugh where we must, be candid where we can;
But vindicate the ways of God to Man.                    *Ib, 1, 15*

9 Hope springs eternal in the human breast;
Man never is, but always to be blest.                    *Ib, 1, 95*

10 Why has not man a microscopic eye?
For this plain reason, man is not a fly.                 *Ib, 1, 193*

11 All are but parts of one stupendous whole,
Whose body Nature is, and God the soul.                  *Ib, 1, 267*

12 All nature is but art, unknown to thee;
All chance, direction which thou canst not see;
All discord, harmony not understood;
All partial evil, universal good:
And, spite of pride, in erring reason's spite,
One truth is clear, whatever is, is right.               *Ib, 1, 289*

13 Know then thyself, presume not God to scan,
The proper study of Mankind is Man.                      *Ib, Epistle 2, 1*

14 Vice is a master of so frightful mien,
As to be hated needs but to be seen;
Yet seen too oft, familiar with her face,
We first endure, then pity, then embrace.                *Ib, 2, 217*

15 O happiness! our being's end and aim!
Good, pleasure, ease, content! whate'er thy name:
That something still which prompts th' eternal sigh,
For which we bear to live, or dare to die.    *Ib, Epistle 4, 1*

16 An honest Man's the noblest work of God.               *Ib, 4, 248*

17 If parts allure thee, think how Bacon shined,
The wisest, brightest, meanest of mankind:
Or, ravished with the whistling of a name,
See Cromwell, damned to everlasting fame.                *Ib, 4, 281*

18 Formed by thy converse happily to steer
From grave to gay, from lively to severe.                *Ib, 4, 379*

19 Thou wert my guide, philosopher, and friend.           *Ib, 4, 390*

20 That true self-love and social are the same;
That virtue only makes our bliss below;
And all our knowledge is, ourselves to know.             *Ib, 4, 396*

21 To observations which ourselves we make,
   We grow more partial for th' observer's sake.
   *Moral Essays, Epistle 1, 11*

22 'Tis education forms the common mind,
   Just as the twig is bent, the tree's inclined.      *Ib, 1, 149*

23 Men, some to business, some to pleasure take;
   But every woman is at heart a rake.      *Ib, Epistle 2, 215*

24 See how the world its veterans rewards!
   A youth of frolics, an old age of cards.      *Ib, 2, 243*

25 And mistress of herself, though China fall.      *Ib, 2, 268*

26 Woman's at best a contradiction still.      *Ib, 2, 270*

27 The ruling passion, be it what it will
   The ruling passion conquers reason still.      *Ib, Epistle 3, 153*

28 Happy the man, whose wish and care
   A few paternal acres bound,
   Content to breathe his native air,
      In his own ground.      *Ode on Solitude*

29 Thus let me live, unseen, unknown,
   Thus unlamented let me die,
   Steal from the world, and not a stone
      Tell where I lie.      *Ib*

30 I am His Highness' dog at Kew;
   Pray tell me sir, whose dog are you?   *On the collar of a dog
         given to His Royal Highness, Frederick, Prince of Wales*

31 I know the thing that's most uncommon;
      (Envy, be silent and attend!)
   I know a reasonable woman,
      Handsome and witty, yet a friend.
                              *On a Certain Lady at Court*

32 Where'er you walk, cool gales shall fan the glade.
   Trees where you sit shall crowd into a shade:
   Where'er you tread, the blushing flowers shall rise,
   And all things flourish where you turn your eyes.
                              *Pastorals, Summer, 73*

33 What dire offence from am'rous causes springs,
   What mighty contests rise from trivial things.
                              *The Rape of the Lock, Canto 1, 1*

34 If to her share some female errors fall,
   Look on her face, and you'll forget 'em all.      *Ib, Canto 2, 17*

35 Fair tresses man's imperial race insnare,
   And beauty draws us with a single hair.      *Ib, 2, 27*

36 At ev'ry word a reputation dies.      *Ib, Canto 3, 16*

37 The hungry judges soon the sentence sign,
   And wretches hang that jury-men may dine.
                          *The Rape of the Lock, Canto 3, 21*

38 Coffee, which makes the politician wise,
   And see through all things with his half-shut eyes.   *Ib, 3, 117*

39 Charms strike the sight, but merit wins the soul.   *Ib, Canto 5, 34*

**PORSON, Richard, 1759–1808**

40 When Dido found Aeneas would not come,
   She mourn'd in silence, and was Di-do-dum.
                          *Epigram on Latin Gerunds*

41 I went to Frankfort, and got drunk
   With that most learned professor, Brunck;
   I went to Worts, and got more drunken
   With that more learn'd professor, Ruhnken.
                          *Facetiae Cantabrigienses*

**PORTER, William Sydney, see HENRY, O.**

**POTTER, Beatrix, 1866–1943**

42 They [*the rabbits*] did not awake because the lettuces had been
   so soporific.                  *The Tale of the Flopsy Bunnies*

**POTTER, Stephen, 1900–1969**

43 Gamesmanship or The Art of Winning Games Without Actually
   Cheating.                              *Title of book*

44 *How to be one up* – how to make the other man feel that something has gone wrong, however slightly.
                          *Lifemanship, Introduction*

45 We work from half a dozen centres co-ordinated, of course, from
   our 'H.Q.' at Station Road, Yeovil.                    *Ib*

46 'Yes, but not in the South', with slight adjustments will do for
   any argument about any place, if not about any person.
                          *Ib, The Canterbury Block*

**POUND, Ezra Loomis, 1885–1972**

47 Winter is icummen in,
   Lhude sing Goddamm,
   Raineth drop and staineth slop
   And how the wind doth ramm!
   Sing: Goddamm.                              *Ancient Music*

48 Bah! I have sung women in three cities,
   But it is all the same;
   And I will sing of the sun.                          *Cino*

**PRESCOTT, William, 1726–1795**

49 Don't fire until you see the whites of their eyes. *Bunker Hill,*
                                    *1775 (Also attributed to Israel Putnam, 1718–1790)*

**PRIOR, Matthew, 1664–1721**

50 Be to her virtues very kind;
   Be to her faults a little blind;
   Let all her ways be unconfined;
   And clap your padlock on her mind.    *An English Padlock, 78*

51 The merchant to secure his treasure,
      Conveys it in a borrowed name;
   Euphelia serves to grace my measure;
   But Chloe is my real flame.
                       *Ode, The Merchant to Secure his Treasure*

52 From ignorance our comfort flows,
   The only wretched are the wise.    *To the Hon. C. Montague*


# PROVERBS

In this selection of familiar proverbs mainly in the English language,
the name and publication date of the Dictionary in which the
proverb was first included has been given, or the century of the first
recorded use of the proverb in literature. Most proverbs were
obviously in common use for many years before they were included
in a dictionary.

The abbreviations shown opposite proverbs refer to the following
Dictionaries:

| | |
|---|---|
| Bohn | *H. G. Bohn, A Handbook of Proverbs, 1855.* |
| Camden | *W. Camden, Remains Concerning Britain, 1614 or later edition.* |
| Clarke | *J. Clarke, Parœmiologia Anglo-Latina, 1639.* |
| Draxe | *T. Draxe, Bibliotheca Scholastica, 1616 or later edition.* |
| Fergusson | *D. Fergusson, Scottish Proverbs, 1641.* |
| Fuller | *T. Fuller, Gnomologia, 1732.* |
| Herbert | *G. Herbert, Outlandish Proverbs, 1640 or later edition.* |
| Heywood | *J. Heywood, A Dialogue containing . . . the Proverbs in the English Tongue, 1546 or later edition.* |
| Howell | *J. Howell, Proverbs, 1659.* |
| Kelly | *J. Kelly, A Complete Collection of Scottish Proverbs, 1721.* |
| Lean | *V. S. Lean, Collectanea, 1902–4.* |
| Ray | *J. Ray, A Collection of English Proverbs, 1670, 1678 or later edition.* |

53 Absence sharpens love, presence strengthens it. *Fuller, 1732*
54 Absent are always in the wrong, The. *Herbert, 1640*
55 Abundance of money ruins youth, The, *Ray, 1670*
56 Accidents will happen in the best-regulated families. *19th c.*
57 Accounting for tastes, There is no. *Latin*
58 Actions speak louder than words. *20th c.*
59 Adversity makes a man wise, not rich. *Ray, 1678*
60 Adversity, Many can bear/ but few contempt. *Fuller, 1732*
61 Advise none to marry or go to war. *Herbert, 1640*
62 After a storm comes a calm. *16th c.*
63 Agree, for the law is costly. *Camden, 1623*
64 All in the day's work, It is. *18th c.*
65 All is fair in love and war. *17th c.*
66 All is not gold that glitters. *Latin*
67 All is over bar (but) the shouting. *19th c.*
68 All is well that ends well. *14th c.*
69 All my eye and Betty Martin. *18th c.*
70 All sorts to make a world, It takes. *17th c.*
71 Any port in a storm. *18th c.*
72 Anything for a quiet life. *17th c.*
73 Apple a day keeps the doctor away, An. *19th c.*
74 Apple-cart, To upset the. *18th c.*
75 Archer is not known by his arrows, but his aim, A good.
*16th c.*
76 Art has no enemy except ignorance. *Latin*
77 Art lies in concealing art. *Latin*
78 Ask no questions and you will be told no lies. *18th c.*
79 Ask thy purse what thou shouldst buy. *Fuller, 1732*
80 Ass of oneself, To make an. *19th c.*
81 *Audi alteram partem* – Hear the other side. *Latin*
82 Aunt had been a man, If my/ she'd have been my uncle.
*Ray, 1813*
83 *Autres temps, autres moeurs* – Other times, other manners.
*French*
84 Axe to grind, To have an. *19th c.*

85 Bachelors' fare: bread and cheese, and kisses. *18th c.*
86 Back again, like a bad penny. *19th c.*

87 Bad excuse is better than none, A.                          *16th c.*
88 Bad workman quarrels with his tools, A.        *Herbert, 1640*
89 Bald as a coot, As.                                           *15th c.*
90 Bald heads are soon shaven.                          *Ray, 1678*
91 Barber shaves so close but another finds work, No.
                                                            *Herbert, 1640*
92 Bark at the moon, To.                                       *15th c.*
93 Bark is worse than his bite, His.                          *17th c.*
94 Bark up the wrong tree, To.                                *19th c.*
95 Barking dogs seldom bite.                                   *16th c.*
96 Bats in the belfry, To have.                               *20th c.*
97 Be sure before you marry of a house wherein to tarry.  *Italian*
98 Bear wealth, poverty will bear itself.        *Fergusson, 1641*
99 Beat about the bush, To.                                    *16th c.*
 1 Beauty is but skin-deep.                                    *17th c.*
 2 Beauty is potent, but money is omnipotent.         *Ray, 1670*
 3 Beauty will buy no beef.                             *Fuller, 1732*
 4 Bee in one's bonnet, To have a.                            *19th c.*
 5 Before one can say Jack Robinson.                         *18th c.*
 6 Beggar can never be bankrupt, A.                  *Clarke, 1639*
 7 Beggars cannot be choosers.                     *Heywood, 1546*
 8 Believe, He does not/ that does not live according to his belief.
                                                             *Fuller, 1732*
 9 Beloved, To be/ is above all bargains.          *Herbert, 1640*
10 Best foot forward, To put one's.                           *16th c.*
11 Best of a bad job, To make the.                            *16th c.*
12 Better a lean peace than a fat victory.                    *17th c.*
13 Better an egg today than a hen tomorrow.               *Italian*
14 Better an open enemy than a false friend.                 *17th c.*
15 Better be alone than in bad company.                       *15th c.*
16 Better be born lucky than rich.                   *Clarke, 1639*
17 Better be envied than pitied.                              *Greek*
18 Better be happy than wise.                     *Heywood, 1546*
19 Better be sure (safe) than sorry.                         *19th c.*
20 Better be the head of a dog than the tail of a lion.      *16th c.*
21 Better buy than borrow.                          *Fergusson, 1641*
22 Better die a beggar than live a beggar.            *Ray, 1670*

23 Better give a shilling than lend a half-crown.  *Howell, 1659*

24 Better go to heaven in rags than to hell in embroidery.
*Fuller, 1732*

25 Better late than never.  *Latin*

26 Better luck next time.  *19th c.*

27 Better never begin than never make an end.  *16th c.*

28 Better some of a pudding than none of a pie.  *Ray, 1670*

29 Better suffer ill than do ill.  *Clarke, 1639*

30 Better the devil you know than the devil you don't know.
*19th c.*

31 Better untaught than ill-taught.  *Ray, 1678*

32 Better wear out shoes than sheets.  *17th c.*

33 Between Scylla and Charybdis.  *Greek*

34 Between two stools one falls to the ground.  *Latin*

35 Between you and me and the (gate) post.  *19th c.*

36 Bird in hand is worth two in the bush, A.  *Latin*

37 Birds of a feather flock together.  *16th c.*

38 Bitter to endure may be sweet to remember, That which was.
*Latin*

39 Black as ink.  *16th c.*

40 Black as soot.  *15th c.*

41 Black as the devil.  *14th c.*

42 Black sheep in every flock, There are.  *19th c.*

43 Blessings are not valued till they are gone.  *Fuller, 1732*

44 Blind as a bat, As.  *16th c.*

45 Blind as those who won't see, None so.  *Heywood, 1546*

46 Blind in their own cause, Men are.  *Heywood, 1546*

47 Blind man will not thank you for a looking-glass, A.
*Fuller, 1732*

48 Blind, In the land of the/ the one-eyed man is king.  *Greek*

49 Blood is thicker than water.  *17th c.*

50 Blow one's own trumpet, To.  *16th c.*

51 Bone in one's leg, To have a.  *Greek*

52 Book that is shut is but a block, A.  *Fuller, 1732*

53 Books and friends should be few and good.  *Spanish*

54 Books, To be in a person's good (or bad).  *19th c.*

55 Boot is on the other leg, The.  *19th c.*

56 Born on the wrong side of the blanket.  *18th c.*

57 Born to be hanged, He that is/ shall never be drowned.  *16th c.*
58 Born with a silver spoon in his mouth, He was.  *Clarke, 1639*
59 Born within the sound of Bow Bells, To be.  *16th c.*
60 Born yesterday, I was not.  *19th c.*
61 Both ends meet, To make.  *Clarke, 1639*
62 Bow at all, If you/ bow low.  *Chinese*
63 Boys will be boys.  *17th c.*
64 Boys will be men.  *17th c.*
65 Bread is buttered on both sides, His.  *Ray, 1678*
66 Bull in a china shop, A.  *19th c.*
67 Bulls the cow must keep the calf, He that.  *16th c.*
68 Bully is always a coward, A.  *19th c.*
69 Burn one's boats, To.  *19th c.*
70 Burn the candle at both ends, To.  *Ray, 1678*
71 Burn the midnight oil, To.  *17th c.*
72 Bury the hatchet, To.  *18th c.*
73 Busiest men have the most leisure, The.  *19th c.*
74 Business is business.  *18th c.*
75 Business before pleasure.  *19th c.*
76 Busy, Who is more/ than he that hath least to do?

*Draxe, 1616*

77 Butter would not melt in his mouth.  *Heywood, 1546*
78 Buy a pig in a poke, To.  *Heywood, 1546*
79 Buy and sell, and live by the loss, To.  *Draxe, 1616*
80 Bygones be bygones, Let.  *Heywood, 1546*

81 Calf love, half love; old love, cold love.  *19th c.*
82 Call a spade a spade, To.  *Latin*
83 Cap fits, If the/wear it.  *18th c.*
84 Care killed a cat.  *16th c.*
85 Carry coals to Newcastle, To.  *16th c.*
86 Cart before the horse, To put the.  *Latin*
87 Cast ne'er a clout till May be out.  *Fuller, 1732*
88 Castles in Spain, To build.  *14th c.*
89 Castles in the air, To build.  *Latin*
90 Cat has nine lives, A.  *Heywood, 1546*
91 Cat jumps, To see which way the.  *19th c.*

92 Cat on hot bricks, Like a. *17th c.*

93 *Caveat emptor* – Let the buyer beware. *Latin*

94 Chalk and cheese. *14th c.*

95 Chanceth in an hour, It/ that happeneth not in seven years.
*Heywood, 1546*

96 Charity begins at home. *14th c.*

97 *Che sera, sera* – Whatever will be, will be. *Italian*

98 Children should be seen and not heard. *19th c.*

99 Chip of the old block, A. *17th c.*

 1 Choose a horse made, and a wife to make. *Herbert, 1640*

 2 Choose a wife rather by your ear than your eye. *Fuller, 1732*

 3 Choose neither a woman nor linen by candle-light. *16th c.*

 4 Chop and change, To. *16th c.*

 5 Christmas comes but once a year
But when it comes it brings good cheer. *16th c.*

 6 Circumstances alter cases. *19th c.*

 7 Civility costs nothing. *19th c.*

 8 Clean as a whistle, As. *19th c.*

 9 Clean breast, To make a. *18th c.*

10 Cleanliness is next to godliness. *Hebrew*

11 Close mouth catcheth no flies, A. *Italian*

12 Cloud has a silver lining, Every. *19th c.*

13 Cloud, To be under a. *16th c.*

14 Coast is clear, The. *17th c.*

15 Cock-a-hoop, To be. *17th c.*

16 Cock-and-bull story, A. *17th c.*

17 Cold as charity. *14th c.*

18 Cold comfort. *16th c.*

19 Cold hand and a warm heart, A. *Lean, 1902*

20 Cold shoulder, To give the. *19th c.*

21 Company makes the feast. The. *17th c.*

22 Comparisons are odious. *15th c.*

23 Confession is good for the soul. *Kelly, 1721*

24 Constant guest is never welcome, A. *Fuller, 1732*

25 Cook one's goose, To. *19th c.*

26 Cook that cannot lick his own fingers, He is an ill.
*Heywood, 1546*

27 Cool one's heels, To.                                              *17th c.*

28 Costs more to do ill than to do well, It.          *Herbert, 1640*

29 Counsel be good, If the/ no matter who gave it.     *Fuller, 1732*

30 Count one's chickens before they are hatched, To.    *16th c.*

31 Couple is not a pair, Every.                                *19th c.*

32 Courtesy on one side only lasts not long.          *Herbert, 1640*

33 Coventry, To send to.                                       *17th c.*

34 Creditors have better memories than debtors.        *Howell, 1659*

35 Crocodile tears.                                            *16th c.*

36 Crooked by nature is never made straight by education.
                                                              *Fuller, 1732*

37 Cross the bridge till you get to it, Don't.              *19th c.*

38 Crowd is not company, A.                                    *17th c.*

39 Cry for the moon, To.                                       *19th c.*

40 Cry 'Wolf', To.                                             *17th c.*

41 Crying over spilt milk, It is no use.               *Howell, 1659*

42 Cupboard love.                                              *17th c.*

43 Curate's egg, good in parts, Like the. (*See Punch, 285:86*)
                                                               *19th c.*

44 Curses are like chickens; they come home to roost.    *14th c.*

45 Custom without reason is but ancient error.             *16th c.*

46 Cut off one's nose to spite one's face, To.             *13th c.*

47 Cut off with a shilling, To.                             *18th c.*

48 Cut the grass from under a person's feet, To.           *16th c.*

49 Cut your coat according to your cloth.             *Heywood, 1546*

50 Dally not with money or women.                    *Herbert, 1640*

51 Daughter win, He that would the/ must with the mother first
   begin.                                                   *Ray, 1670*

52 Day is short and the work is long, The.                 *15th c.*

53 *De gustibus non est disputandum* – There is no disputing about
   tastes.                                                    *Latin*

54 *De mortuis nil nisi bonum* – Concerning the dead (say) nothing
   but good.                                                  *Latin*

55 Dead as a door-nail, As.                                *14th c.*

56 Dead men don't bite.                                      *Greek*

57 Dead men tell no tales.                                 *17th c.*

58 Deaf as a post.                                         *16th c.*

59 Deaf as those who won't hear, None so.   *Heywood, 1546*

60 Death devours lambs as well as sheep.   *17th c.*

61 Death is the grand leveller.   *Fuller, 1732*

62 Death pays all debts.   *17th c.*

63 Debt is the worst poverty.   *Fuller, 1732*

64 Deceives me once, If a man/ shame on him; if he deceives me twice, shame on me.   *Italian*

65 Deceive oneself is very easy, To.   *Herbert, 1640*

66 Deeds are males, and words are females.   *16th c.*

67 Deepest water is the best fishing, In the.   *Draxe, 1616*

68 Delays are dangerous.   *14th c.*

69 Deserves not the sweet that will not taste the sour, He.   *Latin*

70 Desires honour, He that/ is not worthy of honour.   *17th c.*

71 Desperate diseases must have desperate remedies.   *Latin*

72 Devil and the deep sea, Between the.   *17th c.*

73 Devil is not so black as he is painted, The.   *16th c.*

74 Devil take the hindmost, The.   *17th c.*

75 Discreet women have neither eyes nor ears.   *Herbert, 1640*

76 Discretion is the better part of valour.   *16th c.*

77 *Divide et impera* – Divide and rule.   *Latin*

78 Divine grace was never slow.   *Herbert, 1640*

79 Do as you would be done by.   *14th c.*

80 Do as you're bidden and you'll never bear blame.   *Ray, 1678*

81 Dog does not eat dog.   *18th c.*

82 Dog has his day, Every.   *Heywood, 1546*

83 Dog will not howl if you beat him with a bone, A.
   *Howell, 1659*

84 Dogs that bark at a distance never bite.   *Camden, 1623*

85 Done by night appears by day, What is.   *14th c.*

86 Done cannot be undone, Things.   *Heywood, 1546*

87 Door may be shut but death's door, Every.   *Italian*

88 Draw the line somewhere, One must.   *19th c.*

89 Drink wine, and have the gout; drink no wine, and have the gout too.   *16th c.*

90 Drowning man will catch at a straw, A.   *17th c.*

91 Drunk as a fish, As.   *17th c.*

92 Drunk as a lord, As.   *17th c.*

93 Drunk as a mouse, As. *14th c.*

94 Drunk as a wheelbarrow, As. *Ray, 1678*

95 Drunken folks seldom take harm. *17th c.*

96 Drunken night makes a cloudy morning, A. *Fuller, 1732*

97 Dry as dust, As. *16th c.*

98 Ducks and drakes of, To make. *16th c.*

99 Dull as ditchwater, As. *18th c.*

1 Dumb men get no lands. *14th c.*

2 Dying duck in a thunderstorm, Like a. *18th c.*

3 Ears burn, If your/ someone is talking about you.
*Heywood, 1546*

4 Early bird catches the worm, The. *Camden, 1636*

5 Early to bed and early to rise,
Makes a man healthy, wealthy and wise. *Clarke, 1639*

6 Easier said than done. *15th c.*

7 East or west, home is best. *Bohn, 1855*

8 Easy come, easy go. *19th c.*

9 Easy to be wise after the event, It is. *17th c.*

10 Eat, and welcome; fast, and heartily welcome. *Ray, 1678*

11 Eat one's words, To. *16th c.*

12 Eat to live, but do not live to eat. *Latin*

13 Eat your cake and have it, You cannot. *Heywood, 1546*

14 Education begins a gentleman, conversation completes him.
*Fuller, 1732*

15 Eggs in one basket, Do not put all your. *18th c.*

16 Eleventh Commandment: The/ thou shalt not be found out.
*19th c.*

17 Empty purse that is full of other men's money, That is but an.
*Ray, 1678*

18 Empty vessels make the most noise. *16th c.*

19 End justifies the means, The. *17th c.*

20 England is the paradise of women, the hell of horses, and the
purgatory of servants. *16th c.*

21 English never know when they are beaten, The. *19th c.*

22 Englishman's house (home) is his castle, An. *17th c.*

23 Enough is as good as a feast. *15th c.*

24 Enough is enough. *Heywood, 1546*

25 Evening crowns the day, The. *17th c.*

26 Every little helps. *18th c.*

27 Every man for himself, and God for us all. *Heywood, 1562*

28 Every man has his faults. *16th c.*

29 Every man is best known to himself. *Draxe, 1616*

30 Every man to his taste. *16th c.*

31 Everybody's business is nobody's business. *17th c.*

32 Everything comes to him who waits. *16th c.*

33 Everything hath an end, and a pudding hath two. *16th c.*

34 Everything is the worse for wearing. *Clarke, 1639*

35 Everything must have a beginning. *14th c.*

36 Evils, Of two/ choose the least. *14th c.*

37 Example is better than precept. *Latin*

38 Exception proves the rule, The. *17th c.*

39 Experience is good, if not bought too dear. *Kelly, 1721*

40 *Experientia docet* – Experience teaches. *Latin*

41 Extremes meet. *18th c.*

42 Eye sees not, What the/ the heart rues not. *Heywood, 1546*

43 Failing to trust everybody, It is an equal/ and to trust nobody.
*Fuller, 1732*

44 Faint heart never won fair lady. *16th c.*

45 Fair and softly goes far. *14th c.*

46 Fair exchange is no robbery, A. *16th c.*

47 Fair face and a foul heart, A. *Howell, 1659*

48 Fair face is half a fortune, A. *Draxe, 1616*

49 Fair play's a jewel. *19th c.*

50 Fairer the hostess, the fouler the reckoning, The.
*Howell, 1659*

51 Familiarity breeds contempt. *Latin*

52 Far from eye, far from heart. *14th c.*

53 Fast bind, fast find. *Heywood, 1546*

54 Fat in in the fire, The. *Heywood, 1546*

55 Faults are theirs that commit them, The first/ the second theirs
that permit them. *Fuller, 1732*

56 Faults are thick where love is thin. *Howell, 1659*

57 Few lawyers die well, few physicians live well. *16th c.*

58 Few words are best. *Ray, 1678*

59 *Fiat justitia, ruat coelum* – Let justice be done, though heaven fall. *Latin*

60 Fiddle while Rome is burning, To. *17th c.*

61 Finding's keeping. *19th c.*

62 Finger in the pie, To have a. *17th c.*

63 Fire is a good servant but a bad master. *17th c.*

64 First blow is half the battle, The. *18th c.*

65 First catch your hare and then cook it. *18th c.*

66 First come, first served. *16th c.*

67 First impressions are most lasting. *19th c.*

68 First think, and then speak. *Clarke, 1639*

69 Fish out of water, Like a. *Latin*

70 Fish to fry, I have other. *17th c.*

71 Fit as a fiddle, As. *17th c.*

72 Flat as a pancake, As. *16th c.*

73 Fling dirt enough, and some will stick. *Latin*

74 Flog a dead horse, To. *19th c.*

75 Follow the river and you'll get to the sea. *Fuller, 1732*

76 Fool and his money are soon parted, A. *16th c.*

77 Fool like an old fool, No. *Heywood, 1546*

78 Fool that forgets himself, He is a. *14th c.*

79 Fool that is not melancholy once a day, He is a. *Ray, 1678*

80 Fool to the market, Send a/ and a fool he'll return. *16th c.*

81 Fool wanders, The/ the wise man travels. *Fuller, 1732*

82 Fools went not to market, If/ bad wares would not be sold.
*Herbert, 1640*

83 Forewarned, forearmed. *Latin*

84 Forgive and forget. *Heywood, 1546*

85 Fortune favours fools. *Latin*

86 Fortune is blind. *16th c.*

87 Fortune knocks, When/ open the door. *17th c.*

88 Foul water will quench fire. *Heywood, 1546*

89 Four eyes see more than two. *Latin*

90 Fox knows much, The/ but more he that catcheth him.
*Herbert, 1640*

91 Friend at court, A. *17th c.*

92 Friend in need is a friend indeed, A. *Latin*

93 Friend to thyself, Be a/ and others will befriend thee.
Kelly, 1721

94 Friend to everybody is a friend to nobody, A. 17th c.

95 Friends are thieves of time. 17th c.

96 Friends both in heaven and hell, It is good to have some.
Herbert, 1640

97 Friends (The best of friends) must part. 17th c.

98 Friends, Have but few/ though many acquaintances.
Howell, 1659

99 Friendship should not be all on one side. 17th c.

1 Frying-pan into the fire, Out of the. Heywood, 1546

2 Full of courtesy, full of craft. 16th c.

3 Game is not worth the candle, The. 17th c.

4 Geese are swans, All his. 16th c.

5 Gift horse in the mouth, Look not a. Latin

6 Give a dog a bad name and hang him. Kelly, 1721

7 Give him an inch and he'll take an ell. Heywood, 1546

8 Give the devil his due. 16th c.

9 Gives to all, denies all, Who. Herbert, 1640

10 Gives twice who gives quickly, He. Latin

11 Giving much to the poor doth increase a man's store.
Herbert, 1640

12 Glass houses, People who live in/ should never throw stones.
Herbert, 1640

13 Gluttony kills more than the sword. 16th c.

14 Go down the ladder when thou marriest a wife; go up when thou choosest a friend. Ray, 1678

15 Go farther and fare worse. Heywood, 1546

16 Go to bed with the lamb, and rise with the lark. 16th c.

17 God comes at last when we think he is furthest off. Italian

18 God defend me from my friends; from my enemies I can defend myself. 17th c.

19 God heals, and the doctor takes the fee. Herbert, 1640

20 God help the poor, for the rich can help themselves.
Kelly, 1721

21 God help the rich, the poor can beg. Howell, 1659

22 God helps them that help themselves. Herbert, 1640

23 God send me a friend that will tell me of my faults.
*Fuller, 1732*

24 God send you joy, for sorrow will come fast enough.
*Draxe, 1616*

25 God sends fortune to fools. *Heywood, 1546*

26 God tempers the wind to the shorn lamb. *French*

27 God's mill grinds slow but sure. *Greek*

28 Good against evil, Set. *Herbert, 1640*

29 Good and quickly seldom meet. *Herbert, 1640*

30 Good beginning makes a good ending, A. *14th c.*

31 Good example is the best sermon, A. *Fuller, 1732*

32 Good face needs no paint, A. *Fuller, 1732*

33 Good judgement that relieth not wholly on his own, He hath a.
*Fuller, 1732*

34 Good life is the only religion, A. *Fuller, 1732*

35 Good to want and to have, It is not. *Fergusson, 1641*

36 Good turn deserves another, One. *15th c.*

37 Good wife and health are a man's best wealth, A.
*Fuller, 1732*

38 Good wife makes a good husband, A. *Heywood, 1546*

39 Good wine needs no bush. *16th c.*

40 Good workmen are seldom rich. *Herbert, 1640*

41 Grasp all, lose all. *14th c.*

42 Great minds think alike. *20th c.*

43 Great ones if there were no little ones, There would be no.
*Herbert, 1640*

44 Great talkers are great liars. *French*

45 Great trees are good for nothing but shade. *Herbert, 1640*

46 Greater the truth, The/ the greater the libel. *18th c.*

47 Greatest hate springs from the greatest love, The. *16th c.*

48 Greek to me, It is. *16th c.*

49 Grist to the mill, To bring. *16th c.*

50 Hail fellow well met, To be. *16th c.*

51 Half a loaf is better than no bread. *Heywood, 1546*

52 Half the world knows not how the other half lives.
*Herbert, 1640*

53 Half-seas over, To be. *18th c.*

54 Halves, Never do things by. *18th c.*

55 Hand and glove. *17th c.*

56 Handful of good life is better than a bushel of learning, A.
*Herbert, 1640*

57 Hands, Many/ make light work. *Latin*

58 Handsome at twenty, He that is not/ nor strong at thirty, nor rich at forty, nor wise at fifty, will never be handsome, strong, rich or wise. *Herbert, 1640*

59 Handsome is that handsome does. *Ray, 1670*

60 Hanged for a sheep as a lamb, As good be. *Ray, 1678*

61 Hanging and wiving go by destiny. *Heywood, 1546*

62 Happiness takes no account of time. *18th c.*

63 Happy is he that is happy in his children. *Fuller, 1732*

64 Happy is the country which has no history. *19th c.*

65 Happy is the child whose father goes to the devil. *16th c.*

66 Hard as a Flint (stone), As. *14th c.*

67 Hard cases make bad law. *Lean, 1902*

68 Hard cheese. *19th c.*

69 Hard nut to crack, A. *16th c.*

70 Haste, The more/ the less speed. *Heywood, 1546*

71 Hatred is blind, as well as love. *Fuller, 1732*

72 Hatch, match and despatch. *19th c.*

73 Haul over the coals, To. *16th c.*

74 Head, He that hath no/ needs no hat. *Herbert, 1640*

75 Heads I win, tails you lose. *17th c.*

76 Health is better than wealth. *16th c.*

77 Health is not valued till sickness come. *Fuller, 1732*

78 Hear all parties. *15th c.*

79 Hear twice before you speak once. *19th c.*

80 Heard a pin drop, You might have. *19th c.*

81 Heart is in his mouth, His. *16th c.*

82 Heavy purse makes a light heart, A *17th c.*

83 Hell and Chancery are always open. *Fuller, 1732*

84 Hell is paved with good intentions. (The road to) *18th c.*

85 Hell, Hull and Halifax, From/ good Lord deliver us. *16th c.*

86 Higher up, The/the greater the fall. *16th c.*

87 History repeats itself. *19th c.*

88 Hit the nail on the head, To.  *16th c.*
89 Hobson's choice.  *17th c.*
90 Hoist with his own petard.  *17th c.*
91 Hold a candle to the devil, To.  *15th c.*
92 Honest man's word is as good as his bond, An.  *17th c.*
93 Honest men marry soon, wise ones not at all.  *Ray, 1670*
94 Honesty is the best policy.  *16th c.*
95 *Honi soit qui mal y pense* – Evil be to him who evil thinks.
  *French*
96 Honour among thieves, There is.  *18th c.*
97 Hook or by crook, By.  *14th c.*
98 Hope for the best and prepare for the worst.  *16th c.*
99 Hope is as cheap as despair.  *Fuller, 1732*
1 Hot love is soon cold.  *16th c.*
2 Hour in the morning is worth two in the evening, An.  *19th c.*
3 Hour of pain is as long as a day of pleasure, An.
  *Fuller, 1732*
4 Hour today, One/ is worth two tomorrow.  *Fuller, 1732*
5 Hour's sleep before midnight, One/ is worth three after.
  *Herbert, 1640*
6 House on fire, Like a.  *19th c.*
7 *Humanum est errare* – To err is human  *Latin*
8 Hypocrisy is a homage that vice pays to virtue.  *Fuller, 1732*

9 Idle that might be better employed, He is.  *Fuller, 1732*
10 If Ifs and Ans were pots and pans
  There'd be no trade for tinkers.  *19th c.*
11 *Il faut reculer pour mieux sauter* – One must draw back in order
  to leap better.  *French*
12 Ill doers are ill thinkers.  *16th c.*
13 Ill gotten, ill spent,  *Latin*
14 Ill news comes too soon.  *16th c.*
15 Ill wind that blows nobody good, It is an.  *Heywood, 1546*
16 In at one ear and out at the other.  *14th c.*
17 In for a penny, in for a pound.  *17th c.*
18 Insult to injury, To add.  *Latin*
19 Iron entered his soul, The.  *Latin*
20 Iron hand in a velvet glove, An.  *French*

21 Irons in the fire, To have many. *16th c.*

22 Jack has his Jill, Every. *17th c.*

23 Jack of all trades and master of none. *18th c.*

24 Joan is as good as my lady, in the dark. *17th c.*

25 Jolly (happy) as a sandboy, As. *19th c.*

26 Judge from appearances, Never. *16th c.*

27 Keep a dog and bark yourself, Do not. *16th c.*

28 Keep a thing seven years and you will find a use for it.
*17th c.*

29 Keep one's tongue between one's teeth, To. *17th c.*

30 Keep up with the Joneses, To. *20th c.*

31 Keep your eyes wide open before marriage and half shut afterwards. *18th c.*

32 Keep your mouth shut and your eyes open. *18th c.*

33 Kill not the goose that lays the golden eggs. *15th c.*

34 Kill two birds with one stone, To. *17th c.*

35 King can do no wrong, The. *17th c.*

36 King never dies, The. *Latin*

37 King's favour is no inheritance, The. *Fuller, 1732*

38 Kiss and be friends. *14th c.*

39 Kiss the mistress, If you can/ never kiss the maid. *Ray, 1670*

40 Knaves and fools divide the world. *Ray, 1670*

41 Knocked me down with a feather, You might have. *19th c.*

42 Know on which side one's bread is buttered, To.
*Heywood, 1546*

43 Know the ropes, To. *19th c.*

44 Know the worth of water till the well is dry, We never.
*Kelly, 1721*

45 Know which way the wind blows, To. *Heywood, 1546*

46 Knowledge is power. *17th c.*

47 Knows how many beans make nine, He. *19th c.*

48 Knows little, He that/ soon repeats it. *18th c.*

49 Knows nothing, He that/ doubts nothing. *Herbert, 1640*

50 *Laborare est orare* – To work is to pray. *Latin*

51 Large as life, As. *18th c.*

52 Last but not least. *16th c.*

53 Last legs, To be on one's. *16th c.*
54 Last straw breaks the camel's back, The. *17th c.*
55 Laughs best who laughs last, He. *18th c.*
56 Law is a bottomless pit. *18th c.*
57 Law for the rich, One/ and another for the poor. *19th c.*
58 Law makers should not be law breakers. *14th c.*
59 Laws, The more/ the more offenders. *Latin*
60 Lawyers' houses are built on the heads of fools.
*Herbert, 1640*
61 Lay it on with a trowel, To. *16th c.*
62 Lead a horse to the water, A man may/ but he cannot make him drink. *Heywood, 1546*
63 Lean as a rake, As. *14th c.*
64 Learning makes a good man better and an ill man worse.
*17th c.*
65 Least foolish is wise, The. *Herbert, 1640*
66 Least said, soonest mended. *15th c.*
67 Leave in the lurch, To. *16th c.*
68 Leave no stone unturned, To. *Greek*
69 Lend I am a friend, When I/ when I ask I am a foe. *16th c.*
70 Lend your money and lose your friend. *17th c.*
71 Let sleeping dogs lie. *14th c.*
72 Let the cat out of the bag, To. *18th c.*
73 Liar is not believed when he speaks the truth, A. *Latin*
74 Liars should have good memories. *Latin*
75 Lick into shape, To. *15th c.*
76 Lie begets a lie, A. *Fuller, 1732*
77 Lies upon the ground, He that/ can fall no lower. *Latin*
78 Life is half spent before we know what it is. *Herbert, 1640*
79 Life is sweet. *14th c.*
80 Life, While there is/ there is hope. *Latin*
81 Lifeless that is faultless, He is. *Heywood, 1546*
82 Light cares speak, great ones are dumb. *Latin*
83 Light purse makes a heavy heart, A. *16th c.*
84 Lightly come, lightly go. *16th c.*
85 Like father, like son. *Latin*
86 Like it, If you don't/ you can (may) lump it. *19th c.*

87 Like master, like man. *Latin*

88 Line one's pockets, To. *16th c.*

89 Lion is not so fierce as he is painted, The. *17th c.*

90 Listeners hear no good of themselves. *17th c.*

91 Little and often fills the purse. *17th c.*

92 Little things please little minds. *Latin*

93 Live and learn. *Clarke, 1639*

94 Live and let live. *Dutch*

95 Live without our friends, We can/ but not without our neighbours. *Kelly, 1721*

96 Lock, stock, and barrel. *19th c.*

97 Lombard Street to a China orange, All. *18th c.*

98 Long absent, soon forgotten. *Draxe, 1616*

99 Long spoon, He should have a/ that sups with the devil.
*14th c.*

1 Longest day must have an end, The. *17th c.*

2 Look before you leap. *14th c.*

3 Look (at) on the bright side. *19th c.*

4 Lookers-on see most of the game. *16th c.*

5 Losers are always in the wrong. *Spanish*

6 Losers seekers, finders keepers. *19th c.*

7 Lost his taste, To him that has/ sweet is sour. *Draxe, 1616*

8 Love and a cough cannot be hid. *Latin*

9 Love and business teach eloquence. *Herbert, 1640*

10 Love begets love. *Latin*

11 Love best, Whom we/ to them we can say least. *16th c.*

12 Love comes in at the window and goes out at the door.
*Camden, 1614*

13 Love is blind. *14th c.*

14 Love is sweet in the beginning but sour in the ending.
*Draxe, 1616*

15 Love lives in cottages as well as in courts. *16th c.*

16 Love makes one fit for any work. *Herbert, 1640*

17 Love makes the world go round. *17th c.*

18 Love me little, love me long. *Heywood, 1546*

19 Love me, love my dog. *Latin*

20 Love of money and the love of learning rarely meet, The.
*Herbert, 1651*

21 Love too much that die for love, They.                    *17th c.*

22 Love will find a way.                                      *16th c.*

23 Mad as a hatter.                                           *19th c.*

24 Mad as a March hare, As.                                   *14th c.*

25 Maidens should be meek until they be married.
                                                    *Fergusson, 1641*

26 Main chance, Have an eye to the,                           *16th c.*

27 Make hay while the sun shines.                  *Heywood, 1546*

28 Man can only die once, A.                                  *16th c.*

29 Man in the moon.                                           *14th c.*

30 Man in the street, The.                                    *19th c.*

31 Man loveth his fetters, No/ be they made of gold.
                                                    *Heywood, 1546*

32 Man is as old as he feels, and a woman as old as she looks, A.
                                                              *20th c.*

33 Man is known by the company he keeps, A.                  *17th c.*

34 Man lives, As a/ so shall he die.                          *16th c.*

35 Man or mouse.                                              *16th c.*

36 Man proposes, God disposes.                               *Latin*

37 Many a little makes a mickle.                              *13th c.*

38 March comes in like a lion and goes out like a lamb.
                                                         *Ray, 1670*

39 Mare's nest, To find a.                                    *16th c.*

40 Marriage is a lottery.                                     *17th c.*

41 Marriages are made in heaven.                              *16th c.*

42 Marries for wealth, He that/ sells his liberty.   *Herbert, 1640*

43 Marries late, He that/ marries ill.                        *16th c.*

44 Marrieth for love without money, Who/hath good nights and
   sorry days.                                           *Ray, 1670*

45 Marry first and love will follow.                          *17th c.*

46 Marry in haste and repent at leisure.                      *16th c.*

47 Marry late or never, It is good to.               *Clarke, 1639*

48 Marry your daughters betimes, lest they marry themselves.
                                                              *16th c.*

49 Marry your son when you will, your daughter when you can.
                                                    *Herbert, 1640*

50 Measure in all things, There is a.                         *14th c.*

51 Measure thrice before you cut once. *Italian*

52 Meat, One man's/ is another man's poison. *Latin*

53 Meet troubles half-way, Don't. *16th c.*

54 Men who make a city, It is the. *Greek*

55 Meekness of Moses is better than the strength of Samson, The.
*Fuller, 1732*

56 Merry as a cricket, As. *Heywood, 1546*

57 Might is right. *14th c.*

58 Mind your own business. *Clarke, 1639*

59 Mirror, The best/ is an old friend. *Herbert, 1640*

60 Misfortunes never come singly. *14th c.*

61 Miss is as good as a mile, A. *19th c.*

62 Mob has many heads, but no brains, The. *Fuller, 1732*

63 Money be not thy servant, If/ it will be thy master. *17th c.*

64 Money begets money. *Italian*

65 Money is a good servant, but a bad master. *17th c.*

66 Money makes marriage. *Fuller, 1732*

67 Money makes the man. *Greek*

68 Money or your life! Your. *19th c.*

69 Money talks. *17th c.*

70 More the merrier, The/ the fewer the better cheer.
*Heywood, 1546*

71 Mother, Like/ like daughter. *16th c.*

72 Mother-in-law remembers not that she was a daughter-in-law,
The. *Howell, 1659*

73 Mountain out of a molehill, To make a. *16th c.*

74 Much law, but little justice. *Fuller, 1732*

75 Murder will out. *14th c.*

76 Natural folly is bad enough, but learned folly is intolerable.
*Fuller, 1732*

77 Necessity hath no law. *Latin*

78 Necessity is the mother of invention. *16th c.*

79 Neck or nothing. *Ray, 1678*

80 Need makes the old wife trot. *15th c.*

81 Needle in a haystack, To look for a. *15th c.*

82 Needs must when the devil drives. *15th c.*

83 Never a bad day that hath a good night, It is. *17th c.*

84 Never ask pardon before you are accused.        *Bohn, 1855*
85 Never put off till tomorrow what may be done today.   *14th c.*
86 Never refuse a good offer.                      *Ray, 1670*
87 Never say die.                                   *19th c.*
88 Never too late to mend, It is.                   *17th c.*
89 Never too old to learn.                          *17th c.*
90 Never trouble trouble till trouble troubles you.   *19th c.*
91 New broom sweeps clean, A.                  *Heywood, 1546*
92 No fire without some smoke.                 *Heywood, 1546*
93 No man's religion ever survives his morals.    *Fuller, 1722*
94 No mischief but a woman or a priest is at the bottom of it.
                                                    *Latin*
95 No money, no swiss.                              *17th c.*
96 No names, no pack drill.                         *20th c.*
97 No news is good news.                            *Italian*
98 No pleasure without pain.                        *16th c.*
99 No rose without a thorn.                         *15th c.*
 1 No smoke without some fire.                      *15th c.*
 2 No sunshine but has some shadow.           *Ray, 1678*
 3 No taxation without representation.              *18th c.*
 4 Nose to the grindstone, To keep one's.           *16th c.*
 5 Nothing costs so much as what is given us.   *Fuller, 1732*
 6 Nothing for nothing.                             *18th c.*
 7 Nothing is certain but uncertainty.              *Latin*
 8 Nothing is ours, but time.                   *Fuller, 1732*
 9 Nothing questioneth, He that/ nothing learneth.   *16th c.*
10 Nothing seek, nothing find.                      *16th c.*
11 Nothing succeeds like success.                   *French*
12 Nothing that is violent is permanent.            *16th c.*
13 Nothing venture, nothing win.                    *15th c.*
14 Nowadays truth is the greatest news.        *Fuller, 1732*

15 Obedience is much more seen in little things than in great.
                                                *Fuller, 1732*
16 Oil upon the waters, To pour.                    *19th c.*
17 Old as the hills, As.                            *19th c.*
18 Old friends and old wine are best.          *Herbert, 1640*

19 Old head on young shoulders, An.         *Clarke, 1639*

20 Old poacher makes a good game-keeper, An.     *14th c.*

21 Once bitten, twice shy.         *19th c.*

22 One foot in the grave, To have         *16th c.*

23 Opportunity makes the thief.         *13th c.*

24 Ounce of discretion is worth a pound of learning, An.   *17th c.*

25 Out of sight, out of mind.         *13th c.*

26 P's and Q's, To mind one's.         *17th c.*

27 Painters and poets have leave to lie.         *16th c.*

28 Past cure, past care.         *16th c.*

29 Patience is a flower that grows not in everyone's garden.
        *Ray, 1670*

30 Patience, money and time bring all things to pass.
        *Herbert, 1640*

31 Pay a person in his own coin, To.         *16th c.*

32 Pay through the nose, To.         *17th c.*

33 Pays the piper may call the tune, He who.     *17th c.*

34 Peace makes plenty.         *15th c.*

35 Penny and penny laid up will be many.     *Clarke, 1639*

36 Penny for your thoughts, A.         *Heywood, 1546*

37 Penny wise, pound foolish.         *17th c.*

38 Pension never enriched a young man.     *Herbert, 1640*

39 Pigs might fly, but they are very unlikely birds.     *19th c.*

40 Pillar to post, From.         *15th c.*

41 Plain as a pike-staff, As.         *16th c.*

42 Play first (or second) fiddle, To.         *19th c.*

43 Plays best (well) that wins, He.     *Heywood, 1555*

44 Pleased as Punch, As.         *19th c.*

45 Pleased ourselves, When we are/ we begin to please others.
        *Fuller, 1732*

46 Pleasure, There is more/ in loving than in being loved.
        *Fuller, 1732*

47 Pleasure, To overcome/ is the greatest pleasure.   *Fuller, 1732*

48 Pleasure of what we enjoy is lost by coveting more, The.
        *Fuller, 1732*

49 Poor as Job, As.         *14th c.*

50 Poor heart that never rejoices, It is a.     *19th c.*

51 Possession is nine points of the law. *Draxe, 1616*
52 Pot calls the kettle black, The. *17th c.*
53 Poverty breeds strife. *Ray, 1678*
54 Poverty is no sin. *Herbert, 1640*
55 Poverty is not a shame, but the being ashamed of it is.
*Fuller, 1732*
56 Practice makes perfect. *Latin*
57 Practise what you preach. *14th c.*
58 Praise makes good men better and bad men worse.
*Fuller, 1732.*
59 Preaches well that lives well, He. *17th c.*
60 Prevention is better than cure. *Latin*
61 Pride will have a fall. *16th c.*
62 Promises too much, He that/ means nothing. *Draxe, 1616*
63 Proof of the pudding is in the eating, The. *Camden, 1623*
64 Prospect is often better than possession. *Fuller, 1732*
65 Prosperity has damned more souls than all the devils together.
*Fuller, 1732*
66 Proud as Lucifer, As. *14th c.*
67 Proud as a peacock, As. *14th c.*
68 Put on one's thinking cap, To. *17th c.*
69 Pull down than to build, It is easier to. *16th c.*
70 Purse-strings are the most common ties of friendship, The.
*Fuller, 1732*
71 Put that in your pipe and smoke it. *19th c.*
72 Put your shoulder to the wheel. *17th c.*

73 Queen Anne is dead. *18th c.*
74 *Quos Deus vult perdere, prius dementat* – Whom God wishes to
destroy, he first makes mad. *Latin*

75 Rain before seven: fine before eleven. *19th c.*
76 Rain, rain, go to Spain: fair weather come again.
*Howell, 1659*
77 Rains but it pours, It never. *18th c.*
78 Rainy day, Lay it up for a. *16th c.*
79 Rats desert a sinking ship. *17th c.*
80 Red as a rose, As. *14th c.*
81 Red rag to a bull, Like a *16th c.*

82 Redemption from hell, There is no. *17th c.*

83 Religion an ill man is of, It matters not what. *Fuller, 1732*

84 Religion is the best armour in the world, but the worst cloak.
*Fuller, 1732*

85 Remedy for all things but death, There is a. *16th c.*

86 Repentance comes too late. *15th c.*

87 Resolves to deal with none but honest men, He that/ must leave
off dealing. *Fuller, 1732*

88 Respects not is not respected, He that. *Herbert, 1640*

89 Revenge is sweet. *16th c.*

90 Revenge never repairs an injury. *Fuller, 1732*

91 Rich men have no faults. *Fuller, 1732*

92 Rich that is satisfied, He is. *Fuller, 1732*

93 Riches of the mind only that make a man rich and happy, It is.
*Fuller, 1732*

94 Ridicule than commend, It is easier to. *Fuller, 1732*

95 Right as rain, As. *19th c.*

96 Roads lead to Rome, All. *14th c.*

97 Roar like a bull, To. *16th c.*

98 Rob Peter to pay Paul, To. *14th c.*

99 Rod for his own back, He makes a. *14th c.*

1 Rolling stone gathers no moss, A. *Heywood, 1546*

2 Rome was not built in a day. *Latin*

3 Room to swing a cat, Not. *18th c.*

4 Rope enough and he'll hang himself, Give a thief. *Ray, 1670*

5 Rough with the smooth, Take the. *15th c.*

6 Rule the roast (roost), To. *15th c.*

7 Rule youth well, for age will rule itself. *Fergusson, 1641*

8 Run with the hare and hunt with the hounds, To.
*Heywood, 1546*

9 Sadness and gladness succeed each other. *Clarke, 1639*

10 Sail near the wind, To. *19th c.*

11 Same boat, To be all in the. *16th c.*

12 Sauce for the goose is sauce for the gander, What is.
*Ray, 1670*

13 Save one's bacon, To. *17th c.*

14 Say Bo(o) to a goose, He cannot. *16th c.*

15 Say no ill of the year till it be past.               *Herbert, 1640*
16 Saying is one thing and doing another.               *Heywood, 1550*
17 Scot-free, To go.                                              *16th c.*
18 Scratch, To come up to (the).                              *19th c.*
19 Scratch my back and I'll scratch yours, You.         *17th c.*
20 Screw loose somewhere, There is a.                    *19th c.*
21 Second thoughts are best.                                    *Latin*
22 See Naples and die.                                           *Italian*
23 See the wood for the trees, You cannot.          *Heywood, 1546*
24 See what we shall see, We shall.                        *19th c.*
25 Seeing is believing.                                    *Clarke, 1639*
26 Seeks trouble, He that/ never misses.            *Herbert, 1640*
27 Self-praise is no recommendation.                     *17th c.*
28 Self-preservation is the first law of nature.        *17th c.*
29 Set the Thames on fire, To.                              *18th c.*
30 Share and share alike.                                     *17th c.*
31 Shoe pinches, To know where the.                     *14th c.*
32 Short and sweet.                                            *16th c.*
33 Shortest answer is doing, The.                    *Herbert, 1640*
34 Short life and a merry one, A.                          *17th c.*
35 Short pleasure, long lament.                            *15th c.*
36 Sickness is better than sadness.                   *Fuller, 1732*
37 Sight for sore eyes, A.                                    *19th c.*
38 Silence gives consent.                                    *14th c.*
39 Silk purse out of a sow's ear, You cannot make a    *16th c.*
40 Six hours' sleep for a man, seven for a woman, and eight for
   a fool.                                                         *18th c.*
41 Six of one and half a dozen of the other.            *19th c.*
42 Sixes and sevens, To be at.                              *14th c.*
43 Skin of one's teeth, By the.                             *16th c.*
44 Slept well, He hath/ that remembers not he hath slept ill.
                                                            *Fuller, 1732.*
45 Slippery as an eel, As.                                    *15th c.*
46 Slow but sure.                                          *Clarke, 1639*
47 Small profits and quick returns.                       *19th c.*
48 Smell a rat, To.                                            *16th c.*
49 Snake in the grass, There is a.                          *Latin*

50 Sneezed at, Not to be. *19th c.*

51 So far, so good. *Kelly, 1721*

52 Soberness conceals, What/ drunkenness reveals. *Latin*

53 Some are wise and some are otherwise. *Howell, 1659*

54 Soon as a man is born he begins to die, As. *Latin*

55 Soon got, soon spent. *Heywood, 1546*

56 Soon hot, soon cold. *15th c.*

57 Soon ripe, soon rotten. *Latin*

58 Sorrow comes unsent for. *Latin*

59 Soup and love, Of/ the first is the best. *Spanish*

60 Sour grapes can ne'er make sweet wine. *Fuller, 1732*

61 Speak not of my debts unless you mean to pay them.
   *Herbert, 1640*

62 Speak well of your friend, of your enemy say nothing. *18th c.*

63 Speak when you are spoken to. *16th c.*

64 Speaks ill of his wife, He that/ dishonours himself. *Fuller, 1732*

65 Speech is silver, silence is golden. *Persian*

66 Spick and span. *16th c.*

67 Split hairs, To. *16th c.*

68 Spoke in one's wheel, To put a. *17th c.*

69 Sprat to catch a mackerel (whale), To throw a. *19th c.*

70 Spur a free horse, Do not. *Latin*

71 Spur of the moment, On the *19th c.*

72 Stepmother, Take heed of a/ the very name of her sufficeth.
   *Herbert, 1651*

73 Stew (fry) in one's own juice (grease), To. *14th c.*

74 Sticks and stones may break my bones, but words will never
   hurt me. *19th c.*

75 Stiff as a poker. *18th c.*

76 Stiff upper lip, To keep a. *19th c.*

77 Still waters run deep. *14th c.*

78 Sting is in the tail, The. *16th c.*

79 Sting of a reproach is the truth of it, The. *Fuller, 1732*

80 Stir up a hornets' nest, To. *Latin*

81 Stitch in time saves nine, A. *Fuller, 1732*

82 Stone that lieth not in your way need not offend you, The.
   *Fuller, 1732*

83 Storm in a tea-cup, A. *19th c.*

84 Straight trees have crooked roots.                          *16th c.*

85 Strike while the iron is hot.                               *14th c.*

86 Subtlety is better than force.                         *Draxe, 1616*

87 Sun shines upon all alike, The.                             *16th c.*

88 Sure as eggs is eggs, As.                                   *17th c.*

89 Swallow, One/ does not make a summer.                        *Greek*

90 Sweet discourse makes short days and nights.      *Herbert, 1640*

91 Sweet tooth, To have a.                                     *16th c.*

92 Swine, women, and bees cannot be turned.            *Ray, 1678*

93 Take a farthing away from a thousand pounds, it will be a
   thousand pounds no longer.                                  *18th c.*

94 Take a leaf out of one's book, To.                          *19th c.*

95 Take away my good name and take away my life.      *Ray, 1670*

96 Take care of the pence and the pounds will take care of themselves.                                                     *18th c.*

97 Take one down a peg or two, To.                             *16th c.*

98 Take the bull by the horns, To.                             *19th c.*

99 Take the gilt off the gingerbread, To.                      *19th c.*

 1 Take the law into one's own hands, To.                      *17th c.*

 2 Take the wind out of one's sails, To.                       *19th c.*

 3 Take things as you find them.                         *Lean, 1902*

 4 Tales out of school, To tell.                               *16th c.*

 5 Talk the hind leg off a donkey, To.                         *19th c.*

 6 Talk of the devil, and he is sure to appear.                *17th c.*

 7 Talk without thinking, To/ is to shoot without aiming.
                                                        *Fuller, 1732*

 8 Talkers, The greatest/ are (always) the least doers.        *16th c.*

 9 Talks to himself, He that/ speaks to a fool.          *Kelly, 1721*

10 Tarred with the same brush, All.                            *19th c.*

11 Taste of the kitchen is better than the smell, The          *19th c.*

12 Teach an old dog tricks, It is hard to.                     *16th c.*

13 Teach your grandmother to suck eggs.                        *18th c.*

14 Teacheth ill, He/ who teacheth all.                 *Howell, 1659*

15 Tell that to the Marines.                                   *19th c.*

16 Tell the truth and shame the devil.                         *16th c.*

17 Tells his wife news, He that/is but newly married.      *Herbert,
                                                                 1640*

18 *Tempus fugit* – Time flies. *Latin*
19 Tenterhooks, To be on. *18th c.*
20 There's many a slip 'twixt the cup and the lip. *Greek*
21 Thick as thieves, As. *19th c.*
22 Thief to catch a thief, Set a. *Ray, 1670*
23 Thin end of the wedge is to be feared. The. *19th c.*
24 Things are difficult before they are easy, All. *Fuller, 1732*
25 Things at the worst will mend. *17th c.*
26 Think today and speak tomorrow. *Bohn, 1855*
27 Think well of all men. *Howell, 1659*
28 Think with the wise, but talk with the vulgar. *Greek*
29 Thinking is very far from knowing. *18th c.*
30 Though I say it that should not. *16th c.*
31 Thought is free. *14th c.*
32 Thousand pounds of law, In a/ there's not an ounce of love.
   *Ray, 1670*
33 Threadneedle Street, The old lady of. *19th c.*
34 Threatened men live long. *16th c.*
35 Three may keep counsel if two be away. *Heywood, 1546*
36 Three women and a goose make a market. *Italian*
37 Throw good money after bad, To. *19th c.*
38 Time and thinking tame the strongest grief. *Ray, 1670*
39 Time and tide wait for no man. *16th c.*
40 Time for all things, There is a. *14th c.*
41 Time like the present, No. *18th c.*
42 Today, One/ is worth two tomorrows. *17th c.*
43 Tomorrow never comes. *Ray, 1678*
44 Tomorrow is a new day. *16th c.*
45 Tongue, One/ is enough for a woman. *Ray, 1678*
46 Tongue is not steel, yet it cuts, The. *Heywood, 1546*
47 Tongue of idle people is never idle, The. *Fuller, 1732*
48 Too big for one's boots, To be. *19th c.*
49 Too clever by half. *19th c.*
50 Too many cooks spoil the broth. *16th c.*
51 Touch him with a pair of tongs, I would not. *Ray, 1670*
52 Touch wood. *20th c.*

53 *Tout passe, tout casse, tout lasse.* Everything passes, everything perishes, everything palls. *French*
54 Translators, traitors. *Italian*
55 Travels far, He that/ knows much. *Clarke, 1639*
56 Tread on a worm and it will turn. *Heywood, 1546*
57 Tree is known by its fruit, A. *14th c.*
58 True blue will never stain. *Howell, 1659*
59 True word is spoken in jest, Many a. *14th c.*
60 Trust not a new friend nor an old enemy. *Kelly, 1721*
61 Truth fears no colours. *Ray, 1678*
62 Truth is stranger than fiction. *19th c.*
63 Truth is the daughter of God. *Fuller, 1732*
64 Truth never grows old. *Fuller, 1732*
65 Truth, The/ the whole truth, and nothing but the truth. *17th c.*
66 Turn an honest penny, To. *Heywood, 1546*
67 Turn in his grave, To make a person. *19th c.*
68 Turn over a new leaf, To. *Heywood, 1546*
69 Turn the tables, To. *17th c.*
70 Turn up one's nose, To. *16th c.*
71 Turn up trumps, To. *17th c.*
72 Twist round one's little finger, To. *19th c.*
73 Two bites of a cherry, To make. *French*
74 Two black dots do not make a white. *Kelly, 1721*
75 Two can play at that game. *19th c.*
76 Two dogs strive for a bone, and a third runs away with it. *16th c.*
77 Two heads are better than one. *Heywood, 1546*
78 Two is company, three is none. *19th c.*
79 Two negatives make an affirmative. *16th c.*
80 Two sides to every question, There are. *19th c.*
81 Two strings to one's bow, To have. *15th c.*
82 Two to make a quarrel, It takes. *19th c.*
83 Two wrongs don't make a right. *19th c.*

84 Ugly as sin, As. *19th c.*
85 Uncertainty of the law, The glorious. *19th c.*
86 Under the blanket the black one is as good as the white. *Fuller, 1732*

87  Unforeseen (unexpected) that always happens, It is the.  *Latin*
88  Unity is strength.  *French*

89  Variety is pleasing.  *Greek*
90  Vengeance, The noblest/ is to forgive.  *16th c.*
91  Venom to that of the tongue, There is no.  *Howell, 1659*
92  *Verbum sapienti sat est* – A word is enough to the wise.  *Latin*
93  Virtue dwells not in the tongue but in the heart.  *Fuller, 1732*
94  Virtue is its own reward.  *Latin*
95  Virtue never grows old.  *Herbert, 1640*
96  Virtue of necessity, Make a.  *Latin*
97  Vows made in storms are forgotten in calm.  *Fuller, 1732*

98  Wait and see.  *19th c.*
99  Walls have ears.  *17th c.*
 1  Want a thing well done, If you/ do it yourself.  *Draxe, 1616*
 2  Want of wit is worse than want of wealth.  *Kelly, 1721*
 3  War begins, When/ hell opens.  *Herbert, 1651*
 4  Wars bring scars.  *Clarke, 1639*
 5  Warm the cockles of the heart, To.  *17ih c.*
 6  Wash dirty linen in public, To.  *19th c.*
 7  Wash your hands often, your feet seldom, and your head never.
  *Ray, 1670*
 8  Waste not, want not.  *18th c.*
 9  Watched pot never boils, A.  *19th c.*
10  Water in a sieve, To carry.  *Latin*
11  Water off a duck's back, Like.  *19th c.*
12  Water (blood) out of a stone, To get.  *Latin*
13  Way to an Englishman's heart is through his stomach, The
  *19th c.*
14  Way to be safe is never to be secure, The.  *Fuller, 1732*
.15  Weakest goes to the wall, The.  *16th c.*
16  Wealth, The greatest/ is contentment with a little.  *Ray, 1670*
17  Wear one's heart on one's sleeve, To.  *17th c.*
18  Wear the breeches (pants), To.  *15th c.*
19  Wedlock is a padlock.  *Ray, 1678*
20  Welcome is the best cheer.  *Greek*
21  Well begun is half done.  *Latin*

22 Wet one's whistle, To.                                              *14th c.*

23 What can't be cured must be endured.                                *14th c.*

24 What is worth doing is worth doing well.                            *18th c.*

25 What's yours is mine, and what's mine is my own.                    *18th c.*

26 Wheels within wheels, There are.                                    *17th c.*

27 When in doubt, leave out.                                           *20th c.*

28 When the cat is away the mice will play.                            *16th c.*

29 Whispering, Where there is/ there is lying.                         *Ray, 1678*

30 Widows are always rich.                                             *Ray, 1678*

31 Wife, He that has a/ has a master.                                  *Kelly, 1721*

32 Wild oats, To sow one's.                                            *16th c.*

33 Will, Where there's a/ there's a way.                               *Herbert, 1640*

34 Will, Where there's a/ there's trouble.                             *20th c.*

35 Wine and wenches empty men's purses.                                *Clarke, 1639*

36 Wine in the bottle does not quench thirst, The.                     *Herbert, 1640*

37 Wine in, truth out.                                                 *16th c.*

38 Wisdom like silence, No.                                            *Greek*

39 Wise child that knows its own father, It is a.                      *16th c.*

40 Wise man, He is not a/ who cannot play the fool on occasion.
                                                                       *16th c.*

41 Wise men learn by other men's mistakes; fools by their own.
                                                                       *Latin*

42 Wish is father to the thought, The.                                 *Latin*

43 Wive and thrive both in a year, It is hard to.                      *15th c.*

44 Wives must be had, be they good or bad.                             *Clarke, 1639*

45 Wolf from the door, To keep the.                                    *Heywood, 1546*

46 Woman conceals what she knows not, A.                               *16th c.*

47 Woman's work is never done, A.                                      *16th c.*

48 Women and geese, Where there are/ there wants no noise.
                                                                       *Draxe, 1616*

49 Women are always in extremes.                                       *Clarke, 1639*

50 Women are necessary evils.                                          *16th c.*

51 Women look in their glass, The more/ the less they look to their
   house.                                                              *Herbert, 1640*

52 Women must have their wills while they live, because they make
   none when they die.                                                 *17th c.*

53 Women must have the last word.                                      *16th c.*

54 Wonders will never cease.                                           *18th c.*

55 Wool over a person's eyes, To pull the      *19th c.*

56 Work and no play makes Jack a dull boy, All.     *Ray, 1670*

57 World and his wife, All the     *18th c.*

58 Worse things happen at sea.     *19th c.*

59 Worth his weight in gold, He is.     *16th c.*

60 Worth of a thing is best known by the want, The.     *17th c.*

61 Wrong never comes right.     *19th c.*

62 Young man should not marry yet, A/an old man not at all.
    *16th c.*

63 Young men may die, old men must.     *16th c.*

64 Young men think old men fools, and old men know young men
to be so.     *16th c.*

65 Young saint, old devil.     *15th c.*

66 Youth and age will never agree.     *16th c.*

67 Youth will be served.     *19th c.*

68 Youth will have its course (or swing, or fling).     *16th c.*

69 Zeal is fit only for wise men, but is found mostly in fools.
    *Fuller, 1732*

70 Zeal, when it is a virtue, is a dangerous one.     *Fuller, 1732*

71 Zeal without knowledge is fire without light.     *Fuller, 1732*

## PUDNEY, John, 1908–1977

72 Do not despair
For Johnny head-in-air;
He sleeps as sound
As Johnny underground.     *For Johnny*

## PUNCH

73 Advice to persons about to marry. – 'Don't.'     *Vol. 8, Page 1,
1845*

74 You pays your money and you takes your choice.     *Vol. 10,
16, 1846*

75 What is better than Presence of Mind in a Railway accident? –
Absence of Body.     *Vol. 16, 231, 1849*

76 Never do today what you can put off till tomorrow.     *Vol. 17,
241, 1849*

77 What is Matter? – Never Mind.
What is Mind? – No Matter.     *Vol. 29, 19, 1855*

78 Why are Trafalgar Square fountains like Government Clerks? – Because they play from 10 till 4. *Vol. 35, 21, 1858*

79 Mun, a had no' been the-erre abune two hours when – bang – went saxpence!!! *Vol. 55, 235, 1868*

80 Nothink for nothink 'ere, and precious little for sixpence.
*Vol. 57, 152, 1869*

81 Go directly – see what she's doing, and tell her she mustn't.
*Vol. 63, 202, 1872*

82 Here was an old owl liv'd in an oak,
The more he heard the less he spoke:
The less he spoke, the more he heard,
O, if men were all like that wise bird. *Vol. 68, 155, 1875*

83 I never read books – I *write* them. *Vol. 74, 210, 1878*

84 I used your soap two years ago: since then I have used no other.
*Vol. 86, 197, 1884*

85 Nearly all our best men are dead! Carlyle, Tennyson, Browning, George Eliot! I'm not feeling very well myself! *Vol. 104, 210, 1893*

86 I'm afraid you've got a bad egg, Mr Jones.
Oh no, my Lord, I assure you! Parts of it are excellent.
*Vol. 109, 222, 1895*

87 Look here, Steward, if this is coffee, I want tea; but if this is tea, then I wish for coffee. *Vol. 123, 44, 1902*

## QUESNAY, François, 1694–1774

88 *Laissez faire, laissez passer.* – No interference, and complete freedom of movement. [*Of Government interference*]
*Attributed*

## RABELAIS, François, 1494?–1553?

89 *L'appétit vient en mangeant.* Appetite comes with eating.
*Gargantua, 1, 5*

90 *Tirez le rideau, la farce est jouée.* Ring down the curtain, the farce is over. *Last words, attributed*

91 *Je m'en vais chercher un grand peut-être.* I am going in search of a great perhaps. *Last words, attributed*

## RACINE, Jean, 1639–1699

92 *Elle flotte, elle hésite; en un mot, elle est femme.* She wavers, she hesitates; in a word, she is a woman. MATHAN *Athalie, Act 3, Scene 3*

**RALEIGH, Sir Walter, 1552?–1618**

93 Even such is Time, that takes in trust
    Our youth, our joys, our all we have,
And pays us but with age and dust;
    Who in the dark and silent grave,
When we have wandered all our ways,
Shuts up the story of our days;
But from this earth, this grave, this dust,
My God shall raise me up, I trust. *Written the night before*
                                        *his death*

94 Give me my scallop-shell of quiet,
    My staff of faith to walk upon,
My scrip of joy, immortal diet,
    My bottle of salvation,
My gown of glory, hope's true gage,
And thus I'll take my pilgrimage. *The Passionate. Man's*
                                        *Pilgrimage*

95 So the heart be right, it is no matter which way the head lies.
                    *On laying his head on the block*

96 If all the world and love were young,
And truth in every shepherd's tongue,
These pretty pleasures might me move
To live with thee, and be thy love. *The Nymph's Reply to*
                          *the Passionate Shepherd*

**RALEIGH, Sir Walter Alexander, 1861–1922**

97 I wish I loved the Human Race;
I wish I loved its silly face;
I wish I liked the way it walks;
I wish I liked the way it talks;
And when I'm introduced to one
I wish I thought *What Jolly fun*! *The Wishes of an Elderly*
                                        *Man*

**RANKIN, Jeremiah Eames, 1828–1904**

98 God be with you till we meet again. *Hymn*

**RANSOME, Arthur, 1884–1967**

99 Grab a chance and you won't be sorry for a might-have-been.
    COMMANDER WALKER *We didn't Mean to Go to Sea*

**READE, Charles, 1814–1884**

1 *Courage, mon ami, le diable est mort.* Courage, my friend, the
devil is dead. *The Cloister and the Hearth, Ch. 24*

2 Make 'em laugh; make 'em cry; make 'em wait.      *Advice to*
                                                                    *young author on writing novels*

**REED, Henry, 1914–**

3 Today we have naming of parts. Yesterday,
   We had daily cleaning. And tomorrow morning
   We shall have what to do after firing. But today,
   Today we have naming of parts.      *Naming of Parts*

**REMARQUE, Erich Maria, 1898–1970**

4 *Im Westen nichts Neues.* All Quiet on the Western Front.
                                                                    *Title of Novel*

**REYNOLDS, Frederic, 1764–1841**

5 [*Taking out his watch*] How goes the enemy?   ENNUI
                                                                    *The Dramatist, Act 1*

**REYNOLDS, Sir Joshua, 1723–1792**

6 If you have great talents, industry will improve them: if you have
   but moderate abilities, industry will supply their deficiency.
                                                                    *Discourses, 2*

**RHODES, Cecil John, 1853–1902**

7 So little done, so much to do.      *Last words*
8 Educational relations make the strongest tie.      *Will, endowing*
                                                                    *Rhodes Scholarships*

**RICE, Grantland, 1880–1954**

9 For when the one Great Scorer comes
        To write against your name,
   He marks – not that you won or lost –
        But how you played the game.      *Alumnus Football*

**RIPLEY, Robert Leroy, 1893–1949**

10 Believe it or not.      *Title of newspaper feature*

**ROCHE, Sir Boyle, 1743–1807**

11 My love for England and Ireland is so great that I would have
    the two sisters embrace like one brother.      *Reported in Irish*
                                                                    *Parliamentary Register, 11, 294*

12 What has posterity done for us?      *Speech in Irish Parliament,*
                                                                    *1780*

13 Mr Speaker, I smell a rat; I see him forming in the air and darkening the sky; but I'll nip him in the bud. *Attributed*

## ROCHEFOUCAULD, Duc de la, 1613–1680

14 We have all enough strength to bear the misfortunes of others.
*Les Maximes, 19*

15 Everyone complains of his memory, but no one complains of his judgment. *Ib, 89*

16 The intellect is always fooled by the heart. *Ib, 102*

17 Hypocrisy is the homage paid by vice to virtue. *Ib, 218*

18 The height of cleverness is to conceal one's cleverness. *Ib, 245*

19 In the misfortunes of our best friends, we find something that is not displeasing. *Maximes supprimées, 583*

## ROCHEFOUCAULD-LIANCOURT, Duc de La, 1747–1827

20 LOUIS XVI: *C'est une révolte?* Is it a revolt?
THE DUKE: *Non, sire, c'est une révolution.* No, sire it is a revolution. *On hearing of the Fall of the Bastille, 1789*

## ROCHESTER, John Wilmot, 2nd Earl of, 1647–1680

21 Here lies our sovereign lord the King,
    Whose word no man relies on;
He never said a foolish thing,
    Nor ever did a wise one. *Epitaph on Charles II*

## ROGERS, E. W., 1864–1913

22 Ev'ry member of the force
Has a watch and chain, of course;
If you want to know the time,
Ask a P'liceman. *Ask a P'liceman*

## ROGERS, Samuel, 1763–1855

23 When a new book is published, read an old one. *Attributed*

24 Think nothing done while aught remains to do. *Human Life, 49*

25 Sheridan was listened to with such attention that you might have heard a pin drop. *Table Talk*

## ROLAND, Madame Marie Jeanne Philipon, 1754–1793

26 *O Liberté! O Liberté! que de crimes on commet en ton nom!* O liberty, liberty, what crimes are committed in your name!
*Remark from the scaffold, on viewing the Statue of Liberty*

## ROOSEVELT, Franklin Delano, 1882–1945

27 I pledge you, I pledge myself, to a new deal for the American
   people.            *Speech accepting nomination for Presidency,*
                    *Democratic National Convention, Chicago, 2 July*
                                                            *1932*

28 The only thing we have to fear is fear itself.     *First Inaugural*
                                          *Address, 4 March 1933*

29 In the field of world policy, I would dedicate this nation to the
   policy of a good neighbour.                                *Ib*

30 I see one third of a nation ill-housed, ill-clad, ill-nourished.
                    *Second Inaugural Address, 20 Jan. 1937*

31 A radical is a man with both feet firmly planted in the air.
                              *Broadcast, 26 Oct. 1939*

32 We look forward to a world founded upon four essential human
   freedoms. The first is freedom of speech and expression –
   everywhere in the world. The second is freedom of every person
   to worship God in his own way – everywhere in the world. The
   third is freedom from want . . . everywhere in the world. The
   fourth is freedom from fear . . . anywhere in the world.
                        *Speech to Congress, 6 Jan. 1941*

33 We all know that books burn – yet we have the greater knowledge that books cannot be killed by fire. People die, but books
   never die. No man and no force can abolish memory . . . In this
   war, we know, books are weapons.      *Message to American*
                    *Booksellers Association, 23 April 1942*

34 More than an end to war, we want an end to the beginnings of
   all wars.      *Speech written for broadcast, 13 April 1945 (the*
                                          *day after his death)*


## ROOSEVELT, Theodore, 1858–1919

35 I wish to preach, not the doctrine of ignoble ease, but the
   doctrine of the strenuous life.     *Speech, Chicago, 10 April*
                                                            *1899*

36 The first requisite of a good citizen in this Republic of ours is that
   he shall be able and willing to pull his weight.     *Speech, New*
                                          *York, 11 Nov. 1902*

37 A man who is good enough to shed his blood for his country is
   good enough to be given a square deal afterwards. More than
   that no man is entitled to, and less than that no man shall have.
                *Speech, Springfield, Illinois, 4 July 1903*

38 There is no room in this country for hyphenated Americanism.
                    *Speech, New York, 12 Oct. 1915*

39 No man is justified in doing evil on the ground of expediency.
*The Strenuous Life*

**ROSEBERY, Archibald Philip Primrose, 5th Earl of, 1847–1929**

40 The Empire is a Commonwealth of Nations.   *Speech,*
*Adelaide, 18 Jan. 1884*

41 It is beginning to be hinted that we are a nation of amateurs.
*Rectorial Address, Glasgow, 16 Nov. 1900*

**ROSS, Alan Strode Campbell, 1907–1980**

42 U and Non-U, An Essay in Sociological Linguistics.   *Title of*
*Essay included in Noblesse Oblige, 1956*

**ROSSETTI, Christina Georgina, 1830–1894**

43 In the bleak mid-winter
   Frosty wind made moan,
Earth stood hard as iron,
   Water like a stone;
Snow had fallen, snow on snow,
   Snow on snow,
In the bleak mid-winter,
   Long ago.   *Mid-Winter*

44 Remember me when I am gone away,
   Gone far away into the silent land.   *Remember*

45 Better by far you should forget and smile
   Than that you should remember and be sad.   *Ib*

46 'Does the road wind up-hill all the way?'
   'Yes, to the very end.'
'Will the day's journey take the whole long day?'
   'From morn to night, my friend.'   *Up-Hill*

47 When I am dead, my dearest
   Sing no sad songs for me.   *When I am Dead*

48 And if thou wilt, remember,
   And if thou wilt, forget.   *Ib*

**ROSSETTI, Dante Gabriel, 1828–1882**

49 A sonnet is a moment's monument, –
Memorial from the Soul's eternity
To one dead deathless hour.   *The House of Life, Part 1,*
*Introduction*

50 The hour when you too learn that all is vain
   And that Hope sows what Love shall never reap.
*Ib, 44, Cloud and Wind*

51      My name is Might-Have-Been;
I am also called No-More, Too-Late, Farewell.   *The House of*
*Life, Part 2, 97. A Superscription*

52 Unto the man of yearning, thought
And aspiration, to do nought
Is in itself almost an act.                            *Soothsay*

53 I have been here before.
But when or how I cannot tell:
I know the grass beyond the door,
The sweet keen smell,
The sighing sound, the lights around the shore.        *Sudden*
*Light, 1*


**ROUGET DE LISLE, Claude Joseph, 1760–1836**

54 *Allons, enfants, de la patrie,*
*Le jour de gloire est arrivé.*
Come, children of our native land, the day of glory has arrived.
*La Marseillaise*


**ROUSSEAU, Jean Jacques, 1712–1778**

55 *L'homme est né libre, et partout il est dans les fers.* Man was born
free and everywhere he is in chains.        *Du Contrat Social,*
*Ch. 1*


**ROUTH, Martin Joseph, 1755–1854**

56 Always verify your references.                       *Attributed*


**'RED ROWLEY', 20th century**

57 Mademoiselle from Armenteers,
Hasn't been kissed for forty years,
Hinky dinky, parley-voo.     *Mademoiselle from Armentières*


**RUNYON, Damon, 1884–1946**

58 More than somewhat.                                   *Passim*


**RUSKIN, John, 1819–1900**

59 All travelling becomes dull in exact proportion to its rapidity.
*Modern Painters*

60 If a book is worth reading, it is worth buying.   *Sesame and*
*Lilies*

61 Remember that the most beautiful things in the world are the
most useless; peacocks and lilies for instance.   *The Stones of*
*Venice*

62 The purest and most thoughtful minds are those which love colour the most. *The Stones of Venice*

63 Fine art is that in which the hand, the head, and the heart of man go together. *The Two Paths*

64 There is no wealth but life. *Unto this Last*

**RUSSELL, John, 1st Earl, 1792–1878**

65 If peace cannot be maintained with honour, it is no longer peace. *Speech, Greenock, 19 Sept. 1853*

**RUSSELL, Bertrand Arthur William, 3rd Earl, 1872–1970**

66 Men are capable, not only of fear and hate, but also of hope and benevolence. If the populations of the world can be brought to see and to realize in imagination the hell to which hate and fear must condemn them on the one hand, and, on the other, the comparative heaven which hope and benevolence can create by means of new skills, the choice should not be difficult, and our self-tormented species should allow itself a life of joy such as the past has never known. *Common Sense and Nuclear Warfare, 1959*

67 Mathematics possesses not only truth, but supreme beauty – a beauty cold and austere, like that of sculpture. *The Study of Mathematics*

**RUTLAND, John, 7th Duke of, 1818–1906**

68 Let wealth and commerce, laws and learning die,
But leave us still our old nobility. *England's Trust, 3, 227*

**'SAKI' (Hector Hugh Munro), 1870–1916**

69 He's simply got the instinct for being unhappy highly developed. *Chronicles of Clovis, The Match-Maker*

70 The cook was a good cook, as cooks go; and as cooks go she went. *Reginald on Besetting Sins*

**SALINGER, Jerome David, 1919–**

71 If you really want to hear about it, the first thing you'll probably want to know is where I was born, and what my lousy childhood was like, and how my parents were occupied and all before they had me, and all that David Copperfield kind of crap, but I don't feel like going into it. *The Catcher in the Rye, opening words*

**SALISBURY, Robert Cecil, 3rd Marquis of, 1830–1903**

72 By office boys for office boys.  *Remark about the Daily Mail*

**SALLUST, 86–34 B.C.**

73 *Idem velle atque idem nolle, ea demum firma amicitia est.* To like and dislike the same things, that is indeed true friendship.
*Catiline, 20*

74 *Pro patria, pro liberis, pro aris atque focis suis.* On behalf of their country, their children, their altars, and their hearths.  *Ib, 59*

**SAMUEL, Herbert Louis, 1st Viscount, 1870–1963**

75 It takes two to make a marriage a success and only one a failure.
*A Book of Quotations*

76 A truism is on that account none the less true.  *Ib*

**SANDBURG, Carl, 1878–1967**

77 The fog comes
on little cat feet.
It sits looking
over the harbor and city
on silent haunches
and then moves on.  *Fog*

78 Pile the bodies high at Austerlitz and Waterloo.
Shovel them under and let me work –
I am the grass; I cover all.  *Grass*

79 Look out how you use proud words,
When you let proud words go, it is not easy to call them back.
*Primer Lesson*

80 Homestead, Braddock, Birmingham, they make their steel with men,
Smoke and blood is the mix of steel.  *Smoke and Steel*

**SARGENT, Epes, 1813–1880**

81 A life on the ocean wave,
A home on the rolling deep.  *A Life on the Ocean Wave*

**SASSOON, Siegfried, 1886–1967**

82 And when the war is done and youth stone dead
I'd toddle safely home and die – in bed.  *Base Details*

83 Everyone suddenly burst out singing.  *Everyone Sang*

**SAYERS, Henry, 1855–1932**

84 Ta-ra-ra-boom-de-ay!                    *Title of song*

**SCHILLER, Friedrich von, 1759–1805**

85 *Alle Menschen werden Brüder Wo dein sanfter Flügel weilt.* In the shade of your soft wings, all men will be brothers.
*An die Freude*

86 *Die Weltgeschichte ist das Weltgericht.* World history is the world's judgment.                    *Lecture, Jena, 26 May 1789*

**SCHNECKENBURGER, Max, 1819–1849**

87 *Die Wacht am Rhein.* The Watch on the Rhine.    *Title of song*

**SCOTT, Charles Prestwich, 1846–1932**

88 Neither in what it gives, nor in what it does not give, nor in the mode of presentation, must the unclouded face of truth suffer wrong. Comment is free but facts are sacred.    *Manchester Guardian, 6 May 1926*

**SCOTT, Robert Falcon, 1868–1912**

89 Great God! this is an awful place.    [*The South Pole*] *Journal, 17 Jan. 1912*

90 For God's sake look after our people.    *Ib, 25 March 1912*

91 Had we lived, I should have had a tale to tell of the hardihood, endurance, and courage of my companions which would have stirred the hearts of every Englishman. These rough notes and our dead bodies must tell the tale.    *Message to the Public*

**SCOTT, Sir Walter, 1771–1832**

92 Come fill up my cup, come fill up my can,
Come saddle your horses, and call up your men;
Come open the West Port, and let me gang free,
And it's room for the bonnets of Bonny Dundee.
*Bonny Dundee, The Doom of Devorgoil, 2, 3*

93 But answer came there none.    *Bridal of Triermain, 3, 10*

94 The stag at eve had drunk his fill,
Where danced the moon on Monan's rill.    *The Lady of the Lake, 1, 1*

95 Forward and frolic glee was there,
The will to do, the soul to dare.    *Ib, 1, 21*

96 Yet seem'd that tone, and gesture bland,
Less used to sue than to command.    *Ib*

97 Soldier, rest! thy warfare o'er,
   Sleep the sleep that knows not breaking;
Dream of battled fields no more,
   Days of danger, nights of waking. *The Lady of the Lake, 1, 31*

98 Like the dew on the mountain,
   Like the foam on the river,
Like the bubble on the fountain,
   Thou art gone, and for ever! *Ib, 3, 16*

99 The way was long, the wind was cold,
The Minstrel was infirm and old;
His wither'd cheek, and tresses grey,
Seem'd to have known a better day.
   *The Lay of the Last Minstrel, Introduction, 1*

1 If thou would'st view fair Melrose aright,
   Go visit it by the pale moonlight. *Ib, 2, 1*

2 Love rules the court, the camp, the grove,
And men below, and saints above;
For love is heaven, and heaven is love. *Ib, 3, 2*

3 Call it not vain; they do not err,
   Who say, that when the Poet dies,
Mute Nature mourns her worshipper,
   And celebrates his obsequies. *Ib, 5, 1*

4 True love's the gift which God has given
To man alone beneath the heaven. *Ib, 5, 13*

5 Breathes there the man, with soul so dead,
Who never to himself hath said,
   This is my own, my native land! *Ib, 6, 1*

6 The wretch, concentrated all in self,
Living, shall forfeit fair renown,
And, doubly dying, shall go down
To the vile dust, from whence he sprung,
Unwept, unhonour'd, and unsung. *Ib, 6, 1*

7 That day of wrath, that dreadful day,
When heaven and earth shall pass away. *Ib, 6, 31, Hymn for the Dead*

8 November's sky is chill and drear,
November's leaf is red and sear. *Marmion, 1, Introduction*

9 And come he slow or come he fast,
It is but Death who comes at last. *Ib, 2, 30*

10 O, young Lochinvar is come out of the west,
Through all the wide Border his steed was the best. *Ib, 5, 12, Lochinvar*

11 So faithful in love, and so dauntless in war,
There never was Knight like the young Lochinvar.
*Marmion, 5, 12, Lochinvar*

12     And dar'st thou then
To beard the lion in his den,
   The Douglas in his hall?           *Ib, 6, 14*

13 O what a tangled web we weave,
When first we practise to deceive!      *Ib, 6, 17*

14 O Woman! in our hours of ease,
Uncertain, coy, and hard to please,
And variable as the shade,
By the light quivering aspen made;
When pain and anguish wring the brow,
A ministering angel thou!         *Ib, 6, 30*

15 He shook the fragment of his blade,
   And shouted 'Victory!
Charge, Chester, charge! On, Stanley, on!'
Were the last words of Marmion.     *Ib, 6, 32*

16 MRS. BERTRAM: That sounds like nonsense, my dear.
MR BERTRAM: May be so, my dear; but it may be very good law
for all that.          *Guy Mannering, Ch. 9*

17 The hour is come, but not the man.   *The Heart of Midlothian,*
*Ch. 4, Heading*

## SCOTT, William, 1st Baron Stowell, 1745–1836

18 A dinner lubricates business.   *Boswell's Life of Johnson, 1781*

## SEARS, Edmund Hamilton, 1810–1876

19 It came upon the midnight clear,
That glorious song of old.     *That Glorious Song of Old*

## SEEGER, Alan, 1888–1916

20 I have a rendezvous with Death
At some disputed barricade.   *I have a Rendezvous with Death*

## SELDEN, John, 1584–1654

21 Old friends are best. King James used to call for his old shoes;
they were easiest for his feet.      *Table Talk*

22 There is not anything in the world so much abused as this
sentence, Salus populi suprema lex esto.     *Ib*

23 Philosophy is nothing but discretion.     *Ib*

24 Preachers say, Do as I say, not as I do.     *Ib*

25 A king is a thing men have made for their own sakes, for
quietness' sake. Just as if in a family one man is appointed to buy
the meat.                                                    *Table Talk*

26 Every law is a contract between the king and the people, and
therefore to be kept.                                              *Ib*

**SELLAR, Walter Carruthers, 1898–1951, and YEATMAN,
Robert Julian, 1897–1968**

27 1066 And All That.                                    *Title of Book*

28 The Roman Conquest was, however, a *Good Thing*, since the
Britons were only natives at that time.         *1066 And All That,
Ch. 1*

29 Has it never occurred to you that the Romans *counted back-
wards*? (Be honest.)                                *Ib, Test Paper 1*

30 Finding, however, that he was not memorable, he very patrioti-
cally abdicated in favour of Henry IV, Part II.      *Ib, Ch. 26*

31 Shortly after this the cruel Queen died and a post-mortem
examination revealed the word 'CALLOUS' engraved on her
heart.                                                  *Ib, Ch. 32*

32 Williamanmary: England Ruled by an Orange.      *Ib, Heading
to Ch. 38*

33 Napoleon's armies used to march on their stomachs, shouting:
'Vive l'intérieur!'                                     *Ib, Ch. 48*

34 Do not on any account attempt to write on both sides of the
paper at once.                                       *Ib, Test Paper 5*

**SERVICE, Robert William, 1874–1958**

35 This is the Law of the Yukon, that only the strong shall thrive;
That surely the weak shall perish, and only the Fit survive.
*The Law of the Yukon*

36 When we, the Workers, all demand: 'What are we fighting
for?' . . .
Then, then we'll end that stupid crime, that devil's madness –
War.                                                        *Michael*

**SEWARD, William Henry, 1801–1872**

37 There is a higher law than the Constitution.         *Speech, US
Senate, 11 March 1850*

**SHADWELL, Thomas, 1642?–1692**

38 Words may be false and full of art,
Sighs are the natural language of the heart. CUPID      *Psyche
Act 3*

39 He's a wise man that marries a harlot; he's on the surest side.
   Who but an ass would marry an uncertainty? SIR POSITIVE-
   AT-ALL                              *The Sullen Lovers, Act 5*

40 I'll do't instantly, in the twinkling of a bed-staff. SIR SAMUEL
   HEARTY                                    *The Virtuoso, Act 1*


**SHAKESPEARE, William, 1564–1616**

**All's Well that Ends Well**

41          Love all, trust a few,
   Do wrong to none; be able for thine enemy
   Rather in power than use, and keep thy friend
   Under thy own life's key; be check'd for silence,
   But never tax'd for speech. COUNTESS OF ROUSILLON
                                    *Act 1, Scene 1, Line 57*

42 Our remedies oft in ourselves do lie,
   Which we ascribe to heaven. HELENA ·          *1, 1, 202*

43 My friends were poor, but honest. HELENA       *1, 3, 186*

44 A young man married is a man that's marr'd. PAROLLES
                                                *2, 3, 291*

45 No legacy is so rich as honesty. MARIANA       *3, 5, 12*

46 The web of our life is of a mingled yarn, good and ill together.
                                    2ND LORD *4, 3, 67*

47          Praising what is lost
   Makes the remembrance dear. KING OF FRANCE     *5, 3, 19*

48 Th' inaudible and noiseless foot of Time. KING OF FRANCE
                                                *5, 3, 41*


**Antony and Cleopatra**

49 The triple pillar of the world transform'd
   Into a strumpet's fool. PHILO                  *1, 1, 12*

50 There's beggary in the love that can be reckon'd. ANTONY
                                                *1, 1, 15*

51 The nature of bad news infects the teller. MESSENGER
                                                *1, 2, 92*

52 Where's my serpent of old Nile? CLEOPATRA      *1, 5, 25*

53          My salad days,
   When I was green in judgment. CLEOPATRA        *1, 5, 73*

54 The barge she sat in, like a burnish'd throne,
   Burn'd on the water. The poop was beaten gold;
   Purple the sails, and so perfumed that
   The winds were love-sick with them; the oars were silver,

Which to the tune of flutes kept stroke and made
The water which they beat to follow faster,
As amorous of their strokes. For her own person,
It beggar'd all description.   ENOBARBUS        *Antony and*
                                                *Cleopatra, 2, 2, 195*

55 Age cannot wither her, nor custom stale
   Her infinite variety. Other women cloy
   The appetites they feed, but she makes hungry
   Where most she satisfies.   ENOBARBUS           *2, 2, 239*

56 Though it be honest, it is never good
   To bring bad news.   CLEOPATRA                  *2, 5, 85*

57 I will praise any man that will praise me.   ENOBARBUS
                                                   *2, 6, 88*

58 He will to his Egyptian dish again.   ENOBARBUS   *2, 6, 121*

59 Celerity is never more admir'd
   Than by the negligent.   CLEOPATRA             *3, 7, 24*

60            He wears the rose
   Of youth upon him.   ANTONY                    *3, 13, 20*

61 Let's have one other gaudy night.   ANTONY     *3, 13, 183*

62 To business that we love we rise betime,
   And go to't with delight.   ANTONY             *4, 4, 20*

63 O infinite virtue, com'st thou smiling from
   The world's great snare uncaught?   CLEOPATRA  *4, 8, 18*

64 Unarm, Eros; the long day's task is done,
   And we must sleep.   ANTONY                     *4, 14, 35*

65 I am dying, Egypt, dying; only
   I here importune death awhile, until
   Of many thousand kisses the poor last
   I lay upon thy lips.   ANTONY                   *4, 15, 18*

66 O, wither'd is the garland of the war,
   The soldier's pole is fall'n! Young boys and girls
   Are level now with men. The odds is gone,
   And there is nothing left remarkable
   Beneath the visiting moon.   CLEOPATRA         *4, 15, 64*

67            The bright day is done,
   And we are for the dark.   IRAS                 *5, 2, 192*

68 His biting is immortal; those that do die of it do seldom or never
   recover.   CLOWN                                *5, 2, 246*

69 I wish you joy o' th' worm.   CLOWN             *5, 2, 277*

70            I have
   Immortal longings in me.   CLEOPATRA           *5, 2, 278*

71 Dost thou not see my baby at my breast
   That sucks the nurse asleep? CLEOPATRA          *Antony and*
                                             *Cleopatra, 5, 2, 307*

## As You Like It

72 Fleet the time carelessly, as they did in the golden world.
                                          CHARLES  *1, 1, 108*

73 Well said; that was laid on with a trowel.  CELIA    *1, 2, 94*

74 Beauty provoketh thieves sooner than gold.  ROSALIND
                                                   *1, 3, 106*

75 Sweet are the uses of adversity;
   Which, like the toad, ugly and venomous,
   Wears yet a precious jewel in his head;
   And this our life, exempt from public haunt,
   Finds tongues in trees, books in the running brooks,
   Sermons in stones, and good in everything.  DUKE SENIOR
                                                   *2, 1, 12*

76 Sweep on, you fat and greasy citizens.  1ST LORD (quoting
   Jaques)                                          *2, 1, 55*

77 Unregarded age in corners thrown.  ADAM       *2, 3, 42*

78 Therefore my age is as a lusty winter,
   Frosty, but kindly.  ADAM                       *2, 3, 52*

79 O good old man, how well in thee appears
   The constant service of the antique world,
   When service sweat for duty, not for meed!
   Thou art not for the fashion of these times,
   Where none will sweat but for promotion.  ORLANDO  *2, 3, 56*

80 I had rather bear with you than bear you.  TOUCHSTONE
                                                   *2, 4, 9*

81 Ay, now am I in Arden; the more fool I; when I was at home I
   was in a better place; but travellers must be content.
                                    TOUCHSTONE  *2, 4, 13*

82 If thou rememb'rest not the slightest folly
   That ever love did make thee run into,
   Thou hast not lov'd.  SILVIUS                    *2, 4, 31*

83          Under the greenwood tree
              Who loves to lie with me,
              And turn his merry note
              Unto the sweet bird's throat,
   Come hither, come hither, come hither.
              Here shall he see
              No enemy
   But winter and rough weather.  AMIENS            *2, 5, 1*

84 I can suck melancholy out of a song, as a weasel sucks eggs.
JAQUES   *As You Like It, 2, 5, 12*

85 Who doth ambition shun,
And loves to live i' th' sun,
Seeking the food he eats,
And pleas'd with what he gets.   AMIENS, ETC.        *2, 5, 34*

86 I'll rail against all the first-born of Egypt.   JAQUES     *2, 5, 56*

87 A fool! I met a fool i' th' forest,
A motley fool.   JAQUES                             *2, 7, 12*

88 And so, from hour to hour, we ripe and ripe,
And then, from hour to hour, we rot and rot;
And thereby hangs a tale.   JAQUES                 *2, 7, 26*

89                     Whate'er you are
That in this desert inaccessible,
Under the shade of melancholy boughs,
Lose and neglect the creeping hours of time.   ORLANDO
                                                   *2, 7, 109*

90                     All the world's a stage,
And all the men and women merely players;
They have their exits and their entrances;
And one man in his time plays many parts,
His acts being seven ages. At first the infant,
Mewling and puking in the nurse's arms;
Then the whining school-boy, with his satchel
And shining morning face, creeping like snail
Unwillingly to school. And then the lover,
Sighing like furnace, with a woeful ballad
Made to his mistress' eyebrow. Then a soldier,
Full of strange oaths, and bearded like the pard,
Jealous in honour, sudden and quick in quarrel,
Seeking the bubble reputation
Even in the cannon's mouth. And then the justice,
In fair round belly with good capon lin'd,
With eyes severe and beard of formal cut,
Full of wise saws and modern instances;
And so he plays his part. The sixth age shifts
Into the lean and slipper'd pantaloon,
With spectacles on nose and pouch on side,
His youthful hose, well sav'd, a world too wide
For his shrunk shank; and his big manly voice,
Turning again toward childish treble, pipes
And whistles in his sound. Last scene of all,
That ends this strange eventful history,

Is second childishness and mere oblivion;
Sans teeth, sans eyes, sans taste, sans every thing.   JAQUES
*As You Like It, 2, 7, 139*

91       Blow, blow, thou winter wind,
        Thou art not so unkind
          As man's ingratitude;
        Thy tooth is not so keen,
        Because thou art not seen,
          Although thy breath be rude.
Heigh-ho! sing heigh-ho! unto the green holly.
Most friendship is feigning, most loving mere folly.   AMIENS
*2, 7, 174*

92 Run, run, Orlando; carve on every tree,
The fair, the chaste, and unexpressive she.   ORLANDO   *3, 2, 9*

93 He that wants money, means, and content, is without three good
friends.   CORIN   *3, 2, 23*

94 Let us make an honourable retreat; though not with bag and
baggage, yet with scrip and scrippage.   TOUCHSTONE   *3, 2, 150*

95 O wonderful, wonderful, and most wonderful wonderful, and
yet again wonderful, and after that, out of all whooping!
CELIA   *3, 2, 177*

96 Do you not know I am a woman? When I think, I must speak.
ROSALIND   *3, 2, 234*

97 I do desire we may be better strangers.   ORLANDO   *3, 2, 243*

98 Time travels in divers paces with divers persons. I'll tell you who
Time ambles withal, who Time trots withal, who Time gallops
withal, and who he stands still withal.   ROSALIND   *3, 2, 290*

99 Truly, I would the gods had made thee poetical.   TOUCHSTONE
*3, 3, 13*

1 The truest poetry is the most feigning.   TOUCHSTONE   *3, 3, 16*

2 I am not a slut, though I thank the gods I am foul.   AUDREY
*3, 3, 34*

3 Men have died from time to time, and worms have eaten them,
but not for love.   ROSALIND   *4, 1, 94*

4 Men are April when they woo, December when they wed: maids
are May when they are maids, but the sky changes when they
are wives.   ROSALIND   *4, 1, 130*

5 No sooner met but they look'd; no sooner look'd but they lov'd;
no sooner lov'd but they sigh'd; no sooner sigh'd but they ask'd
one another the reason; no sooner knew the reason but they
sought the remedy.   ROSALIND   *5, 2, 29*

6 O, how bitter a thing it is to look into happiness through another
man's eyes! ORLANDO  *As You Like It, 5, 2, 40*

7 It was a lover and his lass,
    With a hey, and a ho, and a hey nonino,
That o'er the green corn-field did pass
    In the spring time, the only pretty ring time,
When birds do sing, hey ding a ding, ding.
Sweet lovers love the spring.  TWO PAGES  *5, 3, 14*

8 An ill-favour'd thing, sir, but mine own.  TOUCHSTONE
*5, 4, 55*

9 I will name you the degrees. The first, the Retort Courteous; the
second, the Quip Modest; the third, the Reply Churlish; the
fourth, the Reproof Valiant; the fifth, the Countercheck
Quarrelsome; the sixth, the Lie with Circumstance; the seventh,
the Lie Direct.  TOUCHSTONE  *5, 4, 86*

10 Your If is the only peace-maker; much virtue in If.
TOUCHSTONE  *5, 4, 97*

11 If it be true that good wine needs no bush, 'tis true that a good
play needs no epilogue.  ROSALIND  *Epilogue, 3*

**The Comedy of Errors**

12 They brought one Pinch, a hungry lean-fac'd villain,
A mere anatomy, a mountebank,
A threadbare juggler, and a fortune-teller,
A needy, hollow-ey'd, sharp-looking wretch,
A living dead man.  ANTIPHOLUS OF EPHESUS  *5, 1, 237*

**Coriolanus**

13 My gracious silence, hail!  CORIOLANUS  *2, 1, 166*

14      Bid them wash their faces
And keep their teeth clean.  CORIOLANUS  *2, 3, 59*

15      Custom calls me to't.
What custom wills, in all things should we do't,
The dust on antique time would lie unswept,
And mountainous error be too highly heap'd
For truth to o'erpeer.  CORIOLANUS  *2, 3, 114*

16 Hear you this Triton of the minnows? Mark you
His absolute 'shall'?  CORIOLANUS  *3, 1, 89*

17 His nature is too noble for the world:
He would not flatter Neptune for his trident,

Or Jove for's power to thunder. His heart's his mouth;
What his breast forges, that his tongue must vent.
MENENIUS  *Coriolanus, 3, 1, 255*

18         Like a dull actor now
I have forgot my part and I am out,
Even to a full disgrace.  CORIOLANUS         *5, 3, 40*

19 If you have writ your annals true, 'tis there
That, like an eagle in a dove-cote, I
Flutter'd your Volscians in Corioli.
Alone I did it.  CORIOLANUS         *5, 6, 114*

## Cymbéline

20 Hark, hark! the lark at heaven's gate sings,
    And Phoebus 'gins arise,
His steeds to water at those springs
    On chalic'd flow'rs that lies;
And winking Mary-buds begin
    To ope their golden eyes.
With everything that pretty bin,
    My lady sweet, arise;
      Arise, arise!  SONG         *2, 3, 19*

21         There be many Caesars
Ere such another Julius. Britain is
A world by itself, and we will nothing pay
For wearing our own noses.  CLOTEN      *3, 1, 11*

22 O for a horse with wings!  IMOGEN      *3, 2, 47*

23           O, this life
Is nobler than attending for a check,
Richer than doing nothing for a bribe,
Prouder than rustling in unpaid-for silk.  BELARIUS  *3, 3, 21*

24 I have not slept one wink.  PISANIO      *3, 4, 99*

25 Hath Britain all the sun that shines?  IMOGEN   *3, 4, 135*

26         Society is no comfort
To one not sociable.  IMOGEN         *4, 2, 12*

27         Though mean and mighty rotting
Together have one dust, yet reverence –
That angel of the world – doth make distinction
Of place 'tween high and low.  BELARIUS    *4, 2, 247*

28 Thersites' body is as good as Ajax',
When neither are alive.  GUIDERIUS      *4, 2, 253*

29 Fear no more the heat o' th' sun
    Nor the furious winter's rages;

Thou thy worldly task hast done,
  Home art gone, and ta'en thy wages.
Golden lads and girls all must,
As chimney-sweepers, come to dust.  GUIDERIUS  *Cymbeline,*
*4, 2, 259*

30 All lovers young, all lovers must
Consign to thee and come to dust.  GUIDERIUS AND ARVIRAGUS
*4, 2, 275*

31 Quiet consummation have,
And renowned be thy grave!  GUIDERIUS AND ARVIRAGUS
*4, 2, 281*

32 He that sleeps feels not the toothache.  GAOLER  *5, 4, 171*

Hamlet

33 For this relief much thanks. 'Tis bitter cold,
And I am sick at heart.  FRANCISCO  *1, 1, 8*

34 What, has this thing appear'd again to-night?  HORATIO
*1, 1, 21*

35 We do it wrong, being so majestical,
To offer it the show of violence.  MARCELLUS  *1, 1, 143*

36 But look, the morn, in russet mantle clad,
Walks o'er the dew of yon high eastward hill.  HORATIO
*1, 1, 166*

37 The memory be green.  CLAUDIUS  *1, 2, 2*

38 A little more than kin, and less than kind.  HAMLET  *1, 2, 65*

39 Not so, my lord; I am too much in the sun.  HAMLET  *1, 2, 67*

40 Thou know'st 'tis common – all that lives must die,
Passing through nature to eternity.  GERTRUDE  *1, 2, 72*

41 But I have that within which passes show –
These but the trappings and the suits of woe.  HAMLET
*1, 2, 85*

42 O, that this too too solid flesh would melt,
Thaw, and resolve itself into a dew!
Or that the Everlasting had not fix'd
His canon 'gainst self-slaughter! O God! God!
How weary, stale, flat, and unprofitable,
Seem to me all the uses of this world!  HAMLET  *1, 2, 129*

43 So excellent a king that was to this
Hyperion to a satyr.  HAMLET  *1, 2, 139*

44       Why, she would hang on him
As if increase of appetite had grown
By what it fed on.  HAMLET  *1, 2, 143*

45 Frailty, thy name is woman!  HAMLET  *Hamlet, 1, 2, 146*

46 It is not, nor it cannot come to good.  HAMLET  *1, 2, 158*

47 A truant disposition, good my lord.  HORATIO  *1, 2, 169*

48 Thrift, thrift, Horatio! The funeral bak'd-meats
Did coldly furnish forth the marriage tables.  HAMLET

*1, 2, 180*

49 'A was a man, take him for all in all,
I shall not look upon his like again.  HAMLET  *1, 2, 187*

50 A countenance more in sorrow than in anger.  HORATIO
*1, 2, 231*

51 Give it an understanding, but no tongue.  HAMLET  *1, 2, 249*

52 　　　　　　All is not well.
I doubt some foul play.  HAMLET  *1, 2, 254*

53 The chariest maid is prodigal enough
If she unmask her beauty to the moon.  LAERTES  *1, 3, 36*

54 Do not, as some ungracious pastors do,
Show me the steep and thorny way to heaven,
Whiles, like a puff'd and reckless libertine,
Himself the primrose path of dalliance treads
And recks not his own rede.  OPHELIA  *1, 3, 47*

55 And these few precepts in thy memory
Look thou character. Give thy thoughts no tongue,
Nor any unproportion'd thought his act.
Be thou familiar, but by no means vulgar.
Those friends thou hast, and their adoption tried,
Grapple them to thy soul with hoops of steel.  POLONIUS
*1, 3, 58*

56 　　　　　　　　　　　　Beware
Of entrance to a quarrel; but, being in,
Bear't that th' opposed may beware of thee.
Give every man thy ear, but few thy voice;
Take each man's censure, but reserve thy judgment.
Costly thy habit as thy purse can buy,
But not express'd in fancy; rich, not gaudy;
For the apparel oft proclaims the man.  POLONIUS  *1, 3, 65*

57 Neither a borrower nor a lender be;
For loan oft loses both itself and friend,
And borrowing dulls the edge of husbandry.
This above all – to thine own self be true,
And it must follow, as the night the day,
Thou canst not then be false to any man.  POLONIUS

*1, 3, 75*

58 Be something scanter of your maiden presence. POLONIUS
*Hamlet, 1, 3, 121*

59 But to my mind, though I am native here
And to the manner born, it is a custom
More honour'd in the breach than the observance. HAMLET
*1, 4, 14*

60 Angels and ministers of grace defend us!
Be thou a spirit of health or goblin damn'd,
Bring with thee airs from heaven or blasts from hell,
Be thy intents wicked or charitable,
Thou com'st in such a questionable shape
That I will speak to thee. HAMLET
*1, 4, 39*

61 I do not set my life at a pin's fee;
And for my soul, what can it do to that,
Being a thing immortal as itself? HAMLET
*1, 4, 65*

62 Something is rotten in the state of Denmark. MARCELLUS
*1, 4, 90*

63      I am thy father's spirit,
Doom'd for a certain term to walk the night. GHOST *1, 5, 9*

64      But that I am forbid
To tell the secrets of my prison-house,
I could a tale unfold whose lightest word
Would harrow up thy soul, freeze thy young blood,
Make thy two eyes, like stars, start from their spheres,
Thy knotted and combined locks to part,
And each particular hair to stand on end,
Like quills upon the fretful porpentine.
But this eternal blazon must not be
To ears of flesh and blood. List, list, O, list! GHOST *1, 5, 13*

65 Revenge his foul and most unnatural murder. GHOST *1, 5, 25*

66 Murder most foul, as in the best it is;
But this most foul, strange, and unnatural. GHOST
*1, 5, 27*

67 O my prophetic soul! My uncle! HAMLET
*1, 5, 40*

68 O Hamlet, what a falling off was there. GHOST
*1, 5, 47*

69 There are more things in heaven and earth, Horatio,
Than are dreamt of in your philosophy. HAMLET
*1, 5, 166*

70 To put an antic disposition on. HAMLET
*1, 5, 172*

71 The time is out of joint. O cursed spite,
That ever I was born to set it right! HAMLET
*1, 5, 189*

72 Brevity is the soul of wit. POLONIUS
*2, 2, 90*

73 More matter with less art. GERTRUDE
*2, 2, 95*

74 That he's mad, 'tis true: 'tis true 'tis pity;
   And pity 'tis 'tis true. POLONIUS *Hamlet*, 2, 2, 97

75 POLONIUS: Do you know me, my lord?
   HAMLET: Excellent well; you are a fishmonger. *2, 2, 172*

76 To be honest, as this world goes, is to be one man pick'd out
   of ten thousand. HAMLET *2, 2, 177*

77 POLONIUS: What do you read, my Lord?
   HAMLET: Words, words, words. *2, 2, 190*

78 Though this be madness, yet there is method in't. POLONIUS
   *2, 2, 204*

79 HAMLET: What news?
   ROSENCRANTZ: None, my lord, but that the world's grown
   honest.
   HAMLET: Then is doomsday near. *2, 2, 235*

80 There is nothing either good or bad, but thinking makes it so.
   HAMLET *2, 2, 248*

81 What a piece of work is a man! How noble in reason! how
   infinite in faculties! in form and moving, how express and
   admirable! in action, how like an angel! in apprehension, how
   like a god! the beauty of the world! the paragon of animals!
   And yet, to me, what is this quintessence of dust? Man delights
   not me – no, nor woman neither. HAMLET *2, 2, 303*

82 He that plays the king shall be welcome. HAMLET *2, 2, 317*

83 I am but mad north-north-west; when the wind is southerly I
   know a hawk from a handsaw. HAMLET *2, 2, 374*

84 The best actors in the world, either for tragedy, comedy, history,
   pastoral, pastoral-comical, historical-pastoral, tragical-historical, tragical-comical-historical-pastoral, scene individable, or
   poem unlimited. POLONIUS *2, 2, 392*

85 The play, I remember, pleas'd not the million; 'twas caviare
   to the general. HAMLET *2, 2, 429*

86 The mobled queen. 1ST PLAYER *2, 2, 496*

87 Let them be well used; for they are the abstract and brief
   chronicles of the time. HAMLET *2, 2, 517*

88 Use every man after his desert, and who shall scape whipping?
   HAMLET *2, 2, 523*

89 O, what a rogue and peasant slave am I! HAMLET *2, 2, 543*

90 What's Hecuba to him or he to Hecuba,
   That he should weep for her? HAMLET *2, 2, 552*

91 A dull and muddy-mettl'd rascal. HAMLET *2, 2, 561*

92  But I am pigeon-liver'd and lack gall
    To make oppression bitter.  HAMLET  *Hamlet, 2, 2, 572*

93                   This is most brave,
    That I, the son of a dear father murder'd,
    Prompted to my revenge by heaven and hell,
    Must, like a whore, unpack my heart with words,
    And fall a-cursing like a very drab.  HAMLET  *2, 2, 578*

94                   The play's the thing
    Wherein I'll catch the conscience of the King.  HAMLET
                                            *2, 2, 600*

95  To be, or not to be – that is the question;
    Whether 'tis nobler in the mind to suffer
    The slings and arrows of outrageous fortune,
    Or to take arms against a sea of troubles,
    And by opposing end them? To die, to sleep –
    No more; and by a sleep to say we end
    The heart-ache and the thousand natural shocks
    That flesh is heir to. 'Tis a consummation
    Devoutly to be wish'd. To die, to sleep;
    To sleep, perchance to dream. Ay, there's the rub;
    For in that sleep of death what dreams may come,
    When we have shuffled off this mortal coil,
    Must give us pause. There's the respect
    That makes calamity of so long life;
    For who would bear the whips and scorns of time,
    Th' oppressor's wrong, the proud man's contumely,
    The pangs of despis'd love, the law's delay,
    The insolence of office, and the spurns
    That patient merit of th' unworthy takes,
    When he himself might his quietus make
    With a bare bodkin? Who would fardels bear,
    To grunt and sweat under a weary life,
    But that the dread of something after death –
    The undiscover'd country, from whose bourn
    No traveller returns – puzzles the will,
    And makes us rather bear those ills we have
    Than fly to others that we know not of?
    Thus conscience does make cowards of us all;
    And thus the native hue of resolution
    Is sicklied o'er with the pale cast of thought,
    And enterprises of great pith and moment,
    With this regard, their currents turn awry
    And lose the name of action.  HAMLET  *3, 1, 56*

96                        For to the noble mind
Rich gifts wax poor when givers prove unkind.   OPHELIA
*Hamlet, 3, 1, 100*

97 Get thee to a nunnery.   HAMLET           *3, 1, 121*

98 Be thou as chaste as ice, as pure as snow, thou shalt not escape
calumny.   HAMLET           *3, 1, 135*

99 I have heard of your paintings too, well enough; God hath given
you one face, and you make yourselves another.   HAMLET
*3, 1, 142*

1 O, what a noble mind is here o'erthrown!
The courtier's, soldier's, scholar's, eye, tongue, sword;
Th' expectancy and rose of the fair state,
The glass of fashion and the mould of form,
Th' observ'd of all observers – quite, quite down!   OPHELIA
*3, 1, 150*

2 Madness in great ones must not unwatch'd go.   CLAUDIUS
*3, 1, 188*

3 Speak the speech, I pray you, as I pronounc'd it to you, trip-
pingly on the tongue; but if you mouth it, as many of our
players do, I had as lief the town-crier spoke my lines. Nor do
not saw the air too much with your hand, thus, but use all
gently.   HAMLET           *3, 2, 1*

4 It out-herods Herod.   HAMLET           *3, 2, 14*

5 Suit the action to the word, the word to the action; with this
specia observance, that you o'erstep not the modesty of nature.
HAMLET   *3, 2, 17*

6                           Give me that man
That is not passion's slave, and I will wear him
In my heart's core, ay, in my heart of heart,
As I do thee.   HAMLET           *3, 2, 69*

7 Here's metal more attractive.   HAMLET      *3, 2, 106*

8 OPHELIA: 'Tis brief, my lord.
HAMLET: As woman's love.           *3, 2, 148*

9 The lady doth protest too much, methinks.   GERTRUDE
*3, 2, 225*

10 We that have free souls, it touches us not. Let the galled jade
wince, our withers are unwrung.   HAMLET    *3, 2, 235*

11 The proverb is something musty.   HAMLET    *3, 2, 334*

12 Very like a whale.   POLONIUS          *3, 2, 372*

13 'Tis now the very witching time of night,
When churchyards yawn, and hell itself breathes out
Contagion to this world.   HAMLET      *3, 2, 378*

14 Let me be cruel, not unnatural:
I will speak daggers to her, but use none. HAMLET *Hamlet,*
*3, 2, 385*

15 O, my offence is rank, it smells to heaven. CLAUDIUS *3, 3, 36*

16 My words fly up, my thoughts remain below.
Words without thoughts never to heaven go. CLAUDIUS
*3, 3, 97*

17 How now! a rat? Dead, for a ducat, dead! HAMLET *3, 4, 23*

18 A king of shreds and patches. HAMLET *3, 4, 102*

19 Assume a virtue, if you have it not. HAMLET *3, 4, 160*

20 I must be cruel only to be kind. HAMLET *3, 4, 178*

21 Diseases desperate grown
By desperate appliance are reliev'd,
Or not at all. CLAUDIUS *4, 3, 9*

22 How all occasions do inform against me,
And spur my dull revenge! What is a man,
If his chief good and market of his time
Be but to sleep and feed? A beast, no more! HAMLET
*4, 4, 32*

23 Some craven scruple
Of thinking too precisely on th' event. HAMLET *4, 4, 40*

24 Rightly to be great
Is not to stir without great argument,
But greatly to find quarrel in a straw,
When honour's at the stake. HAMLET *4, 4, 53*

25 Come, my coach! Good night, ladies; good night, sweet ladies,
good night, good night. OPHELIA *4, 5, 69*

26 When sorrows come, they come not single spies,
But in battalions! CLAUDIUS *4, 5, 75*

27 There's such divinity doth hedge a king
That treason can but peep to what it would. CLAUDIUS
*4, 5, 120*

28 There's rosemary, that's for remembrance; pray you, love,
remember.
And there is pansies, that's for thoughts. OPHELIA *4, 5, 172*

29 A very riband in the cap of youth. CLAUDIUS *4, 7, 77*

30 There is a willow grows aslant the brook
That shows his hoar leaves in the glassy stream. GERTRUDE
*4, 7, 167*

31 Alas, poor Yorick! I knew him, Horatio: a fellow of infinite jest,
of most excellent fancy. HAMLET *5, 1, 179*

32             Lay her i' th' earth;
And from her fair and unpolluted flesh
May violets spring! I tell thee, churlish priest,
A minist'ring angel shall my sister be
When thou liest howling.  LAERTES        *Hamlet*, *5, 1, 232*

33 Sweets to the sweet, farewell!  GERTRUDE         *5, 1, 237*

34 Let Hercules himself do what he may,
The cat will mew, and dog will have his day.  HAMLET *5, 1, 285*

35 There's a divinity that shapes our ends,
Rough-hew them how we will.  HAMLET        *5, 2, 10*

36 A hit, a very palpable hit.  OSRIC        *5, 2, 273*

37 Report me and my cause aright.  HAMLET        *5, 2, 331*

38 If thou didst ever hold me in thy heart,
Absent thee from felicity awhile,
And in this harsh world draw thy breath in pain,
To tell my story.  HAMLET        *5, 2, 338*

39 The rest is silence.  HAMLET        *5, 2, 350*

40 Now cracks a noble heart. Good night, sweet prince,
And flights of angels sing thee to thy rest!  HORATIO *5, 2, 351*

41 For he was likely, had he been put on,
To have prov'd most royal.  FORTINBRAS        *5, 2, 389*


**King Henry the Fourth, Part One**

42 So shaken as we are, so wan with care.  HENRY IV    *1, 1, 1*

43 To chase these pagans in those holy fields
Over whose acres walk'd those blessed feet
Which fourteen hundred years ago were nail'd
For our advantage on the bitter cross.  HENRY IV    *1, 1, 24*

44 See riot and dishonour stain the brow
Of my young Harry.  HENRY IV        *1, 1, 85*

45 Shall there be gallows standing in England when thou art king?
       FALSTAFF *1, 2, 56*

46 O, thou hast damnable iteration, and art indeed able to corrupt
a saint.  FALSTAFF        *1, 2, 88*

47 Why, Hal, 'tis my vocation, Hal; 'tis no sin for a man to labour
in his vocation.  FALSTAFF        *1, 2, 101*

48 There's neither honesty, manhood, nor good fellowship in thee.
       FALSTAFF *1, 2, 133*

49 I know you all, and will awhile uphold
The unyok'd humour of your idleness.  PRINCE    *1, 2, 188*

50 If all the year were playing holidays,
To sport would be as tedious as to work.  PRINCE
*Henry the Fourth, Part One, 1, 2, 197*

51     A certain lord, neat, and trimly dress'd,
Fresh as a bridegroom, and his chin new reap'd
Show'd like a stubble-land at harvest-home.
He was perfumed like a milliner,
And 'twixt his finger and his thumb he held
A pouncet-box, which ever and anon
He gave his nose and took't away again.  HOTSPUR     *1, 3, 33*

52                              He made me mad
To see him shine so brisk, and smell so sweet,
And talk so like a waiting-gentlewoman
Of guns, and drums, and wounds – God save the mark! –
And telling me the sovereignest thing on earth
Was parmaceti for an inward bruise.  HOTSPUR     *1, 3, 53*

53        O, the blood more stirs
To rouse a lion than to start a hare!  HOTSPUR     *1, 3, 197*

54 By heaven, methinks it were an easy leap
To pluck bright honour from the pale-fac'd moon;
Or dive into the bottom of the deep,
Where fathom-line could never touch the ground,
And pluck up drowned honour by the locks.  HOTSPUR
                                                      *1, 3, 201*

55 I know a trick worth two of that.  FIRST CARRIER     *2, 1, 36*

56 I am bewitch'd with the rogue's company. If the rascal have not
given me medicines to make me love him, I'll be hang'd.
                                          FALSTAFF  *2, 2, 16*

57 Have you any levers to lift me up again, being down?  FALSTAFF
                                                      *2, 2, 33*

58 It would be argument for a week, laughter for a month, and a
good jest for ever.  PRINCE                          *2, 2, 91*

59                    Falstaff sweats to death
And lards the lean earth as he walks along.  PRINCE  *2, 2, 104*

60 Out of this nettle, danger, we pluck this flower, safety.
                                          HOTSPUR  *2, 3, 10*

61             Constant you are,
But yet a woman; and for secrecy,
No lady closer; for I well believe
Thou wilt not utter what thou dost not know.  HOTSPUR
                                                      *2, 3, 105*

62 I am not yet of Percy's mind, the Hotspur of the north; he that kills me some six or seven dozen of Scots at a breakfast, washes his hands, and says to his wife 'Fie upon this quiet life! I want work'.   PRINCE          *Henry the Fourth, Part One, 2, 4, 97*

63 A plague of all cowards, I say.   FALSTAFF          *2, 4, 109*

64 There lives not three good men unhang'd in England, and one of them is fat and grows old.   FALSTAFF          *2, 4, 123*

65 I have pepper'd two of them; two I am sure I have paid – two rogues in buckram suits. I tell thee what, Hal, if I tell thee a lie, spit in my face, call me horse. Thou knowest my old ward: here I lay, and thus I bore my point. Four rogues in buckram let drive at me.   FALSTAFF          *2, 4, 183*

66 O monstrous! eleven buckram men grown out of two!   PRINCE
*2, 4, 212*

67 A plague of sighing and grief! it blows a man up like a bladder.
FALSTAFF   *2, 4, 322*

68 That reverend vice, that grey iniquity, that father ruffian, that vanity in years.   PRINCE          *2, 4, 437*

69 Banish plump Jack, and banish all the world.   FALSTAFF
*2, 4, 462*

70 O monstrous! but one halfpenny-worth of bread to this intolerable deal of sack!   PRINCE          *2, 4, 521*

71 I am not in the roll of common men.   GLENDOWER          *3, 1, 43*

72 GLENDOWER: I can call spirits from the vasty deep.
HOTSPUR:      Why, so can I, or so can any man;
              But will they come when you do call for them?
*3, 1, 53*

73 I had rather be a kitten and cry mew
Than one of these same metre ballad-mongers.   HOTSPUR
*3, 1, 129*

74                              Mincing poetry.
'Tis like the forc'd gait of a shuffling nag.   HOTSPUR   *3, 1, 134*

75 I understand thy kisses, and thou mine,
And that's a feeling disputation.   MORTIMER          *3, 1, 204*

76 Swear me, Kate, like a lady as thou art,
A good mouth-filling oath.   HOTSPUR          *3, 1, 254*

77 He was but as the cuckoo is in June,
Heard, not regarded.   HENRY IV          *3, 2, 75*

78 Do I not bate? Do I not dwindle? Why, my skin hangs about me like an old lady's loose gown.   FALSTAFF          *3, 3, 2*

79 Company, villainous company, hath been the spoil of me.
        FALSTAFF  *Henry the Fourth, Part One, 3, 2, 10*

80 I have more flesh than another man, and therefore more frailty.
        FALSTAFF  *3, 3, 167*

81 Doomsday is near; die all, die merrily.  HOTSPUR    *4, 1, 134*

82 I have misused the King's press damnably.  FALSTAFF  *4, 2, 11*

83 The cankers of a calm world and a long peace.  FALSTAFF
        *4, 2, 30*

84 To the latter end of a fray and the beginning of a feast
   Fits a dull fighter and a keen guest.  FALSTAFF    *4, 2, 77*

85 For nothing can seem foul to those that win.  HENRY IV
        *5, 1, 8*

86 Rebellion lay in his way, and he found it.  FALSTAFF  *5, 1, 28*

87 I would 'twere bed-time, Hal, and all well.  FALSTAFF
        *5, 1, 125*

88 Honour pricks me on. Yea, but how if honour prick me off when
   I come on? How then? Can honour set to a leg? No. Or an arm?
   No. Or take away the grief of a wound? No. Honour hath no
   skill in surgery, then? No. What is honour? A word. What is in
   that word? Honour. What is that honour? Air. A trim reckoning! Who hath it? He that died o' Wednesday. Doth he feel it?
   No. Doth he hear it? No. 'Tis insensible then? Yea, to the dead.
   But will it not live with the living? No. Why? Detraction will
   not suffer it. Therefore I'll none of it. Honour is a mere scutcheon. And so ends my catechism.  FALSTAFF    *5, 1, 129*

89               The time of life is short!
   To spend that shortness basely were too long.  HOTSPUR
        *5, 2, 82*

90 Two stars keep not their motion in one sphere.  PRINCE
        *5, 4, 65*

91 But thoughts, the slaves of life, and life, time's fool,
   And time, that takes survey of all the world,
   Must have a stop.  HOTSPUR        *5, 4, 81*

92 What, old acquaintance! Could not all this flesh
   Keep in a little life? Poor Jack, farewell!
   I could have better spar'd a better man.  PRINCE    *5, 4, 102*

93 The better part of valour is discretion; in the which better part
   I have saved my life.  FALSTAFF        *5, 4, 120*

94 Lord, Lord, how this world is given to lying!  FALSTAFF
        *5, 4, 143*

95 I'll purge, and leave sack, and live cleanly, as a nobleman
   should do.  FALSTAFF        *5, 4, 163*

**King Henry the Fourth, Part Two**

96 This man's brow, like to a title-leaf,
   Foretells the nature of a tragic volume. NORTHUMBERLAND
   *1, 1, 60*

97 Yet the first bringer of unwelcome news
   Hath but a losing office, and his tongue
   Sounds ever after as a sullen bell,
   Rememb'red tolling a departing friend. NORTHUMBERLAND
   *1, 1, 100*

98 The brain of this foolish-compounded clay, man, is not able to
   invent anything that tends to laughter, more than I invent or is
   invented on me. I am not only witty in myself, but the cause that
   wit is in other men. I do here walk before thee like a sow that
   hath overwhelm'd all her litter but one. FALSTAFF *1, 2, 7*

99 My lord, I was born about three of the clock in the afternoon,
   with a white head and something a round belly. For my voice –
   I have lost it with hallooing and singing of anthems. FALSTAFF
   *1, 2, 176*

1 Well, I cannot last ever; but it was always yet the trick of our
   English nation, if they have a good thing, to make it too common.
   FALSTAFF *1, 2, 200*

2 I would to God my name were not so terrible to the enemy as
   it is. FALSTAFF *1, 2, 204*

3 I can get no remedy against this consumption of the purse;
   borrowing only lingers and lingers it out, but the disease is
   incurable. FALSTAFF *1, 2, 223*

4 O thoughts of men accurs'd!
   Past and to come seems best; things present, worst.
   ARCHBISHOP *1, 3, 107*

5 Away, you scullion! you rampallian! you fustilarian! I'll tickle
   your catastrophe. FALSTAFF *2, 1, 57*

6 He hath eaten me out of house and home. HOSTESS *2, 1, 71*

7 Now, the Lord lighten thee! Thou art a great fool.
   CHIEF JUSTICE *2, 1, 187*

8 He was indeed the glass
   Wherein the noble youth did dress themselves. LADY PERCY
   *2, 3, 21*

9 Hollow pamper'd jades of Asia. PISTOL *2, 4, 155*

10 Is it not strange that desire should so many years outlive
   performance? POINS *2, 4, 250*

11 Now comes in the sweetest morsel of the night, and we must
   hence, and leave it unpick'd. FALSTAFF *2, 4, 354*

12 You see, my good wenches, how men of merit are sought after;
   the undeserver may sleep, when the man of action is call'd on.
                    FALSTAFF  *Henry the Fourth, Part Two, 2, 4, 361*

13 How many thousands of my poorest subjects
   Are at this hour asleep! O sleep, O gentle sleep,
   Nature's soft nurse, how have I frighted thee,
   That thou no more wilt weigh my eyelids down,
   And steep my senses in forgetfulness?  HENRY IV      *3, 1, 4*

14 Canst thou, O partial sleep, give thy repose
   To the wet sea-boy in an hour so rude;
   And in the calmest and most stillest night,
   With all appliances and means to boot,
   Deny it to a king? Then, happy low, lie down!
   Uneasy lies the head that wears a crown.  HENRY IV   *3, 1, 26*

15 O God! that one might read the book of fate.  HENRY IV
                                                         *3, 1, 45*

16 There is a history in all men's lives,
   Figuring the natures of the times deceas'd.  WARWICK  *3, 1, 80*

17 Death, as the Psalmist saith, is certain to all; all shall die. How
   a good yoke of bullocks at Stamford fair?  SHALLOW  *3, 2, 36*

18 We have heard the chimes at midnight.  FALSTAFF     *3, 2, 210*

19 I care not; a man can die but once; we owe God a death.
                                       FEEBLE  *3, 2, 228*

20 Care I for the limb, the thews, the stature, bulk, and big assemblance of a man! Give me the spirit.  FALSTAFF       *3, 2, 251*

21 Lord, Lord, how subject we old men are to this vice of lying!
                                       FALSTAFF  *3, 2, 294*

22 Against ill chances men are ever merry;
   But heaviness foreruns the good event.  ARCHBISHOP    *4, 2, 81*

23 A peace is of the nature of a conquest;
   For then both parties nobly are subdu'd,
   And neither party loser.  ARCHBISHOP                  *4, 2, 89*

24 I may justly say with the hook-nos'd fellow of Rome – I came,
   saw, and overcame.  FALSTAFF                          *4, 3, 40*

25 He hath a tear for pity and a hand
   Open as day for melting charity.  HENRY IV            *4, 4, 31*

26 Most subject is the fattest soil to weeds.  HENRY IV  *4, 4, 54*

27 O polish'd perturbation! golden care!
   That keep'st the ports of slumber open wide
   To many a watchful night!  PRINCE                     *4, 5, 23*

28 This sleep is sound indeed; this is a sleep
    That from this golden rigol hath divorc'd
    So many English kings. PRINCE
    *Henry the Fourth, Part Two, 4, 5, 35*

29 Thy wish was father, Harry, to that thought. HENRY IV
    *4, 5, 93*

30                                    Commit
    The oldest sins the newest kind of ways. HENRY IV    *4, 5, 126*

31 This is the English, not the Turkish court;
    Not Amurath an Amurath succeeds,
    But Harry Harry. HENRY V                     *5, 2, 47*

32 Under which king, Bezonian?
    Speak, or die. PISTOL                          *5, 3, 112*

33 Let us take any man's horses: the laws of England are at my
    commandment. FALSTAFF                       *5, 3, 134*

34 I know thee not, old man. Fall to thy prayers.
    How ill white hairs become a fool and jester!
    I have long dreamt of such a kind of man,
    So surfeit-swell'd, so old, and so profane. HENRY V   *5, 5, 48*

35 Master Shallow, I owe you a thousand pound. FALSTAFF
    *5, 5, 74*


### King Henry the Fifth

36 O for a Muse of fire, that would ascend
    The brightest heaven of invention. CHORUS      *Prologue, 1*

37                          Can this cockpit hold
    The vasty fields of France? Or may we cram
    Within this wooden O the very casques
    That did affright the air at Agincourt? CHORUS *Prologue, 11*

38 Turn him to any cause of policy,
    The Gordian knot of it he will unloose,
    Familiar as his garter; that, when he speaks,
    The air, a charter'd libertine, is still.
                    ARCHBISHOP OF CANTERBURY *1, 1, 45*

39               For so work the honey bees,
    Creatures that by a rule in nature teach
    The act of order to a peopled kingdom.
    They have a king, and officers of sorts,
    Where some like magistrates correct at home;
    Others like merchants venture trade abroad;
    Others like soldiers, armed in their stings,
    Make boot upon the summer's velvet buds,
    Which pillage they with merry march bring home
    To the tent-royal of their emperor;

Who, busied in his majesty, surveys
The singing masons building roofs of gold,
The civil citizens kneading up the honey,
The poor mechanic porters crowding in
Their heavy burdens at his narrow gate,
The sad-ey'd justice, with his surly hum,
Delivering o'er to executors pale
The lazy yawning drone.   ARCHBISHOP OF CANTERBURY
*Henry the Fifth, 1, 2, 187*

40 Now all the youth of England are on fire,
And silken dalliance in the wardrobe lies;
Now thrive the armourers, and honour's thought
Reigns solely in the breast of every man;
They sell the pasture now to buy the horse,
Following the mirror of all Christian kings
With winged heels, as English Mercuries.
For now sits Expectation in the air.   CHORUS
*2, Prologue, 1*

41 I dare not fight; but I will wink and hold out mine iron.   NYM
*2, 1, 6*

42 Though patience be a tired mare, yet she will plod.   NYM
*2, 1, 24*

43 He's in Arthur's bosom, if ever man went to Arthur's bosom.
'A made a finer end, and went away an it had been any christom
child; 'a parted ev'n just between twelve and one, ev'n at the
turning o' th' tide.   HOSTESS                      *2, 3, 9*

44 His nose was as sharp as a pen, and 'a babbl'd of green fields.
HOSTESS   *2, 3, 17*

45 Once more unto the breach, dear friends, once more;
Or close the wall up with our English dead.
In peace there's nothing so becomes a man
As modest stillness and humility;
But when the blast of war blows in our ears,
Then imitate the action of the tiger:
Stiffen the sinews, summon up the blood,
Disguise fair nature with hard-favour'd rage.   HENRY V   *3, 1, 1*

46            On, on, you noblest English,
Whose blood is fet from fathers of war-proof.   HENRY V
*3, 1, 17*

47 I see you stand like greyhounds in the slips,
Straining upon the start. The game's afoot:
Follow your spirit; and upon this charge
Cry 'God for Harry, England, and Saint George!'   HENRY V
*3, 1, 31*

48 Men of few words are the best men. BOY
*Henry the Fifth, 3, 2, 36*

49 I know the disciplines of war. FLUELLEN 　　　*3, 2, 132*

50 Now entertain conjecture of a time
When creeping murmur and the poring dark
Fills the wide vessel of the universe.
From camp to camp, through the foul womb of night,
The hum of either army stilly sounds,
That the fix'd sentinels almost receive
The secret whispers of each other's watch. CHORUS
*4, Prologue, 1*

51 The King's a bawcock and a heart of gold,
A lad of life, an imp of fame;
Of parents good, of fist most valiant.
I kiss his dirty shoe, and from heart-string
I love the lovely bully. PISTOL 　　　　　　*4, 1, 44*

52 I think the King is but a man as I am: the violet smells to him
as it doth to me. HENRY V 　　　　　　*4, 1, 101*

53 Every subject's duty is the King's; but every subject's soul is
his own. HENRY V 　　　　　　　　*4, 1, 175*

54 　　　　　　　　O that we now had here
But one ten thousand of those men in England
That do no work today! WESTMORELAND 　　*4, 3, 16*

55 If we are mark'd to die, we are enow
To do our country loss; and if to live,
The fewer men, the greater share of honour. HENRY V *4, 3, 20*

56 But if it be a sin to covet honour,
I am the most offending soul alive. HENRY V 　*4, 3, 28*

57 This day is call'd the feast of Crispian.
He that outlives this day, and comes safe home,
Will stand a tip-toe when this day is nam'd,
And rouse him at the name of Crispian. HENRY V 　*4, 3, 40*

58 Old men forget; yet all shall be forgot,
But he'll remember, with advantages,
What feats he did that day. HENRY V 　　*4, 3, 49*

59 We few, we happy few, we band of brothers;
For he to-day that sheds his blood with me
Shall be my brother; be he ne'er so vile,
This day shall gentle his condition;
And gentlemen in England now a-bed
Shall think themselves accurs'd they were not here,
And hold their manhoods cheap whiles any speaks

That fought with us upon Saint Crispin's day.  HENRY V
*Henry the Fifth, 4, 3, 60*

60 There is occasions and causes why and wherefore in all things.
FLUELLEN  *5, 1, 3*

61 For these fellows of infinite tongue, that can rhyme themselves
into ladies' favours, they do always reason themselves out again.
HENRY V  *5, 2, 157*

## King Henry the Sixth, Part One

62 Hung be the heavens with black, yield day to night!  BEDFORD
*1, 1, 1*

63                    Unbidden guests
Are often welcomest when they are gone.  BEDFORD  *2, 2, 55*

64 She's beautiful, and therefore to be woo'd;
She is a woman, therefore to be won.  SUFFOLK  *5, 3, 78*

## King Henry the Sixth, Part Two

65 Smooth runs the water where the brook is deep.  SUFFOLK
*3, 1, 53*

66 I will make it felony to drink small beer.  JACK CADE
*4, 2, 64*

67 The first thing we do, let's kill all the lawyers.  DICK  *4, 2, 73*

68 Thou hast most traitorously corrupted the youth of the realm
in erecting a grammar school; and whereas, before, our forefathers had no other books but the score and the tally, thou hast
caused printing to be us'd, and, contrary to the King, his crown,
and dignity, thou hast built a paper-mill. It will be proved to thy
face that thou hast men about thee that usually talk of a noun
and a verb, and such abominable words as no Christian ear
can endure to hear.  JACK CADE  *4, 7, 30*

69 Away with him, away with him! He speaks Latin.  JACK CADE
*4, 7, 54*

## King Henry the Sixth, Part Three

70 O God! methinks it were a happy life
To be no better than a homely swain;
To sit upon a hill, as I do now,
To carve out dials quaintly, point by point,
Thereby to see the minutes how they run –
How many makes the hour full complete,
How many hours brings about the day,
How many days will finish up the year,
How many years a mortal man may live.  HENRY VI  *2, 5, 21*

71 Gives not the hawthorn bush a sweeter shade
To shepherds looking on their silly sheep,
Than doth a rich embroider'd canopy
To kings that fear their subjects' treachery? HENRY VI
*Henry the Sixth, Part Three, 2, 5, 42*

72 Suspicion always haunts the guilty mind:
The thief doth fear each bush an officer. GLOUCESTER
*5, 6, 11*

73 Down, down to hell; and say I sent thee thither. GLOUCESTER
*5, 6, 67*

**King Henry the Eighth**

74 Heat not a furnace for your foe so hot
That it do singe yourself. We may outrun
By violent swiftness that which we run at,
And lose by over-running. NORFOLK
*1, 1, 140*

75 I swear 'tis better to be lowly born
And range with humble livers in content
Than to be perk'd up in a glist'ring grief
And wear a golden sorrow. ANNE
*2, 3, 19*

76         I would not be a queen
For all the world. ANNE
*2, 3, 45*

77 Orpheus with his lute made trees,
And the mountain tops that freeze,
  Bow themselves when he did sing. SONG
*3, 1, 3*

78 Heaven is above all yet: there sits a Judge
That no king can corrupt. QUEEN KATHARINE
*3, 1, 100*

79 I have touch'd the highest point of all my greatness,
And from that full meridian of my glory
I haste now to my setting. I shall fall
Like a bright exhalation in the evening,
And no man see me more. WOLSEY
*3, 2, 223*

80 Farewell, a long farewell, to all my greatness!
This is the state of man: to-day he puts forth
The tender leaves of hopes; to-morrow blossoms
And bears his blushing honours thick upon him;
The third day comes a frost, a killing frost,
And when he thinks, good easy man, full surely
His greatness is a-ripening, nips his root,
And then he falls, as I do. WOLSEY
*3, 2, 351*

81 Vain pomp and glory of this world, I hate ye;
I feel my heart new open'd. O, how wretched
Is that poor man that hangs on princes' favours!

There is betwixt that smile we would aspire to,
That sweet aspect of princes, and their ruin
More pangs and fears than wars or women have;
And when he falls, he falls like Lucifer,
Never to hope again.   WOLSEY     *Henry the Eighth, 3, 2, 365*

82  A peace above all earthly dignities,
A still and quiet conscience.   WOLSEY          *3, 2, 379*

83  Love thyself last; cherish those hearts that hate thee;
Corruption wins not more than honesty.   WOLSEY   *3, 2, 443*

84  Had I but serv'd my God with half the zeal
I serv'd my King, he would not in mine age
Have left me naked to mine enemies.   WOLSEY     *3, 2, 455*

85  So may he rest; his faults lie gently on him!   KATHARINE
*4, 2, 31*

86  Men's evil manners live in brass: their virtues
We write in water.   GRIFFITH                      *4, 2, 45*

87  He was a scholar, and a ripe and good one;
Exceeding wise, fair-spoken, and persuading;
Lofty and sour to them that lov'd him not,
But to those men that sought him sweet as summer.   GRIFFITH
*4, 2, 51*

88                    Love and meekness, lord,
Become a churchman better than ambition.   CRANMER
*5, 3, 62*


**Julius Caesar**

89  You blocks, you stones, you worse than senseless things!
MARULLUS  *1, 1, 36*

90  Beware the ides of March.   SOOTHSAYER          *1, 2, 18*

91  Well, honour is the subject of my story.
I cannot tell what you and other men
Think of this life; but, for my single self
I had as lief not be as live to be
In awe of such a thing as I myself.   CASSIUS      *1, 2, 92*

92                    Ye gods! it doth amaze me
A man of such a feeble temper should
So get the start of the majestic world,
And bear the palm alone.   CASSIUS                 *1, 2, 128*

93  Why, man, he doth bestride the narrow world
Like a Colossus, and we petty men
Walk under his huge legs, and peep about
To find ourselves dishonourable graves.

Men at some time are masters of their fates:
The fault, dear Brutus, is not in our stars,
But in ourselves, that we are underlings. CASSIUS
*Julius Caesar, 1, 2, 135*

94 Let me have men about me that are fat;
Sleek-headed men, and such as sleep o' nights.
Yond Cassius has a lean and hungry look;
He thinks too much. Such men are dangerous. CAESAR
*1, 2, 192*

95 'Tis very like. He hath the falling sickness. BRUTUS   *1, 2, 253*

96 For mine own part, it was Greek to me. CASCA   *1, 2, 283*

97 And yesterday the bird of night did sit,
Even at noon-day, upon the market-place,
Hooting and shrieking. CASCA   *1, 3, 26*

98 Between the acting of a dreadful thing
And the first motion, all the interim is
Like a phantasma or a hideous dream.
The Genius and the mortal instruments
Are then in council; and the state of man,
Like to a little kingdom, suffers then
The nature of an insurrection. BRUTUS   *2, 1, 63*

99 Let's carve him as a dish fit for the gods. BRUTUS   *2, 1, 173*

1 Cowards die many times before their deaths:
The valiant never taste of death but once. CAESAR   *2, 2, 32*

2 How hard it is for women to keep counsel! PORTIA   *2, 4, 9*

3 Et tu, Brute? CAESAR   *3, 1, 77*

4 Why, he that cuts off twenty years of life
Cuts off so many years of fearing death. CASSIUS   *3, 1, 102*

5                 How many ages hence
Shall this our lofty scene be acted over
In states unborn and accents yet unknown! CASSIUS   *3, 1, 112*

6 O mighty Caesar! dost thou lie so low?
Are all thy conquests, glories, triumphs, spoils,
Shrunk to this little measure? MARK ANTONY   *3, 1, 149*

7 The choice and master spirits of this age. MARK ANTONY
*3, 1, 164*

8 O, pardon me, thou bleeding piece of earth,
That I am meek and gentle with these butchers!
Thou art the ruins of the noblest man
That ever lived in the tide of times. MARK ANTONY   *3, 1, 255*

9 Cry 'Havoc!' and let slip the dogs of war. MARK ANTONY
*3, 1, 274*

10 Not that I lov'd Caesar less, but that I lov'd Rome more.
    BRUTUS  *Julius Caesar, 3, 2, 20*

11 As Caesar lov'd me, I weep for him; as he was fortunate, I
   rejoice at it; as he was valiant, I honour him; but – as he was
   ambitious, I slew him. There is tears for his love; joy for his
   fortune; honour for his valour; and death for his ambition.
   Who is here so base that would be a bondman? If any, speak;
   for him have I offended.  BRUTUS              *3, 2, 24*

12 Friends, Romans, countrymen, lend me your ears;
   I come to bury Caesar, not to praise him.
   The evil that men do lives after them;
   The good is oft interred with their bones.  MARK ANTONY
                                                *3, 2, 73*

13 For Brutus is an honourable man;
   So are they all, all honourable men.  MARK ANTONY  *3, 2, 82*

14 Ambition should be made of sterner stuff.  MARK ANTONY
                                                *3, 2, 92*

15 But yesterday the word of Caesar might
   Have stood against the world: now lies he there,
   And none so poor to do him reverence.  MARK ANTONY
                                                *3, 2, 118*

16 The will, the will! We will hear Caesar's will.  PLEBEIANS
                                                *3, 2, 139*

17 If you have tears, prepare to shed them now.  MARK ANTONY
                                                *3, 2, 169*

18 See what a rent the envious Casca made.  MARK ANTONY
                                                *3, 2, 175*

19 This was the most unkindest cut of all.  MARK ANTONY
                                                *3, 2, 183*

20 O, what a fall was there, my countrymen!  MARK ANTONY
                                                *3, 2, 190*

21 For I have neither wit, nor words, nor worth,
   Action, nor utterance, nor the power of speech,
   To stir men's blood; I only speak right on.  MARK ANTONY
                                                *3, 2, 221*

22 Tear him for his bad verses, tear him for his bad verses!
                                    4TH PLEBEIAN  *3, 3, 30*

23                     You yourself
   Are much condemn'd to have an itching palm.  BRUTUS
                                                *4, 3, 9*

24 I had rather be a dog and bay the moon
   Than such a Roman.  BRUTUS                    *4, 3, 27*

25 Away, slight man!  BRUTUS  *Julius Caesar, 4, 3, 37*

26 A friend should bear his friend's infirmities,
But Brutus makes mine greater than they are.  CASSIUS
*4, 3, 85*

27 There is a tide in the affairs of men
Which, taken at the flood, leads on to fortune;
Omitted, all the voyage of their life
Is bound in shallows and in miseries.
On such a full sea are we now afloat,
And we must take the current when it serves,
Or lose our ventures.  BRUTUS  *4, 3, 216*

28 For ever and for ever farewell, Cassius!
If we do meet again, why, we shall smile;
If not, why then this parting was well made.  BRUTUS
*5, 1, 116*

29         O that a man might know
The end of this day's business ere it come!  BRUTUS  *5, 1, 122*

30 This was the noblest Roman of them all.
All the conspirators save only he
Did that they did in envy of great Caesar.  MARK ANTONY
*5, 5, 68*

31 His life was gentle; and the elements
So mix'd in him that Nature might stand up
And say to all the world 'This was a man!'  MARK ANTONY
*5, 5, 73*


**King John**

32 A strange beginning – 'borrowed majesty'!  ELINOR  *1, 1, 5*

33 Lord of thy presence and no land beside.  ELINOR  *1, 1, 137*

34 For courage mounteth with occasion.  AUSTRIA  *2, 1, 82*

35 Saint George, that swing'd the dragon, and e'er since
Sits on's horse back at mine hostess' door.  BASTARD  *2, 1, 288*

36 Mad world! mad kings! mad composition!  BASTARD  *2, 1, 561*

37 That smooth-fac'd gentleman, tickling commodity,
Commodity, the bias of the world.  BASTARD  *2, 1, 573*

38 Well, whiles I am a beggar, I will rail
And say there is no sin but to be rich;
And being rich, my virtue then shall be
To say there is no vice but beggary.  BASTARD  *2, 1, 593*

39         Here I and sorrows sit;
Here is my throne, bid kings come bow to it.  CONSTANCE
*3, 1, 73*

40 Bell, book, and candle, shall not drive me back,
When gold and silver becks me to come on. BASTARD
*King John, 3, 3, 12*

41 Life is as tedious as a twice-told tale
Vexing the dull ear of a drowsy man. LEWIS *3, 4, 108*

42 Heat me these irons hot. HUBERT *4, 1, 1*

43 To gild refined gold, to paint the lily,
To throw a perfume on the violet,
To smooth the ice, or add another hue
Unto the rainbow, or with taper-light
To seek the beauteous eye of heaven to garnish,
Is wasteful and ridiculous excess. SALISBURY *4, 2, 11*

44 And oftentimes excusing of a fault
Doth make the fault the worse by th' excuse. PEMBROKE
*4, 2, 30*

45 How oft the sight of means to do ill deeds
Make deeds ill done! KING JOHN *4, 2, 219*

46 I beg cold comfort. KING JOHN *5, 7, 42*

47 This England never did, nor never shall,
Lie at the proud foot of a conqueror,
But when it first did help to wound itself. BASTARD *5, 7, 112*

48             Nought shall make us rue,
If England to itself do rest but true. BASTARD *5, 7 117*

**King Lear**

49 Nothing will come of nothing. Speak again. LEAR *1, 1, 89*

50 LEAR: So young and so untender?
CORDELIA: So young, my lord, and true. *1, 1, 105*

51 A still-soliciting eye. CORDELIA *1, 1, 231*

52 These late eclipses in the sun and moon portend no good to us.
GLOUCESTER *1, 2, 99*

53 This is the excellent foppery of the world, that, when we are
sick in fortune, often the surfeits of our own behaviour, we make
guilty of our disasters the sun, the moon, and stars. EDMUND
*1, 2, 112*

54 My cue is villainous melancholy, with a sigh like Tom o' Bedlam.
EDMUND *1, 2, 129*

55 KENT: You have that in your countenance which I would fain
call master.
LEAR: What's that?
KENT: Authority. *1, 4, 28*

56 LEAR: Dost thou call me fool, boy?
FOOL: All thy other titles thou hast given away; that thou wast
born with.                              *King Lear, 1, 4, 147*

57 Ingratitude, thou marble-hearted fiend,
More hideous when thou show'st thee in a child
Than the sea-monster!  LEAR                    *1, 4, 259*

58 How sharper than a serpent's tooth it is
To have a thankless child.  LEAR               *1, 4, 288*

59 Striving to better, oft we mar what's well.  ALBANY  *1, 4, 347*

60 O, let me not be mad, not mad, sweet heaven!
Keep me in temper; I would not be mad!  LEAR   *1, 5, 43*

61 Thou whoreson zed! thou unnecessary letter!  KENT  *2, 2, 58*

62 I have seen better faces in my time
Than stands on any shoulder that I see
Before me at this instant.  KENT               *2, 2, 88*

63 Fortune, good night; smile once more; turn thy wheel.  KENT
                                               *2, 2, 168*

64 Hysterica passio – down, thou climbing sorrow,
Thy element's below.  LEAR                     *2, 4, 56*

65                        You are old;
Nature in you stands on the very verge
Of her confine.  REGAN                         *2, 4, 144*

66 LEAR: I gave you all.
REGAN: And in good time you gave it.           *2, 4, 248*

67 O, reason not the need! Our basest beggars
Are in the poorest thing superfluous.
Allow not nature more than nature needs,
Man's life is cheap as beast's.  LEAR          *2, 4, 263*

68 And let not women's weapons, water-drops,
Stain my man's cheeks!  LEAR                   *2, 4, 276*

69 No, I'll not weep.
I have full cause of weeping; but this heart
Shall break into a hundred thousand flaws
Or ere I'll weep. O fool, I shall go mad!  LEAR  *2, 4, 282*

70 Who's there, besides foul weather?  KENT     *3, 1, 1*

71 Blow, winds, and crack your cheeks; rage, blow.
You cataracts and hurricanoes, spout
Till you have drench'd our steeples, drown'd the cocks.  LEAR
                                               *3, 2, 1*

72 Rumble thy bellyful. Spit, fire; spout, rain.
Nor rain, wind, thunder, fire, are my daughters.
I tax not you, you elements, with unkindness.  LEAR  *3, 2, 14*

73          Here I stand, you slave,
A poor, infirm, weak and despis'd old man.  LEAR
                                        *King Lear, 3, 2, 19*

74 For there was never yet fair woman but she made mouths in a
   glass.  FOOL                               *3, 2, 35*

75          Things that love night
Love not such nights as these.  KENT        *3, 2, 42*

76          I am a man
More sinn'd against than sinning.  LEAR      *3, 2, 59*

77 O, that way madness lies; let me shun that.  LEAR  *3, 4, 21*

78 Poor naked wretches, wheresoe'er you are,
   That bide the pelting of this pitiless storm,
   How shall your houseless heads and unfed sides,
   Your loop'd and window'd raggedness, defend you
   From seasons such as these?  LEAR          *3, 4, 28*

79          Take physic, pomp;
Expose thyself to feel what wretches feel.  LEAR  *3, 4, 33*

80 'Tis a naughty night to swim in.  FOOL     *3, 4, 109*

81 Poor Tom's a-cold.  EDGAR                  *3, 4, 143*

82 Child Rowland to the dark tower came,
   His word was still 'Fie, foh, and fum,
   I smell the blood of a British man'.  EDGAR  *3, 4, 178*

83          Out vile jelly!
Where is thy lustre now?  CORNWALL           *3, 7, 82*

84          The worst is not
So long as we can say 'This is the worst'.  EDGAR  *4, 1, 28*

85 As flies to wanton boys are we to th' gods –
   They kill us for their sport.  GLOUCESTER  *4, 1, 37*

86 Wisdom and goodness to the vile seem vile;
   Filths savour but themselves.  ALBANY      *4, 2, 38*

87          It is the stars,
The stars above us, govern our conditions.  KENT  *4, 3, 32*

88          How fearful
And dizzy 'tis to cast one's eyes so low!
The crows and choughs that wing the mid-way air
Show scarce so gross as beetles.  EDGAR      *4, 6, 11*

89 Ay, every inch a king.  LEAR               *4, 6, 107*

90 The wren goes to't, and the small gilded fly
   Does lecher in my sight.  LEAR             *4, 6, 112*

91 Give me an ounce of civet, good apothecary, to sweeten my
   imagination.  LEAR                        *4, 6, 129*

92 Through tatter'd clothes small vices do appear;
   Robes and furr'd gowns hide all.  LEAR    *King Lear, 4, 6, 164*

93             Get thee glass eyes,
   And, like a scurvy politician, seem
   To see the things thou dost not.  LEAR        *4, 6, 170*

94 When we are born, we cry that we are come
   To this great stage of fools.  LEAR         *4, 6, 183*

95             Mine enemy's dog,
   Though he had bit me, should have stood that night
   Against my fire.  CORDELIA           *4, 7, 36*

96 Thou art a soul in bliss; but I am bound
   Upon a wheel of fire, that mine own tears
   Do scald like molten lead.  LEAR         *4, 7, 46*

97 I am a very foolish fond old man,
   Fourscore and upward, not an hour more nor less;
   And, to deal plainly,
   I fear I am not in my perfect mind.  LEAR    *4, 7, 60*

98             Men must endure
   Their going hence, even as their coming hither:
   Ripeness is all.  EDGAR            *5, 2, 9*

99            Come, let's away to prison.
   We two alone will sing like birds i' th' cage;
   When thou dost ask me blessing, I'll kneel down
   And ask of thee forgiveness; so we'll live,
   And pray, and sing, and tell old tales, and laugh
   At gilded butterflies, and hear poor rogues
   Talk of court news; and we'll talk with them too –
   Who loses and who wins; who's in, who's out –
   And take upon's the mystery of things
   As if we were God's spies.  LEAR         *5, 3, 8*

1 The gods are just, and of our pleasant vices
   Make instruments to plague us:
   The dark and vicious place where thee he got
   Cost him his eyes.  EDGAR          *5, 3, 170*

2 The wheel is come full circle.  EDMUND    *5, 3, 174*

3             But his flaw'd heart –
   Alack, too weak the conflict to support! –
   'Twixt two extremes of passion, joy and grief,
   Burst smilingly.  EDGAR          *5, 3, 196*

4 How, howl, howl, howl! O, you are men of stones!
   Had I your tongues and eyes, I'd use them so
   That heaven's vault should crack.  LEAR    *5, 3, 257*

5          Her voice was ever soft,
Gentle, and low – an excellent thing in woman.  LEAR
                                         *King Lear, 5, 3, 272*

6 And my poor fool is hang'd! No, no, no life!
Why should a dog, a horse, a rat have life,
And thou no breath at all? Thou'lt come no more,
Never, never, never, never, never.
Pray you undo this button.  LEAR          *5, 3, 305*

7 Vex not his ghost. O, let him pass! He hates him
That would upon the rack of this tough world
Stretch him out longer.  KENT             *5, 3, 313*


**Love's Labour's Lost**

8 Spite of cormorant devouring Time.  KING          *1, 1, 4*

9 Why, all delights are vain; but that most vain
Which, with pain purchas'd, doth inherit pain.  BEROWNE
                                                   *1, 1, 72*

10 Small have continual plodders ever won,
Save base authority from others' books.  BEROWNE   *1, 1, 86*

11 At Christmas I no more desire a rose
Than wish a snow in May's new-fangled shows.  BEROWNE
                                                   *1, 1, 105*

12 Remuneration! O, that's the Latin word for three farthings.
                                     COSTARD  *3, 1, 129*

13 He hath never fed of the dainties that are bred in a book; he
hath not eat paper, as it were; he hath not drunk ink; his intellect
is not replenished.  SIR NATHANIEL          *4, 2, 22*

14 For where is any author in the world
Teaches such beauty as a woman's eye?
Learning is but an adjunct to ourself.  BEROWNE   *4, 3, 308*

15 And when Love speaks, the voice of all the gods
Make heaven drowsy with the harmony.  BEROWNE   *4, 3, 340*

16 From women's eyes this doctrine I derive.
They sparkle still the right Promethean fire;
They are the books, the arts, the academes,
That show, contain, and nourish, all the world.  ROSALINE
                                                   *4, 3, 346*

17 A world-without-end bargain.  PRINCESS         *5, 2, 777*

18 A jest's prosperity lies in the ear
Of him that hears it, never in the tongue
Of him that makes it.  BEROWNE             *5, 2, 849*

19 When daisies pied and violets blue
And lady-smocks all silver-white
And cuckoo-buds of yellow hue
Do paint the meadows with delight,
The cuckoo then on every tree
Mocks married men, for thus sings he:
'Cuckoo;
Cuckoo, cuckoo' – O word of fear,
Unpleasing to a married ear!  SPRING
*Love's Labour's Lost, 5, 2, 881*

20 When icicles hang by the wall,
And Dick the shepherd blows his nail,
And Tom bears logs into the hall,
And milk comes frozen home in pail,
When blood is nipp'd, and ways be foul,
Then nightly sings the staring owl:
'Tu-who;
Tu-whit, Tu-who' – A merry note,
While greasy Joan doth keel the pot.

When all aloud the wind doth blow,
And coughing drowns the parson's saw,
And birds sit brooding in the snow,
And Marian's nose looks red and raw,
When roasted crabs hiss in the bowl.  WINTER      *5, 2, 899*

21 The words of Mercury are harsh after the songs of Apollo.
ARMADO   *5, 2, 917*

## Macbeth

22 1ST WITCH: When shall we three meet again?
In thunder, lightning, or in rain?
2ND WITCH: When the hurlyburly's done,
When the battle's lost and won.      *1, 1, 1*

23 Fair is foul, and foul is fair:
Hover through the fog and filthy air.  THREE WITCHES
*1, 1, 10*

24 What bloody man is that?  DUNCAN      *1, 2, 1*

25 So foul and fair a day I have not seen. MACBETH   *1, 3, 38*

26 What are these,
So wither'd, and so wild in their attire,
That look not like th' inhabitants o' th' earth,
And yet are on't?  BANQUO      *1, 3, 39*

27 If you can look into the seeds of time
   And say which grain will grow and which will not,
   Speak then to me, who neither beg nor fear
   Your favours nor your hate.   BANQUO        *Macbeth, 1, 3, 58*

28 This supernatural soliciting
   Cannot be ill; cannot be good.   MACBETH        *1, 3, 130*

29 Come what come may,
   Time and the hour runs through the roughest day.   MACBETH
                                                    *1, 3, 146*

30 Nothing in his life
   Became him like the leaving it: he died
   As one that had been studied in his death
   To throw away the dearest thing he ow'd
   As 'twere a careless trifle.   MALCOLM        *1, 4, 7*

31 Stars, hide your fires.   MACBETH        *1, 4, 50*

32 Yet do I fear thy nature;
   It is too full o' th' milk of human kindness
   To catch the nearest way.   LADY MACBETH        *1, 5, 13*

33 Come, thick night,
   And pall thee in the dunnest smoke of hell.   LADY MACBETH
                                                    *1, 5, 47*

34 O, never
   Shall sun that morrow see!
   Your face, my thane, is as a book where men
   May read strange matters.   LADY MACBETH        *1, 5, 57*

35 If it were done when 'tis done, then 'twere well
   It were done quickly.   MACBETH        *1, 7, 1*

36 That but this blow
   Might be the be-all and the end-all here –
   But here upon this bank and shoal of time –
   We'd jump the life to come.   MACBETH        *1, 7, 4*

37 I have no spur
   To prick the sides of my intent, but only
   Vaulting ambition, which o'er-leaps itself,
   And falls on th' other.   MACBETH        *1, 7, 25*

38 MACBETH: If we should fail?
   LADY MACBETH:                    We fail!
              But screw your courage to the sticking place,
              And we'll not fail.        *1, 7, 59*

39 False face must hide what the false heart doth know.   MACBETH
                                                    *1, 7, 82*

40 Is this a dagger which I see before me,
The handle toward my hand? MACBETH   *Macbeth, 2, 1, 33*

41        The bell invites me.
Hear it not, Duncan, for it is a knell
That summons thee to heaven or to hell. MACBETH   *2, 1, 62*

42 Methought I heard a voice cry 'Sleep no more;
Macbeth does murder sleep' – the innocent sleep,
Sleep that knits up the ravell'd sleave of care,
The death of each day's life, sore labour's bath,
Balm of hurt minds, great nature's second course,
Chief nourisher in life's feast. MACBETH   *2, 2, 35*

43 Will all great Neptune's ocean wash this blood
Clean from my hand? No; this my hand will rather
The multitudinous seas incarnadine,
Making the green one red. MACBETH   *2, 2, 60*

44 I had thought to have let in some of all professions that go the
primrose way to th' everlasting bonfire. PORTER   *2, 3, 18*

45 It provokes the desire, but it takes away the performance. Therefore much drink may be said to be an equivocator with lechery.
                                              PORTER   *2, 3, 28*

46 Had I but died an hour before this chance,
I had liv'd a blessed time; for, from this instant,
There's nothing serious in mortality –
All is but toys. MACBETH   *2, 3, 89*

47          Where we are,
There's daggers in men's smiles; the near in blood,
The nearer bloody. DONALBAIN   *2, 3, 138*

48 Ay, in the catalogue ye go for men;
As hounds, and greyhounds, mongrels, spaniels, curs,
Shoughs, water-rugs, and demi-wolves, are clept
All by the name of dogs. MACBETH   *3, 1, 91*

49 I am one, my liege,
Whom the vile blows and buffets of the world
Hath so incens'd that I am reckless what
I do to spite the world. 2ND MURDERER   *3, 1, 107*

50 Nought's had, all's spent,
Where our desire is got without content.
'Tis safer to be that which we destroy,
Than by destruction dwell in doubtful joy. LADY MACBETH
                                                    *3, 2, 4*

51         Duncan is in his grave;
After life's fitful fever he sleeps well. MACBETH   *3, 2, 22*

52 Things bad begun make strong themselves by ill.  MACBETH
*Macbeth, 3, 2, 55*

53 I had else been perfect,
Whole as the marble, founded as the rock,
As broad and general as the casing air,
But now I am cabin'd, cribb'd, confin'd, bound in
To saucy doubts and fears.  MACBETH                    *3, 4, 21*

54 Now good digestion wait on appetite,
And health on both!  MACBETH                           *3, 4, 38*

55                    The time has been
That when the brains were out the man would die,
And there an end.  MACBETH                             *3, 4, 78*

56 Stand not upon the order of your going,
But go at once.  LADY MACBETH                          *3, 4, 119*

57                    I am in blood
Stepp'd in so far that, should I wade no more,
Returning were as tedious as go o'er.  MACBETH         *3, 4, 136*

58 Double, double toil and trouble;
Fire burn, and cauldron bubble.  THREE WITCHES         *4, 1, 10*

59 Ditch-deliver'd by a drab.  3RD WITCH                *4, 1, 31*

60 How now, you secret, black, and midnight hags!  MACBETH
*4, 1, 47*

61 A deed without a name.  THREE WITCHES                *4, 1, 49*

62 Be bloody, bold, and resolute; laugh to scorn
The pow'r of man, for none of woman born
Shall harm Macbeth.  SECOND APPARITION                 *4, 1, 79*

63 But yet I'll make assurance double sure,
And take a bond of fate.  MACBETH                      *4, 1, 83*

64 What, will the line stretch out to th' crack of doom?  MACBETH
*4, 1, 117*

65 I think our country sinks beneath the yoke;
It weeps, it bleeds; and each new day a gash
Is added to her wounds.  MALCOLM                       *4, 3  39*

66 Stands Scotland where it did?  MACDUFF               *4, 3, 164*

67 The night is long that never finds the day.  MALCOLM *4, 3, 240*

68 Out, damned spot! out, I say!  LADY MACBETH          *5, 1, 33*

69 Here's the smell of the blood still.  All the perfumes of Arabia
will not sweeten this little hand.  LADY MACBETH       *5, 1, 48*

70 To bed, to bed; there's knocking at the gate. Come, come, come,
come, give me your hand. What's done cannot be undone.
LADY MACBETH  *5, 1, 64*

71 I have liv'd long enough. My way of life
Is fall'n into the sear, the yellow leaf;
And that which should accompany old age,
As honour, love, obedience, troops of friends,
I must not look to have. MACBETH *Macbeth, 5, 3, 22*

72 Canst thou not minister to a mind diseas'd,
Pluck from the memory a rooted sorrow,
Raze out the written troubles of the brain,
And with some sweet oblivious antidote
Cleanse the stuff'd bosom of that perilous stuff
Which weighs upon the heart? MACBETH *5, 3, 40*

73 I will not be afraid of death and bane
Till Birnam Forest come to Dunsinane. MACBETH *5, 3, 59*

74 Hang out our banners on the outward walls;
The cry is still 'They come'. MACBETH *5, 5, 1*

75 I have supp'd full with horrors. MACBETH *5, 5, 13*

76 She should have died hereafter;
There would have been a time for such a word.
Tomorrow, and tomorrow, and tomorrow,
Creeps in this petty pace from day to day
To the last syllable of recorded time,
And all our yesterdays have lighted fools
The way to dusty death. Out, out, brief candle!
Life's but a walking shadow, a poor player,
That struts and frets his hour upon the stage,
And then is heard no more; it is a tale
Told by an idiot, full of sound and fury,
Signifying nothing. MACBETH *5, 5, 17*

77 I gin to be aweary of the sun,
And wish th' estate o' th' world were now undone.
Ring the alarum bell. Blow wind, come wrack;
At least we'll die with harness on our back. MACBETH *5, 5, 49*

78 MACBETH: I bear a charmed life, which must not yield
To one of woman born.
MACDUFF: Despair thy charm;
And let the angel whom thou still hast serv'd
Tell thee Macduff was from his mother's womb
Untimely ripp'd. *5, 8, 12*

79 Live to be the show and gaze o' th' time. MACDUFF *5, 8, 24*

80 Lay on, Macduff;
And damn'd be him that first cries 'Hold, enough!'
MACBETH *5, 8, 33*

**Measure for Measure**

81 'Tis one thing to be tempted, Escalus,
   Another thing to fall. I not deny
   The jury, passing on the prisoner's life,
   May in the sworn twelve have a thief or two
   Guiltier than him they try.  ANGELO              *2, 1, 17*

82 Some rise by sin, and some by virtue fall.  ESCALUS   *2, 1, 38*

83 This will last out a night in Russia,
   When nights are longest there.  ANGELO          *2, 1, 128*

84 No ceremony that to great ones longs,
   Not the king's crown nor the deputed sword,
   The marshal's truncheon nor the judge's robe,
   Become them with one half so good a grace
   As mercy does.  ISABELLA                        *2, 2, 59*

85 The law hath not been dead, though it hath slept.  ANGELO
                                                   *2, 2, 90*

86                      O, it is excellent
   To have a giant's strength! But it is tyrannous
   To use it like a giant.  ISABELLA               *2, 2, 107*

87                      But man, proud man,
   Dress'd in a little brief authority,
   Most ignorant of what he's most assur'd,
   His glassy essence, like an angry ape,
   Plays such fantastic tricks before high heaven
   As makes the angels weep.  ISABELLA             *2, 2, 117*

88 That in the captain's but a choleric word
   Which in the soldier is flat blasphemy.  ISABELLA   *2, 2, 130*

89 The miserable have no other medicine
   But only hope.  CLAUDIO                          *3, 1, 2*

90 Ay, but to die, and go we know not where;
   To lie in cold obstruction, and to rot;
   This sensible warm motion to become
   A kneaded clod; and the delighted spirit
   To bathe in fiery floods or to reside
   In thrilling region of thick-ribbed ice.  CLAUDIO   *3, 1, 119*

91 The weariest and most loathed worldly life
   That age, ache, penury, and imprisonment,
   Can lay on nature is a paradise
   To what we fear of death.  CLAUDIO              *3, 1, 130*

92 Take, O, take those lips away,
   That so sweetly were forsworn;

And those eyes, the break of day,
   Lights that do mislead the morn;
But my kisses bring again, bring again;
Seals of love, but seal'd in vain, seal'd in vain. SONG
                        *Measure for Measure, 4, 1, 1*

93 I am a kind of burr; I shall stick.  LUCIO       *4, 3, 173*

94 Haste still pays haste, and leisure answers leisure;
Like doth quit like, and Measure still for Measure. DUKE
                                *5, 1, 408*

95 What's mine is yours, and what is yours is mine.  DUKE
                                *5, 1, 535*

**The Merchant of Venice**

96 I hold the world but as the world, Gratiano –
A stage, where every man must play a part,
And mine a sad one.  ANTONIO        *1, 1, 77*

97 There are a sort of men whose visages
Do cream and mantle like a standing pond.  GRATIANO
                                *1, 1, 88*

98 As who should say 'I am Sir Oracle,
And when I ope my lips let no dog bark'.  GRATIANO  *1, 1, 93*

99 In Belmont is a lady richly left,
And she is fair and, fairer than that word,
Of wondrous virtues.  BASSANIO         *1, 1, 161*

1 By my troth, Nerissa, my little body is aweary of this great
world.  PORTIA                 *1, 2, 1*

2 If to do were as easy as to know what were good to do, chapels
had been churches, and poor men's cottages princes' palaces.
                        PORTIA  *1. 2, 11*

3 How like a fawning publican he looks!
I hate him for he is a Christian;
But more for that in low simplicity
He lends out money gratis, and brings down
The rate of usance here with us in Venice.
If I can catch him once upon the hip,
I will feed fat the ancient grudge I bear him. SHYLOCK *1, 3, 36*

4 The devil can cite Scripture for his purpose.  ANTONIO *1, 3, 93*

5            Many a time and oft
In the Rialto you have rated me.  SHYLOCK      *1, 3, 101*

6 Still have I borne it with a patient shrug,
For suff'rance is the badge of all our tribe;
You call me misbeliever, cut-throat dog,
And spit upon my Jewish gaberdine.  SHYLOCK    *1, 3, 104*

7 I like not fair terms and a villain's mind.  BASSANIO
*The Merchant of Venice*, 1, 3, 174

8 It is a wise father that knows his own child.  LAUNCELOT GOBBO
2, 2, 69

9 There is some ill a-brewing towards my rest,
For I did dream of money-bags tonight.  SHYLOCK    2, 5, 17

10 But love is blind, and lovers cannot see
The pretty follies that themselves commit.  JESSICA    2, 6, 36

11 The ancient saying is no heresy:
Hanging and wiving goes by destiny.  NERISSA       2, 9, 82

12 Let him look to his bond.  SHYLOCK                 3, 1, 39

13 Hath not a Jew eyes? Hath not a Jew hands, organs, dimensions,
senses, affections, passions, fed with the same food, hurt with
the same weapons, subject to the same diseases, healed by the
same means, warmed and cooled by the same winter and
summer, as a Christian is? If you prick us, do we not bleed?
If you tickle us, do we not laugh? If you poison us, do we not
die? And if you wrong us, shall we not revenge?  SHYLOCK
3, 1, 49

14 Tell me where is fancy bred,
Or in the heart or in the head,
How begot, how nourished?  SONG                    3, 2, 63

15 The quality of mercy is not strain'd;
It droppeth as the gentle rain from heaven
Upon the place beneath. It is twice blest:
It blesseth him that gives and him that takes.
'Tis mightiest in the mightiest; it becomes
The throned monarch better than his crown;
His sceptre shows the force of temporal power,
The attribute to awe and majesty,
Wherein doth sit the dread and fear of kings;
But mercy is above this sceptred sway,
It is enthroned in the hearts of kings,
It is an attribute to God himself;
And earthly power doth then show likest God's
When mercy seasons justice. Therefore, Jew,
Though justice be thy plea, consider this —
That in the course of justice none of us
Should see salvation; we do pray for mercy,
And that same prayer doth teach us all to render
The deeds of mercy.  PORTIA                        4, 1, 179

16 Wrest once the law to your authority;
To do a great right do a little wrong.  BASSANIO    4, 1, 210

17 A Daniel come to judgment! Yea, a Daniel! SHYLOCK
                    *The Merchant of Venice, 4, 1, 218*

18 'Tis not in the bond. SHYLOCK               *4, 1, 257*

19 A pound of that same merchant's flesh is thine.
The court awards it and the law doth give it. PORTIA
                                           *4, 1, 294*

20 You take my house when you do take the prop
That doth sustain my house; you take my life
When you do take the means whereby I live. SHYLOCK
                                           *4, 1, 370*

21 He is well paid that is well satisfied. PORTIA    *4, 1, 410*

22 How sweet the moonlight sleeps upon this bank!
Here will we sit and let the sounds of music
Creep in our ears; soft stillness and the night
Become the touches of sweet harmony.
Sit, Jessica. Look how the floor of heaven
Is thick inlaid with patines of bright gold;
There's not the smallest orb which thou behold'st
But in his motion like an angel sings,
Still quiring to the young-ey'd cherubins;
Such harmony is in immortal souls,
But whilst this muddy vesture of decay
Doth grossly close it in, we cannot hear it. LORENZO  *5, 1, 54*

23 I am never merry when I hear sweet music. JESSICA  *5, 1, 69*

24 The man that hath no music in himself,
Nor is not mov'd with concord of sweet sounds,
Is fit for treasons, stratagems, and spoils. LORENZO  *5, 1, 83*

25 How far that little candle throws his beams!
So shines a good deed in a naughty world. PORTIA  *5, 1, 90*

26 For a light wife doth make a heavy husband. PORTIA
                                           *5, 1, 130*

## The Merry Wives of Windsor

27 I will make a Star Chamber matter of it. SHALLOW    *1, 1, 1*

28 I had rather than forty shillings I had my Book of Songs and
Sonnets here. SLENDER                          *1, 1, 179*

29 Here will be an old abusing of God's patience and the King's
English. MISTRESS QUICKLY                     *1, 4, 5*

30 Why, then the world's mine oyster,
Which I with sword will open. PISTOL           *2, 2, 4*

31 I cannot tell what the dickens his name is. MRS PAGE  *3, 2, 15*

32 O, what a world of vile ill-favour'd faults
Looks handsome in three hundred pounds a year! ANNE PAGE
*The Merry Wives of Windsor*, *3, 4, 32*

33 I'll no pullet-sperm in my brewage. FALSTAFF *3, 5, 27*

34 They say there is divinity in odd numbers, either in nativity,
chance, or death. FALSTAFF *5, 1, 3*

**A Midsummer Night's Dream**

35 To live a barren sister all your life,
Chanting faint hymns to the cold fruitless moon. THESEUS
*1, 1, 72*

36　　　　　For aught that I could ever read,
Could ever hear by tale or history,
The course of true love never did run smooth. LYSANDER
*1, 1, 132*

37 O hell! to choose love by another's eyes. HERMIA *1, 1, 140*

38 Love looks not with the eyes, but with the mind;
And therefore is wing'd Cupid painted blind. HELENA
*1, 1, 234*

39 'The most Lamentable Comedy and most Cruel Death of
Pyramus and Thisby.' QUINCE *1, 2, 10*

40 A part to tear a cat in, to make all split. BOTTOM *1, 2, 24*

41 I am slow of study. SNUG *1, 2, 59*

42 Over hill, over dale,
　Thorough bush, thorough brier,
Over park, over pale,
　Thorough flood, thorough fire. FAIRY *2, 1, 2*

43 Ill met by moonlight, proud Titania. OBERON *2, 1, 60*

44 Since once I sat upon a promontory,
And heard a mermaid on a dolphin's back
Uttering such dulcet and harmonious breath
That the rude sea grew civil at her song,
And certain stars shot madly from their spheres
To hear the sea-maid's music. OBERON *2, 1, 149*

45 I'll put a girdle round about the earth
In forty minutes. PUCK *2, 1, 175*

46 I know a bank whereon the wild thyme blows,
Where oxlips and the nodding violet grows,
Quite over-canopied with luscious woodbine,
With sweet musk-roses, and with eglantine. OBERON *2, 1, 249*

47 A lion among ladies is a most dreadful thing; for there is not a
more fearful wild-fowl than your lion living. BOTTOM *3, 1, 27*

48 A calendar, a calendar! Look in the almanack; find out moonshine, find out moonshine.  BOTTOM
*A Midsummer Night's Dream, 3, 1, 46*

49 Bless thee, Bottom, bless thee! Thou art translated.  QUINCE
*3, 1, 109*

50 Lord, what fools these mortals be!  PUCK          *3, 2, 115*

51 I have a reasonable good ear in music. Let's have the tongs and
the bones.  BOTTOM                                *4, 1, 26*

52 The lunatic, the lover, and the poet,
Are of imagination all compact.  THESEUS            *5, 1, 7*

53 The poet's eye, in a fine frenzy rolling,
Doth glance from heaven to earth, from earth to heaven;
And as imagination bodies forth
The forms of things unknown, the poet's pen
Turns them to shapes, and gives to airy nothing
A local habitation and a name.  THESEUS            *5, 1, 12*

54 Very tragical mirth.  THESEUS                     *5, 1, 57*

55 The iron tongue of midnight hath told twelve.
Lovers, to bed; 'tis almost fairy time.  THESEUS   *5, 1, 352*


## Much Ado About Nothing

56 A victory is twice itself when the achiever brings home full
numbers.  LEONATO                                  *1, 1, 7*

57 He wears his faith but as the fashion of his hat.  BEATRICE
*1, 1, 62*

58 BEATRICE: I wonder that you will still be talking, Signior Benedick; nobody marks you.
BENEDICK: What, my dear Lady Disdain! Are you yet living?
*1, 1, 99*

59 Would you have me speak after my custom, as being a professed
tyrant to their sex?  BENEDICK                     *1, 1, 144*

60 Benedick the married man.  BENEDICK               *1, 1, 232*

61 What need the bridge much broader than the flood?
DON PEDRO  *1, 1, 278*

62 Friendship is constant in all other things
Save in the office and affairs of love.  CLAUDIO   *2, 1, 154*

63 She speaks poniards, and every word stabs.  BENEDICK
*2, 1, 220*

64 Silence is the perfectest herald of joy: I were but little happy if I
could say how much.  CLAUDIO                       *2, 1, 275*

65 DON PEDRO: Will you have me, lady?

   BEATRICE: No, my lord, unless I might have another for working-days; your Grace is too costly to wear every day. *Much Ado About Nothing, 2, 1, 293*

66 I was born to speak all mirth and no matter. BEATRICE
   2, 1, 297

67 There was a star danc'd, and under that was I born. BEATRICE
   2, 1, 302

68 Sigh no more, ladies, sigh no more,
   Men were deceivers ever,
   One foot in sea and one on shore,
   To one thing constant never. BALTHASAR    2, 3, 57

69 Doth not the appetite alter? A man loves the meat in his youth
   that he cannot endure in his age. BENEDICK    2, 3, 215

70 The world must be peopled. When I said I would die a bachelor
   I did not think I should live till I were married. BENEDICK
   2, 3, 219

71 Disdain and scorn ride sparkling in her eyes. HERO    3, 1, 51

72 Are you good men and true? DOGBERRY    3, 3, 1

73 To be a well-favoured man is the gift of fortune; but to write
   and read comes by nature. DOGBERRY    3, 3, 13

74 You are thought here to be the most senseless and fit man for
   the constable of the watch. DOGBERRY    3, 3, 19

75 For the watch to babble and to talk is most tolerable and not
   to be endured. DOGBERRY    3, 3, 32

76 I thank God I am as honest as any man living that is an old
   man and no honester than I. VERGES    3, 5, 13

77 Comparisons are odorous. DOGBERRY    3, 5, 16

78 A good old man, sir, he will be talking; as they say 'When the
   age is in the wit is out'. DOGBERRY    3, 5, 32

79 Our watch, sir, have indeed comprehended two aspicious persons. DOGBERRY    3, 5, 42

80 O, what men dare do! What men may do! What men daily do,
   not knowing what they do! CLAUDIO    4, 1, 18

81                    For it so falls out
   That what we have we prize not to the worth
   Whiles we enjoy it, but being lack'd and lost,
   Why, then we rack the value, then we find
   The virtue that possession would not show us
   Whiles it was ours. FRIAR FRANCIS    4, 1, 217

82 Write down that they hope they serve God; and write God first; for God defend but God should go before such villains!
DOGBERRY  *Much Ado About Nothing, 4, 2, 17*

83 Flat burglary as ever was committed.  DOGBERRY          *4, 2, 46*

84 O villain! thou wilt be condemn'd into everlasting redemption for this.  DOGBERRY          *4, 2, 52*

85 O that he were here to write me down an ass!  DOGBERRY
*4, 2, 70*

86 For there was never yet philosopher
That could endure the toothache patiently.  LEONATO  *5, 1, 35*

87 They have committed false report; moreover, they have spoken untruths; secondarily, they are slanders; sixth and lastly, they have belied a lady; thirdly, they have verified unjust things; and to conclude, they are lying knaves.  DOGBERRY  *5, 1, 204*

88 Done to death by slanderous tongues.  CLAUDIO          *5, 3, 3*


**Othello**

89 But I will wear my heart upon my sleeve
For daws to peck at.  IAGO          *1, 1, 65*

90                              Rude am I in my speech,
And little blest with the soft phrase of peace;
For since these arms of mine had seven years' pith,
Till now some nine moons wasted, they have us'd
Their dearest action in the tented field.  OTHELLO  *1, 3, 81*

91 I will a round unvarnish'd tale deliver
Of my whole course of love.  OTHELLO          *1, 3, 90*

92                              My story being done,
She gave me for my pains a world of sighs;
She swore, in faith, 'twas strange, 'twas passing strange;
'Twas pitiful, 'twas wondrous pitiful.
She wish'd she had not heard it; yet she wish'd
That heaven had made her such a man. She thank'd me;
And bade me, if I had a friend that lov'd her,
I should but teach him how to tell my story,
And that would woo her. Upon this hint I spake;
She lov'd me for the dangers I had pass'd;
And I lov'd her that she did pity them.
This only is the witchcraft I have us'd.  OTHELLO          *1, 3, 158*

93 To mourn a mischief that is past and gone
Is the next way to draw new mischief on.  DUKE  *1, 3, 204*

94 The robb'd that smiles steals something from the thief.  DUKE
*1, 3, 208*

95 Look to her, Moor, if thou hast eyes to see:
She has deceiv'd her father, and may thee.  BRABANTIO
*Othello, 1, 3, 292*

96 Put money in thy purse.  IAGO  *1, 3, 338*

97 For I am nothing if not critical.  IAGO  *2, 1, 119*

98 To suckle fools and chronicle small beer.  IAGO  *2, 1, 159*

99 But men are men; the best sometimes forget.  IAGO  *2, 3, 233*

1 Reputation, reputation, reputation! O, I have lost my reputation! I have lost the immortal part of myself, and what remains
is bestial.  CASSIO  *2, 3, 254*

2 Good wine is a good familiar creature if it be well us'd.  IAGO
*2, 3, 299*

3 How poor are they that have not patience!
What wound did ever heal but by degrees?  IAGO  *2, 3, 358*

4 Thereby hangs a tail.  CLOWN  *3, 1, 8*

5 Excellent wretch! Perdition catch my soul
But I do love thee; and when I love thee not
Chaos is come again.  OTHELLO  *3, 3, 91*

6 Good name in man and woman, dear my lord,
Is the immediate jewel of their souls:
Who steals my purse steals trash; 'tis something, nothing;
'Twas mine, 'tis his, and has been slave to thousands;
But he that filches from me my good name
Robs me of that which not enriches him
And makes me poor indeed.  IAGO  *3, 3, 159*

7 O, beware, my lord, of jealousy;
It is the green-ey'd monster which doth mock
The meat it feeds on.  IAGO  *3, 3, 169*

8         O curse of marriage,
That we can call these delicate creatures ours,
And not their appetites! I had rather be a toad,
And live upon the vapour of a dungeon,
Than keep a corner in the thing I love
For others' uses.  OTHELLO  *3, 3, 272*

9 He that is robb'd, not wanting what is stol'n,
Let him not know't, and he's not robb'd at all.  OTHELLO
*3, 3, 346*

10         O, now for ever
Farewell the tranquil mind! farewell content!
Farewell the plumed troops, and the big wars
That make ambition virtue! O, farewell!
Farewell the neighing steed and the shrill trump,
The spirit-stirring drum, th' ear-piercing fife,

The royal banner, and all quality,
Pride, pomp, and circumstance, of glorious war!  OTHELLO
*Othello, 3, 3, 351*

11 They are not ever jealous for the cause,
But jealous for they are jealous.  EMILIA  *3, 4, 161*

12 But yet the pity of it, Iago! O, Iago, the pity of it, Iago!
OTHELLO  *4, 1, 191*

13              But, alas, to make me
The fixed figure for the time of scorn
To point his slow unmoving finger at.  OTHELLO  *4, 2, 54*

14              O thou weed
Who are so lovely fair and smell'st so sweet
That the sense aches at thee!
Would thou had'st never been born!  OTHELLO  *4, 2, 67*

15 'Tis neither here nor there.  EMILIA  *4, 3, 57*

16          If Cassio do remain,
He hath a daily beauty in his life
That makes me ugly.  IAGO  *5, 1, 18*

17          This is the night
That either makes me or fordoes me quite.  IAGO  *5, 1, 128*

18 It is the cause, it is the cause, my soul –
Let me not name it to you, you chaste stars –
It is the cause.  OTHELLO  *5, 2, 1*

19 Put out the light, and then put out the light.
If I quench thee, thou flaming minister,
I can again thy former light restore,
Should I repent me; but once put out thy light,
Thou cunning'st pattern of excelling nature,
I know not where is that Promethean heat
That can thy light relume. When I have pluck'd thy rose,
I cannot give it vital growth again.  OTHELLO  *5, 2, 7*

20 Not Cassio kill'd! Then murder's out of tune,
And sweet revenge grows harsh.  OTHELLO  *5, 2, 118*

21 Here is my journey's end, here is my butt,
And very sea-mark of my utmost sail.  OTHELLO  *5, 2, 270*

22 Soft you; a word or two before you go.
I have done the state some service, and they know't –
No more of that. I pray you, in your letters,
When you shall these unlucky deeds relate,
Speak of me as I am; nothing extenuate,
Nor set down aught in malice. Then must you speak
Of one that lov'd not wisely, but too well;

Of one not easily jealous, but, being wrought,
Perplexed in the extreme; of one whose hand,
Like the base Indian, threw a pearl away
Richer than all his tribe; of one whose subdu'd eyes,
Albeit unused to the melting mood,
Drop tears as fast as the Arabian trees
Their med'cinable gum. Set you down this:
And say besides that in Aleppo once,
Where a malignant and a turban'd Turk
Beat a Venetian and traduc'd the state,
I took by th' throat the circumcised dog,
And smote him – thus.   OTHELLO        *Othello, 5, 2, 341*

23 I kiss'd thee ere I kill'd thee. No way but this –
Killing my self, to die upon a kiss.   OTHELLO        *5, 2, 361*


**Pericles**

24 See where she comes, apparell'd like the spring.   PERICLES
*1, 1, 12*

25 Few love to hear the sins they love to act.   PERICLES   *1, 1, 92*

26 Kings are earth's gods; in vice their law's their will.   PERICLES
*1, 1, 103*

27 3RD FISHERMAN: Master, I marvel how the fishes live in the sea.
1ST FISHERMAN: Why, as men do a-land – the great ones eat up
the little ones.        *2, 1, 27*


**King Richard the Second**

28 Old John of Gaunt, time-honoured Lancaster.   RICHARD II
*1, 1, 1*

29 Let's purge this choler without letting blood.   RICHARD II
*1, 1, 153*

30 The purest treasure mortal times afford
Is spotless reputation; that away,
Men are but gilded loam or painted clay.
A jewel in a ten-times barr'd-up chest
Is a bold spirit in a loyal breast.
Mine honour is my life; both grow in one;
Take honour from me, and my life is done.   MOWBRAY
*1, 1, 177*

31 We were not born to sue, but to command.   RICHARD II
*1, 1, 196*

32 That which in mean men we entitle patience
Is pale cold cowardice in noble breasts.
DUCHESS OF GLOUCESTER   *1, 2, 33*

33                          This must my comfort be —
That sun that warms you here shall shine on me.
               BOLINGBROKE    *Richard the Second, 1, 3, 144*

34 How long a time lies in one little word!
Four lagging winters and four wanton springs
End in a word: such is the breath of Kings.    BOLINGBROKE
                                             *1, 3, 213*

35 Things sweet to taste prove in digestion sour.    GAUNT
                                             *1, 3, 236*

36 All places that the eye of heaven visits
Are to a wise man ports and happy havens.
Teach thy necessity to reason thus:
There is no virtue like necessity.    GAUNT        *1, 3, 275*

37 O, who can hold a fire in his hand
By thinking on the frosty Caucasus?
Or cloy the hungry edge of appetite
By bare imagination of a feast?
Or wallow naked in December snow
By thinking on fantastic summer's heat?
O, no! the apprehension of the good
Gives but the greater feeling to the worse.    BOLINGBROKE
                                             *1, 3, 295*

38 Pray God we may make haste, and come too late!
                              RICHARD II    *1, 4, 64*

39 More are men's ends mark'd than their lives before.
The setting sun, and music at the close,
As the last taste of sweets, is sweetest last,
Writ in remembrance more than things lost past.    GAUNT
                                             *2, 1, 11*

40 Methinks I am a prophet new inspir'd,
And thus expiring do foretell of him:
His rash fierce blaze of riot cannot last,
For violent fires soon burn out themselves;
Small showers last long, but sudden storms are short;
He tires betimes that spurs too fast betimes.    GAUNT    *2, 1, 31*

41 This royal throne of kings, this sceptred isle,
This earth of majesty, this seat of Mars,
This other Eden, demi-paradise,
This fortress built by Nature for herself
Against infection and the hand of war,
This happy breed of men, this little world,
This precious stone set in the silver sea,
Which serves it in the office of a wall,

Or as a moat defensive to a house,
Against the envy of less happier lands;
This blessed plot, this earth, this realm, this England,
This nurse, this teeming womb of royal kings,
Fear'd by their breed, and famous by their birth. GAUNT
*Richard the Second, 2, 1, 40*

42 England, bound in with the triumphant sea,
Whose rocky shore beats back the envious siege
Of wat'ry Neptune, is now bound in with shame,
With inky blots and rotten parchment bonds;
That England, that was wont to conquer others,
Hath made a shameful conquest of itself.
Ah, would the scandal vanish with my life,
How happy then were my ensuing death! GAUNT *2, 1, 61*

43 Can sick men play so nicely with their names? RICHARD II
*2, 1, 84*

44 I count myself in nothing else so happy
As in a soul rememb'ring my good friends. BOLINGBROKE
*2, 3, 46*

45 Grace me no grace, nor uncle me no uncle. YORK *2, 3, 87*

46 The caterpillars of the commonwealth. BOLINGBROKE
*2, 3, 166*

47 Things past redress are now with me past care. YORK
*2, 3, 171*

48 Eating the bitter bread of banishment. BOLINGBROKE *3, 1, 21*

49                            I weep for joy
To stand upon my kingdom once again.
Dear earth, I do salute thee with my hand,
Though rebels wound thee with their horses' hoofs.
RICHARD II *3, 2, 4*

50 Not all the water in the rough rude sea
Can wash the balm from an anointed king;
The breath of worldly men cannot depose
The deputy elected by the Lord. RICHARD II *3, 2, 54*

51 O, call back yesterday, bid time return. SALISBURY *3, 2, 69*

52 Cry woe, destruction, ruin, and decay –
The worst is death, and death will have his day. RICHARD II
*3, 2, 102*

53                    Of comfort no man speak.
Let's talk of graves, of worms, and epitaphs;
Make dust our paper, and with rainy eyes
Write sorrow on the bosom of the earth.
Let's choose executors and talk of wills. RICHARD II *3, 2, 144*

54 For God's sake let us sit upon the ground
   And tell sad stories of the death of kings:
   How some have been depos'd, some slain in war,
   Some haunted by the ghosts they have depos'd,
   Some poison'd by their wives, some sleeping kill'd,
   All murder'd – for within the hollow crown
   That rounds the mortal temples of a king
   Keeps Death his court; and there the antic sits,
   Scoffing his state and grinning at his pomp;
   Allowing him a breath, a little scene,
   To monarchize, be fear'd, and kill with looks;
   Infusing him with self and vain conceit,
   As if this flesh which walls about our life
   Were brass impregnable; and, humour'd thus,
   Comes at the last, and with a little pin
   Bores through his castle wall, and farewell, king! RICHARD II
                          *Richard the Second, 3, 2, 155*

55 What must the King do now? Must he submit?
   The King shall do it. Must he be depos'd?
   The King shall be contented. Must he lose
   The name of king? A God's name, let it go.
   I'll give my jewels for a set of beads,
   My gorgeous palace for a hermitage,
   My gay apparel for an almsman's gown,
   My figur'd goblets for a dish of wood,
   My sceptre for a palmer's walking staff,
   My subjects for a pair of carved saints,
   And my large kingdom for a little grave,
   A little little grave, an obscure grave. RICHARD II   *3, 3, 143*

56 And if you crown him, let me prophesy –
   The blood of English shall manure the ground
   And future ages groan for this foul act;
   Peace shall go sleep with Turks and infidels. CARLISLE
                                   *4, 1, 136*

57 Did they not sometime cry 'All hail!' to me?
   So Judas did to Christ; but he, in twelve,
   Found truth in all but one; I, in twelve thousand, none.
   God save the King! Will no man say amen?
   Am I both priest and clerk? Well then, amen. RICHARD II
                                   *4, 1, 169*

58 I give this heavy weight from off my head,
   And this unwieldy sceptre from my hand,
   The pride of kingly sway from out my heart;

With mine own tears I wash away my balm,
With mine own hands I give away my crown. RICHARD II
*Richard the Second, 4, 1, 204*

59 The woe's to come; the children yet unborn
Shall feel this day as sharp to them as thorn. CARLISLE
4, 1, 322

60    I am sworn brother, sweet,
To grim Necessity; and he and I
Will keep a league till death. RICHARD II   5, 1, 19

61 As in a theatre the eyes of men
After a well-grac'd actor leaves the stage
Are idly bent on him that enters next,
Thinking his prattle to be tedious. YORK   5, 2, 23

62 I have been studying how I may compare
This prison where I live unto the world. RICHARD II 5, 5, 1

63      How sour sweet music is
When time is broke and no proportion kept!
So is it in the music of men's lives. RICHARD II 5, 5, 42

## King Richard the Third

64 Now is the winter of our discontent
Made glorious summer by this sun of York. GLOUCESTER
1, 1, 1

65 Our stern alarums chang'd to merry meetings,
Our dreadful marches to delightful measures. GLOUCESTER
1, 1, 7

66 Deform'd, unfinish'd, sent before my time
Into this breathing world scarce half made up,
And that so lamely and unfashionable
That dogs bark at me as I halt by them. GLOUCESTER 1, 1, 20

67 In this weak piping time of peace. GLOUCESTER  1, 1, 24

68 I am determined to prove a villain. GLOUCESTER 1, 1, 30

69 Was ever woman in this humour woo'd?
Was ever woman in this humour won? GLOUCESTER
1, 2, 227

70 And thus I clothe my naked villainy
With odd old ends stol'n forth of holy writ,
And seem a saint when most I play the devil. GLOUCESTER
1, 3, 336

71 O, I have pass'd a miserable night,
So full of fearful dreams, of ugly sights,
That, as I am a Christian faithful man,

I would not spend another such a night
Though 'twere to buy a world of happy days –
So full of dismal terror was the time!   CLARENCE
*Richard the Third, 1, 4, 2*

72 O Lord, methought what pain it was to drown,
   What dreadful noise of waters in my ears,
   What sights of ugly death within my eyes!
   Methought I saw a thousand fearful wrecks,
   A thousand men that fishes gnaw'd upon,
   Wedges of gold, great anchors, heaps of pearl,
   Inestimable stones, unvalued jewels,
   All scatt'red in the bottom of the sea;
   Some lay in dead men's skulls, and in the holes
   Where eyes did once inhabit there were crept,
   As 'twere in scorn of eyes, reflecting gems,
   That woo'd the slimy bottom of the deep
   And mock'd the dead bones that lay scatt'red by.   CLARENCE
   *1, 4, 21*

73 So wise so young, they say, do never live long.   GLOUCESTER
   *3, 1, 79*

74 My lord of Ely, when I was last in Holborn
   I saw good strawberries in your garden there.   GLOUCESTER
   *3, 4, 32*

75 Talk'st thou to me of ifs? Thou art a traitor.
   Off with his head!   GLOUCESTER        *3, 4, 77*

76 High-reaching Buckingham grows circumspect.   RICHARD III
   *4, 2, 31*

77                But I am in
   So far in blood that sin will pluck on sin.   RICHARD III
   *4, 2, 65*

78 I am not in the giving vein today.   RICHARD III        *4, 2, 120*

79 Their lips were four red roses on a stalk,
   And in their summer beauty kiss'd each other.   TYRREL
   *4, 3, 12*

80 An honest tale speeds best being plainly told.
                                QUEEN ELIZABETH   *4, 4, 358*

81 Harp not on that string.   RICHARD III        *4, 4, 364*

82 Is the chair empty? Is the sword unsway'd?
   Is the King dead, the empire unpossess'd?   RICHARD III
   *4, 4, 470*

83 True hope is swift and flies with swallow's wings;
   Kings it makes gods, and meaner creatures kings.   RICHMOND
   *5, 2, 23*

84 The King's name is a tower of strength.  RICHARD III
                              *Richard the Third, 5, 3, 12*

85 I have not that alacrity of spirit
   Nor cheer of mind that I was wont to have.  RICHARD III
                                         *5, 3, 73*

86 My conscience hath a thousand several tongues,
   And every tongue brings in a several tale,
   And every tale condemns me for a villain.  RICHARD III
                                        *5, 3, 193*

87 A horse! a horse! my kingdom for a horse!  RICHARD III
                                          *5, 4, 7*


**Romeo and Juliet**

88 A pair of star-cross'd lovers.  CHORUS          *Prologue, 6*
89 The two hours' traffic of our stage.  CHORUS        *Ib, 12*
90 Saint-seducing gold.  ROMEO                     *1, 1, 213*
91 For I am proverb'd with a grandsire phrase;
   I'll be a candle-holder and look on.  ROMEO       *1, 4, 37*
92 O, then I see Queen Mab hath been with you.
   She is the fairies' widwife, and she comes
   In shape no bigger than an agate stone
   On the fore-finger of an alderman,
   Drawn with a team of little atomies
   Athwart men's noses as they lie asleep.  MERCUTIO  *1, 4, 53*
93 For you and I are past our dancing days.  CAPULET  *1, 5, 29*
94 O, she doth teach the torches to burn bright!
   It seems she hangs upon the cheek of night
   As a rich jewel in an Ethiop's ear –
   Beauty too rich for use, for earth too dear!  ROMEO  *1, 5, 42*
95 For I ne'er saw true beauty till this night.  ROMEO  *1, 5, 51*
96 My only love sprung from my only hate!  JULIET  *1, 5, 136*
97 He jests at scars that never felt a wound.
   But, soft! What light through yonder window breaks?
   It is the east, and Juliet is the sun.  ROMEO        *2, 2, 1*
98 See how she leans her cheek upon her hand!
   O that I were a glove upon that hand,
   That I might touch that cheek!  ROMEO              *2, 2, 23*
99 O Romeo, Romeo! wherefore art thou Romeo?  JULIET
                                          *2, 2, 33*
 1 What's in a name? That which we call a rose
   By any other name would smell as sweet.  JULIET  *2, 2, 43*

2 O, swear not by the moon, th' inconstant moon,
That monthly changes in her circled orb,
Lest that thy love prove likewise variable.  JULIET
*Romeo and Juliet, 2, 2, 109*

3 This bud of love, by summer's ripening breath,
May prove a beauteous flow'r when next we meet.  JULIET
2, 2, 121

4 Love goes toward love as school-boys from their books;
But love from love, toward school with heavy looks.  ROMEO
2, 2, 156

5 How silver-sweet sound lovers' tongues by night,
Like softest music to attending ears!  ROMEO      2, 2, 166

6 Good night, good night! Parting is such sweet sorrow
That I shall say good night till it be morrow.  JULIET  2, 2, 185

7 Wisely and slow; they stumble that run fast.  FRIAR LAWRENCE
2, 3, 94

8 O flesh, flesh, how art thou fishified!  MERCUTIO      2, 4, 37

9 I am the very pink of courtesy.  MERCUTIO      2, 4, 56

10 Therefore love moderately: long love doth so;
Too swift arrives as tardy as too slow.  FRIAR LAWRENCE
2, 6, 14

11 A plague o' both your houses!
They have made worms' meat of me.  MERCUTIO      3, 1, 103

12 O, I am fortune's fool!  ROMEO      3, 1, 133

13                         Come, civil night,
Thou sober-suited matron, all in black.  JULIET      3, 2, 10

14 Night's candles are burnt out, and jocund day
Stands tiptoe on the misty mountain tops.  ROMEO      3, 5, 9

15 Thank me no thankings, nor proud me no prouds.  CAPULET
3, 5, 152

16 'Tis an ill cook that cannot lick his own fingers.  SERVINGMAN
4, 2, 6

17                         Beauty's ensign yet
Is crimson in thy lips and in thy cheeks,
And death's pale flag is not advanced there.  ROMEO      5, 3, 94

18                         O, here
Will I set up my everlasting rest,
And shake the yoke of inauspicious stars
From this world-wearied flesh. Eyes, look your last.
Arms, take your last embrace.  ROMEO      5, 3, 109

**The Taming of the Shrew**

19 Look in the chronicles: we came in with Richard Conqueror.
CHRISTOPHER SLY  *Induction, 1, 4*

20 No profit grows where is no pleasure ta'en;
   In brief, sir, study what you most affect.  TRANIO        *1, 1, 39*

21 There's small choice in rotten apples.  HORTENSIO      *1, 1, 131*

22 Kiss me, Kate.  PETRUCHIO                               *2, 1, 316*

23 Thereby hangs a tale.  GRUMIO                           *4, 1, 50*

24 This is a way to kill a wife with kindness.  PETRUCHIO
*4, 1, 192*

25 Our purses shall be proud, our garments poor;
   For 'tis the mind that makes the body rich;
   And as the sun breaks through the darkest clouds,
   So honour peereth in the meanest habit.  PETRUCHIO  *4, 3, 167*

26 A woman mov'd is like a fountain troubled –
   Muddy, ill-seeming, thick, bereft of beauty.  KATHERINA
*5, 2, 142*

**The Tempest**

27 He hath no drowning mark upon him; his complexion is perfect
   gallows.  GONZALO                                      *1, 1, 28*

28 The wills above be done, but I would fain die a dry death.
GONZALO  *1, 1, 63*

29                        What seest thou else
   In the dark backward and abysm of time?  PROSPERO  *1, 2, 49*

30 Your tale, sir, would cure deafness.  MIRANDA         *1, 2, 106*

31                My library
   Was dukedom large enough.  PROSPERO                   *1, 2, 109*

32 From the still-vex'd Bermoothes.  ARIEL               *1, 2, 229*

33 You taught me language, and my profit on't
   Is, I know how to curse. The red plague rid you
   For learning me your language!  CALIBAN               *1, 2, 363*

34 Come unto these yellow sands,
      And then take hands.  ARIEL                         *1, 2, 375*

35 Full fathom five thy father lies;
      Of his bones are coral made;
   Those are pearls that were his eyes;
      Nothing of him that doth fade
   But doth suffer a sea-change
   Into something rich and strange.  ARIEL               *1, 2, 396*

36                This swift business
I must uneasy make, lest too light winning
Make the prize light.   PROSPERO      *The Tempest*, *1, 2, 450*

37 He receives comfort like cold porridge.   SEBASTIAN     *2, 1, 10*

38 I' th' commonwealth I would by contraries
Execute all things.   GONZALO                     *2, 1, 141*

39 While you here do snoring lie,
Open-ey'd conspiracy
  His time doth take.   ARIEL                 *2, 1, 291*

40 When they will not give a doit to relieve a lame beggar, they will
lay out ten to see a dead Indian.   TRINCULO     *2, 2, 29*

41 Misery acquaints a man with strange bedfellows.   TRINCULO
                                                    *2, 2, 38*

42 Well, here's my comfort. (*Drinks*)   STEPHANO     *2, 2, 43*

43 The master, the swabber, the boatswain, and I,
The gunner, and his mate,
Lov'd Mall, Meg, and Marian, and Margery,
But none of us car'd for Kate.   STEPHANO     *2, 2, 44*

44 'Ban 'Ban, Ca – Caliban,
Has a new master – Get a new man.   CALIBAN   *2, 2, 173*

45 They say there's but five upon this isle: we are three of them;
if th' other two be brain'd like us, the state totters.   TRINCULO
                                                *3, 2, 4*

46 He that dies pays all debts.   STEPHANO     *3, 2, 126*

47 Be not afeard.   The isle is full of noises,
Sounds, and sweet airs, that give delight, and hurt not.   CALIBAN
                                           *3, 2, 130*

48                Travellers ne'er did lie,
Though fools at home condemn 'em.   ANTONIO     *3, 3, 26*

49               You fools! I and my fellows
Are ministers of Fate; the elements
Of whom your swords are temper'd may as well
Wound the loud winds, or with bemock'd-at stabs
Kill the still-closing waters, as diminish
One dowle that's in my plume.   ARIEL     *3, 3, 60*

50 Our revels now are ended. These our actors,
As I foretold you, were all spirits, and
Are melted into air, into thin air;
And, like the baseless fabric of this vision,
The cloud-capp'd towers, the gorgeous palaces,
The solemn temples, the great globe itself,
Yea, all which it inherit, shall dissolve,

And, like this insubstantial pageant faded,
Leave not a rack behind. We are such stuff
As dreams are made on; and our little life
Is rounded with a sleep. PROSPERO    *The Tempest, 4, 1, 148*

51 Wit shall not go unrewarded while I am king of this country.
STEPHANO  *4, 1, 240*

52 With foreheads villainous low.  CALIBAN    *4, 1, 248*

53          The rarer action is
In virtue than in vengeance.  PROSPERO    *5, 1, 27*

54 Ye elves of hills, brooks, standing lakes, and groves;
And ye that on the sands with printless foot
Do chase the ebbing Neptune, and do fly him
When he comes back.  PROSPERO    *5, 1, 33*

55          I'll break my staff,
Bury it certain fathoms in the earth,
And deeper than did ever plummet sound
I'll drown my book.  PROSPERO    *5, 1, 54*

56   Where the bee sucks, there suck I;
In a cowslip's bell I lie;
There I couch when owls do cry.
On the bat's back I do fly
After summer merrily.
Merrily, merrily shall I live now
Under the blossom that hangs on the bough.  ARIEL   *5, 1, 88*

57 How beauteous mankind is! O brave new world
That has such people in't!  MIRANDA    *5, 1, 183*

58          Retire me to my Milan, where
Every third thought shall be my grave.  PROSPERO   *5, 1, 310*


**Timon of Athens**

59 'Tis not enough to help the feeble up
But to support him after.  TIMON    *1, 1, 110*

60 I wonder men dare trust themselves with men.  APEMANTUS
*1, 2, 42*

61 Uncover, dogs, and lap.  TIMON    *3, 6, 85*


**Titus Andronicus**

62 Sweet mercy is nobility's true badge.  TAMORA    *1, 1, 119*

63 She is a woman, therefore may be woo'd;
She is a woman, therefore may be won;
She is Lavinia, therefore must be lov'd.

What, man! more water glideth by the mill
Than wots the miller of; and easy it is
Of a cut loaf to steal a shive, we know.  DEMETRIUS
*Titus Andronicus, 2, 1, 82*

64 If one good deed in all my life I did,
I do repent it from my very soul.  AARON           *5, 3, 189*

## Troilus and Cressida

65                           Women are angels, wooing:
Things won are done; joy's soul lies in the doing.
That she belov'd knows nought that knows not this:
Men prize the thing ungain'd more than it is.  CRESSIDA
*1, 2, 278*

66 The heavens themselves, the planets, and this centre,
Observe degree, priority, and place,
Insisture, course, proportion, season, form,
Office, and custom, in all line of order.  ULYSSES     *1, 3, 85*

67                    O, when degree is shak'd,
Which is the ladder of all high designs,
The enterprise is sick!  ULYSSES                       *1, 3, 101*

68 Take but degree away, untune that string,
And hark what discord follows!  ULYSSES                *1, 3, 109*

69 I would thou didst itch from head to foot and I had the
scratching of thee.  THERSITES                          *2, 1, 26*

70 To be wise and love
Exceeds man's might.  CRESSIDA                         *3, 2, 152*

71 Time hath, my lord, a wallet at his back,
Wherein he puts alms for oblivion,
A great-siz'd monster of ingratitudes.  ULYSSES       *3, 3, 145*

72 One touch of nature makes the whole world kin.  ULYSSES
*3, 3, 175*

73 There's language in her eye, her cheek, her lip,
Nay, her foot speaks; her wanton spirits look out
At every joint and motive of her body.  ULYSSES       *4, 5, 55*

74 Lechery, lechery! Still wars and lechery! Nothing else holds
fashion.  THERSITES                                    *5, 2, 193*

## Twelfth Night

75 If music be the food of love, play on,
Give me excess of it, that, surfeiting,
The appetite may sicken and so die.
That strain again! It had a dying fall;
O, it came o'er my ear like the sweet sound

That breathes upon a bank of violets,
Stealing and giving odour! Enough, no more;
'Tis not so sweet now as it was before.   DUKE ORSINO
*Twelfth Night, 1, 1, 1*

76 Speaks three or four languages word for word without book.
SIR TOBY BELCH  *1, 3, 24*

77 Is it a world to hide virtues in?   SIR TOBY BELCH        *1, 3, 123*

78 Many a good hanging prevents a bad marriage.   FESTE
*1, 5, 18*

79 A plague o' these pickle-herring!   SIR TOBY BELCH   *1, 5, 114*

80 Make me a willow cabin at your gate,
And call upon my soul within the house;
Write loyal cantons of contemned love
And sing them loud even in the dead of night;
Halloo your name to the reverberate hills,
And make the babbling gossip of the air
Cry out 'Olivia!'   VIOLA                         *1, 5, 252*

81 Farewell, fair cruelty.   VIOLA                  *1, 5, 272*

82 Not to be abed after midnight is to be up betimes.
SIR TOBY BELCH   *2, 3, 1*

83 O mistress mine, where are you roaming?
O, stay and hear; your true love's coming,
That can sing both high and low,
Trip no further, pretty sweeting;
Journeys end in lovers meeting,
Every wise man's son doth know.   FESTE            *2, 3, 38*

84 What is love? 'Tis not hereafter;
Present mirth hath present laughter;
    What's to come is still unsure.
In delay there lies no plenty,
Then come kiss me, sweet and twenty;
    Youth's a stuff will not endure.   FESTE        *2, 3, 46*

85 He does it with a better grace, but I do it more natural.
SIR ANDREW AGUECHEEK  *2, 3, 79*

86 Is there no respect of place, persons, nor time, in you?
MALVOLIO  *2, 3, 89*

87 Dost thou think, because thou art virtuous, there shall be no
more cakes and ale?   SIR TOBY BELCH            *2, 3, 109*

88    Come away, come away, death;
And in sad cypress let me be laid;
    Fly away, fly away, breath,
I am slain by a fair cruel maid.

My shroud of white, stuck all with yew,
    O, prepare it!
My part of death no one so true
    Did share it. FESTE        *Twelfth Night, 2, 4, 50*

89                  She never told her love,
But let concealment, like a worm i' th' bud,
Feed on her damask cheek. She pin'd in thought;
And with a green and yellow melancholy
She sat like Patience on a monument,
Smiling at grief. VIOLA               *2, 4, 109*

90 I am all the daughters of my father's house,
And all the brothers too. VIOLA        *2, 4, 119*

91 Some are born great, some achieve greatness, and some have
greatness thrust upon 'em. MALVOLIO (reading letter)
                                      *2, 5, 129*

92 Remember who commended thy yellow stockings, and wish'd
to see thee ever cross-garter'd. MALVOLIO (reading letter)
                                        *2, 5, 135*

93 O world, how apt the poor are to be proud! OLIVIA *3, 1, 124*

94 Love sought is good, but given unsought is better. OLIVIA
                                      *3, 1, 153*

95 Why, this is very midsummer madness. OLIVIA    *3, 4, 53*

96 If this were play'd upon a stage now, I could condemn it as an
improbable fiction. FABIAN           *3, 4, 121*

97 More matter for a May morning. FABIAN      *3, 4, 136*

98 Still you keep o' th' windy side of the law. FABIAN  *3, 4, 156*

99 Out of my lean and low ability
I'll lend you something. VIOLA          *3, 4, 328*

1 I hate ingratitude more in a man
Than lying, vainness, babbling drunkenness,
Or any taint of vice whose strong corruption
Inhabits our frail blood. VIOLA         *3, 4, 338*

2 And thus the whirligig of time brings in his revenges. FESTE
                                      *5, 1, 363*

3 When that I was and a little tiny boy,
    With hey, ho, the wind and the rain,
A foolish thing was but a toy,
For the rain it raineth every day. FESTE    *5, 1, 375*

**The Two Gentlemen of Verona**

4 Home-keeping youth have ever homely wits. VALENTINE
                                      *1, 1, 2*

5 I have no other but a woman's reason:
   I think him so, because I think him so.   LUCETTA
   *The Two Gentlemen of Verona*, 1, 2, 23

6 O, how this spring of love resembleth
   The uncertain glory of an April day.   PROTEUS    1, 3, 84

7 Dumb jewels often in their silent kind
   More than quick words do move a woman's mind.   VALENTINE
   3, 1, 90

8 Who is Silvia? What is she,
   That all our swains commend her?
   Holy, fair, and wise is she.   SONG    4, 2, 38

9 Is she kind as she is fair?
   For beauty lives with kindness.   SONG    4, 2, 43

10 How use doth breed a habit in a man!   VALENTINE    5, 4, 1

11          O, heaven, were man
   But constant, he were perfect!   PROTEUS    5, 4, 110

## The Winter's Tale

12 Two lads that thought there was no more behind
   But such a day tomorrow as to-day,
   And to be boy eternal.   POLIXENES    1, 2, 63

13 A sad tale's best for winter. I have one
   Of sprites and goblins.   MAMILLIUS    2, 1, 25

14      What's gone and what's past help
   Should be past grief.   PAULINA    3, 2, 219

15 *Exit, pursued by a bear.*   STAGE DIRECTION    3, 3, 58

16 I would there were no age between ten and three and twenty, or
   that youth would sleep out the rest; for there is nothing in the
   between but getting wenches with child, wronging the ancientry,
   stealing, fighting.   SHEPHERD    3, 3, 59

17 When daffodils begin to peer,
   With heigh! the doxy over the dale,
   Why, then comes in the sweet o' the year,
   For the red blood reigns in the winter's pale.   AUTOLYCUS
   4, 3, 1

18 A snapper-up of unconsidered trifles.   AUTOLYCUS    4, 3, 26

19 Jog on, jog on, the footpath way,
   And merrily hent the stile-a;
   A merry heart goes all the day,
   Your sad tires in a mile-a.   AUTOLYCUS    4, 3, 118

20 For you there's rosemary and rue; these keep
   Seeming and savour all the winter long.   PERDITA    4, 4, 74

21                         What you do
Still betters what is done. When you speak, sweet,
I'd have you do it ever. When you sing,
I'd have you buy and sell so; so give alms;
Pray so; and, for the ord'ring your affairs,
To sing them too.  FLORIZEL     *The Winter's Tale*, 4, 4, 135

22 Lawn as white as driven snow.  AUTOLYCUS     *4, 4, 215*

23 The self-same sun that shines upon his court.  PERDITA
                                                     *4, 4, 436*

24 Prosperity's the very bond of love,
Whose fresh complexion and whose heart together
Affliction alters.  CAMILLO                       *4, 4, 565*

25 Though I am not naturally honest, I am so sometimes by chance.
                          AUTOLYCUS   *4, 4, 701*

26 Let me have no lying; it becomes none but tradesmen.
                          AUTOLYCUS   *4, 4, 711*

27 Though authority be a stubborn bear, yet he is oft led by the
nose with gold.  CLOWN                           *4, 4, 790*

## Sonnets

28 To the onlie begetter of these insuing sonnets.     *Dedication*

29 From fairest creatures we desire increase,
That thereby beauty's rose might never die.     *Sonnet 1*

30 Look in thy glass, and tell the face thou viewest.     *Sonnet 3*

31 But wherefore do not you a mightier way
Make war upon this bloody tyrant Time?     *Sonnet 16*

32 Shall I compare thee to a summer's day?
Thou art more lovely and more temperate.
Rough winds do shake the darling buds of May,
And summer's lease hath all too short a date.     *Sonnet 18*

33 But thy eternal summer shall not fade.     *Sonnet 18*

34 So long as men can breathe or eyes can see,
So long lives this, and this gives life to thee.     *Sonnet 18*

35 A woman's face, with Nature's own hand painted,
Hast thou, the Master Mistress of my passion.     *Sonnet 20*

36 For thy sweet love rememb'red such wealth brings
That then I scorn to change my state with kings.     *Sonnet 29*

37 When to the sessions of sweet silent thought
I summon up remembrance of things past,
I sigh the lack of many a thing I sought,
And with old woes new wail my dear time's waste.     *Sonnet 30*

38 But if the while I think on thee, dear friend,
 All losses are restored, and sorrows end.   *Sonnet 30*

39 So true a fool is love that in your will,
 Though you do anything, he thinks no ill.   *Sonnet 57*

40 Like as the waves make towards the pebbled shore,
 So do our minutes hasten to their end.   *Sonnet 60*

41 Some glory in their birth, some in their skill,
 Some in their wealth, some in their body's force;
 Some in their garments, though new-fangled ill;
 Some in their hawks and hounds, some in their horse.
                 *Sonnet 91*

42 For sweetest things turn sourest by their deeds:
 Lilies that fester smell far worse than weeds.   *Sonnet 94*

43 How like a winter hath my absence been
 From thee, the pleasure of the fleeting year!
 What freezings have I felt, what dark days seen! *Sonnet 97*

44 From you have I been absent in the spring,
 When proud-pied April, dress'd in all his trim,
 Hath put a spirit of youth in every thing.   *Sonnet 98*

45 When in the chronicle of wasted time
 I see descriptions of the fairest weights.   *Sonnet 106*

46 For we, which now behold these present days,
 Have eyes to wonder, but lack tongues to praise. *Sonnet 106*

47 Let me not to the marriage of true minds
 Admit impediments. Love is not love
 Which alters when it alteration finds,
 Or bends with the remover to remove.
 O, no! it is an ever-fixed mark,
 That looks on tempests and is never shaken.  *Sonnet 116*

48 Love alters not with his brief hours and weeks,
 But bears it out even to the edge of doom.
 If this be error, and upon me prov'd,
 I never writ, nor no man ever lov'd.   *Sonnet 116*

49 'Tis better to be vile than vile esteemed,
 When not to be receives reproach of being.  *Sonnet 121*

50 Th' expense of spirit in a waste of shame
 Is lust in action; and till action, lust
 Is perjur'd, murd'rous, bloody, full of blame,
 Savage, extreme, rude, cruel, not to trust;
 Enjoy'd no sooner but despised straight.   *Sonnet 129*

51 All this the world well knows; yet none knows well
 To shun the heaven that leads men to this hell. *Sonnet 129*

52 My mistress' eyes are nothing like the sun;
Coral is far more red than her lips' red.         *Sonnet 130*

53 And yet, by heaven, I think my love as rare
As any she belied with false compare.         *Sonnet 130*

54 When my love swears that she is made of truth,
I do believe her, though I know she lies.         *Sonnet 138*

55 Two loves I have, of comfort and despair,
Which like two spirits do suggest me still;
The better angel is a man right fair,
The worser spirit a woman colour'd ill.         *Sonnet 144*

**Poems**

56 Crabbed age and youth cannot live together:
Youth is full of pleasance, age is full of care;
Youth like summer morn, age like winter weather;
Youth like summer brave, age like winter bare.
                    *The Passionate Pilgrim, 12*

57 Age, I do abhor thee; youth, I do adore thee.         *Ib*

58 The first heire of my invention.   *Venus and Adonis, Dedication*

59 Hunting he lov'd, but love he laugh'd to scorn.         *Ib, 1, 4*

60 Beauty itself doth of itself persuade
The eyes of men without an orator.         *The Rape of Lucrece,*
                                                              *1, 29*

## SHAW, George Bernard, 1856–1950

61 Breakages, Limited, the biggest industrial corporation in the
country.   BALBUS         *The Apple Cart, Act 1*

62 You can always tell an old soldier by the inside of his holsters
and cartridge boxes. The young ones carry pistols and cartridges:
the old ones grub.   BLUNTSCHLI         *Arms and the Man, Act 1*

63 You are a very poor soldier: a chocolate cream soldier!
                              RAINA         *Ib, Act 1*

64 It is enough that there *is* a beyond.   LILITH         *Back to*
                              *Methuselah, Part 5, Last words*

65 When a stupid man is doing something he is ashamed of, he
always declares that it is his duty.   APOLLODORUS
                              *Caesar and Cleopatra, Act 3*

66 We have no more right to consume happiness without producing
it than to consume wealth without producing it.   MORELL
                              *Candida, Act 1*

67 The overpaying instinct is a generous one: better than the underpaying instinct, and not so common.   MORELL         *Ib, Act 1*

68 I'm only a beer teetotaller, not a champagne teetotaller.
PROSERPINE   *Candida, Act 3*

69 Martyrdom . . . is the only way in which a man can become
famous without ability.  BURGOYNE     *The Devil's Disciple,*
*Act 3*

70 SWINDON: What will History say?
BURGOYNE: History, sir, will tell lies, as usual.   . *Ib, Act 3*

71 Stimulate the phagocytes.  B. B.  *The Doctor's Dilemma, Act 1*

72 Go anywhere in England where there are natural, wholesome,
contented, and really nice English people; and what do you
always find? That the stables are the real centre of the household.  LADY UTTERWORD     *Heartbreak House, Act 3*

73 Tell me all me faults as man to man, I can stand anything but
flattery.  TIM     *John Bull's Other Island, Act 1*

74 The more a man knows, and the further he travels, the more
likely he is to marry a country girl afterwards.  KEEGAN
*Ib, Act 2*

75 My way of joking is to tell the truth. Its the funniest joke in the
world.  KEEGAN     *Ib*

76 I am a Millionaire. That is my religion.  UNDERSHAFT
*Major Barbara, Act 2*

77 Wot prawce selvytion nah?  BILL WALKER     *Ib*

78 A lifetime of happiness! No man alive could bear it: it would be
hell on earth.  TANNER     *Man and Superman, Act 1*

79 There is no love sincerer than the love of food.  TANNER   *Ib*

80 The true artist will let his wife starve, his children go barefoot,
his mother drudge for his living at seventy, sooner than work
at anything but his art.  TANNER     *Ib*

81 It is a womans business to get married as soon as possible, and a
mans to keep unmarried as long as he can.  TANNER  *Ib, Act 2*

82 An Englishman thinks he is moral when he is only uncomfortable.  THE DEVIL     *Ib, Act 3*

83 There are two tragedies in life. One is to lose your hearts desire.
The other is to gain it.  MENDOZA     *Ib, Act 4*

84 Any person under the age of thirty, who, having any knowledge
of the existing social order, is not a revolutionist, is an inferior.
*Ib, The Revolutionist's Handbook, Foreword*

85 We learn from history that we learn nothing from history.  *Ib*

86 The golden rule is that there are no golden rules.  *Ib, Maxims*
*for Revolutionists*

87 Liberty means responsibility. That is why most men dread it.
*Man and Superman, Maxims for Revolutionists*

88 He who can, does. He who cannot, teaches.                    *Ib*

89 Marriage is popular because it combines the maximum of temptation with the maximum of opportunity.                    *Ib*

90 Ladies and gentlemen are permitted to have friends in the kennel, but not in the kitchen.                    *Ib*

91 Every man over forty is a scoundrel.                    *Ib*

92 There is only one religion, though there are a hundred versions of it.                    *Plays Pleasant, Preface*

93 Remember that you are a human being with a soul and the divine gift of articulate speech: that your native language is the language of Shakespear and Milton and The Bible; and dont sit there crooning like a bilious pigeon.    HIGGINS    *Pygmalion, Act 1*

94 I don't want to talk grammar. I want to talk like a lady.
ELIZA    *Ib, Act 2*

95 Time enough to think of the future when you haven't any future to think of.    HIGGINS                    *Ib*

96 Im one of the undeserving poor: thats what I am. Think of what that means to a man. It means that he's up agen middle class morality all the time.    DOOLITTLE                    *Ib*

97 My aunt died of influenza: so they said . . . But its my belief they done the old woman in.    ELIZA                    *Ib, Act 3*

98 Walk! Not bloody likely.    ELIZA                    *Ib*

99 No eggs! No eggs!! Thousand thunders, man, what do you mean by no eggs?    ROBERT                    *Saint Joan, Scene 1*

1 We want a few mad people now. See where the sane ones have landed us!    POULENGEY                    *Ib*

2 I hear voices telling me what to do. They come from God.
JOAN    *Ib*

3 A miracle, my friend, is an event which creates faith. That is the purpose and nature of miracles.    ARCHBISHOP    *Ib, Scene 2*

4 Do not think you can frighten me by telling me that I am alone. France is alone; and God is alone; and what is my loneliness before the loneliness of my country and my God?    JOAN
*Ib, Scene 5*

5 THE EXECUTIONER: You have heard the last of her.
WARWICK: The last of her? Hm! I wonder!    *Ib, Scene 6*

6 All dress is fancy dress, is it not, except our natural skins?
DUNOIS    *Ib, Epilogue*

7 Well, sir, you never can tell. Thats a principle in life with me,
sir, if youll excuse my having such a thing, sir. WAITER
*You Never Can Tell, Act 2*

8 With the single exception of Homer, there is no eminent writer,
not even Sir Walter Scott, whom I can despise so entirely as I
despise Shakespeare when I measure my mind against his.
*Dramatic Opinions and Essays, Vol. 2, 52*

### SHELLEY, Percy Bysshe, 1792–1822

9 I weep for Adonais – he is dead!
O, weep for Adonais! though our tears
Thaw not the frost which binds so dear a head! *Adonais, 1*

10 Ah, woe is me! Winter is come and gone,
But grief returns with the revolving year. *Ib, 154*

11 Through wood and stream and field and hill and Ocean
A quickening life from the Earth's heart has burst
As it has ever done, with change and motion,
From the great morning of the world when first
God dawned on Chaos. *Ib, 163*

12 Alas! that all we loved of him should be,
But for our grief, as if it had not been,
And grief itself be mortal! *Ib, 181*

13 The Pilgrim of Eternity, whose fame
Over his living head like Heaven is bent,
An early but enduring monument. *Ib, 264*

14 A pardlike Spirit beautiful and swift. *Ib, 280*

15 Live thou, whose infamy is not thy fame!
Live! fear no heavier chastisement from me,
Thou noteless blot on a remembered name! *Ib, 325*

16 He has outsoared the shadow of our night;
Envy and calumny and hate and pain,
And that unrest which men miscall delight,
Can touch him not and torture not again;
From the contagion of the world's slow stain
He is secure, and now can never mourn
A heart grown cold, a head grown gray in vain. *Ib, 352*

17 He lives, he wakes – 'tis Death is dead, not he. *Ib, 361*

18 He is a portion of the loveliness
Which once he made more lovely. *Ib, 379*

19 The One remains, the many change and pass;
Heaven's light forever shines, Earth's shadows fly;
Life, like a dome of many-coloured glass,
Stains the white radiance of Eternity. *Ib, 460*

20    The soul of Adonais, like a star,
     Beacons from the abode where the Eternal are.   *Adonais, 494*

21  I bring fresh showers for the thirsting flowers,
     From the seas and the streams.   *The Cloud, 1*

22  I wield the flail of the lashing tail,
     And whiten the green plains under,
  And then again I dissolve it in rain,
     _And laugh as I pass in thunder.   *Ib, 9*

23  I am the daughter of Earth and Water,
     And the nursling of the Sky;
  I pass through the pores of the ocean and shores;
     I change, but I cannot die.   *Ib, 73*

24  How wonderful is Death,
     Death and his brother Sleep!   *The Daemon of the World, 1, 1*

25  I never was attached to that great sect,
     Whose doctrine is, that each one should select
     Out of the crowd a mistress or a friend,
     And all the rest, though fair and wise, commend
     To cold oblivion.   *Epipsychidion, 149*

26    True Love in this differs from gold and clay,
     That to divide is not to take away.   *Ib, 160*

27  Good-night? ah! no; the hour is ill
     Which severs those it should unite;
  Let us remain together still,
     Then it will be good night.   *Good-Night, 1*

28  The world's great age begins anew,
     The golden years return,
  The earth doth like a snake renew
     Her winter weeds outworn:
  Heaven smiles, and faiths and empires gleam,
  Like wrecks of a dissolving dream.   *Hellas, 1060*

29  Thou Paradise of exiles, Italy!   *Julian and Maddalo, 57*

30  I met Murder on the way –
  He had a mask like Castlereagh.   *The Mask of Anarchy, 5*

31  Shake your chains to earth like dew
  Which in sleep had fallen on you –
  Ye are many – they are few.   *Ib, 153*

32  Swiftly walk o'er the western wave,
     Spirit of Night!
  Out of the misty eastern cave,
  Where, all the long and lone daylight,
  Thou wovest dreams of joy and fear.   *To Night, 1*

33 I ask of thee, belovèd Night —
    Swift be thine approaching flight,
         Come soon, soon!                    *To Night, 33*

34 A glorious people vibrated again
    The lightning of the nations.            *Ode to Liberty, 1*

35 O Wild West Wind, thou breath of Autumn's being,
    Thou, from whose unseen presence the leaves dead
    Are driven, like ghosts from an enchanter fleeing,
    Yellow, and black, and pale, and hectic red,
    Pestilence-stricken multitudes.    *Ode to the West Wind, 1*

36 Wild Spirit, which art moving everywhere;
    Destroyer and preserver; hear, oh, hear!          *Ib, 13*

37 Oh, lift me as a wave, a leaf, a cloud!
    I fall upon the thorns of life! I bleed!
    A heavy weight of hours has chained and bowed
    One too like thee: tameless, and swift, and proud.   *Ib, 53*

38 Scatter, as from an unextinguished hearth
    Ashes and sparks, my words among mankind!
    Be through my lips to unawakened earth
    The trumpet of a prophecy! O, Wind,
    If Winter comes, can Spring be far behind?          *Ib, 66*

39 I met a traveller from antique land
    Who said: Two vast and trunkless legs of stone
    Stand in the desert.                      *Ozymandias, 1*

40 And on the pedestal these words appear:
    'My name is Ozymandias, king of kings:
    Look on my works, ye Mighty, and despair!'
    Nothing beside remains. Round the decay
    Of that colossal wreck, boundless and bare
    The lone and level sands stretch far away.          *Ib, 9*

41 Hell is a city much like London —
    A populous and a smoky city.         *Peter Bell the Third,*
                                           *Part 3, Hell, 1*

42 Crucified 'twixt a smile and whimper.            *Ib, 196*

43 But from these create he can
    Forms more real than living man,
    Nurslings of immortality!       *Prometheus Unbound, 1, 747*

44                          Yet all love is sweet,
    Given or returned. Common as light is love,
    And its familiar voice wearies not ever.       *Ib, 2, 5, 39*

45 Familiar acts are beautiful through love.     *Ib, 4, 403*

46 A Sensitive Plant in a garden grew,
   And the young winds fed it with silver dew,
   And it opened its fan-like leaves to the light,
   And closed them beneath the kisses of Night.    *The Sensitive*
*Plant, 1, 1*

47 It is a modest creed, and yet
   Pleasant if one considers it,
   To own that death itself must be,
   Like all the rest, a mockery.    *Ib, Conclusion, 126*

48 For love, and beauty, and delight,
   There is no death nor change.    *Ib, Ib, 134*

49    Hail to thee, blithe Spirit!
      Bird thou never wert,
   That from Heaven, or near it,
      Pourest thy full heart
In profuse strains of unpremeditated art.    *To a Skylark, 1*

50    We look before and after,
      And pine for what is not:
   Our sincerest laughter
      With some pain is fraught;
Our sweetest songs are those that tell of saddest thought. *Ib, 86*

51    Teach me half the gladness
      That thy brain must know,
   Such harmonious madness
      From my lips would flow
The world should listen then – as I am listening now.    *Ib, 101*

52 Rarely, rarely, comest thou,
   Spirit of Delight!    *Song, Rarely, Rarely, Comest Thou*

53 An old, mad, blind, despised, and dying king.    *Sonnet,*
*England in 1819*

54 Music, when soft voices die,
   Vibrates in the memory –
   Odours, when sweet violets sicken,
   Live within the sense they quicken.
   Rose leaves, when the rose is dead,
   Are heaped for the belovèd's bed;
   And so thy thoughts, when thou art gone,
   Love itself shall slumber on.    *To —, Music, When Soft*
*Voices Die*

55 I fear thy kisses, gentle maiden,
      Thou needst not fear mine;
   My spirit is too deeply laden
      Ever to burthen thine.    *To —, I Fear Thy Kisses*

56 The desire of the moth for the star,
　　Of the night for the morrow,
　The devotion to something afar
　　From the sphere of our sorrow.　　*To —, One Word is too
　　　　　　　　　　　　　　　　　often Profaned*

57 Poetry lifts the veil from the hidden beauty of the world, and
　makes familiar objects be as if they were not familiar.
　　　　　　　　　　　　　　　　　**A Defence of Poetry**

58 Poetry is the record of the best and happiest moments of the
　happiest and best minds.　　　　　　　　　　　　　*Ib*

59 Poets are the unacknowledged legislators of the world.　　*Ib*

**SHENSTONE, William, 1714–1763**

60 Whoe'er has travell'd life's dull round,
　Where'er his stages may have been,
　May sigh to think he still has found
　The warmest welcome, at an inn.　　　*Written at an Inn at
　　　　　　　　　　　　　　　　　　Henley*

**SHERIDAN, Philip Henry, 1831–1888**

61 The only good Indian is a dead Indian.　　　*Attributed*

**SHERIDAN, Richard Brinsley, 1751–1816**

62 Yes, sir, puffing is of various sorts; the principal are, the puff
　direct, the puff preliminary, the puff collateral, the puff collusive,
　and the puff oblique, or puff by implication.　PUFF　*The Critic,
　　　　　　　　　　　　　　　　　　Act, 1, Scene 2*

63 No scandal about Queen Elizabeth I hope.　SNEER　*Ib, Act 2,
　　　　　　　　　　　　　　　　　　Scene 1*

64 An oyster may be crossed in love.　TILBURINA　*Ib, Act 3,
　　　　　　　　　　　　　　　　　　Scene 1*

65 Thought does not become a young woman.　MRS MALAPROP
　　　　　　　　　　　　　　　*The Rivals, Act 1, Scene 2*

66 Illiterate him, I say, quite from your memory.
　　　　　　　　　　　　　　　　MRS MALAPROP　*Ib*

67 'Tis safest in matrimony to begin with a little aversion.
　　　　　　　　　　　　　　　　MRS MALAPROP　*Ib*

68 A circulating library in a town is as an ever-green tree of
　diabolical knowledge! It blossoms through the year.
　　　　　　　　　　　　SIR ANTHONY ABSOLUTE　*Ib*

69 A progeny of learning.　MRS MALAPROP　　　　　　*Ib*

70 A supercilious knowledge in accounts.　MRS MALAPROP　*Ib*

71 If I reprehend any thing in this world it is the use of my oracular tongue and a nice derangement of epitaphs.  MRS MALAPROP
*The Rivals, Act 3, Scene 3*

72 As headstrong as an allegory on the banks of the Nile.
MRS MALAPROP  *Ib*

73 Too civil by half.  ACRES  *Ib, Act 3, Scene 4*

74 You shall see them on a beautiful quarto page, where a neat rivulet of text shall meander through a meadow of margin.
SIR BENJAMIN BACKBITE  *School for Scandal,
Act 1, Scene 1*

75 Though I can't make her love me, there is great satisfaction in quarrelling with her.  SIR PETER TEAZLE  *Ib, Act 2, Scene 1*

76 There is the whole set! a character dead at every word.
SIR PETER TEAZLE  *Ib, Act 2, Scene 2*

77 I'm called away by particular business. But I leave my character behind me.  SIR PETER TEAZLE  *Ib*

78 Here's to the maiden of bashful fifteen;
   Here's to the widow of fifty;
Here's to the flaunting extravagant quean,
   And here's to the housewife that's thrifty.
      Let the toast pass, --
      Drink to the lass,
I'll warrant she'll prove an excuse for a glass.
SIR HARRY BUMPER  *Ib, Act 3, Scene 3*

79 What is principle against the flattery of a handsome, lively young fellow?  SIR PETER TEAZLE  *Ib, Act, 4, Scene 2*

80 The Right Honourable gentleman is indebted to his memory for his jests, and to his imagination for his facts.  *Reply to
Mr Dundas, House of Commons*

**SHERMAN, General William Tecumseh, 1820–1891**

81 There is many a boy here today who looks on war as all glory, but, boys, it is all hell.  *Speech, 1880*

**SIDNEY, Algernon, 1622–1683**

82 Liars ought to have good memories.  *Discourses on
Government, Ch. 2, 15*

**SIDNEY, Sir Philip, 1554–1586**

83 My true love hath my heart, and I have his,
   By just exchange one for another given:
I hold his dear, and mine he cannot miss,
There never was a better bargain driven.  *The Arcadia, 3*

84 Biting my truant pen, beating myself for spite:
'Fool!' said my Muse to me, 'look in thy heart and write.'
*Astrophel and Stella, Sonnet 1*

85 With how sad steps, O Moon, thou climb'st the skies!
How silently, and with how wan a face! *Ib, Sonnet 31*

86 With a tale forsooth he cometh unto you, with a tale which
holdeth children from play, and old men from the chimney
corner. *The Defence of Poesy*

87 Certainly, I must confess mine own barbarousness, I never heard
the old song of Percy and Douglas, that I found not my heart
moved more than with a trumpet. *Ib*

88 Thy necessity is greater than mine. *On giving his water-
bottle to a dying soldier at Zutphen, 1586*

**SIMS, George Robert, 1847–1922**

89 It was Christmas Day in the Workhouse. *Christmas Day
in the Workhouse*

**SITWELL, Edith, 1887–1964**

90 Still falls the Rain –
Dark as the world of man, black as our loss –
Blind as the nineteen hundred and forty nails
Upon the Cross. *Still Falls the Rain*

**SITWELL, Sir Osbert, 1892–1969**

91 The British Bourgeoisie
Is not born,
And does not die,
But, if it is ill,
It has a frightened look in its eyes. *At the House of
Mrs Kinfoot*

**SKELTON, John, 1460?–1529**

92 For though my ryme be ragged,
Tattered and jagged,
Rudely rayne beaten,
Rusty and mothe eaten;
If ye take well therwith,
It hath in it some pyth. *Colyn Cloute, 2, 53*

93 With solace and gladness,
Much mirth and no madness,
All good and no badness. *To Mistress Margaret Hussey*

**SMART, Christopher, 1722–1771**

94 Glorious the northern lights astream;
   Glorious the song, when God's the theme;
     Glorious the thunder's roar.     *Song to David, 85*

95 And now the matchless deed's achieved,
   Determined, dared, and done!     *Ib, 86*

**SMEDLEY, Francis Edward, 1818–1864**

96 You are looking as fresh as paint.   *Frank Fairleigh, Ch. 41*

**SMITH, Adam, 1723–1790**

97 No society can surely be flourishing and happy, of which the far
   greater part of the members are poor and miserable.
            *The Wealth of Nations, 1, 8*

98 To found a great empire for the sole purpose of raising up a
   people of customers, may at first sight appear a project fit only
   for a nation of shopkeepers. It is, however, a project altogether
   unfit for a nation of shopkeepers; but extremely fit for a nation
   that is governed by shopkeepers.     *Ib, 2, 4*

**SMITH, Logan Pearsall, 1865–1946**

99 Happiness is a wine of the rarest vintage, and seems insipid to
   a vulgar taste.    *Afterthoughts, 1, Life and Human Nature*

 1 There are few sorrows, however poignant, in which a good
   income is of no avail.     *Ib*

 2 The wretchedness of being rich is that you live with rich people.
         *Ib, 4, In the World*

 3 People say that Life is the thing, but I prefer Reading.
         *Ib, 6, Myself*

 4 Thank heavens, the sun has gone in, and I don't have to go out
   and enjoy it.     *Last words*

**SMITH, Samuel Francis, 1808–1895**

 5 My country, 'tis of thee,
   Sweet land of liberty,
     Of thee I sing.     *America*

**SMITH, Sydney, 1771–1845**

 6 Poverty is no disgrace to a man, but it is confoundedly inconvenient.     *His Wit and Wisdom*

 7 No furniture so charming as books.   *Lady Holland, Memoir,*
           *Vol. 1, Ch. 9*

8  How can a bishop marry? How can he flirt? The most he can say is, 'I will see you in the vestry after the service.'
*Lady Holland, Memoir, Vol. 1, Ch. 9*

9  As the French say, there are three sexes, – men, women, and clergymen.
*Ib*

10  Praise is the best diet for us, after all.
*Ib*

11  I never read a book before reviewing it; it prejudices a man so.
*H. Pearson, The Smith of Smiths, Ch. 3*

12  I am convinced digestion is the great secret of life.
*Letter to Arthur Kinglake, 30 Sept. 1837*

13  I have no relish for the country; it is a kind of healthy grave.
*Letter to Miss G. Harcourt, 1838*

## SMOLLETT, Tobias George, 1721–1771

14  Hark ye, Clinker, you are a most notorious offender. You stand convicted of sickness, hunger, wretchedness, and want.
*Humphrey Clinker*

15  Some folk are wise, and some are otherwise.
*Roderick Random, Ch. 6*

16  I consider the world as made for me, not me for the world. It is my maxim therefore to enjoy it while I can, and let futurity shift for itself.
*Ib, Ch. 45*

17  True patriotism is of no party.
*Sir Launcelote Greavers*

18  That great Cham of literature, Samuel Johnson.
*Letter to John Wilkes, 16 March 1759, quoted in Boswell's Life of Johnson*

## SNAGGE, John, 1904–

19  I can't see who's ahead – it's either Oxford or Cambridge.
*BBC Commentary on Boat Race, 1949*

## SOCRATES, 469–399 B.C.

20  I am a citizen, not of Athens or Greece, but of the world.
*Plutarch, De Exilio*

21  Other men live to eat, whereas I eat to live.
*Plutarch, Moralia*

## SOLON, 640?–558? B.C.

22  Call no man happy until he dies; he is at best fortunate.
*Herodotus, Histories, 1, 32*

## SOMERVILLE, William, 1675–1742

23          The chase, the sport of kings;
Image of war, without its guilt.
*The Chase, 1, 13*

**SOULE, John Babsone Lane, 1815–1891**

24 Go west, young man. *Terre Haute Express, Indiana, 1851*

**SOUTHEY, Robert, 1774–1843**

25 My days among the Dead are past:
    Around me I behold,
  Where'er these casual eyes are cast,
    The mighty minds of old. *My Days among the Dead*

26 Yet leaving here a name, I trust,
  That will not perish in the dust.

27 It was a summer's evening,
  Old Kaspar's work was done. *The Battle of Blenheim*

28 And by him sported on the green
  His little grandchild Wilhelmine. *Ib*

29 But what they fought each other for,
  I could not well make out. *Ib*

30 'And everybody praised the Duke
  Who this great fight did win.'
  'But what good came of it at last?'
  Quoth little Peterkin.
  'Why that I cannot tell,' said he,
  'But 'twas a famous victory.' *Ib*

**SPENCER, Herbert, 1820–1903**

31 Time: that which man is always trying to kill, but which
  ends in killing him. *Definitions*

32 Science is organized knowledge. *Education, Ch. 2*

33 The Republican form of Government is the highest form of
  government; but because of this it requires the highest type of
  human nature – a type nowhere at present existing. *Essays,
  The Americans*

34 Survival of the fittest. *Principles of Biology*

35 We all decry prejudice, yet are all prejudiced. *Social Statics,
  Part 2*

36 Education has for its object the formation of character. *Ib*

37 Hero-worship is strongest where there is least regard for human
  freedom. *Ib, Part 3*

**SPENSER, Edmund, 1552?–1599**

38 The woods shall to me answer and my Echo ring.
  *Epithalamion, 18*

39 Ah! when will this long weary day have end,
And lend me leave to come unto my love? *Epithalamion, 278*

40 Fierce wars and faithful loves shall moralize my song. *The Fairie Queen, Book 1, Introduction, Stanza 1*

41 A gentle knight was pricking on the plain. *Ib, Book 1, Canto, 1, 1*

42 Sleep after toil, port after stormy seas,
Ease after war, death after life does greatly please. *Ib, Book, 1, Canto 9, 40*

43 And as she looked about, she did behold,
How over that same door was likewise writ,
Be bold, be bold, and everywhere Be bold. *Ib, Book 3, Canto 11, 54*

44 Dan Chaucer, well of English undefiled,
On Fame's eternal beadroll worthy to be filed. *Ib, Book 4, Canto 2, 32*

45 The gentle mind by gentle deeds is known,
For a man by nothing is so well bewrayed
As by his manners. *Ib, Book 6, Canto, 3, 1*

46 Calm was the day, and through the trembling air,
Sweet breathing Zephyrus did softly play. *Prothalamion, 1*

47 Sweet Thames! run softly, till I end my Song. *Ib, 18*

48 So now they have made our English tongue a gallimaufry or hodgepodge of all other speeches. *The Shepherd's Calendar, Letter to Gabriel Harvey*

**SPOONER, Rev. William Archibald, 1844–1930**

49 Kinquering Congs their titles take. *Announcing the hymn in New College Chapel, Oxford, 1879 (See 95:18)*

50 Sir, you have tasted two whole worms; you have hissed all my mystery lectures and been caught fighting a liar in the quad; you will leave by the next town drain. *Attributed*

51 Let us drink to the queer old Dean. *Attributed*

52 I remember your name perfectly, but I just can't think of your face. *Attributed*

**SPRING-RICE, Sir Cecil Arthur, 1858–1918**

53 I vow to thee, my country – all earthly things above –
Entire and whole and perfect, the service of my love.
*I Vow to Thee, My Country*

54 I am the Dean of Christ Church, Sir,
   This is my wife – look well at her.
   She is the Broad: I am the High:
   We are the University. *The Masque of Balliol*

## SQUIRE, Sir John Collings, 1884–1958

55 It did not last: the Devil howling 'Ho,
   Let Einstein be,' restored the status quo. *In Continuation of*
                                      *Pope on Newton (see 248 : 88)*

56 But I'm not so think as you drunk I am. *Ballade of Soporific*
                                              *Absorption*

## STANLEY, Sir Henry Morton, 1841–1904

57 Dr Livingstone, I presume? *On meeting Livingstone in Ujiji,*
                                *Central Africa, 10 Nov. 1871*

## STANTON, Frank Lebby, 1857–1927

58 Sweetest li'l feller, everybody knows;
   Dunno what to call him, but he's mighty lak' a rose.
                                *Mighty Lak' a Rose*

## STEELE, Sir Richard, 1672–1729

59 Among all the diseases of the mind there is not one more
   epidemical or more pernicious than the love of flattery.
                                *The Spectator, No. 238*

60 There are so few who can grow old with a good grace.
                                      *Ib, No. 263*

61 Reading is to the mind what exercise is to the body.
                                  *The Tatler, No. 147*

## STEPHEN, James Kenneth, 1859–1892

62 Two voices are there: one is of the deep . . .
   And one is of an old half-witted sheep
   Which bleats articulate monotony
   And indicates that two and one are three. *Lapsus Calami,*
                      *Sonnet (Parody of Wordsworth, see 412 : 1)*

63 When the Rudyards cease from kipling
   And the Haggards ride no more. *Ib, To R.K.*

## STERNE, Laurence, 1713–1768

64 They order, said I, this matter better in France. *A Sentimental*
                              *Journey, Opening words*

65 As an Englishman does not travel to see Englishmen, I retired
   to my room. *A Sentimental Journey, Preface*

66 I pity the man who can travel from Dan to Beersheba, and cry,
   'tis all barren. *Ib, In the Street, Calais*

67 There are worse occupations in the world than feeling a woman's
   pulse. *Ib, The Pulse*

68 'God tempers the wind,' said Maria, 'to the shorn lamb.'
   *Ib, Maria*

69 So that when I stretched out my hand, I caught hold of the fille
   de chambre's—. *Ib, Last words*

70 'Our armies swore terribly in Flanders,' cried my Uncle Toby,
   'but nothing to this.' *Tristram Shandy, Book 3, Ch. 11*

71 Love, 'an please your honour, is exactly like war in this; that a
   soldier, though he has escaped three weeks complete o' Saturday
   night, – may nevertheless be shot through his heart on Sunday
   morning. *Ib, Book, 8 Ch. 21*

72 'L—d!' said my mother, 'what is all this story about?'
   'A Cock and a Bull,' said Yorick. *Ib, Last words*

## STEVENSON, Robert Louis, 1850–1894

73 Sing me a song of a lad that is gone,
     Say, could that lad be I?
   Merry of soul he sailed on a day
     Over the sea to Skye. *Songs of Travel, 42*

74 Fifteen men on the dead man's chest –
     Yo-ho-ho and a bottle of rum!
   Drink and the devil had done for the rest. SONG
   *Treasure Island, Ch. 1*

75 Many's the long night I've dreamed of cheese – toasted, mostly.
   BEN GUNN *Ib, Ch. 15*

76 This be the verse you grave for me:
     'Here he lies where he longed to be;
   Home is the sailor, home from sea,
     And the hunter home from the hill.' *Underwoods, Book 1,*
   *21, Requiem*

77 Even if we take matrimony at its lowest, even if we regard it as
   no more than a sort of friendship recognised by the police.
   *Virginibus Puerisque, Part 1*

78 Extreme busyness, whether at school or college, kirk or market,
   is a symptom of deficient vitality. *Ib, An Apology for Idlers*

79 There is no duty we so much underrate as the duty of being
   happy. *Ib*

80 To travel hopefully is a better thing than to arrive, and the true success is to labour. *Virginibus Puerisque, El Dorado*

## STEVENSON, William, 1530?–1575

81 I cannot eat but little meat
  My stomach is not good;
  But sure I think that I can drink
  With him that wears a hood. SONG      *Gammer Gurton's Needle, Act 2*

82 I stuff my skin, so full within,
  Of jolly good ale and old. SONG

## STONE, Samuel John, 1839–1900

83 The Church's one foundation
  Is Jesus Christ her Lord;
  She is His new creation
  By water and the Word.      *The Church's One Foundation*

## STOWE, Harriet Elizabeth Beecher, 1811–1896

84 'Never had any mother? What do you mean? Where were you born?' 'Never was born!' persisted Topsy; 'never had no father, nor mother, nor nothin'. I was raised by a speculator.'
  *Uncle Tom's Cabin, Ch. 20*

85 'Do you know who made you?' 'Nobody, as I knows on,' said the child, [*Topsy*] with a short laugh ... 'I 'spect I grow'd. Don't think nobody never made me.'      *Ib*

## SUCKLING, Sir John, 1609–1642

86 Out upon it, I have loved
  Three whole days together;
  And am like to love three more,
  If it prove fair weather.      *A Poem with the Answer*

## SUETONIUS, 75?–150? A.D.

87 *Festina lente*. Hasten slowly.      *Augustus, 25*

88 *Ave, Imperator, morituri te salutant*. Hail, Emperor, those about to die salute you.      *Claudius, 21*

## SURTEES, Robert Smith, 1803–1864

89 The only infallible rule we know is, that the man who is always talking about being a gentleman never is one.      *Ask Mamma, Ch. 1*

90 Hellish dark, and smells of cheese!      *Handley Cross, Ch. 50*

91 Three things I never lends – my 'oss, my wife, and my name.
*Hillingdon Hall, Ch. 33*

92 Women never look so well as when one comes in wet and dirty
from hunting. *Mr Sponge's Sporting Tour, Ch. 21*

93 He was a gentleman who was generally spoken of as having
nothing a-year, paid quarterly. *Ib, Ch. 24*

94 There is no secret so close as that between a rider and his horse.
*Ib, Ch. 31*

**SWIFT, Jonathan, 1667–1745**

95 The two noblest of things, which are sweetness and light.
*The Battle of the Books, Preface*

96 'Tis an old maxim in the schools,
That flattery's the food of fools;
Yet now and then your men of wit
Will condescend to take a bit. *Cadenus and Vanessa*

97 Yet malice never was his aim;
He lash'd the vice, but spared the name;
No individual could resent,
Where thousands equally were meant. *On the Death of
Dr Swift, 512*

98 He put this engine [*a watch*] to our ears, which made an incessant
noise like that of a water-mill; and we conjecture it is either some
unknown animal, or the god that he worships. *Gulliver's Travels,
Voyage to Lilliput, Ch. 2*

99 Big-endians and small-endians. *Ib, Ch. 4*

1 I cannot but conclude the bulk of your natives to be the most
pernicious race of little odious vermin that nature ever suffered
to crawl upon the surface of the earth. *Ib, Voyage to
Brobdingnag, Ch. 6*

2 Whoever could make two ears of corn or two blades of grass
to grow upon a spot of ground where only one grew before
would deserve better of mankind and do more essential service
to his country than the whole race of politicians put together.
*Ib Ch. 7*

3 Proper words in proper places make the true definition of a style.
*Letter to a young clergyman, 9 Jan. 1720*

4 Hail fellow, well met,
All dirty and wet;
Find out, if you can,
Who's master, who's man. *My Lady's Lamentation*

5 So, naturalists observe, a flea
   Hath smaller fleas that on him prey,
   And these have smaller fleas to bite 'em,
   And so proceed *ad infinitum.*                    *On Poetry,* 337

6 Promises and pie-crust are made to be broken.
                                        *Polite Conversation, 1*

7 The sight of you is good for sore eyes.                    *Ib*

8 What though his head be empty, provided his common-place
   book be full.          *A Tale of a Tub, Digression in Praise of
                                                   Digression*

9 We have just enough religion to make us hate, but not enough to
   make us love one another.          *Thoughts on Various Subjects*

10 Few are qualified to shine in company; but it is in most men's
   power to be agreeable.                                    *Ib*

11 A nice man is a man of nasty ideas.                       *Ib*

12 *Ubi saeva indignatio ulterius cor lacerare nequit* – Where burning
   indignation no longer lacerates his heart.          *Swift's Epitaph*

13 I shall be like that tree, I shall die at the top.          *Attributed*

14 Good God! What a genius I had when I wrote that book.
                                        [*A Tale of a Tub*] *Attributed*


## SWINBURNE, Algernon Charles, 1837–1909

15 When the hounds of spring are on winter's traces,
        The mother of months in meadow or plain
   Fills the shadows and windy places
        With lisp of leaves and ripple of rain.          *Atalanta in
                                                          Calydon*

16 Before the beginning of years
        There came to the making of man
   Time, with a gift of tears,
        Grief, with a glass that ran.                          *Ib*

17 Shall I strew on thee rose or rue or laurel,
        Brother, on this that was the veil of thee?  *Ave Atque Vale*

18 Could you hurt me, sweet lips, though I hurt you?
        Men touch them, and change in a trice
   The lilies and languors of virtue
        For the raptures and roses of vice.          *Dolores*

19 I am tired of tears and laughter,
        And men that laugh and weep;
   Of what may come hereafter
        For men that sow to reap.          *The Garden of Proserpine*

20 From too much love of living,
    From hope and fear set free,
We thank with brief thanksgiving
    Whatever gods may be
That no life lives for ever;
That dead men rise up never;
That even the weariest river
    Winds somewhere safe to sea.    *The Garden of Proserpine*

21 Glory to Man in the Highest! for Man is the master of things.
    *Hymn of Man*

22 I have lived long enough, having seen one thing, that love hath
    an end;
Goddess and maiden and queen, be near me now and befriend.
    *Hymn to Proserpine*

23 Laurel is green for a season, and love is sweet for a day;
But love grows bitter with treason, and laurel outlives not May.
    *Ib*

24 Rise ere the dawn be risen;
    Come, and be all souls fed;
From field and street and prison
    Come, for the feast is spread;
Live, for the truth is living; wake, for night is dead.
    *A Marching Song*

25 I will go back to the great sweet mother,
    Mother and lover of men, the sea.
I will go down to her, I and no other,
    Close with her, kiss her and mix her with me.    *The Triumph
    of Time*


**SYNGE, John Millington, 1871–1909**

26 When I was writing 'The Shadow of the Glen' I got more aid
than any learning could have given me from a chink in the
floor of the old Wicklow house where I was staying, that let me
hear what was being said by the servant girls in the kitchen.
    *The Playboy of the Western World, Preface*


**TACITUS, 55?–117? A.D.**

27 *Ubi solitudinem faciunt pacem appellant.* – They create desolation
and call it peace.    *Agricola, 30*

28 *Proprium humani ingenii est odisse quem laeseris.* – It is human
nature to hate the man whom you have hurt.    *Ib*

**TALLEYRAND, Charles Maurice de, 1754–1838**

29 *C'est le commencement de la fin.* – It is the beginning of the end.
*Remark to Napoleon, 1813*

30 *Noir comme le diable,*
*Chaud comme l'enfer,*
*Pur comme un ange,*
*Doux comme l'amour.*

Black as the devil,
Hot as hell,
Pure as an angel,
Sweet as love. *Recipe for coffee*

31 *Ils n'ont rien appris, ni rien oublié.* – They have learnt nothing, and forgotten nothing. *Attributed*

32 *La parole a été donnée à l'homme pour déguiser sa pensée.* – Speech was given to man to disguise his thoughts. *Attributed*

33 *Pas trop de zèle.* – Not too much zeal. *Attributed*

34 War is much too serious a thing to be left to military men.
*Attributed*

**TATE, Nahum, 1652–1715**

35 While shepherds watched their flocks by night,
All seated on the ground,
The Angel of the Lord came down,
And glory shone around.

'Fear not,' said he, for mighty dread
Had seized their troubled mind;
'Glad tidings of great joy I bring
To you and all mankind'. *While Shepherds Watched*

**TAYLOR, Jane, 1783–1827**

36 Twinkle, twinkle, little star,
How I wonder what you are!
Up above the world so high,
Like a diamond in the sky. *The Star*

**TENNYSON, Alfred, 1st Baron, 1809–1892**

37 O for the touch of a vanish'd hand,
And the sound of a voice that is still! *Break, Break, Break*

38 A happy bridesmaid makes a happy bride. *The Bridesmaid, 4*

39 For men may come and men may go
But I go on for ever. *The Brook, 33*

40 Half a league, half a league,
    Half a league onward,
  All in the valley of Death
    Rode the six hundred. *The Charge of the Light Brigade, 1*

41 'Forward the Light Brigade!'
  Was there a man dismay'd? *Ib, 2*

42 Their's not to make reply,
  Their's not to reason why,
  Their's but to do and die. *Ib, 2*

43 Into the jaws of Death
  Into the mouth of Hell. *Ib, 3*

44 Sunset and evening star,
    And one clear call for me!
  And may there be no moaning of the bar
    When I put out to sea. *Crossing the Bar*

45 The spacious times of great Elizabeth
    With sounds that echo still. *A Dream of Fair Women, 7*

46 A daughter of the gods, divinely tall,
    And most divinely fair. *Ib, 87*

47 He clasps the crag with crooked hands;
  Close to the sun in lonely lands,
  Ring'd with the azure world, he stands.

  The wrinkled sea beneath him crawls;
  He watches from his mountain walls,
  And like a thunderbolt he falls. *The Eagle*

48 God made the woman for the man,
  And for the good and increase of the world. *Edwin Morris, 43*

49 Then she rode forth, clothed on with chastity. *Godiva, 53*

50 His honour rooted in dishonour stood,
  And faith unfaithful kept him falsely true. *Idylls of the King,*
                                *Lancelot and Elaine, 871*

51 He makes no friend who never made a foe. *Ib, 1082*

52 For men at most differ as Heaven and Earth,
  But women, worst and best, as Heaven and Hell. *Ib, Merlin*
                                     *and Vivien, 812*

53     The days darken round me, and the years,
  Among new men, strange faces, other minds. *Ib, The Passing*
                                      *of Arthur, 405*

54     And slowly answer'd Arthur from the barge:
  'The old order changeth, yielding place to new,
  And God fulfils himself in many ways.' *Ib, 407*

55 Pray for my soul. More things are wrought by prayer
Than this world dreams of.                   *Idylls of the King,*
*The Passing of Arthur, 415*

56 Our little systems have their day;
They have their day and cease to be.          *In Memoriam*
*A.H.H., Prologue*

57      Men may rise on stepping-stones
Of their dead selves to higher things.             *Ib, 1*

58      For words, like Nature, half reveal
And half conceal the Soul within.                   *Ib, 5*

59 I hold it true, whate'er befall;
I feel it, when I sorrow most;
'Tis better to have loved and lost
Than never to have loved at all.                   *Ib, 27*

60 Be near me when my light is low,
When the blood creeps, and the nerves prick
And tingle; and the heart is sick,
And all the wheels of Being slow.                 *Ib, 50*

61 Oh yet we trust that somehow good
Will be the final goal of ill.                       *Ib, 54*

62 Are God and Nature then at strife
That Nature lends such evil dreams?
So careful of the type she seems,
So careless of the single life.                     *Ib, 55*

63 Nature, red in tooth and claw.                  *Ib, 56*

64      Fresh from brawling courts
And dusty purlieus of the law.                     *Ib, 89*

65      There lives more faith in honest doubt,
Believe me, than in half the creeds.               *Ib, 96*

66 He seems so near and yet so far.               *Ib, 97*

67 Ring out, wild bells, to the wild sky.        *Ib, 106*

68 Ring out the old, ring in the new,
Ring, happy bells, across the snow:
The year is going, let him go;
Ring out the false, ring in the true.             *Ib, 106*

69 Ring out a slowly dying cause,
And ancient forms of party strife;
Ring in the nobler modes of life,
With sweeter manners, purer laws.                 *Ib, 106*

70      Ring out the thousand wars of old,
Ring in the thousand years of peace.              *Ib, 106*

71  Ring in the valiant man and free,
        The larger heart, the kindlier hand;
            Ring out the darkness of the land,
    Ring in the Christ that is to be.   *In Memoriam A.H.H., 106*

72  And thus he bore without abuse
        The grand old name of gentleman,
        Defamed by every charlatan,
    And soil'd with all ignoble use.              *Ib, 111*

73      One God, one law, one element,
        And one far-off divine event,
    To which the whole creation moves.            *Ib, 131*

74  Kind hearts are more than coronets,
        And simple faith than Norman blood.   *Lady Clara Vere
                                                   de Vere*

75  On either side the river lie
    Long fields of barley and of rye,
    That clothe the wold and meet the sky;
    And thro' the field the road runs by
        To many-tower'd Camelot.        *The Lady of Shalott, 1*

76  Willows whiten, aspens quiver,
    Little breezes dusk and shiver.                  *Ib*

77  'The curse is come upon me,' cried
        The Lady of Shalott.                        *Ib, 3*

78  Comrades, leave me here a little, while as yet 'tis early morn:
    Leave me here, and when you want me, sound upon the bugle-
        horn.                              *Locksley Hall, 1*

79  In the Spring a young man's fancy lightly turns to thoughts of
    love.                                          *Ib, 20*

80  For I dipt into the future, far as human eye could see,
    Saw the Vision of the world, and all the wonder that would be.
                                                   *Ib, 116*

81  Till the war-drum throbb'd no longer, and the battle-flags were
        furl'd
    In the Parliament of man, the Federation of the world. *Ib, 127*

82  Knowledge comes, but wisdom lingers.            *Ib, 141*

83  Woman is the lesser man, and all thy passions, match'd with
        mine
    Are as moonlight unto sunlight, and as water unto wine.
                                                   *Ib, 151*

84      They came upon a land
    In which it seemed always afternoon.       *The Lotos-Eaters*

85 Music that gentlier on the spirit lies,
    Than tir'd eyelids upon tir'd eyes.     *The Lotos Eaters*

86 Come into the garden, Maud,
    For the black bat, night, has flown,
Come into the garden, Maud,
    I am here at the gate alone.     *Maud, Part 1, 22*

87 There has fallen a splendid tear
    From the passion-flower at the gate.
She is coming, my dove, my dear;
    She is coming, my life, my fate.     *Ib, 22*

88 O that 'twere possible
After long grief and pain
To find the arms of my true love
Round me once again!     *Ib, Part 2, 4*

89 You must wake and call me early, call me early, mother dear.
    *The May Queen*

90 For I'm to be Queen of the May.     *Ib*

91 Follow the Gleam.     *Merlin and the Gleam*

92 The last great Englishman is low.     *Ode on the Death of the Duke of Wellington, 3*

93 O fall'n at length that tower of strength
    Which stood four-square to all the winds that blew!     *Ib*

94 Not once or twice in our rough island-story,
    The path of duty was the way to glory.     *Ib, 8*

95 With prudes for proctors, dowagers for deans,
    And sweet girl-graduates in their golden hair.     *The Princess, Prologue, 141*

96 Sweet and low, sweet and low,
    Wind of the Western Sea.     *Ib, 3, Song*

97 The splendour falls on castle walls
    And snowy summits old in story.     *Ib, 4, Song*

98 Blow, bugle, blow, set the wild echoes flying,
    Blow, bugle; answer, echoes, dying, dying, dying.     *Ib*

99 Tears, idle tears, I know not what they mean,
    Tears from the depth of some divine despair.     *Ib, 2nd Song*

1 Man is the hunter; woman is his game:
    The sleek and shining creatures of the chase,
We hunt them for the beauty of their skins.     *Ib, 5, 147*

2 Man for the field and woman for the hearth:
  Man for the sword and for the needle she:
  Man with the head and woman with the heart:
  Man to command and woman to obey:
  All else confusion.          *The Princess, 2nd Song, 5, 427*

3 My strength is as the strength of ten,
     Because my heart is pure.          *Sir Galahad*


**TERENCE, 190?–159? B.C.**

4 *Hinc illae lacrimae.* – Hence these tears.          *Andria, 126*

5 *Amantium irae amoris integratio est.* – Lovers' quarrels are the
  renewal of love.          *Ib, 555*

6 *Fortis fortuna adiuvat.* – Fortune favours the brave.          *Phormio,
                                                                  203*

7 *Quot homines tot sententiae.* – So many men, so many opinions.
                                                          *Ib, 454*


**THACKERAY, William Makepeace, 1811–1863**

8 It is impossible, in our condition of society, not to be sometimes
  a Snob.          *The Book of Snobs, Ch. 3*

9 'Tis not the dying for a faith that's so hard, Master Harry –
  every man of every nation has done that – 'tis the living up to it
  that is difficult. RICHARD STEELE  *Henry Esmond, Bk. 1, Ch. 6*

10 'Tis strange what a man may do, and a woman yet think him an
   angel.          *Ib, Ch. 7*

11 The *Pall Mall Gazette* is written by gentlemen for gentlemen.
                                                  *Pendennis, Ch. 32*

12 A woman with fair opportunities and without a positive hump,
   may marry whom she likes.          *Vanity Fair, Ch. 4*

13 Whenever he met a great man he grovelled before him and my-
   lorded him as only a free-born Englishman can do.   *Ib, Ch. 13*

14 Them's my sentiments. FRED BULLOCK          *Ib, Ch. 21*

15 I think I could be a good woman if I had five thousand a year.
                                              BECKY SHARP  *Ib, Ch. 36*


**THOMAS, Brandon, 1857–1914**

16 I'm Charley's aunt from Brazil, where the nuts come from.
            LORD FANCOURT BABERLEY  *Charley's Aunt, Act 1*

**THOMAS, Dylan, 1914–1953**

17 And death shall have no dominion.
   Dead men naked they shall be one
   With the man in the wind and the west moon.
                                        *And Death shall have no Dominion*

18 Do not go gentle into that good night,
   Old age should burn and rave at close of day;
   Rage, rage, against the dying of the light.
                                        *Do not go gentle into that good night*

19 The force that through the green fuse drives the flower
   Drives my green age.        *The Force that through the green*
                                        *Fuse drives the Flower*

20 The hand that signed the treaty bred a fever,
   And famine grew, and locusts came;
   Great is the hand that holds dominion over
   Man by a scribbled name.      *The Hand that Signed the Paper*

21 Light breaks where no sun shines;
   Where no sea runs, the waters of the heart
   Push in their tides.          *Light Breaks where no Sun Shines*

22 After the first death, there is no other.    *A Refusal to Mourn*
                              *the Death, by Fire, of a Child in London*

23 It is spring, moonless night in the small town, starless and
   bible-black.   FIRST VOICE                    *Under Milk Wood*

24 It is night neddying among the snuggeries of babies.
                                           FIRST VOICE  *Ib*

25 You're thinking, you're no better than you should be, Polly, and
   that's good enough for me. Oh, isn't life a terrible thing,
   thank God?  POLLY GARTER                              *Ib*

26 Praise the Lord! We are a musical nation.  REV. ELI JENKINS  *Ib*

27 Organ Morgan, you haven't been listening to a word I said. It's
   organ organ all the time with you.  MRS ORGAN MORGAN    *Ib*

**THOMPSON, Francis, 1859–1907**

28 For the field is full of shades as I near the shadowy coast,
   And a ghostly batsman plays to the bowling of a ghost;
   And I look through my tears on a soundless-clapping host
            As the run-stealers flicker to and fro,
                 To and fro: –
            O my Hornby and my Barlow long ago!    *At Lord's*

29 Nothing begins, and nothing ends,
       That is not paid with moan;
   For we are born in other's pain,
       And perish in our own.                        *Daisy*

30 I fled Him, down the nights and down the days;
   I fled Him, down the arches of the years.        *The Hound of*
                                                     *Heaven*

31 'Tis ye, 'tis your estrangèd faces,
   That miss the many-splendour'd thing.    *The Kingdom of God*

32 Look for me in the nurseries of Heaven.        *To my Godchild*


**THOMSON, James, 1700–1748**

33 When Britain first, at Heaven's command,
   Arose from out the azure main,
   This was the charter of the land,
   And guardian angels sung this strain:
   'Rule, Britannia, rule the waves;
   Britons never will be slaves.'          *Alfred: A Masque, Act 2,*
                                                     *Scene 5*

34 An elegant sufficiency, content,
   Retirement, rural quiet, friendship, books,
   Ease and alternate labour, useful life,
   Progressive virtue, and approving Heaven!        *The Seasons,*
                                                     *Spring, 1161*


**THOMSON, Roy Herbert, 1st Lord, 1894–1976**

35 It is as good as having a Government licence to print money.
        *Remark on the profitability of commercial television*
        *in Great Britain, made during an interview in Canada*


**THOREAU, Henry David, 1817–1862**

36 The mass of men lead lives of quiet desperation.
                                                     *Walden, Economy*

37 Our life is frittered away by detail … Simplify, simplify.
            *Walden, Where I Lived and What I Lived For*

38 The government of the world I live in was not framed, like that
   of Britain, in after-dinner conversations over the wine.
                                                     *Ib, Conclusion*

39 It takes two to speak the truth – one to speak, and another to
   hear.      *A Week on the Concord and Merrimack Rivers,*
                                                     *Wednesday*

40 Not that the story need be long, but it will take a long while to
   make it short.                                      *Letter*

**THUCYDIDES, c. 471–c. 400 B.C.**

41 It is great glory in a woman to show no more weakness than is natural to her sex, and not to be talked of, either for good or evil by men. *History, 2, 45, 2*

**THURBER, James, 1894–1961**

42 Early to rise and early to bed makes a male healthy and wealthy and dead. *Fables for Our Time, The Shrike and the Chipmunks*

43 All right, have it your way – you heard a seal bark. *Title of Cartoon*

44 Well, if I called the wrong number, why did you answer the phone? *Title of cartoon*

45 The War between Men and Women. *Title of series of cartoons*

**TILZER, Harry, 1878–1956**

46 Come, Come, Come and have a drink with me
Down at the old 'Bull and Bush'. *Song*

47 Come, Come, Come and make eyes at me. *Ib*

**TOBIN, John, 1770–1804**

48 The man that lays his hand upon a woman,
Save in the way of kindness is a wretch
Whom 'twere gross flattery to name a coward.
*The Honeymoon, Act 2, Scene 1*

**TOLSTOY, Leo, 1828–1910**

49 All happy families resemble one another, each unhappy family is unhappy in its own way. *Anna Karenina, 1, Ch. 1*

50 Pure and complete sorrow is as impossible as pure and complete joy. *War and Peace, 15, Ch. 1*

**TOPLADY, Augustus Montague, 1740–1778**

51 Rock of Ages, cleft for me,
Let me hide myself in Thee. *Rock of Ages*

**TRAHERNE, Thomas, 1637?–1674**

52 You will never enjoy the world aright, till the sea itself floweth in your veins, till you are clothed with the heavens, and crowned with the stars. *Centuries of Meditation, 1, 29*

53 The corn was orient and immortal wheat, which never should be reaped, nor was ever sown. I thought it had stood from everlasting to everlasting. *Ib, 3, 3*

**TRAPP, Joseph, 1679–1747**

54 The King, observing with judicious eyes,
The state of both his universities,
To Oxford sent a troop of horse, and why?
That learned body wanted loyalty;
To Cambridge books, as very well discerning,
How much that loyal body wanted learning.        *On George I's*
*donation of a library to Cambridge University*
*(For reply, see 72–3:8)*

**TROLLOPE, Anthony, 1815–1882**

55 It's dogged as does it. It ain't thinking about it.    *Last Chronicale*
*of Barset, Ch. 61*

56 Three hours a day will produce as much as a man ought to write.
*Autobiography, Ch. 15*

**TUER, Andrew White, 1838–1900**

57 English as she is Spoke.            *Title of Portuguese-English*
*Conversation Guide*

**TUSSER, Thomas, 1524?–1580**

58 At Christmas play and make good cheer,
For Christmas comes but once a year.    *Five Hundred Points of*
*Good Husbandry, Ch. 12*

**TWAIN, Mark (Samuel Langhorne Clemens), 1835–1910**

59 There was things which he stretched, but mainly he told the
truth.            *The Adventures of Huckleberry Finn, Ch. 1*

60 *Pilgrim's Progress*, about a man that left his family, it didn't say
why. I read considerable in it now and then. The statements was
interesting but tough.            *Ib, Ch. 17*

61 Deep down in me I knowed it was a lie, and He knowed it. You
can't pray a lie – I found that out.            *Ib, Ch. 21*

62 All Kings is mostly rapscallions.            *Ib, Ch. 23*

63 There are three kinds of lies: lies, damned lies, and statistics.
*Autobiography*

64 Soap and education are not as sudden as a massacre, but they
are more deadly in the long run.    *The Facts concerning the*
*Recent Resignation*

65 I must have a prodigious quantity of mind; it takes me as much
as a week, sometimes, to make it up.    *The Innocents Abroad,*
*Ch. 7*

66 They spell it Vinci and pronounce it Vinchy; foreigners always spell better than they pronounce.          *The Innocents Abroad, Ch. 19*

67 Familiarity breeds contempt – and children.          *Notebooks*

68 Adam was but human – this explains it all. He did not want the apple for the apple's sake, he wanted it only because it was forbidden.          *Pudd'nhead Wilson's Calendar, Ch. 2*

69 Training is everything. The peach was once a bitter almond; cauliflower is nothing but cabbage with a college education.
          *Ib, Ch. 5*

70 One of the most striking differences between a cat and a lie is that a cat has nine lives.          *Ib, Ch. 7*

71 When angry, count four; when very angry, swear.          *Ib, Ch. 10*

72 Nothing so needs reforming as other people's habits.          *Ib, Ch. 15*

73 A classic is something that everybody wants to have read and nobody wants to read.          *Speech, The Disappearance of Literature*

74 There ain't-a-going to *be* no core.          *Tom Sawyer Abroad, Ch. 1*

75 Reports of my death are greatly exaggerated.          *Cable to the Associated Press*

## UNITED NATIONS

76 WE THE PEOPLES OF THE UNITED NATIONS DETERMINED
          to save succeeding generations from the scourge of war, which twice in our lifetime has brought untold sorrow to mankind, and
          to reaffirm faith in fundamental human rights, in the dignity and worth of the human person, in the equal rights of men and women and of nations large and small, and
          to establish conditions under which justice and respect for the obligations arising from treaties and other sources of international law can be maintained, and
          to promote social progress and better standards of life in larger freedom,
AND FOR THESE ENDS
          to practise tolerance and live together in peace with one another as good neighbours and
          to unite our strength to maintain international peace and security, and to ensure, by the acceptance of principles and the institution of methods, that armed force shall not be used, save in the common interest, and

to employ international machinery for the promotion of the economic and social advancement of all peoples, HAVE RESOLVED TO COMBINE OUR EFFORTS TO ACCOMPLISH THESE AIMS.

*Preamble to United Nations Charter, 1945*

**UNWIN, Sir Stanley, 1884–1968**

77 Much is written of the power of the Press, a power which may last but a day; by comparison, little is heard of the power of books, which may endure for generations.    *The Truth about Publishing*

**UPTON, Ralph R., 20th century**

78 Stop; look; listen.    *Notice at American railway crossings, 1912*

**USTINOV, Peter, 1921–**

79 THE PHOTOGRAPHER: The prisoners have been brought in, Your Excellency.
THE MARSHALL: Question them, promise them life, and then kill them. Let us have the honour of honourable men. Give them hope before you blacken their world. Lift them high in the air before you drop them.    *The Moment of Truth, Act 3*

80 You will find us only on the very best atlases, because we are the smallest country left in Europe . . . a self-respecting country which deserves and sometimes achieves a colour of its own on the map – usually a dyspeptic mint green, which misses the outline of the frontier by a fraction of an inch, so that one can almost hear the printer saying damn.    THE GENERAL
*Romanoff and Juliet, Act 1*

81 As for being a General, well, at the age of four with paper hats and wooden swords we're all Generals. Only some of us never grow out of it.    THE GENERAL    *Ib*

82 A diplomat these days is nothing but a head-waiter who's allowed to sit down occasionally.    THE GENERAL    *Ib*

**VANBRUGH, Sir John, 1664–1726**

83 The want of a thing is perplexing enough, but the possession of it is intolerable.    CLARISSA    *The Confederacy, Act 1, Scene 3*

84 Much of a muchness.    JOHN MOODY    *The Provok'd Husband, Act 1*

## VAUGHAN, Henry, 1622–1695

85 They are all gone into the world of light,
And I alone sit lingering here.      *Ascension Hymn*

86 Man is the shuttle, to whose winding quest
And passage through these looms
God order'd motion, but ordain'd no rest.      *Man*

87 My soul, there is a country
Far beyond the stars.      *Peace*

## VEGETIUS, 4th century

88 *Qui desiderat pacem, praeparet bellum.* – Let him who desires
peace, prepare for war.      *De re mil., 3, Prologue*

## VERLAINE, Paul, 1844–1896

89 *Et tout le reste est littérature.* – All the rest is just literature.
     *L'Art Poétique*

90 *Il pleure dans mon cœur*
*Comme il pleut sur la ville.* – Tears fall in my heart like rain
on the town.      *Romances sans paroles, 3*

## VICTORIA, Queen, 1819–1901

91 We are not amused.      *Notebooks of a Spinster Lady, 2 Jan.*
     *1900*

92 He [*Gladstone*] speaks to Me as If I was a public meeting.
     *Russell, Collections and Recollections, Ch. 14*

## VIGNY, Alfred de, 1797–1863

93 *Hélas je suis, Seigneur, puissant et solitaire.* – Alas, Lord, I am
powerful but alone.      *Moïse*

94 *Seul le silence est grand; tout le reste est faiblesse.* – Only silence
is great; all else is weakness.      *La Mort du Loup*

## VILLON, François, 1431–1485

95 *Mais où sont les neiges d'antan?* – But where are the snows of
yesteryear?      *Ballade des Dames du Temps Jadis*

## VIRGIL, 70–19 B.C.

96 *Arma virumque cano.* Arms and the man I sing.      *Aeneid, 1, 1*

97 *Furor arma ministrat.* Anger supplies the arms.      *Ib, 1, 150*

98 *Forsan et haec olim meminisse iuvabit.* Perhaps even these things
will some day be pleasant to remember.      *Ib, 1, 203*

99 *Timeo Danaos et dona ferentes.* I fear the Greeks, even when
they bring gifts.                                    *Aeneid, 2, 49*

1            *Varium et mutabile semper*
*Femina.*
Woman is always fickle and changing.              *Ib, 4, 569*

2 *Facilis descensus Averni.* The way down to Hell is easy.
*Ib, 6, 126*

3 *Omnia vincit amor, et nos cedamus amori.* Love conquers all,
and we too succumb to love.                        *Ib, 10, 69*

4            *Labor omnia vicit*
*Improbus et duris urgens in rebus egestas.*
Persistent labour overcame all things, and the stress of need in
a hard life.                                    *Georgics, 1, 145*

5 *Felix qui potuit rerum cognoscere causas.* Happy is he who has
been able to learn the causes of things.          *Ib, 2, 490*

6 *Sed fugit interea, fugit inreparabile tempus.* Meanwhile, time is
flying – flying, never to return.                 *Ib, 3, 284*

## VOLTAIRE, François Marie Arouet, 1694–1778

7 *Tout est pour le mieux dans le meilleur des mondes possibles.* All
is for the best in the best of possible worlds.  *Candide, Ch. 1*

8 *Dans ce pays-ci il est bon de tuer de temps en temps un amiral pour
encourager les autres.* In this country [*England*] it is good to kill
an admiral from time to time, to encourage the others.
*Ib, Ch. 23*

9 *Cela est bien dit, répondit Candide, mais il faut cultiver notre
jardin.* 'That is well said,' replied Candide, 'but we must cultivate
our garden.'                                    *Ib, Ch. 30*

10 *Ils ne se servent de la pensée que pour autoriser leurs injustices, et
n'emploient les paroles que pour déguiser leurs pensées.* Men use
thought only to justify their wrong-doing, and words only to
conceal their thoughts.
*Dialogue 14, Le Chapon et la Poularde*

11 *Le mieux est l'ennemi du bien.* The best is the enemy of the good.
*Dictionnaire Philosophique, Art Dramatique*

12 *Si Dieu n'existait pas, il faudrait l'inventer.* If God did not exist,
it would be necessary to invent Him.
*Épîtres, 96, A L'Auteur du livre des Trois Imposteurs*

13 *L'histoire des grandes événements de ce monde n'est guère que
l'histoire des crimes.* The history of the great events of this world
is scarcely more than the history of crimes.
*Essai sur les Mœurs et L'Esprit des Nations, 23*

14 *Ce corps qui s'appelait et qui s'appelle encore le saint empire
romain n'était en aucune manière ni saint, ni romain, ni empire.*
This agglomeration which was called and which still calls itself
the Holy Roman Empire was neither holy, nor Roman, nor an
empire. *Essai sur les Mœurs et L'Esprit des Nations, 70*

15 *On dit que Dieu est toujours pour les gros bataillons.* It is said
that God is always for the big battalions.
*Letter to M. le Riche, 1770*

16 I disapprove of what you say, but I will defend to the death
your right to say it. *Attributed*


**WALLER, Edmund, 1606–1687**

17 Go, lovely Rose!
   Tell her that wastes her time and me,
That now she knows
    When I resemble her to thee,
    How sweet and fair she seems to be. *Go, Lovely Rose*

18 Poets that lasting marble seek
Must carve in Latin or in Greek. *Of English Verse*


**WALPOLE, Sir Robert, 1st Earl of Orford, 1676–1745**

19 The balance of power. *Speech, House of Commons, 1741*

20 All those men have their price. *W. Coxe, Memoirs of Walpole*

21 Anything but history, for history must be false. *Walpoliana*


**WALPOLE, Horace, 4th Earl of Orford, 1717–1797**

22 It is charming to totter into vogue. *Letter to G. A. Selwyn, 1765*

23 The world is a comedy to those who think, a tragedy to those
who feel. *Letter to Sir Horace Mann 1769*

24 Prognostics do not always prove prophecies, – at least the wisest
prophets make sure of the event first.
*Letter to Thomas Walpole, 1785*


**WALTON, Izaak, 1593–1683**

25 We may say of angling as Dr Boteler said of strawberries,
'Doubtless God could have made a better berry, but doubtless
God never did.' *The Compleat Angler, Ch. 5*


**WARD, Artemus (Charles Farrar Browne), 1834–1867**

26 My pollertics, like my religion, being of an exceedin' accommo-
datin' character. *Artemus Ward His Book, The Crisis*

27 Did you ever have the measels, and if so how many?
                *Artemus Ward His Book, The Census*

28 I prefer temperance hotels – although they sell worse kinds of liquor than any other kind of hotels.  *Artemus Ward's Lecture*

29 Why is this thus? What is the reason of this thusness?    *Ib*

30 I am happiest when I am idle. I could live for months without performing any kind of labour, and at the expiration of that time I should feel fresh and vigorous enough to go right on in the same way for numerous more months.    *Pyrotechny*

31 Let us all be happy and live within our means, even if we have to borrer the money to do it with.  *Science and Natural History*

## WASHINGTON, George, 1732–1799

32 It is our true policy to steer clear of permanent alliances with any portion of the foreign world.
              *Farewell Address, 17 Sept. 1796*

33 Associate yourself with men of good quality if you esteem your own reputation; for 'tis better to be alone than in bad company.
              *Rules of Civility*

34 Father, I cannot tell a lie. I did it with my little hatchet.
              *Attributed*

## WATTS, Isaac, 1674–1748

35 How doth the little busy bee
    Improve each shining hour,
    And gather honey all the day
    From every opening flower.      *Against Idleness*

36 For Satan finds some mischief still
    For idle hands to do.          *Ib*

37 Birds in their little nests agree;
    And 'tis a shameful sight,
  When children of one family
    Fall out, and chide, and fight.
        *Love between Brothers and Sisters*

38 O God, our help in ages past,
    Our hope for years to come,
  Our shelter from the stormy blast,
    And our eternal home.    *O God, our help in ages past*

39 A thousand ages in thy sight
    Are like an evening gone,
  Short as the watch that ends the night
    Before the rising sun.        *Ib*

40 Time, like an ever-rolling stream,
    Bears all its sons away;
They fly forgotten, as a dream
    Dies at the opening day.      *O God, our help in ages past*

41 'Tis the voice of the sluggard, I heard him complain:
'You have waked me too soon, I must slumber again.'
                                  *The Sluggard*

### WEBB, Sidney, 1st Baron Passfield, 1859–1947

42 The inevitability of gradualness.      *Presidential Address to*
                        *Labour Party Conference, 1923*

### WEBSTER, Daniel, 1782–1852

43 Let our object be our country, our whole country and nothing
but our country.      *Speech, Bunker Hill, 17 June 1825*

44 Liberty and Union, now and for ever, one and inseparable.
                        *Speech, 26 Jan. 1830*

45 I was born an American; I will live an American; I shall die an
American.                  *Speech, 17 July 1850*

46 There is always room at the top.    *When advised not to become*
          *a lawyer, as there were already too many*

### WEBSTER, John, 1580?–1625?

47 I am Duchess of Malfi still.
        *The Duchess of Malfi, Act 4, Scene 2*

48 Glories, like glow-worms, afar off shine bright,
But looked to near, have neither heat nor light.   BOSOLA    *Ib*

49 Other sins only speak; murder shrieks out.   BOSOLA    *Ib*

50 Cover her face: mine eyes dazzle: she died young.
                              FERDINAND  *Ib*

51 We are merely the stars' tennis balls, struck and bandied
Which way please them.   BOSOLA      *Ib, Act 5, Scene 4*

52 Is not old wine wholesomest, old pippins toothsomest, old wood
burn brightest, old linen wash whitest? Old soldiers, sweethearts are surest, and old lovers are soundest.   BIRDLIME
                  *Westward Hoe, Act 2, Scene 2*

53 I saw him even now going the way of all flesh, that is to say
towards the kitchen.                 BIRDLIME  *Ib*

54 Call for the robin redbreast, and the wren,
Since o'er shady groves they hover,
And with leaves and flowers do cover
The friendless bodies of unburied men.   CORNELIA
                *The White Devil, Act 5, Scene 4*

55 My soul, like to a ship in a black storm,
Is driven, I know not whither. VITTORIA *The White Devil,*
*Act 5, Scene 6*

56      I have caught
An everlasting cold; I have lost my voice
Most irrecoverably. FLAMINEO *Ib*

**WELLINGTON, Arthur Wellesley, 1st Duke of, 1769–1852**

57 Nothing except a battle lost can be half so melancholy as a battle
won. *Dispatch, 1815*

58 I used to say of him [*Napoleon*] that his presence on the field
made the difference of forty thousand men. *Stanhope, Notes*
*of Conversations with the Duke of Wellington, 2 Nov. 1831*

59 Ours [*our army*] is composed of the scum of the earth.
*Ib, 4 Nov. 1831*

60 Up, Guards, and at 'em. *Waterloo, 18 June 1815, Attributed*

61 The battle of Waterloo was won on the playing fields of Eton.
*Attributed*

62 Publish and be damned. *Attributed*

**WELLS, Herbert George, 1866–1946**

63 He [*Mr Polly*] broke into a quavering song: Roöötten Beëëastly
Silly Hole! *The History of Mr Polly, Ch. 1, 2*

64 'Sesquippledan,' he would say. 'Sesquippledan verboojuice.'
*Ib, Ch. 1, 5*

65 I was thinking jest what a Rum Go everything is.
*Kipps, Book 2, Ch. 3, 8*

66 In England we have come to rely upon a comfortable time-lag
of fifty years or a century intervening between the perception
that something ought to be done and a serious attempt to do it.
*The Work, Wealth and Happiness of Mankind, Ch. 11*

67 The Shape of Things to Come. *Title of Book*

**WESKER, Arnold, 1932–**

68 God in heaven, Mother, you live in the country but you got no
– no – no majesty. You spend your time among green fields, you
grow flowers and you breathe fresh air and you got no majesty.
You go on and you go on talking and talking so your mind's
cluttered up with nothing and you shut out the world. What
kind of life did you give me? BEATIE BRYANT
*Roots, Act 2, Scene 2*

69 Education ent only books and music – it's asking questions, all
the time. There are millions of us, all over the country and no

one, not one of us, is asking questions, we're all taking the easiest way out. Everyone I ever worked with took the easiest way out. We don't fight for anything, we're so mentally lazy we might as well be dead!   BEATIE BRYANT      *Roots, Act 3*

## WESLEY, Charles, 1707–1788

70 Gentle Jesus, meek and mild,
     Look upon a little child;
     Pity my simplicity,
     Suffer me to come to thee.      *Gentle Jesus, Meek and Mild*

71 Hark! the herald Angels sing
     Glory to the new-born King;
     Peace on earth and mercy mild,
     God and sinners reconciled.      *Hark! the Herald Angels sing*

72 Love Divine, all loves excelling,
     Joy of heaven, to earth come down,
     Fix in us thy humble dwelling,
     All thy faithful mercies crown.
     Jesu, thou art all compassion,
     Pure unbounded love thou art;
     Visit us with thy salvation,
     Enter every trembling heart.
      *Love Divine, All Loves Excelling*

## WESLEY, John, 1703–1791

73 I look upon all the world as my parish.    *Journal, 11 June 1739*

## WEST, Mae, 1893–1980

74 Come up and see me sometime.      *Diamond Lil*

## WHISTLER, James Abbott McNeill, 1834–1903

75 I am not arguing with you – I am telling you.
      *The Gentle Art of Making Enemies*

76 OSCAR WILDE: I wish I had said that.
    WHISTLER: You will, Oscar, you will.
      *L. C. Ingleby, Oscar Wilde*

## WHITE, E. B., 1899–

77 Commuter – one who spends his life
     In riding to and from his wife;
     A man who shaves and takes a train,
     And then rides back to shave again.      *The Commuter*

**WHITMAN, Walt, 1819–1892**

78 Women sit or move to and fro, some old, some young,
The young are beautiful – but the old are more beautiful than
the young.                                      *Beautiful Women*

79 I hear it was charged against me that I sought to destroy
institutions,
But really I am neither for nor against institutions.
*I Hear it was Charged Against Me*

80 If anything is sacred the human body is sacred.
*I Sing the Body Electric, 8*

81 O Captain! my Captain! our fearful trip is done,
The ship has weather'd every rack, the prize we sought is won,
The port is near, the bells I hear, the people all exulting.
*O Captain! My Captain!*

82 I celebrate myself, and sing myself,
And what I assume you shall assume.    *Song of Myself, 1*

83 I loafe and invite my soul.                          *Ib, 1*

84 I think I could turn and live with animals, they're so placid
and self-contain'd,
I stand and look at them long and long.              *Ib, 32*

85 Behold, I do not give lectures or a little charity,
When I give I give myself.                          *Ib, 40*

86 I have said that the soul is not more than the body,
And I have said that the body is not more than the soul,
And nothing, not God, is greater to one than one's self is.
*Ib, 48*

87 Do I contradict myself?
Very well then I contradict myself,
(I am large, I contain multitudes).                  *Ib, 51*

**WHITTIER, John Greenleaf, 1807–1892**

88 Oh, rank is good, and gold is fair,
And high and low mate ill;
But love has never known a law
Beyond its own sweet will!              *Amy Wentworth*

89 'Shoot, if you must, this old gray head,
But spare your country's flag,' she said.    *Barbara Frietchie*

90 For all sad words of tongue or pen,
The saddest are these: 'It might have been!'      *Maud Muller*

**WILCOX, Ella Wheeler, 1850–1919**

91 Laugh, and the world laughs with you;
   Weep, and you weep alone,
For the sad old earth must borrow its mirth,
   But has trouble enough of its own.               *Solitude*

92 Feast, and your halls are crowded;
   Fast, and the world goes by.                      *Ib*

93 So many gods, so many creeds,
So many paths that wind and wind,
When just the art of being kind
Is all this sad world needs.               *The World's Need*

**WILDE, Oscar Fingall O'Flahertie Wills, 1856–1900**

94 Yet each man kills the thing he loves,
   By each let this be heard,
Some do it with a bitter look,
   Some with a flattering word.
The coward does it with a kiss,
   The brave man with a sword!
                   *The Ballad of Reading Gaol, 1, 7*

95 Something was dead in each of us,
   And what was dead was Hope.          *Ib, 3, 31*

96 For he who lives more lives than one
   More deaths than one must die.        *Ib, 3, 37*

97 I know not whether Laws be right
   Or whether Laws be wrong;
All that we know who live in gaol
   Is that the wall is strong;
And that each day is like a year,
   A year whose days are long.            *Ib, 5, 1*

98 The man who sees both sides of a question is a man who sees
absolutely nothing at all.        *The Critic as Artist, Part 2*

99 A little sincerity is a dangerous thing, and a great deal of it is
absolutely fatal.                                         *Ib*

1 Ah! don't say you agree with me. When people agree with me I
always feel that I must be wrong.                        *Ib*

2 There is no sin except stupidity.                      *Ib*

3 To love oneself is the beginning of a lifelong romance.
              LORD GORING  *An Ideal Husband, Act 3*

4 Really, if the lower orders don't set us a good example, what
on earth is the use of them?  ALGERNON
                   *The Importance of Being Earnest, Act 1*

5 The truth is rarely pure and never simple. Modern life would be very tedious if it were either, and modern literature a complete impossibility! ALGERNON *The Importance of Being Earnest, 1*

6 I have invented an invaluable permanent invalid called Bunbury, in order that I may be able to go down into the country whenever I choose. ALGERNON *Ib, 1*

7 The amount of women in London who flirt with their own husbands is perfectly scandalous. It looks so bad. It is simply washing one's clean linen in public. ALGERNON *Ib, 1*

8 In married life three is company and two is none. ALGERNON *Ib, 1*

9 I do not approve of anything that tampers with natural ignorance. Ignorance is like a delicate exotic fruit; touch it, and the bloom is gone. LADY BRACKNELL *Ib, 1*

10 To lose one parent, Mr Worthing, may be regarded as a misfortune; to lose both looks like carelessness. LADY BRACKNELL *Ib, 1*

11 JACK: In a hand-bag.
LADY BRACKNELL: A hand-bag?
JACK: Yes, Lady Bracknell. It was in a hand-bag – a somewhat large, black leather hand-bag, with handles to it – an ordinary hand-bag in fact. *Ib, 1*

12 LADY BRACKNELL: The cloak-room at Victoria Station?
JACK: Yes. The Brighton line.
LADY BRACKNELL: The line is immaterial. *Ib, 1*

13 Memory, my dear Cecily, is the diary we all carry about with us. MISS PRISM *Ib, Act 2*

14 I never travel without my diary. One should always have something sensational to read in the train. GWENDOLEN FAIRFAX *Ib, 2*

15 No woman should ever be quite accurate about her age. It looks so calculating. LADY BRACKNELL *Ib, Act 3*

16 It is a terrible thing for a man to find out suddenly that all his life he has been speaking nothing but the truth. JACK *Ib, 3*

17 Please do not shoot the pianist. He is doing his best. *Impressions of America, Leadville*

18 It is absurd to divide people into good and bad. People are either charming or tedious. LORD DARLINGTON *Lady Windermere's Fan, Act 1*

19 I can resist everything except temptation. LORD DARLINGTON *Ib, 1*

20 Scandal is gossip made tedious by morality.   CECIL GRAHAM
*Lady Windermere's Fan, Act 3*

21 CECIL GRAHAM: What is a cynic?
LORD DARLINGTON: A man who knows the price of everything
and the value of nothing.   *Ib, 3*

22 All Art is quite useless.   *The Picture of Dorian Gray, Preface*

23 There is only one thing in the world worse than being talked
about, and that is not being talked about.   *Ib, 1*

24 The only way to get rid of a temptation is to yield to it.   *Ib, 2*

25 MRS ALLONBY: They say, Lady Hunstanton, that when good
Americans die they go to Paris.
LADY HUNSTANTON: Indeed? And when bad Americans die
where do they go?
LORD ILLINGWORTH: Oh, they go to America.
*A Woman of No Importance, Act 1*

26 The youth of America is their oldest tradition. It has been going
on now for three hundred years.   LORD ILLINGWORTH   *Ib, 1*

27 One knows so well the popular idea of health. The English
country gentleman galloping after a fox – the unspeakable in
full pursuit of the uneatable.   LORD ILLINGWORTH   *Ib, 1*

28 We in the House of Lords are never in touch with public opinion.
That makes us a civilized body.   LORD ILLINGWORTH   *Ib, 1*

29 One should never trust a woman who tells one her real age. A
woman who would tell one that, would tell one anything.
LORD ILLINGWORTH   *Ib, 1*

30 LORD ILLINGWORTH: People's mothers always bore me to death.
All women become like their mothers. That
is their tragedy.
MRS ALLONBY: No man does. That is his.   *Ib, 2*

31 Moderation is a fatal thing, Lady Hunstanton. Nothing succeeds like excess.   LORD ILLINGWORTH   *Ib, 3*

32 No woman should have a memory. Memory in a woman is the
beginning of dowdiness.   LORD ILLINGWORTH   *Ib, 3*

33 I have nothing to declare except my genius.
*At New York Custom House*

34 I suppose that I shall have to die beyond my means. [*When asked
a large fee for an operation*]   *Sherard, Life of Wilde*

35 Work is the curse of the drinking classes.   *Attributed*

## WILLIAM III of England, 1650–1702

36 I will die in the last ditch.
*Quoted in Hume's History of England*

37 Every bullet has its billet.   *John Wesley, Journal, 6 June 1765*

**WILLIAM OF WYKEHAM, 1324–1404**
38 Manners maketh man.   *Motto of his foundations, Winchester College and New College, Oxford*

**WILLIAMS, Harry, 1874–1924, and JUDGE, Jack, 1878–1938**
39 It's a long way to Tipperary, it's a long way to go;
It's a long way to Tipperary, to the sweetest girl I know!
Good-bye, Piccadilly, farewell, Leicester Square,
It's a long, long way to Tipperary, but my heart's right there!
   *Tipperary*

**WILLIAMS, W., 1717–1791**
40 Guide me, O thou great Redeemer,
   Pilgrim through this barren land;
I am weak, but thou art mighty,
   Hold me with thy powerful hand:
   Bread of heaven,
Feed me till I want no more.   *Guide me, O thou great Redeemer*

**WILLS, William Gorman, 1828–1891**
41 I'll sing thee songs of Araby,
   And Tales of fair Cashmere.   *Lalla Rookh*

**WILSON, Charles Erwin, 1890–1961**
42 I thought what was good for the country was good for General Motors and vice versa.   *Statement to U.S. Congressional Committee, 23 Jan. 1953*

**WILSON, Harriette, 1789–1846**
43 I shall not say why and how I became, at the age of fifteen, the mistress of the Earl of Craven.   *Memoirs, Opening words*

**WILSON, John, see NORTH, Christopher**

**WILSON, Sandy, 1924–**
44 I could be happy with you.   *The Boy Friend, Title of Song*

**WILSON, Thomas Woodrow, 1856–1924**
45 There is such a thing as a man being too proud to fight.
   *Speech, 10 May 1915*

46 America cannot be an ostrich with its head in the sand.
*Speech, 1 Feb. 1916*

47 The world must be made safe for democracy.
*Speech, 2 April 1917*

**WITHER, George, 1588–1667**

48 I loved a lass, a fair one,
    As fair as e'er was seen;
She was indeed a rare one,
Another Sheba Queen.         *I Loved a Lass*

49 Shall I, wasting in despair,
    Die because a woman's fair?
Or make pale my cheeks with care,
    'Cause another's rosy are?     *The Lover's Resolution*

50 If she love me, this believe,
I will die ere she shall grieve;
If she slight me when I woo;
I can scorn and let her go;
    For if she be not for me,
    What care I for whom she be?     *Ib*

**WODEHOUSE, Pelham Grenville, 1881–1975**

51 He spoke with a certain what-is-it in his voice, and I could see
that, if not actually disgruntled, he was far from being gruntled.
*The Code of the Woosters*

**WOLFE, Charles, 1791–1823**

52 Not a drum was heard, not a funeral note,
    As his corse to the rampart we hurried;
Not a soldier discharged his farewell shot
    O'er the grave where our hero we buried.
*The Burial of Sir John Moore at Corunna, 1*

53 We carved not a line, and we raised not a stone,
    But we left him alone with his glory.     *Ib, 31*

**WOLFE, James, 1727–1759**

54 I would rather have written that poem, [*Gray's Elegy*], gentlemen, than take Quebec.
*The night before he was killed in battle in Quebec*

**WOLSEY, Thomas, Cardinal, 1475?–1530**

55 Had I but served God as diligently as I have served the king, he
would not have given me over in my gray hairs.
*To Sir William Kingston*

**WOOD, Mrs Henry, 1814–1887**

56 Dead! and . . . never called me mother.

*East Lynne, dramatized version*

**WOOLCOTT, Alexander, 1887–1943**

57 I must get out of these wet clothes and into a dry Martini.

*Attributed*

*(Also attributed to Robert Benchley and Billy Wilder)*

**WOOLF, Virginia, 1882–1941**

58 A Room of One's Own.                    *Title of Book*

**WORDSWORTH, Elizabeth, 1840–1932**

59 If all the good people were clever,
    And all clever people were good,
The world would be wiser than ever
    We thought that it possibly could.
But somehow 'tis seldom or never
    The two hit it off as they should;
The good are so harsh to the clever,
    The clever so rude to the good!          *Good and Clever*

**WORDSWORTH, William, 1770–1850**

60 Give all thou canst; high Heaven rejects the lore
    Of nicely-calculated less or more.          *Ecclesiastical Sonnets,*
*Part 3, 43, King's College Chapel*

61 The light that never was, on sea or land,
    The consecration, and the Poet's dream.          *Elegiac Stanzas*
*suggested by a Picture of Peele Castle in a storm, 15*

62 A deep distress hath humanized my Soul.                    *Ib, 39*

63 On Man, on Nature, and on Human Life,
    Musing in solitude.          *The Excursion, Preface, 1*

64        Oh, Sir! the good die first,
And they whose hearts are dry as summer dust
Burn to the socket.                    *Ib, 1, 500*

65 Think you, 'mid all this mighty sum
    Of things for ever speaking,
That nothing of itself will come,
    But we must still be seeking?          *Expostulation and Reply, 25*

66 I travelled among unknown men,
    In lands beyond the sea;
Nor, England! did I know till then
    What love I bore to thee.          *I travelled among unknown men*

67 I wandered lonely as a cloud
That floats on high o'er vales and hills,
When all at once I saw a crowd,
A host, of golden daffodils;
Beside the lake, beneath the trees,
Fluttering and dancing in the breeze.

*I wandered lonely as a Cloud, 1*

68 Continuous as the stars that shine
And twinkle on the milky way.

*Ib, 7*

69 Ten thousand saw I at a glance,
Tossing their heads in sprightly dance.

*Ib, 11*

70 A poet could not but be gay,
In such a jocund company.

*Ib, 15*

71 For oft, when on my couch I lie
In vacant or in pensive mood,
They flash upon that inward eye
Which is the bliss of solitude.

*Ib, 19*

72 There was a time when meadow, grove, and stream,
The earth, and every common sight,
To me did seem
Apparelled in celestial light,
The glory and the freshness of a dream. *Ode, Intimations of
Immortality from Recollections of Early Childhood,
Stanza 1*

73 The Rainbow comes and goes,
And lovely is the Rose.

*Ib, Stanza 2*

74 The sunshine is a glorious birth;
But yet I know, where'er I go,
That there hath past away a glory from the earth.

*Ib*

75 While the young lambs bound
As to the tabor's sound

*Ib, Stanza 3*

76 Whither is fled the visionary gleam?
Where is it now, the glory and the dream?

*Ib, Stanza 4*

77 Our birth is but a sleep and a forgetting:
The Soul that rises with us, our life's Star,
Hath had elsewhere its setting,
And cometh from afar:
Not in entire forgetfulness,
And not in utter nakedness,
But trailing clouds of glory do we come
From God, who is our home:
Heaven lies about us in our infancy!

Shades of the prison-house begin to close
       Upon the growing Boy. *Ode, Intimations of Immortality*
           *from Recollections of Early Childhood, Stanza 5*

78 The Youth, who daily farther from the east
     Must travel, still is Nature's Priest,
     And by the vision splendid
     Is on his way attended;
At length the Man perceives it die away,
And fade into the light of common day.           *Ib*

79 Behold the Child among his new-born blisses,
A six years' Darling of a pigmy size!     *Ib, Stanza 7*

80 O joy! that in our embers
Is something that doth live,
That nature yet remembers
What was so fugitive!          *Ib, Stanza 9*

81 And O, ye Fountains, Meadows, Hills, and Groves,
Forebode not any severing of our loves!   *Ib, Stanza 11*

82 To me the meanest flower that blows can give
Thoughts that do often lie too deep for tears.     *Ib*

83 I heard a thousand blended notes,
While in a grove I sate reclined,
In that sweet mood when pleasant thoughts
Bring sad thoughts to the mind  *Lines written in early Spring, 1*

84 Have I not reason to lament
What man has made of man?         *Ib, 23*

85 I chanced to see at break of day
The solitary child.         *Lucy Gray, 3*

86 The sweetest thing that ever grew
Beside a human door!         *Ib, 7*

87      Meantime Luke began
To slacken in his duty; and, at length,
He in the dissolute city gave himself
To evil courses.         *Michael, 442*

88 There is a comfort in the strength of love;
'Twill make a thing endurable, which else
Would overset the brain, or break the heart.   *Ib, 448*

89 Nuns fret not at their convent's narrow room;
And hermits are contented with their cells.
          *Miscellaneous Sonnets, Part 1, 1*

90      'Twas pastime to be bound
Within the Sonnet's scanty plot of ground.    *Ib*

91 Surprised by joy – impatient as the Wind
I turned to share the transport.     *Ib, 1, 27*

92 It is a beauteous evening, calm and free,
   The holy time is quiet as a Nun
   Breathless with adoration.   *Miscellaneous Sonnets, Part 1, 30*

93 The world is too much with us; late and soon,
   Getting and spending, we lay waste our powers:
   Little we see in Nature that is ours.       *Ib, 1, 33*

94           Great God! I'd rather be
   A Pagan suckled in a creed outworn;
   So might I, standing on this pleasant lea,
   Have glimpses that would make me less forlorn;
   Have sight of Proteus rising from the sea;
   Or hear old Triton blow his wreathèd horn.      *Ib*

95 Scorn not the Sonnet; Critic, you have frowned,
   Mindless of its just honours; with this key
   Shakespeare unlocked his heart.     *Ib, Part 2, 1*

96 Earth has not anything to show more fair:
   Dull would he be of soul who could pass by
   A sight so touching in its majesty:
   This City now doth, like a garment, wear
   The beauty of the morning; silent, bare,
   Ships, towers, domes, theatres, and temples lie
   Open unto the fields, and to the sky;
   All bright and glittering in the smokeless air.   *Ib, 2, 36*

97 Dear God! the very houses seem asleep;
   And all that mighty heart is lying still!      *Ib*

98 My heart leaps up when I behold
   A rainbow in the sky.     *My Heart leaps up*

99 The Child is father of the Man;
   And I could wish my days to be
   Bound each to each by natural piety.     *Ib*

1 Two Voices are there; one is of the sea,
  One of the mountains; each a mighty Voice:
  In both from age to age thou didst rejoice,
  They were thy chosen music, Liberty!   *National Independence*
          *and Liberty, Part 1, 12, Thoughts of a Briton*
            *on the Subjugation of Switzerland*

2 Plain living and high thinking are no more:
  The homely beauty of the good old cause
  Is gone; our peace, our fearful innocence,
  And pure religion breathing household laws.
        *Ib, 1, 13, Written in London, Sept. 1802*

3 Milton! thou shouldst be living at this hour:
  England hath need of thee: she is a fen
  Of stagnant waters.      *National Independence and Liberty,*
                              *Part 1, 14, London, 1802*

4 Thy soul was like a Star, and dwelt apart;
  Thou hadst a voice whose sound was like the sea:
  Pure as the naked heavens, majestic, free,
  So didst thou travel on life's common way,
  In cheerful godliness; and yet thy heart
  The lowliest duties on herself did lay,           *Ib*

5 We must be free or die, who speak the tongue
  That Shakespeare spake; the faith and morals hold
  Which Milton held.                 *Ib, Pt. 1, 16*

6 Another year! – another deadly blow!
  Another mighty Empire overthrown!
  And We are left, or shall be left, alone.      *Ib, 1, 27*

7 Stern Daughter of the Voice of God!
  O Duty! if that name thou love
  Who art a light to guide, a rod
  To check the erring, and reprove.      *Ode to Duty, 1*

8 Give unto me, made lowly wise,
  The spirit of self-sacrifice.              *Ib, 54*

9 Bliss was it in that dawn to be alive,
  But to be young was very Heaven!     *The Prelude, 11, 108*

10                    There is
  One great society alone on earth:
  The noble Living and the noble Dead.      *Ib, 11, 393*

11 There was a roaring in the wind all night;
  The rain came heavily and fell in floods.
               *Resolution and Independence, 1*

12 I thought of Chatterton, the marvellous Boy,
  The sleepless Soul that perished in his pride.     *Ib, 7*

13 Still glides the Stream, and shall for ever glide;
  The Form remains, the Function never dies.
          *The River Duddon, 34, After-Thought*

14 Through love, through hope, and faith's transcendent dower,
  We feel that we are greater than we know.     *Ib*

15 She dwelt among the untrodden ways
  Beside the springs of Dove,
  A Maid whom there were none to praise
    And very few to love.
        *She Dwelt among the Untrodden Ways*

16 She was a Phantom of delight
When first she gleamed upon my sight.
*She was a Phantom of Delight, 1*

17 I saw her upon nearer view,
A Spirit, yet a Woman too! *Ib, 11*

18 A perfect Woman, nobly planned,
To warn, to comfort, and command;
And yet a Spirit still, and bright
With something of angelic light. *Ib, 27*

19 No.motion has she now, no force;
She neither hears nor sees;
Rolled round in earth's diurnal course,
With rocks, and stones, and trees.
*A Slumber did my Spirit seal*

20 Behold her, single in the field,
Yon solitary Highland Lass! *The Solitary Reaper, 1*

21 Will no one tell me what she sings? –
Perhaps the plaintive numbers flow
For old, unhappy, far-off things,
And battles long ago. *Ib, 17*

22 I listened, motionless and still;
And, as I mounted up the hill,
The music in my heart I bore,
Long after it was heard no more. *Ib, 29*

23 Strange fits of passion have I known:
And I will dare to tell. *Strange Fits of Passion, 1*

24 What fond and wayward thoughts will slide
Into a Lover's head!
'O mercy!' to myself I cried,
'If Lucy should be dead!' *Ib, 25*

25 Up! up! my Friend, and quit your books;
Or surely you'll grow double. *The Tables Turned, 1*

26 Books! 'tis a dull and endless strife:
Come, hear the woodland linnet,
How sweet his music! on my life,
There's more of wisdom in it. *Ib, 9*

27 Come forth into the light of things,
Let Nature be your Teacher. *Ib, 15*

28 One impulse from a vernal wood
May teach you more of man,
Of moral evil and of good,
Than all the sages can. *Ib, 21*

29 Come forth, and bring with you a heart
   That watches and receives.                *The Tables Turned, 31*

30 Three years she grew in sun and shower,
   Then Nature said, 'A lovelier flower
   On earth was never sown;
   This Child I to myself will take;
   She shall be mine, and I will make
   A Lady of my own.'                      *Three Years she Grew, 1*

31      That best portion of a good man's life,
   His little, nameless, unremembered, acts
   Of kindness and of love.    *Lines composed a few miles above*
                                                *Tintern Abbey, 33*

32           That blessed mood,
   In which the burthen of the mystery,
   In which the heavy and the weary weight
   Of all this unintelligible world,
   Is lightened.                                *Ib, 37*

33           We are laid asleep
   In body, and become a living soul:
   While with an eye made quiet by the power
   Of harmony, and the deep power of joy,
   We see into the life of things,             *Ib, 45*

34 How oft, in spirit, have I turned to thee,
   O sylvan Wye!                               *Ib, 55*

35           I have learned
   To look on nature, not as in the hour
   Of thoughtless youth; but hearing often-times
   The still, sad music of humanity.           *Ib, 88*

36           Nature never did betray
   The heart that loved her.                   *Ib, 122*

37 O Blithe New-comer! I have heard,
   I hear thee and rejoice.
   O Cuckoo! shall I call thee Bird,
   Or but a wandering Voice?            *To the Cuckoo, 1*

38 Thrice welcome, darling of the Spring!      *Ib, 13*

39 O blessèd Bird! the earth we pace
   Again appears to be
   An unsubstantial, faery place;
   That is fit home for Thee!                  *Ib, 29*

40 'And where are they? I pray you tell.'
   She answered, 'Seven are we;
   And two of us at Conway dwell,
   And two are gone to sea.'           *We are Seven, 17*

41 'You run about, my little Maid,
   Your limbs they are alive;
   If two are in the church-yard laid,
   Then ye are only five.'           *We are Seven, 33*

42 Poetry is the spontaneous overflow of powerful feelings: it takes
its origin from emotion recollected in tranquillity.
                              *Lyrical Ballads, Preface*

## WORK, Henry Clay, 1832–1884

43 But it stopped short – never to go again –
   When the old man died.           *Grandfather's Clock*

44 Bring the good old bugle, boys, we'll sing another song:
   Sing it with a spirit that will start the world along,
   Sing it as we used to sing it – fifty thousand strong,
      As we were marching through Georgia.
                            *Marching through Georgia*

45 'Hurrah! hurrah! we bring the Jubilee!
   Hurrah! hurrah! the flag that makes you free!'
   So they sang the chorus from Atlanta to the sea
      As we were marching through Georgia.      *Ib, Chorus*

## WOTTON, Sir Henry, 1568–1639

46 An Ambassador is an honest man sent to lie abroad for his
country.      *Written in Mr Christopher Fleckamore's Album*

47 He first deceased; she for a little tried
   To live without him, liked it not, and died.
            *Upon the Death of Sir Albertus Morton's wife*

48 How happy is he born and taught,
    That serveth not another's will;
   Whose armour is his honest thought,
    And simple truth his utmost skill!
                *The Character of a Happy Life*

## WREN, Sir Christopher, 1632–1723

49 *Si monumentum requiris, circumspice.* If you seek my monument,
look around you.      *Inscription in St Paul's Cathedral,*
                                  *London, written by his son*

## WYKEHAM, William of, see WILLIAM OF WYKEHAM

## XENOPHON, 435?–354? B.C.

50 The sea! the sea!                         *Anabasis, 4, 7*

YEATMAN, Robert Julian, see SELLAR, Walter Carruthers

YEATS, William Butler, 1865–1939

51      When I was young,
  I had not given a penny for a song
  Did not the poet sing it with such airs
  That one believed he had a sword upstairs.
                              *All Things can Tempt Me*

52 I will arise and go now, and go to Innisfree,
  And a small cabin build there, of clay and wattles made;
  Nine bean rows will I have there, a hive for the honey bee,
  And live alone in the bee-loud glade.   *The Lake Isle of Innisfree*

53 And I shall have some peace there, for peace comes dropping
      slow,
  Dropping from the veils of the morning to where the cricket
      sings.                                          *Ib*

54          The land of faery,
  Where nobody gets old and godly and grave,
  Where nobody gets old and crafty and wise,
  Where nobody gets old and bitter of tongue.
                              *The Land of Heart's Desire*

55 All things uncomely and broken, all things worn out and old,
  The cry of a child by the roadway, the creak of a lumbering cart,
  The heavy steps of the ploughman, splashing the wintry mould,
  Are wronging your image that blossoms a rose in the deeps of
      my heart.        *The Lover Tells of the Rose in his Heart*

56 When I was a boy with never a crack in my heart.
                              *The Meditation of the Old Fisherman*

57 A pity beyond all telling
  Is hid in the heart of love.                    *The Pity of Love*

58 When you are old and grey and full of sleep
  And, nodding by the fire, take down this book,
  And slowly read, and dream of the soft look
  Your eyes had once, and of their shadows deep.
                              *When You are Old*


YOUNG, Edward, 1683–1765

59 Some for renown, on scraps of learning dote,
  And think they grow immortal as they quote.
                              *Love of Fame, 1 89*

60      Be wise with speed,
  A fool at forty is a fool indeed,             *Ib, 2, 281*

61 Be wise today; 'tis madness to defer.
                              *Night Thoughts, Night 1, 390*

62 Procrastination is the thief of time.                    *Ib, 393*

63 At thirty man suspects himself a fool;
   Knows it at forty, and reforms his plan;
   At fifty chides his infamous delay,
   Pushes his prudent purpose to resolve:
   In all the magnanimity of thought
   Resolves; and re-resolves; then dies the same.          *Ib, 417*

64 Man wants but little, nor that little, long.    *Ib, Night 4, 118*

**ZOLA, Émile, 1840–1902**

65 *J'accuse.* I accuse.        *Title of open letter to French President*
                               *about Dreyfus Case, 1898*

# Index

## NOTE TO INDEX

The overriding aims in compiling the index have been to refresh memories by providing fingerposts to half-remembered quotations, and to furnish useful quotations related to given subjects. This being so, in many cases brief and pregnant passages have received particularly thorough analysis.

'A' and 'the' have frequently been omitted from the beginnings of quoted phrases when their presence did not seem essential. The object has been to quote what are, in each case, the most informative words in a phrase. 'Your', 'yours', 'would', 'could', 'should' are the principal abbreviated words; any other isolated abbreviations have been made only when they are unmistakable.

References in the index after a quotation are to the page and to the place on the page. Thus 95:6 after a quotation refers to page 95, quotation 6.

# Index

Ace of trumps up [Gladstone's] sleeve 191:23

Ache, penury and imprisonment 337:91

Aches: the sense a. at thee 346:14

Achieve: my object ... shall a. in time 146:6

Achieving: still a., still pursuing 198:98

Aching: an a. void 113:62

Achitophel: of these the false A. was first 126:38

A-cold: owl, for all his feathers, was a. 181:89

Acquaintance: day ... lost ... do not make a new a. 178:37
hope our a. ... a long 'un 121:69
shd. auld a., be forgot 79:99
what, old a.! ... all this flesh! 315:92

Acquaintances: few friends though many a. 264:98
if a man does not make new a. 174:82

Acquist: he with new a. 223:27

Acres: a few paternal a. 251:28
over whose a. walked those blessed feet 312:43
three a. and a cow 107:85

Act: between the motion and the a. 130:95
every prudent a. ... barter 78:74
future ages groan for this foul a. 350:56
hear the sins they love to a. 347:25
is in itself almost an a. 291:52
unproportion'd thought his a. 306:55

Acting: only ... when ... off he was a. 151:82

Action: a. nor utterance 325:21
dearest a. in the tented field 344:90
I cannot forecast ... the a. of Russia 100:91
in a., how like an angel! 308:81
lose the name of a. 309:95
lust in a., and till a., lust 363:50
man of a. is called on 317:12
rarer a. is in virtue 357:53
suit the a. to the word 310:5

Actions speak louder than words 254:58

Actor: after a well-graced a. leaves 351:61
like a dull a. ... I have forgot 304:18

Actors: best a. ... for tragedy, comedy 308:84
our a. ... were all spirits 356:50
the a. are ... the usual three 209:32

Acts: desires but a. not 69:59
familiar a. are beautiful 369:45
his a. being seven ages 301:90
little, nameless, unremembered a. 415:31

*Ad infinitum:* and so proceed *a.* 382:5

Adam: A. the goodliest man 219:67
A. was but human 394:68
A. was not Adamant! 165:63
in A.'s ear so charming ... his voice 220:85
the old A. in this child 64:94
when A. and Eve were dispossessed 69:68
when A. delved and Eve span 27:50

Adamant: Adam was not A. 165:63

Add: a. insult to injury 267:18
God shall a. ... the plagues 61:35

Adder: deaf a. that stoppeth her ear 42:11

Addington: Pitt is to A. 88:28

Adieu: a. a.! my native shore 83:57
joy ... is ever ... bidding a. 183:22

Adjunct: learning is but an a. to ourself 331:14

Admiral: kill an a. from time to time 397:8

Admiration only of weak minds 221:5

Admire: fools a., but men of sense approve 249:1

Admiring: an a. bog 122:81

Admittance: no a. till ... week after next 94:97

Adonais: O, weep for A.! 367:9
the soul of A. like a star 368:20

Adoption: friends ... and their a. tried 306:55

Adoration: breathless with a. 412:92

Adore: Youth, I do a. thee 364:57

Adorn: nothing that he did not a. 178:38

Adriatic: in the A., an iron curtain 102:8

Adullam: David ... escaped to the cave A. 39:45

Adulteries: all the a. of art 179:52

Adultery: men call gallantry and gods a. 84:66
thou shalt not commit a. 37:89

Advance: retrograde if it does not a. 142:67

Advancement: economic and social a. of all peoples 394–5:76

Advantage: a. of doing one's praising 83:48
for our a. on the bitter cross 312:43

Advantages: remember, with a., what feats 320:58

Adventure: death ... the most beautiful
a. 139:20
  to die will be an awfully big a.
28:61
Adversary: never ... sees her a. 223:39
Adversity: a. ... blessing of the New
24:90
  a. doth best discover virtue 24:92
  a. is not without comforts 24:91
  a. makes ... wise, not rich 254:59
  many can bear a. 254:60
  of fortune's sharp a. 97:51
  sweet are the uses of a. 300:75
Advice: a woman seldom asks a. 9:10
  a. is seldom welcome 98:58
Afar: and cometh from a. 410:77
  the devotion to something a. 371:56
Affair: had an a. with a darky 14:55
Affairs: for the ord'ring yr. a., to sing
362:21
  tide in the a. of men 326:27
  tide in the a. of women 85:80
Affect: study what you most a. 355:20
Affection: to me-wards your a.'s strong
162:20
Affections: hath not a Jew ... a.?
339:13
  woman's ... history is ... of the a.
170:16
Affirmative: two negatives make an a.
281:79
Afflicted: any ways a., or distressed
63:83
Affliction: prosperity ... whose heart
... a. alters 362:24
Afflictions: happy issue out of ... a.
63:84
Affluent: The A. Society 140:42
Affront: a moral ... man will not a. me
112:52
Afraid: a. you've got a bad egg 285:86
  be not a. to do thine office 226:67
  I will not be a. of death 336:73
  it [public] is a. of itself 159:82
  not be a. for the terror by night
43:20
  see all, nor be a. 75–6:46
Afric's sunny fountains 159:86
Africa: always something new out of A.
247:64
  *ex A. semper aliquid novi* 247:64
  silent over A. 74:25
After his head was cut off 15:16
Afternoon: seemed always a. 387:84
Afternoons: slant of light on winter a.
122:83
Afton: flow gently, sweet A. 79:98
Agag came delicately 39:41

Again: and then rides back to shave a.
402:77
  I do it a. and a. 90:48
  we'll fight ... conquer a. and a. 141:48
Against: hand a. every man, every ...
hand a. 35:53
  he said he was a. it [sin] 110:29
  neither for nor a. institutions 403:79
  streams ... a. the wind 84:63
  to live ... all reason is a. it 82:46
  who can be a. us? 57:35
Agate: no bigger than an a. stone
353:92
Age: a, cannot wither her 299:55
  a., I do abhor thee 364:57
  a. is full of care 364:56
  a. is in the wit is out 343:78
  a. like winter bare 364:56
  a. shall not weary them 65:20
  a. will not be defied 26:22
  a. will rule itself 276:7
  but the a. of chivalry is gone 78:78
  choice and master spirits of this a.
324:7
  crabbed a. and youth 364:56
  drives my green a. 390:19
  fetch the a. of gold 215:21
  from a. to a. endure 188:78
  labour of an a. in piled stones
216:23
  lady of a certain age 85:81
  let a. approve of youth 76:47
  most loathed ... life, that a., ache
337:91
  my a. is as a lusty winter 300:78
  not of an a. but for all time 179:57
  old a. a regret 123:95
  old a. shd. burn and rave 390:18
  prefer old a. to the alternative 99:81
  quite accurate about her a. 405:15
  rhyme ... invention of a barbarous a.
216:26
  that which should accompany old a.
336:71
  unregarded a. in corners thrown
300:77
  when a., disease, or sorrows strike
103:27
  woman who tells one her real a.
406:29
  world's great a. begins anew 368:28
  youth of labour ... a. of ease 150:64
Aged: 'certain age' ... certainly a.
85:81
Ages: a thousand a. in thy sight 399:39
  a. of hopeless end 217:50
  future a. groan for this foul act
350:56

Ages (continued)
  gone: aye, a. long ago  181:91
  his acts being seven a.  301:90
  how many a. hence  324:5
  Rock of A., cleft for me  392:51
Agglomeration: this a. ... Holy Roman
  Empire  398:14
Agincourt: did affright the air at A.
  318:37
A-gley: gang aft a.  80:18
Agony: dreadful is the check—intense
  the a.  71:87
  my soul in a.  105:54
Agree: a., for the law is costly
  254:63
  all colours will a.  24:88
  you and I shall never a.  16:75
Agreeable: in most men's power to be
  a.  382:10
  the problems of victory are more a.
  101:5
Agreed: a. to have a battle  92:74
  except they be a.  50:82
Aide-toi, le ciel t'aidera  136:89
Ail: what can a. thee, wretched wight
  182:7
Aim: malice never was his a.  381:97
Aims: sick hurry, its divided a.  21:42
Ain't: as it isn't, it a.  92:75
Air: affright the a. at Agincourt
  318:37
  A. A trim reckoning!  315:88
  all the a. a solemn stillness holds
  155:31
  babbling gossip of the a.  359:80
  both feet firmly planted in the a.
  289:31
  breathing English a.  71:93
  broad and general as the casing a.
  335:53
  castles in the a.  257:89
  diet, humour, a.  72:2
  do not saw the a. too much  310:3
  fairer than the evening a.  204:64
  glittering in the smokeless a.  412:96
  I see him forming in the a.  288:13
  melted into a., into thin a.  356:50
  no stir of a. was there  182:97
  seemed to tread upon the a.  182:3
  take into the a. my quiet breath
  184:29
  the a., a charter'd libertine, is still
  318:38
  the fog and filthy a.  332:23
  we shall fight ... on the seas ... in the
  a.  100–101:94
  wing the mid-way a.  329:88
Airly: A. Beacon, A. Beacon  189:85

Airly (continued)
  shires and towns from A. Beacon
  189:85
Airs: a. from heaven or blasts from hell
  307:60
  said his father, Don't give yourself a.
  90:49
  sing it with such a.  417:51
Airy: gives to a. nothing  342:53
  up the a. mountain  11:22
Ajalon: Moon, in the valley of A.
  38:20
Ajax: Thersites' body is as good as A.
  304:28
Akond of Swat  194:54
Alarms (Alarums): dwell in the midst
  of a.  114:78
  our stern a. ... to merry meetings
  351:65
  used to war's a.  165:57
Alas, poor Yorick!  311:31
Albatross: I shot the a.  105:47
Alderman: on the fore-finger of an a.
  353:92
Aldershot: burnish'd by A. sun
  34:25
Ale: if at the Church ... some a.
  68:45
  jolly good a. and old  380:82
  no more cakes and a.?  359:87
  then to the spicy nut-brown a.
  214:99
Aleppo: in A. once ... took by th'
  throat  346–7:22
Alexander: some talk of A.  18:6
Alibi: vy worn't there a a.!  121:76
Alice: a soldier's life is ... hard, says A.
  211:54
  A. is marrying one of the guard
  211:54
  A.-Mutton; Mutton-A.  94:98
  March Hare said to A.  90:55
  stuff and nonsense! said A.  91:68
  the lion looked at A. wearily  94:94
  time for tea, says A.  211:55
Alike: men's natures are a.  108:2
  million of faces ... none a.  72:3
Alive: a. a. O!  17:89
  bliss ... in that dawn to be a.  413:9
  born into the world a.  144:87
  if I shouldn't be a.  122:85
  officiously to keep a.  103:29
All: ain't it a. a bleedin' shame?
  18:5
  a. for one and one for a.  129:74
  a. is best  222:26
  a. is but toys  334:46
  a. is for the best  397:7

All (*continued*)
a. knowledge... my province  27:39
a. she loves is love  84:73
a. things are artificial  72:1
a. were for the state  201:38
a. ye know on earth  183:20
gives to a., denies a.  264:9
*Goodbye to A. That*  154:21
grasp a., lose a.  265:41
Lord God made them a.  10:17
made and loveth a.  106:64
nor a. that glisters, gold  154:26
ripeness is a.  330:98
teacheth ill, who teacheth a.  279:14
*1066 and A. That*  297:27
we are a. Socialists now  157:62
Allegory: an a. on the banks of the Nile  372:72
life ... a continual a.  187:64
Shakespeare led a life of a.  187:64
Alliances: entangling a. with none  171:29
steer clear of permanent a.  399:32
Alluring: nothing is more a. than a levee  109:15
Almanack: look in the a.; find out moonshine  342:48
Almighty: an arrow from the A.'s bow  66–7:35
the a. dollar, that great object  170:18
Almond: peach was ... a bitter a.  394:69
Alms: a. for oblivion  358:71
if thou hast abundance, give a.  62:39
so give a.; pray so  362:21
Almsman: gay apparel for an a.'s gown  350:55
Alone: all we ask is to be let a.  117:13
a., a., all, all a.  105:54
a. and palely loitering  182:7
a. I did it  304:19
as I was walking all a.  12:40
bear the palm a.  323:92
better be a. than in bad company  255:15, 399:33
but wherefore thou a.?  219:74
France is a.; and God is a.  366:4
here at the gate a.  388:86
how women pass the time when ... a.  161:4
I a. sit lingering here  396:85
I am powerful but a.  396:93
I feel I am a.  192:35
I want to be a.  141:45
leave them a., and they'll come home  234:48

Alone (*continued*)
left him a. with his glory  408:53
not good that the man shd. be a.  35:32
we are left, or shall be left a.  413:6
we two a. will sing like birds  330:99
weep and you weep a.  404:91
who can enjoy a.?  220:87
Alph the sacred river ran  106:71
Alpha: I am A. and Omega  60:19
Alphabet: got to the end of the a.  121:70
Alpine: through an A. village passed  197:93
Altars: on behalf of ... their a. ... their hearths  293:74
Alteration: alters when it a. finds  363:47
Alternative: prefer old age to the a.  99:81
Alters: a. when it alteration finds  363:47
love a. not  363:48
Always (Alway): I am with you a.  53:52
it seemed a. afternoon  387:84
Am: by the grace of God I a. what I a.  57:59
here I a., and here I stay  202:51
I a. that I a.  36:71
I think, therefore I a.  119:31
Amami: Friday night is A. night  11:27
Amaryllis: sport with A. in the shade  215:12
Amateurs: hinted that we are a nation of a.  290:41
Amaze: Ye gods! it doth a. me  323:92
Ambassador: an a. is an honest man sent to lie  416:46
Ambiguity: Seven Types of A.  133:49
Ambition: a. first sprung from yr. blest abodes  248:74
a. shd. be made of sterner stuff  325:14
a. thick-sighted  181:84
become a churchman better than a.  323:88
death for his a.  325:11
let not a. mock  155:34
love ... not with a. join'd  109:14
meaner things to low a.  250:7
to reign is worth a.  216:36
vaulting a. which o'erleaps itself  333:37
wars that makes a. virtue  345:10
who doth a. shun  301:85
Ambitious: as he was a. I slew him  325:11

Amen: will no man say a.? 350:57
America: A. cannot be an ostrich 408:46
  A. ... country of young men 133:46
  A.! God shed His grace 29:67
  ask not what A. will do for you 188:75
  O my A.!, my new-found-land 123–4:9
  Oh, they go to A. 406:25
  the youth of A. 406:26
  wake up, A. 141:46
American: a new deal for the A. people 289:27
  A. system of rugged individualism 166:66
  born an A.; I will live an A. 400:45
  love all mankind, except an A. 177:26
  retreat of the A. Army to our line 102:7
Americanism: no room ... for hyphenated A. 289:38
Americans: a new generation of A. 188:74
  my fellow A., ask not 188:75
  when good A. die 406:25
*Amiral: tuer de temps en temps un a.* 397:2
Ammunition: Praise the Lord and pass the a. 137:95
*Amor: a. che muove il sole* 117:4
  a. vincit insomnia 140:36
  *omnia vincit a.* 397:3
*Amoris: amantium irae a. integratio est* 389:5
Amorous: water ... a. of their strokes 298–9:54
*Amour: absence est à l'a.* 82:34
  *doux comme l'a.* 384:30
  *on ne badine pas avec l'a.* 227:79
Amurath: not A. an A. succeeds 318:31
Amused: we are not a. 396:91
Amusing herself [my cat] more with me 225:55
Anatomy: a mere a., a mountebank 303:12
Ancestral voices prophesying war 107:74
Ancestry: I can trace my a. back 145:97
  mule without pride of a. 124:15
Anchors: great a., heaps of pearl 352:72
Ancient: a. nobility ... act of time 25:6
  a. of days 50:73

Ancient (*continued*)
  did those feet in a. time 67:38
  fear thee, a. Mariner 105:53
  from a. melody have ceased 68:54
  have you left the a. love 68:55
  it is an a. mariner 104:42
Ancientry: wronging the a., stealing 361:16
Anderson: John A. my jo 80:11
*Ange: pur comme un a.* 384:30
Angel: a beautiful and ineffectual a. 21:51
  a minist'ring a. ... my sister be 312:32
  a ministering a. thou 296:14
  A. of the Lord came down 384:35
  a. whom thou still hast serv'd 336:78
  clip an A.'s wings 183:13
  in action, how like an a.! 308:81
  is man an ape or an a.? 122:91
  like an a. sings 340:22
  reverence—that a. of the world 304:27
  she drew an a. down 127:54
  sword of an a. king 66–7:35
  the A. ended 220:85
  the A. of Death has been abroad 70:80
  the better a. is a man 364:55
  who wrote like an a. 141:49
  woman yet think him an a. 389:10
Angelic: something of a. light 414:18
Angels: a. and ministers of grace defend us 307:60
  a band of a. coming 18:8
  fantastic tricks ... as makes the a. weep 337:87
  flights of a. sing thee to thy rest 312:40
  guardian a. sung this strain 391:33
  I ... am on the side of the a. 122:91
  made him a little lower than the a. 41:83
  sing, choirs of A. 241:92
  tears, such as A. weep 217:42
  the glorious fault of a. 248:74
  the herald a. sing 402:71
  where a. fear to tread 249:6
  women are a., wooing 358:65
Anger: a. supplies the arms 396:97
  monstrous a. of the guns 243:16
  more in sorrow than in a. 306:50
Angles: not A. but Angels 156:50
*Angleterre est une nation de boutiquiers* 228:85
*Angli: non A. sed Angeli* 156:50

Angling: ... say of a. as Dr. Boteler said of strawberries 398:25

Anglo-Saxon: he's an A. Messenger 94:92

those are A. attitudes 94:92

Angry: a. for the gourd 50:87

A. Young Man 245:33

be ye a. and sin not 58:71

his glassy essence, like an a. ape 337:87

when a., count four, when very a. 394:71

Anguish: when pain and a. wring the brow 296:14

Animal: are you a.—or vegetable—or mineral? 94:94

man is a noble a. 72:7

man is ... a political a. 20:26

man is ... a religious a. 78:79

man is a tool-making a. 139:17

spiteful, envious ... a. ... the public 159:82

we conjecture ... unknown a. ... or the god 381:98

Animals: all a. are equal but some ... more equal 242:98

a. are such agreeable friends 130:87

cd. ... live with a., they're so placid 403:84

Ann(e) (ie): for bonnie A. Laurie 124:16

Queen A. is dead 275:73

sister A., do you see anyone? 246:47

Annals: if you have writ yr. a. true 304:19

short and simple a. of the poor 155:34

Annihilating all that's made 206:99

Annoy: he only does it to a. 90:51

sewers a. the air 220:93

Annoyance: to his extreme a. tempted him 31:96

Annoys: pernicious weed ... the fair a. 112:53

Annual income twenty pounds ... happiness 119:40

Another: can I see a.'s woe? 68:53

have a. for working-days 343:65

he who wd. do good to a. 67:36

he!l! to choose love by a.'s eyes 341:37

no man truly knows a. 72:4

one religion as true as a. 82:32

who ... king ... that's quite a. thing 83:53

you make yourselves a. [face] 310:99

Answer: blow, bugle, a., echoes 388:98

but a. came there none 93:82, 294:93

give me your a. do 116:99

here is the a. ... to President Roosevelt 101:98

sent an a. back to me 93:90

shortest a. is doing 277:33

soft a turneth away wrath 45:69

the woods shall ... a. 376:38

wd. not stay for an a. 24:85

Ant: go to the a., thou sluggard 44:57

Anthems: hallooing and singing of a. 316:99

loud a. will always be ringing 12:43

Anthony Rowley: Heigh ho! says A. 232:30

Antic: and there the a. sits 350:54

dance an a. hay 204:68

put an a. disposition on 307:70

Antidote: and with some sweet oblivious a. 336:72

she is the a. to desire 109:20

Antipathy: no a. ... in diet, humour 72:2

Antipodes, sheer opposite, a. 182:94

Anybody: is there a. there? said the Traveller 118:23

no one's a.! 143:78

Anything: a. but history 398:21

a. that tampers with ... ignorance 405:9

Earth has not a. ... more fair 412:96

if a. is sacred ... body is 403:80

though you do a., he thinks no ill 363:39

Apart: love is of man's life a thing a. 84:70

others a. sat 218:55

Ape: glassy essence, like an angry a. 337:87

is man an a. or an angel? 122:91

Apes: ivory, and a. and peacocks 207:12

Apollo: after the songs of A. 332:21

burned is A.'s laurel-bough 204:67

musical as is A.'s lute 213:77

Apollos watered 57:46

Apology before you be accused 95:19

Apostles: Cristes lore, and his a. twelve 97:42

Apothecary: an ounce of civet, good a. 329:91

Apparel: a. oft proclaims the man 306:56

gay a. for an almsman's gown 350:55

Apparelled in celestial light 410:72
Appeal: I a. unto Caesar 56:25
Appearance: judge not according to the
a. 55:2
man looketh on the outward a.
39:42
never judge from a. 268:26
Appears: done by night a. by day
260:85
God a., and God is light 66:31
*Appétit vient en mangeant* 285:89
Appetite: a. comes with eating 285:89
as if increase of a. had grown
305:44
cloy the hungry edge of a. 348:37
doth not the a. alter? 343:69
now good digestion wait on a.
335:54
surfeiting the a. may sicken 358:75
Appetites: cloy the a. they feed 299:55
creatures ours, and not their a.!
345:8
Applause: the a.! delight! ... of our
Stage 179:53
Apple: an a. a day ... doctor away
254:73
a. for the a.'s sake 394:68
kept him as the a. of his eye 38:14
my a. trees will never get across
139:26
the a. press'd with specious cant
165:63
Apple-cart: upset the a. 254:74
Apples: comfort me with a. 47:19
Kent ... a., cherries, hops and women
120:61
small choice in rotten a. 355:21
Appliance: by desperate a. are reliev'd
311:21
Appliances: all a. and means to boot
317:14
Apprehension: a. of the good gives ...
feeling 348:37
in a., how like a god! 308:81
Approach: sweet a. of even or morn
218:59
Approve: let age a. of youth 76:47
Approves all forms of competition
103:30
April: a bright cold day in A. 242:99
and after A. 74:22
A. is the cruellest month 131:10
A., June and November 239:77
A. with his shoures sote 96:25
men are A. when they woo 302:4
now that A.'s there 74:21
proud-pied A. 363:44
uncertain glory of an A. day 361:6

Aprons: made themselves a. 35:37
Aquinas: better teacher than ... A.
223:40
Arabia: all the perfumes of A. 335:69
Arabian trees their med'cinable gum
346-7:22
Araby: I'll sing thee songs of A.
407:41
Aram: how Eugene A.. though a thief
87:14
Ararat: upon the mountains of A.
35:46
Arbitrary: accusation of being a.
170:23
*Arcadia: et in A. ego* 19:19
I too am in A. 19:19
Archangel: nor appeared less than A.
ruined 217:41
Arches: fled Him down the a. of the
years 391:30
Architecture: the wondrous a. of the
world 205:76
Arden: am in A.; the more fool I
300:81
Arguing: I am not a. ... I am telling
402:75
no a. with Johnson 152:3
no good in a. with the inevitable
200:27
Argument: any a. about any place
252:46
a. for a week 313:58
furnish ... a. and intellects 152:99
height of this great a. 216:29
in a. with men a woman 222:22
not to stir without great a. 311:24
Tories ... no a. but force 72:8
Whigs ... no force but a. 72:8
Arise: I will a. and go now 417:52
my lady sweet, a. 304:20
Aristotle: bokes ... of A. and his
philosophye 96:33
Arithmetic: branches of A. – Ambition,
Distraction 91:60
Ark: a. rested in the seventh month
35:46
unto Noah into the a. 35:45
Arm: human on my faithless a. 22:60
I bit my a., I sucked the blood
105:51
*Arma: a. virumque cano* 396:96
*cedant a. togae ... laurea laudi*
102:17
Armadas: till the great A. come
230:11
Armageddon: a place called ... A.
61:31
Armies: our a. swore terribly 379:70

Armour: put on ... a. of God   58:73
  religion is the best a.   276:84
  whose a. is his honest thought
    416:48
Armourers: now thrive the a.   319:40
Arms: anger supplies the a.   396:97
  a. against a sea of troubles   309:95
  a. and the man I sing   128:72, 396:96
  a. of mine had seven years' pith
    344:90
  a., take your last embrace   354:18
  imparadised in one another's a.
    219:68
  so he laid down his a.   165:57
  the a. of my true love   388:88
  underneath are the everlasting a.
    38:17
  what a. ... under my head   210:46
Army: an a. marches on its stomach
  228:87
  hum of either a. stilly sounds
    320:50
noble a. of Martyrs   63:69
  terrible as an a. with banners   47:26
Arrive: a better thing than to a.
  380:80
Arrow: an a. from the Almighty's bow
  66–7:35
  I shot an a. into the air   197:91
  the a. that flieth by day   43:20
Arrows: my a. of desire   67:38
*Ars longa, vita brevis*   163:30
Arse upon which everyone has sat
  115:93
*Arsenic and Old Lace*   188:76
Art: all a. is quite useless   406:22
  all nature is but a.   250:12
  all the adulteries of a.   179:52
  a. for a.'s sake   111:38
  a. has no enemy except ignorance
    254:76
  a. is a jealous mistress   132:26
  A. is long, and Time is fleeting
    198:96
  a. is long, but life is short   163:30
  a. is too precise in every part   162:17
  a. lies in concealing a.   254:77
  a. of being kind   404:93
  a. of drawing sufficient conclusions
    82:44
  *a. pour l'a.*   111:38
  aspires ... to the condition of a.
    110:25
  China's gayest a. had dyed   154:23
  clever, but is it a.?   190:96
  fine a. ... hand ... head ... heart
    292:63
  half a trade and half an a.   170:12

Art (*continued*)
  more matter with less a.   307:73
  nature is the a. of God   72:1
  next to Nature, A.   192:34
  source, and end, and test, of A.
    249:92
  squandring ... his peculiar a.
    126:44
  strains of unpremeditated a.   370:49
  true ease in writing ... a., not
    chance   249:99
  what a. can wash her guilt   152:2
Arthur: he's in A.'s bosom   319:43
  slowly answered A. from the barge
    385:54
Article: snuff'd out by an a.   85:83
  these a. subscribed ... I may ...
    dwindle into a wife   109:18
*Artifex: qualis a. pereo!*   230:10
Artificial: all things are a.   72:1
Artisan: merchant, and a., without
  ... meddling   9:6
  to give employment to the a.   31:94
Artist: a. is in danger of death   160:92
  be more of an a.   187:69
  true a. will let his wife starve
    365:80
  what an a. dies with me!   230:10
Arts: a. of every woman false   222:19
  in the inglorious a. of peace   207:2
  the books, the a., the academes
    331:16
Ash on an old man's sleeve   130:97
Ashamed: naked ... and were not a.
  35:35
  she that maketh a.   45:65
Ashes: a. and sparks, my words
  among mankind   369:38
  a. to a., dust to dust   65:15
  for the a. of his fathers   201:36
  man ... splendid in a.   72:7
  slept among his a. cold   182:92
  to give ... beauty for a.   49:53
Asia: hollow pamper'd jades of A.
  316:9
  ye pamper'd jades of A.!   205:78
Ask: we a. and a.   21:44
Asked: nobody a. you, sir, she said
  241:87
  women are glad to have been a.
    243:12
Askelon: in the streets of A.   40:47
Asleep: he thought me a.   244:31
  old ships sail like swans a.   136:85
  the very houses seem a.   412:97
  we are laid a. in body   415:33
Aspect: meet in her a. and her eyes
  86:96

Aspect (*continued*)
  sweet a. of princes 322–3:81
  with grave a. he rose 218:52
Aspen: shade ... light quivering a. made 296:14
Aspens: willows whiten, a. quiver 387:76
Aspicious: comprehended two a. persons 343:79
Ass: an a. wd. marry an uncertainty 298:39
  a. [knoweth] his master's crib 48:29
  average schoolmaster ... essentially an a. 209:29
  bridle for ... a., a rod for the fool's back 46:83
  make an a. of oneself 254:80
  write me down an a. 344:85
Assassination: absolutism tempered by a. 227:75
Assay: th' a. so hard 97:50
Assert: I may a. Eternal Providence 216:29
Asset: healthy citizens are the greatest a. 101:6
Assume: a. a virtue, if you have it not 311:19
  what I a. you shall a. 403:82
Assuming that he's got any [brains] 144:85
Assurance: I'll make a. double sure 335:63
Assured: most ignorant of what he's most a. 337:87
Astonish: things that wd a. you 144:86
Astonished: a. at my own moderation 103:24
  a. Mayor and Corporation 75:39
Asunder: let no man put a. 65:10
Atahualpa: knows ... who strangled A. 202:42
Atheism: a little philosophy inclineth ... to a. 25:10
Athens: a citizen, not of A. 375:20
  Israel, A., Florence 170:13
  maid of A. 86:95
Atkins: it's Thank You, Mr. A. 190:11
Atlanta: from A. to the sea 416:45
Atlases: only on the very best a. 395:80
Atomies: drawn with a team of little a. 353:92
Attached: decidedly and conscientiously a. 115:87
Attachment à la Plato 146:16
Attack: dared a. my Chesterton 32:1
  situation excellent. I shall a. 136:87
Attempt: serious a. to do it 401:66

Attempted: something a., something done 199:8
Attentions: these pleasing a. 23:78
Attic: beauty crieth in an a. 82:47
  mellow glory of the A. stage 20:35
Atticus: if A. were he! 248:84
Attire: in its workaday a. 143:75
  so wild in their a. 332:26
Attitudes: Anglo-Saxon a. 94:92
Attorney: office boy to an A.'s firm 147:26
Attraction and repulsion 68:56
Attribute: an a. to God himself 339:15
  a. to awe and majesty 339:15
  grandest moral a. of a Scotsman 28:64
Auburn: sweet A.! loveliest village 150:61
*Audace: de l'a., ... toujours de l'a.* 117:5
*Audi alteram partem* 254:81
Audible: illiberal ... ill-bred as a. laughter 98:59
August: to recommence [winter] in A. 85:85
Augustus: Fleckno ... like A., young was called 128:68
Auld: a. acquaintance 79:99
  a. lang syne 79:1
  the a. wife sat 87:11
Aunt: if my a. had been a man 254:82
  I'm Charley's a. from Brazil 389:16
  my a. died of influenza 366:97
  written to A. Maud 153:10
Aunts: his cousins and his a. 147:25
Austerlitz: pile the bodies high at A. 293:78
Austin: laboure, as A. bit 96:30
  let A. have his swink 96:30
Austria: Don John of A. is going to the war 99:71
Author: as sincerely from the a.'s soul 169:3
  a. ... of all good things 64:90
  a. who speaks about his own books 122:92
  where is any a. in the world 331:14
Authority: a man under a. 52:28
  a. be a stubborn bear 362:27
  base a. from others' books 331:10
  dress'd in a little brief a. 337:87
  in your countenance ... a. 327:55
  nothing destroys a. so much 25:14
  wrest ... the law to your a. 339:16
Autographs: nuisances who write for a. 145:99
*Autres temps, autres moeurs* 254:83

Autumn: thou breath of A.'s being 369:35

Autumnal: grace ... in one a. face 123:7

Availeth: say not the struggle naught a. 103:32

Avails: what a. the sceptred race! 192:36

Avarice, the spur of industry 168:90

*Ave: a. in perpetuum ... a. atque vale* 94:6

*Averni: facilis descensus A.* 397:2

Aversion: in matrimony to begin with a little a. 371:67

Aves: after thousand a. told 182:92

Avocation: engaging in so puerile an a. 209:29

Avon: sweet Swan of A. 179:58

Awake: a.! for Morning in the Bowl of Night 134:65
    a. my heart, to be loved 70:75
    a., my St. John! 250:7
    lying a. with a dismal headache 144:91
    smiles a. you 118:20

Award: general a. of love 182:4

Aware: England bore, shaped, made a. 71:93

Away: a.! a.! for I will fly to thee 184:26
    a. with him! He speaks Latin 321:69
    a., you rolling river 18:1
    come, dear children, let us a. 20:32
    I wish, I wish he'd stay a. 208:24
    spotless reputation; that a. 347:30
    the little less, and what worlds a. 73:19
    to bear my soul a. 10:13 .
    were t'other dear charmer a. 142:54

Awe: attribute to a. and majesty 339:15
    in a. of such a thing as I 323:91

Awful: felt how a. goodness is 219:73
    nothing ... nobody ... it's a.! 30:74
    that men might shun the a. shops 99:76

Awoke: I a. ... and found myself famous 86:2
    so I a., and behold ... a dream 77:63

Awry: their currents turn a. 309:95

Axe: an a. to grind 254:84
    Lizzie Borden took an a. 15:67
    the a.'s edge did try 207:3

Axiom: long been an a. of mine 124:18

Axis: soft under-belly of the A. 101:4

Azure: arose from out the a. main 391:33
    ring'd with the a. world 385:47

Azure (*continued*)
    robes the mountain in ... a. hue 88:20
    the a. flowers that blow 154:23

Baa, b., black sheep 231:23

Babble: watch to b. and to talk 343:75

Babbled: a' b. of green fields 319:44

Babe: find the b. ... in a manger 54:69

Babel: name of it called B. 35:52

Babes: out of the mouth of b. 41:81

Babies: bit the b. in the cradles 75:37
    putting milk into b. 101:6
    the snuggeries of b. 390:24

Baby: a Mother laid her B. 10:19
    b., cradle, and all 233:38
    every b. born ... finer than the last 120:53
    hush-a-bye b., on the tree top 233:38
    in the oven for b. and me 237:62
    see my b. at my breast? 300:71
    when the first b. laughed 28:59

Babylon: by the rivers of B. ... we sat 44:44
    how many miles to B.? 233:36
    king of B. ... at the parting 49:64

Bacchus: not charioted by B. 184:26

Bachelor: I wd. die a b. 343:70
    now I am a b. 17:95

Bachelors: two old b. ... in one house 194:64

Back: at my b. I always hear 206:94
    die with harness on our b. 336:77
    his wife looked b. from behind 36:56
    mermaid on a dolphin's b. 341:44
    one who never turned his b. 73:16
    rod for his own b. 276:99
    those before cried 'B.!' 201:39

Background: see fit to keep me in the b. 196:72

Backward: dark b. and abysm of time 355:29
    I b. cast my e'e 80:19
    look b. to with pride 139:23

Bacon: think how B. shined 250:17
    to save one's b. 276:13
    when their lordships asked B. 34:20

Bad: altogether irreclaimably b. 89:39
    became ... b. in one step 180:68
    hope ... good breakfast ... b. supper 26:38
    how sad and b. and mad 73:20
    mad, b., and dangerous 191:24
    so much b. in the best of us 163:36
    swans sing ... 'twere no b. thing 106:70

Bad (*continued*)
the b. affright 155:43
things b. begun make strong themselves 335:52
truth told with b. intent 66:29
when she was b. she was horrid
199:5
*Badine: on ne b. pas avec l'amour*
227:79
Badness: all good and no b. 373:93
Baffled to fight better 73:16
Bag: cat out of the b. 269:72
not with b. and baggage 302:94
one and all, b. and baggage, ... clear
out 149:52
Bags: three b. full 231:23
Baked: you have b. me too brown
91:64
Baker Street: the B. irregulars 125:26
Balance: redress the b. of the Old
88:26
the b. of power 398:19
Bald: b. as a coot 255:89
b. heads are soon shaven 255:90
go up thou b. head 40:60
Ball: after the b. 158:71
contenders drive a b. with sticks
172:44
Ballad: woeful b. made to ... eyebrow
301:90
Ballad-mongers: these same metre b.
314:73
Ballads: of b., songs and snatches
145:95
patriotic b. cut and dried 145:96
Ballot is stronger than the bullet
196:74
Balls: the stars' tennis b. 400:51
Balm: a b. upon the world 182:94
b. of hurt minds 334:42
is there no b. in Gilead? 49:55
wash the b. off ... anointed king
349:50
with ... tears I wash away my b.
350:58
without tasting the b. of pity 173:66
Baltic: from Stettin in the B. 102:8
Banbury: cock-horse to B. Cross
237:66
to B. came I 70:74
Band: wearied b. swoons to a waltz
169:5
when the b. begins to play 190:11
Bands: with b. of love 50:77
Bane: I will not be afraid of death and
b. 336:73
Bang: b. went saxpence! 285:79
not with a b. but a whimper 130:96

Banish plump Jack and b. all the
world 314:69
Banishing: worst effect is b. for hours
112:53
Banishment: the bitter bread of b.
349:48
Bank: as I sat on a sunny b. 15:74
b. and shoal of time 333:36
b. whereon the wild thyme blows
341:46
moonlight sleeps upon this b. 340:22
Bankrupt: b. of life yet prodigal of ease
126:40
beggar can never be b. 255:6
Banks: bonnie b. o' Loch Lomon'
18:2
ye b. and braes 81:26
Banner: b. with the strange device
197:93
his b. over me was love 47:18
that b. in the sky 164:46
the royal b. and all quality 345:10
thy b., torn, but flying 84:63
Banners: hang out our b. on the outward walls 336:74
Bar: no moaning at the b. 385:44
when I went to the B. 144:83
Barabbas was a publisher 88:22
Barbara Allen 12:36
Barbarian: dancing ?... certainly a B.
exercise 79:91
Barbarians, Philistines, Populace
21:48
Barbarous: mass of ... people must be
b. 176:3
Barbarousness: I must confess my own
b. 373:87
Barber: no b. shaves so close but
255:91
Bards: ancient love that b. of old
enjoy'd 68:55
B. of Passion and of Mirth 181:83
Bare: the cupboard was b. 236:59
Bargain: a world-without-end b.
331:17
never was a better b. driven 372:83
Bargains: be beloved is above all b.
255:9
here's the rule for b. 120:49
Barge: answer'd Arthur from the b.
385:54
the b. she sat in, like a ... throne
298:54
Bark: all right ... you heard a seal b.
392:43
b. at a distance never bite 260:84
b. at the moon 255:92
b. up the wrong tree 255:94

**Bark** (*continued*)
  b. ... worse than his bite  255:93
  keep a dog and b. yourself  268:27
  when I ope my lips let no dog b.
    338:98
Barkis: 'as true,' said Mr. B., 'as taxes
  is'  120:43
  B. is willin'  119:38
Barley: long fields of b. and of rye
  387:75
Barlow: Councillor B.  33:10
Barrel: lock, stock and b.  270:96
Barren: a b. sister all your life  341:35
  and cry, 'tis all b.  379:66
  nature is b.  69:63
Barricade: at some disputed b.  296:20
Bars: look out through the same b.
  193:38
  nor iron b. a cage  199:15
Barter: founded on compromise and b.
  78:74
Base: so b. that wd. be a bondman
  325:11
Bashful: maiden of b. fifteen  372:78
*Basia: da mi b. mille*  94:4
Basil: steal my B.-pot  182:6
Basingstoke: word ... like B.  148:41
Basket: all yr. eggs in one b.  261:15
Bat: black b., night, has flown  388:86
  blind as a b.  256:44
  twinkle, twinkle, little b.  90:53
*Bataillons: Dieu est ... pour les gros b.*
  398:15
Bate: do I not b.? ... dwindle?  314:78
Bath: I test my b. before I sit  229:96
  sore labour's b.  334:42
Bathe: spirit to b. in fiery floods
  337:90
Bathing: caught the Whigs b.  122:89
Bathing machine: between a large b.
  144:92
Baton of a marshal of France  228:86
Bats: have b. in the belfry  255:96
  suspicions ... like b. amongst birds
  26:23
Batsman: a ghostly b. plays  390:28
Battalions: God is ... for the big b.
  398:15
  not single spies, but in b.  311:26
Battle: agreed to have a b.  92:74
  b. [is not] to the strong  47:8
  b. of Waterloo was won  401:61
  Ben B. was a soldier bold  165:57
  care for him who shall have borne the
    b.  196:81
  first blow is half the b.  263:64
  melancholy as a b. won  401:57
  nothing except a b. lost  401:57

**Battle** (*continued*)
  the b. and the breeze  88:21
  the b. day is past  132:23
  to b. for freedom and truth  169:9
  when the b.'s lost and won  332:22
Battle-flags: till ... the b. were furl'd
  387:81
Battles long ago  414:21
Bauble: what shall we do with this b.?
  115:89
Bays: Britain won her proudest b.
  144:89
Bay-tree: flourishing like a green b.
  42:4
Be: ain't-a-going to b. no core  394:74
  b. not solitary, b. not idle  82:33
  b. strong and of a good courage
    38:18
  fears that I may cease to b.  186:48
  Germany ... will not b. at all  163:32
  God said, Let Newton b.!  248:88
  Ho, let Einstein b.!  378:55
  lest we shd. b. by and by  10:16
  ne'er was, nor is, nor e'er shall b.
    249:96
  nobody is healthy ... nobody can b.
    23:66
  this tree continues to b.  191:20
  to b. or not to b.  309:95
  what will b., shall b.  204:62
  whatever will b., will b.  258:97
  when will that b.? say the bells
    236:61
  ye shall b. as gods  35:36
Be-all and the end-all  333:36
Beach: I shall ... walk upon the b.
  131:4
Beaches: we shall fight on the b.
  100:94
Beachy Head: to Birmingham by way
  of B.  99:73
Beacons from the abode ... Eternal are
  368:20
Beadle: a b. on boxin' day  121:72
Beads: jewels for a set of b.  350:55
Beadsman: the B., after thousand aves
  182:92
Beak: b. holds more than his belican
  209:38
  take thy b. from out my heart
  247:67
Beaker full of the warm South
  184:24
Beale: Miss B. and Miss Buss  15:68
Beam: at the full midday b.  224:43
Beamish: my b. boy!  92:71
Beams: little candle throws his b.!
  340:25

Bean: home of the b. and the cod
69:67
nine b. rows 417:52
not-too-French French b. 146:16
Beans: how many b. make nine 268:47
Bear: a B. of Very Little Brain 212:63
authority be a stubborn b. 362:27
b. those ills we have 309:95
because it gave pain to the b. 202:47
*exit, pursued by a b.* 361:15
funny how a b. likes honey? 211:62
grizzly b is huge and wild 167:78
he has been eaten by the b. 167:78
nothing wd. it b. 233:39
rather b. with you than b. you
300:80
sing Ho! for the life of a b. 212:69
Bear-baiting: the Puritan hated b.
202:47
Beard: b. of formal cut 301:90
b. the lion in his den 296:12
by thy long grey b.  104:42
Old Man with a b. 195:66
singed the Spanish king's b. 125:29
Bearded like the pard 301:90
Bears it out ... to the edge of doom
363:48
Beast: a b., but a just b. 14:59
a b., no more! 311:22
a wild b. or a god 26:20
both man and bird and b. 106:63
man's life is cheap as b.'s 328:67
wee ... cow'rin', tim'rous [beastie]
80:16
when people call this b. to mind
31:89
Beastly: don't let's be B. to the Germans 112:43
how b. the bourgeois is 193:46
Beasts: brute b. that have no understanding 64:4
Beat: b. him when he sneezes 90:51,
52
lion b. the unicorn 234:47
shall b. ... swords into plowshares
48:31
to b. about the bush 255:99
Tom was b. 240:83
ye b. my people to pieces 48:32
Beaten: English never know when ... b.
261:21
Beating: almost hear the b. of his wings
70:80
b. myself for spite 373:84
Beats: truth ... with bad intent b. all the
lies 66:29
Beauteous: a b. evening, calm and free
412:92

Beautified with our feathers 156:49
Beautiful: all heiresses are b. 128:65
as good as she was b. 246:46
b. Soup! 91:65
full b., a faery's child 183:8
how b. upon the mountains 48:46
most b. things ... are the most useless
291:61
old are more b. than the young
403:78
see, not feel, how b. 106:68
she's b. and ... to be woo'd 321:64
stately homes ... how b. they stand
160:90
the good is the b. 247:61
the many men, so b. 105:55
Beauty: a b. cold and austere 292:67
a daily b. in his life 346:16
a thing of b. is a joy for ever 181:85
abstract Idea ... of B. 187:63
as a b. I'm not a ... star 134:53
as b. must be truth 186:50
b. crieth in an attic 82:47
b. draws us with a single hair 251:35
b. is but skin-deep 255:1
b. is ... in the eye of the beholder
168:92
b. is nature's coin; must not be
hoarded 213:79
b. is potent 255:2
b. is truth, truth b. 183:20
b. itself doth of itself persuade
364:60
b. lives with kindness 361:9
b. of a thousand stars 204:64
b. provoketh thieves 300:74
b. stands in the admiration 221:5
b. though injurious, hath strange
power 222:24
b. too rich for use 353:94
b. will buy no beef 255:3
b.'s ensign ... crimson in thy lips
354:17
dress her b. at yr. eyes 117:10
dwells with B.—B. that must die
183:22
extent of its b. and power 202:43
exuberance is b. 69:62
first in b. ... first in might 182:1
have loved the principle of b. 187:68
her B. and her Chivalry 83:59
hidden b. of the world 371:57
homely b. of the good old cause
412:2
humility towards ... Principle of B.
186:58
in their summer b. kiss'd 352:79
Isle of B., fare thee well 29:68

Beauty (*continued*)

like a garment wear the b. 412:96

love built on b., soon as b. dies 123:6

more inviting than b. unadorn'd 31:87

muddy, ill-seeming ... bereft of b. 355:26

needs not June for b.'s heightening 21:46

ne'er saw true b. till this night 353:95

no Spring, nor Summer b. hath such grace 123:7

our saucy ship's a b. 146:19

she walks in b., like the night 86:96

teaches such b. as a woman's eye 331:14

that ... b.'s rose might never die 362:29

the b. of the world! 308:81

to give unto them b. for ashes 49:53

unmask her b. to the moon 306:53

Because: b. he knows, a frightful fiend 106:60

b. I do not hope to turn 130:88

b. we're here b..we're here b. 19:13

we cannot do it, Sir, b. 93:90

Bechstein: if ... we pawn the B. Grand 111:40

Becomes: in peace ... nothing so b. a man 319:45

it hardly b. any of us 163:36

Bed: a b. by night, a chest ... by day 150:70

a manger for His b. 10:19

and so to b. 245:40

b. be blest that I lie on 10:13

candle to light you to b. 236:61

early to b. and early to rise 261:5

early to b. makes a male ... dead 392:42

four angels to my b. 10:13

nicer to lie in b. 193:44

she whipped them ... put them to b. 239:76

to b., to b., there's knocking 335:70

took her into b. and covered up her head 17:96

welcome to yr. gory b. 81:22

Bedecked, ornate and gay 222:18

Bedfellows: misery acquaints ... with strange b. 356:41

Bed-time, Hal, and all well 315:87

Bee: a b. in one's bonnet 255:4

the little busy b. 399:35

where the b. sucks 357:56

Beef: beauty will buy no b. 255:3

roast b. of England 134:61

this little pig had roast b. 239:78

Been: shd. be ... as if it had not b. 367:12

Beer: felony to drink small b. 321:66

life isn't all b. and skittles 168:89

parson, much bemused in b. 248:78

suckle fools and chronicle small b. 345:98

Beer-sheba: from Dan even to B. 39:31

travel from Dan to B. 379:66

Bees: late flowers for the b. 181:79

so work the honey b. 318:39

swine, women and b. cannot be turned 279:92

Beethoven's Fifth Symphony ... most sublime noise 137:97

Beetle wheels his droning flight 155:31

Beetles: scarce so gross as b. 329:88

Before: b., behind, between 123:9

b. you are on with the new 17:93

I have been here b. 291:53

those b. cried 'Back!' 201:39

Befriend: be near me now and b. 383:22

Beg: the poor can b. 264:21

to b. I am ashamed 55:83

Begetter: onlie b. of these ... sonnets 362:28

Beggar: b. can never be bankrupt 255:6

better die a b. than live a b. 255:22

made a b. by banqueting 62:54

not ... a doit to relieve a ... b. 356:40

whiles I am a b. I will rail 326:38

Beggared: her own person it b. all description 298:54

Beggars: basest b. are in ... thing superfluous 328:67

b. cannot be choosers 255:7

Beggary: b. in the love 298:50

no vice but b. 326:38

Begin: b. with certainties ... end in doubts 26:37

content to do b. with doubts 26:37

Beginning: as it was in the b. 63:68

before the b. of years 382:16

b. of a feast fits ... keen guest 315:84

b. of a lifelong romance 404:3

everything must have a b. 262:35

good b. makes a good ending 265:30

I am ... the b. and the ending 60:19

in the b. God created 34:26

in the b. was the Word 55:92

it is the b. of the end 384:29

long choosing and b. late 220:90

Beginning (*continued*)
  memory ... the b. of dowdiness
    406:32
  strange b.—'borrowed majesty'
    326:32
  that was the b. of fairies  28:59
Beginnings: end to the b. of all wars
  259:34
Begins: charity b. at home  258:96
  nothing b. and nothing ends  390:29
Begone dull care ... b. from me  16:75
Begot: how b., how nourished?  339:14
Begun: well b. is half done  282:21
Behaviour: often the surfeits of our
  own b.  327:53
Behest: darkness falls at thy b.  132:24
Behind: and, departing, leave b. us
  198:97
  bring their tails b. them  234:48
  fiend doth close b. him tread  106:60
  get thee b. me, Satan  53:36
  lads that thought there was no more
    b.  361:12
  led his regiment from b.  143:69
  my work is left b.  32:5
  those b. cried 'Forward!'  201:39
Behold: as she looked ... she did b.
  377:43
  b. her, single in the field  414:20
  b., this dreamer cometh  36:63
  mortality, b. and fear  29:71
Being: all the wheels of B. slow
  386:60
  eternal B., the Principle of Beauty
    186:58
  live and move and have our b.  56:20
  receives reproach of b.  363:49
  who wd. lose ... this intellectual b.?
    217:49
Belfry: bats in the b.  255:96
Belgium's capital had gathered then
  83:59
Belial: sons of B., flown with insolence
  217:38
  sons of B. had a Glorious Time
    126:46
Belied: they have b. a lady  344:87
Belief: does not live according to his b.
  255:8
Beliefs: holding two contradictory b.
  242:4
  home of ... forsaken b.  21:49
Believe: b. a woman or an epitaph
  85:91
  b. it or not  287:10
  I do b. her ... know she lies  364:54
  I don't b. in fairies  28:60
  say quick that you b.  28:62

Believe (*continued*)
  some b. they've none [soul]  82:40
Believed: have not seen, yet have b.
  56:14
  liar is not b. ... speaks the truth
    269:73
Believes: he who b. what is wrong
  171:32
  less remote ... who b. nothing
    171:32
  none go ... alike, yet each b. his
    own  249:91
Believing: seeing is b.  277:25
Bell: b. book and candle shall not drive
  327:40
  b. toll for poor Cock Robin  241:89
  for whom the b. tolls  124:14
  in a cowslip's b. I lie  357:56
  ring the alarum b. Blow wind, come
    wrack  336:77
  says the great b. at Bow  236:61
  sexton toll'd the b.  165:59
  the B. at Edmonton  113:55
  the b. invites me. Hear it not, Duncan
    334:41
  tongue sounds ... as a sullen b.
    316:97
  very word is like a b.  184:31
  why people ... do not ring the b.
    27:46
Bells: ring, happy b., across the snow
  386:68
  ring out, wild b.  386:67
  say the b. of St. Clement's  236:61
  silver b. and cockle shells  235:55
  the b. of hell go ting-a-ling-a-ling
    16:76
  the port is near, the b. I hear  403:81
  up so floating many b. down  116:94
Belly: b. (*see also* Under-belly): born
  ... with something a round b.
    316:99
  fair round b. with good capon lin'd
    301:90
  I mind my b. very studiously  175:91
  whose God is their b.  58:76
  wd. fain have filled his b.  55:81
Bellyful: rumble thy b.  328:72
Belmont: In B. is a lady richly left
  338:99
Beloved: be b. ... is above all bargains
  255:9
  heaped for the b.'s bed  370:54
  Oh sleep! ... b. from pole to pole!
    105:57
Below: down and away b.  20:32
Bends: he who b. himself a joy  66:34
  though she b. him, she obeys  198:3

Benedick: B. the married man 342:60
Signior B., nobody marks you 342:58
Benevolence: comparative heaven ... b. can create 292:66
Bent: politics ... are not our b. 148:35
though on pleasure she was b. 113:56
Bermoothes: the still-vex'd B. 355:32
Bermudas: remote B. ride 206:89
Berries: pluck your b. harsh and crude 215:8
Berry: God, cd. have made a better b. 398:25
O sweeter than the b. 141:51
Berth: his death ... happened in his b. 165:59
Beset: idols which b. men's minds 27:41
Best: all is for the b. 397:7
all that's b. of dark and bright 86:96
b. and distinguished above others 165:55
b. is ... enemy of the good 397:11
b. is yet to be 75:46
b. of friends must part 19:11
b. of life is but intoxication 84:71
b. of possible worlds 397:7
b. portion of a good man's life 415:31
b. thing ... between France and England 171:38
b. to be off with the old love 17:93
b. words in their b. order 107:82
hope for the b. 267:98
make the b. of a bad job 255:11
past and to come seems b. 316:4
prayeth best who loveth b. 106:64
so much bad in the b. of us 163:36
stolen sweets are b. 102:13
tort'ring hour ... afflict the b. 155:43
where the b. is like the worst 190:8
Bestial: what remains is b. 345:1
Bestride: he doth b. the narrow world 323:93
Bet: I b. my money on de bob-tail 137:1
three ... farmers once b. a pound 118:26
Bethlehem: O come ye to B. 241:91
O little town of B. 72:95
Betimes: he tires b. that spurs too fast b. 348:40
Better: a far, far b. thing ... I do 121:79
baffled to fight b. 73:16

Better (continued)
b. ... alone than in bad company 399:33
b. book ... b. sermon ... b. mousetrap 133:48
b. is a dinner of herbs 45:71
b. man than I am, Gunga Din 190:1
b. part of valour is discretion 315:93
b. rest ... I go to 121:79
b. than a play 96:23
b. that ten guilty ... escape 66:26
b. to err with Pope 85:92
b. to have loved and lost 83:50, 386:59
b. to have no opinion 25:11
b. to marry than to burn 57:50
b. to wear out than to rust out 115:92
ending is b. than mending 168:98
for b. for worse 64:7
former days ... b. than these 46:5
good name ... b. than precious ointment 46:3
how can man die b.? 201:36
he is no b. ... much the same 24:83
I am getting b. and b. 111:37
I cd. have b. spar'd a b. man 315:92
if you knows of a b. 'ole 27:47
it is b. to trust in the Lord 43:34
nae b. than he shd. be 80:5
no b. than you shd. be, Polly 390:25
open rebuke is b. than secret love 46:86
poetry ... had b. not come at all 186:55
seen b. faces in my time 328:62
striving to b. ... mar what's well 328:59
thy love is b. than wine 47:15
to a b. land I know 138:7
wd. deserve b. of mankind 381:2
you shall now give place to b. men 115:90
Betters: order myself lowly ... to all my b. 64:97
still b. what is done 362:21
Between: no age b. ten and three and twenty 361:16
Bevy: a b. of fair women 221:99
Beware: b. the fury of a patient man 127:48
b. the Ides of March 323:90
Bewitched with the rogue's company 313:56
Beyond: enough that there *is* a b. 364:64

Bitter: and shed a b. tear  92:79
  b. groan of a martyr's woe  66–7:35
  b. ... on itself [revenge] recoils
    220:91
  b. to endure ... sweet to remember
    256:38
  children ... make misfortunes more
    b.  24:95
  eating the b. bread of banishment
    349:48
  lack gall to make oppression b.
    309:92
  love grows b. with treason  383:23
  old and b. of tongue  417:54
  peach was once a b. almond  394:69
  sadden after none or b. fruit  135:75
Bitterness: ills have no weight, and tears
  no b.  201:33
  little sweet doth kill much b.  182:4
  no hatred or b. towards anyone  95:7
Black: b. as ink  256:39
  b. as soot  256:40
  b. as the devil  256:41
  b. as the devil, hot as hell  384:30
  b. as the pit from pole to pole  160:93
  b. one ... good as the white  281:86
  b. sheep in every flock  256:42
  dark as the world ... b. as our loss
    373:90
  hung be the heavens with b.  321:62
  I am b. but comely  47:16
  I am b. ... my soul is white  68:51
  not so b. as he is painted  260:73
  one b., and one white, and two khaki
    14:55
  pot calls the kettle b.  275:52
  ravens ... as b. as they might
    · be  12:39
  secret, b., and midnight hags!
    335:60
  ship in a b. storm  401:55
  sober-suited matron all in b.  354:13
  two lovely b. eyes  104:37
Blackbird: there came a little b.  238:70
Blackbirds: four-and-twenty b.  238:70
Bladder: blows a man up like a b.
  314:67
Blade: shook the fragment of his b.
  296:15
  vorpal b. went snicker-snack!  92:70
Blame: murd'rous, bloody, full of b.
  363:50
  poor wot gets the b.  18:5
  scarcely can ... b. it too much
    151:78
  what they b. at night  249:2
Blanket: under the b. the black ... as
  good  281:86

Blanket (*continued*)
  wrong side of the b.  256:56
Blasphemy: in the soldier is flat b.
  337:88
Blast: our shelter from the stormy b.
  399:38
  with contrary b. proclaims most deeds
    222:23
Blaze: his rash fierce b. of riot cannot
  last  348:40
Blazon: this eternal b. must not be
  307:64
Bleats articulate monotony  378:62
Bleed: if you prick us, do we not b.?
  339:13
  upon the thorns of life! I b.!  369:37
Bleeding: thou b. piece of earth  324:8
Bleeds: our country ... weeps it b.
  335:65
Bless: b. the turf that wraps their clay
  107–8:90
  God b. the moon and God b. me
    234:43
  'God b. us every one!' said Tiny Tim
    119:36
  with thee at hand to b.  201:33
Blessed: b. are the horny hands of toil
  200:22
  judge none b. before his death  62:52
  more b. to give  56:22
Blesseth: it b. him that gives ... that
  takes  339:15
Blessing: a boon and a b. to men  11:32
  b. of the Old Testament  24:90
  God bless—no harm in b.  83:53
  prophetick b. – Be thou dull  127:49
  set before you ... b. and cursing
    38:13
  when thou dost ask me b.  330:99
Blessings: all the b. of this life  64:85
  b. are not valued till ... gone  256:43
Blest: always to be b.  250:9
  thou art b. compared with me  80:19
Blind: be to her faults a little b.  253:50
  b. as a bat  256:44
  b. as the nineteen hundred and forty
    nails  373:90
  b., despised, and dying king  370:53
  b. man will not thank you  256:47
  b. mouths! that scarce ... know how
    215:15
  Cupid painted b.  341:38
  discomforts ... accompany my being
    b.  246:45
  hatred is b.  266:71
  if the b. lead the b.  52:33
  in the land of the b.  256:48
  love is b.  270:13, 339:10

# Blind

**Blind** (*continued*)

men are b. in their own cause
256:46

none so b. as those who won't see
256:45

the maimed, and the halt, and the b.
54:79

three b. mice  240:80

**Blindly**: never lov'd so b.  79:97

**Bliss**: b. was it in that dawn to be alive
413:9

inward eye ... the b. of solitude
410:71

perfect b. and sole felicity  205:76

thou art a soul in b.  330:96

though thou hast not thy b.  183:18

virtue only makes our b. below
250:20

where ignorance is b.  154:29

**Blisses**: child among his new-born b.
411:79

**Blithe**: no lark more b. than he  65:16

O b. Newcomer ... O Cuckoo!
415:37

**Block**: a chip of the old b.  258:99

big black b.  145:3

he was ... the old b. itself  78:76

**Blockhead**: bookful b., ignorantly read
249:5

no man but a b. ever wrote  177:21

**Blockheads** of all ages  109:8

**Blocks**: you b., you stones!  323:89

**Blood**: all great Neptune's ocean wash
this b.  334:43

b. and iron  66:23

b. is fet from fathers of war-proof
319:46

b. is nipp'd and ways be foul
332:20

b. is thicker than water  25:49

b. of English shall manure the ground
350:56

b. of this just person  53:51

b. out of a stone  282:12

by man shall his b. be shed  35:49

corruption inhabits our frail b.
360:1

freeze thy young b.  307:64

guiltless of his country's b.  155:38

here's the smell of the b. still  335:69

he today that sheds his b. with me
320:59

I am in b. stepp'd in so far  335:57

I smell the b. of a British man
329:82

I sucked the b.  105:51

in so far in b. that sin will pluck
352:77

**Blood** (*continued*)

nothing to offer but b., toil, tears and
sweat  100:92

O, the b. more stirs  313:53

purge this cholar without letting b.
347:29

red b. reigns ... winter's pale  361:17

simple faith than Norman b.  387:74

smoke and b. is the mix of steel
293:80

some moment when the moon was b.
98:67

speech to stir men's b.  325:21

summon up the b.  319:45

sunset ran one glorious b.-red  74:24

the b. of Jesus whispers peace  65:19

the near in b. the nearer bloody
334:47

who thicks man's b. with cold
105:52

whoso sheddeth man's b.  35:49

young b. must have its course
189:89

**Bloody**: be b., bold and resolute
335:62

if you break the b. glass  203:55

my head is b. but unbowed  160:94

often wipe a b. nose  142:58

walk! not b. likely  366:98

what b. man is that?  332:24

wrong with our b. ships  29:69

**Bloom**: how can ye b. sae fresh and
fair?  81:26

you seize the flow'r, its b. is shed
81:25

**Blooming**: last rose ... left b. alone
226:63

like a b. Eastern bride  127:50

**Blossom** that hangs on the bough
357:56

**Blot**: noteless b. on a remembered
name  367:15

**Blots**: inky b. and rotten parchment
bonds  349:42

**Blow**: another deadly b.!  413:6

b., b., thou winter wind  302:91

b., bugle, b., set ... echoes flying
388:98

b. out, you bugles, over the rich
Dead  71:88

b. wind, come wrack  336:77

b. your pipe ... till you burst  75:42

hear old Triton b. his wreathed horn
412:94

liberty's in every b.  81:23

that but this b. might be the be-all
333:36

to take one b. and turn  164:45

Blows: heal the b. of sound  164:44
  the wild thyme b.  341:46
Bludgeonings: under the b. of chance
  160:94
Blue: Little Boy B.  234:49
  their hands are b.  194:58
  true b. will never stain  281:58
Blunder: wonder at so grotesque a b.
  33–4:19
  youth is a b.  123:95
Blunders: one of Nature's agreeable b.
  112:48
Blush: wd. it bring a b.?  120:59
Blushing: bears his b. honours  322:80
*Blut und Eisen*  66:23
Board: wasn't any b. ... isn't any
  trade  161:8
Boards: all the b. did shrink  105:50
Boast of heraldry ... pomp of power
  155:34
Boasts two soul-sides  74:34
Boat: all in the same b.  276:11
  beautiful pea-green b.  195:60
Boatman do not tarry  88:19
Boats: burn one's b.  257:69
  messing about in b.  153:13
Boatswain and I, the gunner and his
  mate  356:43
Bobby Shafto: bonny B.  231:24
Bodies: friendless b. of unburied men
  400:54
  pile the b. high  293:78
  rough notes and our dead b.  294:91
  their b. are buried in peace  62:62
Bodkin: quietus make with a bare b.
  309:95
Body: absent in b., ... present in spirit
  57:47
  asleep in b., ... become a living soul
  415:33
  b. is not more than the soul  403:86
  b. of a feeble woman  132:20
  carry ... b. around ... its sentimental
  value  140:31
  every joint and motive of her b.
  358:73
  fretted the pigmy b. to decay  126:39
  gin a b. meet a b.  79:3
  mind that makes the b. rich  355:25
  my little b. is aweary  338:1
  need a b. cry?  79:3
  perfect little b., without fault  70:78
  Presence of Mind ... Absence of B.
  284:75
  reading is to ... mind what exercise
  ... to the b.  378:61
  some in their b.'s force  363:41
  soul not more than the b.  403:86

Body (*continued*)
  sound mind in a sound b.  180:71
  that learned b. wanted loyalty
  393:54
  the corruptible b.  62:44
  Thersites' b. is as good as Ajax'
  304:28
  we ... are one b. in Christ  57:36
  we therefore commit his b.  65:15
  with my b. I thee worship  65:9
Bog: tell your name ... to an admiring
  b.  122:81
Boil: we b. at different degrees  133:45
Bold: be bloody, b. and resolute
  335:62
  be b., be b. ... everywhere Be b.
  377:43
Boldness, and again b., and always b.
  117:5
Bond: let him look to his b.  339:12
  take a b. of fate  335:63
  'tis not in the b.  340:18
  the very b. of love  362:24
  word is as good as his b.  267:92
Bondage: out of the house of b.  37:81
Bondman: so base that wd. be a b.?
  325:11
Bonds: inky blots and rotten parchment
  b.  349:42
Bone: a b. to pick with fate  228:92
  beat him with a b.  260:83
  b. of my bones  35:34
  fetch her poor dog a b.  236:59
  have a b. in one's leg  256:51
  two dogs strive for a b.  281:76
Bones: as rottenness in his b.  45:65
  good ... interred with their b.
  325:12
  let's have the tongs and the b.
  342:51
  mock'd the dead b. ... scatt'red by
  352:72
  my Shakespeare for his honoured b.
  216:23
  o ye dry b., hear the word  49:65
  of his b. are coral made  355:35
Bonfire: primrose way to th' everlasting
  b.  334:44
Bong-tree: land where the B. grows
  195:61
Bonnet: a bee in one's b.  255:4
Bonnets: the b. of Bonny Dundee
  294:92
Bonnie (Bonny): b., b. banks o' Loch
  Lomon'  18:2
  braes o' b. Doon  81:26
  bring back my B.  17:94
  for b. Annie Laurie  124:16

**Bonnie** (*continued*)
  is b. and blithe and good  235–6:56
  my B. is over the ocean  17:94
Bons mots: not enough b. in existence
  169:2
*Bonum: Summum b.*  102:16
Bo(o): cannot say B. to a goose
  276:14
Booby: give her b. for another  142:57
Book: a bad b. is as much labour
  169:3
  a b. ... amusing with numerous
    errors  152:95
  a b.'s a b. although  85:89
  a good b. is the precious life-blood
    223:38
  a leaf out of one's b.  279:94
  bell, b. and candle shall not drive me
    back  327:40
  b. ... shut is but a block  256:52
  b. that furnishes no quotations
    245:36
  but where's the b.?  100:84
  dainties ... bred in a b.  331:13
  damned, thick, square b.!  149:56
  do not throw this b. about  31:88
  go, litel b.  98:52
  half a library to make one b.
    176:11
  he who destroys a good b.  223:37
  his common-place b. ... full  382:8
  if a b. is worth reading ... worth
    buying  291:60
  I'll drown my b.  357:55
  is no b. – it is a plaything  245:36
  my B. of Songs and Sonnets  340:28
  never read a b. before reviewing
    375:11
  never read ... b. ... not a year old
    133:42
  seldom read a b. ... given to them
    176:5
  take down this b.  417:58
  that one might read the b. of fate!
    317:15
  upon a b. in cloistre ... to poure
    96:30
  use of a b. without pictures?  89:42
  what genius ... when I wrote that b.
    382:14
  when a new b. is published  288:23
  word for word without b.  359:76
  write a better b.  133:48
  your face, my thane, is as a b.
    333:34
Books: as school-boys from their b.
  354:4
  at his beddes heed twenty b.  96:33

Books (*continued*)
  author who speaks about his own b.
    122:92
  base authority from others' b.
    331:10
  b. and friends ... few and good
    256:53
  b. cannot always please  114:80
  b. cannot be killed by fire  289:33
  b. from which the lectures are taken
    175:95
  b. in the running brooks  300:75
  b. think for me  192:29
  b.! 'tis a dull and endless strife
    414:26
  borrowers of b.  192:26
  deep-versed in b. and shallow
    221:8
  his sins ... scarlet ... his b. ... read
    31:93
  I keep my b. at the British Museum
    82:42
  I never read b.—I *write* them  285:83
  I'll burn my b.!  204:66
  in a person's bad [good] b.  256:54
  in this war ... b. are weapons
    289:33
  learning ... gained most by those b.
    140:40
  needed not the spectacles of b.
    127:59
  no furniture so charming as b.
    374:7
  of making many b. ... is no end
    47:13
  old b. maken us memorie  97:47
  old b., old wine  151:83
  quit your b.  414:25
  read any good b. lately?  227:76
  read of in b., or dreamt of  28:53
  rural quiet, friendship, b.  391:34
  some b. are to be tasted  26:32
  the b., the arts, the academes
    331:16
  to Cambridge b.  393:54
  to Cambridge b. he sent  72–3:8
  true University ... collection of b.
    89:37
  we all know that b. burn  289:33
Boom: strong gongs groaning ... guns
  b. far  99:71
Boon: a b. and a blessing to men  11:32
  is life a b.?  148:44
Boot: b. is on the other leg  256:55
  make b. upon the summer's ... buds
    318:39
Boots: b., b., b.  190:95
  too big for one's b.  280:48

Boots (*continued*)
what b. it with incessant care?
215:11

Bo-peep has lost her sheep 234:48

Border: through all the wide B. 295:10

Bore: every hero ... a b. at last 133:41
people's mothers ... b. me 406:30

Bored: two mighty tribes, the *Bores*
and *B.* 85:86

Boring: something ... b. about somebody else's happiness 169:1

Born: a sucker b. every minute 28:58
better to be lowly b. 322:75
b., bred, and hanged ... same parish
13:47
b. for the Universe 151:78
b. out of my due time 227:71
b. to be hanged 256:57
b. to speak all mirth 343:66
b. with silver spoon 256:58
b. within the sound of Bow Bells
256:59
b. ... wrong side of the blanket
256:56
I was b. about three of the clock
316:99
I was not b. yesterday 257:60
is not b., and does not die 373:91
man that is b. of a woman 65:13
native here, and to the manner b.
307:59
'Never was b.!' persisted Topsy
380:84
none of woman b. shall harm Macbeth 335:62
not b. to sue, but to command
347:31
one b. out of due time 57:58
powerless to be b. 20:36
some are b. great 360:91
that ever I was b. to set it right
307:71
then surely I was b. 98:67
under that [star] I was b. 343:67
we are b. in other's pain 390:29
when we are b. we cry 330:94
who are b. of thee 33:13
wd. thou had'st never been b.
346:14
ye must be b. again 55:97
yield to one of woman b. 336:78

Borne it with a patient shrug 338:6

Borogoves: mimsy were the b. 91:69

Borrow: better buy than b. 255:21
earth must b. its mirth 404:91
even if we have to b. 399:31
Sorrow, why dost b.? 181:87
the men who b. 191:25

Borrower: neither a b. nor a lender be
306:57

Borrowers of books—those mutilators
192:26

Borrowing: beggar by banqueting upon
b. 62:54
b. dulls the edge of husbandry
306:57
b. only ... lingers it out 316:3

Bosom: b. of his Father and his God
155:42
. cleanse the stuff'd b. 336:72

Bosom-friend: close b. of the maturing
sun 180:78

Bosoms: to men's business, and b.
24:84

Boston: and this is good old B. 69:67
readers of the B. Evening Transcript 130:89

Boteler: as Dr B. said of strawberries
398:25

Both: money ... life; women require b.
83:51
much might be said on b. sides 9:8
to lose b. [parents] ... carelessness
405:10

Bottle: my b. of salvation 286:94
she found a little b. on it 89:43

Bottles: new wine into old b. 54:73

Bottom: bless thee, B. ... thou art
translated 342:49

Bottomless: the b. pit 61:28

Bough: blossom that hangs on the b.
357:56
when the b. breaks 233:38

Boughs: incense hangs upon the b.
184:27
lowest b. and the brushwood sheaf
74:21
my soul into the b. does glide
206:1
shade of melancholy b. 301:89

Bought: until she has b. her wedding
clothes 9:10

Boulogne: a young man of B. 13:53

Bound upon a wheel of fire 330:96

Bounty: large was his b. 155:41

Bourgeois: how beastly the b. is
193:46

Bourgeoisie: British B. is not born
373:91

Bourn: from whose b. no traveller
returns 309:95
to see beyond our b. 181:88

*Boutiquiers: une nation de b.* 228:85

Bow: arrow from the Almighty's b.
66–7:35
as unto the b. the cord is 198:3

Brother (*continued*)
  two sisters embrace like one b. 287:11
Brotherhood: crown thy good with b. 29:67
Brotherly: let b. love continue 60:2
Brothers: all men will be b. 294:85
  and all the b. too 360:90
  two b. and their murder'd man 182:5
Brow: b. like to a title-leaf 316:96
  on Ida's shady b. 68:54
  yr. bonnie b. was brent 80:11
Brown: baked me too b. 91:64
Bruce: Scots whom B. has ... led 81:22
*Brüder: alle Menschen werden B.* 294:85
Bruise: parmaceti for an inward b. 313:52
Brunck: most learned professor, B. 252:41
Brush: all tarred with the same b. 279:10
Brute beasts that have no understand-ing 64:4
*Brute: et tu, B.?* 87:9, 324:3
Brutish: life ... nasty, b., and short 163:34
Brutus: for B. is an honourable man 325:13
  the fault, dear B. 323–4:93
  you too, B.? 87:9
Bubble: fire burn and cauldron b. 335:58
  like the b. on the fountain 295:98
  seeking the b. reputation 301:90
Bubbles: beaded b. winking 184:24
Bucket: nations are as a drop of a b. 48:43
Buckingham: Palace, changing the guard at B. 211:54
  high-reaching B. grows circumspect 352:76
Buckram: rogues in b. 314:65
Bud: concealment, like a worm i' th' b. 360:89
  this b. of love 354:3
Buds: gather the flowers, but spare the b. 207:5
  shake the darling b. of May 362:32
Buffets: blows and b. of the world 334:49
Buffoon: a private b. 149:49
  statesman and b. 126:43
Bugle: blow, b.; answer, echoes 388:98
  bring the good old b., boys 416:44

Bugles: blow out, you b., over the rich Dead 71:88
Build: easier to pull down than to b. 275:69
  except the Lord b. the house 44:41
  on this rock ... b. my church 53:34
Building: don't clap too hard ... very old b. 242:6
Built: houses are b. to live in 26:28
  Rome was not b. in a day 276:2
Bulbul: Abdul the B. Amir 18:7
Bull: b. in a china shop 257:66
  in time the savage b. 191:22
  red rag to a b. 275:81
  roar like a b. 276:97
  take the b. by the horns 279:98
Bull and Bush: down at the old B. 392:46
Bullet: ballot is stronger than the b. 196:75
  every b. has its billet 407:37
Bullfighting is the only art in which 160:92
Bullocks: good yoke of b. at Stamford 317:17
  he ... whose talk is of b. 62:58
Bulls the cow must keep the calf 257:67
Bully: I love the lovely b. 320:51
Bumbast out a blank verse 156:49
Bunbury: a ... permanent invalid called B. 405:6
Bunk: Gert's poems are b. 14:57
  history is b. 137:91
Buns: hot cross b.! 233:35
Burden: take up the White Man's B. 190:12
Burdens: bear ye one another's b. 58:69
  heavy b. at his narrow gate 318–9:39
Burglar: enterprising b.'s not a-burgling 148:34
Burglary: flat b. as ever was committed 344:83
Buried: half-b. in the snow was found 198:94
  the old Adam ... so b. 64:94
Burlington: I'm B. Bertie 158:69
Burn: better to marry than to b. 57:50
  b. ... candle at both ends 257:70
  b. one's boats 257:69
  b. the midnight oil 257:71
  hearts are dry ... b. to the socket 409:64
  I'll b. my books! 204:66
  old age shd. b. and rave 390:18
  violent fires soon b. out 348:40
  we all know that books b. 289:33

Caesar (*continued*)
  in envy of great C.  326:30
  not that I lov'd C. less  325:10
  O mighty C., dost thou lie so low?
    324:6
  regions C. never knew  112:50
  unto C. shalt thou go  56:26
  unto C. the things which are C.'s
    53:43
Caesars: there be many C.  304:21
Café: laughter ... in every street c.
  157:58
Cage: a robin redbreast in a c.  66:28
  marriage is like a c.  225:56
  nor iron bars a c.  199:15
  will sing like birds i' th' c.  330:99
Cain: the first city C. [made]  112:46
  the Lord set a mark upon C.  35:42
Caitiff: rude c. smite the other too
  164:45
Cake: bake me a c.  237:62
  eat yr. c. and have it  261:13
  let them eat c.  204:61
  some gave them plum c.  234:47
Cakes: no more c. and ale?  359:87
Calais: find C. lying in my heart
  207:10
Calamity: makes c. of so long life
  309:95
*Calamus saevior ense patet*  81:30
Calculated: nicely-c. less or more
  409:60
Calculating: accurate about her age.
  It looks so c.  405:15
Calculation of the expense of ... bow-
  windows  119:39
Calculators: age of ... sophisters ... c.
  78:78
Calendar: a c., a c.! ... find out moonshine!  342:48
Calf: bring hither the fatted c.  55:82
  c. love, half love  257:81
  c. ... young lion ... fatling together
    48:37
Caliban: 'ban, 'ban, Ca-C.  356:44
Call: a wild c. and a clear c.  207:15
  c. me early, mother dear  388:89
  c. of the running tide  207:15
  Death ... must c. too soon  148:44
  dost thou c. me fool, boy?  328:56
  go, for they c. you, Shepherd  21:39
  I can c. spirits from the ... deep
    314:72
  one clear c. for me!  385:44
  that ... I wd. fain c. master  327:55
Called: he c. for his pipe ... his bowl
  236:58
**Callooh! Callay!**  92:71

Callous engraved on her heart  297:31
Calm of mind, all passion spent
  223:27
Calumny: envy and c. and hate  367:16
  thou shalt not escape c.  310:98
Camberwell: a long way east of C.
  32:4
Cambridge: to C. books, as ... wanted
  learning  393:54
  to C., books he sent  72–3:8
  who's ahead ... either Oxford or C.
  375:19
Came: for yr. pleasure you c. here
  113:60
  I c., I saw, I conquered  87:8
  I c. like Water, and like Wind I go
  135:72
  I c., saw, and overcame  317:24
  tell them I c. and no one answered
  118:24
Camel: c. ... through the eye of a
  needle  53:41
  last straw breaks the c.'s back
  269:54
  strain at a gnat and swallow a c.
  53:44
Camelot: many-tower'd C.  387:75
Camp: from c. to c., through ... night
  320:50
  love rules ... court ... c. ... grove
  295:2
Campbells are coming  16:77
Can: fill up my cup ... my c.  294:92
  he who c., does ... cannot, teaches
  366:88
Canary: mine host's C. wine  183:14
Cancel: lure it back to c. half a line
  136:79
Cancels: debt which c. all others
  108:1
Candid: be c. where we can  250:8
  save me from the c. friend  88:27
Candide: '... Well said,' replied C.
  397:9
Candle: bell, book and c. shall not
  drive me back  327:40
  burn the c. at both ends  257:70
  c. to light you to bed  236:61
  game is not worth the c.  264:3
  hold a c. to the devil  267:91
  little c. throws his beams  340:25
  my c. burns at both ends  210:45
  out, out, brief c.!  336:76
  this day light such a c.  193:40
Candle-holder: I'll be a c. and look on
  353:91
Candle-light: can I get there by c.?
  233:36

**Candle-light** (*continued*)
choose ... woman nor linen by c.
258:3
Candles: night's c. are burnt out
354:14
Candy is dandy 229:95
Cankered: heart ... grief hath c. 87:12
Cankers: the c. of a calm world 315:83
Cannon: even in the c.'s mouth 301:90
Cannon-ball: a c. took off his legs
165:57
Cannons: where the thundering c. roar
151:86
Canoe: paddle his own c. 206:88
Canon: his c. 'gainst self-slaughter
305:42
Canopy: rich embroider'd c. to kings
322:71
*Canossa: nach C. gehen wir nicht* 65:22
We will not go to C. 65:22
Cant: apple press'd with specious c.
165:63
clear yr. mind of c. 177:34
Cantons: loyal c. of contemned love
359:80
Cap: if the c. fits 257:83
put on one's thinking c. 275:68
riband in the c. of youth 311:29
stuck a feather in his c. 241:90
Capability: Negative C. 186:52
Capon: belly with good c. lined 301:90
Captain! a right good c., too! 147:21
a train-band c. eke was he 112:54
C., art tha sleepin' there below?
230:11
c.'s hand on his shoulder smote
230:14
in the c.'s but a choleric word
337:88
O C.! my C.! 403:81
the c. of my soul 160:95
Captains: the c. and the kings depart
190:9
Captive: weak minds led c. 221:5
Caravan: put up yr. c. just for one day
163:37
Cardinal: C. Lord Archbishop of
Rheims 28:53
jackdaw sat on the C.'s chair 28:52
Cards: an old age of c. 251:24
can pack the c. ... cannot play
25:15
played at c. for kisses 201:29
Care: begone, dull c. 16:75
c. killed a cat 257:84
I c. for nobody 65:17
I c. not whether a man is good 67:37
nor for itself hath any c. 67:43

**Care** (*continued*)
past my help is past my c. 29:72
past redress ... with me past c.
349:47
polish'd perturbation! golden c.!
317:27
ravell'd sleave of c. 334:42
sae weary, fu' o' c. 81:26
so shaken ... wan with c. 312:42
sport that wrinkled C. derides
214:94
this life if full of c. 117:11
what boots it with incessant c.
215:11
what c. I for whom she be? 408:50
Career: which might damage his c.
28:64
Careful: be very c. o' vidders ... Sammy
121:67
Careless: first fine c. rapture 74:23
sitting c. on a granary floor 181:80
so c. of the single life 386:62
Cares: if no one c. for me 65:17
light c. speak, great ones are dumb
269:82
Carew: the grave of Mad C. 159:76
Cargo of ivory and apes 207:12
Caricature of a face 146:11
Carlyle, Tennyson, Browning 285:85
Carouse: for ... marriage I did make c.
135:76
*Carpe diem, quam minimum ... postero*
166:74
Carpenter: Walrus and the C.
92–3:78–82
Carriage: a very small second-class c.
144:92
I can't afford a c. 116:99
the c. held but just ourselves 122:84
Cart: creak of a lumbering c. 417:55
put the c. before the horse 257:86
*Carthago: delenda est C.* 94:2
Carve: c. on every tree the fair ... she
302:92
c. out dials quaintly 321:70
let's c. him as a dish 324:99
must c. in Latin or in Greek 398:18
Carved: we c. not a line 408:53
Casca: the envious C. 325:18
Case: c. is still before the courts 166:70
nothing to do with the c. 146:11
there to attend to the c. 144:84
Cased: yr. hare when it is c. 149:55
Casement ope at night 185:33
Casements: magic c. opening on the
foam 184:30
Cases: circumstances alter c. 258:6
hard c. make bad law 266:67

Cash: he takes yr c., but where's the book? 100:84
Cashmere: tales of fair C. 407:41
Casques: within this wooden O the very c. 318:37
Cassio: if C. do remain 346:16
   not C. kill'd! 346:20
Cassius: for ever ... farewell, C.l 326:28
   yond C. has a lean and hungry look 324:94
Cast: I backward c. my e'e 80:19
   pale c. of thought 309:95
   the die is c. 87:7
Castle: a c. called Doubting C. 77:62
   a man's house is his c. 104:39
   Englishman's house is his c. 261:22
   I'm the king of the c. 233:41
   splendour falls on c. walls 388:97
   the rich man in his c. 10:18
Castlereagh: a mask like C. 368:30
Castles: build c. in Spain 257:88
   c. in the air 257:89
Cat: a c. and a lie 394:70
   care killed a c. 257:84
   c. has nine lives 257:90
   c. is away the mice will play 283:28
   c. out of the bag 269:72
   c. will mew, and dog will have his day 312:34
   fog comes on little c. feet 293:77
   hanging of his c. 70:74
   he bought a crooked c. 239:74
   like a c. on hot bricks 258:92
   more ways of killing a c. 189:91
   part to tear a c. in 341:40
   room to swing a c. 276:3
   runcible c. with crimson whiskers 195:63
   the c. and the fiddle 232:33
   what c.'s averse to fish? 154:24
   when I play with my c. 225:55
   which way the c. jumps 257:91
Cataclysm: out of their c. but one poor Noah 169:4
Catalogue: in the c. ye go for men 334:48
Cataracts: you c. and hurricanoes, spout 328:71
Catastrophe: I'll tickle yr. c. 316:5
Catch: c. a falling star 124:11
   c. a nigger by his toe 232:29
   c. him once upon the hip 338:3
   perdition c. my soul 345:5
   set a thief to c. a thief 280:22
Catechism: and so ends my c. 315:88
Categorical: in order c. 147:31
Caterpillars of the commonwealth 349:46

Cats: killed the c. and bit the babies 75:37
Caucasus: thinking on the frosty C. 348:37
Caught: maidens ... are ever c. by glare 83:56
   one c. a Muffin, the other c. a Mouse 195:64
Cauldron: fire burn and c. bubble 335:58
*Causas: felix qui potuit rerum cognoscere c.* 397:5
Cause: an effect whose c. is God 114:74
   beauty of the good old c. 412:2
   blind in their own c. 256:46
   great c. of cheering us all up 33:10
   it is the c., it is the c., my soul 346:18
   jealous for the c. 346:11
   know c., or just impediment 64:3
   report me and my c. aright 312:37
   ring out a slowly dying c. 386:69
   'what great c. ... identified with?' 33:10
Causes: able to learn the c. of things 397:5
   c. why and wherefore in all 321:60
   home of lost c. ... beliefs 21:49
   of all the c. which conspire 249:93
Cavaliero: he was a perfect c. 83:54
*Cave canem* 246:49
Cave: her vacant interlunar c. 221:14
   Idols of the C. 27:41
   in Stygian c. forlorn 213–14:91
   out of the misty eastern c. 368:32
Cave (of) Adullam: escaped to the C. 39:45
   retired into ... his political C. 71:82
*Caveat emptor* 258:93
Cavern: happy field or mossy c. 183:14
   in a c. in a canyon 225:59
Caverns measureless to man 106:71
Caves: dark unfathom'd c. of ocean 155:37
   pleasure-dome with c. of ice 107:75
Caviare to the general 308:85
Cavity: filling his last c. 13:49
Cease: I will not c. from mental fight 67:38
   poor shall never c. 38:11
   seedtime ... harvest ... shall not c. 35:48
   warm days will never c. 181:79
Ceases: love c. to be a pleasure 30:85
Ceiling: stood up and spat on the c. 14:56
Celebrate: I c. myself 403:82

Chapels had been churches ... cottages ... palaces 338:2

Chaps: biography is about c. 33:15

Character: a c. dead at every word 372:76
  education ... formation of c. 376:36
  I leave my c. behind me 372:77
  precepts ... look thou c. 306:55
  she gave me a good c. 91:67

Characteristics: vanity and love; ... their universal c. 98:62

Charge: c. Chester, c.! 296:15
  take thou in c this day 201:40

Charged with the grandeur of God 166:67

Charing-Cross: full tide of ... existence is at C. 176:9

Chariot: bring me my c. of fire 67:38
  swing low, sweet c. 18:8
  Time's winged c. hurrying near 206:94

Charioted: not c. by Bacchus 183:16

Chariots: some trust in c., and some in horses 42:90

Charity: c. begins at home 258:96
  c. shall cover ... sins 60:11
  cold as c. 258:17
  doings without c. are nothing worth 64:87
  greatest of these is c. 57:55
  hand open as day for melting c. 317:25
  I do not give ... c., ... I give myself 403:85
  in c. there is no excess 25:4
  living need c. more than the dead 20:29
  with c. for all 196:81

Charity-boy: as the c. said 121:70

Charlatan: defamed by every c. 387:72

Charles the First: King C. walked and talked 15:66

Charm: despair thy c. 336:78
  what c. can soothe her melancholy? 152:2

Charmed: I bear a c. life, which must not yield 336:78

Charmer: were t'other dear c. away 142:54

Charming: c. to totter into vogue 398:22
  how c. is divine Philosophy! 213:77
  people are either c. or tedious 405:18
  the rabbit has a c. face 15:70

Charms: c. strike the sight, but merit wins 252:39
  do not all c. fly? 183:12
  music has c. to soothe 108:5

Charms (continued)
  solitude! Where are the c.? 114:78

Charter: this was the c. of the land 391:33

Charybdis: between Scylla and C. 256:33

Chase: the c., the sport of kings 375:23

Chasing the wild deer 81:20

Chassis: whole worl's in a state of c. 241:94

Chaste: be thou as c. as ice 310:98

Chasteneth: c. his son, so the Lord ... c. thee 38:8
  loveth him c. him betimes 45:67
  whom the Lord loveth he c. 60:1

Chastisement: fear no heavier c. from me 367:15

Chastity: c. and continence, but not yet 22:63
  clothed on with c. 385:49
  'tis c., my brother, c. 212:76

Chatterton, the marvellous Boy 413:12

Chaucer: Dan C., well of English undefiled 377:44

Che sera sera 258:97

Che sera sera: what doctrine ... C.? 204:62

Cheap: flesh and blood so c. 166:65
  man's life is c. as beast's 328:67

Cheating: Winning Games Without Actually C. 252:43

Check: alas! I wd. not c. 192:35
  O dreadful is the c. 71:87

Checked: I c. him while he spoke 192:35

Cheek: bring a blush to the c. 120:59
  feed on her damask c. 360:89
  leans her c. upon her hand 353:98
  pale grew thy c. and cold 86:99
  she hangs upon the c. of night 353:94
  smite thee on thy right c. 52:13
  take one blow and turn the other c. 164:45
  that I might touch that c.! 353:98
  there's language in her eye, her c. 358:73
  wither'd c. and tresses grey 295:99

Cheeks: beauty's ensign ... crimson ... in thy c. 354:17
  blow winds, and crack yr. c. 328:71
  make pale my c. with care 408:49
  rosy c. and flaxen curls 75:43
  stain my man's c. 328:68

Cheer: Christmas ... brings good c. 258:5
  cd. scarce forbear to c. 202:41
  cups that c. 114:73

Cheer (*continued*)
  so I piped with merry c.  68:49
  the fewer the better c.  272:70
  welcome is the best c.  282:20
Cheerful: God loveth a c. giver  58:63
  merry heart ... c. countenance  45:70
  more c. ... than to be forty  164:52
Cheerfully: how c. he seems to grin
  89–90:45
Cheerfulness was always breaking in
  129:82
Cheering: great cause of c. us all up
  33:10
Cheerio my deario  205:83
Cheers: three c. and one cheer more
  147:24
Cheese: chalk and c.  258:94
  dreamed of c.—toasted mostly
  379:75
  hard c.  266:68
  hellish dark, and smells of c.!
  380:90
Cheltenham: killed by drinking C.
  waters  12:41
Chemist (Chymist): was c., fiddler,
  statesman  126:43
Chequer-board: a c. of Nights and
  Days  135:78
Cherish: c. those hearts that hate thee
  323:83
  to love and to c., till death  64:7
  to love, c., and to obey  64:8
Cherries: c. ... which none may buy
  88:25
  Kent ... apples, c., hops  120:61
Cherry: c. ripe, ripe ... I cry  162:15
  make two bites of a c.  281:73
  ruddier than the c.  141:51
  there's the land, or c.-isle  162:15
  till 'C. Ripe' themselves do cry
  88:25
Cherubins: quiring to the young-ey'd c.
  340:22
Chess: life's too short for c.  86:3
Chest: a c. of drawers by day  150:70
  on the dead man's c.  379:74
  ten-times barred-up c.  347:30
Chester: charge, C., charge!  296:15
Chesterton: dared attack my C.  32:1
Chestnut-tree: under a spreading c.
  199:6
Chevalier: the young C.  227:80
Chewing little bits of string  31:90
Chicken: Some c.! Some neck!  101:1
Chickens: count one's c. before ...
  hatched  259:30
  curses are like c. ... home to roost
  259:44

Chides: at fifty c. his infamous delay
  418:63
Chief: brilliant c., irregularly great
  76:53
Child: a little c. shall lead them  48:37
  an it had been any christom c.
  319:43
  at break of day the solitary c.  411:85
  C. among his new-born blisses
  411:79
  C. I do not throw this book  31:88
  C. Rowland to the dark tower came
  329:82
  c. says 'I don't believe in fairies'
  28:60
  c. whose father goes to the devil
  266:65
  divide the ... c. in two  40:50
  even a c. is known by his doings
  45:76
  get with c. a mandrake root  124:11
  has devoured the infant c.  167:78
  Heaven-born C. all meanly wrapt
  215:20
  Jesus Christ her little c.  10:19
  Monday's c. is fair of face  235:56
  more hideous ... in a c.  328:57
  on a cloud I saw a c.  68:48
  the cry of a c. by the roadway
  417:55
  the old Adam in this c.  64:94
  this c. I to myself will take  415:30
  to have a thankless c.  328:58
  train up a c. in the way  45:80
  unto us a c. is born  48:36
  wise c. ... knows its own father
  283:39
  wise father ... knows his own c.
  339:8
  with that the wretched c. expires
  31:92
Childhood: companions, in my days of
  c.  192:32
  my careless c. stray'd  154:27
  the c. shows the man  221:6
  what my lousy c. was like  292:71
Childishness: second c. and mere
  oblivion  301–2:90
Children: artist will let ... his c. go
  barefoot  365:80
  as c. fear ... the dark  24:86
  become as little c.  53:37
  c., dear, was it yesterday?  20:33
  c. of one family fall out  399:37
  c. of this world ... wiser ... c. of light
  55:84
  c. shd. be seen and not heard  258:98
  c.'s teeth are set on edge  49:58

**Children** (*continued*)
c. sweeten labours  24:95
c. ... with nothing to ignore  228:93
c. yet unborn shall feel this day  351:59
come, c. of our native land  291:54
come, dear c., let us away  20:32
do you hear the c. weeping?  73:11
familiarity breeds ... c.  394:67
father pitieth his c.  43:22
had borne him three c.  169:7
happy ... that is happy in his c.  266:63
he that hath wife and c.  24:96
men ... c. of a larger growth  127:56
more careful of ... dogs than ... c.  245:39
Rachel weepeth for her c.  51:3
she had so many c.  239:76
stars ... are my c.  187:63
tale which holdeth c. from play  373:86
voices of c. are heard on the green  68:52
your c. all gone  234:46
**Chill**: Ah, bitter c. it was  181:89
Chills the finger not a bit  229:96
**Chilly**: although the room grows c.  153:11
**Chime**: higher than the sphery c.  213:81
merry village c.  148:34
**Chimes**: heard the c. at midnight  317:18
**Chimney**: old men from the c. corner  373:86
**Chimney-sweepers**: as c., come to dust  304–5:29
**Chin**: his c. new reap'd  313:51
his c. upon an orient wave  216:22
**China**: bull in a c. shop  257:66
C.'s gayest art had dyed  154:23
mistress of herself, though C. fall  251:25
**China orange**: Lombard Street to a C.  270:97
**Chinamen**: birds in ... nests agree with C.  32:99
**Chink**: aid ... from a c. in the floor  383:26
**Chip**: a c. of the old block  258:99
not merely a c. of the old block  78:76
**Chirche-dore**: housbondes at c.  97:39
**Chivalry**: age of c. is gone  78:73
her Beauty and her C.  83:59
**Chloe**: but C. is my real flame  253:51
**Chocolate cream soldier**  364:63

**Choice**: Hobson's c.  267:89
pays yr. money ... takes yr. c.  284:74
small c. in rotten apples  355:21
**Choir**: sweet singing in the c.  16–17:87
**Choler**: purge ... c. without letting blood  347:29
**Choleric**: in the captain's but a c. word  337:88
**Choose**: c. life, that ... thy seed may live  38:13
to c. love by another's eyes  341:37
to c. time is to save time  26:18
where to c. their place of rest  221:3
**Choosing**: subject for ... song ... long c.  220:90
**Chop and change**  258:4
**Chopper**: cheap and chippy c.  145:3
here comes a c.  236:61
**Chops and Tomata sauce** ... Pickwick  121:74
**Chortled in his joy**  92:71
**Chorus**: a c.-ending from Euripides  73:17
**Chosen**: many are called, but few are c.  53:42
**Choughs**: the crows and c. that wing  329:88
**Christ**: beseech you, in the bowels of C.  115:88
C. is thy strength ... thy right  225:53
so Judas did to C.  350:57
the C. that is to be  387:71
we ... are one body in C.  57:36
**Christ Church**: I am the Dean of C., Sir  378:54
**Christendom**: the wisest fool in C.  160:98
**Christian**: a C. faithful man  351:71
assume the honourable style of C.  72:99
good C. men, rejoice  229:2
hate him for he is a C.  338:3
if possible ... C. men for C. boys  22:55
in what peace a C. can die  10:12
mirror of all C. kings  319:40
persuadest me to be a C.  56:28
warmed and cooled ... as a C. is  339:13
words ... no C. ear can endure  321:68
**Christians**: C. awake, salute  83:52
profess and call themselves C.  63:82
**Christmas**: at C. I no more desire a rose  331:11

Christmas (*continued*)

C. comes but once a year 258:5, 393:58

C. Day in the Workhouse 373:89

eating a C. pie 235:50

on C. Day in the morning 15:74, 233-4:42

the first day of C. 238:72

the twelfth day of C. 238:73

Christopher Robin: C. is saying his prayers 211:61

C. went down with Alice 211:54

Chronicle: in the c. of wasted time 363:45

suckle fools and c. small beer 345:98

Chronicles: abstract and brief c. 308:87

look in the c.: we came in 355:19

Church: if at the C. ... give us some ale 68:45

new and great period in His C. 224:42

some to c. repair, ... for ... the music 249:98

the C.'s one foundation 380:83

the C.'s Restoration in 1883 34:24

wish from the C. to stray 68:45

Churches: chapels had been c. 338:2

let yr. women keep silence in the c. 57:56

Churchman: become a c. better than ambition 323:88

Church-yard: if two are in the c. laid 416:41

Churchyards: when c. yawn 310:13

Cigar: a good cigar is a smoke 190:94

Circle: weave a c. round him thrice 107:76

wheel is come full c. 330:2

Circumcised: took by th' throat the c. dog 346-7:22

Circumlocution office was beforehand 120:47

Circumspect: high-reaching Buckingham grows c. 352:76

Circumstances alter cases 258:6

Cities: sung women in three c. 252:48

towered c. please us then 214:1

Citizen: c. of no mean city 56:23

first requisite of a good c. 289:36

I am a c. ... of the world 375:20

John Gilpin was a c. 112:54

Citizens: civil c. kneading up the honey 318-19:39

healthy c. are the greatest asset 101:6

my fellow c. of the world 188:75

Citizens (*continued*)

sing, all ye c. of heaven 241:92

you fat and greasy c. 300:76

City: a populous and a smoky c. 369:41

c. now doth like a garment wear 412:96

c. with her dreaming spires 21:46

her in the dissolute c. 411:87

in Dublin's fair c. 17:89

it is the men who make a c. 272:54

long in c. pent 186:47

once in royal David's c. 10:19

one ... in populous c. pent 220:93

rose-red c. half as old as time 77:70

the first c. Cain [made] 112:46

without a c. wall 11:20

City Road: up and down the C. 203:60

Civet: an ounce of c. 329:91

Civil: over violent or over c. 126:44

too c. by half 372:73

Civilises: the sex whose presence c. ours 112:53

Civility: C. costs nothing 258:7

I see a wild c. 162:17

Civilized: woman will be the last thing c. 209:35

*Civis Romanus sum* 102:20

Clad: she that has [chastity] is c. in ... steel 212:76

Clap: don't c. too hard 242:6

if you believe, c. yr. hands 28:62

Claret is the liquor for boys 177:31

Class: not [happiness] of any one c. 247:62

Classes: the masses against the c. 149:53

the three great c. ... our society 21:48

to prove the upper c. 111:39

Classic: a c. ... nobody wants to read 394:73

Clay: as the c. is in the potter's hand 49:57

cabin ... of c. and wattles made 417:52

men ... gilded loam or painted c. 347:30

tenement of c. 126:39

turf that wraps their c. 107-8:90

Clean: as c. as a whistle 258:8

halo? ... one more thing to keep c. 140:32

make a c. breast 258:9

Cleaning: yesterday, we had daily c. 287:3

Cleanliness is next to godliness 258:10

Cleanly: thus so c. I myself can free 125:34

Cleanse the stuff'd bosom 336:72

Cleared: if this were only c. away 92:78

Clearing-house of the world 95:13

Clementine: oh my darling C. 225:59

Cleopatra: had C.'s nose been shorter 244:27

*Cléopâtre: le nez de C.* 244:27

Clergy: as the c. are, or are not 23:69

Clergymen: three sexes—men, women, and c. 375:9

Clerk: am I both priest and c. ? 350:57
   c. foredoom'd his father's soul to cross 248:78

Clerks: fountains like Government C. ? 285:78

Clever: c. of the turtle 229:98
   c. so rude to the good 409:59
   if all the good people were c. 409:59
   it's c., but is it art? 190:96
   let who will be c. 189:86
   our c. young poets 107:82
   too c. by half 280:49

Cleverness: height of c. ... to conceal one's c. 288:18

Climate: common where the c.'s sultry 84:66

Climax: that c. of all human ills 84:76

Climb: teach you how to c. 213:81

Climbing after knowledge infinite 205:76

Climbs: sun c. slow, how slowly 104:34

Clive: what I like about C. 33:17

Cloak: religion is ... the worst c. 276:84

Cloakroom: the c. at Victoria Station 405:12

Clock: mouse ran up the c. 232:34
   stand the church c. at ten to three? 71:91

Clocks: morning c. will ring 167:80
   the c. were striking thirteen 242:99

Clod: warm motion to become a kneaded c. 337:90

Cloke: Knyf under the c. 97:44

Close: breathless hush in the C. tonight 230:13
   c. yr. eyes with holy dread 107:76
   fiend doth c. behind him tread 106:60
   no barber shaves so c. but 255:91
   now ... c. the shutters fast 114:73
   porpoise c. behind us 91:62

Close (*continued*)
   the setting sun, and music at the c. 348:39

Closet: one by one back in the c. lays 135:78

Cloth: cut yr. coat according to ... c. 259:49
   on a c. untrue 146:8

Clothe: long fields ... that c. the wold 387:75

Clothed: she rode ... c. on with chastity 385:49

Clothes: fine c., rich furniture 31:87
   hanging out the c. 238:70
   kindles in c. a wantonness 162:16
   out of ... wet c. and into a dry Martini 409:57
   that liquefaction of her c. 162:23
   through tatter'd c. small vices 330:92
   walked away with their c. 122:89

Clothing: false prophets ... in sheep's c. 52:27

Cloud: a fiend hid in a c. 67–8:44
   but c. instead ... surrounds me 218:59
   every c. has a silver lining 258:12
   I wandered lonely as a c. 410:67
   on a c. I saw a child 68:48
   set my bow in the c. 35:50
   there ariseth a little c. 40:57
   through the dark c. shining 137:94
   to be under a c. 258:13
   turn the dark c. inside out 137:94

Clouds: never doubted c. wd. break 73:16
   O c., unfold! 67:38
   sun breaks through the darkest c. 355:25
   trailing c. of glory do we come 410:77

Clout: cast ne'er a c. 257:87

Clown: heard ... by emperor and c. 184:30

Cloy the hungry edge of appetite 348:37

Clutching the inviolable shade 21:43

Coals: carry c. to Newcastle 257:85
   haul over the c. 266:73
   heap c. of fire 45:81

Coarse: one of them is rather c. 15:64

Coast: the c. is clear 258:14

Coaster: dirty British c. 207:13

Coat: a riband to stick in his c. 74:28
   c. of many colours 36:62
   cut yr. c. according to yr. cloth 259:49

Cock: a C. and a Bull, said Yorick
379:72
before the c. crow twice  54:65
C. a doodle doo!  231:26
c. that crowed in the morn  239:79
Cock Robin: heard the bell toll for
poor C.  241:89
I killed C.  241:88
Cock-a-hoop: to be c.  258:15
Cock-and-bull story  258:16
Cockles: c. and mussels ... alive O!
17:89
warm the c. of the heart  282:5
Cockpit: can this c. hold ... fields of
France?  318:37
Cocks: drench'd our steeples, drown'd
the c.  328:71
Cocksure ... as Tom Macaulay  208:27
Cod: home of the bean and the c.
69:67
*Coeur: le c. a ses raisons*  244:28
Coffee: c. which makes the politicians
wise  252:38
if this is c., I want tea  285:87
*Cogito ergo sum*  119:31
Coil: shuffled off this mortal c.  309:95
Coin: beauty is nature's c.  213:79
pay ... in his own c.  274:31
Cold: caught an everlasting c.  401:56
c. comfort  258:18
comfort like c. porridge  356:37
I beg c. comfort  327:46
pale grew thy cheek and c.  86:99
poor Tom's a-c.  329:81
seedtime ... harvest ... c. and heat
35:48
slept among his ashes c.  182:92
'tis bitter c. and I am sick at heart
305:33
to lie in c. obstruction  337:90
to shelter me from the c.  32:6
we called a c. a c.  32:9
who thicks man's blood with c.
105:52
Colder thy kiss  86:99
Coliseum: when falls the C.  84:64
while stands the C.  84:64
College: I am Master of this C.  30:80
Colossus: bestride the ... world like a
C.  323:93
Colour: a c. of its own on the map
395:80
purest ... minds ... love c. the most
292:62
Coloured: see the c. counties  167:82
worser spirit a woman c. ill  364:55
Colours: all c. will agree in the dark
24:88

Colours (*continued*)
coat of many c.  36:62
truth fears no c.  281:61
Column: urn throws up a steamy c.
114:73
Columns: enormous fluted Ionic c.
203:56
Combine: love and marriage rarely can
c.  84:74
Come: but will they c. when you do
call?  314:72
c. and trip it as you go  214:94
c. back, Peter! C. back, Paul!
240:84
c., c. and have a drink  392:46
c., c. and make eyes at me  392:47
c., c., give me yr. hand  335:70
c. forth into the light of things
414:27
c., he slow or c. he fast  295:9
c., Helen, give me my soul  204:63
c. here often? ... in the mating
season  210:48
c., into the garden, Maud  388:86
c., knit hands  212:75
c., landlord, fill the flowing bowl
16:78
c., lasses and lads  16:79
c., let's away to prison  330:99
c., my coach!  311:25
c. not, Lucifer!  204:66
c. up and see me sometime  402:74
easy c., easy go  261:8
lightly c., lightly go  269:84
nothing of itself will c.  409:65
O c., all ye faithful ... c. ye  241:91
rise up, my love ... c. away  47:20
suffer me to c. to thee  402:70
the cry is still 'They c.'  336:74
thou'lt c. no more  331:6
will ye no c. back again?  228:81
Comedies: all c. are ended by a marriage  84:75
Comedy: most Lamentable C. ... of
Pyramus  341:39
world is a c. to those who think
398:23
Comes: c. from the heart, goes to the
heart  107:84
c. silent, flooding in, the main
103:33
here she c. ... full sail ... fan spread
109:10
knowledge c. but wisdom lingers
387:82
nobody c., nobody goes  30:74
repentance c. too late  276:86
tomorrow never c.  280:43

Comparisons: c. are odious 258:22
c. are odorous 343:77
Compassion: shutteth up his bowls of
c. 60:15
thou art all c. 402:72
Compassions: his c. fall not ... new
every morning 49:61
Competition: tradition approves all
forms of c. 103:30
Complain: moping owl ... to the
moon c. 155:32
sluggard, I heard him c. 400:41
Complaining: woods have no voice
but ... c. 227:72
Complete: let ... death c. the same
76:47
Complexion: his c. is perfect gallows
355:27
that schoolgirl c. 11:30
whose fresh c. and whose heart
362:24
Complies against his will 82:39
Comprehended: our watch ... have
indeed c. 343:79
Compromise: All ... founded on c. and
barter 78:74
Comrades, leave me here a little
387:78
Conceal: cleverness is to c. one's
cleverness 288:18
knowing anything, shd. c. it 23:73
use ... words ... to c. ... thoughts
397:10
Concealment, like a worm i' th' bud
360:89
Conceit: infusing him with self and
vain c. 350:54
Conceits: wise in yr. own c. 57:39
Concentrates: it c. his mind wonderfully 177:24
Concessions of the weak, ... c. ... of
fear 77:71
Conclusions: life ... art of drawing ...
c. 82:44
Condemn: age shall not weary ...
years c. 65:20
travellers ... fools at home c. 'em
356:48
Condemned: much c. to have an itching palm 325:23
Condemns: Johnson c. whatever he
disapproves 79:93
Condescend: your men of wit will c.
381:96
Condition: the c. of man ... c. of war
163:33
Conditions: stars above us, govern
our c. 329:87

Cones: eat the c. under his pines
139:26
Conference [maketh] a ready man
26:33
Confession is good for the soul 258:23
Confidence: we shall fight with growing c. 100:94
Confident: never glad c. morning
again 74:29
Conflict: never in the field of human c.
101:96
too weak the c. to support 330:3
Confound: Lord did ... c. the language
35:52
Confusion: all else, c. 389:2
c. to his enemies 16:85
levee from a couch in some c.
109:15
Congregation: latter has the largest c.
118:18
Conjecture: now entertain c. of a time
320:50
we c. ... animal or ... god 381:98
Conjunction: is the c. of the mind
206:98
Connect: only c. 137:96
Conquer: England ... wont to c.
others 349:42
we'll c. again and again 141:48
Conquered: I came, I saw, I c. 87:8
nation ... perpetually to be c. 78:72
Conquering: see the c. hero comes
226:68
so sharp the c. 97:50
went forth c., and to conquer 61:25
Conqueror: came in with Richard C.
355:19
lie at the proud foot of a c. 327:47
Conquers: love c. all and we too succumb 397:3
Conquest: a shameful c. of itself
349:42
peace is of the nature of a c. 317:23
Conquests: all thy c., glories, triumphs,
spoils 324:6
Conscience: a still and quiet c. 323:82
argue freely according to c. 224:44
catch the c. of the king 309:94
c. does make cowards of us all
309:95
my c. hath a thousand ... tongues
353:86
Consciousness: this growth of national
c. 203:53
Consecration: the c. and the poet's
dream 409:61
Consent: govern another man without
... c. 196:73

Consent *(continued)*
  'I will ne'er c.' – consented 84:67
  silence gives c. 277:38
Consented: whispering 'I will ne'er
  consent – c. 84:67
Consequence: business of c., *do it yourself* 27:51
Conservatism: what is c.? 196:77
Conservative: a c. government ...
  organised hypocrisy 122:90
  or else a little C. 144:87
  with more propriety be called the C.
  115:87
Consider: though justice be thy plea, c.
  339:15
Considereth: blessed is he that c. the
  poor 42:6
Consign to thee and come to dust
  305:30
Consolation: with peace and c. ... dismissed 223:27
Consorts: constitution ... c. ... with
  all things 72:2
Conspiracy: a c. to cheat the world
  176:6
  open-ey'd c. his time doth take
  356:39
Conspirators: all the c. save only he
  326:30
Conspiring ... how to load and bless
  with fruit 180:78
Constable: fit man for the c. of the
  watch 343:74
Constabulary duty's to be done
  148:33
Constancy: c. lives in realms above
  106:67
  hope c. in wind 85:91
  in c. follow the Master 77:64
Constant: a woman c. ... argues a
  decay 109:9
  c. you are, but yet a woman 313:61
  friendship is c. in all ... things
  342:62
  merciful as c., c. as various 154:22
  to one thing c. never 343:68
  were man but c. 361:11
Constitution: higher law than the C.
  297:37
  I am of a c. so general 72:2
  our C. is in ... operation 139:16
  principle of the English c. 66:25
Consul: Rome, born when I was c.
  103:21
Consults: neither c. ... nor trusts
  [women] 98:60
Consume: no more right to c. happiness 364:66

Consumed: bush burned ... was not c.
  36:69
Consummation: a c. devoutly to be
  wish'd 309:95
  quiet c. have 305:31
Consumption: remedy against ... c. of
  the purse 316:3
Contagion: breathes out c. to this
  world 310:13
  c. of the world's slow stain 367:16
  rot inwardly, and foul c. spread
  215:16
Contemplate: let us c. existence
  120:48
Contemplation: for c. he 219:66
  left for c. not what ... used to be
  34:24
Contempt: familiarity breeds c. 262:51
  familiarity breeds c. ... children
  394:67
  few [can bear] c. 254:60
  means ... for c. too high 112:47
Content: be c. with yr. wages 54:73
  but if I'm c. with a little 65:18
  c. to breathe his native air 251:28
  c. to have them ... course by course
  100:90
  farewell c.! 345:10
  in whatsoever state ... to be c.
  58:80
  let us draw upon c. 152:98
  where our desire is got without c.
  334:50
Consented: hermits are c. with their
  cells 411:89
Contentment: all enjoying, what c.
  find? 220:87
  where wealth and freedom ... c. fails
  151:92
Contests: what mighty c. rise from
  trivial things 251:33
Continence: chastity and c., but not
  yet 22:63
Continent: every man ...: a piece of
  the c. 124:13
Continued: how long so ever ... c. ...
  no force in law 104:38
Continuous as the stars that shine
  410:68
Contract between the king and the
  people 297:26
Contradict: very well, ... I c. myself
  403:87
Contradiction: woman's at best a c.
  still 251:26
Contraries: without c. is no progression 68:56
  wd. by c. execute all things 356:38

'Contrariwise',. continued Tweedledee 92:75

Contrary (Contrairy): everything goes c. with me 119:37
Mary, Mary, quite c. 235:55

Contrive to write so even 23:77

Contumely: the proud man's c. 309:95

Convent's narrow room 411:89

Conversation: our c. is in heaven 58:77

Conversationalist: to provide any industrious c. 169:2

Conversations: after-dinner c. over the wine 391:38

Converse: formed by thy c. 250:18

Conversing: with thee c. I forget all time 219:70

Converted: except ye be c. 53:37

Convicted of sickness, hunger 375:14

Convicts: they [Americans] are a race of c. 176:7

Convince: persuading others we c. ourselves 180:67

Cook: ill c. ... cannot lick his own fingers 258:26, 354:16
to c. one's goose 258:25

Cookery: kissing don't last: c. do! 209:36

Cooking: no c., or washing, or sewing 12:43

Cooks: as c. go she went 292:70
too many c. spoil the broth 280:50

Coolibah: shade of a c. tree 244:30

Coot: bald as a c. 255:89

Copulation: birth, and c., and death 131:9

Coral: c. is far more red 364:52
of his bones are c. made 355:35

Corbies: twa c. making a mane 12:40

Cord: a threefold c. is not quickly broken 46:99

Cords of a man, with bands of love 50:77

Corioli: flutter'd yr. Volscians in C. 304:19

Cormorant: c. devouring Time 331:8
sat like a c. 219:64

Corn: as soon ... hope ... c. in chaff 85:91
c. in Egypt 36:64
c. was orient and immortal wheat 392:53
cow's in the c. 234:49
farmer sowing his c. 239:79
in tears amid the alien c. 184:30
readers ... sway ... like ... ripe c. 130:89
when he treadeth out the c. 38:12

Corner: Jack Horner sat in the c. 235:50
keep a c. in the thing I love 345:8
some c. of a foreign field 71:92

Corners: unregarded age in c. thrown 300:77

Cornfield: down in de c. 138:3
o'er the green c. did pass 303:7

Cornish men: here's twenty thousand C. 158–9:74

Coromandel: on the Coast of C. 194:55

Coronets: kind hearts are more than c. 387:74

Corpse : he'd make a lovely c. 120:50

Correct: like magistrates, c. at home 318:39

Correcteth: whom the Lord loveth he c. 44:55

Corrupt: a people generally c. 78:86
art ... able to c. a saint 312:46
judge that no king can c. 322:78
power tends to c. 9:11
unlimited power is apt to c. 246:55

Corrupted the youth of the realm 321:68

Corrupteth: wanton love c. 25:99

Corruption: c. wins not more than honesty 323:83
vice whose ... c. inhabits 360:1

Corse: his c. to the rampart we hurried 408:52

Cortez: like stout C. 185:41

Cost: defend our island, whatever the c. may be 100–1:94

Costly: c. thy habit 306:56
Your Grace is too c. 343:65

Costs: nothing c. so much as what is given 273:5
victory at all c. 100:93

Cottage: wherever there's a c. small 244:24

Cottages: love lives in c. ... courts 270:15
poor men's c. princes' palaces 338:2

Cottleston, C. Pie 212:65

Cotton: from the c. fields away 138:7

'Couch: a levee from a c. 109:15
oft, when on my c. I lie 410:71
there I c. when owls do fly 357:56

Cough cannot be hid 270:8

Coughing drowns the parson's saw 332:20

Counsel: hard ... for women to keep c. 324:2
if the c. be good 259:29
justice, c., and treasure 25:7

Cover: c. her face: mine eyes dazzle
400:50
  c. thee with his feathers 43:19
  with leaves and flowers do c. 400:54
Covet: thou shalt not c.; but tradition
103:30
Coveting: pleasure ... is lost by c.
274:48
Cow: couple-colour as a brindled c.
166:68
  c. jumped over the moon 232:33
  c.'s in the corn 234:49
  c. with the cumpled horn 239:79
  .c., proportion, season 358:66
  I never saw a Purple C. 77:68
  I wrote the 'Purple C.' 77:69
  three acres and a c. 107:85
Coward: bully is always a c. 257:68
  c. does it with a kiss 404:94
  gross flattery to name a c. 392:48
  no c. soul is mine 71:84
Cowardice: pale cold c. in noble
breasts 347:32
Cowards: a plague of all c. 314:63
  conscience does make c. of us all
309:95
  c. die many times before ... deaths
324:1
  it [public] is the greatest of c. 159:82
  though c. flinch, and traitors jeer
109–10:21
Cowslip: in a c.'s bell I lie 357:56
Coy: be not c. but use yr. time 162:25
Coyness: this c., lady, were no crime
206:92
Crabs: roasted c. hiss in the bowl
332:20
Crack: stretch out to th' c. of doom?
335:64
  that heaven's vault shd. c. 330:4
  winds ... c. yr. cheeks 328:71
Cracked: it c. and growled and roared
105:46
Crackling of thorns under a pot 46:4
Cracks: now c. a noble heart 312:40
Cradle: the c. will rock 233:38
Cradles: bit the babies in the c. 75:37
Craft: c. so long to lerne 97:50
  gentlemen of the gentle c. 118:21
Cramp: when I heard she'd died of c.
153:10
Cravat: the one [robin] in red c.
122:85
Crawling: whereunder c. coop't we
live 136:80
Crazy: checkin' the c. ones 154:19
  I'm half c. 116:99
Creak of a lumbering cart 417:55

Cream: choking her with c. 189:91
  visages do c. and mantle 338:97
Created: about ... to be c. like to us
218:53
  c. man in his own image 34:28
  God c. the heaven 34:26
Creation: O fairest of c. 220:94
  our c. preservation 64:85
  she is His new c. 380:83
  to which the whole c. moves 387:73
Creature: God's first c., which was
light 27:40
  lone lorn c. 119:37
  she is an excellent c., but 123:1
  though the most beautiful C. ...
waiting 187:63
  wine is a good familiar c. 345:2
Creatures: all c. great and small
10:17
  call these delicate c. ours 345:8
  from fairest c. we desire 362:29
  the meanest of his c. 74:34
  true hope ... makes ... meaner c.
kings 352:83
Credit: citizen of c. and renown
112:54
  my c. in men's eyes 136:82
  stories ... not to thy c. 87:15
  to his c. ... is an Englishman!
147:29
Creditors have better memories 259:34
Creed: a modest c. and yet 370:47
Creeds: honest doubt ... than in half
the c. 386:65
  so many gods, so many c. 404:93
  vain are the thousand c. 71:85
Creeks: far back through c. and inlets
103:33
Creep: let the sounds of music c.
340:22
Creeping like snail ... to school
301:90
Creeps: when the blood c. ... nerves
prick 386:60
Crew: Mirth, admit me of thy c.
214:96
  we were a ghastly c. 105:58
Cricket: c. – a sport at which the contenders 172:44
  merry as a c. 272:56
  save the c. on the hearth 213:86
  to where the c. sings 417:53
Crime: atrocious c. of being ... young
246:54
  bigamy, sir, is a c.! 224–5:52
  cut-throat isn't occupied in c.
148:34
  for my wilful c. art banished 221:2

Crime (*continued*)

in heaven, a c. to love too well? 248:73

no c.'s so great as ... to excel 100:83

nor any c. so shameful as poverty 134:55

the Napoleon of c. 125:22

the punishment fit the c. 146:6

this coyness, lady, were no c. 206:92

treason was no c. 126:46

Crimes: c., follies and misfortunes of mankind 142:66

history of the great events ... history of c. 397:13

*l'histoire des c.* 397:13

*liberté, que de c. ... en ton nom* 288:26

liberty, what c. ... in yr. name 288:26

Crimson in thy lips and in thy cheeks 354:17

Cripple: comfort's a c. 125:32

Crispian: this day is call'd the feast of Crispian 320:57

Critic: first attribute of a good c. 200:26

scorn not the sonnet; C., you have frowned 412:95

Critical: I am nothing if not c. 345:97

Criticism: ask ... for c. ... only want praise 208:20

my own definition of c. 21:50

Criticisms: animals ... pass no c. 130:87

Critics: before you trust in c. 85:91

c. all are ready made 85:90

Crocodile: c. tears 259:35

how doth the little c. 89:45

Cromek: O! Mr. C., how do ye do? 67:42

Cromwell: restless C. cd. not cease 207:2

ruins that C. knocked about 197:87

see C., damned to everlasting fame 250:17

some C. guiltless 155:38

Crooked: c. by nature is never ... straight 259:36

straight trees have c. roots 279:84

strive to set the c. straight? 227:71

there was a c. man 239:74

Crop: a-watering the last year's c. 130:85

Cross: a little marble c. below the town 159:76

blind as the ... nails upon the C. 373:90

c. the bridge ... get to it 259:37

Cross (*continued*)

e'en though it be a c. 9:3

for our advantage on the bitter c. 312:43

one more river to c. 15:73

with the C. of Jesus 28:57

Cross-bow: with my c. I shot the albatross 105:47

Crosses: between the c., row on row 202:48

Cross-gartered: wishes to see thee ever c. 360:92

Crow: there is an upstart c. 156:49

Crowd: all at once I saw a c. 410:67

c. is not company 259:38

madding c.'s ignoble strife 155:39

out of the c. a mistress or a friend 368:25

trees ... shall c. into a shade 251:32

Crowded: feast, and yr. halls are c. 404:92

Crowds without company 142:65

Crowed: cock that c. in the morn 239:79

Crown: all thy faithful mercies c. 402:72

c. thy good with brotherhood 29:67

fighting for the c. 234:47

I give away my c. 350–1:58

I will give thee a c. of life 60:20

if you c. him, let me prophesy 350:56

let us c. ourselves with rosebuds 62:41

not the king's c. ... deputed sword 337:84

sweet fruition of an earthly c. 205:76

the holly bears the c. 16–17:87

this I count the glory of my c. 132:21

throned monarch better than his c. 339:15

uneasy ... head that wears a c. 317:14

virtuous woman ... c. to her husband 45:65

with the ... c. ... keeps Death his court 350:54

Crowns: evening c. the day 262:25

give c. and pounds and guineas 167:81

who c. ... a youth of labour 150:64

Crows: the c. and choughs that wing 329:88

Crucified: c. 'twixt a smile and a whimper 369:42

the dear Lord was c. 11:20

Crucify him 54:66

Cruel: I must be c. only to be kind
311:20

let me be c., not unnatural 311:14

more c. the pen is than the sword
81:30

Cruelly: I am c. used 23:79

Cruelty: farewell, fair c. 359:81

O c., to steal my Basil-pot 182:6

Crumb: a memorial c. 122:85

who craved no c. 148–9:46

Crumbs ... from the rich man's table
55:86

Cruse: neither shall the c. of oil fail
40:55

Crustimoney Proseedcake: what does
C. mean? 212:63

Cry: c. for the moon 259:39

c. 'Havoc!' 324:9

c. not when his father dies 172:56

c. out 'Olivia!' 359:80

c. woe, destruction, ruin 349:52

c. 'Wolf' 259:40

did they not sometime c. 'All hail'?
350:57

kissed the girls and made them c.
232:31

need a body c.? 79:3

the c. is still 'They come' 336:74

Crying over spilt milk 259:41

Cuckoo: but as the c. is in June 314:77

c., c. – O word of fear 332:19

lhude sing c. 15:71

O C., shall I call thee bird? 415:37

the c. then on every tree 332:19

the weather the c. likes 158:67

Cuckoo-buds of yellow hue 332:19

Cue: my c. is villainous melancholy
327:54

with a twisted c. 146:8

Cultivate: we must c. our garden
397:9

*Cultiver: il faut c. notre jardin* 397:9

Culture, the acquainting ourselves with
the best 21:53

Cunning: my right hand forget her c.
44:48

Cup: ah, fill the C. 135:74

C. that clears TO-DAY of past Regrets
135:69

kiss but in the c. 178:49

'twixt the c. and the lip 280:20

we'll tak' a c. o' kindness 79:1

Cupboard: c. love 259:42

Mother Hubbard went to the c.
236:59

Cupid: C. and my Campaspe 201:29

C. painted blind 341:38

C.'s darts do not feel 15:68

Cups that cheer but not inebriate
114:73

Curate: like the C.'s egg 259:43

Curb: you might c. yr. magnanimity
187:69

Curds: eating her c. and whey 235:51

Cure: past c., past care 274:28

prevention is better than c. 275:60

there is no c. for this disease 31:91

Cured: can't be c. must be endured
283:23

Curfew tolls the knell of parting day
155:30

Curiosity: newspapers always excite c.
192:31

Curious: that was the c. incident
125:23

'Curiouser and c.!' cried Alice 89:44

Curled: he ... c. up on the floor
158:73

Curls: rosy cheeks and flaxen c. 75:43

Curly locks, c. 231:27

Current: take the c. when it serves
326:27

Currents: their c. turn awry 309:95

Curs: mongrels, spaniels, c. 334:48

Curse: I know how to c. 355:33

O c. of marriage 345:8

the c. is come upon me! 387:77

work ... c. of the drinking classes
406:35

Curses are like chickens 259:44

Cursing: fall a-c. like a very drab
309:93

Curst be the verse 248:85

Curtain: ring down the c., the farce is
over 285:90

Curtained with cloudy red 216:22

Curtains: let fall the c., wheel the sofa
114:73

Curve: dear red c. of her lips 207:11

*Custodiet: quis c. ipsos custodes?*
180:69

Custom: a c. loathsome ... hateful ...
harmful 170:19

c. calls me to't 303:15

c. without reason ... ancient error
259:45

what c. wills ... shd. we do 303:15

Customary: said Owl, the c. procedure
212:63

Customers: a people of c. 374:98

Customs: the c., politics, and tongue
245:32

Cut: c. is the branch that might have
grown 204:67

c. it without a knife? 235:52

easy ... of a c. loaf to steal 357–8:63

Darjeeling: there was an old man from
   D.  14:56
Dark: a great leap in the d.  163:35
   all colours will agree in the d.  24:88
   all that's best of d. and bright  86:96
   as children fear to go in the d.  24:86
   creeping murmur and the poring d.
   320:50
   d. as the world of man  373:90
   d. backward and abysm of time
   355:29
   don't want to go home in the d.
   161:5
   ever-during d.  218:59
   good as my lady in the d.  268:24
   hellish d. and smells of cheese
   380:90
   in the morning's d.  117:14
   Joan as my Lady is as good i' th' d.
   162:21
   never to refuse a drink after d.
   209:30
   O d., d., d., amid the blaze  221:13
   the sun to me is d.  221:14
   we are for the d.  299:67
   what in me is d. illumine  216:29
Darken: the days d. round me
   385:53
Darkeneth: who is this that d. counsel?
   41:76
Darkling I listen  184:29
Darkly: see through a glass, d.  57:54
Darkness: a distant voice in the d.
   198:4
   and d. Night be named  220:84
   and light from d. ... divided  220:84
   d. again and a silence  198:4
   d. falls at they behest  132:24
   d. which may be felt  36:75
   in d. and with dangers compassed
   219–20:83
   leaves the world to d. and to me
   155:30
   lighten our d.  63:74
   men loved d. rather than light  55:1
   pestilence that walketh in d.  43:21
   ring out the d. of the land  387:71
   rulers of the d. of this world  58:74
   the d. deepens; Lord, with me abide!
   201:31
   the d. silvers away  70:75
   the people that walked in d.  48:35
Darling: Charlie is my d.  227:80
   d. buds of May  362:32
   d. of the Spring  415:38
   in thy green lap was Nature's d.
   156:44
   oh my d. Clementine  225:59

Darling (*continued*)
   Six years' d. of a pigmy size  411:69
   the d. of my heart  89:31
Darts: Cupid's d. do not feel  15:68
Dated: women and music shd. never
   be d.  151:88
Daughter: d. of Earth and Water
   368:23
   d. of Jove, relentless Power  155:43
   d. of the gods divinely tall  385:46
   D. of the Vine to Spouse  135:76
   don't put your d. on the stage
   112.44
   he that wd. the d. win  259:51
   like mother, like d.  272:71
   marry ... yr. d. ... when you can
   270:18
   skipper had taken his little d.  199:9
   stern D. of the Voice of God  413:7
   the King of Spain's d.  233:39
   truth is the d. of God  281:63
Daughter-in-law: remembers not ...
   she was a d.  272:72
Daughters: all the d. of my father's
   house  360:90
   d. of the Philistines rejoice  40:47
   d. of the uncircumcised triumph
   40:47
   here lie I and my four d.  12:41
   marry yr. d. betimes  271:48
   nor rain, wind ... are my d.  328:72
   sweet her artless d.  185:44
   the fairest of her d. Eve  219:67
   words are the d. of earth  172:41
David: D. ... escaped to the cave
   Adullam  39:45
   D. [hath slain] his ten thousands
   39:44
   D. took an harp and played  39:43
   once in royal D.'s city  10:19
   D. Copperfield kind of crap  292:71
Davy: Sir Humphrey D. detested gravy
   33:18
Dawn: till the dappled d. doth rise
   214:97
Daws: heart ... for d. to peck at
   344:89
Day: a thousand years as one d.  60:14
   a tip-toe when this d. is named
   320:57
   ah! when will this long weary d.
   377:39
   and those eyes, the break of d.
   337–8:92
   arrow that flieth by d.  43:20
   as morning shows the d.  221:6
   calm was the d.  377:46
   chanced to see at break of d.  411:85

**Day** (*continued*)

compare thee to a summer's d. 362:32
d. and night shall not cease 35:48
d. as sharp to them as thorn 351:59
d. for a man to afflict his soul 49:52
d. is short and the work is long 259:52
d. of death ... d. of ... birth 64:3
d. of Empires has come 95:14
d. of wrath, that dreadful d. 295:7
d. returns too soon 86:98
d.'s at the morn 75:44
d.'s journey take the whole long d.? 290:46
d.'s out and the labour done 73:9
d. thou gavest, Lord, is ended 132:24
d. unto d. uttereth speech 41:87
death of each d.'s life 334:42
death will have his d. 349:52
deficiencies of the present d. 173:61
dies at the opening d. 400:40
dog will have his d. 312:34
drinka pinta milka d. 11:26
dwell in realms of d. 66:31
each d. is like a year 404:97
eclipse without all hope of d.! 221:13
every d., in every way ... better 111:37
every d. to be lost 178:37
every dog has his d. 260:82
every dog its d. 189:89
from this d. forward, for better for worse 64:7
good morning to the d. ... my gold! 179:59
he that outlives this d. 320:57
how many hours bring about the d. 321:70
if every d. ... last d. but one 194:50
in the d. of judgement 63:79
in the shade on a fine d. 23:70
jocund d. stands tiptoe 354:14
known a better d. 295:99
lay it up for a rainy d. 275:78
light the D. ... He named 220:84
live to fight another d. 14:61
longest d. ... have an end 270:1
merry heart goes all the d. 361:19
murmur of a summer's d. 21:40
never a bad d. ... hath a good night 272:83
night is long that never finds the d. 335:67
not to me returns d. 218:59
now the d. is over 28:56

**Day** (*continued*)

O frabjous d.! 92:71
old age ... at close of d. 390:18
one d. is with the Lord as a thousand years 60:14
our little systems have their d. 386:56
power of the press ... last but a d. 395:77
rain it raineth every d. 360:3
remember the sabbath d. 37:86
Rome was not built in a d. 276:2
sailed ... for a year and a d. 195:61
seize the present d. 166:74
sing ... pray all the livelong d. 68:45
so foul and fair a d. 332:25
so rare as a d. in June? 200:25
sufficient unto the d. ... evil thereof 52:22
sweet d., so cool, so calm 161:14
the bright d. is done 299:67
the d. of small things 51:96
the light of common d. 411:78
this d. our daily bread 52:18
time ... runs through the roughest d. 333:29
uncertain glory of an April d. 361:6
until the d. break, ... shadows flee 47:24
yield d. to night! 321:62
**Daylight:** all the long and lone d. 368:31
when d. comes, comes in the light 104:34
**Days:** all the d. of Methuselah 35:43
Ancient of d. 50:73
as thy d. ... thy strength 38:16
chequer-board of nights and d. 135:78
d. of danger, nights of waking 295:97
d. seem lank and long 148:40
ere half my d. in this dark world 223:29
former d. ... better than these 46:5
good nights and sorry d. 271:44
how many d. will finish ... year 321:70
in good Queen Bess's glorious d. 144:89
in the belly of the fish three d. 50:86
in the mad March d. 207:13
King Charles's golden d. 17:91
loved three whole d. 380:86
my d. among the dead 376:25
my salad d. 298:53
now behold these present d. 363:46
of few d. and full of trouble 41:69

Days (*continued*)
 past our dancing d. 353:93
 shalt find it after many d. 47:9
 six d. shalt thou labour 37:86
 teach us to number our d. 43:18
 that has twenty-eight d. clear 239:77
 that thy d. may be long 37:87
 the d. of our years 43:17
 then, if ever, come perfect d. 200:25
 think warm d. will never cease
  181:79
 though fallen on evil d. 219–20:83
 what dark d. seen! 363:43
 while the evil d. come not 47:11
 world of happy d. 351–2:71
 year whose d. are long 404:97
Dazzle: mine eyes d.: she died young
  400:50
Dead: a character d. at every word
  372:76
 and they all d. did lie 105:55
 beside the wench is d. 204:71
 blow ... bugles, over the rich D.
  71:88
 concerning the d. [say] ... good
  259:54
 courage ... the devil is d. 286:1
 d.! and never called me mother!
  409:56
 d. as a door-nail 259:55
 d. for a ducat, d.! 311:17
 dew on the face of the d. 30:84
 doctors found when she was d.
  150:74
 down among the d. men 129:78
 faith without works is d. 60:4
 great deal to be said for being d.
  33:17
 healthy and wealthy and d. 392:42
 it struck him d.: and serve him right
  31:94
 just as d. as if he'd been wrong 13:50
 little fairy ... falls down d. 28:60
 my days among the d. 376:25
 nearly all our best men are d.!
  285:85
 need charity more than the d. 20:29
 on stepping-stones of their d. selves
  386:57
 Queen Anne is d. 275:73
 say I'm sick, I'm d. 248:78
 something ... d. in each of us 404:95
 soul is d. that slumbers 198:95
 that d. men rise up never 383:20
 the law hath not been d. 337:85
 the noble D. 413:10
 'tis Death is d., not he 367:17
 to see a d. Indian 356:40

Dead (*continued*)
 two worlds, one d. 20:36
 view halloo wd. awaken the d.
  154:20
 wake, for night is d. 383:24
 we might as well be d. 401–2:69
 weep for Adonais, he is d. 367:9
 when I am d. and opened 207:10
 when I am d., my dearest 290:47
Deadener: habit is a great d. 30:76
Deadlock: Holy D. 161:10
Deadly: soap ... more d. in the long
  run 393:64
Deaf: d. as a post 259:58
 none so d. as those who won't hear
  260:59
Deafness: your tale ... wd. cure d.
  355:30
Deal: a new d. for the American
  people 289:27
 d. with none but honest men 276:87
 good enough to be given a square d.
  289:37
Dean: I am the D. of Christ Church
  378:54
 queer old D. 377:51
Deans: with ... dowagers for d. 388:95
Dear: a man ... to all the country d.
  150:66
 beauty ... for earth too d. 353:94
 d. to me as light and life 80:9
 God! that bread shd. be so d.!
  166:65
 Plato is d. to me 20:28
 the d. God who loveth us 106:64
Dearie: flew o'er me and my d. 80:9
Deario: its cheerio my d. 205:83
Death: a rendezvous with D. 296:20
 a sunset-touch, a fancy ... some one's
  d. 73:17
 after the first d. ... no other 390:22
 all in the valley of D. 385:40
 all tragedies are finished by a d.
  84:75
 and d. complete the same 76:47
 and d. shall have no dominion
  390:17
 and now to d. devote 220:94
 Angel of D. has been abroad 70:80
 any man's d. diminishes me 124:14
 as one that had been studied in his d.
  333:30
 be thou faithful unto d. 60:20
 because I cd. not stop for D. 122:84
 birth, and copulation, and d. 131:9
 brood over ... the hour of my d.
  187:65
come away, d. 359:88

**Death** (*continued*)

day of d. [is better] 46:3

d. after life does greatly please 377:42

d., as the Psalmist saith, is certain 317:17

d., be not proud 124:10

d. devours lambs as well 260:60

d. for his ambition 325:11

d. hath no more dominion 56:31

d. is an ende of every ... sore 97:45

d. is the grand leveller 260:62

d. ... like all the rest, a mockery 370:47

d. of each day's life 334:42

d. pays all debts 260:62

d.'s pale flag is not advanced 354:17

D., whene'er he call ... too soon 148:44

die not, poor d. 124:10

die the d. of the righteous 38:4

disappointed by that stroke of d. 178:43

dread of something after d. 309:95

every door ... shut but d.'s door 260:87

fear and danger of violent d. 163:34

for love, and beauty ... no d. 370:48

give me liberty or give me d. 161:6

half in love with easeful D. 184:29

happy ... were my ensuing d. 349:42

his d., which happened in his berth 165:59

how wonderful ... D. and ... Sleep! 368:24

I have set before you life and d. 38:13

I here importune d. awhile 299:65

I will not be afraid of d. and bane 336:73

I'll ... condemn you to d. 90:46

if ought but d. part 39:34

in nativity, chance, or d. 341:34

in that sleep of d. what dreams? 309:95

in the hour of d. 63:79

in the ranks of d. 226:64

in their d. ... not divided 40:48

into the jaws of D. 385:43

it is but D. who comes at last 295:9

judge none blessed before his d. 62:52

keep a league till d. 351:60

love is strong as d. 47:27

men fear d., as children ... dark 24:86

midst of life we are in d. 65:14

most cruel d. of Pyramus 341:39

**Death** (*continued*)

my part of d. no one so true 359–60:88

never taste of d. but once 324:1

no one till his d. ... unhappy 73:9

nothing is certain but d. and taxes 139:16

O D., where is thy sting? 57:60, 247:71

pale D. with impartial foot 166:73

pale horse ... that sat on him was D. 61:26

paradise to what we fear of d. 337:91

precious ... the d. of his saints 43:33

rashly importunate, gone to her d. 165:56

remedy for all ... but d. 276:85

reports of my d. ... exaggerated 394:75

sad stories of the d. of kings 350:54

so many years of fearing d. 324:4

the way to dusty d. 336:76

there is d. in the pot 40:61

there shall be no more d. 61:34

thou wast not born for d. 184:30

through envy of the devil came d. 62:42

till d. us do part 64:7

'tis D. is dead, not he 367:17

useless life is an early d. 150:59

valley of the shadow of d. 42:93

vasty Hall of D. 21:38

wages of sin is d. 56:32

we owe God a d. 317:19

Webster ... much possessed by d.. 131:13

what sights of ugly d. 352:72

when d. to either shall come 70:79

where is d.'s sting? 201:33

whose mortal taste brought d. 216:27

within the hollow crown keeps D. his court 350:54

worst is d. and d. will have his day 349:52

wd. fain die a dry d. 355:28

**Deaths:** cowards die many times before ... d. 324:1

more d. than one must die 404:96

**Debate:** Rupert of D. 76:53

**Debonair:** so buxom, blithe and d. 214:92

**Debt:** contrived a double d. to pay 150:70

d. is the worst poverty 260:63

the d. which cancels all others 108:1

Debts: and forgive us our d. 52:18
death pays all d. 260:62
he that dies pays all d. 356:46
speak not of my d. unless 278:61
Decay: be sincere ... argues a d. 109:9
d. of that colossal wreck 369:40
energies of our system will d. 27:48
fretted the ... body to d. 126:39
this muddy vesture of d. 340:22
wealth accumulates, and men d.
150:62
Deceased: he first d.; she for a little
tried 416:47
Deceive: Oh, don't d. me 16:80
to d. oneself is very easy 260:65
when first we practise to d. 296:13
Deceived: by bad women been d.
222:15
d. her father, and may thee 345:95
Deceivers: men were d. ever 343:68
Deceives me once ... d. me twice
260:64
December: as soon seek roses in D.
85:91
D. when they are wed 302:4
wallow naked in D. snow 348:37
Decent: d. godless people 131:8
d. means poor 245:35
Decently: things done d. and in order
57:57
Deck: boy stood on the burning d.
160:89
Declare: nothing to d. except my
genius 406:33
Decoration: deserves some sort of d.
242:9
Decoyed into our condition 245:42
Decreed: soul has to itself d. 185:36
Dee: lived on the river D. 65:16
Deed: a d. without a name 335:61
a good d. in a naughty world 340:25
if one good d. ... I did 358:64
now the matchless d.'s achieved
374:95
so I may do the d. ... my soul ...
decreed 185:36
Deeds: d. are males, and words are
females 260:66
means to do ill d. ... d. ill done
327:45
these unlucky d. relate 346:22
turn sourest by their d. 363:42
Deep: call spirits from the vasty d.
314:72
d. and crisp and even 229:3
in the lowest d., a lower d. 218:62
thoughts ... too d. for tears 411:82
two voices ... one is of the d. 378:62

Deep (*continued*)
very singularly d. young man 146:15
Deeper than did ever plummet sound
357:55
Deer: in the Highlands, a-chasing the
d. 81:20
the running of the d. 16–17:87
Defaced, deflowered 220:94
Defamed by every charlatan 387:72
Defeat: in D.: Defiance 102:10
the problems of victory ... of d.
101:5
Defect: chief d. of Henry King 31:90
Defence or apology before ... accused
95:19
Defend: d. ... yr. right to say it 398:16
from my enemies ... d. myself
264:18
they [newspapers] never d. anyone
208:28
we shall d. our island 100–1:94
Defender: I mean the Faith's D. 83:53
Defiance: in Defeat: D. 102:10
Defied: age will not be d. 26:22
Definition: true d. of a style 381:3
Definitions: homely d. of prose and
poetry 107:82
Deflowered: defaced, d. 220:94
Deformed, unfinish'd, sent before my
time 351:66
Degree: a d. of delight ... in ... misfortunes 78:88
O, when d. is shak'd 358:67
observe d., priority and place 358:66
people ... a d. or two lower 23:64
take but d. away 358:68
Degrees: did ever heal but by d.?
345:3
we boil at different d. 133:45
Delay: in d. ... lies no plenty 359:84
in me is no d. 221:2
Delayed till ... I cannot enjoy ...
impart it 174:78
Delays are dangerous 260:68
Deliberate: where both d., the love is
slight 205:81
Deliberates: woman that d. 9:5
Deliberation: deep on his front engraven d. sat 218:52
Delicate: we can call these d. creatures
ours 345:8
Delicately: Agag came ... d. 39:41
Delight: a Phantom of d. 414:16
d. in ... misfortunes ... of others
78:88
d. ... ornament ... ability 26:30
energy is eternal d. 68:57
go to't with d. 299:62

**Destroy:** doth the wingèd life d. 66:34
I sought to d. institutions 403:79
'tis safer to be that which we d.
334:50
whom God wishes to d. 275:74
**Destroyer** and preserver; hear, oh,
hear! 369:36
**Destruction:** by d. dwell in doubtful
joy 334:50
d. that wasteth at noonday 43:21
pride goeth before d. 45:72
**Detail:** our life is frittered away by d.
391:37
**Determined,** dared and done! 374:95
**Detest:** but they d. at leisure 85:84
**Detraction** will not suffer it 315:88
*Deutschland über alles* 164:38
**Device:** banner with the strange d.
197:93
miracle of rare d. 107:75
**Devil:** abashed the D. stood 219:73
better the d. you know 256:30
between the d. and the deep sea
260:72
black as the d. 256:41, 384:30
courage ... the d. is dead 286:1
d. ... builds a chapel 118:18
d. can cite Scripture 338:4
d., having nothing else to do 31:96
d. is not so black 260:73
d. shd. have all the good tunes
163:29
d.'s walking parody 99:68
d. take the hindmost 260:74
d. was sick ... a monk wd. be 227:74
d. was well ... a monk he'd be
227:74
d. whoops, as he whooped 190:96
drink and the d. had done for 379:74
every man ... god or d. 126:44
first Whig was the D. 177:28
give the d. his due 264:8
he ... that sups with the d. 270:99
heaviest stone ... d. can throw
159:84
hold a candle to the d. 267:91
needs must when the d. drives
272:82
renounce the d. ... his works 64:95
resist the d. and he will flee 60:6
saint when most I play the d. 351:70
shame the d. 279:16
talk of the d. ... sure to appear 279:6
the D., howling Ho! 378:55
the world, the flesh, and the d. 63:78
through envy of the d. came death
62:42
who cleft the d.'s foot 124:11

**Devil** (*continued*)
young saint, old d. 284:65
your adversary the d., as a roaring
lion 60:12
**Devils:** prosperity has damned more ...
than ... d. 275:65
*Devoir: faites votre d. et laissez faire
aux dieux* 111:33
**Devon,** glorious D. 69:68
*Dévot: pour être d. ... pas moins
homme!* 224:50
**Devotion:** dollar ... object of universal
d. 170:18
the d. to something afar 371:56
**Devour:** threat'ning to d. me opens
wide 218:62
**Devout:** d. but ... human 224:50
miserable, but not ... d. 173:65
**Dew:** d. on the face of the dead 30:84
foggy, foggy d. 17:96
hill-side's d.-pearled 75:44
like the d. on the mountain 295:98
resolve itself into a d. 305:42
walks o'er the d. of yon ... hill
305:36
**Dew-drop:** fragile d. on its perilous
way 185:35
*Diable: courage ... le d. est mort* 286:1
*noir comme le d.* 384:30
**Dials:** carve out d. quaintly 321:70
**Diamond:** d. and safire bracelet lasts
199:11
like a d. in the sky 384:36
**Diana** of the Ephesians 56:21
**Diary:** I never travel without my d.
405:14
memory ... is the d. 405:13
**Dick** the shepherd blows his nail
332:20
**Dickens:** what the d. his name is
340:31
**Dictate:** not presume to d., but broiled
fowl 120:60
**Dictator:** the German d., instead of
snatching 100:90
**Did:** d. nothing ... d. it very well
144:90
d. that they d. in envy of great
Caesar 326:30
nor ever d. a wiser one 288:21
sang his didn't he danced his d.
116:94
**Dido** found Aeneas wd. not come
252:40
**Di-do-dum:** Dido ... was D. 252:40
**Die:** a man can d. but once 317:19
and shall Trelawny d.? 158:74
appointed unto men once to d. 59:97

Die (*continued*)

as a man lives, so shall he d.   271:34
as natural to d.   24:87
beauty's rose might never d.   362:29
beauty that must d.   183:22
beneath its shade we'll live and d.
  109:21
break faith with us who d.   202:49
cowards d. many times   324:1
crawling coop't we live and d.
  136:80
d. a dry death   355:28
d. all, d. merrily   315:81
d. and go we know not where   337:90
d. because a woman's fair   408:49
d. beyond my means   406:34
d. in the last ditch   79:90
d. not, poor death   124:10
d. ... the last thing I shall do!   243:21
do d. of it do seldom ... recover
  299:68
how can man d. better?   201:36
I shall d. at the top   382:13
I will d. ere she shall grieve   408:50
I will d. in the last ditch   406:36
if I shd. d. think only this   71:92
if we are mark'd to d.   320:55
in what peace a Christian can d.
  10:12
lay me down and d.   124:16
leave me there to d.   17:88
let me d. the death of the righteous
  38:4
let us do or d.   81:23
look about us and to d.   250:7
love her till I d.   18:9
love too much ... d. for love   271:21
lovers ... d. as soon as one pleases
  109:13
man can only d. once   271:28
more deaths than one must d.
  404:96
never say d.   273:87
no young man believes he shall ... d.
  159:80
Oh, Sir! the good d. first   409:64
people d., but books never d.   289:33
said I wd. d. a bachelor   343:70
see Naples and d.   277:22
seemly ... to d. for one's country
  167:77
seems it rich to d.   184:29
shd. certain persons d. before they
  sing   106:70
soon as ... born, he begins to d.
  278:54
swans sing before they d.   106:70
Tamburlaine ... must d.   205:79

Die (*continued*)

the d. is cast   87:7
the Man perceives it d. away   411:78
theirs but to do and d.   385:42
they ... d. by famine, d. by inches
  161:1
those about to d. salute you   380:88
to d. ... awfully big adventure   28:61
to d., to sleep   309:95
to d. upon a kiss   347:23
toddle ... home and d. in bed   293:82
we must be free or d.   413:5
when good ... bad ... Americans d.
  406:25
who wd. wish to d.?   69:65
with my little eye, I saw him d.
  241:88
you asked this man to d.   22:58
young men may d., old men must
  284:63

Died: d. maintaining his right of way
  13:49
d. when his prospects ... brightening
  12:42
in the odour of sanctity d.   28:54
laugh! I thought I shd. have d.   99:79
liked it not, and d.   416:47
men have d. ... but not for love
  302:3
queens have d. young and fair
  229:99
she damned near d.   17:96
she had d. of cramp   153:10
she shd. have d. hereafter   336:76
since Maurice d.   70:77
stopped short ... when the old man
  d.   416:43
the dog it was that d.   151:77
to the North-west d. away   74:24
who d. to save us all   11:20
wd. God I had d. for thee   40:51
wd. to God we had d. ... in ...
  Egypt   36:79

Dies: flower ... once has blown for
  ever d.   135:71
he that d. pays all debts   356:46
light of the bright world d.   69:70
love ... soon as beauty d.   123:6
no man happy until he d.   375:22
not how a man d., but how he lives
  175:98
person who either marries or d.
  23:67
say that when the Poet d.   295:3
the king never d.   66:24, 268:36
what an artist d. with me!   230:10

Diet: all necessaries ... d. unparalleled
  120:52

Diet (*continued*)
no ... idiosyncrasy in d.   72:2
praise is the best d.   375:10
*Dieu: D. est ... pour les gros bataillons* 398:15
*si D. n'existait pas*   397:12
Differ: men ... d. as Heaven and Earth 385:52
Different: how d. from us, Miss Beale 15:68
Difficult: all things are d. before ... easy   280:24
d. ..., Sir? I wish it were impossible 178:40
problems of victory ... no less d. 101:5
Dig: I cannot d.; to beg I am ashamed 55:83
Digest: mark, learn, and inwardly d. 64:86
Digestion: d. ... great secret of life 375:12
now good d. wait on appetite 335:54
things sweet ... prove in d. sour 348:35
Diggeth: whoso d. a pit shall fall   46:85
Dignities: peace above all earthly d. 323:82
Dignity and worth of the human person   394:76
Diminish one dowle ... in my plume 356:49
Diminished: stars hide their d. heads 218:61
Diminishes: any man's death d. me 124:14
Dimmed: glory of the sun will be d. 27:48
Dine: and go to inns to d.   99:76
I shd. d. at Ware   113:59
if wife shd. d. at Edmonton   113:59
Noah ... when he sat down to d. 99:77
'whar shall we ... d. the day? 12:40
Dined on mince and ... quince   195:62
Ding: d. dong, bell   232:28
sing hey d. a d. d.   303:7
Dinner: a d. lubricates business   296:18
best number for a d. party   157:54
d. of herbs where love is   45:71
good d. enough to be sure   175:92
good d. upon his table   178:45
people who want d. do not ring 27:46
Diplomat these days ... a head-waiter 395:82
Direction: all chance, d.   250:12

Directions: rode madly off in all d. 194:51
Dirge: by forms unseen their d. is sung 107:90
Dirt: fling d. enough ... will stick 263:73
Dirty: hail fellow ... all d. and wet 381:4
Disadvantage: ship has ... d. of ... danger   177:16
Disappointments: I have been too familiar with d.   196:72
Disapprove: I d. ... but will defend ... yr. right   398:16
Disapproves: condemns whatever he d. 79:93
Disaster: meet with Triumph and D. 190:4
valiant ... 'gainst all d.   77:64
Disasters: day's d. in his morning face 150:68
we make guilty of our d.   327:53
Disbelief: willing suspension of d. 107:79
Disciplines: I know the d. of war 320:49
Discobolus: the D. standeth ... dusty ... maimed   82:47
Discommendeth: he who d. others 72:98
Discontent: winter of our d.   351:64
Discord: all d., harmony not understood   250:12
hark what d. follows!   358:68
Discount: sells us life at a d.   140:33
Discouragement: no d. shall make him ... relent   77:64
Discover: doth ... d. vice ... d. virtue 24:92
Discretion: an ounce of d. is worth 274:24
being now come to the years of d. 64:2
better part of valour is d.   315:93
d. is the better part of valour   260:76
fair woman ... without d.   45:64
philosophy ... nothing but d.   296:33
Disdain: d. and scorn ride sparkling 343:71
what, my dear Lady D.!   342:58
Disease: d. [consumption of purse] is incurable   316:3
remedy ... worse than the d.   25:9
strange d. of modern life   21:42
'There is no cure for this d.'   31:91
this long d., my Life   248:81
when age, d., or sorrows strike him 103:27

Diseases: among all the d. of the mind
378:59

    desperate d. ... desperate remedies
260:71

    d. desperate grown 311:21

    subject to the same d. 339:13

Disgrace: am out, even to a full d.
304:18

    its private life is a d. 15:70

    my learned profession ... never d.
144:84

Disgruntled: if not ... d., ... far from
... gruntled 408:51

Dish: a d. fit for the gods 324:99

    butter in a lordly d. 39:23

    d. ran away with the spoon 232:33

    goblets for a d. of wood 350:55

    he will to his Egyptian d. 299:58

    was not that a dainty d. 238:70

Dishes: no washing of d. 12:43

    thou shalt not wash d. 231–2:27

    washed the d. with his wife 226:70

Dishonour: d. stain the brow of my
young Harry 312:44

    his honour rooted in d. 385:50

Dishonourable: find ourselves d. graves
323:93

Dislike what I fancy I feel 13:51

Dismay: let nothing you d. 16:82

Dismayed; was there a man d.? 385:41

Disobedience: of Man's first d. 216:27

Disobedient: for a drudge, d. 151:79

    not d. unto the heavenly vision
56:27

Disobey: naughty girl to d. 236:57

Disorder: a sweet d. in the dress
162:16

    her last d. mortal 150:74

Dispose: unsearchable d. of Highest
Wisdom 222:26

Disposes: man proposes, God d.
271:36

Disposition: a truant d. 306:47

    put an antic d. on 307:70

Disputation: a feeling d. 314:75

Dispute: my right there is not to d.
114:77

Dissimulation: let love be without d.
57:37

Dissipation without pleasure 142:65

Dissolute: in the d. city 411:87

Dissolve: all which it inherit shall d.
356:50

    and then ... I d. it in rain 368:22

Distance: d. lends enchantment 88:20

    sixty seconds' worth of d. 190:5

Distinction: reverence ... doth make d.
304:27

Distress: a deep d. hath humanised
409:62

Distressed: mind quite vacant is a
mind d. 113:67

Distributed: dollars ... will not be d.
103:23

Ditch: both shall fall into the d. 52:33

    die in the last d. 79:90

    I will die in the last d. 406:36

Ditchwater: as dull as d. 261:99

Ditties of no tone 183:17

Dive into the bottom of the deep
313:54

Diver: don't forget the d. 180:74

Diverse, sheer opposite 182:94

Diversion: walking ... a country d.
109:16

*Divide et impera* 260:77

Divide: d. and rule 260:77

    d. the living child in two 40:53

    to d. is not to take away 368:26

Divine: depth of some d. despair
388:99

    one far-off d. event 387:73

    study the past ... d. the future 108:3

Divinely tall and most d. fair 385:46

Divinity: by these we reach d. 123:5

    d. in odd numbers 341:34

    d. that shapes our ends 312:35

    such d. doth hedge a king 311:27

Divorced old barren Reason 135:76

Dizzy 'tis to cast one's eyes 329:88

Do: as I wad d., were I Lord God
202:50

    business of consequence, d. it your-
self 27:51

    can I d. you now, sir? 180:73

    d. as I say, not as I d. 296:24

    d. as you're bidden 260:80

    d. as you wd. be done by 260:79

    d. nothing ... damage his career
28:64

    d. other men ... they wd. d. you
120:49

    d. ... that one can pay others to d.
208:23

    d. thou but thine 220:88

    d. what seemeth him good 39:37

    d. ye even so to them 52:25

    from having too little to d.
190–1:15

    I am to d. what I please 139:19

    I don't mind if I d. 180:75

    knows not what to d. 231:26

    let us d. or die 81:23

    never d. today what you can put off
284:76

    the Lord d. so to me 39:34

Do (*continued*)

    we never d. anything well till 159:85

    what men dare d. ... daily d. 343:80

    what you can d. for yr. country 188:75

Doch-an'-dorris 193:42

Dock: in a dull, dark d. 145:3

Doctor: God heals ... d. takes the fee 264:19

Doctrine: d. is that each one shd. select 368:25

    d. of a strenuous life 289:35

    from women's eyes this d. I derive 331:16

    not for the d., but the music 249:98

Doctrines: makes all d. plain and clear 82:38

Dodger: sobriquet of 'The artful D.' 120:56

Dog: as a d. returneth to his vomit 46:84

    beware of the d. 246:49

    d. did nothing in the night-time 125:23

    d. does not eat d. 260:81

    d. is turned to his own vomit 60:13

    d. it was that died 151:77

    d.'s walking on his hind legs 175:90

    d., to gain some private ends 151:76

    d. will have his day 312:34

    d. will not howl if you beat 260:83

    every d. has his d. 260:82

    every d. its day 189:89

    fetch her poor d. a bone 236:59

    give a d. a bad name 264:6

    I am His Highness' d. at Kew 251:30

    if you call a d. Hervey 174:73

    keep a d. and bark yourself 268:27

    let no d. bark 338:98

    love me, love my d. 270:19

    mine enemy's d., though he had bit me 330:95

    misbeliever, cut-throat d. 338:6

    pray tell me sir, whose d. are you? 251:30

    rather be a d. and bay the moon 325:24

    teach an old d. tricks 279:12

    the little d. laughed 232:33

    the young man's d. with them 62:40

    they grin like a d., and run 42:12

    took by th' throat the circumcised d. 346–7:22

    when a d. bites a man 116:1

    why should a d. ... have life? 331:6

Dogged: it's d. as does it 393:55

Dogs: barking d. seldom bite 255:95

    clept all by the name of d. 334:48

Dogs (*continued*)

    d. bark at me as I halt 351:66

    fought the d. and killed the cats 75:37

    let sleeping d. lie 269:71

    let slip the d. of war 324:9

    mad d. and Englishmen 112:42

    two d. strive ... a third runs ... with [bone] 281:76

    uncover, d., and lap 357:61

Doing: joy's soul lies in the d. 358:65

    let us then be up and d. 198:98

    nothing – half so much worth d. 153:13

    saying is one thing and d. another 277:16

    see what she's d. and tell her she mustn't 285:81

    shortest answer is d. 277:33

    what was he d. ... god Pan? 73:13

    worth d. at all is worth d. well 98:55

    worth d. is worth d. well 283:24

Doings: all our d. without charity 64:87

    even a child is known by his d. 45:76

Doit: a d. to relieve a lame beggar 356:40

Dollar: almighty d. ... object of ... devotion 170:18

Dollars: however plenty ... d. may become 103:23

Dolore: *nessun maggior d. che ricordarsi* 116:3

Dolphin: a mermaid on a d.,s back 341:44

Dome: a d. of many-coloured glass 367:19

Dominion: death hath no more d. 56:31

    death shall have no d. 390:17

    hand that holds d. over man 390:20

    I'm truly sorry man's d. 80:17

Dominions on which the sun never sets 230:18

Don: remote and ineffectual d. 32:1

Done: do as you wd. be d. by 260:79

    d. those things ... we ought not 63:67

    easier said than d. 261:6

    nothing d. while aught remains to do 288:24

    put off ... what may be d. today 273:85

    so little d., so much to do 287:7

    something ought to be d. 401:66

    surprised to find it d. 175:90

    thank God I have d. with him 174:79

**Done** (*continued*)
    they d. the old woman in  366:97
    things d. cannot be undone  260:86
    to have loved ... thought ... d.  20:31
    'twere well it were d. quickly  333:35
    well begun is half d.  282:21
    what have I d. for you, England?
      160:96
    what's d. cannot be undone  335:70
**Dong** with a luminous Nose  194:56
**Donkey:** talk the hind leg off a d.
    279:5
**Donne:** another Newton, a new D.
    169:4
    D.'s verses ... the peace of God
    170:20
**Doom:** even to the edge of d.  363:48
    stretch out to th' crack of d.  335:64
**Doomed** for a ... term to walk the
    night  307:63
**Doomsday:** d. is near; die ... merrily
    315:81
    then is d. near  308:79
**Doon:** banks and braes o' bonnie D.
    81:26
**Door:** a beaten path to his d.  133:48
    a d. must be ... open or shut  227:78
    a D. to which ... no key  135:73
    at her ivied d.  87:11
    every d. ... shut but death's d.
      260:87
    fortune knocks, open the d.  263:87
    keep the d. of my lips  44:51
    keep the wolf from the d.  283:45
    knocking at Preferment's d.  21:41
    knocking on the moonlit d.  118:23
    love ... goes out at the d.  270:12
    stand at the d., and knock  61:24
    three, four, knock at the d.  236:60
    thy form from off my d.  247:67
**Doorkeeper:** I had rather be a d.  43:15
**Doors:** d. ... being as yet shut upon me
    187:60
    pale Death ... knocks at the d.
    166:73
**Dotheboys Hall:** at ... D. Youth are
    boarded  120:52
**Dots:** what those damned d. meant
    100:87
**Double:** d., d., toil and trouble  335:58
    surely you'll grow d.  414:25
**Double entendre:** the horrible d.  13:53
**Doubled** him up for ever  143:73
**Doublethink** means ... two contradic-
    tory beliefs  242:4
**Doubt:** 'I d. it,' said the Carpenter
    92:79
    more faith in honest d.  386:65

**Doubt** (*continued*)
    new philosophy calls all in d.  123:3
    no probable ... possible d. whatever
    143:72
    when in d., leave out  283:27
    when in d., win the trick  168:87
**Doubted:** never d. clouds wd. break
    73:16
**Doubtful:** by destruction dwell in d.
    joy  334:50
**Doubting:** a castle called D. Castle
    77:62
**Doubts:** begin with d., ... end in
    certainties  26:37
    he shall end in d.  26:37
    knows nothing, d. nothing  268:49
    saucy d. and fears  335:53
**Douglas:** Judge D. and myself  196:76
    old song of Percy and D.  373:87
    the D. in his hall  296:12
**Dove:** beside the springs of D.  413:15
    d. came ... in the evening  35:47
    my d., my dear ... my life  388:87
    Oh that I had wings like a d.!  42:10
**Dove-cote:** like an eagle in a d.  304:19
**Doves:** grass is as soft as the breast of
    d.  111:34
**Dowagers:** with ... d. for deans  388:95
**Dowdiness:** memory ... beginning of d.
    406:32
**Dower:** faith's transcendent d.  413:14
**Down:** d., d. to hell  322:73
    d. will come baby, cradle  233:38
    easier to pull d. than to build  275:69
    get d. you dirty rascal  233:41
    he that is d. ... fear no fall  77:66
    I don't think one 'comes d.'  242:10
    levers to lift me ... being d.  313:57
    never go d. to the end of the town
    211:57
    quite, quite d.  310:1
**Downstairs:** be off, or I'll kick you d.
    90:49
**Doxy** over the dale  361:17
**Drab:** a-cursing like a very d.  309:93
    ditch-deliver'd by a d.  335:59
**Dragon:** Saint George, that swing'd
    the d.  326:35
**Drain:** leave by the next town d.
    377:50
**Drake** he's in his hammock  230:11
**Draughts:** shallow d. intoxicate the
    brain  249:94
**Draw:** d. back ... to leap better  267:11
    d. but twenty miles a-day?  205:78
    must d. the line somewhere  260:88
**Drawers:** hewers of wood and d. of
    water  38:19

Dread: close your eyes with holy d. 107:76
doth walk in fear and d. 106:60
d. and fear of kings 339:15
d. of something after death 309:95
Dreadful: dancing? Oh, d. 79:91
death ... mighty and d. 124:10
O! d. is the check 71:87
the acting of a d. thing 324:98
Dream: a sight to d. of 106:66
a vision or a waking d.? 184:32
and slowly read, and d. 417:58
awoke ... from a deep d. of peace 168:94
behold it was a d. 77:63
consecration, and the poet's d. 409:61
d. of battled fields no more 295:97
d. of money-bags to-night 339:9
d. you are crossing the Channel 144:92
fly, forgotten, as a d. dies 400:40
glory and the freshness of a d. 410:72
if you can d. 190:3
life is but an empty d. 198:95
lust of fame was but a d. 71:86
not d. them, all day long 189:86
oaks ... d., and so d. all night 182:98
old men shall d. dreams 50:80
perchance to d. Ay, there's the rub 309:95
phantasma or a hideous d. 324:98
the glory and the d. 410:76
they d. of home 137:94
wrecks of a dissolving d. 368:28
Dreamed: d. of cheese—toasted, mostly 379:75
I d. that Greece might ... be free 84–5:78
Dreamer: behold, this d. cometh 36:63
d. of dreams 227:71
poet and the d. 182:94
Dreaming: city with her d. spires 21:46
d. arl the time o' Plymouth Hoe 230:11
Dreams: fanatics have their d. 182:93
into the land of my d. 189:84
more things ... than this world d. 386:55
nature lends such evil d. 386:62
not make d. yr. master 190:3
read of ... or dreamt of in d. 28:53
so full of fearful d. 351:71
such stuff as d. are made on 356–7:50
wovest d. of joy and fear 368:32

Dreamt: d. of in yr. philosophy 307:69
d. that I dwelt in marble halls 76:55
I have long d. of such a ... man 318:34
read of ... or d. of 28:53
Dreary: how d. to be somebody 122:81
world am sad and d. 138:6
Drenched with dew, Old Nod the shepherd 118:25
Dress: a sweet disorder in the d. 162:16
all d. is fancy d. 366:6
noble youths did d. themselves 316:8
Drill: no names, no pack d. 273:96
Drink: a rule never to d. by daylight 209:30
d. and the devil had done for the rest 379:74
d. 'a pinta milka day 11:26
d. deep, or taste not the Pierian spring 249:94
'D. ME' beautifully printed 89:43
d. no longer water 59:90
d. to me only with thine eyes 178:49
d. with him that wears a hood 380:81
five reasons we shd. d. 10:16
lead a horse ... cannot make him d. 269:62
man wants but little d. 164:47
much d. ... equivocator with lechery 334:45
nor any drop to d. 105:50
shall sit and d. with me 32:7
taste for d., combined with gout 143:73
that I might d., and leave the world 184:24
what shd. we do for d.? 15:65
Drinking: continual d. of Knowledge 186:59
diverted by every means but d. 177:20
d. Cheltenham waters 12:41
d. is the soldier's pleasure 127:53
d. largely sobers us again 249:94
d. the blude red wine 12:37
there are two reasons for d. 245:37
Drinks his wine 'mid laughter free 19:10
Driven: soul ... d., I know not whither 401:55
Drives the flower ... d. my green age 390:19
Driving: d. of Jehu ... he driveth furiously 40:62

Driving (*continued*)
  spend my life in d. briskly  177:23
Drone: the lazy, yawning d. 318–19:39
Drop: every d. of the Thames  79:94
  nor any d. to drink  105:50
  raineth d. and staineth slop  252:47
Drops: little d. of water  89:41
  women's weapons, water-d.  328:68
Dross: all is d. that is not Helena 204:63
Drought of March hath perced  96:25
Drown: I'll d. my book  357:55
  what paid ... to d.  352:72
Drowned: drench'd our steeples, d. the cocks  328:71
  d. in the depth of the sea  53:38
  d. my Honour in a shallow Cup 136:82
  pluck up d. honour by the locks 313:54
Drowning: d. man ... catch at a straw 260:90
  no d. mark upon him  355:27
Drowns things weighty and solid  26:35
Drudge: for a d., disobedient  151:79
  *lexicographer*—a harmless d.  172:46
Drum: listenin' for the d.  230:11
  not a d. was heard  408:52
  the spirit-stirring d.  345:10
  war-d. throbbed no longer  387:81
Drummed them out of town  234:47
Drummers: nine d. drumming  238:73
Drums: hearts ... like muffled d. are beating  198:96
  sound the trumpets, beat the d. 127:52
Drunk: d. as a fish  260:91
  d. as a lord  260:92
  d. as a mouse  260:93
  d. as a wheelbarrow  260:94
  d. the milk of Paradise  107:76
  man ... must get d.  84:71
  never [happy] but when he is d. 176:13
  not so think as you d.  378:56
  stag at eve had d. his fill  294:94
  this meeting is d.  121:73
Drunkard: the rolling English d. made the rolling English road  99:72
Drunken: do with the d. sailor  19:14
  d. folks seldom take harm  260:95
  d. night ... cloudy morning  261:96
  went to Worts and got more d. 252:41
Drunkenness: babbling d.  360:1
Dry: a d. brain in a d. season  130:93
  as d. as dust  261:97

Dry (*continued*)
  but oh, I am so d.  17:88
  die a d. death  355:28
  hearts ... d. as summer dust  409:64
  old man in a d. month  130:92
Dublin: in D.'s fair city  17:89
Duchess: I am D. of Malfi still  400:47
  the D.! Oh, my dear paws!  90:47
  the D. said, in a hoarse growl  90:50
Duck: dying d. in a thunderstorm 261:2
  water off a d.'s back  282:11
Duckling: The Ugly D.  11:24
Ducks and drakes: to made d. of 261:98
Due: to give the devil his d.  264:8
  one born out of d. time  57:58
Duke: became a most important d. 32:4
  everybody praised the D.  376:30
Dukedom: library was d. large enough 355:31
*Dulce et decorum est pro patria mori* 167:77
Dull: as d. as ditchwater  261:99
  d. in himself, ... cause of dullness 11:12
  d. wd. he be of soul  412:96
  prophetick blessing—Be thou d. 127:49
Dullness: Shadwell ... mature in d. 128:69
Dumb: d. men get no lands  261:1
  great [cares] are d.  269:82
Duncan is in his grave  334:51
Dunce: a d. ... kept at home  113:65
  a d. ... sent to roam  113:65
  a d. with wits  247:69
Dundee: bonnets of Bonny D.  294:92
Dunfermline: king sits in D. town 12:37
Dungeon: live upon the vapour of a d. 345:8
Dunsinane: till Birnam Forest come to D.  336:73
Dusk: in the d. ... light behind her 148:42
  little breezes d. and shiver  387:76
Dust: a d. whom England bore  71:93
  all lovers must ... come to d.  305:30
  as chimney-sweepers, come to d. 304–5:29
  as dry as d.  261:97
  ashes to ashes, d. to d.  65:15
  before we too into the D. descend 135:70
  cinders, ashes, d.  183:11
  d. hath closed Helen's eye  229:99

Dust (*continued*)

d. in the air suspended 130:97

D. into D., and under D. to lie 135:70

d. on antique time wd. lie unswept 303:15

d. thou art, and unto d. 35:39

d. thou art, to d. returnest 198:95

guilty of d. and sin 161:12

hearts are dry as summer d. 409:64

make d. our paper 349:53

name ... not perish in the d. 376:26

not without d. and heat 223:39

pays us but with age and d. 286:93

pride that licks the d. 248:86

rotting together have one d. 304:27

vile d. from whence he sprung 295:6

what is the quintessence of d.? 308:81

Dust-heap: great d. called history 65:21

Dusty: d. cobweb-covered, maimed 82:47

the way to d. death 336:76

what a d. answer gets the soul 209:34

Dutch: my dear old D. 99:80

Duties: embark ... on the d. of the day 143:75

let us ... brace ourselves to our d. 101:95

lowliest d. on herself did lay 413:4

property has its d. 126:35

Duty: ashamed of ... declares it is his d. 364:65

do yr. d. and leave the rest to the Gods 111:33

every man will do his d. 229:7

man's first d.? ... To be himself 169:11

my d. in that state of life 64:99

no d. we so ... underrate 379:79

O D! if that name thou love 413:7

picket's off d. forever 30:84

Thank God, I have done my d. 230:8

the path of d. was the way 388:94

the whole d. of man 47:14

when constabulary d.'s to be done 148:33

when service sweat for d. 300:79

Dwell: poor souls who d. in night 66:31

those who d. in realms of day 66:31

Dwelling: fix in us thy humble d. 402:72

Dwelt: she d. among the untrodden ways 413:15

Dwindle into a wife 109:18

Dying: a most unconscionable time d. 96:20

a slowly d. cause 386:69

doubly d. shall go down 295:6

echoes, d., d., d. 388:98

I am d., Egypt, d. 299:65

it had a d. fall 358:75

'tis not the d. for a faith 389:9

to-morrow will be d. 162:24

truth sits upon the lips of d. men 21:45

unmoved see thee d. ... frog! 121:64

Eagle: an e. mewing her mighty youth 224:43

does the E. know? 66:32

in and out the E. 203:60

like an e. in a dove-cote 304:19

the way of an e. 46:91

Eagles: where his e. never flew 112:50

Ealing: boarded a bus bound for E. 14:56

Ear: a rich jewel in an Ethiop's e. 353:94

choose a wife ... by yr. e. 258:2

deaf adder that stoppeth her e. 42:11

every man thy e., but few thy voice 306:56

give e. unto my song 150:75

in at one e. and out at the other 267:16

more is meant than meets the e. 213:87

not to the sensual e. 183:17

O, it came o'er my e. 358:75

reasonable good e. in music 342:51

silk purse out of a sow's e. 277:39

softly her warm e. lays 200:25

vexing the dull e. of a drowsy man 327:41

when the e. begins to hear 71:87

wd. have won the e. of Pluto 215:6

Earl: an e. by right, by courtesy a man 24:82

Earl of Craven: mistress of the E. 407:43

Early: call me e., mother dear 388:89

e. one morning, just as the sun 16:80

e. to bed and e. to rise 261:5

e. to rise ... wealthy and dead 392:42

get up e. ... to take in God 200:20

she was one of the e. birds 110:23

vain ... to rise up e. 44:42

Earnest: Live is real, Life is e. 198:95

Earnings: equal division of unequal e. 132:25

Earns: he e. whate'er he can 199:7

Ears: e. burn, someone is talking 261:3
    have e., but they hear not 43:31
    he that hath e. to hear 54:56
    lend me your e. 325:12
    make two e. of corn ... to grow
        381:2
    music creep in our e. 340:22
    noise of waters in my e. 352:72
    put this engine to our e. 381:98
    softest music to attending e. 354:5
    there was a shout about my e. 99:69
    to e. of flesh and blood 307:64
    walls have e. 282:99
Earth: a girdle round about the e.
        341:45
    a Heaven on E. 219:65
    a ladder set up on the e. 36:61
    a new heaven and a new e. 61:32
    all people that on e. do dwell 188:77
    created the heaven and the e. 34:26
    daughter of E. and Water 368:23
    dear e., I do salute thee 349:49
    differ as Heaven and E. 385:52
    dim spot which men call E. 212:73
    e. has not anything ... more fair
        412:96
    e. is the Lord's, and the fulness
        42:94
    e.'s diurnal course 414:19
    e.'s sweet flowing breast 188–9:81
    e.'s the right place for love 139:21
    e. to e., ashes to ashes 65:15
    e. was without form, and void 34:26
    firm place ... I will move the e. 20:24
    from this e., this grave, this dust
        286:93
    heaven to e., from e. to heaven
        342:53
    Heaven tries e. if it be in tune 200:25
    Judge of all the e. 35:54
    kings are e.'s gods 347:26
    lards the lean e. as he walks 313:59
    lay her i' th' e. 312:32
    multiply and replenish the e. 34:29
    old sad e. must borrow its mirth
        404:91
    past away a glory from the e. 410:74
    poetry of e. is never dead 135:42
    shall not perish from the e. 196:79
    the e. abideth for ever 46:95
    the e. and every common sight
        410:72
    the e. ... appear ... [a] faery place
        415:39
    the e. doth like a snake renew 368:28
    the e., tideless and inert 27:48
    the meek shall inherit the e. 42:2
    there were giants in the e. 35:44

Earth (*continued*)
    this e. of majesty, this seat of Mars
        348:41
    this e., this realm, this England
        348–9:41
    thou bleeding piece of e. 324:8
    through my lips to unawakened e.
        369:38
    while the e. remaineth, seedtime
        35:48
    write sorrow on the bosom of the e.
        349:53
    yours is the E. and everything 190:5
Ease: bankrupt of life, ... prodigal of e.
        126:40
    done with so much e. 126:37
    for another gives its e. 67:43
    not the doctrine of ignoble e.
        289:35
    O Woman! in our hours of e. 296:14
    through the air with the greatest of e.
        196:71
    true e. in writing comes from art
        249:99
    youth of labour ... age of e. 150:64
Easiest: the e. way out 401–2:69
Easy come, e. go 261:8
East: a long way e. of Camberwell
        32:4
    E. is E., and West is West 189:92
    gorgeous E. with richest hand
        217:45
    in the chambers of the E. 68:54
    it is the e. and Juliet is the sun
        353:97
    somewhere E. of Suez 190:8
    we have seen his star in the e. 51:2
Eastern: like a blooming E. bride
        127:50
    not by e. windows only 104:34
Eat: dare to e. a peach 131:4
    did e. bread to the full 36:79
    dog does not e. dog 260:81
    e. and welcome 261:10
    e. one's words 261:11
    e. to live ... not live to e. 261:12
    e. yr. cake and have it 261:13
    great ones e. up the little ones
        347:27
    I always e. peas with honey 15:63
    I cannot e. but little meat 380:81
    let us e. and drink; for tomorrow
        we ... die 48:40
    my apple trees will never ... e.
        139:26
    so I did sit and e. 161:13
    some ... canna e., ... some wad e.
        81:24

'Elementary,' said he [Holmes] 124:21
Elements: e. of whom yr. swords are
    temper'd 356:49
    framed us of four e. 205:76
    I tax not you, you e. 328:72
    our torments also may ... become
    our e. 217:51
    the e. so mix'd in him 326:31
Eleven: e. buckram men ... out of two
    314:66
    rain before seven, fine before e.
    275:75
Eleventh Commandment ... not be
    found out 261:16
Elf: a servant's ... an impudent e.
    27:51
Elijah ... cast his mantle 40:59
Eliminated: when you have e. the im-
    possible 125:25
Elinor: 'I am afraid,' replied E.
    23:80
Elizabeth: no scandal about Queen E.
    371:63
    spacious times of great E. 385:45
Eloquence: love and business teach e.
    270:9
Elsewhere: when e., live as they live e.
    11:23
Elves of hills, brooks, ... groves 357:54
Ely: my Lord of E., when I was ... in
    Holborn 352:74
Elysium: what E. have ye known?
    183:14
*Embarras des richesses* 11:21
Embarrassing: the e. young 141:50
Embers: glowing e. through the room
    213:86
    O joy! that in our e. ... doth live
    411:80
Embodiment: the Law is the true e.
    143:81
Embody: I, my Lords, e. the Law
    143–4:81
Embrace: arms, take your last e.
    354:18
    none, I think, do there e. 206:95
Eminence: by merit raised to that bad
    e. 217:45
Emotion recollected in tranquillity
    416:42
Emperor: heard ... by e. and clown
    184:30
    to the tent-royal of their e. 318:39
Empire: all the loungers of the E.
    125:27
    another mighty E. overthrown!
    413:6
    how is the E.? 142:63

Empire (*continued*)
    if the British E. ... last for a thousand
    years 101:95
    King dead, the e. unpossess'd?
    352:82
    Mother E. stands splendidly isolated
    137:99
    neither holy, nor Roman, nor an e.
    398:14
    preside over the liquidation of the
    British E. 101:3
    the E. is a Commonwealth of Nations
    290:40
    to found a great e. 374:98
    young was called to E. 128:68
Empires: day of E. has come 95:14
    vaster than e. and more slow
    206:93
Employment: give e. to the artisan
    31:94
    the pleasantness of an e. 23:80
Empty vessels make the most noise
    261:18
Enchanted: as holy and e. 106:72
Enchanter: ghosts from an e. fleeing
    369:35
Enchantment: lends e. to the view
    88:20
Encourage: kill an admiral ... to e. the
    others 397:8
*Encourager: pour e. les autres* 397:8
Encumbers: Patron ... e. him with help
    174:78
End: a loud noise at one e. 191:21
    'a made a finer e. 319:43
    ages of hopeless e. 217:50
    attempt the e. 162:22
    beginning of the e. 384:29
    big e.-ians and small e.-ians 381:99
    boys get at one e. ... lose at the other
    176:15
    e. justifies the means 261:19
    everything hath an e. 262:33
    found no e., in wandering mazes lost
    218:55
    four ... winters ... springs e. in a
    word 348:34
    he shall e. in certainties 26:37
    long weary day have e. 377:39
    longest day must have an e. 270:1
    Lord, make me to know mine e.
    42:5
    more than an e. to war, we want
    289:34
    my last e. be like his! 38:4
    not even the beginning of the e. ...
    but ... the e. of the beginning
    101:2

End (*continued*)
  our minutes hasten to their e.  363:40
  seen one thing, that love hath an e. 383:22
  the e. of this day's business  326:29
  the man would die ... and there an e. 335:55
  the right true e. of love  123:8
  Sans Wine ... Song ... E. 1  135:70
  vegetate and wish ... an e.  79:92
  yes, to the very e.  290:46
Endeavour: a disinterested e. to learn 21:50
Ending: e. is better than mending 168:98
  love is ... sour in the e.  270:14
Endowed by their Creator with ... rights  171:26
Ends: divinity that shapes our e. 312:35
  dog, to gain some private e.  151:76
  make both e. meet  257:61
  odd old e. stol'n forth of holy writ 351:70
  to serve our private e.  100:84
Endurable: love [will] make a thing e. 411:88
Endure: cannot e. in his age  343:69
  cd. e. the toothache patiently  344:86
  first e., then pity, then embrace 250:14
  from age to age e.  188:78
  youth's a stuff will not e.  359:84
Endured: can't be cured, must be e. 283:23
  much is to be e.  173:64
  tolerable and not to be e.  343:75
Enemies: confusion to his e.  16:85
  left me naked to mine e.  323:84
  love your e.  52:14
Enemy: best ... e. of the good  397:11
  better an open e.  255:14
  here shall he see no e.  300:83
  how goes the e.?  287:5
  if thine e. be hungry  45:81
  mine e.'s dog  330:95
  my name ... terrible to the e.  316:2
  of yr. e. say nothing  278:62
  the e. faints not  103:32
  trust not ... an old e.  281:60
Energetic: our speech ... e. without rules  172:40
Energies of our system will decay 27:48
Energy: e. is eternal delight  68:57
  reason and e., love and hate  68:56
*Enfants: les e. terribles*  141:50
*Enfer: chaud comme l'e.*  384:30

Engine: e. that moves in determinate grooves  158:68
  put this e. to our ears  381:98
England: a body of E.'s, breathing English air  71:93
  a dust whom E. bore  71:93
  a time there was, ere E.'s griefs 150:63
  be E. what she will  100:82
  between France and E. is the sea 171:38
  E., bound in with the triumphant sea 349:42
  E. expects every man  229:7
  E. has saved herself ... save Europe 247:57
  E. hath need of thee  413:3
  E. ... hell for horses  81:31, 261:20
  E. is a nation of shop-keepers 228:85
  E. is the mother of parliaments 71:81
  E. is the paradise of women  81:31, 136:86, 261:20
  E., my E.? E. my own  160:96
  E.'s green and pleasant land  67:38
  E. will have her neck wrung  101:1
  E., with all thy faults  114:70
  E. ... wont to conquer others  349:42
  Florence, Elizabethan E.  170:13
  for E.'s the one land  71:90
  foreign field ... forever E.  71:92
  gallows standing in E. when thou art king?  312:45
  gentlemen in E., now abed  320:59
  Happy is E.! I cd. be content  185:43
  heart and stomach of ... King of E. 132:20
  high road that leads him to E. 175:85
  history of E. is ... history of progress 202:45
  I know the kings of E.  147:31
  if E. to itself do rest but true  327:48
  in E. – now!  74:21
  in E. we ... rely on ... time-lag 401:66
  know of E. who only E. know? 190:97
  laws of E. are at my commandment 318:33
  light such a candle ... in E.  193:40
  men in E. that do no work today 320:54
  my love for E. and Ireland  287:11
  nor, E., did I know till then  409:66
  not three good men unhang'd in E. 314:64

England (*continued*)
  *Oats.* – ... in E. ... given to horses
    172:48
  Oh, to be in E.   74:21
  on E.'s pleasant pastures seen
    67:38
  people of E. that never have spoken
    yet 99:75
  roast beef of E.  134:61
  Stately Homes of E.   111:39, 40
  stately homes of E.!   160:90
  there'll always be an E.   244:24
  this earth, this realm, this E.
    348–9:41
  this E. never did ... lie at the ... foot
    327:47
  'Tis for the honour of E.   109:8
  wake up, E.   142:62
  walk upon E.'s mountains   67:38
  ye mariners of E.   88:21
  youth of E. are on fire   319:40
English: a body of England's, breath-
    ing E. air   71:93
  be among the E. Poets after my death
    187:62
  blood of E. shall manure the ground
    350:56
  Chaucer, well of E. undefiled   377:44
  E. are ... the least ... pure philo-
    sophers   27:45
  E. as she is Spoke   393:57
  E. never know when ... beaten
    261:21
  E. winter—ending in July   85:85
  grave where E. oak and holly   158:72
  on, on, you noblest E.   319:46
  our E. tongue a gallimaufry   377:48
  principle of the E. constitution
    66:25
  the E. ... a foul-mouthed nation
    159:79
  the E. country gentleman   406:27
  the E. have hot-water bottles   209:40
  the rolling E. drunkard made the
    rolling E. road   99:72
  the sort of E. up with which   102:9
  trick of our E. nation   316:1
  under an E. heaven   71:94
  wholesome ... really nice E. people
    365:72
  winged heels, as E. Mercuries
    319:40
  with our E. dead   319:45
Englishman: an E., even ... alone,
    forms a ... queue   209:41
  an E. thinks he is moral   365:82
  E. does not travel to see Englishmen
    379:65

Englishman (*continued*)
  E. ... enjoys himself ... for a noble
    purpose   161:9
  E.'s home is his castle   261:22
  my-lorded as only a free-born E. can
    389:13
  rights of an E.   180:65
  stirred the hearts of every E.   294:91
  the last great E. is low   388:92
  to his credit ... an E.!   147:29
  way to an E.'s heart   282:13
Englishmen: mad dogs and E.   112:42
  reveal Himself ... first to his E.
    224:42
  when two E. meet ... talk of the
    weather   172:51
Engross: pens a stanza when he shd. e.
    248:78
Enigma: a riddle wrapped in a mystery
    inside an e.   100:91
Enjoy: can thoroughly e. the pepper
    90:52
  e. themselves so well, as at ... tavern
    177:17
  prize not ... whiles we e. it   343:81
  who can e. alone?   220:87
  you will never e. the world   392:52
Enjoyed: e. no sooner but despised
    363:50
  human life ... little to be e.   173:64
  that bards of old e.   68:55
  to have e. the sun   20:31
  what peaceful hours I once e.   113:62
Enjoyment: variety is the mother of e.
    123:99
Enjoys: the Englishman never e. him-
    self   161:9
Enough: e. is as good as a feast   65:18,
    261:23
  e. is e.   261:24
  e. that there *is* a beyond   364:64
  grant me ... more than e.   203:59
  wore e. for modesty   76:15
Enriched: pension never e. a young
    man   274:38
Enriches: robs me ... not e. him   345:6
*Ense: calamus saevior e. patet*   81:30
Ensign: beauty's e. yet is crimson
    354:17
  tear her tattered e. down   164:46
  th' imperial e. ... high advanced
    217:39
Enter: abandon hope all ye who e.
    116:2
  e. ye in at ... strait gate   52:26
  ye shall not e. into ... Kingdom
    53:37
Enterprise: the e. is sick   358:67

Enterprises: e. of great pith and moment 309:95
impediments to great e. 24:96
Entertaining: more e. than half the novels 208:22
Enthroned in the hearts of kings 339:15
Enthusiasm: considering that e. moves the world 27:49
long for a little ordinary e. 242:8
'nothing great ... without e. 132:28
Enthusiasts: so few e. ... speak the truth 27:49
Entire and whole and perfect 377:53
Entrance: beware of e. to a quarrel 306:56
Entrances: have their exits and their e. 301:90
Envied: better be e. than pitied 255:17
Envious: rent the e. Casca made 325:18
Envy: e. and calumny and hate and pain 367:16
e., hatred, and malice 63:77
in e. of great Caesar 326:30
means ... too low for e. 112:47
the e. of less happier lands 348–9:41
Ephesians: Diana of the E. 56:21
Epilogue: a good play needs no e. 303:11
Epitaph: believe a woman or an e. 85:91
Epitaphs: a nice derangement of e. 372:71
graves and worms and e. 349:53
Epithet: fair is too foul an e. for thee 205:77
Epitome: all mankind's e. 126:43
*Eppur si muove* 141:44
Epsom Salts: had we but stuck to E. 12:41
Equal: all animals are e. but some are more e. 242:98
e. division of unequal earnings 132:25
far from ... true ... naturally e. 175:96
inferiors revolt ... be e. 20:27
that all men are created e. 171:26
Equals [revolt] that they may be superior 20:27
Eros: unarm, E.; the ... task is done 299:64
Err: better to e. with Pope 85:92
not e., who say ... when the Poet dies 295:3
the most may e. as grossly 127:47
to e. is human 267:7

Err (*continued*)
to e. is human, to forgive divine 249:4
Errand: in thy joyous e. reach the spot 136:83
Errands for the Ministers of State 143:76
Erred: we have e. and strayed 63:66
Erring: a rod to check the e. 413:7
Error: custom without reason ... ancient e. 259:45
e. of opinion may be tolerated 171:28
gross e. held in schools 142:59
if this be e. and upon me prov'd 363:48
ignorance is preferable to e. 171:32
mountainous e. ... highly heap'd 303:15
Errors: amusing with numerous e. [book] 152:95
e., like straws, upon the surface 127:55
if to her share some female e. 251:34
Esau: E. my brother ... a hairy man 36:59
the hands of E. 36:60
Escape: e. me?—never 74:27
thou shalt not e. calumny 310:98
who shall e. whipping? 308:88
Essence: his glassy e., like an angry ape 337:87
Estate: become a fourth e. of the realm 202:44
ordered their e. 10:18
Esteem: riches I hold in light e. 71:86
Esteemed: better to be vile than vile e. 363:49
Esther: loved E. above all ... women 40:64
*État: l'É. c'est moi* 199:12
Eternal: abode where the E. are 368:20
condition ... liberty ... e. vigilance 116:98
energy is e. delight 68:57
e. summer gilds them yet 84:77
on Fame's e. beadroll 377:44
thought ... to be boy e. 361:12
Eternity: damned from here to E. 190:99
deserts of vast e. 206:94
e. in an hour 66:27
lives in e.'s sunrise 66:34
make the mighty ages of e. 89:41
memorial from the soul's e. 290:49
passing through nature to e. 305:40
stains the white radiance of E. 367:19

Eternity (*continued*)
thoughts that wander through e. 217:49

Etherised: evening is spread out ... like a patient e. 130:98

Ethiop: a rich jewel in an E.'s ear 353:94

Ethiopian: can the E. change his skin? 49:56

Eton: Waterloo ... won on the playing fields of E. 401:61

Euphelia serves to grace my measure 253:51

Euripides: a chorus-ending from E. 73:17

Europe: all E. shd. know that we have blockheads 109:8
glory of E. is extinguished 78:78
lamps are going out all over E. 156:51
last territorial claim ... in E. 163:31
part of the community of E. 149:54
save E. by her example 247:57
Soviet power into heart of Western E. 102:7
splendidly isolated in E. 137:99
we are ... smallest country left in E. 395:80

Eurydice: half-regained E. 215:6

Eve: fairest of her daughters E. 219:67
from noon to dewy e. 217:44
when Adam delved and E. span 27:50
when E. upon the first of Men 165:63

Even: contrive to write so e. 23:77

*Événements: l'histoire des grands é.* 397:13

Evening: bright exhalation in the e. 322:79
e. crowns the day 262:25
e. is spread out against the sky 130:98
I light my lamp in the e. 32:5
it is a beauteous e. 412:92
It was a summer's e. 376:27
like an e. gone 399:39
now came still e. on 219:69
shadows of the e. steal 28:56
the winter e. settles down 131:7
whoso turns as I, this e. 74:25

Event: heaviness foreruns the good e. 317:22
one far-off divine e. 387:73
wise after the e. 261:9
wisest prophets make sure of the e. 398:44

Ever: but I go on for e. 384:39

Ever (*continued*)
do nothing for e. and e. 12:43
for e. and for e. farewell, Cassius! 326:28
for e. hold his peace 64:5
if for e., still for e. 85:93
left lonely for e. 20:34
that no life lives for e. 383:20
thou art gone, and for e. 295:98
what, *never*? Hardly e.! 147:22
wished him to talk on for e. 159:78

Everlasting: caught an e. cold 401:56
condemn'd into e. redemption 344:84
had stood [wheat] from e. to e. 392:53
primrose way to th' e. bonfire 334:44
that the E. had not fix'd 305:42

Everybody: e. praised the Duke 376:30
e. wants to have read 394:73
friend to e. ... friend to nobody 264:94

Everyman, I will go with thee 14:58

Everyone: e. ... put his whole wit 29:70
e. suddenly burst out singing 293:83
war of e. against e. 163:33

Everything: a smattering of e. 121:78
can resist e. except temptation 405:19
e. by starts and nothing long 126:43
e.'s got a moral 91:57
God saw e. ... he had made 35:30
sans taste, sans e. 301-2:90
sermons in stones, and good in e. 300:75
with e. that pretty bin 304:20

Everywhere: e. be bold 377:43
e. that Mary went 157:55
water, water e. 105:50

Eves: on summer e. by haunted stream 214:3

Evidence of things not seen 59:99

Evil: abhor that which is e. 57:37
all partial e., universal good 250:12
be not overcome of e. 57:41
care not whether ... good or e. 67:37
decide ... for the good or e. side 200:24
deliver us from e. 52:18
doing e. on the ground of expediency 290:39
E., be thou my Good 218:63
e. be to him who e. thinks 267:95
e. is wrought by want of Thought 165:62

**Evil** .490

Evil (*continued*)
e. that men do lives after them 325:12
e. which I wd. not, that I do 56:33
government ... a necessary e. 243:20
I will fear no e. 42:93
knowing good and e. 35:36
love of money ... root of all e. 59:92
loved darkness ... their deeds were e. 55:1
Luke ... gave himself to e. courses 411:87
maketh ... sun to rise on the e. 52:15
nature lends such e. dreams 386:62
of moral e. and of good 414:28
on e. days ... fallen, and e. tongues 219–20:83
out of good ... find means of e. 216:32
overcome e. with good 57:41
purer eyes than to behold e. 51:92
resist not e. 52:13
root of all e. The want of money 82:41
set good against e. 265:28
supernatural source of e. 110:27
the tongue ... is an unruly e. 60:5
them that call e. good 48:33
Evils: he ... must expect new e. 26:17
of two e. choose the least 262:36
women are necessary e. 283:50
Exact: an e. man 26:33
*Exactitude ... politesse des rois* 199:14
Exactness: with e. grinds he all 198:99
Exaggerated: reports of my death ... e. 394:75
Exalteth: righteousness e. a nation 45:68
Examination: post-mortem e. revealed ... 'Callous' 297:31
Examinations are formidable even to the best 108:99
Example: e. is better than precept 262:37
e. is the school of mankind 78:82
good e. is the best sermon 265:31
Excavating for a mine 225:59
Exceed: reach shd. e. his grasp 73:15
Excel: daring to e. 100:83
unstable ... thou shalt not e. 36:66
Excellent: an e. thing in woman 331:5
embodiment of everything ... e. 143:81
e. to have a giant's strength 337:86
Excels: how much a dunce ... e. 113:65
Excelsior: the strange device, E.! 197:93
Exception proves the rule 262:38

Excess: e. leads to wisdom 69:58
e. of glory obscured 217:41
give me e. of it 358:75
in charity there is no e. 25:4
nothing in e. 19:17
nothing succeeds like e. 406:31
surprise by a fine e. 186:55
wasteful and ridiculous e. 327:43
Exchange: by just e. one for another given 372:83
fair e. is no robbery 262:46
novels gain by the e. 85:87
Exciting: he found it less e. 143:69
Exclamation: 'fifty thousand!' was the e. 75:39
Excommunicate: unbaptized, or e. 65:12
Excuse: a bad e. is better than none 255:87
make the fault the worse by the e. 327:44
no longer e. for ... playing the rake 226:65
she'll prove an e. for a glass 372:78
Execution: their [of laws] stringent e. 153:16
Executioner: I am mine own e. 124:12
Executors: delivering o'er to e. pale 318–19:39
let's choose e. and talk of wills 349:53
Exercise: dancing? ... a barbarian e. 79:91
what e. is to the body 378:61
Exhalation: I shall fall like some bright e. 322:79
Exhausted worlds ... imagin'd new 173:58
Exiles: thou Paradise of e., Italy 368:29
Exist: if God did not e. 397:12
Existence: contraries ... are necessary to ... e. 68:56
E. saw him spurn her ... reign 173:58
love ... 'tis woman's whole e. 84:70
Exits: they have their e. and their entrances 301:90
Expands: work e. ... to fill the time available 244:25
Expatiate free o'er all this scene of man 250:7
Expectancy and rose of the fair state 310:1
Expectation: however certain our e. 132:18
now sits E. in the air 319:40

Expediency: doing evil on the ground of e. 290:39

Expedient: all things ... lawful ... but ... not e. 57:49

too fond of the *right* to pursue the *e.* 151:79

Expense: at the e. of two [Gods] 103:28

Expensive: did ... from e. sins refrain 126:45

Experience: an e. of women which extends 125:24

e. ... if not bought too dear 262:39

e. teaches 262:40

till old e. do attain ... prophetic 213:89

travel ... part of e. 25:12

triumph of hope over e. 176:1

true e. from this great event 223:27

*Experientia docet* 262:40

Expires: with that the Wretched Child e. 31:92

Expiring: thus e. do foretell of him 348:40

Expose thyself to feel what wretches feel 329:79

Expressed: oft was thought, but ne'er so well e. 249:97

Expresses himself in terms too deep 146:15

Extensive: knowledge of London ... e. and peculiar 121:66

Extent of [our language's] beauty and power 202:43

Extenuate: speak ... as I am; nothing e. 346:22

Extinguished: glory of Europe is e. 78:78

nature is ... seldom e. 26:25

Extinguishes the small, ... inflames the great 82:34

Extremes: e. meet 262:41

two e. of passion, joy and grief 330:3

women are always in e. 283:49

Extremity: a daring pilot in e. 126:39

Exuberance: e. is beauty 69:62

e. of his own verbosity 123:94

Exulting: the people all e. 403:81

Eye: a custom loathsome to the e. 170:19

a still-soliciting e. 327:51

all my e. and Betty Martin 254:69

all places that the e. of heaven visits 348:36

an e. for an e. 52:12

an e. made quiet by ... harmony 415:33

Eye (*continued*)

as the apple of his e. 38:14

camel ... through the e. of a needle 53:41

courtier's, soldier's, scholar's e. 310:1

e. for e., tooth for tooth 37:93

e. sees not, ... heart rues not 262:42

e. to the main chance 271:26

far from e., far from heart 262:52

flash upon that inward e. 410:71

has not man a microscopic e.? 250:10

holds him with his glittering e. 104:43

I backward cast my e. 80:19

if thine e. offend thee 53:39

in the e. of the beholder 168:92

keep me as the apple of the e. 41:85

long grey beard and glittering e. 104:42

many an e. has danced to see 164:46

my credit in men's e. 136:82

now mine e. seeth thee 41:79

poet's e. in a fine frenzy rolling 342:53

teaches such beauty as a woman's e. 331:14

the e. begins to see 71:87

the ... e. of heaven to garnish 327:43

there's language in her e. 358:73

what immortal hand or e. 68:46

with his keener e. the axe's edge 207:3

with my little e., I saw him die 241:88

Eyebrow: ballad ... to his mistress' e. 301:90

Eyeless in Gaza 221:12

Eyelids: no more wilt weigh my e. down 317:13

tir'd e. upon tir'd eyes 388:85

with e. heavy and red 166:64

Eyes: and her e. were wild 183:8

and those e., the break of day 337–8:92

as in a theatre the e. of men 351:61

as 'twere in scorn of e. 352:72

choose love by another's e. 341:37

close yr. e. with holy dread 107:76

cost him his e. 330:1

discreet women ... neither e. nor ears 260:75

disdain and scorn ride ... in her e. 343:71

Eyes (*continued*)

dress her beauty at yr. e.   117:10

drink to me only with thine e.
178:49

e. have they but they see not   43:30

e., look your last   354:18

e. of all wait upon thee   44:52

e. wide open before marriage 268:31

flourish where you turn yr. e.
251:32

four e. see more than two   263:89

from women's e. this doctrine
331:16

get thee glass e.   330:93

golden slumbers kiss your e.   118:20

had I your tongues and e.   330:4

handkerchief before his streaming e.
93:81

happiness through another man's e.
303:6

have e. to wonder but lack tongues
363:46

her aspect and her e.   86:96

holes where e. did once inhabit
352:72

how fearful ... to cast one's e. so low
329:88

I was e. to the blind   41:74

if thou hast e. to see   345:95

justice ... with e. severe   301:90

kindling her undazzled e.   224:43

love looks not with the e.   341:38

make thy two e. ... start from ...
spheres   307:64

mine e. dazzle 400:50

my mistress' e. ... nothing like the
sun   364:52

night has a thousand e.   69:70

not all that tempts yr. wand'ring e.
154:26

one whose subdu'd e. ... drops tears
346–7:22

pearls that were his e.   355:35

pull the wool over ... e.   284:55

rapt soul sitting in thine e.   213:84

right in his own e.   39:32

see through all things with his half-
shut e.   252:38

set my e. on sweet Molly Malone
17:89

sight for sore e.   277:37

sight ... good for sore e.   382:7

sights of ... death within my e.
352:72

so long as ... e. can see   362:34

soft look your e. had once   417:58

sparkling e., ... teeth like pearls
75:43

Eyes (*continued*)

stout Cortez ... with eagle e.   185:41

strike mine e. but not my heart
179:52

take a pair of sparkling e.   143:77

thou art of purer e.   51:92

tired eyelids upon tired e.   388:85

to ope their golden e.   304:20

two lovely black e.   104:37

until you see the whites of their e.
253:49

very few e. can see the Mystery
187:64

where'er these casual e. are cast
376:25

whose bright e. rain influence 214:2

with e. up-rais'd, as one inspired
108:92

with rainy e. write sorrow   349:53

yr. mouth shut and yr. e. open
268:32

Fabric: baseless f. of this vision
356:50

Face: a caricature of a f.   146:11

a garden in her f.   88:24

and with how wan a f.!   373:85

but then f. to f.   57:54

cover her f.: mine eyes dazzle
400:50

dew on the f. of the dead   30:84

disasters in his morning f.   150:68

Discobolus ... turneth his f. to the
wall   82:47

f. that launch'd a thousand ships
204:63

f. with nature's own hand painted
362:35

fair and open f. of heaven   186:47

fair f. ... foul heart   262:47

fair f. half a fortune   262:48

false f. must hide   333:39

God hath given you one f.   310:99

good f. needs no paint   265:32

grace,... seen in one autumnal f.
123:7

grace to get ... red in the f.   34:20

honour the f. of the old man   38:1

human f. divine   218:59

I wish I loved its silly f.   286:97

in the sweat of thy f.   35:38

just can't think of yr. f.   377:52

look on her f. and you'll forget
251:34

looks the whole world in the f.   199:7

Monday's child is fair of f.   235:56

my f.—I don't mind it   134:53

my f. is my fortune, sir   241:87

Face (*continued*)
  never f. so pleased my mind  18:9
  painting a f. and not washing  140:37
  princely counsel in his f. yet shone  218:52
  principles ... f. to f. from ... beginning  196:76
  satchel and shining morning f.  301:90
  seen too oft, familiar with her f.  250:14
  smile on the f. of the tiger  13:52
  tell the f. thou viewest  362:30
  the air on his f. unkind  117:14
  the unclouded f. of truth  294:88
  with her f. upturned  193:48
  your f., my thane ... a book  333:34
Faces: grind the f. of the poor  48:32
  heavily jowled or hawk-like ... f.  203:56
  seen better f. in my time  328:62
  so many millions of f. ... none alike  72:3
  strange f., other minds  385:53
  the old familiar f.  192:32
  'tis ye, 'tis yr. estranged f.  391:31
*Facilis descensus Averni*  397:2
Facing: Mr. F.-both-ways  77:61
Facts: all the f. when ... brass tacks  131:9
  f. are sacred  294:88
  indebted to ... imagination for his f.  372:80
  irritable reaching after f.  186:52
Faculties: our souls, whose f. can comprehend  205:76
Fade: f. away into the forest dim  184:24
  f. into the light of common day  411:78
  old soldiers ... only f. away  18:99
  she cannot f.  183:18
  thy eternal summer shall not f.  362:33
Faded: like this insubstantial pageant f.  356–7:50
Fades: now f. the glimmering landscape  155:31
Faery: full beautiful, a f.'s child  183:8
  in f. lands forlorn  184:30
  the land of f.  417:54
*Faiblesse: tout le reste est f.*  396:94
Fail: if we shd. f.? We f.!  333:38
  neither shall ... cruse of oil f.  40:55
  sooner f. than not be among the greatest  187:61
  we shall not flag or f.  100:94
Failed: The Light that F.  191:17

Faileth: enemy faints not, nor f.  103:32
Failing: f. to trust everybody ... nobody  262:43
  true ... she had one f.  80:12
Failure: only one [to make a marriage] a f.  293:75
Faint, yet pursuing  39:25
Faints: the enemy f. not  103:32
Fair: all is f. in love and war  254:65
  brave deserves the f.  127:51
  f. is foul and foul is f.  332:23
  f. is too foul an epithet for thee  205:77
  f. stood the wind for France  125:31
  for ever shalt thou love and she be f.  183:18
  holy, f. and wise is she  361:8
  how sweet and f. she seems to be  398:17
  is she kind as she is f.?  361:9
  like not f. terms and a villain's mind  339:7
  most divinely f.  385:46
  pernicious weed! ... the f. annoys  112:53
  she is f. and, fairer  338:99
  she is not f. to outward view  104:41
  so foul and f. a day  332:25
Fair play's a jewel  262:49
Fairer: and f. than that word  338:99
  I can't say no f. than that  120:45
  thou art f. than the evening air  204:64
Fairest: O, f. of creation  220:94
Fairies: do you believe in f.?  28:62
  f. at the bottom of our garden  140:41
  I don't believe in f.  28:60
  She is the f. midwife  353:92
  that was the beginning of f.  28:59
Fair-spoken and persuading  323:87
Fairy: a little f. ... falls down dead  28:60
  by f. hands their knell is rung  107:90
  light she was and like a f.  225:60
  'tis almost f. time  342:55
Faith: an event which creates f.  366:3
  break f. with us who die  202:49
  f. and morals ... Milton held  413:5
  f. ... as the fashion of his hat  342:57
  f. is ... substance of things  59:99
  f. shines equal, arming me  71:84
  f.'s transcendent dower  413:14
  f. unfaithful kept him falsely true  385:50
  f. without works is dead  60:4

## Fate (continued)

f. so enviously debars  206:98
fixed f., free will  218:55
Foreknowledge, Will, and F.  218:55
hanging breathless on thy f.!  197:92
I am the master of my f.  160:95
I and my fellows are ministers of F.
356:49
limits of a vulgar f.  156:45
my dear ... my life, my f.  388:87
take a bond of f.  335:63
that one might read the book of f.!
317:15
when F. summons, Monarchs must
obey  128:68
will in us is over-rul'd by f.  205:80
with a heart for any f.  198:98
**Fates**: masters of their f.  323–4:93
**Father**: as a f. pitieth his children
43:22
child whose f. goes to the devil
266:65
cry not when his f. dies  172:56
foredoom'd his f.'s soul to cross
248:78
full fathom five thy f. lies  355:35
gave her f. forty-one  15:67
hath the rain a f.?  41:77
have we not all one f.?  51:98
honour thy f. and thy mother  37:87
like f., like son  269:85
my mother groan'd, my f. wept
67:44
shall a man leave his f.?  58:72
she has deceived her f.  345:95
so were her f. and mother before
17:90
son of a dear f. murder'd  309:93
take example by your f.  121:67
wise child that knows its own f.
283:39
wise f. that knows his own child
339:8
wise son maketh a glad f.  45:61
wish is f. to the thought  283:42
**Fathers**: blood is fet from f. of war-
proof  319:46
f. have eaten a sour grape  49:58
iniquity of the f. upon the children
37:84
**Fathom**: full f. five thy father lies
355:35
**Fathom-line** cd. never touch the ground
313:54
**Fathoms**: bury it certain f. in the earth
357:55
**Fatigued** ... tie up the knocker  248:77
**Fatter**: valley sheep are f.  245:38

**Fault**: a f. ... grows two thereby
161:11
body without f. or stain  70:78
excusing of a f. ... make f. worse
327:44
f., dear Brutus, is not in our stars
323–4:93
glorious f. of angels and of gods
248:74
**Faultless**: lifeless that is f.  269:81
**Faults**: be to her f. a little blind  253:50
England, with all thy f.  114:70
Every man has his f.  262:28
f. are theirs that commit ... permit
262:55
f. are thick ... love is thin  262:56
friend that will tell me ... f.  265:23
his f. lie gently on him!  323:85
rich men have no f.  276:91
tell me all my f.  365:73
with all her f., ... my country  100:82
**Favour**: I hold with those who f. fire
139:25
king's f. is no inheritance  268:37
truths in and out of f.  139:22
**Favourite**: a f. has no friend  154:25
**Favours**: hangs on princes' f.  322:81
neither beg ... your f.  333:27
**Fawning**: how like a f. publican he
looks!  338:3
**Fear**: capable not only of f. and hate
292:66
concessions of the weak are ... of f.
77:71
doth walk in f. and dread  106:60
faith ... arming me from f.  71:84
f. ... God, ... walk in ... his ways
38:9
f. no more the heat o' th' sun  304:29
f. not, said he, for mighty dread
384:35
for f. of little men  11:22
freedom from f. ... anywhere  289:32
from hope and f. set free  383:20
having little to f. ... from censure
172:43
I f. the Greeks, even when  397:99
I f. thee, ancient Mariner  105:53
I f. thy kisses, gentle maiden  370:55
I guess an' f.  80–1:19
I'll f. not what men say  77:65
irrational f. of life  110:22
many things to f.  25:13
men f. death, as children f. dark
24:86
mortality, behold and f.  29:71
needs f. no fall ... no pride  77:66
no f. in love  60:17

**Fear** (*continued*)
O word of f.  332:19
only thing ... to f. is f. itself  289:28
perfect love casteth out f.  60:17
quite unaccustomed to f.  18:7
who neither beg not f.  333:27
wise f. ... forbids the robbing  100:84
with f. and trembling  58:75
with hope, farewell f.  218:63
yet do I f. thy nature  333:32

**Fearful**: a lovely and a f. thing  84:72
our f. innocence  412:2
our f. trip is done  403:81
snatch a f. joy  154:28
thy f. symmetry  68:46
'tis melancholy and a f. sign  84:74

**Fears**: bound in to saucy doubts and f.  335:53
enough for fifty hopes and f.  73:17
have f. that I may cease to be  186:48
humanity with all its f.  197:92
not without ... f. and distastes  24:91
past Regrets and future F.  135:69
so are their griefs and f.  24:94

**Feast**: as good as a f.  65:18
as you were going to a f.  179:51
bare imagination of a f.  348:37
chief nourisher in life's f.  334:42
company makes the f.  258:21
enough is as good as a f.  261:23
f., and yr. halls are crowded  404:92
perpetual f. of nectared sweets  213:17

**Feather**: birds of a f.  256:37
he stuck a f. in his cap  241:90
knocked me down with a f.  268:41

**Feathers**: cover thee with his f.  43:19
crow, beautified with our f.  156:49

**Feats**: 'twas one of my f.  86:94

**February**: excepting F. alone  239:77

**Fed**: appetite ... grown by what it f. on  305:44
bite the hand that f. them  78:83
f. with the same food  339:13
he on honey-dew hath f.  107:76
hungry sheep look up and are not f.  215:16

**Federation**: the F. of the world  387:81

**Fee**: taking a f. with a grin  144:84

**Feeble**: not enough to help the f. up  357:59

**Feed**: f. fat the ancient grudge  338:3
f. me till I want no more  407:40
f. me with food convenient  46:90
f. upon strawberries, sugar and cream  231–2:27

**Feel**: I f. it when I sorrow most  386:59
I f. no pain, dear mother  17:88

**Feel** (*continued*)
see, not f., how beautiful  106:68
to f. what wretches f.  329:79
we uncomfortable f.  148:32
what I fancy I f.  13:51
world ... a tragedy to those who f.  398:23

**Feels**: man is as old as he f.  271:32

**Fees**: as they took their f.  31:91

**Feet**: at the f. of Gamaliel  56:24
chase the ... Hours with flying f.  83:60
did those f. in ancient time  67:38
f. of him that bringeth good tidings  48:46
f. was I to the lame  41:74
palms before my f.  99:69
walked those blessed f.  312:43
what flowers are at my f.  184:27

**Feigning**: most friendship is f.  302:91
truest poetry ... most f.  302:1

**Felicity**: absent thee from f. awhile  312:38
our own f. we make or find  152:94
perfect bliss and sole f.  205:76
tavern chair ... throne of human f.  178:44

*Felix qui potuit ... cognoscere causas*  397:5

**Fell**: bowed himself ... and the house f.  39:30
I do not love thee, Dr F.  72:96
it f. to earth, I know not where  197:91

**Fellow**: hail f., well met  381:4
you're a f. Sir ..., you're another  121:65
you threaten us, f.?  75:42

**Fellow-creatures**: make his f. wise  149:47

**Fellow-men**: one that loves his f.  168:95

**Fellowship**: manhood, nor good f. in thee  312:48
right hands of f.  58:67

**Felony**: make it a f. to drink ... beer  321:66

**Felt**: darkness which may be f.  36:75

**Female**: f. of sex it seems  222:18
f. of the species is more deadly  190:98
into the ark the male and the f.  35:45
male and f. created he them  34:28
what f. heart can gold despise?  154:24

*Femina*: *varium et mutabile semper f.*  397:1

*Femme: en un mot, elle est f.* 285:92
Fen: a f. of stagnant waters 413:3
Fences: good f. make good neighbours 139:26
Ferry: to row us o'er the f. 88:19
Fertile: in such a fix to be so f. 229:98
Fester: lilies that f. 363:42
*Festina lente* 380:87
Fettered: so f. fast we are! 73:14
Fetters: no man loveth his f. 271:31
*Feu: ce qu'est au f. le vent* 82:34
Fever: after life's fitful f. he sleeps well 334:51
   bred a f. ... famine grew 390:20
Février: Generals Janvier and F. 230:17
Few: far and f., are the lands 194:58
   let thy words be f. 46:1
   miserable ... to have f. things to desire 25:13
   most may err as grossly as the f. 127:47
   so f. enthusiasts can be trusted 27:49
   some f. [books] to be ... digested 26:32
   the sound is forc'd, the notes are f. 68:55
   we f., we happy f. 320:59
Fewer: the f. men, the greater ... honour 320:55
*Fiat justitia, ruat coelum* 263:59
Fibs: I'll tell you no f. 151:87
Fickle: woman ... f. and changing 397:1
Fiction: condemn it as an improbable f. 360:96
   truth is stranger than f. 281:62
   truth ... stranger than f. 85:87
Fiddle: f. while Rome is burning 263:60
   fit as a f. 263:71
   play first (or second) f. 274:42
   the cat and the f. 232:33
Fiddler: f. statesman and buffoon 126:43
   the f.'s standing by 16:79
Fiddlers: called for his f. three 236:58
Fiddlestick: my master's lost his f. 231:26
Fidele: to fair F.'s grassy tomb 107:87
Fie upon this quiet life! 314:62
Field: action in the tented f. 344:90
   behold her, single in the f. 414:20
   cottage small beside a f. of grain 244:24
   for the f. is full of shades 390:28
   happy f. or mossy cavern 183:14
   in the f. after the reapers 39:35

Field (*continued*)
   man for the f. 389:2
   never in the f. of human conflict 101:96
   some corner of a foreign f. 71:92
   thro' the f. the road runs by 387:75
   what though the f. be lost? 216:30
Fields: 'a babbl'd of green f. 319:44
   cockpit hold the vasty f. of France? 318:37
   dream of battled f. no more 295:97
   f. where joy for ever dwells 216:34
   from the cotton f. away 138:7
   pagans in those holy f. 312:43
   tyrant of his f. withstood 155:38
   walk through the f. in gloves 111:34
   we shall fight in the f. 100–1:94
   your time among green f. 401:68
Fiend: a f. hid in a cloud 67–8:44
   a frightful f. ... behind him 106:60
   ingratitude, thou marble-hearted f. 328:57
Fierce: lion is not so f. as ... painted 270:89
Fiery: Shadrach ... into the burning f. furnace 49:67
Fife: stirring drum, th' ear-piercing f. 345:10
Fifteen: at ... f., the mistress of the Earl 407:43
   f. men on the dead man's chest 379:74
   the maiden of bashful f. 372:78
Fifth of November: please to remember the f. 15:69
Fifty: care f. times more for a marriage 27:44
   enough for f. hopes and fears 73:17
   f. different sharps and flats 75:38
   here's to the widow of f. 372:78
   in Sodom f. righteous 36:55
   one? – f. thousand! [guilders] 75:39
   time-lag of f. years 401:66
Fig: they sewed f. leaves together 35:37
Fight: f. in France ... seas ... beaches 100:94
   f. the good f. of faith 59:93
   fought the better f. 219:82
   I dare not f.; but I will wink 319:41
   I have fought a good f. 59:95
   man being too proud to f. 407:45
   not cease from mental f. 67:38
   through the perilous f. 188:79
   warned them that Britain would f. on alone 101:1
   we ... are baffled to f. better 73:16
   we don't f. for anything 401–2:69

**Fight** (*continued*)

we don't want to f., but by jingo 168:93

we'll f. and we'll conquer 141:48

when the f. begins within himself 73:18

you cannot f. against the future 149:51

**Fighter:** fits a dull f. 315:84

**Fighting:** f. a liar in the quad 377:50

not conquering but f. well 111:36

were f. for the crown 234:47

**Fights:** he that f. and runs away 14:61

I quote the f. historical 147:31

**Figs** grew upon thorn 98:67

**Figurative:** cuts a figure – but he is not f. 187:64

**Figure:** fixed f. for the time of scorn 346:13

**Filches** from me my good name 345:6

**Fill** the unforgiving minute 190:5

**Fille de chambre:** caught hold of the f.'s 379:69

**Filling:** is f. his last cavity 13:49

**Filths** savour but themselves 329:86

**Filthy lucre** 59:87

**Finchley:** Lord F. tried to mend the ... light 31:94

**Find:** can't tell where to f. them 234:48

nothing seek, nothing f. 273:10

take things as you f. them 279:3

they shall f. him ware and wakin' 230:12

**Finding's** keeping 232:61

**Finds** too late that men betray 152:2

**Fine arts:**, murder ... as one of the F. 119:30

**Finer:** no f. investment than ... milk in babies 101:6

**Finest:** men will still say, 'This was their f. hour' 101:95

· this was our f. shower 242:7

**Finger:** have a f. in the pie 263:62

Moving F. writes: and, having writ 136:79

point his slow unmoving f. at 346:13

this is the f. of God 36:74

twist round one's little f. 281:72

**Fingers:** and with forced f. rude 215:8

ill cook ... cannot lick his own f. 258:26, 354:16

with f. weary and worn 166:64

**Finish:** tools and we will f. the job 101:98

**Finished:** I have f. my course 59:95

**Fire:** a clear f., a clean hearth 192:27

brand plucked out of ... f. 51:95

bring me my chariot of f. 67:38

**Fire** (*continued*)

element of f. is ... put out 123:3

fat is in the f. 262:54

fell in the f. ... burned to ashes 153:11

f. burn and cauldron bubble 335:58

f. is a good servant ... bad master 263:63

f. our souls to regale 68:45

foul water will quench f. 263:88

frying-pan into the f. 264:1

heap coals of f. upon his head 45:81

in the F. of Spring 135:66

like a house on f. 267:6

many irons in the f. 268:21

no f. without some smoke 273:92

no smoke without some f. 273:1

nor rain, wind, thunder, f. 328:72

now stir the f., ... close ... shutters 114:73

shd. have stood that night against my f. 330:95

spit f., spout rain 328:72

the right Promethean f. 331:16

upon a wheel of f. 330:96

warmed ... hands before the f. of life 192:34

we proceed to light the f. 143:75

what wind is to f. 82:34

who can hold a f. in his hand? 348:37

world will end in f. 139:25

**Fires:** keep the home f. burning 137:94

stars, hide your f. 333:31

violent f. soon burn out themselves 348:40

**Firing:** we shall have what to do after f. 287:3

**Firmament:** f. showeth his handywork 41:86

the spacious f. on high 9:9

**Firmness:** with f. in the right 196:81

**First:** f. baby laughed ... f. time 28:59

f. come, f. served 263:66

f. fine careless rapture 74:23

God's f. creature ... light 27:40

last of life, for which the f. was made 75:46

the f. that ever burst into ... sea 105:48

there is no last nor f. 75:45

when f. we practice to deceive 296:13

**First-born:** I'll rail against all the f. 301:86

the Lord smote all the f. 36:77

**Fish:** he has gone to f. 195:63

I sent a message to the f. 93:89

Fish (*continued*)
 in the belly of the f.  50:86
 like a f. out of water  263:69
 other f. to fry  263:70
 what cat's averse to f.?  154:24
Fish-ball: no bread with one f.  192:37
Fishers of men  51:8
Fishes: if you were to make little f.
  talk  152:4
 men that f. gnaw'd upon  352:72
 the little f. of the sea  93:90
 waiting for ... invasion. So are the f.
  101:97
 welcome little f. in  89–90:45
 when f. flew and forests walked
  98:67
Fishified: flesh, flesh, how art thou f.!
  354:8
Fishing: deepest water ... best f.
  260:67
Fishmonger: she was a f. ... 'twas no
  wonder  17:90
 you are a f.  308:75
Fit: all the news that's f. to print
  242:95
 f. for the kingdom of God  54:74
 f. for treasons, stratagems  340:24
 love makes one f. for any work
  270:16
 men ... not f. to live on land  177:16
 not f. that you shd. sit ... longer
  115:90
Fits: if the cap f., wear it  257:83
 strange f. of passion have I known
  414:23
Fittest: survival of the f.  376:34
Five: but f. upon this isle  356:45
 f. reasons why we shd. drink  10:16
 full fathom f. thy father lies  355:35
 stand f. minutes with that man
  178:46
 then ye are only f.  416:41
Five-pound note: as the gen'l'm'n said
  to the f.  121:69
 wrapped up in a f.  195:60
Fix: f. in us thy humble dwelling
  402:72
 in such a f. to be so fertile  229:98
Fixed the where and when  158:74
Flag: death's pale f. is not advanced
  354:17
 f. has braved a thousand years
  88:21
 keep the Red F. flying here!
  109–10:21
 spare yr. country's f.  403:89
 the old f. flyin'  230:12
 we shall not f. or fail  100:94

Flagons: stay me with f.  47:19
Flail: the f. of the lashing hail  368:22
Flame: adding fuel to the f.  222:25
 burn always with ... gem-like f.
  244:29
 Chloe is my real f.  253:51
 words ... full of subtle f.  29:70
Flanders: armies swore terribly in F.
  379:70
 in F. fields the poppies blow  202:48
Flash: he might have cut a f.  12:42
 they f. upon that inward eye  410:71
Flask: a F. of Wine, a Book of Verse
  137:67
Flat: your life extremely f.  148:40
Flatter: Mr Lely, f. me not  115:91
Flattered: I have not f. its rank breath
  83:61
Flatterer: scoundrel, hypocrite, and f.
  67:36
Flattering: talent for f. with delicacy
  23:78
Flattery: f.'s the food for fools  381:96
 gained by every sort of f.  98:63
 gross f. to name a coward  392:48
 I can stand anything but f.  365:73
 imitation ... sincerest form of f.
  108:98
 pernicious ... love of f.  378:59
 supports with insolence ... paid with
  f.  172:49
 what is principle against ... f.  372:79
Flavour: gives it [life] all its f.  114:71
Flaw: it is a f. in happiness  181:88
Flaws: break into a hundred thousand
  f.  328:69
Flax: smoking f. shall he not quench
  48:44
Flea: a f. hath smaller fleas  382:5
Fleas: great f. have little f.  226:69
 little f. have lesser f.  226:69
Fleckno(e) ... who like Augustus
  128:68
Fled: I f. Him down the nights  391:30
 whence all but he had f.  160:89
Flee from the wrath to come  51:6
Fleece was white as snow  157:55
Fleet-Street ... very animated appearance  176:9
Flesh: a pound of that same merchant's
  f.  340:19
 a thorn in the f.  58:65
 all f. is as grass  60:8
 all f. is grass  48:42
 all this f. keep in a little life  315:92
 and f. and blood so cheap  166:65
 bring me f. and bring me wine  229:4
 f., f., how art thou fishified  354:8

Fly (*continued*)

I will f. to thee  184:26

man is not a f.  250:10

pigs might f.  274:39

small gilded f. does lecher  329:90

they f. forgotten, as a dream  400:40

up above the world you f.  90:54

which way I f. is Hell  218:62

Flying-fishes play  190:7

Foam: f. of perilous seas  184:30

like the f. on the river  295:98

the white f. flew  105:48

Foe: I fear no f. with thee at hand  201:33

make one worthy man my f.  248:85

overcome but half his f.  217:43

the robbing of a f.  100:84

when I ask I am a f.  269:69

who never made a f.  385:51

Foeman bares his steel, tarantara  148:32

Foes: judge a man by his f.  110:24

Fog: a London particular ... A f.  119:33

f. comes on little cat feet  293:77

hover through the f. and filthy air  332:23

yellow f. that rubs its back  131:1

Folds: tinklings lull the distant f.  155:31

Follies: the pretty f. that ... commit  339:10

Follow: f. me, and I will make you fishers  51:8

f. the Gleam  388:91

f. the river ... get to the sea  263:75

f. thy fair sun  88:23

Followed: the furrow f. free  105:48

Follows: though she draws him, yet she f.  198:3

Folly: all my joys to this are f.  81:29

brood of F. without father bred  213:82

deem it not ... presumptuous f.  158:72

fool returneth to his f.  46:84

frailty, f., also crime  84:74

learned f. is intolerable  272:76

lovely woman stoops to f.  131:12, 152:2

most loving mere f.  302:91

natural f. is bad enough  272:76

rememb'rest not the slightest f.  300:82

shunn'st the noise of f.  213:85

where ignorance ... 'tis f. to be wise  154:29

Fond: not over-f. of resisting temptation  30:77

Fonder: absence makes the heart grow f.  15:72, 29:68

Food: Continent ... good f.; ... England ... good ... manners  209:39

flattery's the f. for fools  381:96

if music be the f. of love  358:75

minds are not ever craving ... f.  114:80

no love sincerer than ... of f.  365:79

nothing to eat but f.  189:83

seeking the f. he eats  301:85

Fool: a child, not yet a f. to fame  248:80

a f. at forty ... f. indeed  417:60

a f. his whole life long  200:28

a f. sees not the same tree  69:60

a f. the rest of his dull life  29:70

a wise man or a f.  67:37

and my poor f. is hang'd!  331:6

at thirty man suspects himself a f.  418:63

cannot play the f. on occasion  283:40

dost thou call me f., boy?  328:56

eight [hours' sleep] for a f.  277:40

even a f. ... is counted wise  45:73

f. and his money are soon parted  263:76

f. ... ask more than wisest ... answer  108:99

f. hath said in his heart  41:84

f. returneth to his folly  46:84

f. some of the people  197:82

f. that forgets himself  263:78

f. that is not melancholy  263:79

f. to the market ... f. he'll return  263:80

f. wanders ... wise man travels  263:81

how ill white hairs become a f.  318:34

I am fortune's f.  354:12

I met a f. i' th' forest  301:87

laughter of the f.  46:4

more of the f. than of the wise  25:2

no creature smarts so little as a f.  248:79

no f. like an old f.  263:77

O f., I shall go mad  328:69

rod for the f.'s back  46:83

so true a f. is love  363:39

talks to himself, speaks to a f.  279:9

the f. of love, unpractis'd  128:70

the wisest f. in Christendom  160:98

thou art a great f.  316:7

Forget (*continued*)
  better ... you shd. f. and smile 290:45
  don't f. the diver  180:74
  forgive and f.  263:84
  lest we f.  190:10
  look on her face and you'll f.  251:34
  old men f., yet all shall be forgot 320:58
  smile at us, pay us, pass us, but do not quite f.  99:75
  the best sometimes f.  345:99
Forgetfulness: sleep my senses in f. 317:13
Forgets: is a fool that f. himself  263:78
Forgetting: our birth is but a sleep and a f.  410:77
  world f., by the world forgot  248:76
Forgive: Father, f. them  55:91
  f. and forget  263:84
  noblest vengeance is to f.  282:90
  to err is human, to f. divine  249:4
Forgiveness: and ask of thee f.; so we'll live  330:99
  mutual f. of each vice  66:33
Forgot: shd. auld acquaintance be f.? 79:99
Forgotten: learnt nothing, f. nothing 384:31
  long absent, soon f.  270:98
  they fly, f., as a dream  400:40
Forlorn: f.! the very word is like a bell 184:31
  glimpses that wd. make me less f. 412:94
Form: ah, what the f. divine!  192:36
  earth was without f.  34:26
  his f. had not yet lost ... brightness 217:41
  in f. and moving, how ... admirable! 308:81
  the F. remains  413:13
  thy f. from off my door!  247:67
Forms: by f. unseen ... dirge is sung 107:90
  f. more real than living man  369:43
  f. of things unknown  342:53
  hope from outward f. to win  106:69
Fornication: but ... in another country  204:71
Forsake not an old friend  62:51
Fortitude: that was great f. of mind 174:72
Fortress: this f. built by Nature for herself  348:41
*Fortuna: fortis f. adiuvat*  389:6
Fortunate: as he was f., I rejoice 325:11

Fortunate (*continued*)
  be f. without adding ... felicity 173:66
Fortune: a youth to f. and to fame unknown  155:40
  children ... hostages to f.  24:96
  fair face is half a f.  262:48
  f. always favours fools  142:59
  f. favours fools  263:85
  f. favours the brave  389:6
  f., good night; smile once more 328:63
  f. is blind  263:86
  God sends f. to fools  265:25
  I am f.'s fool  354:12
  method of making a f.  156:46
  my face is my f., sir  241:87
  of f.'s sharp adversity  97:51
  possession of f. ... in want of a wife 23:75
  slings and arrows of outrageous f. 309:95
  taken at the flood, leads on to f. 326:27
  well-favoured ... the gift of f.  343:73
  when f. knocks, open  263:87
  when we are sick in f.  327:53
Fortune-teller: threadbare juggler and a f.  303:12
Forty: every man over f. is a scoundrel 366:91
  fool at f. is a fool indeed  417:60
  f. centuries look down on you 228:83
  f. years on, growing older  70:72
  gave her mother f. whacks  15:67
  girdle round ... earth in f. minutes 341:45
  he that is ... not rich at f.  266:58
  his death ... at f. odd befell 165:59
  I had rather than f. shillings  340:28
  passing rich with f. pounds  150:66
  together now for f. years  99:80
Forty-niner: dwelt a miner, f.  225:59
Forward: f. the Light Brigade!  385:41
  f. tho' I canna see  80–1:19
  look f. to with hope  139:23
  those behind cried 'F.!'  201:39
Foster-child: thou f. of silence  183:16
Fought: better to have f. and lost 103:31
  but what they f. each other for 376:29
  f. with us upon St Crispin's day 320–21:59
Foul: blood is nipp'd and ways be f. 332:20

Freedom (*continued*)
  f. and Whisky   79:2
  f. from fear ... anywhere   289:32
  f. from want—everywhere   289:32
  F. is Slavery   242:2
  f. of speech and expression   289:32
  F. shall a-while repair   107–8:90
  f. ... to worship God   289:32
  f. with which Dr Johnson condemns
    79:93
  least regard for human f.   376:37
  love not f., but licence   224:46
  none can love f. ... but good men
    224:46
  those who deny f. to others   196:75
  whose service is perfect f.   63:71
  yet, F.! yet thy banner   84:63
Freedoms: world ... upon four essential
  human f.   289:32
Freezings: what f. have I felt   363:43
French: F. are wiser than they seem
  26:19
  F. of Paris was to hir unknowe
    96:28
  F., or Turk, or Proosian   147:30
  F. say, there are three sexes   375:9
  F. she spak ful faire   96:28
  he's gone to fight the F.   179:63
  how it's improved her F.   153:12
  not too F. F. bean   146:16
Frenchmen: fifty million F. can't be
  wrong   156:53
Frenzy: demonic f., moping melan-
  choly   220:97
  poet's eye in a fine f. rolling   342:53
Fresh: bloom sae f. and fair   81:26
  f. as in the month of May   96:27
  I shd. feel f. and vigorous   309:30
  looking as f. as paint   374:96
Freshness: glory and ... f. of a dream
  410:72
Fret: nuns f. not   411:89
Frets: that struts and f. his hour
  336:76
Fretted the ... body to decay   126:39
Friday: F. night is Amami night   11:27
  F.'s child is loving and giving   235:56
  worse on F.   238:71
Friend: a faithful f. is ... medicine
  62:47
  a fav'rite has no f.!   154:25
  a f. ... the masterpeice of Nature
    132:29
  (all he wished) a f.   155:41
  best mirror ... old f.   272:59
  faithful are the wounds of a f.   46:87
  forsake not an old f.   62:51
  f. at court   263:91

Friend (*continued*)
  f., go up higher   54:78
  f. in need ... f. indeed   263:92
  f. shd. bear his f.'s infirmities   326:26
  f. that will tell ... my faults   265:23
  f. to everybody ... f. to nobody
    264:94
  f. to thyself ... others will befriend
    264:93
  good wine – a f. – or being dry
    10:16
  handsome and witty, yet a f.   251:31
  if I had a f. that loved her   344:92
  keep thy f. under ... life's key   298:41
  keep wel thy tonge ... keep thy f.
    97:49
  lend yr. money and lose yr. f.   269:70
  loan ... loses ... itself and f.   306:57
  makes no f. who never made a foe
    385:51
  my guide, philosopher and f.   250:19
  of every friendless name the f.
    172:53
  only way to have a f.   132:30
  open enemy than a false f.   255:14
  save me from the candid f.   88:27
  speak well of your f.   278:62
  tolling a departed f.   316:97
  trust not a new f.   281:60
  up the ladder ... choosest a f.   264:14
  when I lend I am a f.   269:69
Friends: a soul remembering my good
  f.   349:44
  animals are such agreeable f.   130:87
  best of f. must part   19:11, 264:97
  can live without our f.   270:95
  expectation of finding many f.
    175:94
  f. are thieves of time   264:95
  f. begin to compliment him   170:15
  f. in heaven and in hell   264:96
  f. of the mammon of unrighteousness
    55:85
  f., Romans, countrymen   325:12
  f. shd. be few and good   256:53
  God defend me from my f.   264:18
  golden f. I had   167:84
  have but few f.   264:98
  How to Win F. and Influence
    People   89:40
  I love ... old f., old times   151:83
  in the misfortunes of our best f.
    288:19
  judge ... man by his foes as well as
    ... f.   110:24
  kiss and be f.   268:38
  laughter learnt of f.   71:94
  lay down his life for his f.   56:10

**Fury** (*continued*)
civil f. first grew high 82:35
cunning old F. 90:46
nor hell a f. like a woman scorned
108:6
tale ... full of sound and f. 336:76
**Fuse**: through the green f. drives the
flower 390:19
**Fustian**: whose f.'s so sublimely bad
248:82
**Fustilarian**: you f.! 316:5
**Future**: for I dipt into the f. 387:80
haven't any f. to think of 366:95
I never think of the f. 129:83
if you wd. divine the f. 108:3
you cannot fight ... the f. 149:51
**Futurity**: let f. shift for itself 375:16

**Gaiety**: eclipsed the g. of nations
178:43
**Gain**: broke the Sabbath but for g.
126:45
no painful inch to g. 103:33
**Gales**: cool g. shall fan the glade
251:32
**Gallantly** streaming 188:79
**Gallantry**: what men call g. 84:66
**Gallery** in which the reporters sit
202:44
*Gallia ... in partes tres* 87:6
**Gallimaufry**: made our English tongue
a g. 377:48
**Galloped**: I g., Dirck g., we g.
74:26
**Galloping** after a fox 406:27
**Gallows**: his complexion is perfect g.
355:27
shall there be g. standing 312:45
**Galumphing**: he went g. back 92:70
**Gamaliel**: brought up ... at the feet of
G. 56:24
**Game**: a rich man's g. 18:3
but how you played the g. 287:9
g. is not worth the candle 264:3
golf ... not being a g. 194:52
lookers-on see most of the g. 270:4
rigour of the g. 192:27
the g.'s afoot 319:47
win this g. ... thrash the Spaniards
too 125:30
woman is his g. 388:1
**Game-keeper**: old poacher ... good g.
274:20
*Gamesmanship or ... Winning Games
Without ... Cheating* 252:43
**Gang**: the old g. 100:85
**Gaol**: all ... we know who live in g.
404:97

**Gaol** (*continued*)
in a g. better air, better company
177:16
**Garden**: a g. in her face 88:24
a g. is a lovesome thing 72:97
come into the g., Maud 388:56
dispossessed of the g. hard by
Heaven 69:68
fairies at the bottom of our g.
140:41
g. ... purest of human pleasures
26:29
God Almighty first planted a g.
26:29
God the first g. made 112:46
good strawberries in yr. g. 352:74
how does your g. grow 235:55
patience ... not in everyone's g.
274:29
put him into the g. of Eden 35:31
redbreast whistles from a g. croft
181:82
we must cultivate our g. 397:9
**Garland**: immortal g. is to be run for
223:39
wither'd is the g. of the war 299:66
**Garment**: City now doth like a g. wear
412:96
Winter G. of Repentance 135:66
**Garments**: g. though new-fangled ill
363:41
our purses ... proud, our g. poor
355:25
**Garnish**: the ... eye of heaven to g.
327:43
**Garrick**: here lies David G. 151:80
**Garrulity**: my crime, shameful g.
222:17
**Garter**: he will unloose, familiar as his
g. 318:38
I like the G. ... no damned merit
208:25
**Gas** smells awful 243–4:23
**Gash**: each new day a g. is added
335:65
**Gasp**: at the last g. 63:64
**Gate**: aged man, a-sitting on a g. 94:95
at the strait g. 52:26
heavy burdens at his narrow g.
318–19:39
I am here at the g. alone 388:86
lark at heaven's g. sings 304:20
passion-flower at the g. 388:87
the poor man at his g. 10:18
there's knocking at the g. 335:70
willow cabin at your g. 359:80
**Gatepost**: you and me and the g.
256:35

Gates: such are the g. of paradise
66:33

the Gaul is at her g.! 112:49

Gath: tell it not in G. 40:47

Gather ye rosebuds while ye may
162:24

Gathering nuts in May 16:86

*Gaudeamus igitur* 19:20

Gaudy: express'd in fancy; rich, not g.
306:56

one other g. night 299:61

Gaul: G. is divided into three parts
87:6

hark! the G. is at her gates! 112:49

Gave: I g. you all ... And in good time
you g. it 328:66

the Lord g. and ... hath taken away
41:65

Gay: a poet cd. not but be g. 410:70

her heart was young and g. 157:58

Gaza: eyeless in G. 221:12

Gaze: show and g. o' th' time 336:79

Gazed: and still they g. ... the wonder
grew 150:69

Gazes: yellow god forever g. down
159:76

Geese: all his g. are swans 264:4

six g. a-laying 238:73

where there are women and g.
283:48

Gem: of purest ray serene 155:37

General: as for being a G. 395:81

caviare to the g. 308:85

of a constitution so g. 72:2

Generals: all G. ... some never grow
out of it 395:81

*bite* some of my other g. 142:61

g. are already poring over maps
22:59

Russia has two g. 213:17

Generation: O g. of vipers, who hath
warned? 51:6

one g. passeth ... another g. cometh
46:95

unto the third and fourth g. 37:84

Generations: no hungry g. tread thee
down 184:30

power of books ... may endure for g.
395:77

save succeeding g. from ... war
394:76

Genius: g. (... capacity of taking
trouble) 89:33

g. does what it must 209:37

g. is ... inspiration ... perspiration
129:79

good Edmund, whose g. was such
[Burke] 151:78

Genius (*continued*)
Good God! what a g. I had
382:14

nothing to declare except my g.
406:33

since when was g. found respectable? 73:10

the G. and the mortal instruments
324:98

Gentle: a g. knight was pricking on the
plain 377:41

do not go g. 390:18

his life was g. 326:31

humane and g. virtue 78:89

meek and g. with these butchers
324:8

sleep! it is a g. thing 105:57

the g. mind by g. deeds is known
377:45

this day shall g. his condition 320:59

verray parfit g. knight 96:26

Gentleman: almost a definition of a g.
230:15

always talking about being a g.
380:89

education begins a g., conversation
completes 261:14

grand old name of g. 387:72

smooth-fac'd g., tickling commodity
326:37

the English country g. galloping
406:27

who was then the g. ? 27:50

Gentlemanly: we must look for ... g.
conduct 22:54

Gentlemen: by g. for g. 389:11

g. in England, now abed 320:59

g. of the gentle craft 118:21

G. Prefer Blondes 199:10

g. rankers out on the spree 190:99

God rest you merry, g. 16:82

not a religion for g. 96:21

we are g. of Japan 145:94

Gentleness, in hearts at peace 71:94

Gentlier: music that g. on the spirit lies
388:85

Geography is about maps 33:15

Geometry: no royal road to g. 133:52

George: any good of G. the Third
192:33

G. the First was ... reckoned vile
192:33

G. the Third ought never to have
occurred 33:19

King G. upon the throne 179:63

viler G. the Second 192:33

Georgia: marching through G.
416:44, 45

Georgie Porgie, pudding and pie
232:31

German: I speak ... G. to my horse
96:24

the G. dictator, instead of snatching
100:90

Germans: Don't let's be Beastly to the
G. 112:43

Germany: G. G. above all 164:38

G. will be ... world power or will not
be 163:32

Gert and ... Epp and ... Ein 14:57

Get: g. thee glass eyes 330:93

g. thee to a nunnery 310:97

Getting and spending, we lay waste
412:93

Ghastly: we were a g. crew 105:58

Ghost: plays to the bowling of a g.
390:28

vex not his g. 331:7

what beckoning g. ... invites my
steps? 248:72

Ghosts: g. from an enchanter fleeing
369:35

haunted by the g. they have depos'd
350:54

rain is full of g. tonight 210:46

Ghoulies: from g. and ghosties and ...
beasties 14:60

Giant: g.'s strength ... use it like a g.
337:86

owner whereof was G. Despair
77:62

Giants: there were g. ... in those days
35:44

Giant's-Causeway worth seeing?
177:32

Gibbon: scribble ! Eh, Mr G.?
149:56

Gibeon: sun, stand thou still upon G.
38:20

Gift: time with a g. of tears 382:16

Gifts, even when they bring g. 397:99

man's work or his own g. 223:30

rich g. wax poor 310:96

Gilded: men are but g. loam 347:30

Gilead: is there no balm in G. ? 49:55

Gilpin: and G. long live he 113:61

away went G.–who but he ? 113:57

John G. was a citizen 112:54

said G., so am I 113:58

Gilt off the gingerbread 279:99

Gimble: gyre and g. in the wabe 91:69

Gingerbread: gilt off the g. 279:99

Girdle: I'll put a g. round ... the earth
341:45

Girl: a g. ... cheeks are covered with
paint 228:88

Girl (*continued*)
little g. who had a little curl 199:5

marry a country g. afterwards
365:74

naughty g. to disobey 236:57

Poor Little Rich G. 112:45

sweet g.-graduates 388:95

to the sweetest g. I know 407:39

Girlish: filled ... with g. glee 145:2

Girls: a set of wretched un-idea'd g.
174:75

all the g. ... so smart 89:31

passes at g. who wore glasses 243:22

secrets with g. ... guns with boys
114:82

servant g. in the kitchen 383:26

what are little g. made of? 240:85

where the g. are so pretty 17:89

Give: better g. a shilling 256:23

g. all thou canst 409:60

g. me an ounce of civet 329:91

g. me back my legions 86:4

g. me my soul again 204:63

g. not thy soul unto a woman
62:50

g., oh g. me back my heart 86:95

g. one man a lecture ... another a
shilling 175:87

g. us the luxuries of life 227:73

it is more blessed to g. 56:22

Mother, g. me the sun 169:10

no more g. the people straw 36:72

such as I have g. I thee 56:15

these pleasures, Melancholy, g.
213:90

when I g., I g. myself 403:85

Given: costs so much as what is g.
273:5

unto ... one that hath shall be g.
53:46

Giver; a cheerful g. 58:63

Givers: when g. prove unkind 310:96

Gives: blesseth him that g. 339:15

g. twice who g. quickly 264:10

who g. to all, denies all 264:9

Giving: g. much to the poor 264:11

not in the g. vein today 352:78

Glad: and I am g., yea g. 125:34

never g. confident morning 74:29

Glade: alone in the bee-loud g. 417:52

Gladly wolde he lerne ... teche 97:34

Gladness: sadness and g. succeed each
other 276:9

teach me half the g. 370:51

Gladsome: let us with a g. mind
221:10

Gladstone's always having the ace of
trumps 191:23

Go (continued)

let him g. for a scapegoat 37:96
let my people g. 36:73
the lamb was sure to g. 157:55
train ... child in the way he shd. g. 45:80
what a Rum G. everything is 401:65
whither thou goest I will g. 39:33
with thee to g. is to stay here 221:2
year is going, let him g. 386:68
Goal: good ... the final g. of ill 386:61
grave is not its g. 198:95
Goat: with their g.-feet dance an antic hay 204:68
Goblets: my figur'd g. for a dish of wood 350:55
Goblin: spirit of health or g. damn'd 307:60
Goblins: tales ... of sprites and g. 361:13
God: a contrite heart, O G. 42:9
a lovesome thing, G. wot 72:97
a wild beast or a g. 26:20
all scripture ... inspiration of G. 59:94
all service is the same with G. 75:35
an old abusing of G.'s patience 340:29
and G. said, Let there be light 34:27
and G. said to Jonah 50:87
and G. saw everything ... he had made 35:30
and the Word was G. 55:92
are G. and Nature ... at strife ? 356:62
as G. gives us to see the right 196:81
as if we were G.'s spies 330:99
being blind, the good G. prepare me 246:45
better to have no opinion of G. 25:11
Cabots talk only to G. 69:67
cannot serve G. and mammon 52:20
charged with the grandeur of G. 166:67
cry, G. for Harry, England! 319:47
destroys ... book, kills the image of G. 223:37
doorkeeper in the house of my G. 43:15
doubtless G. could have made a better berry 398:25
earthly power doth then show likest G.'s 339:15
eternal G. is thy refuge 38:17
every man ... g. or devil 126:44

God (continued)

fear G. and keep his commandments 47:14
fear G. Honour the king 60:9
fit for the kingdom of G. 54:74
fool hath said ... There is no G. 41:84
for the greater glory of G. 19:18
freedom ... to worship G. 289:32
got up airly ... to take in G. 200:20
glorious the song, when G.'s the theme 374:94
glory be to G. for dappled things 166:68
glory to G. in the highest 54:70
G. Almighty first planted a garden 26:29
G. and sinners reconciled 402:71
G. appears, and G. is light 66:31
G. be praised, the Georges ended 192:33
G. be thanked ... two soul-sides 74:34
G. be with you till we meet again 286:98
G. bless ... Faith's Defender 83:53
G. bless the moon and G. bless me 234:43
G. chasteneth thee 38:8
G. comes at last 264:17
G. defend me from my friends 264:18
G. disposes 188:71
G. doth not need ... man's work 223:30
G. erects a house of prayer 118:18
G. ... esteems the growth ... of one virtuous person 224:41
G. for us all 262:27
G. fulfils himself in many ways 385:54
G. gave the increase 57:46
G. hath given liberty 116:98
G. hath given you one face 310:99
G. heals ... doctor takes the fee 264:19
G. help the poor 264:20
G. help the rich 264:21
G. helps them that help themselves 264:22
G. is alone 366:4
G. is decreeing to begin 224:42
G. is ... for the big battalions 398:15
G. is in heaven and thou upon earth 46:1
G. is love 60:16
G. is no respecter of persons 56:19
G. is not mocked 58:70

God (*continued*)

G. is our refuge and our strength 42:7

G. is thy law, thou mine 219:70

G. loveth a cheerful giver 58:63

G. made the country 114:69

G. made the wicked Grocer 99:76

G. made the woman for the man 385:48

G. made them, high or lowly 10:18

G. make me able to pay 245:41

G. moves in a mysterious way 113:63

G. must think it ... odd 191:20

g. of our idolatry, the press 113:66

G. order'd motion but ordain'd no rest 396:86

G. our help in ages past 399:38

G. ... put him into ... Eden 35:31

G. rest you merry 16:82

G. said, Let Newton be! 248:88

G. save our Gracious King 88:29

G. save the mark! 313:52

G. saw the light was good 220:84

G. send you joy 265:24

G.'s first creature ... light 27:40

G. shall add unto him 61:35

G. shall wipe away all tears 61:34

G. shed his grace on thee 29:67

G. shd. go before such villains 344:82

G.'s in his heaven 75:44

G.'s mill grinds slow 265:27

'G. tempers the wind,' said Maria 379:68

G. tempers the wind ... shorn lambs 265:26

G. the first garden made 112:46

G. who is our home 410:77

G. who made thee mighty 33:13

hath not one G. created us? 51:98

he for G. only, she for G. in him 219:66

heavens declare the glory of G. 41:86

honest G. ... noblest work of man 170:14

honest Man's the noblest work of G. 250:16

I am the Lord thy G. 37:81

I reflect that G. is just 171:33

I speak Spanish to G. 96:24

I the Lord your G. am holy 37:97

I ... thy G. am a jealous G. 37:84

if G. be for us 57:35

if G. did not exist 397:12

in apprehension, how like a g.! 308:81

God (*continued*)

in the beginning G. created 34:26

in the image of G. created He him 34:28

inclines to think there is a G. 103:27

into the hands of the living G. 59:98

isn't life ... terrible ... thank G.? 390:25

it shall please G. to call me 64:99

just are the ways of G. 222:16

justify the ways of G. to men 216:29

knowledge ... make a G. of me 182:2

knowledge of G. ... burnt offerings 50:75

land which the Lord thy G. giveth 37:87

last and best of all G.'s works 220:94

Lord G. made them all 10:17

love, we are in G.'s hands 73:14

make a joyful noise unto G. 43:13

malt ... to justify G.'s ways to man 167:85

man proposes, G. disposes 271:36

name of the Lord thy G. in vain 37:85

nature is the art of G. 72:1

nearer, my G., to thee 9:3

new Jerusalem, coming ... from G. 61:33

not G. is greater ... than ... self 403:86

O G., O Montreal! 82:47

of such is the kingdom of G. 54:61

Oh! G.! that bread shd. be so dear 166:65

one G., one law, one element 387:73

one on G.'s side is a majority 246:51

only G. can make a tree 189:82

out of the mouth of G. 51:7

peace of G., which passeth 58:78

powers ... ordained of G. 57:42

pray G. we may make haste 348:38

prepare to meet thy G. 50:83

presume not G. to scan 250:13

pretence that G. had put it [ace] there 191:23

pure in heart ... shall see G. 52:10

remember the name of the Lord our G. 42:90

resistance ... is obedience to G. 171:31

rib which ... G. had taken 35:33

rich man ... into the kingdom of G. 53:41

sabbath of the Lord thy G. 37:86

God (*continued*)

Sarah Battle, now with G.   192:27

servant of G., well done!   219:82

serv'd my G. with half the zeal 323:84

shall ... man be more just than G.? 41:66

shalt love the Lord thy G.   38:6

so G. created man   34:28

so lonely 'twas, that G. himself 106:62

souls ... in the hand of G.   62:43

stern daughter of the voice of G. 413:7

taken at the flood, leads – G. knows 85:80

thank G. we're normal   242:7

the dear G. who loveth us   106:64

the Lord our G. is one Lord   38:5

the Lord thy G. chasteneth thee 38:8

the sacrifices of G. are   42:9

there, but for the grace of G.   70:73

they [voices] come from G.   366:2

this is the finger of G.   36:74

those whom G. hath joined   65:10

thou shalt have one G. only   103:28

though G. hath raised me high 132:21

though the mills of G. grind slowly 198:99

thy G. my G.   39:33

to walk humbly with thy G.   51:91

true love's the gift which G.   295:4

turn to G. to praise   74:25

unto G. the things that are G.'s 53:43

vindicate the ways of G. to Man 250:8

voice of the people is the voice of G. 10:15

was the holy Lamb of G.   67:38

we owe G. a death   317:19

what therefore G. hath joined   54:60

when first G. dawned on Chaos 367:11

who think not G. at all   222:16

whole armour of G.   58:73

whom G. wishes to destroy   275:74

whose G. is their belly   58:76

Wonderful, Counsellor, The mighty G.   48:36

wd. G. I had died ... O Absalom 40:51

would to G. we had died   36:79

yellow g. forever gazes down   159:76

youth shows but half; trust G. 75–6:46

Goddess: g. and maiden and queen 383:22

g. excellently bright   178–9:50

Godliness: in cheerful g.   413:4

Gods: a daughter of the g.   385:46

as flies ... are we to th' g.   329:85

as g., knowing good and evil   35:36

by the Nine G. he swore   201:35

carve him as a dish for the g.   324:99

for the ... temples of his G.   201:36

I thank whatever g. may be   160:93

kings are earth's g.   347:26

kings it makes g.   352:83

leave the rest to G.   111:33

men call gallantry and g. adultery 84:66

no other g. before me   37:82

so many g., so many creeds 404:93

thank the g. I am foul   302:2

the darling of the G. was born   207:4

the g. are just   330:1

voice of all the g. make heaven drowsy   331:15

we thank ... whatever g. may be 383:20

wd. the g. had made thee poetical 302:99

Goest: whither thou g. I will go   39:33

Gog, the land of Magog   49:66

Going: as I was g. to St. Ives   231:22

at the g. down of the sun   65:20

Cross of Jesus g. on before   28:57

g. one knows not where   208:17

I am just g. outside   241:93

I don't feel like g. into it   292:71

men must endure their g. hence 330:98

the Lord shall preserve thy g.   .44:39

where are you g. to, my pretty maid? 241:86

Gold: all is not g. that glitters   254:66

beauty provoketh ... sooner than g. 300:74

building roofs of g.   318–19:39

fetters, be they made of g.   271:31

floor of heaven ... with patines of bright g.   340:22

g. in phisik is a cordial   97:38

hadde he but litel g. in cofre   96:33

her locks were yellow as g.   105:52

if g. ruste, what shall iren do?   97:41

king's ... a heart of g.   320:51

led by the nose with g.   362:27

my bow of burning g.   67:38

my g.!—open the shrine   179:59

nor all, that glisters, g.   154:26

rank is good, and g. is fair   403:88

**Gold** (*continued*)

run back and fetch the age of g. 215:21

saint-seducing g. 353:90

showers ... barbaric pearl and g. 217:45

the poop was beaten g. 298:54

to gild refined g. 327:43

travell'd in the realms of g. 185:40

true love ... differs from g. 368:26

weakness to resist Philistian g. 222:20

wedges of g., great anchors 352:72

what female heart can g. despise? 154:24

when g. and silver becks me 327:40

worth his weight in g. 284:59

**Golden**: as they did in the g. world 300:72

from this g. rigol 318:28

girl-graduates in their g. hair 388:95

g. friends I had 167:84

g. lads and girls 304–5:29

g. rule ... there are no g. rules 365:86

g. slumbers kiss yr. eyes 118:20

love in a g. bowl 66:32

O polished perturbation! g. care! 317:27

silver nutmeg and a g. pear 233:39

the g. years return 368:28

waters of the Nile on every g. scale 89–90:45

wear a g. sorrow 322:75

**Goldsmith**: here lies Nolly G. ... called Noll 141:49

**Golf** may be played on Sunday 194:52

**Golf-balls**: a thousand lost g. 131:8

**Gondolier**: a highly respectable g. 143:71

**Gone**: if she's not g. ... there still 239:75

now thou art g., and never must return 215:10

thou art g., and for ever 295:98

thy thoughts, when thou art g. 370:54

what's g. ... shd. be past grief 361:14

**Gongs**: strong g. groaning as the guns boom far 99:71

**Good**: a g., unless counterbalanced by evil 177:29

all g. and no badness 373:93

all g. to me is lost 218:63

all partial evil, universal g. 250:12

all things work together for g. 56:34

and for the g. and increase 385:48

any g. of George the Third? 192:33

apprehension of the g. gives ... feeling 348:37

are you g. men and true? 343:72

**Good** (*continued*)

as gods, knowing g. and evil 35:36

as g. as she was beautiful 246:46

as g. be out of the world 102:12

be g., sweet maid 189:86

behold, it was very g. 35:30

beneath the g. how far 156:45

best is the enemy of the g. 397:11

but what g. came of it? 376:30

care not whether man is g. or evil 67:37

chief g. and market of his time 311:22

cleave to that which is good 57:37

Continent ... g. food ... England ... g. table manners 209:39

crown thy g. with brotherhood 29:67

curate's egg, g. in parts 259:43

enough is as g. as a feast 65:18

Evil, be thou my G. 218:63

general g. ... plea of the scoundrel 67:36

giver of all g. things 64:90

go about doing g. 115:85

gone whar de g. niggers go 138:9

g. are so harsh to the clever 409:59

g., but not religious-g. 158:66

g. enough to govern another 196:73

g. enough to shed his blood 289:37

g. fences make g. neighbours 139:26

g. for the country was g. for General Motors 407:42

g. is oft interred with their bones 325:12

g. that I wd. I do not 56:33

g. ... the final goal of ill 386:61

g., the more communicated 219:76

g. to be merry ... honest and true 17:93

g. to be out on the road 208:17

Guinness is g. for you 11:28

he [Time] ... our g. will sever 179:61

he who wd. do g. to another 67:36

hear no g. of themselves 270:90

hold fast that which is g. 59:85

if all the g. people were clever 409:59

ill wind that blows nobody g. 267:15

it is not, nor it cannot come to g. 306:46

Joan is as g. as my lady 268:24

let him do what seemeth him g. 39:37

little of what you fancy does you g. 197:86

money... not g. unless ... spread 25:8

never g. to bring bad news 299:56

never had it so g. 202:52

Good (*continued*)

not g. that man shd. be alone 35:32

nothing ... g. or bad, but thinking makes 308:80

Oh, Sir! the g. die first 409:64

only g. Indian is a dead Indian 371:61

out of g. still to find means of evil 216:32

sermons in stones, and g. in everything 300:75

she was very, very g. 199:5

so much g. in the worst of us 163:36

some said it might do g. 76:56

the g. is the beautiful 247:61

the greatest g. 102:16

to the public g. private respects must yield 222:21

wives must be had, ... g. or bad 283:44

Good night: fortune, g. 328:63

g.? ah! no; the hour is ill 368:27

g. g.! Parting is such sweet sorrow 354:6

say g. till it be morrow 354:6

sweet ladies, g. 311:25

Goodbye to All That 154:21

Goodness: felt how awful g. is 219:73

g., what is she a-doin' of? 18:4

Goods: with all my worldly g. 65:9

Goose: g. that lays the golden eggs 268:33

sauce for the g. ... the gander 276:12

say Bo(o) to a g. 276:14

three women and a g. 280:36

Goosey, goosey gander 232:32

Gordian: the G. knot ... he will unloose 318:38

Gormed: I'm G. – I can't say no fairer 120:45

Gossip, babbling g. of the air 359:80

scandal is g. made tedious 406:20

Got: vicious place where thee he g. 330:1

Gourd: to be angry for the g. 50:87

Gout: drink, combined with g. 143:73

wine ... the g.; ... no wine ... the g. too 260:89

*Gouvernement: le g. qu'elle mérite* 203:58

Govern: g. another man without that other's consent 196:73

he that wd. g. others 208:18

Governed: a nation is not g. 78:72

Government: all g. ... founded on compromise 78:74

every nation has the g. it deserves 203:58

Government (*continued*)

g. ... a necessary evil 243:20

g. ... framed ... in after-dinner conversations 391:38

g. of the people, by the people 196:79

g. shall be upon his shoulder 48:36

having looked to g. for bread 78:83

if any ask me what a free g. is 78:84

one form of G. rather than another 176:2

only legitimate object of good g. 171:31

Gower: O moral G. 98:53

Gown: g. of glory, hope's true gage 286:94

like an old lady's loose g. 314:78

Gowns: robes and furr'd g. hide all 330:92

Grace: an inward and spiritual g. 64:1

divine g. was never slow 260:78

God shed his g. 29:67

g. me no g. 349:45

grow old with a good g. 378:60

he does it with a better g. 359:85

he had at least the g. 34:20

my g. is sufficient for thee 58:66

no ... beauty hath such g. 123:7

sweet attractive g. 219:66

Tuesday's child is full of g. 235:56

with one half so good a g. 337:84

ye are fallen from g. 58:68

Graced with polished manners 114:75

Gradualness: the inevitability of g. 400:42

Graduates, sweet girl-g. in their golden hair 388:95

Grain: which g. will grow ... will not 333:27

Grammar: erecting a g. school 321:68

*Grammatici certant ... sub iudice lis est* 166:70

Gramophone: puts a record on the g. 131:12

Granary: sitting careless on a g. floor 181:80

Grand: they said, 'it wd. be g.' 92:78

Grandchild: his little g. Wilhelmine 376:28

Grandeur: g. hear with a disdainful smile 155:34

g. that was Rome 247:66

Grandmother: teach yr. g. to suck eggs 279:13

Grandsire: proverb'd with a g. phrase 353:91

Grape: fathers have eaten a sour g. 49:58

Grape (*continued*)

 merry with the fruitful g. 135:75

 neither shalt thou gather every g.
  37:98

 the g. that can with Logic absolute
  135:77

Grapes: our vines have tender g. 47:23

 sour g. can ne'er make sweet wine
  278:60

Grapeshot: a whiff of g. 89:34

Grapple them to thy soul 306:55

Grasp: a man's reach shd. exceed his g.
 73:15

Grass: a snake in the g. 277:49

 all flesh is as g. 60:8

 all flesh is g. 48:42

 cut the g. from under … feet 259:48

 g. … as soft as … breast of doves
  111:34

 Guests star-scattered on the G.
  136:83

 hare limp'd trembling through the
  frozen g. 181:89

 his days are as g. 43:23

 I am the g.; I cover all 293:78

 I know the g. beyond the door
  291:53

 seed from the feather'd g. 182:97

 two blades of g. to grow 381:2

Grate on their scrannel pipes 215:16

Gratis: he lends out money g. 338:3

Grave: a little g., an obscure g. 350:55

 body lies a mould'ring in the g.
  157:57

 country … a kind of healthy g.
  375:23

 Duncan is in his g. 334:51

 eat our pot of honey on the g.
  209:33

 every third thought … my g. 357:58

 from g. to gay, from lively to severe
  250:18

 funeral marches to the g. 198:96

 g. is not its goal 198:95

 g. of Mike O'Day 13:50

 g. where English oak and holly
  158:72

 g. where our hero we buried 408:52

 g.'s a fine and private place 206:95

 in the dark and silent g. 286:93

 lead but to the g. ·155:36

 make … turn in his g. 281:67

 man … pompous in the g. 72:7

 my large kingdom for a little g.
  350:55

 O g., where is thy victory? 57:60

 O G., where is thy Victory? 247:71

 one foot in the g. 274:22

Grave (*continued*)

 renowned be thy g.! 305:31

 see myself go into my g. 246:45

 where, g., thy victory? 201:33

Graves: find ourselves dishonourable
 g. 323:93

 talk of g., of … epitaphs 349:53

Gravity: approach this spot with g.!
 13:49

Gravy: rich wot gets the g. 18:5

 Sir Humphrey Davy detested g.
  33:18

Great: all things both g. and small
 106:64

 brilliant chief, irregularly g. 76:53

 but far above the g. 156:45

 even g. men have … poor relations
  119:35

 g. is Diana of the Ephesians 56:21

 g. is Truth, and mighty 31:37

 g. men are almost always bad men
  9:1

 g. men … not commonly … g.
  scholars 164:51

 g. ones eat up the little ones 347:27

 madness in g. ones 310:2

 rightly to be g. … g. argument
  311:24

 rule of men entirely g. 76:54

 some are born g., some achieve greatness 360:91

 such g. men as these 18:6

 to be g. is to be misunderstood
  133:37

Great War: what did you do in the
 G.? 11:25

Greater: feel that we are g. than we
  know 413:14

 there is no g. sorrow 116:3

 thy necessity is g. than mine 373:88

Greatest: g. happiness of the g. number
  33:14

 g. talkers … least doers 279:8

 sooner fail than not be among the g.
  187:61

Greatness: farewell, to all my g. 322:80

 highest point of all my g. 322:79

 some achieve g. 360:91

 some have g. thrust upon them
  360:91

 thinks … his g. is a-ripening 322:80

Greece: citizen not of Athens or G.
  375:20

 dream'd that G. … be free 84–5:78

 G., Italy and England did adorn
  128:66

 the glory that was G. 247:66

 the isles of G., the isles of G.! 84:77

Greedy: not g. of filthy lucre 59:87
Greek: it is G. to me 265:48
it was G. to me 324:96
must carve in Latin or in G. 398:18
paid at the G. Kalends 86:5
small Latin and less G. 179:56
when his wife talks G. 178:45
Greeks: G. had a word for it 10:14
I fear the G. 397:99
when G. joined G. 195:67
which came first, the G. or the Romans 123:1
Green: a dyspeptic mint g. 395:80
a g. and yellow melancholy 360:89
and all the trees are g. 189:88
drives my g. age 390:19
flourishing like a g. bay-tree 42:4
g. grow the rashes O 80:7
g. thought in a g. shade 206:99
in England's g. and pleasant land 67:38
laurel is g. for a season 383:23
making the g. one red 334:43
salad days, when I was g. 298:53
the memory be g. 305:37
their heads are g. 194:58
there is a g. hill far away 11:20
through the g. fuse drives the flower 390:19
upon England's mountains g. 67:38
voices of children are heard on the g. 68:52
when woods are getting g. 93:88
whiten the g. plains under 368:22
Greenery-yallery ... young man 146:18
Greenland: from G.'s icy mountains 159:86
Greensleeves: G. was all my joy 16:83
who but Lady G.? 16:83
Greet: how shd. I g. thee? 86:1
Grenadier: for the British G. 18:6
Grew: where only one g. before 381:2
Grey: by thy long g. beard 104:42
lend me yr. g. mare 19:12
that g. iniquity 314:68
Greyhounds: stand like g. in the slips 319:47
Grief: after long g. and pain 388:88
but for our g., as if it had not been 367:12
g. and pain for promis'd joy. 80:18
g. itself be mortal 367:12
g. returns with the revolving year 367:10
g., with a glass that ran 382:16
hopeless g. is passionless 73:12
past help shd. be past g. 361:14
silent manliness of g. 150:71

Grief (*continued*)
smiling at g. 360:89
time and thinking tame the g. 250:38
when thou art old ... g. enough 156:48
Griefs: of all the g. that harass 172:54
secret ... are their g. and fears 24:94
Grin: g. like a dog, and run about 42:12
taking a fee with a g. 144:84
Grind: my life is one demd horrid g. 120:54
[ye] g. the faces of the poor 48:32
Grinds: with exactness g. he all 198:99
Grindstone: one's nose to the g. 273:4
Grinning; antic sits ... g. at his pomp 350:54
Grist: bring g. to the mill 265:49
Groan: bitter g. of a martyr's woe 66–7:35
future ages g. for this foul act 350:56
Groaned: my mother g., my father wept 67:44
Groaning: strong gongs g. 99:71
Grocer: God made the wicked G. 99:76
Groomed: nicely g., like a mushroom 193:47
Grosvenor Gallery ... young man 146:18
Grotesque: so g. a blunder 33–4:19
Ground: betwixt the stirrup and the g. 87:16
blood of English shall manure the g. 350:56
children of Israel ... upon the dry g. 36:78
commit his body to the g. 65:15
fathom-line cd. never touch the g. 313:54
let us sit upon the g. 350:54
massa's in de cold, cold g. 138:3
native air, in his own g. 251:28
upon the g., can fall no lower 269:77
when every rood of g. maintained 150:63
Grovel: souls that g. 87:13
Grovelled: he g. ... and my-lorded 389:13
Groves: o'er shady g. they hover 400:54
Grow: ask me where they do g. 162:15
g. up with the country 156:47
Growed: I 'spect I g. 380:85
Growled: cracked and g. and roared and howled 105:46

Growth: I cannot give it vital g. again 346:19

*Grubstreet* ... near Moorfields 172:45

Grudge: feed fat the ancient g. 338:3

Grumble: nothing whatever to g. at 148:40

Grumbling: the g. grew to a ... rumbling 75:40

Grundy, the end of Solomon G. 238:71

Grunt and sweat under a weary life 309:95

Gruntled: he was far from being g. 408:51

Gryphon: called lessons, the G. remarked 91:61

Guard: Alice is marrying one of the g. 211:54

    g. the guards themselves? 180:69

Guards: up, G., and at 'em 401:60

*Guerre: la g. ... industrie nationale* 224:47

Guess: I g. an' fear 80–1:19

Guest: constant g. is never welcome 258:24

    dull fighter and a keen g. 315:84

Guests: the G. star-scattered on the Grass 136:83

    unbidden g. ... welcomest when ... gone 321:63

Guide: custom ... the great g. 168:91

    g. me, O thou great Redeemer 407:40

    my g., philosopher and friend 250:19

Guilders: 'will you give me a thousand g.?' 75:39

Guilt: other pens dwell on g. and misery 23:71

    what art can wash her g.? 152:2

Guilty: better that ten g. ... escape 66:26

    my soul ... g. of dust and sin 161:12

    suspicion ... haunts the g. mind 322:72

    we make g. of our disasters the sun 327:53

Guinea: worth a g. a box 11:34

Guinness is good for you 11:28

Gulf: a great g. fixed 55:87

Gull's way and the whale's way 208:16

Gum: Arabian trees their med'cinable g. 346–7:22

Gummidge: Mrs G.'s words 119:37

Gunga Din 190:1

Gunner and his mate lov'd Mall 356:43

**Gunpowder treason and plot 15:69**

Guns: g. aren't lawful, nooses give 243:23

    g. will make us powerful; butter ... fat 149:58

    loaded g. with boys 114:82

    strong gongs groaning as the g. boom far 99:71

*Gustibus: de g. non est disputandum* 259:53

Gypsies: play with the g. in the wood 236:57

Gyre and gimble in the wabe 91:69

Ha, ha, ha, you and me 16:84

Habit: costly thy h. as thy purse can buy 306:56

    h. is a great deadener 30:76

    h. with him was all the test of truth 114:79

    honour ... in the meanest h. 355:25

Habitation: local h. and a name 342:53

Habits: h. ... carry them far apart 108:2

    needs reforming as other people's h. 394:72

Hackney: see to H. ('A) Marshes 29:66

Haggards ride no more 378:63

Hags: secret, black, and midnight h. 335:60

Hail: h. and farewell 94:6

    h., divinest Melancholy! 213:83

    h., Holy Light 218:58

    h., horrors! h. 216:34

    h., wedded Love 219:71

    my gracious silence, h.! 303:13

    the flail of the lashing h. 368:22

    to be h. fellow well met 265:50

Hailed at the twilight's last gleaming 188:79

Hair: beauty draws us with a single h. 251:35

    each particular h. to stand on end 307:64

    graduates in their golden h. 388:95

    her h. was long, her foot was light 183:8

    I must sugar my h. 91:64

    if a woman have long h. 57:52

    Jeanie with the light brown h. 138:2

    [letters] serve ... to pin up one's h. 109:11

    shall I part my h. behind? 131:4

    smooths her h. with automatic hand 131:12

    train of thy amber-dropping h. 213:80

Hairs: given me over in my grey h. 408:55

how ill white h. become a ... jester 318:34

to split h. 278:67

Hairy: Esau, my brother, is a h. man 36:59

Hal: why, H., 'tis my vocation, H. 312:47

Half: h. a league onward 385:40

h. a trade and h. an art 170:12

h. as much as ... Mr Toad 153:14

h.-seas over 265:53

knows not how the other h. lives 265:52

the h. that's got my keys 153:9

too civil by h. 372:73

too clever by h. 280:49

yr. servant's cut in h. 153:9

youth shows but h. 75–6:46

Half-a-crown: if I fling h. to a beggar 175:84

Half-a-dozen of the other 206:87, 277:41

Half-way: don't meet trouble h. 272:53

Halifax: from Hell, Hull and H. ... deliver us 266:85

Hall: bride hath paced into the h. 104:45

the Douglas in his h. 296:12

Tom bears logs into the h. 332:20

Hallelujah: h.! I'm alive 242:8

here lies my wife, h.! 13:44

Hallowed: place of justice is an h. place 26:36

Halo? ... one more thing to keep clean 140:32

Halt: how long h. ye between two opinions 40:56

Halves: never do things by h. 266:54

Hamelin town's in Brunswick 75:36

Hamlet: I saw H. Prince of Denmark played 134:54

O H., what a falling off! 307:68

rude forefathers of the h. 155:33

Hamlets brown, and dim-discover'd spires 107:88

Hammock: Drake he's in his h. 230:11

Hampden: some village H. 155:38

Hand: bite the h. that fed them 78:83

captain's h. on his shoulder smote 230:14

cold h. ... warm heart 258:19

come, give me your h. 335:70

discern between ... right h. ... left h. 50:88

Hand (continued)

earth, I do salute thee with my h. 349:49

every man's h. against him 35:53

great is the h. that holds dominion 390:20

h. and glove 266:55

h. for h., foot for foot 37:93

h. ... head ... heart of man go together 292:63

h. in h., on ... edge of the sand 195:62

h. open as day for ... charity 317:25

h. that signed the treaty 390:20

have still the upper h. 111:39

having put his h. to the plough 54:74

her h. on his thick skull 127:49

I fear thy skinny h. 105:53

infinity in the palm of your h. 66:27

iron h. in a velvet glove 267:20

leans her cheek upon her h. 353:98

lend thy guiding h. 221:11

let not thy left h. know 52:16

O that I were a glove upon that h. 353:98

one whose h. ... threw a pearl away 346–7:22

our times are in His h. 75:46

reason is our soul's left h. 123:5

smooths ... hair with automatic h. 131:12

the h. of war 348:41

the handle toward my h. 334:40

the larger heart, the kindlier h. 387:71

this blood clean from my h. 334:43

this my h. will rather 334:43

touch of a vanish'd h. 384:37

we are in God's h. 73:14

what immortal h. or eye 68:46

whatsoever thy h. findeth to do 47:7

when I stretched out my h. 379:69

who will stand on either h.? 201:37

will not sweeten this little h. 335:69

Handbag: an ordinary h. in fact 405:11

yes, Lady Bracknell ... a h. 405:11

Handful: just for a h. of silver he left us 74:28

Handle: and I polished up the h. 147:26

the h. toward my hand 334:40

Hands: and then take h. 355:34

by fairy h. their knell is rung 107:90

fall into the h. of the living God 59:98

Haunt (*continued*)
  our life, exempt from public h.
  300:75

Haunted: beneath a waning moon was
  h.  106:72
  on summers eves by h. stream
  214:3

Have: not good to want and to h.
  265:35
  to h. and to hold  64:7
  what we h. we prize not  343:81

Havens: ports and happy h.  348:36

Haves: the *H.* and the *Have-Nots*
  95:10

Havoc: Cry 'H.!' and let slip the dogs
  of war  324:9

Hawk: I know a h. from a handsaw
  308:83

Hawks: all haggard h. will stoop
  191:22

Hawthorn: gives not the h. bush a
  sweeter shade?  322:71
  under the h. in the dale  214:98

Hay: dance an antic h.  204:68
  make h. while the sun shines  271:27

Haystack: needle in a h.  272:81

He: every h. has ... a she  16:79

Head: a h. grown gray in vain  367:16
  better be the h. of a dog  255:20
  born about three ... with a white h.
  316:99
  four angels round my h.  10:13
  frost which binds so dear a h.  367:9
  hath no h., needs no hat  266:74
  heavy weight from off my h.  350:58
  here rests his h. upon the lap of earth
  155:40
  I ... covered up her h.  17:96
  I will make you shorter by a h.
  132:19
  if you can keep yr. h. when all about
  you  190:2
  in the heart or in the h.  339:14
  incessantly stand on your h.  90:48
  lay your sleeping h., my love  22:60
  left it dead and with its h.  92:70
  my h. is bending low  138:8
  my h. is bloody, but unbowed  160:94
  old h. on young shoulders  274:19
  on the ... hands little gold h.  211:61
  one small h. cd. carry all he knew
  150:69
  precious jewel in his h.  300:75
  rise up before the hoary h.  38:1
  shoot ... this old gray h.  403:89
  shouting 'Off with his h.!'  91:56
  talked ... after his h. was cut off
  15:66

Head (*continued*)
  thou art a traitor. Off with his h.!
  352:75
  turns no more his h.  106:60
  uneasy lies the h. that wears a crown
  317:14
  wash ... yr. h. never  282:7
  weak h. with strongest bias rules
  249:93
  what though his h. be empty  382:8
  which way the h. lies  286:95
  with intention to break his h.  175:84

Headache: awake with a dismal h.
  144:91

Heads: bald h. are soon shaven  255:90
  h. I win, tails you lose  115:86,
  266:75
  houseless h. and unfed sides  329:78
  mob has many h., but no brains
  272:62
  stars hide their diminished h.  218:61
  their h. are green  194:58
  two h. are better than one  281:77

Headstone: become the h. of the corner
  44:35

Headstrong: as h. as an allegory
  372:72

Head-waiter who's allowed to sit
  395:82

Heal: ever h. but by degrees?  345:3

Healed: they have h. also the hurt
  49:54

Healing: arise with h. in his wings
  51:1

Health: a h. unto his Majesty  16:85
  and h. on both!  335:54
  good wife and h. ... best wealth
  265:37
  h.! h.! the blessing of the rich!
  179:60
  h. is better than wealth  266:76
  h. is not valued till sickness
  266:77
  he that will not drink his h.  16:85
  he that will this h. deny  129:78
  me? In my state of h.?  180:77
  the popular idea of h.  406:27

Healthy: all h. instinct for it  82:46
  h. and wealthy and dead  392:42
  h. citizens ... greatest asset  101:6
  h., wealthy and wise  261:5
  imagination of a boy is h.  181:84
  nobody is h. in London  23:66

Hear: chink in the floor ... let me h.
  383:26
  deaf as those who won't h.  260:59
  destroyer and preserver, h., oh h.!
  369:36

Hear (*continued*)

do you h. the children weeping?
73:11

few love to h. the sins   347:25

grossly close it in, we cannot h.
340:22

h. a voice in every wind   154:28

h. dat mournful sound   138:3

h. twice before you speak   266:79

I h. thee and rejoice   415:37

never merry when I h. sweet music
340:23

the ear begins to h.   71:87

time ... when you will h. me   122:88

to h. the lark begin his flight   214:97

Heard: cuckoo is in June, h., not
regarded   314:77

h. a thousand blended notes   411:83

h. melodies are sweet   183:17

I h. a maid singing in the valley
16:80

more he h. the less he spoke   285:82

not a drum was h.   408:52

voice I h. this passing night was h.
184:30

Hearing: I have heard of thee by the h.
41:79

Hears: she neither h. nor sees   414:19

Heart: a broken and a contrite h.
42:9

a h. grown cold ... in vain   367:16

a man after his own h.   39:40

absence makes h. grow fonder
15:72, 29:68

all that mighty h. is lying still   412:97

as well as want of H.!   165:62

awake, my h., to be loved   70:75

ay, in my h. of h.   310:6

because my h. is pure   389:3

blessed are the pure in h.   52:10

bring with you a h. that watches
415:29

bringing Soviet power into the h. of
Western Europe   102:7

but [give] not yr. h. away   167:81

but his flaw'd h. ... too weak   330:3

cold hand ... warm h.   258:19

comes from the h., goes to the h.
107:84

enter every trembling h.   402:72

faint h. never won fair lady   263:44

fair face ... foul h.   262:47

find Calais lying in my h.   207:10

fool hath said in his h.   41:84

give me back my h.   86:95

Greensleeves was my h. of gold
16:83

hardened Pharaoh's h.   36:76

Heart (*continued*)

h. and stomach of a king   132:20

h. of oak are our ships   141:48

h. shall break into ... flaws   328:69

h.'s lightness from ... May   181:87

h. to poke poor Billy   153:11

h. upon my sleeves for daws
344:89

h. which grief hath cankered   87:12

heavy purse ... light h.   266:82

her h. was young and gay   157:58

his h. is in his mouth   266:81

his h.'s his mouth   303–4:17

his tiger's h. wrapped in ... hide
156:49

holiness of the h.'s affection   186:50

hope deferred maketh ... h. sick
45:66

how my h. grows weary   138:6

I feel my h. new open'd   322:81

I said to H., 'How goes it?'   31:97

I shall light a candle ... in thine h.
61:38

I sleep but my h. waketh   47:25

if thou didst ever hold me in thy h.
312:38

in the h., not in the knees   171:37

in the h. or in the head   339:14

intellect ... fooled by the h.   288:16

inward fragrance of each other's h.
182:3

it's Oh! in my h.   179:63

language of the h.   248:87

light purse ... heavy h.   269:83

like music on my h.   106:61

·look in thy h. and write   373:84

love the Lord ... with all thine h.
38:6

many a h. is aching   158:71

meditation of my h. be acceptable
42:89

merry h. ... cheerful countenance
45:70

merry h. goes all the day   361:19

my h. aches and a drowsy numbness
184:23

my h. leaps up when I behold   412:98

my h. untravelled ... turns to thee
151:90

my true love hath my h.   372:83

nation ... that had the lion h.
102:11

natural language of the h.   297:38

never a crack in my h.   417:56

no longer lacerates his h.   382:12

now cracks a noble h.   312:40

open not thine h. to every man
62:49

Heart (*continued*)

overset the brain, or break the h. 411:88

perilous stuff which weighs upon the h. 336:72

pity ... in the h. of love 417:57

poor h. that never rejoices 274:50

pourest thy full h. 370:49

quickening life from the earth's h. 367:11

rend yr. h. and not yr. garments 50:78

rose in the deeps of my h. 417:55

serve the Lord ... with all thy h. 38:9

Shakespeare unlocked his h. 412:95

shall command my h. and me 115:84

shot through his h. on Sunday 379:71

so the h. be right 286:95

strike mine eyes but not my h. 179:52

strings, said Mr. Tappertit, in the ... h. 119:32

take thy beak from out my h. 247:67

tears fall in my h. 396:90

the h. has its reasons 244:28

the larger h., the kindlier hand 387:71

the laughter of her h. 157:58

the Lord looketh on the h. 39:42

the waters of the h. 390:21

them that are of a broken h. 42:1

through the sad h. of Ruth 184:30

to lose your h.'s desire ... to gain it 365:83

warm the cockles of the h. 282:5

way to an Englishman's h. 282:13

wear him in my h.'s core 310:6

wear one's h. on one's sleeve 282:17

what female h. can gold despise? 154:24

what the false h. doth know 333:39

when my h. was young and gay 138:7

where my h. lies 74:33

whose ... complexion and whose h. 362:24

wine that maketh glad the h. 43:24

with a h. for any fate 198:98

with h., and soul, and voice 229:2

with rue my h. is laden 167:84

woman with the h. 389:2

word 'Callous' engraved on her h. 297:31

Heart-ache: to say we end the h. 309:95

Hearts: agonies, the strife of human h. 185:37

apply our h. unto wisdom 43:18

enthroned in the h. of kings 339:15

grows old with their sick h. 180:70

h. are dry as summer dust 409:64

h. at peace, under an English heaven 71:94

kind h. are more than coronets 387:74

men with splendid h. 71:90

our h., though stout and brave 198:96

thousand creeds ... move men's h. 71:85

two h. that beat as one 200:18

wand'ring eyes and heedless h. 154:26

while yr. h. are yearning 137:94

Heat: fear no more the h. o' th' sun 304:29

have neither h. nor light 400:48

h. me these irons hot 327:42

h. not a furnace for your foe 322:74

I know not where is that Promethean h. 346:19

thinketh on fantastic summer's h. 348:37

Heath: a wind on the h. 69:65

Heathen: why do the h. rage? 41:80

Heaven: a h. in a wild flower 66:27

a H. on Earth 219:65

a new h. and a new earth 61:32

all this and h. too 161:2

brightest h. of invention 318:36

builds a h. in hell's despair 67:43

created the h. and the earth 34:26

differ as H. and earth 385:52

droppeth as the gentle rain from h. 339:15

every purpose under the h. 46:98

fallen from h., O Lucifer 48:38

fantastic tricks before high h. 337:87

first h. ... passed away 61:32

floor of h. is thick inlaid 340:22

friends ... in h. and hell 264:96

gain'd from h. ... a friend 155:41

garden hard by H. 69:68

God is in h. and thou upon earth 46:1

God's in his h. 75:44

h. and earth shall pass away 295:7

h. has no rage like love to hatred turned 108:6

h. is in these lips 204:63

Heaven (*continued*)
H. itself wd. stoop to her [Virtue]
213:81
H. lies about us in our infancy
410:77
H. tries earth if it be in tune 200:25
Hell I suffer seems a H. 218:62
high H. rejects the lore 409:60
how long ... permit to H. 220:98
I see H.'s glories shine 71:84
in earth ... as it is in h. 52:18
in the nurseries of H. 391:32
joy shall be in h. 54:80
justice be done, though h. fall
263:59
keys of the kingdom of h. 53:35
kingdom of h. is at hand 51:4
leave to H. the measure ... choice
174:71
love is h. and h. is love 295:2
make h. drowsy with the harmony
331:15
marriages are made in h. 274:41
mind ... can make a H. of Hell
216:35
more things in h. and earth 307:69
new Jerusalem ... out of h. 61:33
not mad, sweet h.! 328:60
O h., were men but constant 361:11
open face of h. 186:47
or what's a h. for? 73:15
our conversation is in h. 58:77
over his living head like H. 367:13
parting is all we know of h. 122:82
places that the eye of h. visits
348:36
praise my soul, the King of H.
201:34
progressive virtue, and approving
H.! 391:34
puts all H. in a rage 66:28
reign in Hell than serve in H. 216:36
shun the h. that leads men to this hell
363:51
steep and thorny way to h. 306:54
summons thee to h. or to hell
334:41
that from H., or near it 370:49
that h.'s vault shd. crack 330:4
there was silence in h. 61:27
to be young was very H.! 413:9
to seek the ... eye of h. to garnish
327:43
top ... reached to h. 36:61
under an English h. 71:94
watered h. with their tears 68:47
when Britain first, at H.'s command
391:33

Heavens: pure as the naked h. 413:4
spangled h., a shining frame 9:9
the h. declare the glory of God 41:86
the h. themselves, the planets ...
observe 358:66
till you are clothed with the h.
392:52
Heaviness foreruns the good event
317:22
Heavy: a light wife doth make a h.
husband 340:26
Hebrew: called in the H. tongue Armageddon 61:31
Hector: of H. and Lysander 18:6
Hecuba: what's H. to him or he to H.?
308:90
Hedge: a voice ... from h. to h. 185:42
Heels: if yr. h. are nimble and light
233:36
to cool one's h. 259:27
Heigh! the doxy over the dale 361:17
Heigh-ho: h.! says Rowley 232:30
sing h. unto the green holly 302:91
Height: happiness makes up in h.
139:28
to the h. of this great argument
216:29
Heir: dear son of memory, great h. of
fame 216:24
first h. of my invention 364:58
Heiresses: all h. are beautiful 128:65
Helen: dust hath closed H.'s eye
229:99
sweet H., make me immortal 204:63
Helena: all is dross that is not H.
204:63
Hell: a shout that tore H.'s concave
217:40
airs from heaven or blasts from h.
307:60
all H. broke loose 219:74
all we need of h. 122:82
and H. followed with him 61:26
better to reign in H. 216:36
boys, it [war] is all h. 372:81
builds a Heaven in H.'s despair
67:43
down to h.; and say I sent thee
322:73
dunnest smoke of h. 333:33
England ... h. for horses 81:31
gates of h. shall not prevail 53:34
go ... to h. in embroidery 256:24
heaven that leads men to this h.
363:51
h. and Chancery are always open
266:83
h. is a city ... like London 369:41

**Hell** (*continued*)
h. itself breathes out contagion 310:13
h. to which hate and fear ... condemn 292:66
into the mouth of H. 385:43
Italy ... h. for women 81:31
jealousy ... injured lover's h. 219:79
lifetime of happiness! ... h. on earth 365:78
make a Heaven of H., a H. of Heaven 216:35
myself am H. 218:62
no redemption from h. 276:82
nor h. a fury like a woman scorned 108:6
prompted ... by heaven and h. 309:93
road to h. is paved ... intentions 266:84
summons thee to heaven or to h. 334:41
the bells of h. go ting-a-ling 16:76
to reign ... though in H. 216:36
though h. shd. bar the way 231:21
ugly h., gape not! come not, Lucifer! 204:66
way down to H. is easy 397:2
way ... that out of H. leads 218:54
when war begins, h. opens 282:3
which way I fly is H. 218:62
women ... as Heaven and H. 385:52
**Hellish** dark, and smells of cheese! 380:90
**Helmsman**: so the h. answered 198:1
**Help**: a very present h. 42:7
H. of the helpless 201:31
h. yourself, heaven will h. you 136:89
hills, from whence cometh my h. 44:37
many of yr. countrymen cannot h. 174:83
not enough to h. the feeble up 357:59
O God, our h. in ages past 399:38
past h. shd. be past grief 361:14
past my h. is past my care 29:72
since there's no h. ... kiss and part 125:34
the rich can h. themselves 264:20
**Helpers**: when other h. fail 201:31
**Helpless**: Help of the h., O Abide with me 201:31
h., naked, piping loud 67–8:44
**Hemlock**: as though of h. I had drunk 184:23

**Hen**: two Owls and a H. 195:66
yaf nat of that text a pulled h. 96:29
**Henry**: the chief defect of H. King 31:90
**Henry IV Part II**: abdicated in favour of H. 297:30
**Hens**: three French h. 238:73
**Heraldry**: the boast of h., the pomp of power 155:35
**Herbert Spencer**: expression ... used by Mr H. 117:8
**Herbs**: dinner of h. where love is 45:71
**Hercules**: and some of H. 18:6
let H. ... do what he may 312:34
**Herd**: lowing h. winds slowly 155:30
**Here**: h. he lies where he longed to be 379:76
h. is my journey's end, h. is my butt 346:21
h. lie I and ... daughters 12:41
h. lies a man who was killed 12:42
h. lies a poor woman 12:43
h. lies ... Mary Ann Lowder 13:46
h. lies my wife ... hallelujee! 13:44
h. lies my wife: h. let her lie! 127:60
h. lies ... Richard Hind 13:45
h. lies Will Smith 13:47
h. we come gathering nuts in May 16:86
I have been h. before 291:53
the ice was h., the ice was there 105:46
'tis neither h. nor there 346:15
we're h. because we're h. 19:13
**Hereafter**: she shd. have died h. 336:76
what is love? 'Tis not h. 359:84
what may come h. 382:19
**Heresies**: begin as h. ... end as superstitions 169:6
**Heresy**: ancient saying is no h. 339:11
there is no worse h. 9:1
**Heretics**: Jews, Turks, Infidels, and H. 64:88
**Heritage**: Americans ... proud of our ancient h. 188:74
**Hermit**: dwell a weeping h. there! 107–8:90
**Hermitage**: my gorgeous palace for a h. 350:55
**Hermits** are contented with their cells 411:89
**Hero**: be a h. ... must drink brandy 177:31
every h. becomes a bore 133:41
no man is a h. to his valet 111:35
see the conquering h. comes 226:68

History (*continued*)
 world h. ... world's judgment
  294:86
Hit: a h., a very palpable h. 312:36
 h. the nail on the head 267:88
Hitch yr. wagon to a star 133:43
Hither: come h., come h. 300:83
Hitler has missed the bus 95:17
Hive: a h. for the honey bee 417:52
Hoarded: beauty is nature's coin; must
  not be h. 213:79
Hobson's choice 267:89
Hodgepodge: our ... tongue a galli-
  maufry or h. 377:48
Hoist with his own petard 267:90
Holborn: when I was last in H. 352:74
Hold: for ever h. his peace 64:5
 h. fast that which is good 59:85
 to have and to h. 64:7
Hole: a better 'ole 27:47
 Roöötten, Beëëastly, Silly H.!
  401:63
Holes where eyes did once inhabit
  352:72
Holidays: if ... year were playing h.
  313:50
Holiness: go! put off H.! 67:37
 h. of the Heart's affection 186:50
Hollow: we are the h. men 130:94
Holly: heigh-ho unto the green h.
  302:91
 the h. and the ivy 16:87
 the h. bears the crown 16–17:87
Holy: an h. and a good thought 63:65
 H. Deadlock 161:10
 h., divine, good, amiable 220:94
 h., fair and wise is she 361:8
 h., h., h., all the Saints adore thee
  160:88
 hunters been nat h. men 96:29
 sabbath day – to keep it h. 37:86
 savage place! As h. and enchanted
  106:72
 the h. city, new Jerusalem 61:33
 was the h. Lamb of God 67:38
 ye shall be h. ... for I the Lord ... am
  h. 37:97
Holy Roman Empire was neither holy,
  nor Roman, nor an Empire
  398:14
Holy writ: odd old ends ... of h.
  351:70
Homage: hypocrisy ... h. paid by vice
  288:17
Home: as much like h. as we can
  140:35
 at h. I was in a better place 300:81
 blest by suns of h. 71:93

Home (*continued*)
 charity begins at h. 258:96
 comin' for to carry me h. 18:8
 don't want to go h.. in the dark
  161:5
 dunce that has been kept at h.
  113:65
 east or west, h. is best 261:7
 fools at h. condemn 'em 356:48
 God, who is our h. 410:77
 his first, best country ... h. 151:91
 h. art gone, and ta'en thy wages
  304–5:29
 h. is heaven 228:90
 h. is the sailor, h. from sea 379:76
 h. life of our own dear Queen 14:62
 h. of the bean and the cod 69:67
 h. on the rolling deep 293:81
 h ... they have to take you in
  139:24
 hunter h. from the hill 379:76
 I am far from h. 230:16
 it's h. and it's h. ... fain wad I be
  116:97
 keep the h. fires burning 137:94
 ladybird, ladybird, fly away h.
  234:46
 leave them alone, and they'll come h.
  234:48
 man goeth to his long h. 47:12
 our eternal h. 399:38
 pillage ... with merry march bring h.
  318:23
 pleasure never is at h. 182:95
 returned h. the previous night 76:52
 sick for h., she stood in tears
  184:30
 Sublimity to welcome me h. 187:63
 sweet h. of ... fears and hopes and
  joys 183:15
 that is fit h. for thee 415:39
 the old Kentucky H. 138:4
 there's no place like h. 245:34
 they dream of h. 137:94
 this little pig stayed at h. 239:78
 what's the good of a h.? 156:52
Homely: home-keeping youth hath ...
  h. wits 360:4
Homer: seven cities warred for H.,
  being dead 163:26
 shame when the worthy H. nods
  166:71
 with the single exception of H.
  367:8
*Homerus: quandoque ... dormitat H.*
  166:71
Homes: the stately h. of England!
  111:39, 160:90

Homestead, Braddock, Birmingham
293:80

*Homines: quot h. tot sententiae* 389:7

Honest: armour is his h. thought
416:48

   deal with none but h. men 276:87

   good to be h. and true 17:93

   h. God is the noblest work of man
170:14

   h. man sent to lie abroad 416:46

   h. man's the noblest work of God
250:16

   I am not naturally h. 362:25

   she was poor but she was h. 18:3

   the world's grown h. 308:79

   to be h. ... is to be one man pick'd
out 308:76

Honesty: corruption wins not more
than h. 323:83

   for saving of thine h. 226:67

   h. is the best policy 267:94

   neither h., manhood, nor ... fellowship 312:48

   no legacy is so rich as h. 298:45

Honey: and is there h. still for tea?
71:91

   civil citizens kneading up the h.
318–19:39

   eat our pot of h. on the grave
209:33

   flowing with milk and h. 36:70

   funny how a bear likes h.? 211:62

   gather h. all the day 399:35

   I always eat peas with h. 15:63

   in the parlour eating bread and h.
238:70

   it's no go my h. love 203:55

   some h., and plenty of money
195:60

   sweeter than h. and the h.-comb
41:88

   Tiggers don't like h. 210:50

Honey-dew: he on h. hath fed 107:76

Honeyed middle of the night 181:90

*Honi soit qui mal y pense* 267:95

Honour: as h., love, obedience 336:71

   brilliance ... left to the fighter's h.
160:92

   can h. set to a leg? 315:88

   desires h. ... not worthy of h.
260:70

   drown'd my H. in a shallow Cup
136:82

   fewer men, the greater share of h.
320:55

   giving h. unto the wife 60:10

   his h. rooted in dishonour 385:50

   h. a physician with the h. due 62:57

Honour (*continued*)

   h. all men ... h. the king 60:9

   H. comes, a pilgrim grey 107–8:90

   h. for his valour 325:11

   h. hath no skill in surgery 315:88

   h. is a mere scutcheon 315:88

   h. is the subject of my story 323:91

   h. of honourable men 395:79

   h. peereth in the meanest habit
355:25

   h. pricks me on 315:88

   h. sinks where commerce ... prevails
151:92

   h.'s thought reigns solely 319:40

   h. the face of the old man 38:1

   h. thy father and thy mother 37:87

   I believe it is ... peace with h.
95:16

   if I give thee h. due 214:96

   if it be a sin to covet h. 320:56

   if peace cannot be ... with h.
292:65

   jealous in h. 301:90

   loss of h. was a wrench 153:12

   loved I not H. more 200:17

   mine h. is my life 347:30

   pledge ... our fortunes, and our
sacred h. 171:27

   pluck bright h. from the ... moon
313:54

   pluck up drowned h. 313:54

   take h. from me ... life is done
347:30

   the louder he talked of his h. 132:27

   there is h. among thieves 267:96

   'tis for the h. of England 109:8

   to h. we call you 141:48

   what is h.? A word 315:88

   when h.'s at the stake 311:24

Honourable: Brutus is an h. man
325:13

Honoured: more h. in the breach than
the observance 307:59

Honours: bears his blushing h. thick
upon him 322:80

   mindless of its just h. 412:95

Hood: can drink with him that wears a
h. 380:81

Hoofs: wound ... with their horses' h.
349:49

Hook: by h. or by crook 267:97

   draw out leviathan with an h.
41:78

   he for subscribers baits his h.
100:84

Hook-nos'd fellow of Rome 317:24

Hooks: silken lines and silver h.
123:4

Hooting: bird of night ... h. and shrieking 324:97

Hope: abandon h. all ye who enter 116:2

because I do not h. to turn 130:88

condemned to h.'s delusive mine 172:52

from h. and fear set free 383:20

give ... h. before you blacken ... world 395:79

h. deferred maketh the heart sick 45:66

h. for the best 267:98

h. from outward forms to win 106:69

h. is a good breakfast 26:38

H. sows what Love shall never reap 290:50

h. springs eternal in the human breast 250:9

in trembling h. repose 155:42

land of h. and glory 33:13

like Lucifer, never to h. again 322-3:81

look forward to with h. 139:23

my gown of glory, h.'s true gage 286:94

no other medicine but only h. 337:89

nursing the unconquerable h. 21:43

our h. for years to come 399:38

pursue ... the phantoms of h. 173:61

reinforcement we may gain from h. 216:33

so farewell h. 218:63

they h. they serve God 344:82

triumph of h. over experience 176:1

true h. is swift and flies 352:83

what was dead was h. 404:95

while there is life, there is h. 269:80

worldly H. ... turns Ashes 135:68

Hopeful: hey, but I'm h. 146:17

Hopefully: to travel h. 380:80

Hopeless grief is passionless 73:12

Hopes: all the h. of future years 197:92

enough for fifty h. and fears 73:17

many the h. that have vanished 158:71

the tender leaves of h. 322:80

vanity of human h., ... public library 173:60

what are the h. of man! 178:43

Hops: Kent – apples, ... h. and women 120:61

Horatio: poor Yorick! I knew him, H. 311:31

there are more things ... H. 307:69

Horde: society is now one polished h. 85:86

Horn: Boy Blue, come blow your h. 234:49

cow with the crumpled h. 239:79

Triton blow his wreathèd h. 412:94

Hornby: my H. and my Barlow long ago! 390:28

Hornets: stir up a h.' nest 278:80

Horns: take the bull by the h. 279:98

Horrible: the h. *double entendre* 13:53

Horrid: sure they are all h.? 23:72

when she was bad, she was h. 199:5

Horrors: I have supp'd full with h. 336:75

Horse: a dog, a h., a rat have life 331:6

behold a pale h. 61:26

cart before the h. 257:86

do not spur a free h. 278:70

fine lady upon a white h. 237:66

flog a dead h. 263:74

h. made ... wife to make 258:1

I speak ... German to my h. 96:24

king ... sent a troop of h. 72:8

know two things about the h. 15:64

lene was his h. as is a rake 96:32

looks a gift h. in the mouth 264:5

may lead a h. to the water 269:62

my kingdom for a h.! 352:87

O for a h. with wings! 304:22

on's h. back at mine hostess' door 326:35

putting money on a h. 32:3

secret ... between a rider and his h. 381:94

sell the pasture now to buy the h. 319:40

some [glory] in their h. 363:41

spit in my face, call me h. 314:65

to Oxford sent a troop of h. 393:54

where's the bloody h.? 87:17

whip for the h., a bridle for the ass 46:83

Horses: all the king's h. 93:84, 233:37

careful of the breed of their h. 245:39

England ... hell of h. 136:86, 261:20

H. and Power and War 189:93

let us take any man's h. 318:33

not hanged for stealing h. 157:56

rebels wound ... with their h.' hoofs 349:49

saddle yr. h. and call up yr. men 294:92

Horses (*continued*)

some trust in chariots and some in h. 42:90

swap h. in mid-stream 196:80

that h. may not be stolen 157:56

Hose: youthful h. ... a world too wide 301:90

Host: a h. of golden daffodils 410:67

a soundless-clapping h. 390:28

Hostages: given h. to fortune 24:96

Hostess: fairer the h., the fouler the reckoning 262:50

sits on's horse back at mine h.' door 326:35

Hot: h. as hell 384:30

H., Cold, Moist and Dry 218:57

soon h., soon cold 278:56

Hotel: living in a vile h. 32:4

Hotspur: the H. of the north 314:62

Hound: a traveller, by the faithful h. 198:94

Hounds: cry of his h. 154:20

h. of spring are on winter's traces 382:15

hunt with the h. 276:8

with his h. and his horn in the morning? 154:20

Hour: but one bare h. to live 204:65

dusky h. friendliest to sleep 219:80

Eternity in an h. 66:27

fools! for I also had my h. 99:69

fourscore ... not an h. more nor less 330:97

from h. to h. we ripe ... rot 301:88

he rose in less than half an h. 32:4

how many makes the h. ... complete 321:70

I have known the lightning's h. 117:15

improve each shining h. 399:35

it chanceth in an h. 258:95

memorial ... to one dead deathless h. 290:49

one far fierce h. and sweet 99:69

that struts and frets his h. 336:76

the h. is come, but not the man 296:17

the h. is ill which severs 368:27

the wish'd, the trysted h. 80:15

this was their finest h. 101:95

wet sea-boy in an h. so rude 317:14

Hours: a heavy weight of h. has chained 369:37

golden h. on angel wings 80:9

lazy, leaden-stepping h. 223:34

lose and neglect the creeping h. 301:89

Hours (*continued*)

love alters not with his brief h. 363:48

six h. in sleep, in ... study six 104:40

sweetest h. that e'er I spend 80:7

three h. a day will produce 393:56

to chase the glowing H. 83:60

two h.' traffic of our stage 353:89

worst effect is banishing for h. 112:53

House: a h. where help wasn't hired 12:43

a h. wherein to tarry 255:97

a man's h. is his castle 104:39

as a moat defensive to a h. 348–9:41

call upon my soul within the h. 359:80

daughters of my father's h. 360:90

eaten me out of h. and home 316:6

glory of this latter h. 51:94

h. fell upon the lords, and ... people 39:30

h. is a machine for living in 110:31

h. that Jack built 239:79

I will build a h. with deep thatch 32:6

if a h. be divided ... h. cannot stand 53:55

in a little crooked h. 239:74

in my Father's h. are many mansions 56:9

in that H. M.P.'s divide 144:88

like a h. on fire 267:6

my h. in the high wood 32:7

my h. ... the h. of prayer 54:62

out of the h. of bondage 37:81

prop that doth sustain my h. 340:20

set thine h. in order 48:41

shalt not covet thy neighbour's h. 37:92

the h. where I was born 165:60

wounded in the h. of my friends 51:97

you take my h. when you do take the prop 340:20

yr. h. is on fire and yr. children all gone 234:46

House of Lords are never in touch 406:28

House of Peers throughout the war 144:90

Household: breathing h. laws 412:2

stables ... real centre of h. 365:72

Houses: a plague o' both your h. 354:11

h. are built to live in 26:28

h. thick and sewers annoy 220:93

Houses (*continued*)

if it wasn't for the h. in between
29:66

lawyers' h. ... on the heads of fools
269:60

Housewife: here's to the h. that's
thrifty 372:78

Hovel: *prefer* ... a h. to ... marble halls
87:13

Hover through the fog and filthy air
332:23

How: a pretty h. town 116:94

How-de-do: here's a h.! 145:5

Howl, h., h., h., ... men of stones!
330:4

Howled: cracked and growled and
roared and h. 105:46

Howling: churlish priest ... when thou
liest h. 312:32

Tom went h. down the street 240:83

Hubbard: old Mother H. 236:59

Hubbub increases more they call out
'Hush!' 182:99

Hue: add another h. unto the rainbow
327:43

native h. of resolution 309:95

Huffy: not h. or stuffy, nor tiny
161:7

Hull: from Hell, H. and Halifax ...
deliver us 266:85

Hum: busy h. of men 214:1

h. of either army stilly sounds
320:50

sad-ey'd justice, with his surly h.
318–19:39

Human: a fearful sign of h. frailty
84:74

Adam was but h. 394:68

all h. things are subject to decay
128:68

all that is h. must retrograde 142:67

climax of all h. ills 84:76

dignity and worth of the h. person
394:76

every h. benefit and enjoyment
78:74

full tide of h. existence ... Charing-
Cross 176:9

[God] ... does a h. form display
66:31

h. on my faithless arm 22:60

h. kind cannot bear ... much reality
130:91

h. race to which ... readers belong
99:78

I may be devout, but I am h.
224:50

I wish I loved the H. Race 286:97

Human (*continued*)

in h. nature ... more of the fool
25:2

purest of h. pleasures 26:29

requires the highest type of h. nature
376:33

the field of h. conflict 101:96

to err is h. 249:4, 267:7

where ... least regard for h. freedom
376:37

women—one half the h. race 27:44

Human being: remember that you are a
h. 366:93

Humane: every h. and gentle virtue
78:89

Humanized: distress hath h. my soul
409:62

Humanity: h. i love you because
116:95

h. with all its fears 197:92

still, sad music of h. 415:35

*Humanum est errare* 267:7

Humble: neither too h. nor too great
203:59

we are so very h. 119:41

you are *not* his most h. servant
177:34

Humbly: walk h. with thy God
51:91

Humility: h. towards the Public
186:58

modest stillness and h. 319:45

Humour: deficient in a sense of h.
107:83

unyok'd h. of yr. idleness 312:49

was ever woman in this h. woo'd ...
won? 351:69

Hump: a woman ... without a positive
h. 389:12

camel's h. is an ugly lump 190:15

uglier yet is the h. we get 190–91:15

Humpty Dumpty: 93:84–6, 233:37

Hundred: about two h. pounds a year
82:38

only one religion ... a h. versions
366:92

uttered it a h. times 164:49

Hunger ... is highly indelicate 148:39

Hungry: if thine enemy be h. 45:81

makes h. where most she satisfies
299:55

Hunter: h. home from the hill 379:76

Lo! the H. of the East 134:65

man is the h. 388:1

mighty h. before the Lord 35:51

Hunter Dunn: Miss J. H. 34:25

Hunters: seith ... h. been nat holy men
96:29

Intellectual: a tear is an i. thing 66:35
  being i., was amongst the noblest
  87:14
  I am an i. chap 144:86
  the word i. suggests 22:61
  thirdly, i. ability 22:54
Intelligence: pawn your i. to buy a
  drink 116:95
Intelligent: i. Mr Toad 153:14
  on the whole ... not i. 148:35
Intent: his first avowed i. 77:64
  truth told with bad i. 66:29
Intentions: paved with good i. 266:84
Intents: be thy i. wicked or charitable
  307:60
Interchange of power pressed too far
  25:14
Interest: *du* [believe] in i. 200:21
Interested: whatever he is most i. in
  28:63
Interesting: those ... in i. situations
  23:67
Interference: no i., and freedom of
  movement 285:88
Interim: acting ... first motion, all the i.
  324:98
Interrupt: you shdn't i. my interrup-
  tions 131:15
Interstices between the intersections
  172:47
Intolerable: possession of [a thing] is i.
  395:83
  this i. deal of sack! 314:70
Intoxication: best of life is but i. 84:71
Introduced: when I'm i. to one 286:97
Intrudes: society where none i. 84:65
Invariable: double glass of the i.
  121:71
Invasion: waiting for the long-promised
  i. 101:97
Invent: all the lies you can i. 66:29
  more than I i. or invented 316:98
  necessary to i. Him 397:12
Invented: I have i. an ... invalid
  405:6
Invention: ascend the brightest heaven
  of i. 318:36
  first heire of my i. 364:58
  necessity is the mother of i. 272:78
  rhyme ... i. of a barbarous age
  216:26
Inverse proportion to the sum 244:26
Investment: no finer i. ... than putting
  milk into babies 101:6
Invincible: none i. as they 112:50
Invisibly: silently, i., he took her 67:41
  wind does move silently, i. 67:40
Involved: I am i. in mankind 124:14

Inward: flash upon that i. eye 410:71
  i. and spiritual grace 64:1
Inwards: he looked i., and found her
  [nature] there 127:59
*Iohannes fac totum:* an absolute *I.*
  156:49
Ireland: my love for England and I.
  287:11
*Irene:* ill success of his tragedy [*I.*]
  174:74
Irish: the I. are a fair people 176:6
  the I. are not in a conspiracy 176:6
Iron: earth stood hard as i. 290:43
  he shall rule them with a rod of i.
  60:21
  if gold ruste, what shall i. do?
  97:41
  i. tongue of midnight 342:55
  strike while the i. is hot 279:85
  the i. entered his soul 267:19
  the i. entered into his soul 43:25
  wink and hold out my i. 319:41
Iron curtain: i. between us and ...
  eastward 102:7
  i. has descended across the Continent
  102:8
Irons: heat me these i. hot 327:42
  many i. in the fire 268:21
Irregulars: the Baker Street i. 125:26
Is: whatever i., i. right 250:12
Island: no man is an i. 124:13
  our rough i.-story 388:94
  we shall defend our i., whatever the
  cost 100–101:94
  Zuleika, on a desert i. 30:82
Isle: but five upon this i. 356:45
  I. of Beauty, fare thee well 29:68
  this i. is full of noises 356:47
  this sceptr'd i. 348:41
Isles: the i. of Greece 84:77
Isolation: stood alone in ... our
  splendid i. 152–3:8
Israel: as the clay ... O house of I.
  49:57
  children of I. ... said ... It is manna
  37:80
  hear, O I. 38:5
  I arose a mother in I. 39:21
  I., Athens, Florence 170:13
  I., what doth ... God require 38:9
  the children of I. ... upon the dry
  ground 36:78
  the sweet psalmist of I. 40:52
It: Greeks had a word for i. 10:14
  I. rolls impotently on 136:80
  lift not thy hands to *I.* 136:80
Italian: I. to women, French to men
  96:24

Joy (*continued*)
  he chortled in his j.  92:71
  he who bends himself a J.  66:34
  impossible as pure ... complete j.
    392:50
  j. cometh in the morning  42:95
  j. of heaven, to earth come down
    402:72
  j. shall be in heaven  54:80
  j.'s soul lies in the doing  358:65
  j. whose hand is ever at his lips
    183:22
  kisses the j. as it flies  66:34
  let j. be unconfined  83:60
  man was made for j. and woe  66:30
  my scrip of j.  286:94
  O j.! that in our embers  411:80
  pledges of Heaven's j.  212:71
  shd. allow itself a life of j.  292:66
  sow in tears ... reap in j.  44:40
  surprised by j. ,... I turned  411:91
  the deep power of j.  415:33
  the oil of j. for mourning  49:53
  there is ... j. for his fortune  325:11
  thy j. and crown eternally  225:53
  weep for j. to stand upon my kingdom
    349:49
  wish you the j. o' th' worm  299:69
Joyful: j. and triumphant  241:91
  make a j. noise unto God  43:13
Joyous hour, we give thee greeting!
    145:4
Joys: all my j. to this are folly  81:29
  can I ever bid these j. farewell?
    185:37
  hence, vain deluding J.  213:82
  j. of parents are secret  24:94
  minds me o' departed j.  81:27
  our youth, our j., our all we have
    286:93
  their homely j. and destiny obscure
    155:34
  unfriendly to society's chief j.
    112:53
Jubilee: we bring the J.  416:45
Judas: so J. did to Christ  350:57
Judge: a j. ... no king can corrupt
    322:78
  a perfect j. will read  249:95
  as sober as a j.  134:60
  I'll be j., I'll be jury  90:46
  j. none blessed before his death
    62:52
  j. not  52:23
  j. of a man by his foes  110:24
  J. of all the earth  35:54
  marshal's truncheon nor the j.'s robe
    337:84

Judge (*continued*)
  never j. from appearances  268:26
Judg(e)ment: a Daniel come to j.
    340:17
  but reserve thy j.  306:56
  causes ... blind man's erring j.
    249:93
  good j. ... relieth not ... on his own
    265:33
  hour of death, ... day of j.  63:79
  no one complains of his j.  288:15
  nor is the People's j. always true
    127:47
  right j. in all things  64:89
  world history is the world's j.
    294:86
  wd. not give his j. rashly  9:8
Judges: hungry j. soon the sentence
    sign  252:37
Judging: want of skill appear ... in j. ill
    249:90
Judgments: with our j. as our watches
    249:91
Jug: little brown j.  16:84
Juggler: a threadbare j.  303:12
Juice (Grease):stew (fry) in one's own j.
    278:73
Julia: where my J.'s lips do smile
    162:15
Juliet: it is the east and J. is the sun
    353:97
Julius: many Caesars ere such another
    J.  304:21
July: English winter—ending in J.
    85:85
Jumblies: lands where the J. live
    194:58
Jump: we'd j. the life to come  333:36
Jumping from the chair  168:96
Jumps: which way the cat j.  257:91
June: cuckoo is in J., heard, not re-
    garded  314:77
  ice in J.  85:91
  rose that's newly sprung in J.  81:21
  she needs not J.  21:46
  so rare as a day in J.?  200:25
Jungle: this is the Law of the J.  190:6
Junk: Epp's statues are j.  14:57
Juno: haughty J.'s unrelenting hate
    128:72
Jury: the j. passing on the prisoner's life
    337:81
  trial by j. ... will be a delusion
    119:28
Jury-men: wretches hang that j. may
    dine  252:37
Just: a beast, but a j. beast  14:59
  cause or j. impediment  64:3

**Kin:** more than k., and less than kind
305:38

one's own k. and kith   228:89

one touch of nature ... whole world
k.   358:72

**Kind:** be to her virtues very k.   253:50

cruel only to be k.   311:20

dumb jewels ... in their silent k.
361:7

just the art of being k.   404:93

k. as she is fair   361:9

k. hearts are more than coronets
387:74

more than kin and less than k.
305:38

neither ingenious, sober, nor k.
13:45

what k. of people do they think we
are?   101:99

**Kindly:** is sure of being k. spoken of
23:67

**Kindness:** A Woman Killed with K.
163:27

beauty lives with k.   361:9

kill a wife with k.   355:24

k. in another's trouble   152:7

save in the way of k.   392:48

tak' a cup o' k.   79:1

too full o' th' milk of human k.
333:32

unremembered acts of k., love
415:31

**Kinds:** soft maids and village k.   107:87

**King:** a little pin bores ... farewell, k.!
350:54

a new k. over Egypt   36:67

all the k.'s horses ... men   93:84,
233:37

as I have served the king.   408:55

ay, every inch a k.   329:89

catch the conscience of the K.
309:94

dainty dish, to set before the K.?
238:70

deny it (repose) to a k.   317:14

discharge my duties as K.   129:81

divinity doth hedge a k.   311:27

glory to the new-born K.   402:71

God save the K.! Will no man say
amen?   350:57

have a k., and officers of sorts   318:39

he that plays the k. ... be welcome
308:82

here lies our sovereign lord the k.
288:21

I'm the k. of the castle   233:41

is the k. dead, the empire unpossess'd?   352:82

**King** (*continued*)

Judge that no k. can corrupt   322:78

k. is a thing men have made   297:25

k. is but a man as I am   320:52

K., observing with judicious eyes
393:54

k. of shreds and patches   311:18

K. shall do it ... shall be contented
350:55

k.'s name is a tower of strength
353:84

lad that's born to be k.   69:69

let us sing, Long live the K.   113:61

mortal temples of a k.   350:54

no bishop, no K.   170:21

Old K. Cole   236:58

old, mad, blind ... dying k.   370:53

one-eyed man is k.   256:48

our Gracious K. ... noble K.   88:29

passing brave to be a k.   205:75

so excellent a k.   305:43

sword of an angel k.   66:35

the K. asked the Queen and   211:59

the k. can do no wrong   66:25

the k. himself has followed her
150:73

the K. is strongest   61:36

the k. loved Esther   40:64

the k. never dies   66:24

the k.'s a bawcock ... heart of gold
320:51

the k. sits in Dunfermline   12:37

the K. to Oxford sent   72:8

think the K. knows about me?
211:55

wash the balm off from an anointed
k.   349:50

we will go by the k.'s high way   38:3

whatsoever K. shall reign   17:92

who Pretender is, or who is K.   83:53

with half the zeal I serv'd my k.
323:84

**King Charles:** in good K.'s golden days
17:91

**King James** ... call for his old shoes
296:21

**King of the Jews:** he that is born K.
51:2

**Kingdom:** for thine is the k.   52:18

keys of the k. of heaven   53:35

k. of heaven is at hand   51:4

my k. for a horse!   353:87

my large k. for a little grave   350:55

my mind to me a k. is   129:77

my new-found land, my k.   123–4:9

of such is the k. of God   54:61

stand upon my k. once again   349:49

state of man, like to a little k.   324:98

Knew (*continued*)

I k. almost as much at eighteen 175:18

I k. him well, and every truant k. 150:68

men fell out they k. not why 82:35

new king ... which k. not Joseph 36:67

one small head cd. carry all he k. 150:69

Knife: cut it without a k. 235:52

cut off their tails ... carving k. 240:80

honey ... keeps them on the k. 15:63

smyler with the k. 97:44

Knight: a verray parfit gentle k. 96:26

gentle k. was pricking on the plain 377:41

k. of the sorrowful countenance 95:8

Knit: k. hands, and beat the ground 212:75

stuff of life to k. me 167:83

Knits up the ravell'd sleave of care 334:42

Knitting: in twisted braids of lilies k. 213:80

Knocked: k. 'em in the Old Kent Road 99:79

k. me down with a feather 268:41

Knocker: tie up the k., say ... I'm dead 248:77

Knocking: k. at Preferment's door 21:41

k. on the moonlit door 118:23

there's k. at the gate 335:70

Knocks you down with the butt end 152:3

Know: all Europe should k. we have blockheads 109:8

all ye need to k. 183:20

and when this we rightly k. 66:30

believe her, though I k. she lies 364:54

but I k. what I like 30:83

do you k. me, my lord? 308:75

does your mother k. you are out? 28:55

every wise man's son doth k. 359:83

he replied, Yes, I k. 13–14:54

I don't know anything ... really 30:83

I k. a bank ... wild thyme blows 341:46

I k. a reasonable woman 251:31

I k. the kings of England 147:31

I k. thee not, old man 318:34

I k. two things about the horse 15:64

Know (*continued*)

I k. you all, and will ... uphold 312:49

I thought so once; but now I k. it 142:60

k. a subject ... k. where ... information 176:14

k. all that there is to be knowed 153:14

k. cause, or just impediment 64:3

k. then thyself 250:13

k. where the shoe pinches 277:31

little do we k. what lays afore us! 120:51

mad, bad, and dangerous to k. 191:24

no knowledge but I k. it 30:80

not to k. me ... yourselves unknown 219:72

not utter what thou dost not k. 313:61

O, that a man might k. the end 326:29

ol' man river ... must k. sumpin' 157:59

pleasant to k. Mr Lear 194:59

she didn't k. what to do 239:76

than the devil you don't k. 256:30

they k. not what they do 55:91

this alone I k. full well 72:96

to k. that which before us lies 220:86

to k. this only, that he nothing knew 221:7

we are greater than we k. 413:14

what I don't k. isn't knowledge 30:80

what shd. they k. of England? 190:97

what the false heart doth k. 333:39

whom truly to k. is everlasting life 64:91

Knoweth: talketh what he k. 24:93

Knowing: as gods, k. good and evil 35:36

k. what shd. not be known 136:84

the misfortune of k. anything 23:73

thinking ... far from k. 280:29

Knowledge: a supercilious k. in accounts 371:70

all k. to be my province 27:39

all our k. is ourselves to know 250:20

conscious ... ignorant is a great step to k. 123:97

continual drinking of K. 186:59

darkeneth counsel by words without k. 41:76

Knowledge *(continued)*

ever-green tree of diabolical k.
371:68

fear of the Lord ... beginning of k.
44:54

having any k. of ... social order
365:84

his k. of life ... so hazy  242:9

increaseth k. increaseth sorrow
46:97

k. comes, but wisdom lingers  387:82

k. enormous makes a God  182:2

k. is of two kinds  176:14

k. is power  268:46

k. of God more than burnt offerings
50:75

night unto night showeth k.  41:87

science is organized k.  376:32

smattering of everything ... k. of
nothing  121:78

still climbing after k. infinite  205:76

Thou ... art still, out-topping k.
21:44

to know no more is woman's happiest k.  219:70

Zeal without k. is fire without light
284:71

Known: best that has been k. and said
21:53

best that is k. and thought  21:50

I am k. and do not want [patronage]
174:78

k. by the company he keeps  271:33

Knows: a woman conceals what she k.
not  283:46

I never k. the children  206:87

if you k. of a better 'ole  27:47

k. nought that k. not this  358:65

no man truly k. another  72:4

nobody k. how to write letters
109:11

the more a man k.  365:74

travels far, k. much  281:55

wise father that k. his own child
339:8

Kubla: in Xanadu did K. Khan
106:71

K. heard from far ancestral voices
107:74

Kyd: Lyly outshine, or sporting K.
179:55

*Labor omnia vicit ... egestas*  397:4

*Laborare est orare*  268:50

Labour: crowns a youth of l.  150:64

ease and alternate l.  391:34

l., and do all thy work  37:86

l. and the wounds are vain  103:32

Labour *(continued)*

l. night and day to be a pilgrim
77:65

l. of an age in piled stones  216:23

months without ... any kind of l.
399:30

persistent l. overcame all things
397:4

six days shalt thou l.  37:86

sore l.'s bath  334:42

true success is to l.  380:80

votes L., ought to be locked up
225:58

yr. work of faith ... l. of love
59:83

Labourer: l. is worthy of his hire  54:75

now the l.'s task is o'er  132:23

Labours: children sweeten l,  24:95

Lack: sigh the l. of many a thing
362:37

Lacked: being l. and lost ... rack the
value  343:81

*Lacrimae: hinc illae l.*  389:4

Lad: and many a lightfoot l.  167:84

cd. that l. be I?  379:73

l. that's born to be king  69:69

song of a l. that is gone  379:73

when I was a l. I served a term
147:26

Ladder: a l. set up on the earth  36:61

down the l. when thou marriest
264:14

l. of all high designs  358:67

wiv a l. and some glasses  29:66

Ladies: a lion among l. ... dreadful
341:47

eleven l. dancing  238:73

good night, sweet l.  311:25

rhyme themselves into l.' favours
321:61

sigh no more, l.  343:68

store of l., whose bright eyes  214:2

Lads: golden l. and girls ... come to
dust  304–5:29

though yr. l. are far away  137:94

two l. that thought ... to be boy
eternal  361:12

Lady: a l. of a certain age  85:81

a l. sweet and kind  18:9

and in my l.'s chamber  232:32

courting his l. in the spring  70:76

faint heart never won fair l.  262:44

fine l. upon a white horse  237:66

for secrecy, no l. closer  313:61

I met a l. in the meads  183:8

I want to talk like a l.  366:94

make a l. of my own  415:30

my l. sweet, arise  304:20

**Lady** (*continued*)
old l. of Threadneedle Street 280:33
returned ... with the l. inside 13:52
sighed for the love of a l. 148–9:46
swear ... like a l. as thou art 314:76
the elder unto the elect l. 60:18
the l. doth protest too much 310:9
there ain't a l. livin' 99:80
there was a young lady named Bright 76:52
they have belied a l. 344:87
went ... to tempt My L. Poltagrue 31:96

**Lady Disdain! Are you yet living?** 342:58

**Ladybird**, fly away home 234:46

**Ladylike:** the birch, most ... l. of trees 200:23

**Lady-smocks** all silver white 332:19

**Lag:** in England ... a comfortable time-l. 401:66

**Laid:** in sad cypress ... l. 359:88

*Laissez faire, laissez passer* 285:88

**Lake:** beside the l., beneath the trees 410:67

**Lamb:** brought as a l. to the slaughter 48:49
did he who made the L., make thee 68:47
go to bed with the l. 264:16
little l., who made thee? 68:50
Mary had a little l. 157:55
pipe a song about a l. 68:49
tempers the wind to the shorn l. 265:26, 379:68
was the holy l. ... on England's ... pastures seen? 67:38
wolf ... shall dwell with the l. 48:37

**Lambs:** death devours l. as well as sheep 260:60
little hills [skipped] like l. 43:29
while the young l. bound 410:75

**Lament:** have I not reason to l. 411:84
short pleasure, long l. 277:35

**Lamp:** I light my l. in the evening 32:5

**Lamps:** bright the l. shone o'er fair women 83:59
l. are going out all over Europe 156:51
who will change old l.? 20:22

**Land:** a traveller from an antique l. 369:39
a woman is a foreign l. 245:32
England's green and pleasant l. 67:38
gone far away into the silent l. 290:44
ill fares the l. 150:62

**Land** (*continued*)
l. flowing with milk and honey 36:70
l. of hope and glory 33:13
l. of the free ... home of the brave 188:80
l. where the Bong-tree grows 195:61
my America, my new-found l. 123–4:9
my native L. – Good Night! 83:58
my own, my native l. 295:5
o'er all the pleasant l. 160:90
ring out the darkness of the l. 387:71
stranger in a strange l. 36:68
sweet l. of liberty 374:5
they are not fit to live on l. 177:16
they came upon a l. ... always afternoon 387:84
westward, look, the l. is bright 104:34
whistles o'er the furrowed l. 214:98

**Landing grounds:** we shall fight on the l. 100–101:94

**Landlord;** come l., fill the ... bowl 16:78

**Lands:** close to the sun in lonely l. 385:47
l. where the Jumblies live 194:58

**Landscape:** now fades the glimmering l. on the sight 155:31

**Lane:** an England while ... a country l. 244:24
little boy who lives down the l. 231:23

**Language:** if everything else in our l. shd. perish 202:43
l. in her eye, her cheek 358:73
Lord did ... confound the l. 35:52
natural l. of the heart 297:38
no l. but the l. of the heart 248:87
no tracing ... but by l. 178:39
plague rid you for learning me yr. l. 355:33
sorry when any l. is lost 178:39
stability or enlargement of the l. 172:42
sure in l. strange she said 183:10
thunder in such lovely l. 194:49
use any l. you choose 144:91
you taught me l., and my profit on't 355:33
yr. ... l. is the l. of Shakespeare 366:93

**Languages:** all l. living and dead 120:52
three or four l. ... without book 359:76

**Languid:** the l. strings do scarcely move 68:55

Lap: his head upon the l. of earth 155:40

 in thy green l. was Nature's Darling 156:44

Lards the lean earth as he walks 313:59

Large as life, and twice as natural 94:93

Largest: shout with the l. [mob] 121:63

Lark: no l. more blithe than he 65:16

 rise with the l. 264:16

 the l.'s on the wing 75:44

 to hear the l. begin his flight 214:97

Larks: hear the l. so high about us 167:82

 two Owls ... four L. and a Wren 195:66

Lars Porsena of Clusium 201:35

Lashed the vice, but spared the name 381:97

Lass: I loved a l., a fair one 408:48

 yon solitary Highland L. 414:20

Lasses: come, l. and lads 16:79

 he dearly lov'd the l. 80:8

 hours ... spent among the l. 80:7

Last: die ... the l. thing I shall do! 243:21

 filling his l. cavity 13:49

 heard the l. of her ... I wonder! 366:5

 it will not l. the night 210:45

 kissing don't l.: cookery do! 209:36

 l. but not least 268:52

 L. of the Mohicans 110:30

 l. out a night in Russia 337:83

 l. taste of sweets, is sweetest l. 348:39

 might be the l., my Mary! 114:76

 of many thousand kisses the poor l. 299:65

 rash ... blaze of riot cannot l. 348:40

 the l. of life, for wh. the first was made 75:46

 there is no l. nor first 75:45

 well, I cannot l. ever 316&1

Late: better l. than never 256:25

 good to marry l. or never 271:47

 make haste, and come too l. 348:38

 marries l., marries ill 271:43

 never too l. to mend 273:88

 too l. to save the stamp 153:10

Lately: read any good books l.? 227:76

Latin: away with him! He speaks L. 321:69

 must carve in L. or in Greek 398:18

 small L. and less Greek 179:56

Latter: meeter to carry off the l. 245:38

Laugh: and l. at gilded butterflies 330:99

 if I l. at any mortal thing 85:79

 l. and the world l. with you 404:91

 l. as I pass in thunder 368:22

 l. to scorn the pow'r of man 335:62

 l. where we must, be candid 250:8

 loud l. that spoke the vacant mind 150:65

 love I l. to scorn 71:86

 make 'em l. ... cry ... wait 287:2

 men that l. and weep 382:19

 the l. broke into ... pieces 28:59

 who but must l.? 248:84

Laughed: little dog l. to see such sport 232:33

 no man who has ... wholly l. 89:39

 when the first baby l. 28:59

Laughing is heard on the hill 68:52

Laughs: flabby hands and irritating l. 145:99

 he l. best who l. last 269:55

Laughter: drinks his wine 'mid l. free 19:10

 I heard the l. of her heart 157:58

 invent anything that tends to l. 316:98

 it wd. be ... l. for a month 313:58

 L. holding both his sides 214:94

 l., learnt of friends 71:94

 nothing so ... ill-bred as audible l. 98:59

 present mirth hath present l. 359:84

 ran ... after the ... music with ... l. 75:43

 sincerest l. with some pain is fraught 370:50

 so is the l. of the fool 46:4

 tired of tears and l. 382:19

Laundry: general idea ... in any ... l. 194:53

Laurel: burned is Apollo's l.-bough 204:67

 l. is green for a season 383:23

 l. outlives not May 383:23

Laurels: the l. all are cut 167:79

 yet once more, O ye l. 215:8

Lavinia: she is L. ... must be loved 357:63

Law: against reason, ... of no force in l. 104:38

 agree, for the l. is costly 254:63

 and the l. doth give it 340:19

 and this is l. that I'll maintain 17:92

 dusty purlieus of the l. 386:64

 every l. is a contract 297:26

 glorious uncertainty of the l. 281:85

 God is thy l., thou mine 219:70

Law (continued)

good of the people ... chief l. 102:15
hard cases make bad l. 266:67
higher l. than the Constitution 297:37
I ... embody the L. 143–4:81
in l.'s grave study 104:40
in vice their l.'s their will 347:26
l. is a bottomless pit 269:56
l. is an ass—a idiot 120:58
l. makers shd. not be l. breakers 269:58
love ... fulfilling of the l. 57:43
love has never known a l. 403:88
may be ... good l. for all that 296:16
much l., but little justice 272:74
nature's l. that man was made to mourn 80:13
necessity hath no l. 272:77
one God, one l., one element 387:73
one l. for the rich 269:57
other sources of international l. 394:76
ought l. to weed it out 24:89
possession is nine points of the l. 275:51
pounds of l., ... not an ounce of love 280:32
rich men rule the l. 151:93
self-preservation is the first l. 277:28
take the l. into one's own hands 279:1
the l. hath not been dead 337:85
the L. is the true embodiment 143:81
the l. of the Yukon 297:35
the L. of Triviality 244:26
the l.'s delay 309:95
the more l., the more offenders 269:59
these ... a l. unto themselves 56:30
this is the l. and the prophets 52:25
this is the L. of the Jungle 190:6
wedded Love, mysterious l. 219:71
windy side of the l. 360:98
wrest once the l. to yr. authority 339:16
Lawn as white as driven snow 362:22
Laws: know not whether l. be right 404:97
l. grind the poor and rich men rule the law 151:93
l. of England are at my command-ment 318:33
l. of the Persians ... Medes 40:63
l. were made to be broken 230:19
let ... l. and learning die 292:68
Nature's L. lay hid in Night 248:88

Laws (continued)

religion breathing household l. 412:2
repeal of bad or obnoxious l. 153:16
sweeter manners, purer l. 386:69
Lawyers: few l. die well 262:57
let's kill all the l. 321:67
Lay on, Macduff 336:80
Lazy: liftin' the l. ones on 154:19
mentally l. ... as well be dead 401–2:69
Lead: do scald like molten l. 330:96
l., Kindly Light ... l. thou me on 230:16
strange ... the life he makes us l. 73:14
Leaden-eyed despairs 184:25
Leadeth me beside the still waters 42:92
Leaf: fall'n into the sear, the yellow l. 336:71
lowest boughs ... are in tiny l. 74:21
November's l. is red 295:8
take a l. out of one's book 279:94
turn over a new l. 281:68
where the dead l. fell ... did it rest 182:97
League: half a l. onward 385:40
keep a l. till death 351:60
Lean: his wife cd. eat no l. 234:45
l. and slipper'd pantaloon 301:90
Leap: a great l. in the dark 163:35
methinks it were an easy l. 313:44
Leaps: morn doth break ... l. in the sky 70:75
my heart l. up when I behold 412:98
Leapt: into the dangerous world I l. 67:44
Leap-year: twenty-nine in each l. 239:77
Lear: how pleasant to know Mr L. 194:59
Learn: gladly wolde he l. 97:34
l. by other men's mistakes 283:41
l. to labour and to wait 198:98
live and l. 270:93
they will l. at no other 78:82
we l. nothing from history 365:85
Learned: he was naturally l. 127:59
loads of l. lumber in his head 249:5
that ... grew within this l. man 204:67
that l. body wanted loyalty 393:54
Learning: a little l. is a dangerous thing 249:94
better than a bushel of l. 266:56
l. is but an adjunct to ourself 331:14
l. makes ... better ... worse 269:64

Learning (*continued*)
 l.'s triumph o'er her barb'rous foes
   173:58
 l. without thought ... thought without l.   108:4
 love of money and love of l.   270:20
 loyal body wanted l.   393:54
 more aid than any l.   383:26
 on scraps of l. dote   417:59
 whence is thy l.?   142:56
Learnt nothing, and forgotten nothing
   384:31
Lease: summer's l. ... too short a date
   362:32
Leave: comrades, l. me here a little
   387:78
 fare thee well, for I must l. thee
   19:11
 l. me there to die   17:88
 l. this barren spot to me   88:18
 l. us nought but grief an' pain   80:18
 Oh, never l. me!   16:80
Leaven: a little l. leaveneth ... lump
   57:48
Leaves: generation of l. ... is that of
   men   165:54
 his hoar l. in the glassy stream
   311:30
 l. dead are driven, like ghosts   369:35
 life out of the dead l.   193:47
 lisp of l.   382:15
 puts forth the tender l. of hope
   322:80
 they sewed fig l. together   35:37
 with forced fingers rude shatter your
   l.   215:8
 with l. and flowers do cover   400:54
*Leben: unnütz L. ... früher Tod*   150:59
Lecher: gilded fly does l. in my sight
   329:90
Lechery: an equivocator with l.   334:45
 l., l.! still wars and l.!   358:74
Lectures: cannot see that l. can do so
   much good   175:95
 I do not give l. or ... charity   403:85
Led by the nose with gold   362:27
Leer: assent with civil l.   248:83
Left: a lady richly l.   338:99
 ah! he l. the thorn with me   81:28
 l. for contemplation not what ... used
   34:24
 l. him alone with his glory   408:53
 sun came up upon the l.   104:44
 we that are l. grow old   65:20
Leg: can honour set to a l.?   315:88
 have a bone in one's l.   256:51
 here I leave my second l.   165:58
Legion: my name is L.   54:57

Legions: give me back my l.   86:4
Legislators: poets are the unacknowledged l.   371:59
Legs: a cannon-ball took off his l.
   165:57
 on one's last l.   269:53
 vast and trunkless l. of stone   369:39
 walk under his huge l.   323:93
Leicester Square: farewell, L.   407:39
Leisure: busiest men ... most l.   257:73
 detest at l.   85:84
 l. answers l.   338:94
Lely: Mr L. ... paint my picture
   115:91
Lend: give a shilling than l. a half-
   crown   256:23
 I'll l. you something   360:99
 men who borrow ... men who l.
   191:25
 when I l. I am a friend   269:69
Lender: neither a borrower nor a l. be
   306:57
Lends: he l. out money gratis   338·3
 three things I never l.   381:91
Length: what [happiness] lacks in l.
   139:28
Leopard: can the ... l. [change] his
   spots?   49:56
 l. shall lie down with the kid   48:37
Leprosy: her skin was as white as l.
   105:52
Lesbia: let us live, my L.   94:3
 *vivamus, mea L., atque amemus*   94:3
Less: I love not man the l.   84:65
 l. than [square deal] no man shall
   have   289:37
 one failing, had a woman ever l.?
   80:12
 stand ... l. betwn. me and the sun
   122:86
 the little l., and what worlds away
   73:19
 you mean you can't take *l.*   90:55
Lessen: they l. from day to day
   91:61
Lessons: reason they're called l.   91:61
Lethe: no. no, go not to L.   183:21
Letter: the l. killeth   58:61
 thou unnecessary l.!   328:61
Letters: his sayings ... like women's l.
   159:77
 I am persecuted with l.   109:11
 I pray you, in yr. l.   346:22
 l. get in the wrong places   212:67
 nobody knows how to write l.
   109:11
Lettuces had been so soporific   252:42
Leveller: death is the grand l.   260:61

Levellers: yr. l. wish to level down 175:89

Levers to lift me up ... being down? 313:57

Leviathan: canst thou draw out l.? 41:78

*Lexicographer.*—a harmless drudge 172:61

Lexicography: not yet so lost in l. 172:41

Liar ... when he speaks the truth 269:73

Liars: all men are l. 43:32
    great talkers are great l. 265:44
    l. ought to [should] have good memories 269:74, 372:82

Libel: greater the truth, the greater the l. 265:46

Liberal: is either a little L. 144:87

*Liberté: l., égalité, fraternité* 19:15
    *O L.! que de crimes ... en ton nom!* 288:26

Libertine: puff'd and reckless l. 306:54
    the air, a charter'd l. 318:38

Liberty: give me l. or ... death 161:6
    God hath given l. to man 116:98
    L., and Union, now and for ever 400:44
    l. cannot long exist 78:86
    l., equality, fraternity 19:15
    l. is precious ... must be rationed 195:69
    l. means responsibility ... men dread it 366:87
    l. ... must be limited 78:85
    L. of the Press ... the *Palladium* 180:65
    l.'s in every blow 81:23
    l. to know, to utter 224:44
    marries for wealth, sells his l. 271:42
    mountain-nymph, sweet L. 214:95
    O l., l., what crimes ... in yr. name! 288:26
    sweet life of l. 374:5
    thy chosen music, L. 412:1

Liberty Hall: this is L. 151:85

Library: a circulating l. in a town 371:68
    my l. was dukedom ... enough 355:31
    vanity of ... hopes ... public l. 173:60

*Libre: l'homme est né l. ... est dans les fers* 291:55

Licence: Government l. to print money 391:35
    the rest love not freedom, but l. 224:46

*Licht: mehr L.!* 150:60

Lick: ill cook that cannot l. his own fingers 258:26, 354:16
    to l. into shape 269:75

Licked: they l. the platter clean 234:45

Lie: a cat and a l. 394:70
    a l. begets a l. 269:76
    after all, what is a l.? 85:82
    and they all dead did l. 105:55
    Father, I cannot tell a l. 399:44
    honest man sent to l. abroad 416:46
    I knowed it was a l. 393:61
    not a stone tell where I l. 251:29
    nothing can need a l. 161:11
    oft when on my couch I l. 410:71
    painters and poets have leave to l. 274:27
    seventh, the L. Direct 303:9
    the L. with Circumstance 303:9
    where my heart lies, let my brain l. 74:33
    while you here do snoring l. 356:39
    who loves to l. with me 300:83

Lied: Heart replied ... but it l. 31:97

Lies: ask no questions ... be told no l. 254:78
    beats all the l. you can invent 66:29
    believe her, though I know she l. 364:54
    one of the social l. 169:8
    one thing is certain ... Rest is L. 135:71
    three kinds of l. 393:63
    where my heart l. 74:33

Life: a daily beauty in his l. 346:16
    a handful of good l. 266:56
    a keen observer of l. 22:61
    a lad of l., an imp of fame 320:51
    a l. like the scriptures 187:64
    a l. on the ocean wave 293:81
    a space of l. between 181:84
    a useless l. is an early death 150:59
    after l.'s fitful fever he sleeps well 334:51
    all his l. ... speaking the truth 405:16
    all the blessings of this l. 64:85
    all the voyage of their l. is bound 326:27
    all this flesh keeps in a little l. 315:92
    and l. is thorny 106:67
    any practical part of l. 9:6
    anything for a quiet l. 121:77, 254:72
    art is long, but l. is short 163:30
    as large as l. 268:51
    bankrupt of l., yet prodigal of ease 126:40
    before us lies in daily l. 220:86

Life (*continued*)

best of l. is but intoxication 84:71

best portion of a good man's l. 415:31

brief l. is here our portion 229:1

cannot tell what you ... think of this l. 323:91

care of human l. ... not their destruction 171:30

commuter—one who spends his l. 402:77

compare human l. to ... Mansion 187:60

custom ... great guide of ... l. 168:91

dear ... as light and l. 80:9

death after l. doth greatly please 377:42

digestion is the great secret of l. 375:12

doth the wingèd l. destroy 66:34

each change of many-colour'd l. 173:58

essential thing in l. is not conquering 111:36

expect more from l. than l. will afford 176:99

fie upon this quiet l.! 314:62

giveth his l. for the sheep 55:6

he that cuts off twenty years of l. 324:4

his name out of the book of l. 61:22

I bear a charmed l. 336:78

I do not set my l. at a pin's fee 307:61

I fall upon the thorns of l. 369:37

I will give thee a crown of l. 60:20

in London all that l. can afford 177:25

in the midst of l. we are in death 65:14

is l. a boon? 148:44

isn't l. a terrible thing? 390:25

its private l. is a disgrace 15:70

I've done it all my l. 15:63

large as l. and twice as natural 94:93

last of l., for which the first 75:46

lay hold on l. 225:53

letter killeth ... spirit giveth l. 58:61

l. for l., eye for eye 37:93

l., force and beauty must ... impart 249:92

l. ... is a continual allegory 187:64

l. is a jest 142:60

l. is as tedious as a twice-told tale 327:41

l. is but a day; a ... dew-drop 185:35

l. is but an empty dream 198:95

Life (*continued*)

l. is just one damned thing after another 168:88

l. is mostly froth and bubble 152:7

l. is ... process of getting tired 82:43

L. is real! L. is earnest 198:95

l. is sweet 269:79

l. is the art of drawing ... conclusions 82:44

l. is very sweet, brother 69:65

l. isn't all beer and skittles 168:89

l., liberty ... pursuit of happiness 171:26

l., like a dome of many-coloured glass 367:19

l. protracted is protracted woe 174:70

l. ... solitary, poor, nasty, brutish 163:34

l., time's fool 315:91

l.'s too short for chess 86:3

live a barren sister all yr. l. 341:35

love is of man's l. a thing apart 84:70

make l., death ... for-ever one ... song 189:86

makes calamity of so long l. 309:95

man's l. is cheap as beast's 328:67

married to a single l. 115:83

measured out my l. with coffee spoons 131:2

mine honour is my l. 347:30

modern l. ... tedious, ... and modern literature 405:5

most of the change ... in l. 139:22

no, no, no l. 331:6

nor love thy l., nor hate 220:98

not so much l. as on a summer's day 182:97

nothing in his l. became him 333:30

O for a L. of Sensations! 186:51

on human l., musing in solitude 409:63

on the Tree of L. ... sat 219:64

one good deed in all my l. 358:64

our l., exempt from public haunt 300:75

our l. is frittered away by detail 391:37

our little l. is rounded ... sleep 356–7:50

my l. is one demd horrid grind 120:54

my way of l. ... the yellow leaf 336:71

pass them for a nobler l. 185:37

people say that L. is the thing 374:3

preach ... doctrine of strenuous l. 289:35

Life (*continued*)

promise them l. and then kill them 395:79

quickening l. from the Earth's heart 367:11

saw l. steadily and ... whole 20:35

sells us l. at a discount 140:33

she is coming, my l., my fate 388:87

short l. and a merry one 277:34

shd. ... have everlasting l. 55:99

so careless of the single l. 386:62

soldier's l. is terrible hard 211:54

spare all I have and take my l. 134:57

spend my l. in driving briskly 177:23

strange disease of modern l. 21:42

stuff of l. to knit me 167:83

sucking his l. out of the dead leaves 193:47

take away my good name ... my l. 279:95

take honour ... and my l. is done 347:30

that a man lay down his l. 56:10

that no l. lives for ever 383:20

that state of l., unto which 64:99

the death of each day's l. 334:42

the l. he makes us lead! 73:14

the l. so short, the craft so long to lerne 97:50

the nobler modes of l. 386:69

the passion and the l. 106:69

the rest of his dull l. 29:70

there are two tragedies in l. 365:83

there is no wealth but l. 292:64

therefore choose l. 38:13

this gives l. to thee 362:34

this long disease, my L. 248:81

those with irrational fear of l. 110:22

thoughts, the slaves of l. 315:91

to the vagrant gypsy l. 208:16

travel on l.'s common way 413:4

travelled l.'s dull round 371:60

treasured up ... to a l. beyond l. 223:38

upright l., unstained by guilt 166:75

useful l., progressive virtue 391:34

variety's ... spice of l. 114:71

warmed both hands before the fire of l. 192:34

way of l. uncertain 181:84

we see into the l. of things 415:33

weariest and most loathed worldly l. 337:91

what is this l. if, full of care 117:11

what kind of l. did you give me? 401:68

while ... l. there is hope 269:80

Life (*continued*)

whom ... to know is everlasting l. 64:91

yr. l. extremely flat 148:40

yr. money or yr. l.! 272:68

yr. money or yr. l.; women require 83:51

Life-in-death: the Night-mare L. was she 105:52

Lifeless: he is l. that is faultless 269:81

Lifetime: lamps ... lit again in our l. 156:51

Lift: l. not thy hands to It 136:80

l. them high ... before you drop them 395:79

oh, l. me as a wave, a leaf 369:37

Light: a certain slant of l. 122:83

apparelled in celestial l. 410:72

casting a dim religious l. 213:88

clear, unchang'd, and universal l. 249:92

come forth into the l. of things 414:27

common as l. is love 369:44

dear ... as l. and life 80:9

God appears, and God is l. 66:31

God said, Let there be l. 34:27

God saw the l. was good 220:84

God's first creature ... l. 27:40

gone into the world of l. 396:85

hail, Holy L., offspring of Heaven 218:58

Heaven's l. forever shines 367:19

Hesperus entreats thy l. 178–9:50

how my l. is spent 223:29

I can again thy former l. restore 346:19

in a Noose of L. 134:65

it gives a lovely l. 210:45

lead, Kindly L. 230:16

Let Newton be! and all was L. 248:88

l. breaks where no sun shines 390:21

l. that never was, on sea or land 409:61

l. the Day ... he named 220:84

more l.! 150:60

out of Hell leads up to l. 218:54

passion for sweetness and l. 21:52

Promethean heat that can thy l. relume 346:19

pursuit of sweetness and l. 21:47

put out the l., and then put out the l. 346:19

shower of l. is poesy 185:38

teach l. to counterfeit a gloom 213:86

the dying of the l. 390:18

Light (*continued*)
   the l. of common day  411:78
   the l. of the world  55:4
   The L. that Failed  191:17
   The people ... have seen a great l.
   48:35
   things l. and swoln ... weighty  26:35
   too l. winning, make the prize l.
   356:36
   true l. which lighteth every man
   55:93
   two noblest ... sweetness and l.
   381:95
   what l. through yonder window?
   353:97
   when my l. is low  386:60
   who art a l. to guide, a rod  413:7
   wiser than the children of l.  55:84
   with a l. behind her  148:42
Light Brigade: forward, the L.  385:41
Lighten: l. our darkness  63:74
   now, the Lord l. thee!  316:7
Lighter than vanity  77:60
Lighthouse: took the sitivation at the l.
   121:77
Lighting a little Hour or two  135:68
Lightly come, l. go  269:84
Lightning: I have known the l.'s hour
   117:15
   man who was killed by l.  12:42
   the l. of the nations  369:34
   thunder, l., or in rain  332:22
Lights: l. that do mislead the morn
   337–8:92
   turn up the l. ... home in the dark
   161:5
Like: a God, or something very l. Him
   103:27
   I know what I l.  30:83
   I l. two months of every year  83:55
   I shall not look upon his l. again
   306:49
   l. and dislike the same things  293:73
   l. doth quit l., and Measure still for
   Measure  338:94
   l. to be Beside the Seaside  149:57
   people who l. this sort of thing
   197:83
Liked it not, and died  416:47
Liking: I have a l. old for thee  87:15
Lilac: down to Kew in l.-time  230–31:20
   just now the l. is in bloom  71:89
Lilacs out of the dead land  131:10
Lilies: consider the l. of the field
   52:21
   in twisted braids of l. knitting
   213:80
   l. that fester smell far worse  363:42

Lilies (*continued*)
   peacocks and l.  291:61
   the l. and languors of virtue  382:18
   where roses and white l. grow  88:24
Lily: I am the ... l. of the valleys
   47:17
   to paint the l.  327:43
Limb: care I for the l., the thews ...
   bulk?  317:20
Limbo: into a L. large and broad
   218:60
Limbs: your l. they are alive  416:41
Limericks; whose l. never wd. scan
   13:54
Lime-tree Bower my prison  107:77
Limited in order to be possessed  78:85
Limits: beyond the l. of a vulgar fate
   156:45
Line: l. stretch out to th' crack of
   doom?  335:64
   must draw the l. somewhere  260:88
   the Brighton l. ... the l. is immaterial
   405:12
   to cancel half a l.  136:79
   to l. one's pockets  270:88
   we carved not a l.  408:53
Linen: choose neither ... l. by candle-
   light  258:3
   old l. wash whitest  400:52
Lines: with silken l. and silver hooks
   123:4
Lingering: something l., with boiling oil
   146:10
Lingers: borrowing only l. and l. it
   out  316:3
Linguistics: An Essay in Sociological
   L.  290:42
Lining: there's a silver l.  137:94
Linnet: a l. courting his lady  70:76
   come, hear the woodland l.  414:26
Lion: a l. among ladies  341:47
   dar'st ... beard the l. ... The Douglas
   296:12
   in like a l. ... out like a lamb  271:38
   l. is not so fierce as ... painted
   270:89
   nation ... had the l. heart  102:11
   not a more fearful wildfowl than ... l.
   341:47
   rouse a l. than to start a hare  313:53
   the devil, as a roaring l.  60:12
   the l. and the unicorn  234:47
   the l. looked at Alice wearily  94:94
Lions: cast him into the den of l.
   50:72
   Saul and Jonathan ... stronger than
   l.  40:48
Lip: keep a stiff upper l.  94:99, 278:76

Lips: beauty's ensign is crimson in thy
l.   354:17
  cd. you hurt me, sweet l.?   382:18
  dear red curve of her l.   207:11
  her l. suck forth my soul   204:63
  her l. were red, her looks were free
    105:52
  take, O, take, those l. away   337:92
  their l. were four red roses   352:79
  through my l. to unawakened earth
    369:38
  truth sits upon the l. of dying men
    21:45
  what l. my l. have kissed   210:46
  when I ope my l. let no dog bark
    338:98
  where my Julia's l. do smile   162:15
Liquefaction of her clothes   162:23
Liquid: Thames is l. history   79:94
Liquidation: preside over the l. of the
    British Empire   101:3
Liquor: l. is quicker   229:95
  they sell worse kinds of l.   399:28
Lisp of leaves and ripple of rain   382:15
List: I've got a little l.   145:99
  I wd. not enter on my l. of friends
    114:75
  l., l., O, l.!   307:64
Listen: darkling I l.   184:29
  l. with credulity to ... fancy   173:61
  the world shd. l. then   370:51
Listened: I l., motionless and still
    414:22
Listeners hear no good of themselves
    270:90
Lit again in our lifetime   156:51
Literature: he has raised the price of l.
    174:80
  itch of l. comes over a man   200:19
  l. flourishes best when it is half a
    trade   170:12
  that great Cham of l.   375:18
  the rest is just l.   396:89
  to produce a little l.   170:24
Litter: all her l. but one   316:98
Littérature: tout le reste est l.   396:89
Little: a l. of what you fancy   197:86
  a l. still she strove   84:67
  comrades, leave me here a l.   387:78
  every l. helps   262:26
  give according to that l.   62:39
  goin' through so much to learn so l.
    121:70
  great ones eat up the l. ones   347:27
  having too l. to do   190-1:15
  I thought so l. they rewarded me
    147:27
  if I'm content with a l.   65:18

Little (continued)
  it was a very l. one   206:86
  knows l., soon repeats it   268:48
  knows l. who will tell his wife all
    140:39
  l. breezes dusk and shiver   387:76
  l. drops ... l. grains ... l. minutes
    89:41
  l. things please l. minds   270:92
  l. things ... the most important
    124:18
  l. we see in nature that is ours   412:93
  love me l., love me long   270:18
  man wants but l. drink below   164:47
  man wants but l., nor that l. long
    418:64
  many a l. makes a mickle   271:37
  no great ones if ... no l. ones   265:43
  nor wants that l. long   150:72
  obedience is ... seen in l. things
    273:15
  so l. done, so much to do   287:7
  such a l. tail behind   31:89
  the l. less, and what worlds away
    73:19
  the l. more, and how much   73:19
  think too l. ... talk too much   126:42
  through so much to learn so l.
    121:70
  wealth is contentment with a l.
    282:16
Live: a bachelor, I l. by myself   17:95
  anything but – l. for it [religion]
    108:96
  bear to l. or dare to die   250:15
  better to l. rich   177:27
  but a short time to l.   65:13
  but one bare hour to l.   204:65
  come l. with me and be my love
    123:4, 205:82
  crabbed age and youth cannot l.
    together   364:56
  desire ... to l. beyond its income
    82:45
  eat to l. ... not l. to eat   261:12
  I had as lief not be as l.   323:91
  I marvel how the fishes l.   347:27
  I with thee will choose to l.   213:90
  in our embers is something that doth
    l.   411:80
  let me l. unseen, unknown   251:29
  l. a fool the rest of his dull life   29:70
  l. and learn   270:93
  l. and let l.   270:94
  l., and move, and have our being
    56:20
  l. as the Romans do   11:23
  l., for the truth is living   383:24

**Live** (*continued*)

loves to l. i' th' sun   301:85

may l. to fight another day   14:61

Mirth, with thee I mean to l.   215:7

not l. by bread only   38:7

not suffer a witch to l.   37:94

other men l. to eat   375:21

rogues ... want to l. for ever?   139:18

she ... tried to l. without him   416:47

so we'll l., and pray, and sing   330:99

so wise, so young, ... never l. long   352:73

take the means whereby I l.   340:20

threatened men l. long   280:34

to l. is like love   82:46

to l. with her and l. with thee   214:96

to l. with thee and be thy love   286:96

we that l. to please   173:59

what thou liv'st l. well   220:98

will it not l. with the living?   315:88

you might as well l.   243–4:23

**Lived**: for I have l. to-day   128:71

I have l. long enough   383:22

l. in the odium ... sodium   33:18

l. on, and so did I   105:55

who has never loved has never l.   142:55

**Liver**: open and notorious evil l.   64:93

**Livery**: in her sober l. all things clad   219:69

**Lives**: a history in all men's l.   317:16

all that l. must die   305:40

as a man l., so shall he die   271:34

cat has only nine l.   394:70

constancy l. in realms above   106:67

he l. ... 'tis Death is dead   367:17

he preaches well that l. well   275:59

he who l. more l. than one   404:96

l. in eternity's sunrise   66:34

l. of great men all remind us   198:7

love l. in cottages ... courts   270:15

men lead l. of quiet desperation   391:36

not how a man dies, but how he l.   175:98

one really l. nowhere   79:92

so long l. this, and this gives life   362:34

the music of men's l.   351:63

there l. more faith in ... doubt   386:65

**Living**: from too much love of l.   383:20

Homer ... who, l., had no roof   163:26

Lady Disdain, are you yet l.?   342:58

live, for the truth is l.   383:24

**Living** (*continued*)

l. ... eight years with a strange man   169:7

l., shall forfeit fair renown   295:6

plain l. and high thinking   412:2

the l. need charity   20:29

the mother of all l.   35:40

the noble L.   413:10

'tis the l. up to [faith]   389:9

we have gone on l., l. and partly l.   131:16

**Livingstone**, Dr L., I presume   378:57

**Lizzie Borden** took an axe   15:67

**Load**: how to l. and bless with fruit   180:78

**Loaf**: half a l. is better   265:51

of a cut l. to steal a shive   357–8:63

**Loafe**: I l. and invite my soul   403:83

**Loan** oft loses both itself and friend   306:57

**Lobster**: the voice of the l.   91:64

**Lochinvar**: never was Knight like ... L.   296:11

young L. is come out of the west   ·295:10

**Lock**: l., stock and barrel   270:96

prison with a life-long l.   145:3

**Locks**: her l. were yellow as gold   105:52

knotted and combined l. to part   307:64

pluck up ... honour by the l.   313:54

shaking her invincible l.   224:43

yr. l. were like the raven   80:11

**Locust**: years that the l. hath eaten   50:79

**Lodge**: where thou lodgest, I will l.   39:33

**Loftiness**: in l. of thought surpass'd   128:66

**Lofty** and sour to them that lov'd him not   323:87

**Log**: on a l., expiring frog   121:64

**Logic**: as it isn't, it ain't. That's l.   92:75

grape that can with L. absolute   135:77

l. and rhetoric [make] able to contend   26:34

un-to l. hadde longe y-go   96:31

**Logs**: bring me pine l. hither   229:4

Tom bears l. into the hall   332:20

**Loitering**: alone and palely l.   182:7

**Lombard Street** to a China orange   270:97

**London**: a L. particular ... A fog   119:33

as L. is to Paddington   88:28

London (*continued*)
  citizen ... of famous L. town  112:54
  hell is ... much like L.  369:41
  it isn't far from L.  230–1:20
  L., ... flower of Cities all  129:75
  L., that great cesspool  125:27
  L., ... the Clearing-house of the
    World  95:13
  Mr Weller's knowledge of L.  121:66
  no man ... willing to leave L.  177:25
  nobody is healthy in L.  23:66
  our scene is L.  178:47
  to L. to look at the queen  237:64
  when a man is tired of L.  177:25
London Bridge is broken down  235:53
Loneliness of my country and my God
    366:4
Lonely: close to the sun in l. lands
    385:47
  left l. for ever the kings  20:34
  so l. 'twas, that God himself  106:62
  wandered l. as a cloud  410:67
Lonesome: one that on a l. road
    106:60
Long: a l., l. trail a-winding  189:84
  a l. way to Tipperary  407:39
  by thy l. grey beard  104:42
  has been l. in city pent  186:47
  he l. lived the pride  28:54
  how l. or short permit to Heaven
    220:98
  I have lived l. enough  383:22
  it cannot hold you l.  150:75
  it shall be witty and it shan't be l.
    98:64
  l. after it was heard no more  414:22
  l., dark, boggy, dirty ... way  151:84
  l. is the way and hard  218:54
  l. live the king, and Gilpin l. live he
    113:61
  look at them l. and l.  403:84
  love me little, so you love me l.
    162:20
  man goeth to his l. home  47:12
  nor wants that little l.  150:72
  not that the story need be l.  391:40
  Shenandoah, I l. to hear you  18:1
  star-spangled banner! O l. may it
    wave  188:80
  the night is l. that never finds the day
    335:67
  victory however l. ... the road
    100:93
  waiting for the l.-promised invasion
    101:97
Longed: lies where he l. to be  379:76
Longest: hatred is by far the l. pleasure
    85:84

Longest (*continued*)
  Russia, when nights are l. there
    337:83
Longings: I have immortal l. in me
    299:70
Longitude: a l. with no platitude
    140:34
Look; but westward, l., the land is
    bright  104:34
  Cassius has a lean and hungry l.
    324:94
  do it with a bitter l.  404:94
  has a frightened l. in its eye  373:91
  houses are built ... not to l. on  26:28
  I'll be a candle-holder and l. on
    353:91
  just to l. about us and to die  250:7
  let him l. to his bond  339:12
  l. at [animals] long and long  403:84
  l. before you leap  270:2
  l. thy last on all things lovely  118:22
  mountains l. on Marathon  84:78
  only a l. and a voice  198:4
  shall not l. upon his like again
    306:49
  to l. upon verdure ... perfect refresh-
    ment  23:70
  we l. before and after  370:50
Looked: having l. to government for
    bread  78:83
  no sooner l. but they lov'd  302:5
  she l. at me as she did love  183:9
Lookers-on see most of the game
    270:4
Looking-glass: not thank you for a l.
    256:47
Looks: her l. were free  105:52
  how like a ... publican he l.  338:3
  l. the whole world in the face
    199:7
  love l. not with the eyes  341:38
  toward school with heavy l.  354:4
  woman as old as she l.  107:86
Looms: quest and passage through
    these l.  396:86
Loon: private buffoon is a light-hearted
    l.  149:49
  sung ... by a love-lorn l.  148:45
Lord: a ... l., neat, and trimly dress'd
    313:51
  bread which the L. ... hath given
    37:80
  deputy elected by the L.  349:50
  foundation is Jesus Christ her L.
    380:83
  from ghoulies ... good L. deliver us!
    14:60
  I thought ... a L. among wits  174:76

Lord (*continued*)

L. Finchley tried to mend ... light 31:94

L. Hippo suffered fearful loss 32:3

L. Lucky, by a curious fluke 32:4

l. of thy presence and no land 326:33

now, the L. lighten thee! 316:7

O L., thou lover of souls 62:45

one day is with the L. 60:14

praise the L. for he is kind 221:10

sing to the L. with cheerful voice 188:77

speak, L.; for thy servant heareth 39:36

the Angel of the L. came down 384:35

the day thou gavest, L. 132:24

the L. bless thee and keep thee 38:2

the L. ... chasteneth thee 38:8

the L. do so to me 39:34

the L. gave and the L. hath taken 41:65

the L. hardened Pharaoh's heart 36:76

the L. is my shepherd 42:91

the L. ... is one L. 38:5

the L. lift up his countenance 38:2

the L. make his face shine 38:2

the L. our God is good 188:78

the L. set a mark upon Cain 35:42

the L., whom ye seek 51:99

where the dear L. was crucified 11:20

whom the L. loveth he chasteneth 60:1

Lords: twelve l. a-leaping 238:73

Lose: grasp all, l. all 265:41

heads I win, tails you l. 115:86, 266:75

l. and neglect the creeping hours 301:89

l. by over-running 322:74

l. myself in other men's minds 192:29

who wd. l. ... this intellectual being 217:49

Losers: l. are ... in the wrong 270:5

l. seekers, finders keepers 270:6

Loss: buy and sell, and live by the l. 257:79

enow to do our country's l. 320:55

Lord Hippo suffered fearful l. 32:3

l. of honour was a wrench 153:12

Losses: all l. are restor'd 363:38

Lost: and she l. her maiden name 18:3

better to have fought and l. 103:31

better to have loved and l. 83:50, 386:59

Lost (*continued*)

books by which the printers have l. 140:40

field be l.? All is not l. 216:30

how art thou l.! 220:94

I have l. all the names 177:33

I have l. my reputation 345:1

I look upon every day to be l. 178:37

learning without thought is labour l. 108:4

l. causes, forsaken beliefs 21:49

never to have l. at all 83:50

praising ... l. makes the remembrance dear 298:47

sorry when any language is l. 178:39

thou art l. and gone for ever 225:59

wherever we're l. in 140:35

woman that deliberates is l. 9:5

Lot: policeman's l. is not a happy one 148:33

remember L.'s wife 55:88

the l. fell upon Jonah 50:85

Lots: so they cast l. 50:85

Lottery: marriage is a l. 271:40

Loud: I said it very l. and clear 93:91

Louder: the l. he talked of his honour 132:27

Loungers: all the l. of the Empire 125:27

Love: a little l. and good company 134:56

absence sharpens l. 254:53

ah, dearest l., sweet home of all 183:15

Alas! the l. of women 84:72

all is fair in l. and war 254:65

all l. is sweet 369:44

all mankind l. a lover 132:32

all she loves is l. 84:73

am like to l. three more 380:86

an oyster may be crossed in l. 371:64

and when l. speaks 331:15

as honour, l., obedience 336:71

be wise and l. exceeds man's might 358:70

brief ... as woman's l. 310:8

but l. is blind, and lovers cannot see 339:10

choose l. by another's eyes 341:37

comfort in the strength of l. 411:88

corner in the thing I l. 345:8

course of true l. never ... smooth 341:36

cupboard l. 259:42

dinner of herbs where l. is 45:71

dislike ... the l. of a woman ... treacle 187:66

drew them ... with bands of l. 50:77

Love (*continued*)

earth's the right place for l. 139:21

familiar acts are beautiful through l. 369:45

faults are thick where l. is thin 262:56

fear the Lord ... and to l. him 38:9

few l. to hear the sins they l. to act 347:25

folly ... l. did make thee run into 300:82

for ever wilt thou l. 183:18

for I am sick of l. 47:19

for ... them that l. God 56:34

for thy sweet l. rememb'red 362:36

friendly l. perfecteth 25:99

friendship is constant ... save in ... l. 342:62

from too much l. of living 383:20

gave, once, her flowers to l. 71:93

general award of l. 182:4

God is l. 60:16

greater l. hath no man 56:10

greatest hate ... from the greatest l. 265:47

hail, wedded L. 219:71

half in l. with easeful Death 184:29

his banner over me was l. 47:18

hot l. is soon cold 267:1

how have you left the ancient l. 68:55

I cd. not l. thee, Dear, so much 200:17

I do not l. thee, Dr Fell 72:96

I hate and l. ... and am in torment 94:5

I l. a lassie 193:41

I l. everything that's old 151:83

I l. not man the less 84:65

I l. sixpence 233:40

I l. thee true 183:10

I never shall l. the snow 70:77

I think my l. as rare 364:53

if music be the food of l. 358:75

is it ... a crime to l. too well 248:73

leave to come unto my l. 377:39

lest that thy l. prove variable 354:2

let brotherly l. continue 60:2

let l. be without dissimulation 57:37

lightly turns to thoughts of l. 387:79

little brown jug ... I l. thee 16:84

live with me and be my l. 123:4, 205:82

live with thee and be thy l. 286:96

look'd at me as she did l. 183:9

l. all, trust a few 298:41

l. alters not 363:48

Love (*continued*)

l. and a cough cannot be hid 270:8

l. and business teach eloquence 270:9

l. and fame to nothingness 186:49

l. and hate are necessary 68:56

l. and marriage rarely can combine 84:74

l. and meekness ... become a churchman 323:88

l. bade me welcome: yet my soul drew back 161:12

l. begets l. 270:10

l. built on beauty 123:6

l. but her and l. for ever 79:96

l. ceases to be a pleasure 30:85

l. conquers all 397:3

l. ... differs from gold and clay 368:26

l. Divine, all loves excelling 402:72

L. forgive us—cinders, ashes 183:11

l., free as air, at sight of ... ties 248:75

l. goes toward l. ... but l. from l. 354:4

l. grows bitter with treason 383:23

l. has never known a law 403:88

l. he laughed to scorn 364:59

l. her till I die 18:9

l. I laugh to scorn 71:86

l. in a golden bowl 66:32

l. in a hut with water 183:11

l. in a palace 183:11

l. is blind 270:13

l. is enough 227:72

l. ... is exactly like war 379:71

l. is heaven and heaven is l. 295:2

l. is like the measles 171:34

l. is my religion—I cd. die 187:67

l. is not l. which alters 363:47

l. is ... sour in the ending 270:14

l. is strong as death 47:27

l. is sweet for a day 383:23

l. is the fulfilling of the law 57:43

l. itself shall slumber on 370:54

l. looks not with the eyes 341:38

l. me little, l. me long 270:18

l. me little, so you l. me long 162:20

l. me, l. my dog 270:19

l. of flattery 378:59

l. of money ... root of all evil 59:92

l. rules the court, the camp 295:2

l.'s but the frailty of the mind 109:14

l. seeketh not itself to please 67:43

l. sought is good 360:94

l.'s the noblest frailty of the mind 128:63

l. that moves the sun 117:4

Love (continued)
1. that never told can be   67:40
1. the brotherhood   60:9
1. the Lord ... with all thine heart
   38:6
1. thy neighbour as thyself   37:99
1. thyself last   323:83
1. too much that die for 1.   271:21
1., we are in God's hand   73:14
1. will find a way   271:22
1. worketh no ill   57:43
1. ye therefore the stranger   38:10
1. you because ... hard up you pawn
   116:95
1. your enemies   52:14
lovers' quarrels ... renewal of 1.
   389:5
loyal cantons of contemned 1.   359:80
man's 1. ... a thing apart   84:70
many waters cannot quench 1.   47:28
marry first and 1. will follow   271:45
master-passion ... 1. of news   114:81
me and my true 1.   18:2
medicines to make me 1. him   313:56
men have died ... but not for 1.
   302:3
men 1. in haste ... detest at leisure
   85:84
my dear 1. sits him down   19:10
my 1. and I wd. lie   167:82
my 1. climbed up to me   189:85
my 1. is like a red red rose   81:21
my 1. is like the melodie   81:21
my L. is of a birth as rare   206:97
my 1. lies underground   193:48
my only 1. sprung from my only hate
   353:96
my true 1. hath my heart   372:83
my true 1. sent to me   238:72, 73
my vegetable 1. shd. grow   206:93
my whole course of 1.   344:91
nameless ... acts of kindness and of
   1.   415:31
never seek to tell thy 1.   67:40
no 1. sincerer than the 1. of food
   365:79
no rage like 1. to hatred turned 108:6
none to praise ... few to 1.   413:15
nor 1. thy life, nor hate   220:98
not enough [religion] to make us 1.
   382:9
not in our power to 1. or hate 205:80
nuptial 1. maketh mankind   25:99
O L.; has she done this to thee?
   201:30
of soup and 1., the first   278:59
off with the old 1.   17:93
office and affairs of 1.   342:62

Love (continued)
old 1., cold 1.   257:81
one does not 1. a place less   23:74
one must not trifle with 1.   227:79
open rebuke is better than secret 1.
   46:86
passing the 1. of women   40:49
perfect 1. casteth out fear   60:17
pity ... in the heart of 1.   417:57
politicians neither 1. nor hate   126:41
pounds of law, not an ounce of 1.
   280:32
pray you, 1., remember   311:28
prosperity's the very bond of 1.
   362:24
prove ... the sports of 1.   179:61
regain 1. once possessed   222:24
rise up, my 1.   47:20
said that the 1. of money is the root
   82:41
saying 'Farewell, blighted 1.'   18:4
seals of 1., but seal'd in vain
   337–8:92
seen ... that 1. hath an end   383:22
she never told her 1.   360:89
sighed for the 1. of a ladye   148–9:46
so faithful in 1.   296:11
so true a fool is 1.   363:39
some are fou o' 1. divine   80:10
something ... doesn't 1. a wall
   139:27
support of the woman I 1.   129:81
that true self-1. and social are the
   same   250:20
that ye 1. one another   56:8
the arms of my true 1.   388:88
the fool of 1., unpractis'd   128:70
the 1. that can be reckon'd   298:50
the 1. which doth us bind   206:98
the pangs of despis'd 1.   309:95
the right true end of 1.   123:8
the service of my 1.   377:53
there is no fear in 1.   60:17
there is tears for his 1.   325:11
things that 1. might   329:75
this bud of 1. may prove a ... flower
   354:3
this spring of 1. resembleth   361:6
though I can't make her 1. me   372:75
through 1., through hope, and faith's
   413:14
thy 1. is better than wine   47:15
thy 1. to me was wonderful   40:49
tired of 1. ... tired of rhyme   32:98
to do justly and to 1. mercy   51:91
to hold my wealth of 1.   149:48
to let the warm L. in   185:33
to live is like 1.   82:46

Lying (*continued*)
to conclude, they are l. knaves 344:87
world is given to l.! 315:94
Lyly: didst our L. outshine 179:55
Lyme: an old party of L. 224:52
Lysander: of Hector and L. 18:6

Mab: I see Queen M. hath been with you 353:92
Macaroni: and called it m. 241:90
Macaulay: as cocksure ... as Tom M. is 208:27
Macavity: no one like M. 131:6
Machine: house is a m. for living in 110:31
*maison est une m.-à-habiter* 110:31
Mackerel: sprat to catch a m. 278:69
Mad: but m. north-north-west 308:83
how sad and bad and m. 73:20
I wd. not be m.! 328:60
m. as a hatter 271:23
m. as a March hare 271:24
m., bad and dangerous to know 191:24
m. world! m. kings! m. composition! 326:36
made me m. to see him shine 313:52
O, fool, I shall go m.! 328:69
O, let me not be m. 328:60
Oh, he is m., is he? 142:61
that he's m., 'tis true 308:74
to destroy, he first makes m. 275:74
we want a few m. people now 366:1
went m. and bit the man 151:76
Madding crowd's ignoble strife 155:39
Made: did he who m. the Lamb make thee? 68:47
dost thou know who m. thee? 68:50
fearfully and wonderfully m. 44:50
m. and loveth all 106:64
m. him a coat of many colours 36:62
nobody never m. me. 380:85
Mademoiselle from Armenteers 291:57
Madness: devil's m.—War 297:36
great wits ... to m. near allied 126:39
m. in great ones ... not unwatch'd 310:2
m., yet there is method in't 308:78
melancholy and moon-struck m. 220:97
much mirth and no m. 373:93
such harmonious m. from my lips 370:51
that way m. lies 329:77
this is ... midsummer m. 360:95
**work like m. in the brain** 106:67

Magdalen: fourteen months at M. College 142:64
Magistrates: some like m. correct at home 318:39
Magnanimity: in all his m. of thought 418:63
in Victory: M. 102:10
you might curb yr. m. 187:69
Magnificence comes after 192:30
Magnificent: it is m., but it is not war 69:66
*Magnifique: c'est m. ... pas la guerre* 69:66
Magog: Gog, the land of M. 49:66
Mahomet: hill will not come to M. 25:3
Maid: a fair m. dwellin' 12:36
be good, sweet m. 189:86
chariest m. is prodigal enough 306:53
I heard a m. singing 16:80
m. whom there were none to praise 413:15
Music, heavenly m., was young 108:91
O Music, sphere-descended M. 108:93
slain by a fair cruel m. 359:88
the m. was in the garden 238:70
way of a man with a m. 46:91
where are you going to, my pretty m.? 241:86
woo a fair young m. 17:95
Maiden: for many a rose-lipt m. 167:84
kissed the m. all forlorn 239:79
m. of bashful fifteen 372:78
m. ... must be slaughtered too 145:5
prithee, pretty m., will you marry me? 146:17
use a poor m. so 16:80
when a merry m. marries 143:74
Maidens: m. like moths, are ever caught 83:56
twenty lovesick m. we 146:13
Maids: eight m. a-milking 238:73
m. are May when ... m. 302:4
pretty m. all in a row 235:55
seven m. with seven mops 92:79
three little m. from school 145:2
Maimed and set at naught 82:47
Main: every man ... part of the m. 124:13
Maintaining: died m. his right of way 13:50
Majestic: his face ... m. though in ruin 218:52
Majestical: we do it wrong, being so m. 305:35

Majesty: a strange beginning—'borrowed m.'] 326:32
  attribute to awe and m. 339:15
  busied in his m., surveys 318–19:39
  sight so touching in its m. 412:96
  the next in M. 128:66
  then our M. adorning 143:75
  this earth of m., this seat of Mars 348:41
  you got no-no-no m. 401:68
Major-General: model of a modern M. 147:31
Majority: m. never has right on its side 169:8
  one on God's side is a m. 246:51
  who makes up the m.? 169:8
Make: m. him an help meet 35:32
  makes no mistakes does not m. anything 246:50
  one of them said to his m. 12:39
Makes: the night that either m. me or fordoes 346:17
Male: into the ark ... m. and ... female 35:45
  m. and female created he them 34:28
  more deadly than the m. 190:98
Males: deeds are m. and words are females 260:66
Malice: m. never was his aim 381:97
  nor set down aught in m. 346:22
  with m. toward none 196:81
Malignant: a m. and a turban'd Turk 346–7:22
Malt: m. does more than Milton can 167:85
  rat that ate the m. 239:79
Mammon: and M. wins his way 83:56
  m. of unrighteousness 55:85
Man: a better m. than I am 190:1
  a Christian faithful m. 351:71
  a good old m. sir 343:78
  a hairy m. ... a smooth m. 36:59
  a living dead m. 303:12
  a m. after his own heart 39:40
  a m. can die but once 317:19
  a m. can raise a thirst 190:8
  a m. leave his father and mother 58:72
  a m. more sinn'd against 329:76
  a m. must serve his time 85:90
  a m. of sorrows 48:47
  a m. of such a feeble temper 323:92
  a m.'s a m. for a' that 80:6
  a m.'s [business] to keep unmarried 365:81
  a m.'s first duty? ... To be himself 169:11

Man (*continued*)
  a m.'s friendships ... are invalidated 83:49
  a m.'s reach should exceed his grasp 73:15
  a m.'s worth something 73:18
  a m. severe he was 150:68
  a m. so various 126:43
  a m. that is young in years 26:26
  a m. that left his family 393:60
  a m. under authority 52:28
  a m. who cd. make so vile a pun 119:29
  a m. who has not been in Italy 177:22
  a m. who said 'God' 191:20
  a m. who shaves and takes a train 402:77
  a m. who's untrue to his wife 22:61
  a m. will ne'er quite understand 245:32
  a moral, sensible and well-bred m. 112:52
  a nice m. ... a m. of nasty ideas 382:11
  a ready m. 26:33
  a sadder and a wiser m. 106:65
  a single-m. ... a good fortune 23:75
  a strong m. after sleep 224:43
  a stupid m. is doing something 364:65
  a very unclubbable m. 175:93
  'A was a m. 306:49
  a weak m. who marries for love 177:19
  Adam, the goodliest m. 219:67
  all my faults as m. to m. 365:73
  all that was pleasant in m. 151:80
  an aged aged m. 94:95
  an elder m. not at all 25:98
  an exact m. 26:33
  an honest God ... noblest work of m. 170:14
  an old m. and no honester 343:76
  an old m. in a dry month 130:92
  and the last m. in 230:13
  Angry Young M. 245:33
  any m.'s death diminishes me 124:14
  apparel oft proclaims the m. 306:56
  as for m., his days are as grass 43:23
  ash on an old m.'s sleeve 130:97
  at thirty m. suspects 418:63
  away, slight m.] 326:25
  beauty crieth ... no m. regardeth 82:47
  became a m., I put away childish things 57:53
  Benedick the married m. 342:60

Man (*continued*)

better angel is a m. right fair   364:55
better spar'd a better m.   315:92
big assemblance of a m.!   317:20
both m. and bird and beast   106:63
brothers and their murder'd m. 182:5
Brutus is an honourable m.   325:13
busiest m. who has time to spare 244:25
business of the wealthy m.   31:94
by courtesy a m.   24:82
by m. shall his blood be shed   35:49
came to the making of m.   382:16
care not whether a m. is good 67:37
caverns measureless to m.   106:71, 73
child is father of the m.   412:99
cloud ... like a m.'s hand   40:57
condition of m. ... condition of war 163:33
conference [maketh] a ready m. 26:33
crumbs ... from the rich m.'s table 55:86
daring young m. on the flying trapeze   196:71
Darwinian M. ... well-behaved 148:38
deep young m.   146:15
each m. kills ... thing he loves 404:94
every m. did that which was right 39:32
every m. for himself   262:27
every m. has his faults   262:28
every m. is as Heaven made him 95:9
every m. is best known to himself 262:29
every m. is wanted, no m. ... much 133:34
every m. meets his Waterloo   246:52
every m. must play a part   338:96
every m. over forty   366:91
every m.'s hand against him   35:53
every m. that cometh into ... world 55:93
every m. to his taste   262:30
every m. under his vine   50:89
every m. was ... god or devil   126:44
every woman shd. marry ... no m. 123:96
everyone has sat except a m.   115:93
expects every m. ... do his duty 229:7
face of the old m.   38:1
foolish fond old m.   330:97

Man (*continued*)

foolishly-compounded clay, m. 316:98
foot-in-the-grave young m.   146:18
get a new m.   356:44
glory to M. in the highest!   383:21
God created m. in his own image 34:28
God doth not need ... m.'s work 223:30
God made the woman for the m. 385:48
God took the m. and put him   35:31
good for a m. that he bear the yoke 49:62
good name in m. and woman   345:6
greater love hath no m.   56:10
greatest m. you had ... yet seen 178:46
he thinks, good easy m.   322:80
heaven had made her such a m. 344:92
her m. ... he done her wrong   16:81
honest m. sent to lie abroad   416:46
honest m.'s the noblest work of God 250:16
how use doth breed a habit in a m. 361:10
I hate ingratitude ... in a m.   360:1
I love not m. the less   84:65
ideal m. ... non-attached m.   168:99
if a m. will begin with certainties 26:37
if any m. shall add   61:35
if I ever become a rich m.   32:6
if such a m. there be   248:84
if the m. who turnips cries   172:56
I'm truly sorry m.'s dominion   80:17
in the Parliament of m.   387:81
in the spring a young m.'s fancy 387:79
in wit a m.: simplicity a child   248:89
is m. an ape or an angel?   122:91
it is the number of a m.   61:30
It's That M. Again   180:76
laugh to scorn the pow'r of m. 335:62
let no m. despise thy youth   59:89
let no m. put asunder   65:10
let not m. put asunder   54:60
like master, like m.   270:87
looking for a m.'s footprint   30:82
m. and wife together   65:11
m. ... bears in his bodily frame 117:6
m. being too proud to fight   407:45
m. ... born free ... is in chains 291:55

Man (*continued*)

m. delights not me ... nor woman 308:81

m. for the field ... the sword 389:2

m. goeth to his long home 47:12

m. has his will, – but woman 164:48

m. in the moon 271:29

m. in the street 271:30

m. is a noble animal 72:7

m. is ... a political animal 20:26

m. is ... a religious animal 78:79

m. is a tool-making animal 139:17

m. is born unto trouble 41:67

m. is Nature's sole mistake 148:37

m. is not a fly 250:10

m. is the hunter 388:1

m. is the master of things 383:21

m. is the shuttle 396:86

m. ... killed by lightning 12:42

m. looketh on ... outward appearance 39:42

m. made the town 114:69

m. ... must get drunk 84:71

m. of upright life unstained 166:75

m. or mouse 271:35

m. proposes ... God disposes 188:71, 271:36

m., proud m. 337:87

m.'s a ribald ... a rake 148:37

m.'s inhumanity to m. 80:14

m. shall not live by bread 51:7

m. that is born of a woman 41:69, 65:13

m. that lays his hand upon a woman 392:48

m. to afflict his soul 49:52

m. wants but little 418:64

m. wants but little here below 150:72

m. was made for joy and woe 66:30

m. who knows the price 406:21

m. who sees absolutely nothing 404:98

m. who sees both sides 404:98

m. who ... sets foot upon a worm 114:75

m. with the head ... to command 389:2

manners maketh m. 407:38

met a m. who wasn't there 208:24

met a m. with seven wives 231:22

money makes the m. 272:67

Nature might ... say ... 'This was a m.!' 326:31

new m. ... raised up in him 64:94

no great m. lives in vain 89:36

no m. can serve two masters 52:19

no m. dieth to himself 57:44

Man (*continued*)

no m. does [become like his mother] 406:30

no m. ever talked poetry 121:72

no m., having put ... hand to plough 54:74

no m. is an island 124:13

no m. is good enough to govern 196:73

no m. putteth new wine 54:73

no m. truly knows another 72:4

nor no m. ever loved 363:48

not a dinner to ask a m. to 175:92

no-wher so bisy a m. 97:35

O good old m., how well in thee 300:79

o'er all this scene of m. 250:7

of M.'s first disobedience 216:27

old m. in a hurry 100:86

on m., on nature ... life 409:63

one m. ... appointed to buy the meat 297:25

one m. ... plays many parts 301:90

one m.'s meat is another m.'s poison 272:52

only m. is vile 160:87

open not ... heart to every m. 62:49

poor, infirm ... despis'd old m. 329:73

poor m. that hangs on princes' favours 322:81

proper study of Mankind is M. 250:13

reading maketh a full m. 26:33

rejoice, O young m., in ... youth 47:10

reminds a m. he is mortal 117:14

rich m., poor m., beggar m. 240:81

ruins of the noblest m. 324:8

sabbath was made for m. 53:54

safeliest when with one m. m.'d 123–4:9

same tree ... a wise m. sees 69:60

say to ... world, This was a m.! 326:31

shall mortal m. be more just than God 41:66

sleep of a labouring m. 46:2

so can I, or so can any m. 314:72

so unto the m. is woman 198:3

some new race, called M. 218:53

son of m., set thy face against Gog 49:66

stagger like a drunken m. 43:27

state of m., like to a ... kingdom 324:98

style is the m. himself 76:51

that a m. lay down his life 56:10

Man (*continued*)

that m. was made to mourn   80:13
the blood of a British m.   329:82
the childhood shows the m.   221:6
the fury of a patient man   127:48
the hour is come, but not the m.
   296:17
the m. all tattered and torn   239:79
the m. hath penance done   105:59
the m. of action is called on   317:12
the m. perceives it die away   411:78
the m. that hath no music   340:24
the m., with soul so dead   295:5
the most senseless and fit m.   343:74
the proud m.'s contumely   309:95
the tongue can no m. tame   60:5
the whole duty of m.   47:14
the young m.'s dog with them   62:40
there came to the making of m.
   382:16
There once was a m. who said
   'Damn'   158:68
there was an old m. from Darjeeling
   14:56
there was an Old M. who said
   'Hush!'   195:65
there was an Old M. with a beard
   195:66
there was a young m. of Boulogne
   13:53
there was a young m. of Japan   13:54
there was a young m. of Montrose
   33:12
thinking m. is bound to rebel   169:8
this is the state of m.   322:80
till one greater M. restore us   216:27
'tis strange what a m. may do   389:10
to be a well-favoured m.   343:73
to every m. a damsel or two   39:24
true love's the gift ... to m. alone
   295:4
valiant m. and free   387:71
vexing the dull ear of a drowsy m.
   327:41
wager ... m. ... is absolutely fixed on
   134:59
was there a m. dismayed   385:41
water-drops stain my m.'s cheeks
   328:68
way of a m. with a maid   46:91
were m. but constant!   361:11
what a piece of work is a m.!   308:81
what bloody m. is that?   332:24
what is m., that thou art mindful
   41:82
what m. has made of m.   411:84
what shall it profit a m.?   54:58
whatsoever a m. soweth   58:70

Man (*continued*)

when a m. bites a dog   116:1
when a m. shd. marry   25:98
when no m. can work   55:5
when the brains were out the m.
   would die   335:55
whenever he met a great m.   389:13
where m. is not, nature is barren
   69:63
whether ... wise m. or a fool
   67:37
who kills a m.   223:37
who sheddeth m.'s blood   35:49
who's master, who's m.   381:4
who thicks m.'s blood with cold
   105:52
whoso wd. be a m.   133:36
wine ... maketh glad ... heart of m.
   43:24
wisest m. the warl' saw   80:8
with cords of a m.   50:77
woman is the lesser m.   387:83
wd. this m. ... ask why?   22:58
you asked this m. to die   22:58
you'll be a M., my son   190:5
Man Friday: I takes my M. with me
   118:17
Mandalay: on the road to M.   190:7
Mandrake: get with child a m. root
   124:11
Manger: in a m. for His bed   10:19
in the rude m. lies   215:20
the babe ... lying in a m.   54:69
Manhood: m. full and fair   70:78
neither ... m., nor good fellowship
   312:48
Manhoods: and hold their m. cheap
   320:59
Manifold stories ... told not to thy
   credit   87:15
Man-in-the-street ... a keen observer of
   life   22:61
Mankind: amongst the noblest of m.
   87:14
example is the school of m.   78:82
gave up what was meant for m.
   151:78
how beauteous m. is!   357:57
I am involved in m.   124:14
love all m., except an American
   177:26
m. and posterity ... in their debt
   170:13
not retreat but exclusion from m.
   173:66
nuptial love maketh m.   25:99
proper study of M. is Man   250:13
seems to be all m.'s epitome   126:43

Mankind (*continued*)

survey m. from China to Peru 173:67

to you and all m. 384:35

wd. deserve better of m. 381:2

wisest, brightest, meanest of m. 250:17

Manliness: the silent m. of grief 150:71

Manna: said one to another. It is m. 37:80

though his tongue dropped m. 217:48

Manner: cease to think about the m. 159:85

native here, and to the m. born 307:59

Manners: by nothing ... as by his m. 377:45

graced with polished m. 114:75

m. maketh man 407:38

m. of a dancing-master 174:77

men's evil m. live in brass 323:86

old m., old books, old wine 151:83

sweeter m., purer laws 386:69

Manservant: nor his m., nor his maid-servant 37:92

Mansion: life ... M. of many Apart-ments 187:60

Mansions: build thee more stately m. 164:50

in my Father's house are many m. 56:9

Mantle: cast his m. upon him 40:59

cream and m. like a standing pond 338:97

morn, in russet m. clad 305:36

twitched his m. blue 215:18

Manure: blood of English shall m. the ground 350:56

Many: have the measels? ... how m.? 399:27

m. are called, but few are chosen 53:42

m. things to fear 25:13

owed by so m. to so few 101:96

the m. change and pass 367:19

the m. men, so beautiful 105:55

ye are m.—they are few 368:31

Many-splendour'd: miss the m. thing 391:31

Maps: generals are already poring over m. 22:59

Mar: oft we m. what's well 328:59

Marathon: from M. to Waterloo 147:31

M. looks on the sea 84:78

Marble: I dreamt ... I dwelt in m. halls 76:55

Marble (*continued*)

poets that lasting m. seek 398:18

whole as the m., founded as the rock 335:53

your dreary m. halls 87:13

March: beware the Ides of M. 323:90

droghte of M. hath perced 96:25

M. comes in like a lion 271:38

Marched breast forward 73:16

Marches: dreadful m. to delightful measures 351:65

funeral m. to the grave 198:96

Marching: as we were m. through Georgia 416:44, 45

his soul is m. on! 157:57

m. as to war 28:57

Mare: lend me yr. grey m. 19:12

patience ... tired m. ... will plod 319:42

to find a m.'s nest 271:39

*Maréchal: le bâton de m. de France* 228:86

Margin: through a meadow of m. 372:74

Marian: Mall, Meg, and M., and Margery 356:43

M.'s nose looks red and raw 332:20

Mariner: I fear thee, ancient M. 105:53

it is an ancient M. 104:42

Mariners: ye m. of England 88:21

Marines: tell that to the M. 279:15

Mark: God save the m.! 313:52

love ... an ever-fixed m. 363:47

Matthew, M., Luke, and John 10:13

no drowning m. upon him 355:27

read, m., learn 64:86

Market: chief good and m. of his time 311:22

if fools went not to m. 263:82

school or college, kirk or m. 379:78

send a fool to the m. 263:80

women ... goose make a m. 280:36

Market-place: at noon-day, upon the m. 324:97

Idols of the M. 27:41

Marks: Signior Benedick; nobody m. you 342:58

Marlowe: M.'s mighty line 179:55

neat M. 125:33

Marmion: last words of M. 296:15

Marquis: abducted by a French m. 153:12

Marred: young man married ... man that's m. 298:44

Marriage: care ... more for a m. than a ministry 27:44

coldly furnish ... m. tables 306:48

Marriage (*continued*)

comedies are ended by a m.  84:75

exclaim ... against second m.  134:59

eyes wide open before m.  268:31

friendships are ... invalidated by m.
83:49

hanging prevents a bad m.  359:78

happiness in m. ... matter of chance
23:76

love and m. rarely can combine
84:74

m. has many pains but celibacy has
no pleasures  173:66

m. is a lottery  271:40

m. is like a cage  225:56

m. is popular because  366:89

m. is the best state for a man  177:18

m. of true minds  363:47

O curse of m.  345:8

takes two to make a m. a success
293:75

won't be a stylish m.  116:99

Married: a woman's business to get m.
365:81

as wellbred as if ... not m.  109:17

Benedick the m. man  342:60

cuckoo ... mocks m. men  332:19

how ... be m. without a wife?  235:52

how to be happy though m.  157:63

if ever we had been m.  141:52

live till I were m.  343:70

man who m. ... did more service
152:96

m. three wives at a time  224:52

unpleasing to a m. ear  332:19

wen you're a m. man, Samivel
121:70

what delight we m. people have
245:42

wd. be m. but I'd have no wife
115:83

wd. be m. to a single life  115:83

young man m. is ... marr'd  298:44

Marries: m. late, m. ill  271:43

person who either m. or dies  23:67

Marry: advise none to m.  254:61

be sure before you m. of a house
255:97

better to m. than to burn  57:50

every woman should m. – and no
man  123:96

he'll come back and m. me  231:24

honest men m. soon  267:93

I can't m. you, my pretty maid
241:87

if men knew ... they'd never m.
161:4

may m. whom she likes  389:12

Marry (*continued*)

now that you are going to m.  176:99

to persons about to m.—Don't
284:73

when a man shd. m.  25:98

while ye may, go m.  162:25

young man shd. not m. yet  284:62

Mars: this seat of M.  348:41

Marshal: the m.'s truncheon nor the
judge's robe  337:84

Martin Elginbrode: here lie I, M.
202:50

Martini: get ... into a dry M.  409:57

Martyr: bitter groan of a m.'s woe
66–7:35

Martyrdom ... in which ... can become
famous  365:69

Martyrs: noble army of M.  63:69

Marvel: I m. how the fishes live  347:27

match me such m.  77:70

they m. more and more  31:89

Marvellous: Chatterton, the m. boy
413:12

Mary: M. had a little lamb  157:55

M., M., quite contrary  235:55

M. was that Mother mild  10:19

might be the last, my M.!  114:76

my sweet Highland M.  80:9

O M., at thy window be  80:15

Mary Ann: M. has gone to rest  13:48

nuts for M.  13:48

Mary Ann Lowder: here lies the body
of M.  13:46

Mary Jane: *What* is the matter with
M.?  211:58

Mary-buds: winking M. begin  304:20

Masons: singing m. building roofs of
gold  318–19:39

Masquerade: the truth in m.  85:82

Mass: Paris is well worth a m.  160:97

Massacre: not as sudden as a m.
393:64

Masses: the m. against the classes
149:53

Mast: bends the gallant m.  116:96

Master: has a new m., get a new man
356:44

has a wife, has a m.  283:31

I am the M. of this College  30:80

in constancy follow the M.  77:64

like m., like man  270:87

man is the m. of things  383:21

M. Mistress of my passion  362:35

money is ... a bad m.  272:65

money ... will be thy m.  272:63

my m.'s lost his fiddlestick  231:26

one for the m.  231:23

that ... I wd. fain call m.  327:55

Memory (*continued*)

m. of the just is blessed   45:62
m. ... the beginning of dowdiness
   406:32
mixing m. and desire   131:10
no man ... force can abolish m.
   289:33
no woman shd. have a m.   406:32
peaceful hours ... how sweet their m.
   113:62
pluck from the m. a rooted sorrow
   336:72
shorter in wind, as in m. long   70:72
the m. be green   305:37
the M. of great Men   186:58
vibrates in the m.   370:54

Men: a sort of m. whose visages
   338:97
a tide in the affairs of m.   326:27
all sorts and conditions of m.   63:81
all things to all m.   57:51
among new m., strange faces   385:53
appointed unto m. once to die   59:97
are you good m. and true?   343:72
ay, in the catalogue ye go for m.
   334:48
best m. are dead   285:85
bodies of unburied m.   400:54
boon and a blessing to m.   11:32
busiest m. ... most leisure   257:73
busy hum of m.   214:1
but m. are m. ... sometimes forget
   345:99
common wonder of all m.   72:3
daggers in m.'s smiles   334:47
dead m. don't bite   259:56
dead m. naked shall be one   390:17
dead m. rise up never   383:20
dead m. tell no tales   259:57
deal with none but honest m.   276:87
despised and rejected of m.   48:47
destiny with m. for pieces plays
   135:78
down among the dead m.   129:78
dumb m. get no lands   261:1
England ... purgatory of m.   136:86
equal rights of m. and women
   394:76
Eve upon the first of M.   165:63
even great m. have ... poor relations
   119:35
evil that m. do lives after them
   325:12
fair women and brave m.   83:59
fifteen m. on ... dead man's chest
   379:74
finds too late that m. betray   152:2
for fear of little m.   11:22

Men (*continued*)

for m. must work   189:87
give place to better m.   115:90
glory of young m. is their strength
   45:78
going to dine with some m.   33:16
good will toward m.   54:70
great m. are almost always bad m.
   9:1
great m. are not always wise   41:75
great m. ... not commonly ... great
   scholars   164:51
have m. about me that are fat   324:94
heaven ... leads m. to this hell
   363:51
histories make m. wise   26:34
I said ... All m. are liars   43:32
I speak ... French to m.   96:24
I will make you fishers of m.   51:8
idols which beset m.'s minds   27:41
in mean m. we entitle patience
   347:32
in most m.'s power to be agreeable
   382:10
it is the m. who make a city   272:54
jolly tars are our m.   141:48
let us now praise famous m.   62:59
lives not three good m. unhang'd
   314:64
m. alone ... capable of every wickedness   110:27
m. and women merely players
   301:90
m. are April when they woo   302:4
m. are but gilded loam   347:30
m. are capable ... of ... benevolence
   292:66
m. are children of a larger growth
   127:56
m. at some time are masters of their
   fates   323–4:93
m. below and saints above   295:2
m. ... differ as heaven and earth
   385:52
m. fear death as children ... dark
   24:86
m. fell out ... knew not why   82:35
m. have died from time to time
   302:3
m. in great places are thrice servants
   25:1
m. love in haste ... detest at leisure
   85:84
m. may bleed and m. may burn
   148:43
m. may come and m. may go   384:39
m. may rise on stepping-stones
   386:57

Men (*continued*)

m. must endure their going hence 330:98

m. of few words ... best m. 320:48

m. of good quality 399:33

m. prize the thing ungain'd 358:65

m. seldom make passes 243:22

m. that laugh and weep 382:19

m. that sow to reap 382:19

m. that were boys when I was 32:7

m. were deceivers ever 343:68

m. who borrow and m. who lend 191:25

m. will still say ... their finest hour 101:95

m. will wrangle ... write ... fight 108:96

m. with splendid hearts 71:90

m.'s natures are alike 108:2

mocks married m. 332:19

mother and lover of m. 383:25

my object ... to form Christian m. 22:55

new m., strange faces, other minds 385:53

nor yet favour to m. of skill 47:8

nor yet riches to m. of understanding 47:8

not as other m. are 55:89

not in the roll of common m. 314:71

old m. shall dream dreams 50:80

praise makes ... bad m. worse 275:58

praise makes good m. better 275:58

quit yourselves like m. 39:38

reputed one of the wise m. 25:98

rich m. furnished with ability 62:60

rich m. have no faults 276:91

rule of m. entirely great 76:54

schemes o' mice an' m. 80:18

sleek-headed m., and such as sleep 324:94

so are they all, all honourable m. 325:13

so long as m. can breathe 362:34

so many m., so many opinions 389:7

sons of the prophet ... brave m. 18:7

such m. are dangerous 324:94

talk of censorious old m. 94:3

that all m. are created equal 171:26

that all m. everywhere cd. be free 196:78

the breath of worldly ... m. 349:50

the clever m. at Oxford 153:14

the many m., so beautiful 105:55

the most mighty m. ... in his army 49:67

Men (*continued*)

The War between M. and Women 392:45

they make their steel with m. 293:80

thousand creeds ... move m.'s hearts 71:85

to m.'s business, and bosoms 24:84

to put confidence in m. 43:34

truth ... on the lips of dying m. 21:45

two m. look out through the same bars 193:38

we are the hollow m. ... the stuffed m. 130:94

we cannot be free m. if ... slavery 196:75

we petty m. walk under his huge legs 323:93

wealth accumulates and m. decay 150:62

what m. call gallantry 84:66

whatsoever ye wd. that m. shd. do 52:25

wisest m. have erred 222:15

wives are ... old m.'s nurses 24:97

wives are young m.'s mistresses 24:97

women are more like each other than m. 98:62

wonder m. dare trust th'selves with m. 357:60

you are m. of stones 330:4

young m. shall see visions 50:80

Mend: tried to m. the electric light 31:94

Mended: least said, soonest m. 269:66

Mene, mene, tekel, upharsin 49:68

*Mens: m. cuiusque is est quisque* 102:18

*ut sit m. sana in corpore sano* 180:71

Mentioned: and m. me to him 91:67

Merchant: m. to secure his treasure 253:51

that same m.'s flesh 340:19

Merchants: like m., venture trade abroad 318:39

Mercies: all thy faithful m. crown 402:72

His m. ay endure 221:10

Merciful as constant 154:22

Mercuries: as English M. 319:40

Mercury: words of M. are harsh 332:21

Mercy: desired m., and not sacrifice 50:75

doing justice ... leaving m. to heaven 134:63

half so good a grace as m. 337:84

have m. upon us ... sinners 63:76

Midsummer: this is very m. madness 360:95

Midwife: she is the fairies' m. 353:92
the m. laid her hand on ... Skull 127:49

Mid-winter: bleak m., long ago 290:43

*Mieux: le m. est l'ennemi du bien* 397:11
*tout est pour le m.* 397:7

Might: first in beauty shd. be first in m. 182:1
m. is right 272:57
saddest [words] ... It m. have been 403:90
'tis m. half-slumbering 185:38

Might-have-been: my name is M. 291:51
you won't be sorry for a m. 286:99

Mightier: God ... make thee m. yet 33:13
in word m. than they in arms 219:82

Mightiest: 'tis m. in the m. 339:15

Mighty: a m. man is he 199:6
death ... some have called thee m. 124:10
fear not, said he, for m. dread 384:35
God who made thee m. 33:13
how are the m. fallen! 40:46
I am weak, but thou art m. 407:40
look on my works, ye M., and despair 369:40
mean and m. rotting together 304:27
m. hunter before the Lord 35:51
this m. sum of things 409:65
Truth ... m. above all things 61:37

Mike O'Day: this is the grave of M. 13:50

Milan: retire me to my M. 357:58

Mile: he walked a crooked m. 239:74
miss is as good as a m. 272:61
yr. sad [heart] tires in a m.-a 361:19

Miles: can ye draw but twenty m. a day 205:78
how many m. to Babylon? 233:36
people come m. to see it 146:9

*Miles gloriosus* 247:63

Military: war ... too serious ... to be left to m. men 384:34

Milk: crying over spilt m. 259:41
drunk the m. of Paradise 107:76
flowing with m. and honey 36:70
m. comes frozen home in pail 332:20
no finer investment than ... m. in babies 101:5
too full o' th' m. of human kindness 333:32

Milking: going a-m., sir, she said 241:86

Milkmaid singeth blithe 214:98

Milky way: twinkle on the m. 410:68

Mill: bring grist to the m. 265:49
God's m. grinds slow but sure 265:27
in Gaza at the m. with slaves 221:12
more water glideth by the m. 357–8:63

Millar: I respect M., Sir 174:80
last sheet [*Johnson's Dictionary*] to M. 174:79

Miller: more water ... than wots ... m. of 357–8:63
there was a jolly m. once 65:16

Milliner: perfumed like a m. 313:51

Million: a m. m. spermatozoa 169:4
among so many m. of faces 72:3
the play ... pleas'd not the m. 308:85

Millionaire: I am a M. That is my religion 365:76

Millions: there are m. of us 401:69

Mills: the m. of God grind slowly 198:99

Millstone ... hanged about his neck 53:38

Milton: faith and morals ... M. held 413:5
malt does more than M. can 167:85
M.! thou shdst. be living 413:3
some mute inglorious M. 155:38

Mimsy were the borogoves 91:69

Mince: they dined on m. and ... quince 195:62

Mind: a m. not to be changed 216:35
a m. quite vacant is a m. distressed 113:67
a miserable state of m. 25:13
a prodigious quantity of m. 393:65
among all the diseases of the m. 378:59
better than P. of M. 284:75
blind ... judgment, and misguide the m. 249:93
born for the Universe, narrowed his m. 151:78
cheer of m. ... I was wont to have 353:85
clap yr. padlock on her m. 253:50
distressed, in m., body, or estate 63:83
dread had seized their troubled m. 384:35
education forms the common m. 251:22
fair terms and a villain's m. 339:7
farewell the tranquil m. 345:10

Mind (*continued*)

four seasons in the m. of man 185:45
great hills ... come back into my m. 32:5
he who does not m. his belly 175:91
I don't m. if I do 180:75
incline man's m. to atheism 25:10
it concentrates his m. wonderfully 177:24
last infirmity of noble m. 215:13
loud laugh ... spoke the vacant m. 150:65
love looks ... with the m. 341:38
love's but the frailty of the m. 109:14
love's the noblest frailty of the m. 128:63
m. ... deficient in ... humour 107:83
m. one's P's and Q's 274:26
m. that makes the body rich 355:25
m. yr. own business 272:58
minister to a m. diseased 336:72
my m. to me a kingdom is 129:77
never face so pleased my m. 18:9
no m. is thoroughly well organized 107:83
noble m. is here o'erthrown 310:1
not in my perfect m. 330:97
out of sight, out of m. 274:25
reading is to the m. 378:61
riches of the m. ... make ... rich 276:93
she had a frugal m. 113:56
sound m. in a sound body 180:71
that ... was great fortitude of m. 174:72
the gentle m. by gentle deeds 377:45
the m. is its own place 216:35
think my m. is maturing late? 228:92
'tis strange the m., that fiery particle 85:83
to the noble m., rich gifts 310:96
what is M.? No Matter 284:77
when I measure my m. against his [Shaw on Shakespeare] 367:8
when people call this beast to m. 31:89
whether 'tis nobler in the m. 309:95
with a gladsome m. 221:10
worst [tyranny] ... persecutes the m. 127:62
your m.'s cluttered up 401:68
Minds: balm of hurt m. 334:42
bringeth ... m. about to religion 25:10
great m. think alike 265:42

Minds (*continued*)

happiest moments of the ... best m. 371:58
lose myself in other men's m. 192:29
m. are not ever craving ... food 114:80
Nature ... doth teach ... to have aspiring m. 205:76
purest and most thoughtful m. 292:62
strange faces, other m. 385:53
the mighty m. of old 376:25
the refuge of weak m. 98:61
the religion of feeble m. 78:80
to the marriage of true m. 363:47
Mine: be m., as I yours for ever 154:22
Curly locks, wilt thou be m.? 231:27
hope's delusive m. 172:52
thou needest not fear m. [kisses] 370:55
'twas m., 'tis his 345:6
what's m. is my own 283:25
what's m. is yours, ... yours is m. 338:95
Miner: dwelt a m., forty-niner 225:59
Minister: canst thou not m. to a mind diseas'd? 336:72
quench thee, thou flaming m. 346:19
Ministers: angels and m. of grace defend us! 307:60
errands for the M. of State 143:76
my fellows are m. of Fate 356:49
Ministries: *The Times* has made many m. 27:43
Ministry: more for a marriage than a m. 27:44
the merit of a m. 180:66
Minnehaha, Laughing Water 198:2
Minnows: Triton of the m. 303:16
Minstrel: a wandering m. I 145:95
the M. Boy to the war is gone 226:64
the M. was infirm and old 295:99
Minute: a sucker born every m. 28:58
fill the unforgiving m. 190:5
must do [good] in m. particulars 67:36
Minutes: our m. hasten to their end 363:40
round ... the earth in forty m. 341:45
see the m. how they run 321:70
Miracle: a m. ... event which creates faith 366:3
a m. of loveliness 146:9
a m. of rare device 107:75
Miranda: do you remember an inn, M.? 32:8

Mirror: best m. is an old friend  272:59
 m. of all Christian kings  319:40
Mirth: all m. and no matter  343:66
 bards of passion and of M.  181:83
 far from all resort of m.  213:86
 M., admit me of thy crew  214:96
 M., with thee I mean to live  215:7
 much m. and no madness  373:93
 no country's m. is better than our
  own  178:47
 old earth must borrow its m.  404:91
 present m. hath present laughter
  359:84
 very tragical m.  342:54
Miscarriage: success and m. are empty
 172:43
Mischief: no m. but a woman ... priest
 is at the bottom  273:94
 Satan finds some m. still  399:36
 to draw new m. on  344:93
 to mourn a m. ... past  344:93
Miserable: a m. state of mind  25:13
 me m.!  218:62
 m. have no other medicine  337:89
Miseries: bound in shallows and in m.
 326:27
 hopes, and joys, and panting m.
  183:15
Misery: dwell on guilt and m.  23:71
 fallen ... into m. and endeth
  wrecchedly  97:47
 gave to m. all he had, a tear  155:41
 man ... is full of m.  65:13
 m. acquaints ... with strange bedfellows  356:41
 my m., the wormwood ... gall  49:60
 recall ... happiness when in m.  116:3
Misfortune: the m. of knowing anything  23:73
 to lose one parent ... a m.  405:10
Misfortunes: children ... make m. more
 bitter  24:95
 m. never come singly  272:60
 m. of our best friends ... not displeasing  288:19
 strength to bear the m. of others
  288:14
Misgivings: I view with profound m.
 the retreat  102:7
Mislead: lights that do m. the morn
 337–8:92
Miss: and mine [heart] he cannot m.
 372:83
 m. is as good as a mile  272:61
Missed: how I m. my Clementine!
 225:61
 society offenders ... who never wd.
  be m.  145:99

Mist: the rank m. they draw  215:16
Mistake: any m. about it in any quarter
 101:3
 man is Nature's sole m.  148:37
Mistakes: learn by other men's m.
 283:41
 the man who makes no m.  246:50
Mistress: art is a jealous m.  132:26
 if you can kiss the m.  268:39
 Master M. of my passion  362:35
 m. of herself, though China fall
  251:25
 m. of the Earl of Craven  407:43
 O m. mine  359:83
 select ... a m. or a friend  368:25
Mistresses: wives are young men's
 m.  24:27
Mists: season of m. and ... fruitfulness
 180:78
Misunderstood: to be great is to be m.
 133:37
Misused the King's press  315:82
Mix: I m. them with my brains, sir
 242:97
Moan: is not paid with m.  390:29
Moaning: no m. at the bar  385:44
Moat: as a m. defensive to a house
 348–9:41
Mob: best ... to do what the m. do
 121:63
 m. has ... no brains  272:62
Mobled queen  308:86
Mobs: suppose there are two m.?
 121:63
Mock: green-ey'd monster wh. doth m.
 345:7
 m. on, m. on, Voltaire  67:39
Mock Turtle: said the M. angrily
 91:59
 the M. replied  91:60
Mocked: be not deceived; God is not
 m.  58:70
Mockery: death itself ... a m.  370:47
Model of a modern Major-General
 147:31
Moderately: love m.; long love doth so
 354:10
Moderation: astonished at my own m.
 103:24
 m. is a fatal thing  406:31
Modes: ring in the nobler m. of life
 386:69
Modesty: O m.! 'twas strictly kept
 244:31
 o'erstep not the m. of nature  310:5
 wore enough for m.  76:50
Mohicans: The Last of the M.  110:30
Mole: wilt thou go ask the m.  66:32

Molehill: mountain out of a m.
272:73
Molly Malone 17:89
Mome raths outgrabe 91:69
Moment: all my possessions for a m. of
time 132:22
   happy in the m. that was present
176:13
   m. foreseen may be unexpected
132:18
   pleasing attentions ... impulse of the
m. 23:78
   snow falls ... a m. white then melts
81:25
   some m. when the moon was blood
98:67
   sonnet is a m.'s monument 290:49
   spur of the m. 278:71
   to every ... nation comes the m.
200:24
Monan's rill: the moon on M. 294:94
Monarch: becomes the ... m. better
than his crown 339:15
   I am m. of all I survey 114:77
Monday: hanging ... cat on M. 70:74
   M.'s child is fair of face 235:56
*Monde: se mêler à corriger le m.* 224:49
*Mondes: meilleur des m. possibles*
397:7
Money: abundance of m. ruins youth
254:55
   borrer the m. to do it with 399:31
   business ... may bring m. 23:68
   by any means make m. 166:72
   dally not with m. or women 259:50
   did dream of m.-bags to-night 339:9
   fool ... m. are soon parted 263:76
   Government licence to print m.
391:35
   he lends out m. gratis 338:3
   he that wants m., means 302:93
   I have spent all the m. 177:33
   if m. be not thy servant 272:63
   innocently employed ... getting m.
176:8
   lend yr. m. and lose yr. friend
269:70
   love of m. ... root of all evil 59:92
   marrieth for love without m. 271:44
   merit will not serve ... as m. 175:87
   m. begets m. 272:64
   m. gives me pleasure 32:98
   m. is like muck 25:8
   m. makes marriage 272:66
   m. talks 272:69
   no man ... wrote, except for m.
177:21
   no m., no swiss 273:95

Money (*continued*)
   pays yr. m. ... takes yr. choice
284:74
   purse ... full of other men's m.
261:17
   put m. in thy purse 345:96
   putting m. on a horse 32:3
   remember when ... m. not scarce
133:47
   said that love of m. is the root 82:41
   some honey, and plenty of m.
195:60
   that's the way the m. goes 203:60
   the want of m. is so [root of evil]
82:41
   throw good m. after bad 280:37
   thy m. perish with thee 56:16
   your m. or your life 83:51
Mongrels: greyhounds, m., spaniels,
curs 334:48
Monk: the devil a m. wd. be 227:74
Monkey: only a m. shaved 148:38
Monotony: bless articulate m. 378:62
   to chase m. 144:85
Monster: great-siz'd m. of ingratitudes
358:71
   green-ey'd m. wh. doth mock 345:7
Montezuma: knows who imprisoned
M. 202:42
Month: April is the cruellest m. 131:10
   ark rested in the seventh m. 35:46
   laughter for a m. ... jest for ever
313:58
   this is the m. ... the happy morn
215:19
Months: cd. live for m. without ...
labour 399:30
   go right on ... for numerous more m.
399:30
Montreal: in a M. lumber room 82:47
   O God! O M.! 82:47
Montrose: young man of M. 33:12
Monument: a sonnet is a moment's m.
290:49
   an early but enduring m. 367:13
   he replied, 'Like the M.' 174:74
   if you seek my m. 416:49
   Patience on a m. 360:89
   their only m. the asphalt road 131:8
   thou art a m. 179:54
*Monumentum: si m. requiris, circum-
spice* 416:49
Mood: albeit unused to the melting m.
346–7:22
   in vacant or in pensive m. 410:71
   sweet m. when pleasant thoughts
bring sad 411:83
   that blessed m. 415:32

Moon: a-roving by the light of the m.
86:98
  beneath a waning m. was haunted
106:72
  beneath the visiting m.   299:66
  course of one revolving m.   126:43
  cry for the m.   259:39
  danced by the light of the m.   195:62
  danced the m. on Monan's Rill
294:94
  honour from the pale-fac'd m.
313:54
  hymns to the cold fruitless m.
341:35
  I see the m. ... m. sees me   234:43
  late eclipses in the sun and m.
327:52
  lustres slake the o'ertaken m.   70:75
  make guilty ... the m.   327:53
  man in the m.   271:29
  man in the m. ... down too soon
235:54
  m. in the valley of Ajalon   38:20
  m. when she deserts the night   221:14
  moving M. went up the sky   105:56
  nor the m. [smite thee] by night
44:38
  one with ... the west m.   390:17
  Queen-M. is on her throne   184:26
  rather be a dog and bay the m.
325:24
  slowly, silently, now the m.   118:27
  sung to the m. by a ... loon   148:45
  swear not by the m., th' inconstant
m.   354:2
  the cow jumped over the m.   232:33
  the m. be still as bright   86:97
  the m. doth shine as bright as day
231:25
  the m. lies fair   20:30
  to bark at the m.   255:92
  unmasked her beauty to the m.
306:53
  with how sad steps, O M.   373:85
Moonlight: ghost along the m. shade
248:72
  go visit it by the pale m.   295:1
  how sweet the m. sleeps   340:22
  I'll come to thee by m.   231:21
  ill met by m., proud Titania   341:43
  look for me by m.   231:21
  passions ... as m. unto sunlight
387:83
Moonlit: knocking on the m. door
118:23
Moons: some nine m. wasted   344:90
Moonshine: look in the almanack;
find out m.   342:48

Mops: seven maids with seven m.
92:79
Moral: a m., if only you can find it
91:57
  a m., sensible, and well-bred man
112:52
  golf ... a form of m. effort   194:52
  grandest m. attribute of a Scotsman
28:64
  let us be m. ... contemplate existence
120:48
  O m. Gower   98:53
  point a m. or adorn a tale   174:69
Morality: give ... a lecture on m. ... a
shilling   175:87
  gossip made tedious by m.   406:20
  m. of an action depends   175:84
  periodical fits of m.   202:46
  up agen middle class m.   366:96
Moralize: faithful loves shall m.
377:40
Morals: foundation of m. and legislation   33:14
  no man's religion ... survives his m.
273:93
  teach the m. of a whore   174:77
More: and penance m. will do   105:59
  easy to take *m.* than nothing   90:55
  enough for modesty—no m.   76:50
  m. than somewhat   29:58
  Oliver Twist has asked for m.   120:55
  you get no m. of me   125:34
*Morituri te salutant*   380:88
Morn: awake, the m. will never rise
117:10
  healthy breath of m.   182:96
  lights that do mislead the m.
337–8:92
  now M., her rosy steps   219:75
  sang from m. till night   65:16
  the m., in russet mantle clad   305:36
  this the happy m.   215:19
Morning: beauty of the m.; silent,
bare   412:96
  day's at the morn. M.'s at seven
75:44
  early one m. ... sun was rising
16:80
  glad, confident m.   74:29
  great m. of the world   367:11
  hour in the m. is worth two   267:2
  in his m. face   150:68
  in the m. we will remember them
65:20
  it's nice to get up in the m.   193:44
  Lucifer, son of the m.   48:38
  M. in the Bowl of Night   134:65
  on a cold and frosty m.   16:86

Morning (*continued*)

peace ... dropping from the veils of the m.   417:53

sees some m., unaware   74:21

Morrow: good night till it be m.   354:6

never shall sun that m. see   333:34

trusting the m. as little as you can   166:74

*Mors: pallida M. aequo ... pede*   166:73

Morsel: sweetest m. of the night   316:11

Mortal: he raised a m. to the skies   127:54

her last disorder m.   150:74

reminds a man he is m.   117:14

shall m. man be more just than God?   41:66

Mortality: m., behold and fear   29:71

there's nothing serious in m.   334:46

Mortals: not in m. to command success   9:4

what fools these m. be!   342:50

*Mortuis: de m. nil nisi bonum*   259:54

Moses: meekness of M. ... strength of Samson   272:55

M. said, ... This is the bread   37:80

persuaded to leave M. out   34:21

Moss: a rolling stone gathers no m.   276:1

Most may err as greatly as the few   127:47

Moth: desire of the m. for the star   371:56

Mother: call me early, m. dear   388:89

dead! and ... never called me m.   409:56

disclaim her for a m.   142:64

does your m. know ... you are out?   28:55

England ... m. of parliaments   71:81

foolish son ... heaviness of his m.   45:61

gave her m. forty whacks   15:67

home to his m.'s house   221:9

I arose a m. in Israel   39:21

I feel no pain, dear m.   17:88

let ... his m. drudge ... at seventy   365:80

like m., like daughter   272:71

Mary was that M. mild   10:19

m. of the free, how shall we extol?   33:13

m., who'd give her booby for another   142:57

m. who talks about her own children   122:92

my m. bore me in ... wild   68:51

my m. said that I never shd.   236:57

Mother (*continued*)

never had any m.?   380:84

the m. of all living   35:40

the m. of months in meadow   382:15

took great care of his m.   211:56

variety ... m. of enjoyment   123:99

where a M. laid her Baby   10:19

whether his m. wd. let him or no   232:30

with the m. first begin   259:51

Mother-in-law remembers not   272:72

Mothers: all women become like their m.   406:30

people's m. always bore me   406:30

Moths ... ever caught by glare   83:56

Motion: between the m. and the act   130:95

in his m. like an angel sings   340:22

in our proper m. we ascend   217:47

no m. has she now, no force   414:19

sensible warm m. to become ... clod   337:90

Motive: morality ... depends on the m.   175:84

Motley: a m. fool   301:87

Mould: splashing the wintry m.   417:55

the m. of form   310:1

Mount: yet shall he m. [Milton]   156:45

Mountain: m. out of a molehill   272:73

robes the m. in its azure hue   88:20

tiptoe on the misty m. tops   354:14

up the airy m.   11:22

Mountains: from Greenland's icy m.   159:86

m. skipped like rams   43:29

the m. look on Marathon   84:78

two voices ... one of the m.   412:1

upon the m. of Ararat   35:46

walk upon England's m. green   67:38

Mountebank: a mere anatomy, a m.   303:12

Mourn: don't m. for me never   12:43

in summer skies to m.   181:88

makes countless thousands m.   80:14

secure, and now can never m.   367:16

that man was made to m.   80:13

to m. a mischief ... past   344:93

Mourning: with my m. very handsome   246:44

Mouse: caught a crooked m.   239:74

frightened a little m. under her chair   237:64

killing of a m. on Sunday   70:74

man or m.   271:35

the m. ran up the clock   232:34

the other caught a m.   195:64

Mouse-trap: make a better m.   133:48

Mouth: a close m. catcheth no flies
258:11
   burnt his m. with ... cold plum
      porridge 235:54
   gift horse in the m. 264:5
   heart is in his m. 266:81
   her m. unclosed in ... kiss 193:48
   if you m. it as many ... players do
      310:3
   into the m. of Hell 385:43
   lo, in her m. ... an olive leaf 35:47
   out of thine own m. ... I judge thee
      55:90
   purple-stained m. 184:24
   set a watch ... before my m. 44:51
   spue thee out of my m. 61:23
   tree whose hungry m. is pressed
      188–9:81
   wd. not melt in his m. 257:77
Mouths: blind m. that scarce ... know
      how 215:15
   have m. but ... speak not 43:30
   made m. in a glass 329:74
*Moutons: revenons à nos m.* 19:16
Move: but it does m. 141:44
   do m. a woman's mind 361:7
   I will m. the earth 20:24
   languid strings do scarcely m. 68:55
   m. him into the sun 243:17
Moved: not m. with concord of sweet
      sounds 340:24
Moves: and having writ, m. on 136:79
   m., and mates, and slays 135:78
   m. in determinate grooves 158:68
Moving: always m. as the restless
      spheres 205:76
   m. Moon went up the sky 105:56
Mower whets his scythe 214:98
Much: missing so m. and so m. 111:34
   m. may be made of a Scotchman
      176:4
   m. of a muchness 395:84
   m. ... said on both sides 9:8
   so m., to learn so little 121:70
Muck: money is like m. 25:8
Mud: two men look out ... one sees
      the m. 193:38
Muddy, ill-seeming, thick, bereft
      355:26
Mudie's: I keep my books at ... M.
      82:42
Muffet: little Miss M. sat on a tuffet
      235:51
Muffin: one caught a m. 195:64
Multiply: be fruitful, and m. 34:29
Multitudes: against revolted m. 219:82
   I contain m. 403:87
   m. in the valley of decision 50:81

Multitudes (*continued*)
   pestilence-stricken m. 369:35
Multitudinous: the m. seas incarnadine
      334:43
Munch on, crunch on 75:41
Murder: foul and most unnatural m.
      307:65
   I met M. on the way 368:30
   m. most foul ... unnatural 307:66
   m. ... one of the Fine Arts 119:30
   m. shrieks out 400:49
   m. will out 97:48, 272:75
   then m.'s out of tune 346:20
Murdered: death of kings ... all m.
      350:54
   two brothers and their m. man 182:5
Murderer: Aram ... thief ... liar ... m.
      87:14
Murmur: creeping m. and the poring
      dark 320:50
   live m. of a summer's day 21:40
Muse: Fool, said my M. to me 373:84
   O for a M. of fire 318:36
   strictly meditate the thankless M.
      215:11
   the M. but served to ease 248:81
Mushroom: nicely groomed, like a m.
      193:27
Mushrooms: broiled fowl and m.—
      capital! 120:60
Music: a reasonable good ear in m.
      342:51
   and let the sounds of m. creep
      340:22
   deep sea ... m. in its roar 84:65
   fled is that m. 184:32
   have m. wherever she goes 237:66
   how sour sweet m. is! 351:63
   if m. be the food of love 358:75
   like m. on my heart 106:61
   linnet, how sweet his m.! 414:26
   man that hath no m. 340:24
   m. and women I ... give way to
      245:43
   m. has charms to soothe 108:5
   m. that gentlier on the spirit lies
      388:85
   m., when soft voices die 370:54
   never merry when I hear sweet m.
      340:23
   O M., sphere-descended Maid
      108:93
   ran ... after the wonderful m. 75:43
   still, sad m. of humanity 415:35
   the m. in my heart I bore 414:22
   the setting sun, and m. at the close
      348:49
   the soul of m. shed 226:62

Music (*continued*)
thou hast thy m. too 181:81
thy chosen m., Liberty! 412:1
to church ... not for the doctrine, but the m. 249:98
to hear the sea-maid's m. 341:44
uproar's your only m. 186:53
when M., heavenly maid, was young 108:91
women and m. shd. never be dated 151:88
Musical: most m., most melancholy! 213:85
we are a m. nation 390:26
Musing there an hour alone 84–5:78
Musty: proverb is something m. 310:11
Mutilators: borrowers of books ... m. of collections 192:26
Muttering: the m. grew to a grumbling 75:40
Mutton: Alice—M.; M.—Alice 94:98
Muzzle: shall not m. the ox 38:12
Myriad-minded: our m. Shakespeare 107:80
Myrtles: ye m. brown, with ivy never sere 215:8
Myself: awe of such a thing as I m. 323:91
best image of m. 219:77
deliver me from m. 72:6
I celebrate m., and sing m. 403:82
I like to go by m. 159:81
made m. a speculative statesman 9:6
said I to m.—said I 144:83
thought of thinking for m. 147:27
very well then I contradict m. 403:87
when I give I give m. 403:85
Mysteries: capable of being in uncertainties, m. 186:52
Mysterious: God moves in a m. way 113:63
Mystery: brave its [sea's] dangers comprehend its m. 198:1
hissed all my m. lectures 377:50
riddle ... in a m. inside an enigma 100:91
[sea's] works ... are wrapped in m. 110:26
take upon's the m. of things 330:99
the wicked grocer ... m. and a sign 99:76

Nag: forc'd gait of a shuffling n. 314:74
Nail: and Dick the shepherd blows his n. 332:20

Nail (*continued*)
dead as a door-n. 259:55
hit the n. on the head 267:88
Nailed: blessed feet which ... years ago were n. 312:43
Nails: nineteen hundred and forty n. 373:90
Naked: both n. ... and were not ashamed 35:35
dead men n. they shall be one 390:17
helpless, n., piping loud 67–8:44
left me n. to mine enemies 323:84
n. came I out of ... womb 41:65
Nakedness: and not in utter n. 410:77
Name: a deed without a n. 335:61
a good n. ... rather than great riches 45:79
a rose by any other n. 353:1
and she lost her maiden n. 18:3
conveys it in a borrowed n. 253:51
dominion ... by a scribbled n. 390:20
gathered together in thy N. 63:73
give a dog a bad n. 264:6
good n. in man and woman 345:6
good n. is better than precious ointment 46:3
halloo yr. n. to the reverberate hills 359:80
hallowed be thy n. 52:18
he that filches from me my good n. 345:6
her n. was Barbara Allen 12:36
I remember yr. n. perfectly 377:52
I will not blot out his n. 61:22
I wd. ... my n. were not so terrible 316:2
it beareth the n. of Vanity Fair 77:60
lash'd the vice but spared the n. 381:97
let me not n. it to you, you chaste stars 346:18
local habitation and a n. 342:53
must he lose the n. of king? 350:55
my n. is Legion 54:57
my n. is Might-Have-Been 291:51
my 'oss, my wife, and my n. 381:91
n., at which the world grew pale 174:69
n. to all succeeding ages curst 126:38
nature ... a n. for an effect 114:74
not take the n. of ... God in vain 37:85
noteless blot on a remembered n. 367:15
of every friendless n. the friend 172:53

Name (*continued*)

    rouse him at the n. of Crispian 320:57

    such weak witness of thy n.  216:24

    take ... my good n. ... my life  279:95

    tell your n. the livelong day  122:81

    the gentleman's n. ... Worldly Wise-man  77:59

    the grand old n. of gentleman 387:72

    the n. of it called Babel  35:52

    the n. of the slough was Despond 77:58

    the very n. of [stepmother] sufficeth 278:72

    the whistling of a n.  250:17

    their n. liveth for evermore  62:62

    to see one's n. in print  85:89

    tranquility! thou better n.  107:78

    what's in a n.?  353:1

    what the dickens his n. is  340:31

    whose n. was writ in water  187:70

    write against your n.  287:9

    yet leaving here a n.  376:26

Names: call'd him soft n.  184:29

    I have lost all the n.  177:33

    no n., no pack drill  273:96

    sick men play ... with their n.  349:43

    such great n. as these  18:6

    unpopular n. and impossible loyalties 21:49

Naming: today we have n. of parts 287:3

Naples: see N. and die  277:22

Napoleon: N.'s armies used to march 297:33

    N.'s presence ... forty thousand men 401:58

    the N. of crime [Moriarty]  125:22

*Narr: blebt ein N. sein Lebelang*  200:28

Nasty: a nice man ... of n. ideas 382:11

    something n. in the woodshed 142:68

Nation: as the clergy ... so ... rest of the n.  23:69

    bind up the n.'s wounds  196:81

    dedicate this n. to the policy  289:29

    every n. has the govt. it deserves 203:58

    hinted that we are a n. of amateurs 290:41

    inspired the n. It was the n.  102:11

    n. of shopkeepers  228:85, 374:98

    n. ... perpetually to be conquered 78:72

    n. shall not lift up sword agst. n. 48:31

Nation (*continued*)

    no n. was ever ruined by trade 138:11

    noble and puissant n. rousing herself 224:43

    once to every man and n.  200:24

    one third of a n. ill-housed  289:30

    righteousness exalteth a n.  45:68

    that this n. ... shall have a new birth 196:79

    we are a musical n.  390:26

Nations: day of small n. ... passed away  95:14

    eclipsed the gaiety of n.  178:43

    equal rights ... of n., large and small 394:76

    happiest n. have no history  130:86

    in thy seed shall all the n. ... blessed 36:57

    languages are the pedigree of n. 178:39

    lasting peace ... with all n.  196–7:81

    lightning of the n.  369:34

    many n. and three continents  125:24

    n. are as a drop of a bucket  48:43

    n. which have put mankind ... in their debt  170:13

    Privileged ... People ... Two N. 123:98

Native: content to breathe his n. air 251:28

    fast by their n. shore  113:64

    my n. Land—Good Night  83:58

    n. hue of resolution  309:95

    though I am n. here  307:59

Natives: the bulk of your n. ... vermin 381:1

Nativity: in n., chance, or death 341:34

Natural: as n. to die as to be born 24:87

    I do it more n.  359:85

    in him alone, 'twas n. to please 126:37

    n., simple, affecting  151:82

Natural Philosophy [makes men] deep 26:34

Natural Selection: called this principle ... N.  117:7

Naturalists: so, n. observe, a flea 382:5

Naturally: if Poetry come not as n. as the Leaves  186:56

    not n. honest  362:25

Nature: a friend ... masterpiece of N. 132:29

    accuse not N.!  220:88

    all n. is but art  250:12

Nature (*continued*)

allow not n. more than n. needs 328:67

are God and N. then at strife? 386:62

as old and new ... as N.'s self 73:17

broken N.'s social union 80:17

creatures that by a rule in n. teach 318:39

cunning'st pattern of excelling n. 346:19

disguise fair n. with ... rage 319:45

first follow N. 249:92

Force of N. cd. no farther go 128:66

fortress built by N. for herself 348:41

great n.'s second course 334:42

his n. is too noble 303:17

human n. is so well disposed 23:67

I have learned to look on n. 415:35

I love not Man the less, but N. more 84:65

in human n. ... more of the fool 25:2

in thy green lap was N.'s darling 156:44

let N. be your teacher 414:27

little we see in N. 412:93

loathed ... life that age ... can lay on n. 337:91

man is N.'s sole mistake 148:37

mute N. mourns her worshipper 295:3

N. always does contrive 144:87

N. and N.'s Laws lay hid 248:88

N. I loved 192:34

n. in you stands on the very verge 328:65

n. is but a name for an effect 114:74

n. is often hidden, sometimes overcome 26:25

n. is the art of God 72:1

n. lends such evil dreams 386:62

N. might stand up and say 326:31

n. ... must be obeyed 27:42

n. never did betray the heart 415:36

n. of a tragic volume 316:96

n., red in tooth and claw 386:63

n.'s law ... man was made to mourn 80:13

n.'s soft nurse 317:13

N. that framed us 205:76

o'erstep not the modesty of n. 310:5

on N., and on human life, musing 409:63

one touch of n. ... whole world kin 358:72

passing through n. to eternity 305:40

Nature (*continued*)

scenery is fine ... human n. is finer 186:57

spectacles of books to read n. 127:59

that N. yet remembers ... fugitive 411:80

the more man's n. runs to 24:89

the n. of an insurrection 324:98

the purpose and n. of miracles 366:3

the rest [hours] on N. fix 104:40

then N. said, 'A lovelier flower' 415:30

to write and read comes by n. 343:73

true wit is n. to advantage dress'd 249:97

unerring N., still divinely bright 249:92

where man is not, n. is barren 69:63

whose body N. is, and God the soul 250:11

woman ... one of N.'s agreeable blunders 112:48

words, like N., half reveal 386:58

yet do I fear thy n. 333:32

youth ... still is N.'s priest 411:78

Natures: men's n. are alike 108:2

Naught: it is n., it is n., saith the buyer 45:77

Naughty: a n. night to swim in 329:80

good deed in a n. world 340:25

n. girl to disobey 236:57

Navy: Ruler of the Queen's N. 147:26, 27

Nazareth: can ... any good thing come out of N.? 55:96

Neaera: tangles of N.'s hair 215:12

Near: call ... while he is n. 48:50

he seems so n. and yet so far 386:66

Nearer, my God, to thee 9:3

Neat: still to be n. ... be drest 179:51

Necessary: is yr. journey really n.? 11:5

Necessities: give us the luxuries ... will dispense with ... n. 227:73

Necessity: by n. ... we all quote 133:40

make a virtue of n. 282:96

n. hath no law 272:77

n. ... is the argument of tyrants 246:56

n. is the mother of invention 272:78

no virtue like n. 348:36

sworn brother ... to grim N. 351:60

teach thy n. to reason thus 348:36

thy n. is greater than mine 373:88

Neck: a n. God made for other use 167:80

**Neck** (*continued*)
England will have her n. wrung 101:1
my n. is very short 226:67
n. or nothing 272:79
some chicken! Some n.! 101:1

**Need:** all we n. of hell 122:82
friend in n. is a friend indeed 263:92
in thy most n. ... by thy side 14:58
n. to pray for fair weather 25:7
O, reason not the n. 328:67

**Needle:** man for the sword and for the n. she 389:2
plying her n. and thread 166:64
through the eye of a n. 53:41

**Needlessly** sets foot upon a worm 114:75

**Needs:** all this sad world n. 404:93
more than nature n. 328:67
to each according to his n. 207:6

**Negative Capability** 186:52

**Negatives:** two n. make an affirmative 281:79

**Neglect:** n. the creeping hours 301:89
such sweet n. more taketh me 179:52

**Negligent:** celerity ... admir'd than by the n. 299:59

*Neiges: où sont les n. d'antan?* 396:95

**Neighbour:** false witness against thy n. 37:91
lov'd his wicked n. as himself 126:46
love thy n. as thyself 37:99
policy of a good n. 289:29
thy n.'s wife ... manservant ... ox ... ass 37:92
worketh no ill to his n. 57:43

**Neighbours:** good fences make good n. 139:26
in peace ... as good n. 394:76
live without friends ... not without ... n. 270:95

**Nelly:** let not poor N. starve 96:22

**Neptune:** do choose the ebbing N. 357:54
envious siege of wat'ry N. 349:42
he wd. not flatter N. 303:17
will all great N.'s ocean wash this blood? 334:43

**Nerissa,** my little body is aweary 338:1

**Nerves:** when ... the n. prick 386:60

**Nervous:** Bradshaw—n. and terse but limited 125:28

**Nest:** to find a mare's n. 271:39

**Nests:** birds in their little n. agree 399:37
birds in their ... n. agree with China-men 32:99
built their n. in my beard 195:66

**Nettle:** out of this n., danger 313:60

**Never:** and ... n. called me mother 409:56
better late than n. 256:25
books n. die 289:33
dead men rise up n. 383:20
don't mourn for me n. 12:43
I n. shall love the snow again 70:77
limericks n. wd. scan 13:54
love that n. told can be 67:40
me and my true love will n. meet 18:2
my apple trees will n. 139:26
n. a spray of yew 21:37
n. begin than n. make an end 256:27
n. broke the Sabbath, but for gain 126:45
n. glad confident morning again 74:29
n., I ween, was a prouder 28:53
n. lov'd ... met ... parted 79:97
n., n., n., n., n. 331:6
n., n. thinks of me 19:10
n. seek to tell thy love 67:40
n. send to know for whom the bell 124:14
n. the time and the place 74:31
n. the twain shall meet 189:92
n. to have lost at all 83:50
n. to have loved at all 386:59
n. turned his back ... n. doubted 73:16
seldom or n. the two hit it off 409:59
This England n. did nor n. shall 327:47
what, n.? No, n.! 147:22
who n. made a foe 385:51

**Nevermore:** quoth the Raven, N. 247:67

**New:** a n. broom sweeps clean 273:91
a n. commandment I give 56:8
a n. heaven and a n. earth 61:32
a n. master—get a n. man 356:44
among n. men, strange faces 385:53
as old and n. ... as Nature's self 73:17
before you are on with the n. 17:93
called the N. World into existence 88:26
[compassions] are n. every morning 49:61
conservatism? ... is ... against the n. 196:77
how strange it seems, and n.! 74:30
n. king ... knew not Joseph 36:67
n. man ... raised up in him 64:94
n. nobility ... act of power 25:6

New (*continued*)

  n. philosophy calls all in doubt 123:3

  n. wine into old bottles 54:73

  no n. thing under the sun 46:96

  old lamps for n: 20:22

  old order ... yielding place to n. 385:54

  piping songs for ever n. 183:19

  ring in the n. 386:68

  sing unto him a n. song 42:98

  will not apply n. remedies 26:17

New Way to Pay Old Debts 208:19

Newcastle: coals to N. 257:85

Newcomer: O, blithe N.!...415:37

New-fangled: May's n. shows 331:11

  their garments, though n. ill 363:41

News: all the n. that's fit to print 242:95

  first bringer of unwelcome n. 316:97

  for there is good n. yet to hear 99:74

  good n. from a far country 45:82

  he that tells his wife n. 279:17

  ill n. comes too soon 267:14

  man bites a dog; that is n. 116:1

  master-passion ... love of n. 114:81

  nature of bad n. infects 298:51

  never good to bring bad n. 299:56

  no n. is good n. 273:97

  nowadays truth ... greatest n. 273:14

  talk of court n. 330:99

Newspapers: n. always excite curiosity 192:31

  successful n. are ceaselessly querulous 208:28

Newton: another N., a new Donne 169:4

  God said, Let N. be! 248:88

Nice: a n. man ... of nasty ideas 382:11

  n. to get up in the mornin' 193:44

  sugar and spice and all that's n. 240:85

  too n. for a statesman 151:79

Nicely: n.-calculated less or more 409:60

  sick men play so n. with their names 349:43

Nickname: a n. is the heaviest stone 159:84

Nigh: the Lord is n. 42:1

Night: a braw, bricht, moonlicht n. 193:42

  a casement ope at n. 185:33

  a naughty n. to swim in 329:80

  afraid for the terror by n. 43:20

  all n. long ... on sentry-go 144:85

Night (*continued*)

  and darkness N. he named 220:84

  a-roving so late into the n. 86:97

  as a watch in the n. 43:16

  beneath the kisses of n. 370:46

  calmest and most stillest n. 317:14

  come, civil n. 354:13

  come, thick n. 333:33

  desire ... of the n. for the morrow 371:56

  dog in the n.-time 125:23

  done by n. appears by day 260:85

  doom'd ... to walk the n. 307:63

  Friday n. is Amami n. 11:27

  from morn to n., my friend 290:46

  gentle into that good n. 390:18

  gwine to run all n. ... all day 137:1

  honey'd middle of the n. 181:90

  I ask of thee, beloved N. 369:33

  I read much of the n. 131:11

  in the Bowl of N. 134:65

  in the forests of the n. 68:46

  it [candle] will not last the n. 210:45

  labour n. and day to be a pilgrim 77:65

  let's have one other gaudy n. 299:61

  like the n. of cloudless climes 86:96

  moonless n. in the small town 390:23

  my delight on a shining n. 18:98

  ne'er saw true beauty till this n. 353:95

  n. cometh, when no man can work 55:5

  n. is drawing nigh 28:56

  n. is long that never finds the day 335:67

  n. makes no difference 162:21

  n. neddying among the snuggeries 390:24

  n.'s candles are burnt out 354:14

  n. unto n. sheweth knowledge 41:87

  odd ... it was the middle of the n. 92:76

  out of the n. that covers me 160:93

  pass'd a miserable n. 351:71

  perils and dangers of this n. 63:75

  poor souls who dwell in N. 66:31

  reign of Chaos and old N. 217:40

  remain together ... it will be good n. 368:27

  returned home the previous n. 76:52

  shades of n. were falling fast 197:93

  she hangs upon the cheek of n. 353:94

  ships that pass in the n. 198:4

  silver-sweet ... lovers' tongues by n. 354:5

Noise (*continued*)
.never valued till they make a n.
114:82
Noises: like n. in a swound 105:46
this isle is full of n. 356:47
Noll: for shortness called N. 141:49
No-More, Too-Late, Farewell 291:51
Nonconformist: whoso wd. be a man
must be a n. 133:36
None: n. of us liveth to himself 57:44
n. that ... trust in him shall be overcome 63:63
so the poor dog had n. 236:59
some believe they've n. at all 82:40
then n. was for a party 201:38
this little pig had n. 239:78
Nonsense: sounds like n., my dear
296:16
through ... realms of N. absolute
128:68
Noon: dark, amid the blaze of n.
221:13
far from the fiery n. 182:96
from morn to n. he fell 217:44
sun has not attained his n. 162:18
Noon-day, upon the market-place
324:97
Noose: in a N. of Light 134:65
naked to the hangman's n. 167:80
Normal, yes, thank God, we're n.
242:7
Norman: simple faith than N. blood
387:74
North-north-west: am but mad n.
308:83
Nor(o)way: to N., N. ... o'er the faem
12:38
Norwich: asked his way to N. 235:54
Nose: custom ... hateful to the n.
170:19
cut off one's n. to spite one's face
259:46
Dong with a luminous N. 194:56
ever and anon he gave his n. 313:51
had Cleopatra's n. been shorter
244:27
led by the n. with gold 362:27
Marian's n. looks red and raw
332:20
n. was as sharp as a pen 319:44
one's n. to the grindstone 273:4
pay through the n. 33:12, 274:32
ring at the end of his n. 195:61
snapped off her n. 238:70
to turn up one's n. 281:70
wipe a bloody n. 142:58
Noses: athwart men's n. as they lie
asleep 353:92

Noses (*continued*)
n., ... but they smell not 43:31
nothing pay for wearing our own n.
304:21
Note: as the gen'l'm'n said to the fi'
pun' n. 121:69
his merry n. unto ... bird's throat
300:83
not a funeral n. 408:52
when found, make a n. 120:46
Notes: I heard a thousand blended n.
411:83
the sound is forced, the n. are few
68:55
Nothing: book although there's n. in't
85:89
certain of n. but ... holiness 186:50
civility costs n. 258:7
days ... when ... n. goes wrong
148:40
devil, having n. else to do 31:96
did n. in particular 144:90
do n. for ever and ever 12:43
doing n. for a bribe 304:23
doings without charity are n. worth
64:87
easy to take *more* than n. 90:55
everything by starts and n. long
126:43
gives to airy n. ... habitation 342:53
he n. common did or mean 207:3
he that knows n., doubts n. 268:49
I am n. if not critical 345:97
I do n. upon myself 124:12
is it n. to ... ye that pass by? 49:59
know this only, that he n. knew
221:7
learnt n., and forgotten n. 384:31
let n. you dismay 16:82
looked at for n. Nohow! 92:73
mind's cluttered up with n. 401:68
neck or n. 272:79
n. a year, paid quarterly 381:93
n – absolutely n. – half so much
worth doing 153:13
n. begins and n. ends 390:29
n. beside remains. Round the decay
369:40
n. can bring you peace 133:38
n. destroyeth authority so much
25:14
n. except a battle lost 401:57
n. for n. 273:6
n. for n. 'ere 285:80
n. great ... without enthusiasm
132:28
n. happens, nobody comes 30:74
n. in excess 19:17

**Nothing** (*continued*)

n. in his life became him   333:30

n. is certain but death and taxes   139:16

n. is certain but uncertainty   273:7

n. is had for n.   103:25

n. is ours but time   273:8

n. of him that doth fade   355:35

n. of itself will come   409:65

n. pay for wearing our own noses   304:21

n. seek, n. find   273:10

n. so absurd but some philosopher has said it   102:14

n. so sharply reminds   117:14

n.'s truer than them [taxes]   120:43

n. succeeds like excess   406:31

n. succeeds like success   273:11

n. to declare except my genius   406:33

n. to do but work   189:83

n. to eat but food   189:83

u. to look backward [forward] to   139:23

n. to say—say n.   108:97

n. to wear but clothes   189:83

n. venture, n. win   273:13

n. ... violent.is permanent   273:12

n. went unrewarded but Desert   126:44

n. whatever to grumble at   148:40

n. will come of n.   327:49

questioneth n., n. learneth   273:9

sea ... n. but to make him sick   123:8

smattering of everything ... knowledge of n.   121:78

sound and fury signifying n.   336:76

speak ... as I am; n. extenuate   346:22

think n. done while aught remains   288:24

'tis something, n.   345:6

we brought n. into this world   59:91

yeomanry ... with whom ... n. to do   23:64

**Nothingness:** love and fame to n.   186:49

will never pass into n.   181:85

**Notice** ... you have been pleased to take   174:78

**Notorious:** open and n. evil liver   64:93

**Nought:** knows n. that knows not this   358:65

**Noun:** talk of a n. and a verb   321:68

**Nourished:** how begot, how n.   339:14

**Novel:** I've read in many a n.   87:13

**Novel** (*continued*)

only obligation to which ... we may hold a n.   170:23

when I want to read a n.   123:2

**Novels:** catalogue ... more entertaining than ... n.   208:22

how much wd. n. gain   85:87

**November's** sky ... November's leaf   295:8

**Novice:** young, a N. in the Trade   128:70

**Now:** in England – n.!   74:21

**Nowhere:** and n. did abide   105:56

one really lives n.   79:92

**Nude:** keep one from going n.   189:83

**Nuisances** who write for autographs   145:99

**Number:** count the n. of the beast   61:30

greatest happiness of the greatest n.   33:14

so teach us to n. our days   43:18

**Numbers:** achiever brings home full n.   342:56

divinity in odd n.   341:34

I lisp'd in n., for the n. came   248:80

perhaps the plaintive n. flow   414:21

tell me not, in mournful n.   198:95

**Numbness:** drowsy n. pains my sense   184:23

**Nun:** holy time is quiet as a n.   412:92

**Nuncheon:** crunch on, take your n.   75:41

**Nunnery:** get thee to a n.   310:97

n. of thy chaste breast   199:16

**Nuns** fret not at ... narrow cell   411:89

**Nuptials:** prone to any iteration of n.   109:19

**Nurse:** baby ... that sucks the n. asleep   300:71

nature's soft n.   317:13

this n., this teeming womb of ... kings   348–9:41

**Nurseries:** in the n. of Heaven   391:32

n. of all vice and immorality   134:62

**Nurses:** wives are ... old men's n.   24:97

**Nursing** the unconquerable hope   21:43

**Nursling:** I am ... the n. of the Sky   368:23

**Nurslings** of immortality   369:43

**Nut:** hard n. to crack   266:69

I had a little n. tree   233:39

**Nutmeg:** silver n. and a golden pear   233:39

**Nuts:** Brazil, where the n. come from   389:16

Nuts (*continued*)
 gathering n. in May  16:86
 may be n. for Mary Ann  13:48
Nymph: haste thee, N.  214:93
 mountain-n., sweet Liberty  214:95

O: cram within this wooden O  318:37
Oak: bend a knotted o.  108:5
 grave where English o. and holly 158:72
 hearts of o. are our ships  141:48
Oaks: tall o., branch-charmed 182:98
Oars: the o. were silver  298:54
 with falling o. ... kept the time 206:91
Oath: a good mouth-filling o.  314:76
Oaths: full of strange o.  301:90
 o. are but words  82:37
Oats: *o.* ... in England ... given to horses  172:48
 sow one's wild o.  283:32
Obedience: as honour, love, o.  336:71
 o. is ... seen in little things  273:15
 resistance to tyrants is o. to God 171:31
Obey: safer to o. than to rule  188:73
 to love, cherish, and to o.  64:8
 woman to o.  389:2
Object: my o. all sublime  146:6
 only legitimate o. of government 171:30
 'tis for o. strange and high  206:97
Obligation: only o. to which ... we may hold a novel  170:23
Obligations: nobility imposes its own o.  196:70
 respect for the o. arising from treaties 394:76
Oblivion: put alms for o.  358:71
 second childishness and mere o. 301-2:90
 the rest ... commend to cold o. 368:25
Oblivious: some sweet o. antidote 336:72
Obsequies: Nature ... celebrates his o. 295:3
Observance: more honour'd in the breach than the o.  307:59
 with this special o.  310:5
Observation: let o. with extensive view 173:67
Observations which ourselves we make 251:21
Observed: the o. of all observers 310:1
Obstruction: to lie in cold o. and to rot 337:90

Occasion: courage mounteth with o. 326:34
Occasions: all o. do inform against me 311:22
 there is o. and causes  321:60
Occupation: absence of o. is not rest 113:67
 line of o. in the central sector  102:7
Occupations: worse o. in the world 379:67
Occupied: how my parents were o. and all  292:71
Ocean: a life on the o. wave  293:81
 dark unfathom'd caves of o.  155:37
 great Neptune's o. wash this blood 334:43
 in the o.'s bosom unespied  206:89
 make the mighty o.  89:41
 on the o. of life we pass  198:4
 painted ship upon a painted o. 105:49
 pores of the o. and shores  368:23
 we sail the o. blue  146:19
Odd: creators of o. volumes  192:26
 divinity in o. numbers  341:34
 o. because ... middle of the night 92:76
 scarcely o. because they'd eaten every one  93:82
 think it exceedingly o.  191:20
Odds: die better than facing fearful o. 201:36
 the o. is gone  299:66
*Odi et amo. Quare ... nescio*  94:5
Odium: the o. of having discovered sodium  33:18
Odorous: comparisons are o.  343:77
Odour: in the o. of sanctity died  28:54
 stealing and giving o.  358-9:75
Odours, when sweet violets sicken 370:54
O'erpeer: for truth to o.  303:15
Off: o. with his head!  91:56
 o. with the old love  17:93
 only that when ... o. [stage] he was acting  151:82
Offence: beauty ... after o. returning 222:24
 dire o. from am'rous causes springs 251:33
 my o. is rank  311:15
Offend: if thine eye o. thee  53:39
 o. one of these little ones  53:38
Offended: for him have I o.  325:11
Offender: Clinker ... a most notorious o.  375:14
Offenders: little list of Society o. 145:99

Offenders (*continued*)
the more laws, the more o.  269:59
Offer: never refuse a good o.  273:86
nothing to o. but blood, toil, tears 100:92
Office: hath but a losing o.  316:97
heresy ... that ... o. sanctifies  9:1
o. and affairs of love  342:62
o. and custom, in all line  358:66
the insolence of o.  309:95
Office boy: as o. to an Attorney's firm 147:26
Officers: a King, and o. of sorts  318:39
Official: what is o. is incontestable 140:33
Officious, innocent, sincere  172:53
Officiously to keep alive  103:29
Offspring: o. of Heaven first-born! 218:58
true source of human o.  219:71
Oft: many a time and o.  338:5
o., when on my couch I lie  410:71
Oil: lingering, with boiling o.  146:10
o'er books consumed the midnight o. 142:56
pour o. upon the waters  273:16
Ointment: good name ... better than precious o.  46:3
Old: a liking o. for thee  87:15
adherence to the o. and tried  196:77
all things worn out and o.  417:55
an o. abusing of ... patience  340:29
an o. man in a dry month  130:92
an o. man in a hurry  100:86
an o. maxim in the schools  381:96
as o. and new ... as Nature's self 73:17
call for his o. shoes  296:21
grow o. along with me  75:46
grow o. with a good grace  378:60
half as o. as time  77:70
I grow o. ... I grow o.  131:3
I love everything that's o.  151:83
if I ever grow to be o.  32:6
man ... as o. as he's feeling 107:86
never too o. to learn  273:89
new book is published, read an o. one  288:23
o. age shd. burn  390:18
o. and godly and grave  417:54
o. as he feels ... o. as she looks 271:32
o. as the hills  273:17
o. books, o. wine  151:83
o. friends and o. wine are best 273:18
o. friends are best  296:21

Old (*continued*)
o. friends, o. times, o. manners 151:83
o. head on young shoulders  274:19
o. lamps for new  20:22
o. men forget  320:58
o. poacher ... good game-keeper 274:20
o. soldiers ... only fade away  18:99
o. soldiers, sweethearts ... lovers 400:52
o., unhappy, far-off things  414:21
o. wine ... o. pippins ... o. wood 400:52
one of them is fat and grows o. 314:64
ring out the o.  386:68
so o., and so profane  318:34
summits o. in story  388:97
tell me the o., o. story  157:61
the grand o. name of gentleman 387:72
the mighty minds of o.  376:25
the o. gang  100:85
the o. order changeth  385:54
the thousand wars of o.  386:70
they shall grow not o.  65:20
they think he is growing o.  170:15
when thou art o. ... grief enough 156:48
when you are o. and grey  417:58
woman as o. as she looks  107:86
young in years ... o. in hours  26:26
Old Bailey: say the bells of O.  236:61
Old Kent Road: knock'd 'em in the O. 99:79
Old Testament: prosperity is the blessing of the O.  24:90
Olive-leaf: an o. he brings, pacific sign 221:1
in her mouth was an o.  35:47
Oliver Twist has asked for more 120:55
Olivia: air cry out 'O.!'  359:80
*Olympiades: l'important dans ces o.* 111:36
Olympic Games: important thing in the O. is  111:36
*Omnia vincit amor ... cedamus*  397:3
On: before you are o. with the new 17:93
o. o., you noblest English  319:46
o., Stanley, o.!  296:15
Once: children ... call yet o.  20:33
One: all for o., and o. for all 129:74
animals went in o. by o.  15:73
but the O. was Me  169:4

Other: after the first death ... no o. 390:22

    bunch of o. men's flowers 225:57

    or any o. reason why 10:16

    o. times, o. manners 254:83

    since then I have used no o. 285:84

Others: a corner ... for o.' uses 345:8

    be not false to to o. 25:16

    best and distinguished above o. 165:55

    England ... wont to conquer o. 349:42

    fly to o. that we know not of 309:95

    misfortunes and pains of o. 78:88

    o. abide our question 21:44

    pleased ourselves, we ... please o. 274:45

    some ... are more equal than o. 242:98

    to encourage the o. 397:8

Otherwise: some ... wise, and some ... o. 278:53, 375:15

Ounce: an o. of discretion 274:24

Ours: little we see in nature that is o. 412:93

Ourselves: fault ... not in our stars, but in o. 323–4:93

    praise o. in other men 249:3

Out: include me o. 152:6

    mordre wol o. 97:48

    murder will o. 272:75

    O., damned spot! o., I say! 335:68

    o. of sight, o. of mind 274:25

    o., o., brief candle! 336:76

    o., o., hyaena! 222:19

    who's in, who's o. 330:99

Outgrabe: mome raths o. 91:69

Outlive: desire shd. so ... o. performance? 316:10

Outrun: we may o. by violent swiftness 322:74

Outside: I am just going o. 241:93

Outsoared: he has o. the shadow of our night 367:16

Outward: hope from o. forms to win 106:69

    o. and visible sign 64:1

Oven: in the o. for baby and me 237:62

Over: now the day is o. 28:56

    'O. the hills and far away' 240:82

    until it doth run o. 16:78

Over much: be not righteous o. 47:6

Over-canopied with luscious woodbine 341:46

Overcast: since first our sky was o. 114:76

Overcoat: only argument ... put on yr. o. 200:27

Overcome: nature ... sometimes o. 26:25

    o. evil with good 57:41

    to o. pleasure ... greatest pleasure 274:47

    what is else not to be o.? 216:30

Overcomes: who o. by force 217:43

O(v)erjoyed was he to find 113:56

Overpaid: high official ... grossly o. 161:8

Overset the brain, or break the heart 411:88

Overthrow: those ... thou thinkest thou dost o. 124:10

Overwhelm myself in poesy 185:36

Overwhelmed all her litter but one 316:98

Owed: so much o. by so many to so few 101:96

Owes: he o. not any man 199:7

    o. its pleasure to another's pain 114:72

Owl: moping o. does to the moon complain 155:32

    nightly sings the staring o. 332:20

    old o. lived in an oak 285:82

    o., for all his feathers, was a-cold 181:89

    the O. and the Pussy-Cat 195:60

Owls: I couch when o. do fly 357:56

    two O. and a Hen 195:66

Own: came unto his o. and his o. received him not 55:94

    every country but his o. 145:1

    our watches ... each believes his o. 249:91

    room of one's o. 409:58

    we mean to hold our o. 101:3

Owner: the o. whereof was Giant Despair 77:62

    the ox knoweth his o. 48:29

Ox: a stalled o. and hatred 45:71

    nor his o., nor his ass 37:92

    o. knoweth his owner 48:29

    thou shalt not muzzle the o. 38:12

Oxenford: a Clerk ther was of O. 96:31

Oxford: ahead ... either O. or Cambridge 375:19

    the clever men at O. 153:14

    the king to O. sent a troop 72:8

    to ... O. I acknowledge no obligation 142:64

    to O. sent a troop of horse 393:54

Oxlips and the nodding violet 341:46

Oyster: an o. may be crossed in love
371:64
   the world's mine o. 340:30
Oysters: 'O, O.,' said the Carpenter
93:82
   poverty and o. 121:68
Ozymandias, king of kings 369:40

P's and Q's: to mind one's P. 274:26
Pace: creeps in this petty p. 336:76
Paced: bride hath p. into the hall
104:45
*Pacem: qui desiderat p.* 396:88
Paces about her room ... alone 131:12
Pacific: he stared at the P. 185:41
Pack: can p. the cards 25:15
Paddington: as London is to P. 88:28
Paddle: every man p. his own canoe
206:88
Padlock: clap yr. p. on her mind
253:50
   wedlock is a p. 282:19
Pagan suckled in a creed outworn
412:94
Pagans: to chase these p. in those holy
fields 312:43
Page: on a beautiful quarto p. 372:74
Pageant: this insubstantial p. faded
356-7:50
Paid: at cards for kisses – Cupid p.
201:29
   p. at the Greek Kalends 86:5
   two I am sure I have p. 314:65
   well p. that is well satisfied 340:21
Pail: to fetch a p. of water 234:44
Pain: a stranger yet to p. 154:27
   although p. isn't real 13:51
   cease upon the midnight with no p.
184:29
   hour of p. ... long as a day 267:3
   I feel no p., dear mother 17:88
   I love to give p. 109:12
   laughter with some p. is fraught
370:50
   long grief and p. 388:88
   neither shall there be any more p.
61:34
   not because it gave p. to the bear
202:47
   not in pleasure, but in rest from p.
128:64
   one who never inflicts p. 230:15
   owes its pleasure to another's p.
114:72
   p. clings cruelly to us 181:86
   sweet is pleasure after p. 127:53
   we are born in others' p. 390:29
   what p. it was to drown! 352:72

Pain (*continued*)
   when p. and anguish wring the brow
296:14
   who wd. lose, though full of p., this
... being 217:49
   with p. purchas'd, doth inherit p.
331:9
Painful: no p. inch to gain 103:33
   one ... as p. as the other 24:87
Pains: for my p. a world of sighs
344:92
Paint: cheeks are covered with p.
228:88
   good face needs no p. 265:32
   looking as fresh as p. 374:96
   p. my picture truly like me 115:91
   p. the meadows with delight 332:19
   to p. the lily 327:43
Painted: face with nature's own hand p.
362:35
   idle as a p. ship upon a p. ocean
105:49
   not so young as ... p. 30:81
Painters and poets ... lie 274:27
Painting a face ... not washing 140:37
Paintings: I have heard of your p.
310:99
Palace: a p. and a prison on each hand
84:62
   love in a p. 183:11
   my gorgeous p. for a hermitage
350:55
Palaces: cottages, princes' p. 338:2
Pale: p. cold cowardice 347:22
   p. grew thy cheek and cold 86:99
Palestine: to haven in sunny P. 207:12
*Pall Mall Gazette* is written by gentle-
men 389:11
*Palladium* of all the ... rights 180:65
Palm: an itching p. 325:23
   bear the p. alone 323:92
Palms before my feet 99:69
Palpable: a very p. hit 312:36
Pan: what ... doing, the great god P.?
73:13
Pancake: as flat as a p. 263:72
Pangs: more p. ... than wars or women
have 322–3:81
   p. of despis'd love 309:95
Panic: what a p.'s in thy breastie 80:16
Pansies, that's for thoughts 311:28
Pantaloon: lean and slipper'd p.
301:90
Paper: both sides of the p. at once
297:34
   he hath not eat p. 331:13
   if all the world were p. 15:65
   make dust our p. 349:53

Paper-mill: thou hast built a p.  321:68
Paradise: a p. to what we fear of death
  337:91
  called the P. of Fools  218:60
  drunk the milk of P.  107:76
  England ... p. of women, the hell of
    horses  81:31, 261:20
  P. of exiles, Italy  368:29
  such are the gates of P.  66:33
  this other Eden, demi-p.  348:41
  to P. by way of Kensal Green  99:74
  weave a p. for a sect  182:93
  Wilderness is P. enow  135:67
Paragon: the p. of animals!  308:81
Parchment: inky blots and rotten p.
  bonds  349:42
Pard: bearded like the p.  301:90
Pardon: bret-ful of p. ... from Rome
  97:43
  never ask p. before ... accused
    273:84
Parent: to lose one p., Mr Worthing
  405:10
Parents: joys of p. are secret  24:94
  of p. good, of fist most valiant
    320:51
  p. we can have but once  175:94
  what p. were created for  228:93
Paris: good Americans ... go to P.
  406:55
  P. is well worth a mass  160:97
  P. vaut bien une messe  160:97
  the last time I saw P.  157:58
Parish: all the world as my p.  402:73
  born ... hanged ... in the same p.
    13:47
Parliament: in the P. of man  387:81
Parliaments: England ... mother of p.
  71:81
Parlour: 'tis the prettiest little p.
  168:86
  will you walk into my p.?  168:86
Parmaceti for an inward bruise  313:52
Parochial: worse than provincial – he
  was p.  170:25
Parody: the devil's walking p.  99:68
Parole ... donnée à l'homme pour
    déguiser  384:32
Paroles ... pour déguiser leures pensées
  397:10
Parson: a p. much bemused in beer
  248:78
  coughing drowns the p.'s saw  332:20
Part: every man must play a p.  338:96
  I have forgot my p.  304:18
  if ought but death p. thee and me
    39:34
  kiss and p.  125:34

Part (continued)
  p. of education ... p. of experience
    25:12
  till death us do p.  64:7
Parted: when we two p.  86:99
Partial: more p. for the observer's sake
  251:21
Particle: very fiery p. ... snuff'd out
  85:83
Particular: a London p. – fog, miss
  119:33
  called away by p. business  372:77
Particulars: [do good] in Minute P.
  67:36
Parties: both p. nobly are subdu'd
  317:23
  hear all p.  266:78
Parting: do not let this p. grieve thee
  19:11
  p. is all we know of heaven  122:82
  p. is such sweet sorrow  354:6
  stood at the p. of the way  49:64
  this p. was well made  326:28
Partitions: thin p. do their bounds
  divide  126:39
Partridge in a pear tree  238–9:73
Parts: one man ... plays many p.
  301:90
Party: ancient forms of p. strife  386:69
  best number for a dinner p. is two
    157:54
  neither p. loser  317:23
  then none was for a p.  201:38
  there was an old p. of Lyme  224:52
  to p. gave up what was ... for man-
    kind  151:78
  true patriotism is of no p.  375:17
Pass: his ghost. O, let him p.  331:7
  I p. through the pores of the ocean
    368:23
  she may ... p. for forty-three  148:42
  they shall not p.  246:48
Passed: he p. by on the other side
  54:77
  so he p. over  77:67
  [time] wd. have p. in any case  30:75
Passeront: ils ne p. pas  246:48
Passes: everything p. ... perishes ...
  palls  281:53
  p. at girls who wear glasses  243:22
Passing: did but see her p. by  18:9
  P. of the Third Floor Back  171:36
  p. the love of women  40:49
Passing-bells for those who die as
  cattle  243:16
Passion: a master-p. is the love of news
  114:81
  calm of mind, all p. spent  223:27

Passion (*continued*)
  in her first p. woman  84:73
  man that is not p.'s slave  310:6
  master mistress of my p.  362:35
  Queen was in a furious p.  91:56
  ruling p. conquers reason still 251:27
  strange fits of p.  414:23
  the p. and the life  106:69
Passion-flower: the p. at the gate 388:87
Passionless: hopeless grief is p.  73:12
Passions: all thy p., match'd with mine 387:83
  hath not a Jew ... p.?  339:13
  in truth but two p., vanity and love 98:62
Past: a mischief that is p. and gone 344:93
  leave thy low-vaulted p.  164:50
  p. and to come seems best  316:4
  p. cure, p. care  274:28
  p. help ... p. grief  361:14
  p. my help ... p. my care  29:72
  remembrance of things p.  362:37
  study the p. ... divine the future 108:3
'Pastern' as the 'knee of a horse' 174:81
Pastoral-comical, historical-p.  308:84
Pastors: as some ungracious p. do 306:54
Pasture: sell the p. now to buy the horse  319:40
Pastures: fresh woods, and p. new 215:18
  lie down in green p.  42:92
  on England's pleasant p. seen  67:38
Pat-a-cake, baker's man  237:62
Path: a beaten p. to his door  133:48
  p. of duty ... way to glory  388:94
Pathetic: That's what it is, P.  212:64
Pathless: pleasure in the p. woods 84:65
Paths: so many p. that wind  404:93
Patience: abusing of God's p.  340:29
  how poor ... that have not p.! 345:3
  in mean men we entitle p.  347:32
  p. is a flower  274:29
  p., money ... bring all ... to pass 274:30
  p. under ... sufferings  63:84
  sat like P. on a monument  360:89
  though p. be a tired mare  319:42
  though with p. He stands waiting 198:99
  ye have heard of the p. of Job  60:7

Patient: a p. etherized upon a table 130:98
  fury of a p. man  127:48
Patines: inlaid with p. of bright gold 340:22
*Patria: dulce et decorum est pro p. mori* 167:77
  *pro p. ... liberis ... aris*  293:74
*Patrie: allons, enfants de la p.*  291:54
Patriot: for a p., too cool  151:79
  such is the p.'s boast  151:91
Patriotic: if p. sentiment is wanted 145:96
Patriotism: I realize ... p. is not enough 95:7
  p. ... last refuge of a scoundrel 176:12
  true p. is of no party  375:17
Patriots: true p. we  29:65
Patron: a P., ... looks with unconcern 174:78
  p. ... a wretch ... with insolence 172:49
Pattern: thou cunning'st p. of ... nature  346:19
Paul: one named Peter, the other named P.  240:84
  rob Peter to pay P.  276:98
Pause: what dreams ... must give us p. 309:95
Pawn: p. the Bechstein Grand  111:40
  you p. your intelligence  116:95
Pay: God make me able to p.  245:41
  p. ... in his own coin  274:31
  p. through the nose  274:32
  what one can p. others to do  208:23
  when will you p. me?  236:61
  you ought to p., you know  92:73
Pays: he who p. the piper  274:33
  p. yr. money ... takes yr. choice 284:74
Peace: a hard and bitter p.  188:74
  a p. above all earthly dignities 323:82
  a p. I hope with honour  122:93
  all her paths are p.  44:56
  better a lean p.  255:12
  blood of Jesus whispers p.  65:19
  calm world and a long p.  315:83
  cherish a just and lasting p.  196–7:81
  create desolation, call it p.  383:27
  for ever hold his p.  64:5
  for p. comes dropping slow  417:53
  give p. in our time, O Lord  63:70
  I am for p. ... they ... for war  44:36
  I shall have some p. there  417:53
  if p. cannot be ... with honour 292:65

Peace (*continued*)
  in P., Goodwill  102:10
  in what p. a Christian can die  10:12
  inglorious arts of p.  207:2
  live together in p. ... as good neighbours  394:76
  never was ... a bad p.  138:15
  no p. ... unto the wicked  48:45
  nothing can bring you p. but yourself  133:38
  on earth p., good will  54:70
  our p., our fearful innocence  412:2
  p., commerce, and honest friendship  171:29
  p. for our time ... p. with honour  95:16
  p. hath her victories  223:32
  p. is indivisible  197:84
  p. is of the nature of a conquest  317:23
  p. is poor reading  158:64
  p. makes plenty  274:34
  p. of God ... passeth all understanding  58:78
  p. on earth and mercy mild  402:71
  p., p., when there is no p.  49:54
  p., perfect p.  65:19
  p. shall go sleep with Turks  350:56
  the Lord ... give thee p.  38:2
  the Prince of P.  48:36
  the soft phrase of p.  344:90
  the thousand years of p.  386:70
  their bodies are buried in p.  62:62
  weak piping time of p.  351:67
  when ... p. he was for p.  22:62
  who desires p., prepare for war  396:88
Peaceably: living p. in their habitations  62:60
Peaceful: p. hours I once enjoyed  113:62
  welcome p. evening in  114:73
Peace-maker: yr. If is the only p.  303:10
Peach: do I dare to eat a p.?  131:4
  p. was once a bitter almond  394:69
Peacock: as proud as a p.  275:67
Peacocks and lilies for instance  291:61
Pear: and a gold p.  233:39
Pearl: barbaric p. and gold  217:45
  heaps of p., inestimable stones  352:72
  hillside's dew-p.'d  75:44
  like the base Indian, threw a p. away  346–7:22
  one p. of great price  52:31
  sowed the earth with orient p.  219:75

Pearls: he who wd. search for p. must dive  127:55
  neither cast ... p. before swine  52:24
  p. that were his eyes  355:35
  teeth like p.  75:43
Peas: I always eat p. with honey  15:63
*Peccavi* [I have Sind]  228:82
*Pêcher en silence*  224:51
Pedigree: languages ... p. of nations  178:39
Peep about to find ... graves  323:93
Peeping: came p. in at morn  165:60
Peepshow: a ticket for the p.  203:54
Peer: a rhyming p.  248:78
  when daffodils begin to p.  361:17
Peg: take one down a p.  279:97
Pelican: wonderful bird is the p.  209:38
Pelting: bide the p. of this pitiless storm  329:78
Pen: before my p. has glean'd  186:48
  biting my truant p.  373:84
  more cruel ... p. is than ... sword  81:30
  p. is mightier than the sword  76:54
  poet's p. turns them to shapes  342:53
Pennance: hath p. done and p. more will do  105:59
Pence: take care of the p.  279:96
Penny: back again, like a bad p.  254:86
  I spent a p. ... I lent a p.  233:40
  in for a p., in for a pound  267:17
  not given a p. for a song  417:51
  p. and p. laid up  274:35
  p. for yr. thoughts  274:36
  p. wise, pound foolish  274:37
  shall have but a p. a day  237:68
  show me first yr. p.  237:69
  turn an honest p.  281:66
  two a p., hot cross buns  233:35
Pens: let other p. dwell on guilt  23:71
*Pensée: se servent de la p. ... pour autoriser ... injustices*  397:10
*Pensées: paroles ... pour déguiser ... p.*  397:10
Pension: p. never enriched a young man  274:38
  p. ... pay given to a state hireling  172:50
Pensive: in vacant or in p. mood  410:71
Pent: long in city p.  186:47
  long in populous city p  220:93
Penury: age, ache, p., and imprisonment  337:91

Pleased (*continued*)
p. with what he gets 301:85
when ... p. ourselves, we ... please 274:45
Pleases: every prospect p. 160:87
one makes lovers ... as one p. 109:13
Pleasing: art of p. ... being pleased 159:83
Pleasure: a p. in the pathless woods 84:65
business before p. 257:75
but the privilege and p. 143:76
dissipation without p. 142:65
drinking is the soldier's p. 127:53
every p. is of itself a good 177:29
friend of P., Wisdom's aid 108:93
gave p. to the spectators 202:47
good, p., ease, content! 250:15
great source of p. is variety 178:42
happiness ... not in p. but in rest from pain 128:64
hatred ... the longest p. 85:84
love ceases to be a p. 30:85
money gives me p. 32:98
more p. in loving than ... loved 274:46
no p. without pain 273:98
no profit ... where is no p. 355:20
owes its p. to another's pain 114:72
p. ... is lost by coveting more 274:48
p. is oft a visitant 181:86
p. never is at home 185:95
p. of the fleeting year 363:43
p.'s a sin ... sin's a p. 84:69
public stock of harmless p. 178:43
refrain from the unholy p. 31:88
short p., long lament 277:35
some to business, some to p. take 251:23
sweet is p. after pain 127:53
though on p. she was bent 113:56
to overcome p. is the greatest p. 274:47
'twas for your p. you came 113:60
variety ... soul of p. 30:86
when Youth and P. meet 83:60
written without effort ... read without p. 178:41
Pleasure-dome: a stately p. 106:71
sunny p. with caves of ice 107:75
Pleasures: all the p. prove 205:82
cannot understand the p. 23:65
can sympathise ... not with their p. 169:1
in unreproved p. free 214:96
'mid p. and palaces 245:34
no man is a hypocrite in his p. 178:36

Pleasures (*continued*)
p. are like poppies spread 81:25
the purest of human p. 26:29
these p., Melancholy, give 213:90
these pretty p. might me move 286:96
we will some new p. prove 123:4
Pledge: I will p. with mine 178:49
p. to each other our lives, our fortunes 171:27
Plenty: however p. silver dollars may become 103:23
in delay there lies no p. 359:84
p. makes me 243:13
wasna fou, but just had p. 79:4
*Pleure: il p. dans mon cœur* 396:90
Plodders: small have continual p. ... won 331:10
Plot: the sonnet's scanty p. of ground 411:90
this blessed p., this earth 348–9:41
Plough: having put his hand to the p. 54:74
Ploughman: heavy steps of the p. 417:55
the p., near at hand 214:98
Plowman homeward plods 155:30
Pluck: p. from the memory a rooted sorrow 336:72
sin will p. on sin 352:77
we p. this flower, safety 313:60
Plucked: when I have p. thy rose 346:19
Plum: and pulled out a p. 235:50
supping cold p. porridge 235:54
Poacher: a p. is a keeper 189:90
old p. makes a good game-keeper 274:20
Pocket: a p. full of posies 237:67
a p. full of rye 238:70
Pocket borough: by a p. into Parliament 147:27
Pocket-handkerchief: holding his p. 93:81
Pockets: p. in none of his clothes 33:12
to line one's p. 270:88
Poem: I would rather have written that p. 408:54
ought himself to be a true p. 223:36
p. lovely as a tree 188:81
p. must ride on ... melting 139:29
p. ... worked ... not worried 139:29
Poems: dictionaries, and temporary p. 172:45
Gert's p. are bunk 14:57
p. are made by fools like me 189:82
Poesy: drainless shower of light is p. 185:38

Poesy (*continued*)
    great end of p. ... shd. be a friend
      185:39
    on the viewless wings of P.  184:26
    overwhelm myself in p.  185:36
Poet: a p. cd. not but be gay
    410:70
    business of a p., said Imlac  173:63
    consecration, and the p.'s dream
      409:61
    lunatic, the lover, and the p.  342:52
    p. and the dreamer, are distinct
      182:94
    p.'s eye, in a fine frenzy rolling
      342:53
    p.'s pen turns ... to shapes  342:53
    say that when the P. dies  295:3
    Swift, you will never be a p.  128:67
    the p. sing it with such airs  417:51
    the p.'s inward pride  117:15
Poetess: a maudlin p., a rhyming peer
    248:78
Poetic: which constitutes p. faith
    107:79
Poetical: gods had made thee p.
    302:99
Poetry: Fleshly School of P.  76:49
    homely definitions of prose and p.
      107:82
    if P. comes not as naturally  186:56
    in p. ... in life ... ineffectual angel
      21:51
    mincing p.  314:74
    not P., but prose run mad  248:82
    p. is in the pity  243:18
    p. is the record of the best  371:58
    p. is the spontaneous overflow
      416:42
    p. lifts the veil  371:57
    p. of earth is never dead  185:42
    p. shd. be great and unobtrusive
      186:54
    p. shd. surprise by ... excess  186:55
    p.'s unnat'ral; no man ever talked
      p.  121:72
    truest p. is the most feigning  302:1
Poets: I shall be among the English P.
    187:62
    our clever young p.  107:82
    painters and p. ... lie  274:27
    p. are the unacknowledged legis-
      lators  371:59
    p. [make men] witty  26:34
    p. that lasting marble seek  398:18
    souls of p. dead and gone  183:14
    such sights as youthful p. dream
      214:3
    three p. in three distant Ages  128:66

Poets (*continued*)
    translunary things ... first p. had
      125:33
Point: missed the p. completely, Julia
    131:14
    p. his slow unmoving finger  346:13
    thus I bore my p.  314:65
    touch'd the highest p. of all my great-
      ness  322:79
Poison: if you p. us, do we not die?
    339:13
*Poissons: nous attendons ... les p. aussi*
    101:97
Poke: buy a pig in a p.  257:78
    p. poor Billy  153:11
Poker: stiff as a p.  278:75
Pole: beloved from p. to p.  105:57
    soldier's p. is fall'n!  299:66
Police: friendship recognized by the p.
    379:77
Policeman: a p.'s lot is not a happy one
    148:33
    want to know the time, ask a P.
      288:22
Policemen: sadists ... p. or butchers
    110:22
Policy: honesty is the best p.  267:94
    p. of a good neighbour  289:29
    turn him to any cause of p.  318:38
Polished up the silver plate  226:70
Politely: hang you ... most p.  148:36
Political: man is ... a p. animal  20:26
    retired into ... p. Cave of Adullam
      71:82
Politician: coffee, which makes the p.
    wise  252:38
    like a scurvy p. seem  330:93
    p. is an arse  115:93
Politicians: for P. neither love nor hate
    126:41
    whole race of p. put together  381:2
Politics: confound their p.  88:30
    holy, mistaken zeal in p.  180:67
    my p. like my religion ... accom-
      modatin'  398:26
    p. we bar ... not our bent  148:35
Poll: but talked like poor P.  141:49
Polly-wolly-doodle all the day  18:97
Poltagrue: My Lady P.  31:96
Polygamy: before p. was made a sin
    126:36
Pomp: grinning at his p.  350:54
    p., and circumstance, of ... war
      345–6:10
    take physic, p.  329:79
    the p. of power  155:35
    vain p. and glory of this world
      322:81

Pompous: man is ... p. in the grave 72:7

Pomps and vanity of ... world 64:96

Poniards: she speaks p. 342:63

Pony: to town riding on a p. 241:90

Pooh: three cheers for P.! 212:70

Pooh-Bah (Lord High Everything Else) 144:93

Poor: a certain p. widow 54:63
  as p. as Job 274:49
  decent means p. 245:35
  leave [grapes] for the p. and stranger 37:98
  grind the faces of the p. 48:32
  he that considereth the p. 42:6
  how apt the p. are to be proud 360:93
  how p ... that have not patience! 345:3
  Im one of the undeserving p. 366:96
  inconvenient to be p. 112:51
  it's the p. wot gets 18:5
  laws grind the p. 151:93
  makes me p. indeed 345:6
  my friends were p. but honest 298:43
  none so p. to do him reverence 325:15
  plenty makes me p. 243:13
  p. ... maimed ... halt ... blind 54:79
  p. old Joe 138:8
  poverty consists in feeling p. 133:44
  simple annals of the p. 155:34
  the p. man at his gate 10:18
  the p. shall never cease 38:11
  the riches of the p.! 179:60
  to be p. and independent 104:35
  too p. for a bribe 156:46
  ye have the p. always 53:49

Poor relations: even great men have their p. 119:35

Pop goes the weasel 203:60

Pope: better to err with P. 85:92

Poppies: in Flanders fields the p. blow 202:48
  pleasures are like p. spread 81:25

Populace: Barbarians, Philistines, P. 21:48

Population: only talked of p. 152:96

Porpentine: quills upon the fretful p. 307:64

Porpoise: there's a p. close behind us 91:62

Porridge: comfort like cold p. 356:37
  supping cold plum p. 235:54

Port: any p. in a storm 254:71
  p. after stormy seas 377:42
  p. for men 177:31

Port (continued)
  the p. is near, the bells I hear 403:81

Porte: il faut qu'une p. soit ouverte ou fermée 227:78

Portend: late eclipses ... p. no good 327:52

Porter: Oh, mister P. 197:88

Porters: mechanic p. crowding in 318–19:39

Portion: any p. of the foreign world 399:32
  best p. of a good man's life 415:31
  he is a p. of the loveliness 367:18

Portrait of the Artist as a Young Man 179:64

Ports: all places ... are ... p. and happy havens 348:36
  p. of slumber open wide 317:27

Possessed: liberty ... limited ... to be p. 78:85
  Webster was much p. by death 131:13

Possession: have p. of them both 187:65
  p. ... is intolerable 395:83
  p. is nine points of the law 275:51
  prospect is ... better than p. 275:64
  virtue that p. wd. not show us 343:81

Possessions: all my p. for a moment of time 132:22

Possible: O that 'twere possible after long grief 388:88
  think ... p. you may be mistaken 115:88

Post: deaf as a p. 259:58
  from pillar to p. 274:40
  p. o'er land and ocean 223:30

Post-chaise: driving briskly in a p. 177:23

Posterity: see p. do something for us 10:11
  think of yr. p.! 9:2
  thy p. shall sway 112:50
  what has p. done for us? 287:12
  without ... hope of p. 124:15

Postscript: pith is in the p. 159:77

Postumus: alas P., P., the fleeting years 167:76

Pot: a useful p. to put things in 212:68
  crackling of thorns under a p. 46:4
  death in the p. 40:61
  greasy Joan doth keel the p. 332:20
  p. calls the kettle black 275:52
  watched p. never boils 282:9
  who is the potter ... who the p.? 136:81

Potato: bashful young p. 146:16
Potomac: all quiet along the P. 30:84
Potter: as the clay is in the p.'s hand 49:57
  who is the p., pray? 136:81
Pouch: spectacles on nose and p. on side 301:90
Poultice: silence like a p. 164:44
Pouncet-box: he held a p. 313:51
Pound: a p. of ... merchant's flesh 340:19
  I'll give thee a silver p. 88:19
Pounds: about two hundred p. a year 82:38
  handsome in three hundred p. a year 341:32
  p. ... take care of themselves 279:96
  with forty p. a year 150:66
*Pour encourager les autres* 397:8
Poverty: debt is the worst p. 260:63
  give me neither p. nor riches 46:90
  her p. was glad, her heart content 127:57
  in p., hunger, and dirt 166:64
  nor any crime so shameful as p. 134:55
  p. and oysters ... go together 121:68
  p. breeds strife 275:53
  p. consists in feeling poor 133:44
  p. is an anomaly to rich 27:46
  p. is no disgrace ... is ... inconvenient 374:6
  p. is no sin 275:54
  p. is not a shame 275:55
  p. will bear itself 255:98
  slow rises worth by p. depressed 172:55
Power: accursed p. ... stands on privilege 31:95
  beauty ... injurious ... hath strange p. 222:24
  earthly p. ... likest God's 339:15
  force of temporal p. 339:15
  greater the p. the more dangerous the abuse 78:87
  knowledge is p. 268:46
  like us, though less in p. 218:53
  new nobility ... act of p. 25:6
  not in our p. to love or hate 205:80
  p. gradually extirpates ... virtue 78:89
  p. of the press ... p. of books 395:77
  p. tends to corrupt 9:1
  riches, dignity and p. 32:4
  the balance of p. 398:19
  the certainty of p. 117:15
  unequal and untimely interchange of p. 25:14

Power (*continued*)
  unlimited p. is apt to corrupt 246:55
Powerful: Lord, I am p., but alone 396:93
Powers: p. that be are ordained of God 57:42
  we lay waste our p. 412:93
Practical: meddling with any p. part of life 9:6
Practice makes perfect 275:56
Practise what you preach 275:57
Praise: a song in thy p. 79:98
  give them ... the garment of p. 49:53
  let us now p. famous men 62:59
  maid whom there were none to p. 413:15
  p. any man that will p. me 299:57
  p. at morning ... blame at night 249:2
  p. is the best diet 375:10
  p. makes good men better 275:58
  p. the Lord, for he is kind 221:10
  p. the Lord ... pass the ammunition 137:95
  p. the Lord! We are ... musical 390:26
  to bury Caesar, not to p. him 325:12
  we but p. ourselves in other men 249:3
  we ... lack tongues to p. 363:46
  we scarcely can p. it, or blame 151:78
  you p. the firm restraint 87:17
Praised: everybody p. the Duke 376:30
Praising: doing one's p. for oneself 83:48
Prattle: thinking his p. to be tedious 351:61
Pray: after this manner ... p. ye 52:18
  came to scoff, remained to p. 150:67
  I p. it be first to me 70:79
  need to p. for fair weather 25:7
  one to watch and one to p. 10:13
  p. all the livelong day 68:45
  p. without ceasing 59:84
  so give alms; p. so 362:21
  to God, to praise and p. 74:25
  watch and p. 53:50, 54:64
  we do p. for mercy 339:15
  you can't p. a lie 393:61
Prayer: four [hours] spend in p. 104:40
  God erects a house of p. 118:18
  more things are wrought by p. 386:55
Prayeth: p. best, who loveth best 106:64
  p. well, who loveth well 106:63
Preach: practise what you p. 275:57

Preacher: vanity of vanities, saith the
P. 46:93

Preaches: he p. well that lives well
275:59

Preaching: a woman's p. is like 175:90

Precept: example is better than p.
262:37

Precepts: these few p. in thy memory
306:55

Precise: too p. in every part 162:17

Precisely: thinking too p. on th' event
311:23

Prefer: folks *p.* ... a hovel to ... marble
halls 87:13

Preferment: and so I got p. 17:91
tired of knocking at P.'s door
21:41

Prejudice: we all decry p., yet 376:35

Prejudices: it p. a man so [reading ...
before reviewing] 375:11

Premises: sufficient conclusions from
insufficient p. 82:44

Prepare to meet Thy God 50:83

Preposterous? A thorough-paced absurdity 146:14

Presbyter: new P. is but old Priest
223:31

Presence: from whose unseen p. the
leaves dead 369:35
lord of thy p. and no land 326:33
p. strengthens [love] 254:53
scanter of yr. maiden p. 307:58

Present: a very p. help in trouble 42:7
both perhaps p. in time future
130:90
no time like the p. 280:41
p. mirth hath p. laughter 359:84
p. only toucheth thee 80:19
things p., worst 316:4
un-birthday p. 93:85

Presents ... endear Absents 192:28

Preservation: creation, p., and all the
blessings 64:85

President: rather be right than be P.
103:22

Press: god of our idolatry, the p.
113:66
misused the King's p. damnably
315:82
written of the power of the p. 395:77

Pressed: if it were p., would run 32:3
power p. too far and relaxed too
much 25:14

Pretender: who P. is, or who is King
83:53

Pretty: where the girls are so p. 17:89

Prevail: gates of hell shall not p. 53:34
passion for making them p. 21:52

Prevention is better than cure 245:37,
275:60

Prey: have they not divided the p.?
39:24
smaller fleas that on him p. 382:5
to hastening ills a p. 150:62

Price: all those men have their p.
398:20
p. of everything ... value of nothing
406:21
p. of wisdom is above rubies 41:73
virtuous woman ... p. ... above
rubies 46:92

Prick: how if honour p. me off? 315:88
if you p. us, do we not bleed? 339:13
no spur to p. the sides of my intent
333:37
pat it and p. it 237:62
when ... the nerves p. 386:60

Pricking: a gentle knight was p. on the
plain 377:41

Pricks: kick against the p. 56:18

Pride: he that is low, no p. 77:66
look backward to with p. 139:23
perished in his p. 413:12
p. goeth before destruction 45:72
p. of kingly sway from out my heart
350:58
p., pomp, and circumstance, of ...
war 345–6:10
p. that licks the dust 248:86
p., the ... vice of fools 249:93
p. will have a fall 275:61
the poet's inward p. 117:15
the p. of that country side 28:54

Priest: am I both p. and clerk? 350:57
free me of this turbulent p. 160:99
I tell thee, churlish p. 312:32
p. all shaven and shorn 239:79
p. is at the bottom of it [mischief]
273:94
youth ... still is Nature's p. 411:78

Priest-craft: ere p. did begin 126:36

Priests: of p. ... a charmin' variety
154:18

Prime: having lost but once yr. p.
162:25

Primrose: p. path of dalliance treads
306:54
p. way to th' everlasting bonfire
334:44
rathe p. that forsaken dies 215:17

Prince: the P. of Peace 48:36

Princes: hangs on p.' favours 322:81
put not yr. trust in p. 44:53
that sweet aspect of p. 322–3:81

Principalities: against p., against
powers ... rulers 58:74

Principle: a p. in life with me, sir 367:7
   don't believe in p. ... *do* in interest 200:21
   fundamental p. of ... constitution 66:25
   what is p. against ... flattery? 372:79
Principles: first, religious and moral p. 22:54
   these two p.—right and wrong 196:76
   they speak of p.—look out 22:59
Print: some said, John, p. it 76:56
   to see one's name in p. 85:89
Printer: almost hear the p. saying damn 395:80
Printers: books by which the p. have lost 140:40
Printing: barbarous where there is no p. 176:3
   cogent reasons for not p. ... subscribers 177:33
   thou hast caused p. to be used 321:68
Priority: observe degree, p., and place 358:66
Prison: come, let's away to p. 330:99
   dock in a pestilential p. 145:3
   Lime-tree Bower my p. 107:77
   palace ... p. on each hand 84:62
   stone walls do not a p. make 199:15
   this p. where I live 351:62
Prisoner: the jury, passing on the p.'s life 337:81
Prison-house: secrets of my p. 307:64
   shades of the p. begin to close 410-11:77
Prithee, pretty maiden 146:17
Private: to the public good p. respects ... yield 222:21
Privilege: accursed power which stands on p. 31:95
   but the p. and pleasure ... little errands 143:76
Privileged: the p. and the people ... two nations 123:98
Prize: men p. the thing ungain'd 358:65
   not all that tempts ... is lawful p. 154:26
   rain influence, and judge the p. 214:2
   the p. we sought is won 403:81
   too light winning make the p. light 356:36
   what we have we p. not 343:81
Problem: quite a three-pipe p. 124:19
Problems: the p. of victory are more agreeable 101:5

Proceedings: subsequent p. interested him no more 158:73
Process: one long p. of getting tired 82:43
Procrastination is the thief of time 418:62
Procreate: we might p. like trees 72:5
Proctors: with prudes for p. 388:95
Prodigal: chariest maid is p. enough 306:53
Shimei, though not p. of pelf 126:46
Profane: O p. one! 70:74
   so old, and so p. 318:34
Profaned: province ... desolated and p. 149:52
Profess: all who p. ... themselves Christians 63:82
Professions: let in some of all p. 334:44
Profit: my p. on't is, I know how to curse 355:33
   no p. ... where ... no pleasure 355:20
   the winds will blow the p. 203:55
   what p. hath a man of ... labour 46:94
   what shall it p. a man? 54:58
Profits: small p. and quick returns 277:47
Progeny: a p. of learning 371:69
Prognostics do not ... prove prophecies 398:24
Progress: all p. ... desire ... to live beyond ... income 82:45
   history of England ... history of p. 202:45
   to promote social p. 394:76
Promethean: I know not where is that P. heat 346:19
Promise of strength and manhood 70:78
Promises: he p. himself too much 175:94
   p. and pie-crust ... to be broken 382:6
   p. too much ... means nothing 275:62
Promising: pretty Thomasina ... once ... so p. 140:30
Promontory: I sat upon a p. 341:44
Promotion: none will sweat but for p. 300:79
Prone to any iteration of nuptials 109:19
Pronounce: spell better than they p. 394:66
**Proof of the pudding** 275:63

Prop: you take my house ... take the p.
340:20

Propagate: endeavour to ... p. the best
21:50

Proper words in p. places 381:3

Properties: general p. and large appearances 173:63

Property has its duties ... rights 126:35

Prophecies: prognostics do not always
prove p. 398:24

Prophecy: the trumpet of a p. 369:38

Prophesy: if you crown him, let me p.
350:56

Prophesying: ancestral voices p. war
107:74

Prophet: a p. is not without honour
52:32
methinks I am a p. new inspir'd
348:40
sons of the p. were brave 18:7

Prophetess: more than a p. ... uncommon pretty 129:84

Prophetic: O my p. soul 307:67
to something like p. strain 213:89

Prophets: beware of false p. 52:27
is Saul ... among the p. 39:39
wisest p. ... sure of the event first
398:24

Proportion: time is broke and no p.
kept! 351:63

Propose: whoever loves ... do not p.
123:8

Propriety: pleasantness ... does not ...
evince p. 23:80

*Proprium humani ingenii ... odisse*
383:28

Prose: homely definitions of p. and
poetry 107:82
in p. and verse was own'd ... absolute
128:68
*je dis de la p.* 224:48
p. run mad 248:82
talking p. for over forty years 224:48
unattempted yet in p. or rhyme
216:28

Prospect: noblest p. ... Scotchman ever
sees 175:85
p. is ... better than possession
275:64
though every p. pleases 160:87

Prospects: died when his p. ... brightening 12:42
on p. drear 80:19

Prosper: treason doth never p. 158:70

Prosperity: a jest's p. lies in the ear
331:18
a man to have been in p. 97–8:51
him that stood in great p. 97:47

Prosperity (*continued*)
p. doth best discover vice 24:92
p. has damned more ... than ...
devils 275:65
p. is the blessing of the Old Testament 24:90
p.'s the very bond of love 362:24
you will see a state of p. 202:52

Prospers: Hope ... turns Ashes—or it
p. 135:68

Protest: the lady doth p. too much
310:9

Proteus rising from the sea 412:94

Protracted: life p. is p. woe 174:70

Proud: Americans ... p. of ... ancient
heritage 188:74
as p. as Lucifer 275:66
as p. as a peacock 275:67
being too p. to fight 407:45
death, be not p. 124:10
how apt the poor are to be p. 360:93
I might grow p. the while 162:19
p. me no prouds 354:15
too p. for a wit 151:79
too p. to importune 156:46

Prouder: never, I ween, was a p. seen
28:53

Prove: might p. anything by figures
89:32
prov'd true before, p. false again
82:38

Proved: likely ... to have p. most royal
312:41
p. true before, prove false again
82:38
which was to be p. 133:51

Proverb: a p. is much matter 140:38
the p. is something musty 310:11

Providence: assert Eternal P. 216:29
P. their guide 221:3
reasoned high of P., Foreknowledge
218:55

Province: all knowledge to be my p.
27:39
p. they [Turks] have desolated
149:52

Provincial: worse than p.—he was
parochial 170:25

Prudes: with p. for proctors 388:95

Pruning-hooks: swords into plowshares, ... spears into p. 48:31

Prussia: war ... national industry of P.
224:47

Prussian: French, or Turk, or P.
147:30

Psalmist: the sweet p. of Israel 40:52

Psaltery: sing unto him with the p.
42:97

Public: British p. in one of its ... fits
202:46

deliberation sat, and p. care 218:52

dislike the favour of the p. 187:66

how p., like a frog 122:81

mean, stupid, dastardly, ... p.
159:82

never in touch with p. opinion
406:28

reasons for ... not speaking in p.
176:10

the sound of p. scorn 220:96

wash dirty linen in p. 282:6

washing ... clean linen in p. 405:7

Public house: vidders ... if they've kept
a p. 121:67

Public meeting: speaks ... as if I was a
p. 396:92

Public opinion: researchers into p.
22:62

Public schools are the nurseries of vice
134:62

Publican: how like a fawning p. 338:3

Publish: I'll p., right or wrong 85:88

p. and be damned 401:62

p. it not in the streets 40:47

Publisher: now Barabbas was a p.
88:22

Publishers: with irrational fear of life
become p. 110:22

Pudding: a p. hath two [ends] 262:33

better some of a p. 256:28

proof of the p. is in the eating 275:63

Puff direct ... preliminary ... collateral
371:62

Puffing is of various sorts 371:62

*Puissant et solitaire* 396:93

Puking: infant, mewling and p. 301:90

Pullet-sperm: no p. in my brewage
341:33

Pulse: feeling a woman's p. 379:67

two people with one p. 203:57

when the p. begins to throb 71:87

Pumpkins: where the early p. blow
194:55

Punch: as pleased as P. 274:44

Punctuality is the politeness of kings
199:14

Punctures: pin ... p. my skin 13:51

Punishment: as I deserve, pay on my p.
222:17

the p. fit the crime 146:6

Puppets: God, whose p. ... are we
75:45

Purchased: thought ... gift of God may
be p. 56:16

Pure: as p. as snow 310:98

because my heart is p. 389:3

Pure (*continued*)

blessed are the p. in heart 52:10

more p. than his Maker 41:66

p. as an angel 384:30

p. as the naked heavens 413:4

p. unbounded love thou art 402:72

things are p. ... lovely ... of good
report 58:79

unto the p. all things are p. 59:96

Purest: garden ... p. of human
pleasures 26:29

Purgatory: England ... p. of men
136:86

no other p. but a woman 29:73

Purge: I'll p., and leave sack 315:95

p. me with hyssop 42:8

Puritan: saw a P.-one hanging of his
cat 70:74

the P. hated bear-baiting 202:47

Purlieus: dusty p. of the law 386:64

Purple: I never saw a P. Cow 77:68

I wrote the 'P. Cow' 77:69

p. the sails, and so perfumed 298:54

Purpose: cite Scripture for his p.
338:4

Purse: ask thy p. what thou shdst. buy
254:79

heavy p. ... light heart 266:82

light p. ... heavy heart 269:83

little and often fills the p. 270:91

p. ... full of other men's money
261:17

put money in thy p. 345:96

remedy against ... consumption of
the p. 316:3

silk p. out of a sow's ear 277:39

who steals my p. steals trash 345:6

Purses: our p. shall be proud 355:25

wine and wenches empty ... p.
283:35

Purse-strings are ... common ties
275:70

Pursuing: faint, yet p. 39:25

Pursuit of perfection ... is the p. of
sweetness 21:47

Pussy: Owl and the P.-cat 195:60

P cat, where have you been? 237:64

P.'s in the well 232:28

Put: p. off holiness and p. on intellect
67:37

up with which I will not p. 102:9

Putting milk into babies 101:6

Pye: than shine with P. 85:92

*Pyramides: du haut de ces p.* 228:83

Pyramids: from the summit of these p.
228:83

Pyramus: Death of P. and Thisby
341:39

Quires and places where they sing 63:72

Quiring to the young-ey'd cherubins 340:22

Quit: like doth q. like 338:94
  q. yourselves like men 39:38

Quiver: willows whiten, aspens q. 387:76

*Quod erat demonstrandum* 133:51

Quotation: every q. contributes something 172:42

Questions: a book that furnishes no q. 245:36

Quote: by necessity ... delight, we all q. 133:40
  grow immortal as they q. 417:59
  I'll kill you if you q. it 77:69
  I q. the fights historical 147:31

Quoter: next to originator ... is the first q. 133:39

Rabbit: the r. has a charming face 15:70

Race: earth ... will no longer tolerate the r. 27:48
  he rides a r. 113:57
  pernicious r. ... of odious vermin 381:1
  slow and steady wins the r. 197:89
  some new r., called Man 218:53
  the human r., to which so many ... belong 99:78
  the r. dwelling all round the globe 102:11
  the r. is not to the swift 47:8
  whole r. of politicians 381:2

Races: human species ... two distinct r. 191:25

Rachel weeping for her children 51:3ᶜ

Rack: leave not a r. behind 356–7:50
  ship has weather'd every r. 403:81
  the r. of this tough world 331:7
  then we r. the value 343:81

Radical ... with both feet ... in the air 289:31

Rage: disguise ... nature with hard-favour'd r. 319:45
  puts all Heaven in a r. 66:28
  r., r., against the dying 390:18

Ragged: though my ryme be r., tattered 373:92

Raggedness: loop'd and window'd r. 329:78

Rags: heaven in r., than to hell in embroidery 256:24
  no scandal like r. 134:55
  sat in unwomanly r. 166:64

Rail: I'll r. against ... first-born 301:86
  whiles I am a beggar, I will r. 326:38

Rain: being read to ... waiting for r. 130:92
  droppeth as the gentle r. from heaven 339:15
  hath the r. a father? 41:77
  I dissolve it in r. 368:22
  in thunder, lightning, or in r. 332:22
  nor r., wind, thunder ... my daughters 328:72
  r. before seven, fine before eleven 275:75
  r., r., go to Spain 275:76
  right as r. 276:95
  ripple of r. 382:15
  rudely r. beaten ... moth-eaten 373:92
  sendeth r. on ... just ... unjust 52:15
  still falls the r. 373:90
  stirring ... roots with spring r. 131:10
  the r. came heavily ... in floods 413:11
  the r. is full of ghosts 210:46
  the r. is over and gone 47:21
  the r. it raineth every day 360:3
  the r. it raineth on the just 70:71
  the wind and the r. 360:3

Rainbow: a r. in the sky 412:98
  add another hue unto the r. 327:43
  the r. comes and goes 410:73

Rains: it never r. but it pours 275:77

Rainy: lay it up for a r. day 275:78
  the weather when it is not r. 83:55

*Raisons que la raison ne connaît point* 244:28

Rake: every woman is at heart a r. 251:23
  excuse for thus playing the r. 226:65
  lean as a r. 269:63
  lene was his hors as is a r. 96:32
  man's a ribald ... a r. 148:37

Rampallion, you r.! 316:5

Rampart: his corse to the r. we hurried 408:52

Ramparts: o'er the r. we watched 188:79

Ran: Georgie Porgie r. away 232:31
  grief with a glass that r. 382:16
  the sacred river r. 106:71, 73

Ranged with humble livers in content 322:75

Rank is good, and gold is fair 403:88

Rankers: gentlemen r. 190:99

Ranks: all service r. the same with God 75:45
  even the r. of Tuscany 202:41

Rap and knock and enter in our soul
73:17
Rapidity: travelling ... dull in ... pro-
portion to its r. 291:59
Rapidly: yes, but not so r. 30:75
Rapscallions: all kings is mostly r.
393:62
Rapture: a r. on the lonely shore 84:65
first fine careless r. 74:23
Raptures: the r. and roses of vice
382:18
Rare: I think my love as r. 364:53
she was indeed a r. one 408:48
Rarely, rarely, comest thou 370:52
Rascal: a dull and muddy-mettl'd r.
308:91
get down you dirty r. 233:41
Rashes: green grow the r. 80:7
Rasselas, prince of Abyssinia 173:61
Rat: a dog, a horse, a r. have life
331:6
a r.? Dead, for a ducat 311:17
cat that killed the r. 239:79
Mr Speaker, I smell a r. 288:13
to smell a r. 277:48
Rate: brings down the r. of usance
338:3
Rated: in the Rialto you have r. me
338:5
Rather: he had r. have a turnip 172:56
I live ... r. as a Spectator 9:6
Rationed: liberty ... so precious ... it
must be r. 195:69
Rats: out ... the r. came tumbling
75:40
r. desert a sinking ship 275:79
r. I they fought the dogs 75:37
rid your town of r. 75:39
Rattle: spoiled his nice new r. 92:74
Rave: old age shd. burn and r. 390:18
Raven: quoth the R., Nevermore
247:67
yr. locks were like the r. 80:11
Ravens: there were three r. 12:39
Ray: gem of purest r. serene 155:37
Raze out the ... troubles of the brain
336:72
Reach: man's r. shd. exceed his grasp
73:15
Read: classic ... everybody wants to
have r. 394:73
classic ... nobody wants to r. 394:73
I r. much of the night 131:11
I've r. in many a novel 87:13
r. ... as inclination leads him 175:86
r., mark, learn 64:86
sins were scarlet ... books were r.
31:93

Read (*continued*)
sooner r. a time-table ... than
nothing 208:22
what do you r., my lord? 308:77
without an intention to r. it
176:5
Reader: last r. reads no more 164:43
Readers: the human race, to which ...
r. belong 99:78
Reading: I prefer r. 374:3
peace is poor r. 158:64
r. is to the mind 378:61
r. maketh a full man 26:33
when ... not walking, I am r. 192:29
writer's time is spent in r. 176:11
Ready: conference [maketh] a r. man
26:33
we always are r. 141:48
Real: although pain isn't r. 13:51
Realistic: when statesmen ... say ... r.
22:59
Reality: between the idea and the r.
130:95
cannot bear very much r. 130:91
Realm: this earth, this r., this England
348–9:41
Realms: constancy lives in r. above
106:67
who dwell in r. of day 66:31
Reap: men that sow to r. 382:19
shall r. the whirlwind 50:76
Reaped: wheat which never shd. be r.
392:53
Reason: all r. is against it 82:46
Cornish men will know the r. why
158–9:74
divorced old barren R. 135:76
do ... r. themselves out again
321:61
have I not r. to lament 411:84
in erring r.'s spite 250:12
no other but a woman's r. 361:5
O, r. not the need 328:67
or any other r. why 10:16
r. and energy, love and hate 68:56
r. is left free to combat it 171:28
r. is our soul's left hand 123:5
r. why I cannot tell 72:96
reasons which r. does not know
244:28
right deed for the wrong r. 132:17
ruling passion conquers r. still
251:27
teach thy necessity to r. thus 348:36
theirs not to r. why 385:42
worse appear the better r. 217:48
Reasonable: a r. good ear in music
342:51

Reasoned high of Providence 218:55
Reasons: the heart has its r. 244:28
Rebel: thinking man is bound to r. 169:8
Rebellion lay in his way 315:86
Rebels: dear earth ... though r. wound thee 349:49
Rebuke: boldly r. vice 64:92
   open r. is better than secret love 46:86
Recapture: think he never could r. 74:23
Reckless what I do to spite the world 334:49
Recommendation: self-praise is no r. 277:27
Recompense: heaven did a r. ... send 155:41
Record: puts a r. on the gramophone 131:12
Recover: die of it do seldom ... r. 299:68
*Recte: si possis r., si non, quocumque modo rem* 166:72
*Reculer: il faut r. pour mieux sauter* 267:11
Red: coral is far more r. than her lips' r. 364:52
   grace to get ... r. in the face 34:20
   her lips were r., her looks were free 105:52
   keep the R. Flag flying 109–10:21
   like a r. r. rose 81:21
   making the green one r. 334:43
   nature, r. in tooth and claw 386:63
   r. as a rose 275:80
   r. as a rose is she 104:45
   r. rag to a bull 275:81
   sun ... curtained with cloudy r. 216:22
   sunset ... one glorious blood-r. 74:24
   the one in r. cravat 122:85
   the r. plague rid you 355:33
   the R. Queen 94:96, 98
Red brick: not even r., but white tile 242:10
Red-breast: the r. whistles 181:82
Rede: recks not his own r. 306:54
Redeemer: I know that my r. liveth 41:72
Redemption: condemn'd into everlasting r. 344:84
   no r. from hell 276:82
Redress: things past r. ... past care 349:47
Reed: a bruised r. shall he not break 48:44

Reed (*continued*)
   r. shaken with the wind 52:29
Reeds: down in the r. by the river 73:13
Reeking into Cadiz Bay 74:24
Reeling and Writhing 91:60
References: always verify yr. r. 291:56
Reflect: when I r. that God is just 171:33
Reformation: reforming of R. itself 224:42
Reforming: nothing so needs r. as ... habits 394:72
Refrain: did ... from expensive sins r. 126:45
Refreshment: the most perfect r. 23:70
Refuge: eternal God is thy r. 38:17
   God is our r. and strength 42:7
   idleness ... r. of weak minds 98:61
Refugees: the guttural sorrow of the r. 203:56
Regard: where ... least r. for human freedom 376:37
Regiment: four elements warring ... for r. 205:76
   led his r. from behind 143:69
   Monstrous R. of Women 191:19
Region: in thrilling r. of thick-ribbed ice 337:90
Regions: double lived in r. new 181:83
   r. Caesar never knew 112:50
Regret: youth is a blunder ... old age a r. 123:95
Regrets: past R. and future Fears 135:69
Reign: r. in this horrible place 114:78
   whatsoever King shall r. 17:92
Reigned: I have r. with your loves 132:21
Reinforcement: what r. we may gain from hope 216:33
Rejoice: as he was fortunate, I r. 325:11
   daughters of the Philistines r. 40:47
   from age to age thou didst r. 412:1
   good Christian men, r. 229:2
   I hear thee and r. 415:37
   r. with them that do r. 57:38
Rejoices: a poor heart that never r. 274:50
Rejoicing: went on his way r. 56:17
Relative: set out ... in a r. way 76:52
Relaxed: power ... r. too much 25:14
Relaxes: damn braces, bless r. 69:61
Relent: shall make him once r. 77:64
Relief: for this r. much thanks 305:33
Religion: bringeth ... minds about to r. 25:10

Religion (*continued*)
    enough r. to make us hate   382:9
    good life is the only r.   265:34
    love is my r.—I cd. die for that
        187:67
    men will wrangle for r.   108:96
    Millionaire. That is my r.   365:76
    my pollertics, like my r.   398:26
    no man's r. ... survives his morals
        273:93
    not a r. for gentlemen   96:21
    one r. is as true as another   82:32
    one's r. is whatever he is ... inter-
        ested in   28:63
    only one r., though ... a hundred ver-
        sions   366:92
    pure r. breathing household laws
        412:2
    r. but a childish toy   204:69
    r. is allowed to invade   208:26
    r., justice, counsel, and treasure
        25:7
    r. of an ill man   276:83
    r. is the best armour ... worst cloak
        276:84 .
    r.'s in the heart, not ... knees   171:37
    r. ... the opium of the people   207:7
    superstition ... r. of feeble minds
        78:80
Religious: casting a dim r. light   213:88
    good, but not r. good   158:66
    man is ... a r. animal   78:79
Rely upon a comfortable time-lag
    401:66
Remain: as things have been, things r.
    103:32
Remained: came to scoff, r. to pray
    150:67
Remains: what r. is bestial   345:1
Remarkable: nothing left r. beneath the
    moon   299:66
Remedies: desperate diseases ... des-
    perate r.   260:71
    he that will not apply new r.   26:17
    our r. oft in ourselves   298:42
Remedy: a r. for all ... but death
    276:85
    force is not a r.   71:83
    knew the reason ... sought the r.
        302:5
    one unfailing r.—the Tankard   87:12
    r. is worse than the disease   25:9
Remember: and if thou wilt, r.   290:48
    bitter to endure ... sweet to r.   256:38
    do you r. an inn, Miranda?   32:8
    forget and smile ... r. and be sad
        290:45
    he'll r., with advantages   320:58

Remember (*continued*)
    I r., I r.   165:60, 61
    I r. your name perfectly   377:52
    I wish our ... poets wd. r.   107:82
    if I do not r. thee   44:49
    in the morning we will r. them
        65:20
    it r., whan it passed is   97–8:51
    please to r. the fifth of November
        15:69
    r. ... best of friends must part   19:11
    r. Lot's wife,   55:88
    r. me when I am gone away   290:44
    r. now thy Creator   47:11
    r. when ... money not scarce?   133:47
    some day ... pleasant to r.   396:98
Remembered: r. tolling a departed
    friend   316:97
    when we r. Zion   44:44
    wd. have made myself r.   187:68
Remembering: a soul r. my good
    friends   349:44
    r. mine affliction ... misery   49:60
Remembers: nature yet r. what was so
    fugitive   411:80
Remembrance: appear almost a r.
    186:55
    praising ... lost makes the r. dear
        298:47
    rosemary, that's for r.   311:28
    summon up r. of things past .  362:37
    writ in r. more than things long
        past   348:39
Reminds a man he is mortal   117:14
Remorse: farewell fear, farewell r.
    218:63
Remote: r. and ineffectual don   32:1
    r., unfriended, melancholy, slow
        151:89
Remover: bends with the r. to remove
    363:47
Remuneration: Latin word for three
    farthings   331:12
Rend yr. heart and not yr. garments
    50:78
Render therefore unto Caesar   53:43
Rendezvous: I have a r. with Death
    296:20
Renounce the devil ... his works   64:95
Renown: a citizen of credit and r.
    112:54
    living, shall forfeit fair r.   295:6
Renowned for larnin' and piety   154:18
Rent: what a r. the envious Casca
    made   325:18
Repair unto the Bell at Edmonton
    113:55
Repay: I will r., saith the Lord   57:40

Repeal of bad or obnoxious laws 153:16

Repent: I do r. it from my very soul 358:64

Repentance: r. comes too late 276:86
    Winter Garment of R. fling 135:66

Repented: she strove, and much r. 84:67

Repetitions: use not vain r. 52:17

Replenish: be fruitful ... r. the earth 34:29

Reply: third, the R. Churlish 303:9

Report me and my cause aright 312:37

Reporters: gallery in which the r. sit 202:44

Repose: earned a night's r. 199:8
    O partial sleep, give thy r.? 317:14
    r. is taboo'd by anxiety 144:91

Reposes: in quiet she r. 21:37

Reprehend: if I r. any thing in this world 372:71

Representation: no taxation without r. 273:3

Reproach: receives r. of being 363:49
    sting of a r. ... truth of it 278:79

Reproof: fourth, the R. Valiant 303:9

Reprove: check the erring, and r. 413:7

Republican form of Government is the highest 376:33

Reputation: at every word a r. dies 251:36
    if you esteem your own r. 399:33
    purest treasure ... spotless r. 347:30
    r., r., r., ... lost my r.! 345:1
    seeking the bubble r. 301:90
    sold my R. for a Song 136:82

Reputations: murdered r. of the week 108:7

Requests: thou wilt grant their r. 63:73

Require: what doth the Lord r.? 51:91

Requires: all the human frame r. 31:92

Researchers: our r. into public opinion 22:62

Resemble: when I r. her to thee 398:17

Resent: no individual cd. r. ... thousands ... meant 381:97

Resist: can r. everything except temptation 405:19
    r. the devil and he will flee 60:6

Resisting: not over-fond of r. temptation 30:77

Resolute: be bloody, bold and r. 335:62

Resolution: in War: R. 102:10
    native hue of r. 309:95
    what r. from despair 216:33

Resolved to live a fool 29:70

Resolves: and re-resolves; then dies the same 418:63

Resort: far from all r. of mirth 213:86

Resource: infinite— r.— and— sagacity 191:16

Respect: is there no r. of place ... time? 359:86
    the r. that makes calamity 309:95

Respectable: r. means rich 245:35
    when was genius found r.? 73:10

Respecter of persons 56:19

Respects: he that r. not is not respected 276:88

Responsibility: liberty means r. ... men dread it 366:87
    no sense of r. (baby) 191:21

Rest: absence of occupation is not r. 113:67
    angels sing thee to thy r. 312:40
    far better r. that I go to 121:79
    God ... ordain'd no r. 396:86
    run far faster than the r. 32:3
    set up my everlasting r. 354:18
    she's at r. and so am I 127:60
    so may he r. 323:85
    some ill a-brewing towards my r. 339:9
    the r. is silence 312:39
    the r. of his dull life 29:70
    wear ourselves and never r. 205:76

Restoration: the Church's R. in 1883 34:24

Restraint: firm r. with which they write 87:17.

Resumed: democracy r. her reign 31:95

Reticulated or decussated 172:47

Retire me to my Milan 357:58

Retired into ... political Cave of Adullam 71:82

Retirement: short r. urges sweet return 220:92

Retort: first the R. Courteous 303:9

Retreat: let us make an honourable r. 302:94

Return: art gone and never must r. 215:10
    departed never to r. 81:27
    short retirement urges sweet r. 220:92
    unto dust shalt thou r. 35:39

Returns: and the day r. too soon 86:98
    small profits and quick r. 277:47

Reveal: words ... half r. ... half conceal 386:58

Reveals: soberness conceals what drunkenness r. 278:52

Revelry: sound of r. by night 83:59

Revels: our r. now are ended 356:50

Revenge: prompted to my r. by heaven 309:93

r., at first though sweet 220:91

r. his foul ... unnatural murder 307:65

r. is a kind of wild justice 24:89

r. is sweet 276:89

r. never repairs 276:90

shall we not r.? 339:13

spur my dull r. 311:22

study of r., immortal hate 216:30

sweet is r.—especially to women 84:68

sweet r. grows harsh 346:20

Revenges: time brings in his r. 360:2

Reverence: none so poor to do him r. 325:15

yet r. ... doth make distinction 304:27

Reviewing: read a book before r. it 375:11

Revolt: a r.? No, Sire, ... a revolution 288:20

inferiors r. in order that 20:27

*Révolte: c'est une r.? non ... une révolution* 288:20

Revolution: a revolt? No, sire, ... a r. 288:20

*Révolution: une révolte? Non ... une r.* 288:20

Revolutionist: not a r., is an inferior 365:84

Revolutions: state of mind which creates r. 20:27

Reward: only r. of virtue is virtue 132:30

r. of a thing well done 133:33

the Lord shall r. thee 45:81

virtue is its own r. 282:94

Rheims: Cardinal Lord Archbishop of R. 28:53

Rhetorician: a sophistical r. inebriated [Gladstone] 123:94

Rheumatic of shoulder 70:72

Rhodope: brighter than is ... R. 204:73

Rhyme: build the lofty r. 215:9

r. being no necessary adjunct 216:26

r. themselves into ladies' favours 321:61

soft names in many a mused r. 184:29

still more tired of r. 32:98

though my r. be ragged 373:92

Rialto: in the R. you have rated me 338:5

Rib: r. ... made he a woman 35:33

smote him under the fifth r. 40:50

Riband: just for a r. ... in his coat 74:28

r. in the cap of youth 311:29

Ribstone pippin: right as a R. 31:97

Rich: adversity makes ... not r. 254:59

being r., my virtue ... shall be 326:38

better to live r. than to die r. 177:27

born lucky than r. 255:16

good workmen are seldom r. 265:40

God help the r. 264:21

grew so r. that I was sent 147:27

he is r. that is satisfied 276:92

health! the blessing of the r.! 179:60

if I ever become a r. man 32:6

maketh haste to be r. 46:88

never be handsome, strong, r. 266:58

no sin but to be r. 326:38

one law for the r. 369:57

over the r. Dead 71:88

passing r. with forty pounds a year 150:66

Poor Little R. Girl 112:45

poverty is an anomaly to r. people 27:46

respectable means r. 245:35

r. can help themselves 264:20

r. man to enter ... kingdom of God 53:41

r. men have no faults 276:91

r. men rule the law 151:93

r. not gaudy 306:56

r. what gets the gravy 18:5

seems it r. to die 184:29

the r. man in his castle 10:18

victim of a r. man's game 18:3

when I grow r., say the bells 236:61

widows are always r. 283:30

wretchedness of being r. 374:2

Richard: body of R. Hind 13:45

we came in with R. Conqueror 355:19

Richer: for r. or for poorer 64:7

r. than doing nothing for a bribe 304:23

Riches: infinite r. in a little room 204:70

of great r. ... no real use 26:24

r. are for spending 26:21

r. I hold in light esteem 71:86

r. of the mind ... make ... rich 276:93

to r., dignity and power 32:4

Richly: a lady r. left  338:9
Rickshaw: it's no go the r.  203:54
Rid: idea of getting r. of it [work]
    171:35
    if I can r. your town  75:39
Riddle: a r. wrapped in a mystery
    100:91
Ride: a poem must r.  139:29
    Haggards r. no more  378:63
    r. a cock-horse  237:66
    r. in triumph through Persepolis
    205:75
    went for a r. on a tiger  13:52
    when he next doth r. abroad  113:61
*Rideau: tirez le r., la farce est jouée*
    285:90
Rider: secret ... between a r. and his
    horse  381:94
Rides: and r. upon the storm  113:63
Ridicule: easier to r. than commend
    276:94
Ridiculous: is not this r.?  146:14
    one step above the r.  243:19
    sublime to the r.  228:84
    the sublime and the r. ... nearly
    related  243:19
Riding: r. to and from his wife  402:77
    Yankee Doodle ... r. on a pony
    241:90
Ridley: be of good comfort, Master R.
    193:40
*Rien appris ... oublié*  384:31
Rifle all the breathing spring  107:87
Rift: load every r. of yr. subject  187:69
Riga: young lady of Riga  13:52
Right: a r. judgement in all things
    64:89
    all goes r. and nothing ... wrong
    148:40
    all's r. with the world  75:44
    an earl by r., by courtesy a man
    24:82
    defend to the death your r.  398:16
    do the r. deed for the wrong reason
    132:17
    earth's the r. place for love  139:21
    great r. ... a little wrong  339:16
    I'll publish r. or wrong  85:88
    it must be r. I've done it from my
    youth  114:79
    know not whether laws be r.  404:97
    majority never has r. on its side
    169:8
    my r. there is none to dispute  114:77
    never dreamed, though r. were
    worsted  73:16
    no r. to strike against the public
    safety  110:28

Right (*continued*)
    our country, r. or wrong  118:16
    rather be r. than be President  103:22
    r. as a Ribstone Pippin  31:97
    r. as rain  276:95
    r. divine of kings to govern wrong
    247:70
    r. in his own eyes  39:32
    shall not the Judge ... do r.?  35:54
    think at yr. age, it is r.?  90:48
    think the last opinion r.  249:2
    too fond of the r.  151:79
    two wrongs don't make a r.  281:83
    with firmness in the r.  196:81
Righteous: be not r. over much  47:6
    die the death of the r.  38:4
    if I find ... fifty r.  36:55
    judge r. judgment  55:2
    souls of the r. are in the hand of God
    62:43
Righteousness: r. exalteth a nation
    45:68
    the Sun of r. arise  51:1
Rights: endowed ... with certain un-
    alienable r.  171:26
    property has its duties ... its r.
    126:35
    reaffirm faith in fundamental ... r.
    394:76
Rigol: from this golden r. hath
    divorc'd  318:28
Rigour of the game  192:27
Ring: r. at the end of his nose  195:61
    spring ... the only pretty r. time
    303:7
    with this r. I thee wed  65:9
Ring-a-ring o' roses  237:67
Rings: my true love sent ... five gold r.
    238:73
    r. on her fingers  237:66
Riot: rash fierce blaze of r. cannot last
    348:40
    r. and dishonour stain the brow
    312:44
Ripe: from hour to hour, we r. and r.
    301:88
    scholar ... r. and good one  323:87
Ripeness is all  330:98
Rise: r. up before the hoary head
    38:1
    r. up, my love, my fair one  47:20
    some r. by sin ... by virtue fall
    337:82
Rises: hoo-ray and up she r.  19:14
    while Jove's planet r. yonder  74:25
Rising: in his r. seemed a pillar  218:52
River: Alph, the sacred r., ran  106:71
    away, you rolling r.  18:1

Rome (*continued*)
  I lov'd R. more   325:10
  pardoun come from R.   97:43
  R. shall fall; and when R. falls   84:64
  R. was not built in a day   276:2
  the grandeur that was R.   247:66
  the hook-nos'd fellow of R.   317:24
  when in R., live as the Romans do
    11:23
Romeo: wherefore art thou R.?
    353:99
Ronald: Lord R. said nothing ... rode
    ... off   194:51
Rood: when every r. ... maintained its
    man   150:63
Roofs: masons building r. of gold
    318–19:39
Room: all before my little r.   71:89
  although the r. grows chilly   153:11
  always r. at the top   400:46
  convent's narrow r.   411:89
  infinite riches in a little r.   204:70
  no r. ... for hyphenated American-
    ism   289:38
  no r. for them in the inn   54:67
  not r. to swing a cat   276:3
  r. of one's own   409:58
  r. with a view—and you   112:41
Roosevelt: here is the answer ... to
    President R.   101:98
Roost (Roast): to rule the r.   276:6
Root of all evil, The want of money
    82:41
Rooted: pluck from the memory of r.
    sorrow   336:72
Roots: stirring dull r. with spring rain
    131:10
  straight trees have crooked r.   279:84
Rope: a r. to hang himself   16:85
  give a thief r. enough   276:4
Ropes: know the r.   268:43
Rose: a sadder ... man he r.   106:65
  and lovely is the r.   410:73
  as red as a r.   275:80
  At Christmas I no more desire a r.
    331:11
  beauty's r. might never die   362:29
  go, lovely r.   398:17
  he's mighty lak' a r.   378:58
  I am the r. of Sharon   47:17
  in a twilight dim with r.   118:25
  my fause lover stole my r.   81:28
  my love ... like a red red r.   81:21
  no r. without a thorn   273:99
  not to me returns ... summer's r.
    218:59
  red as a r. is she   104:45
  r. by any other name   353:11

Rose (*continued*)
  r. leaves, when the r. is dead   370:54
  r. of the fair state   310:1
  r. or rue or laurel   382:17
  the last r. of summer   226:63
  the r. of youth upon him   299:60
  when I have pluck'd thy r.   346:19
  your image that blossoms a r.   417:55
Rosebuds: gather ye r. while ye may
    162:24
  r., before they be withered   62:41
Rosemary: for you there's r. and rue
    361:20
  r., that's for remembrance   311:28
Rose-moles all in stipple upon trout
    166:68
Rose-red city half as old as time   77:70
Roses: as soon seek r. in December
    85:91
  ash the burnt r. leave   130:97
  it was r., r., all the way   74:35
  raptures and r. of vice   382:18
  strew on her r., r.   21:37
  their lips were four red r.   352:79
  twin r. by the zephyr blown apart
    182:3
  where r. and white lilies grow   88:24
Rosy cheeks and flaxen curls   75:43
Rot: from hour to hour, we r. and r.
    301:88
  lie in cold obstruction and to r.
    337:90
  r. inwardly, and foul contagion
    spread   215:16
Rotted: do you think my mind ... r.
    early?   228:92
Rotten: something is r. in the state of
    Denmark   307:62
  soon ripe, soon r.   278:57
Rotting: mean and mighty r. together
    304:27
Rough: take the r. with the smooth
    276:5
Rough-hew them how we will   312:35
Round: in a light fantastic r.   212:75
Rounded: our little life is r. with a sleep
    356–7:50
Rousseau: mock on, Voltaire, R.
    67:39
Roving: we'll go no more a r.   86:97,98
Rowland: Child R., to the dark tower
    329:82
Rowley, powley, gammon and spinach
    232:30
Royal: likely ... to have prov'd most r.
    312:41
  no r. road to geometry   133:52
Rub: Ay, there's the r.   309:95

Safest: just when we are s. ... a sunset-
　touch 73:17
Safety: in ... multitude of counsellors
　... is s. 45:63
　our s. is in our speed 133:35
　strike against the public s. 110:28
　we pluck this flower, s. 313:60
Sagacious, bold and turbulent of wit
　126:38
Sagacity: infinite—resource—and—s.
　191:16
Sage: thou Goddess s. and holy 213:83
Sages: teach you more ... than all the s.
　414:28
Said: best ... known and s. in the world
　21:53
　I hope it may be s. 'His sins' 31:93
Sail: and cried, A s.! A s.! 105:51
　full s. ... fan spread ... streamers
　109:10
　s. near the wind 276:10
　s. on, O Ship of State! 197:92
　very sea-mark of my utmost s.
　346:21
　white and rustling s. 116:96
Sailed: they s. away ... year and a day
　195:61
Sailing: three ships come s. by 15:74,
　233-4:42
　what thing ... comes this way s.
　222:18
Sailor: drunken s. early in the morning
　19:14
　home is the s. 379:76
Sails: purple the s., and so perfumed
　298:54
　when we our s. advance 125:31
　wind out of one's s. 279:2
Saint: and never a s. took pity on
　105:54
　art ... able to corrupt a s. 312:46
　my late espoused s. 223:35
　open the shrine, that I may see my s.
　179:59
　s.-seducing gold 353:90
　seem a s. when ... play the devil
　351:70
　young s., old devil 284:65
St. Agnes Eve—Ah, bitter chill 181:89
St. Clement's: say the bells of S.
　236:61
St. Crispin: fought ... upon S.'s day
　320-21:59
Saint Empire Romain ... ni saint, ni
　romain, ni empire 398:14
St. George: for Harry, England, and
　S.! 319:47
　S., that swing'd the dragon 326:35

St. Ives: as I was going to S. 231:22
St. John: awake, my S. 250:7
St. Martin's: say the bells of S. 236:61
St. Paul's: 'Say I am designing S.'
　33:16
Saint Vincent: nobly, nobly, Capt. S.
　74:24
Saints: a pair of carved s. 350:55
　all the S. adore thee 160:88
Sal: down South for to see my S.
　18:97
Salad: my s. days 298:53
Salisbury: Lord S. ... brought back
　peace 122:93
Sally: there's none like pretty S. 89:31
Salt: became a pillar of s. 36:56
　coaster with a s.-caked smoke-stack
　207:13
　ye are the s. of the earth 52:11
Salus populi suprema est lex 102:15
Salute: s. the happy morn 83:52
　s. thee with my hand 349:49
Salvation: my bottle of s. 286:94
　none of us shd. see s. 339:15
　visit us with thy s. 402:72
　work out yr. own s. 58:75
　wot prawce s.? 365:77
Samarkand: the Golden Road to S.
　136:84
Same: it's the s. the whole world over
　18:5
　Jesus Christ the s. ... for ever 60:3
　more they are the s. 180:72
　no better ... much the s. 24:83
Sammy: vy worn't there a alleybi!
　121:76
Samson: better than the strength of S.
　272:55
Sanctity: in the odour of s. died 28:54
Sand: a world in a grain of s. 66:27
　little grain of s. 89:41
　on the edge of the s. 195:62
　roll down their golden s. 159:86
　such quantities of s. 92:78
　throw the s. against the wind 67:39
Sandals were for Clementine 225:60
Sandalwood, cedarwood, ... white
　wine 207:12
Sandboy: jolly as a 268:25
Sands: come unto these yellow s.
　355:34
　golden s., and crystal brooks 123:4
　lone and level s. stretch far away
　369:40
　on the s. with printless foot 357:54
　wd. steer too nigh the s. 126:39
Sane: see where the s. ... have landed
　us! 366:1

Sang: he worked and s. 65:16
  s. his didn't ... danced his did 116:94
Sank: but oh! the silence s. 106:61
Sans teeth, sans eyes 301–2:90
Sappho: where burning S. loved 84:77
Sarah: old S. Battle 192:27
Sashes: one of his nice new s. 153:11
Sat: as I s. on a sunny bank 15:74
  we s. by the flesh pots 36:79
Satan: get thee behind me, S. 53:36
  S. exalted sat, by merit raised 217:45
  S. finds some mischief still 399:36
Satchel: school-boy with his s. 301:90
Satire: let s. be my song 85:88
Satisfaction: great s. in quarrelling with her 372:75
Satisfied: well paid that is well s. 340:21
Satisfies: makes hungry where she most s. 299:55
Saturday: died on S. 238:71
  escaped three weeks ... o' S. 379:71
  S.'s child works hard 235–6:56
Saturn: grey-hair'd S., quiet as a stone 182:96
Satyr: Hyperion to a s. 305:43
Satyrs: my men, like s. grazing 204:68
Sauce for the goose is s. for the gander 276:12
Saul: is S. also among the prophets? 39:39
  S. and Jonathan were lovely 40:48
  S. hath slain his thousands 39:44
Sautrye: fithele, or gay s. 96:33
Savage: dancing? ... of s. origin 79:91
  s., extreme, rude, cruel 363:50
  s. place, as holy and enchanted 106:72
  so s. and Tartarly 86:94
Save: choose time ... s. time 26:18
  died to s. us all 11:20
  s. her from the foggy, foggy dew 17:96
  s. one's bacon 276:13
Saviour: the S. of the world was born 83:52
Savour: filths s. but themselves 329:86
  keep seeming and s. all the winter 361:20
  salt have lost his s. 52:11
Saw: all at once I s. a crowd 410:67
  coughing drowns the parson's s. 332:20
  do not s. the air too much 310:3
  s. the Vision of the world 387:80
  ten thousand s. I at a glance 410:69
  who s. him die? 241:88

Saws: wise s. and modern instances 301:90
Say: do as I s., not as I do 296:24
  he may have nothing to s. 176:10
  I s. that shd. not 280:30
  my people ... to s. what they please 139:19
  never s. die 273:87
  s. it with flowers 242:96
  s. not the struggle naught availeth 103:32
  s. now Shibboleth 39:26
  we love best, to them ... s. least 270:11
  when you have nothing to s. 108:97
Saying: ancient s. is not heresy 339:11
  s. is one thing 277:16
Scald: tears do s. like molten lead 330:96
Scallop-shell of quiet 286:94
Scan: whose limericks never wd. s. 13:54
Scandal: no s. about Queen Elizabeth 371:63
  public s. that gives offence 224:51
  s. ... is gossip made tedious 406:20
  there's no s. like rags 134:55
  would the s. vanish with my life 349:42
*Scandale: la s. du monde* 224:51
Scanter of yr. maiden presence 307:58
Scapegoat: let him go for a s. 37:96
Scarlet: raise the s. standard high 109:21
  though your sins be as s. 48:30
Scars: wars bring s. 282:4
Scatter as from ... hearth ... my words 369:38
Scattered: dead bones ... s. by 352:72
  s. in the bottom of the sea 352:72
Scene: our lofty s. be acted over 324:5
  s. individable, or poem unlimited 308:84
  upon that memorable s. 207:3
Scenery is fine, but human nature 186:57
Scenes: busy s. of crowded life 173:67
Scepticism: a wise s. ... attribute of a good critic 200:26
Sceptre: my s. for a palmer's ... staff 350:55
  s. shows the force of ... power 339:15
  this unwieldy s. from my hand 350:58
Sceptred: what avails the s. race? 192:36

Sea (*continued*)

devil and the deep s.  260:72
down to a sunless s.  106:71
down to the s. in ships  43:26
England ... with the triumphant s.  349:42
first ... into that silent s.  105:48
from s. to shining s.  29:67
into the midst of the s.  36:78
learn the secret of the s.?  198:1
mother and lover ... the s.  383:25
my Bonnie is over the s.  17:94
never, never sick at s.!  147:22
not all the water in the rough, rude s.  349:50
on such a full s. are we now afloat  326:27
one foot in s.  343:68
one that goes to s. for nothing  123:8
out of the s. came he  104:44
over the s. to Skye  69:69, 379:73
plants His footsteps in the s.  113:63
precious stone set in the silver s.  348:41
sailed the wintry s.  199:9
scatter'd in the bottom of the s.  352:72
the kings of the s.  20:34
the rude s. grew civil  341:44
the s. is calm to-night  20:30
the s. never changes  110:26
the s.! the s.!  416:50
the wrinkled s. beneath him crawls  385:47
there is Society ... by the deep s.  84:65
till the s. ... floweth in yr. veins  392:52
to s. for nothing but to make him sick  123:8
to s. in a ... pea-green boat  195:60
two Voices ... one is of the s.  412:1
went down into the s.  104:44
went to s. in a sieve  194:57
when I put out to s.  385:44
where no s. runs  390:21
whose sound was like the s.  413:4
why the s. is boiling hot  93:80
wind of the Western S.  388:96
winds somewhere safe to s.  383:20
within a walk of the s.  32:7
worse things happen at s.  284:58
Sea-boy: wet s. in an hour so rude  317:14
Seagreen Incorruptible  89:35
Seal: all right ... you heard a s. bark  392:43
opened the seventh s.  61:27

Sealing-wax: ships and s.  93:80
Seals of love, but seal'd in vain  337–8:92
Sea-maid: to hear the s.'s music  341:44
Sea-mark: very s. of my utmost sail  346:21
Sea-monster: ingratitude ... more hideous ... than the s.  328:57
Search will find it out  162:22
Seas: foam of perilous s.  184:30
guard our native s.  88:21
I must down to the s. again  207–8:14–16
port after stormy s.  377:42
the multitudinous s. incarnadine  334:43
we shall fight on the s. and oceans  100:94
Seaside: I do like to be beside the s.  149:57
Season: a dry brain in a dry s.  130:93
givest ... meat in due s.  44:52
in the s. of the year  18:98
to every thing ... a s.  46:98
Seasons: as the swift s. roll  164:50
defend you from s. such as these  329:78
four s. fill the measure  185:45
four s. in the mind of man  185:45
thus with the year s. return  218:59
when mercy s. justice  339:15
Seat: regain the blissful s.  216:27
this s. of Mars  348:41
Seats: you want the best s.; we have them  11:35
Seconds: sixty s.' worth of distance run  190:5
Secrecy: for s., no lady closer  313:61
Secret: bread eaten in s. is pleasant  45:60
digestion ... great s. of life  375:12
it [love] ceases to be a s.  30:85
joys of parents are s.  24:94
learn the s. of the sea?  198:1
s., black, and midnight hags!  335:60
there is no s. so close  381:94
Secrets: s. with girls ... never valued  114:82
tell the s. of my prison-house  307:64
Sect: attached to that great s.  368:25
paradise for a s.  182:93
Sects: two-and-seventy jarring s. confute  135:77
Secure: safe ... never to be s.  282:14
s., and never now can mourn  367:16
Sedge is wither'd from the lake  182:7
See: and no man s. me more  322:79
blind as those who won't s.  256:45

See (*continued*)
  come up and s. me sometime  402:74
  content to s. no other verdure
    185:43
  did you once s. Shelley plain?  74:30
  ever s. such a thing in yr. life?
    240:80
  forward tho' I canna s.  80–1:19
  I did but s. her passing by  18:9
  I s. the moon ... moon sees me
    234:43
  if thou hast eyes to s.  345:95
  may I be there to s.  113:61
  O! say you can s.  188:79
  rather s. than be one  77:68
  s. all, nor be afraid  75–6:46
  s. her on the bridge at midnight
    18:4
  s., not feel, how beautiful  106:68
  s. what we shall s.  277:24
  shall never s. a billboard  229:97
  the eye begins to s.  71:87
  to s. beyond our bourn  181:88
  to s. her was to love her  79:96
  wait and s.  22:57, 282:98
  we s. through a glass darkly  57:54
Seed: groweth s. and bloweth med
  15:71
  in thy s. ... all nations ... blessed
    36:57
  robs not one light s.  182:97
  s. begging their bread  42:3
Seeds: if you can look into the s. of
  time  333:27
Seeing: s. is believing  277:25
  worth s.? Yes; but not ... going
    177:32
Seek: nothing s., nothing find  273:10
  s. ye the Lord  48:50
Seeking: s. the food he eats  301:85
  s. whom he may devour  60:12
  we must still be s.  409:65
Seeks: he that s. trouble  277:26
  whoever s. abroad may find  181:80
Seem: free we s. ... fettered ... are
  73:14
  s. here no painful inch to gain
    103:33
  s. wiser than they are  26:19
  things are not what they s.  198:95
Seeming: keep s. ... all the winter
  361:20
Seems: he s. so near and yet so far
  386:66
  how sweet and fair she s. to be
    398:17
  so careful of the type she s.  386:62
Seen: because thou art not s.`  302:91

Seen (*continued*)
  s. and not heard  258:98
  to be hated needs but to be s.  250:14
  who hath not s. thee?  181:80
See-saw, Margery Daw  237:68
Seidlitz powder: burst while drinking
  a s.  13:46
Seize the flow'r, its bloom is shed
  81:25
Self: from thee to my sole s.  184:31
  nothing ... greater to one than ... s.
    403:86
  to thine own s. be true  306:57
  wretch, concentred all in s.  295:6
Self-evident: we hold these truths to
  be s.  171:26
Self-praise is no recommendation
  227:27
Self-preservation ... first law of nature
  277:28
Self-sacrifice: the spirit of s.  413:8
Self-sufficient: know how to be s.
  225:54
Seldom: a woman s. asks advice  9:10
  s. or never the two hit it off  409:59
Sempronius: we'll do more, S.  9:4
Senators: green-rob'd s. of mighty
  woods  182:98
Sensation of a short sharp shock  145:3
Sensations: Life of S. rather than of
  Thoughts  186:51
Sense: devoid of s. and motion  217:49
  fools admire, but men of s. approve
    249:1
  live within the s. they quicken
    370:54
  man of s. ... trifles with [women]
    98:60
  Shadwell never deviates into s.
    128:69
  so sweet that the s. aches  346:14
  sound ... an echo to the s.  249:99
  take care of the s.  91:58
Sense of humour: mind ... deficient in
  a s.  107:83
Senseless: the most s. and fit man
  343:74
Senses: steep my s. in forgetfulness
  317:13
Sensibility: fine sense, yet wanting s.
  114:75
Sensible: moral, s., and well-bred
  112:52
Sentence: my s. is for open war  217:46
  originator of a good s.  133:39
  s. first—verdict afterwards  91:68
Sentimental: carry ... body around
  because of its s. value  140:31

Shadrach, Meshach, and Abed-nego 49:67

Shadwell: S. ... my perfect image bears 128:69

S. never deviates into sense 128:69

Shady: on Ida's s. brow 68:54

Shafto: Bobby S.'s gone to sea 231:24

Shaken: looks on tempests and is never s. 363:47

so s. as we are, so wan 312:42

when taken to be well s. 108:95

Shake-scene: is the only s. 156:49

Shakespeare: fashionable topics ... pictures ... S. 152:1

immortal S. rose 173:58

might have chanced to be S. 169:4

our myriad-minded S. 107:80

S. led a life of allegory 187:64

S. unlocked his heart 412:95

sweetest S., Fancy's child 214:4

the tongue that S. spake 413:5

what needs my S. for his ... bones 216:23

when I read S. 194:49

Shall: mark you his absolute 's.' 303:16

Shallow: Master S., I owe you 318:35

s. in himself 221:8

Shallows: bound in s. and in miseries 326:27

Shalott: the Lady of S. 387:77

Shame: ain't it all a bleedin' s.? 18:5

England ... now bound in with s. 349:42

in a waste of s. 363:50

poverty is not a s. 275:55

whose glory is their s. 58:76

Shank: too wide for his shrunk s. 301:90

Shape: com'st in such a questionable s. 307:60

S. of Things to Come 401:67

the other S.—if s. it might be 218:56

to lick into s. 269:75

virtue in her s. how lovely 219:73

Share: no one so true did s. it 359–60:88

s. and s. alike 277:30

Sharon: I am the rose of S. 47:17

Sharper: a s. played with a dupe 115:86

s. than a serpent's tooth 328:58

Sharps: fifty different s. and flats 75:38

Shatter yr. leaves before the mellowing year 215:8

Shaven: bald heads are soon s. 255:90

if I be s. ... strength will go 39:29

Shaves: a man who s. and takes a train 402:77

She: has got him a s. 16:79

that not impossible s. 115:84

the fair ... and unexpressive s. 302:92

Sheba: another S. Queen 408:48

Shed: a lowly cattle s. 10:19

by man shall his blood be s. 35:49

tears, prepare to s. them now 325:17

with ... [Edmund Burke] beneath a s. 178:46

Sheep: an old half-witted s. 378:62

baa, baa, black s. 231:23

black s. in every flock 256:42

divideth ... s. from ... goats 53:47

hanged for a s. as a lamb 266:60

hungry s. look up, and are not fed 215:16

Little Bo-peep has lost her s. 234:48

looking on their silly s. 322:71

mountain s. are sweeter 245:38

noble ensample to his s. he yaf 97:40

return to our s. 19:16

strayed from thy ways like lost s. 63:66

the s.'s in the meadow 234:49

Sheep-hook: know how to hold a s. 215:15

Sheet: a wet s. and a flowing sea 116:96

Sheets: better wear out shoes than s. 256:32

Shelley: did you once see S. plain? 74:30

Shelter: I will build a house ... to s. me 32:6

our s. from the stormy blast 399:38

Shenandoah: O, S. I long to hear you 18:1

Shepherd: as a s. divideth his sheep 53:47

Dick the s. blows his nail 332:20

every s. tells his tale 214:98

go, for they call you, S. 21:39

good s. giveth his life 55:6

homely, slighted, s.'s trade 215:11

Old Nod the s. goes 118:25

truth in every s.'s tongue 286:96

Shepherds: a sweeter shade to s. 322:71

s. abiding in the field 54:68

while s. watched their flocks 384:35

Sheridan was listened to 288:25

Shibboleth: say now S. 39:26

Shift: let me s. for myself 226:66

Shilling: better give a s. 256:23

cut off with a s. 259:47

Shillings: rather than forty s. ... Book of Songs 340:28

Shimei, though not prodigal of pelf 126:46

Shine: err with Pope ... s. with Pye 85:92

few are qualified to s. 382:10

I see Heaven's glories s. 71:84

moon doth s. as bright as day 231:25

s. so brisk, and smell so sweet 313:52

sun that warms you ... s. on me 348:33

Shines: light ... where no sun s. 390:21

Shining: from sea to s. sea 29:67

s. with all his might 92:76

Ship: a s. in a black storm 401:55

a s. is worse than a gaol 177:16

a stately s. of Tarsus 222:18

all I ask is a tall s. 207:14

as idle as a painted s. 105:49

our saucy s.'s a beauty 146:19

rats desert a sinking s. 275:79

sail on, O S. of State 197:92

the s. has weathered every rack 403:81

Ships: face that launch'd a thousand s. 204:63

I saw three s. come sailing by 233–4:42

our bloody s. today 29:69

seen old s. sail like swans 136:85

s. that pass in the night 198:4

s., towers, domes, theatres 412:96

spied three s. come sailing by 15:74

we've got the s., we've got the men 168:93

Shires and towns from Airly Beacon 189:85

Shirt: no s. or collar ... comes back twice 194:53

Shive: cut loaf to steal a s. 357–8:63

Shiver: little breezes dusk and s. 387:76

Shivering: grass ... s.-sweet to the touch 111:34

Shoal: a s. of fools for tenders 109:10

bank and s. of time 333:36

Shock: short sharp s. 145:3

Shock-headed Peter 164:42

Shocks: natural s. that flesh is heir to 309:95

Shoe: I kiss his dirty s. 320:51

know where the s. pinches 277:31

my dame has lost her s. 231:26

old woman ... lived in a s. 239:76

one, two, buckle my s. 236:60

Shoemakers: brave s. ... of the gentle craft 118:21

Shoe-string: a careless s. in whose tie 162:17

Shoes: better wear out s. than sheets 256:32

her s. were number nine 225:60

old s. ... easiest for his feet 296:21

s. – and ships – and sealing-wax 93:80

Shone like a meteor streaming 217:39

Shoot: do not s. the pianist 405:17

s., if you must, this old gray head 403:89

Shopkeepers: England is a nation of s. 228:85

fit only for a nation of s. 374:98

nation that is governed by s. 374:98

Shops: that men might shun the awful s. 99:76

Shore: adieu, my native s. 83:57

fast by their native s. 113:64

now upon the farther s. 132:23

rapture on the lonely s. 84:65

rocky s. beats back the envious siege 349:42

s. of the wide world 186:49

the lights around the s. 291:53

waves make towards the pebbled s. 363:40

Shoreditch: say the bells of S. 236:61

Short: if you find it wond'rous s. 150:75

s. and sweet 277:32

sweet discourse makes s. days 279:90

take a long while to make it s. 391:40

Shorter: had Cleopatra's nose been s. 244:27

make you s. by a head 132:19

Shortly: I expect a judgment. S. 119:34

Shortness: to spend that s. basely 315:89

Shot: I s. the albatross 105:47

not a soldier discharged his farewell s. 408:52

Shoulder: give the cold s. 258:20

put yr. s. to the wheel 275:72

Shoulder-blade: I have a left s. ... a miracle 146:9

Shoulders: old head on young s. 274:19

Shout: s. that tore Hell's concave 217:40

's. with the largest' [mob] 121:63

there was a s. about my ears 99:69

Shouting: after the ... music with s.
and laughter 75:43
all is over bar the s. 254:67

Shovel them [bodies] under and let me
work 293:78

Show: s. and gaze o' th' time 336:79
that within which passes s. 305:41
to offer it the s. of violence 305:35

Shower: drainless s. of light is poesy
185:38
this was our finest s.! 242:7

Showers: Aprille with his s. sote 96:25
fresh s. for thirsting flowers 368:21
small s. last long 348:40

Shows: May's new-fangled s. 331:11

Shreds: king of s. and patches 311:18
thing of s. and patches 145:95

Shrieking: with s. and squeaking 75:38

Shrink: all the boards did s. 105:50

Shroud: my s. ... stuck all with yew
359–60:88

Shrug: borne it with a patient s. 338:6

Shuffled off this mortal coil 309:95

Shun: s. the heaven that leads ... to ...
hell 363:51
that men might s. the awful shops
99:76

Shut, shut the door, good John 248:77

Shutters: now ... close the s. fast
114:73

Shy: once bitten, twice s. 274:21
you look a little s. 94:98

Sick: can s. men play so nicely? 349:43
for I am s. of love 47:19
hope deferred maketh the heart s.
45:66
I am s. at heart 305:33
never, never s. at sea! 147:22
s. hurry ... divided aims 21:42
the devil was s. 227:74
the enterprise is s.! 358:67
tie up the knocker, say I'm s. 248:77
to sea for nothing but to make him s.
123:8
when ... the heart is s. 386:60
when we are s. in fortune 327:53

Sicklied o'er with the pale cast 309:95

Sickness: he hath the falling s. 324:95
in s. and in health 64:7
s. is better than sadness 277:36

Side: courtesy on one s. only 259:32
hear the other s. 254:81
look on the bright s. 270:3
nobody is on my s. 23:79
trumpets sounded ... on the other s.
77:67
which s. one's bread is buttered
268:42

Sides: buttered on both s. 257:65
laughter holding both his s. 214:94
your ... unfed s. 329:78

*Siècles: quarante s. vous contemplent*
228:83

Siege: rocky shore beats back the
envious s. 349:42

Sieve: carry water in a s. 282:10
in a s. they went to sea 194:57

Sigh: a s. is the sword 66:35
a s. like Tom o' Bedlam 327:54
s. no more, ladies, s. no more 343:68
s. the lack of many a thing 362:37
something ... prompts th' eternal s.
250:15

Sighed: no sooner s. but they ask'd
302:5
she s., she cried 17:96
s. for ... love of a ladye 148–9:46

Sighing: a plague of s. and grief!
314:67
fell a-s. and a-sobbing 241:89

Sighs: for my pains a world of s.
344:92
s. are the natural language 297:38

Sight: a s. to dream of 106:66
and 'tis a shameful s. 399:37
every common s. to me did seem
410:72
Oh the pleasant s. to see 189:85
she gleamed upon my s. 414:16
s. for sore eyes 277:37
s. ... good for sore eyes 382:7
s. of means to do ill deeds 327:45
s. of vernal bloom 218:59
s. so touching in its majesty 412:96
to s. or thought be formed 220:94
who ever lov'd that lov'd not at first
s.? 205:81

Sights: such s. as youthful poets dream
214:3
what s. of ugly death! 352:72

Sign: an olive-leaf ... pacific s. 221:1
an outward and visible s. 64:1
God made the wicked Grocer for a
... s. 99:76

Signal: only a s. shown 198:4

Silence: but oh! the s. sank 106:61
darkness again and a s. 198:4
dusky hour friendliest to ... s.
219:80
foster-child of s. 183:16
greet thee? With s. and tears 86:1
let yr. women keep s. in ... churches
57:56
mourn'd in s. and was Di-do-Dum
252:40
my gracious s., hail! 303:13

Sing (*continued*)
    when you s., I'd have you buy
    362:21
Singe: so hot ... it doth s. yourself
    322:74
Singed: I have s. ... king's beard
    125:29
Singing: everyone suddenly burst out s.
    293:83
    I'll be quit of the s.   12:43
    maid s. in the valley below   16:80
    s. in the Wilderness   135:67
    sweet s. in the choir   16–17:87
Single: continued s. ... only talked of
    population 152:96
Sings: chaffinch s. on the orchard
    bough 74:21
    in his motion like an angel s.   340:22
    in me [summer] s. no more   210:47
    lark at heaven's gate s.   304:20
    s. for his supper   235:52
    tell me what she's.   414:21
    thrush, he s. each song twice over
    74:23
Singularity: surprise by ... excess ...
    not by S.   186:55
Sinks: it s., and I am ready   192:34
Sinner: joy ... over one s. that repenteth
    54:80
Sinners: God and s. reconciled   402:71
    mercy upon us miserable s.   63:76
Sinning: more sinn'd against than s.
    329:76
Sins: did ... from expensive s. refrain
    126:45
    few love to hear the s. they love to
    act 347:25
    his s. were scarlet, but his books
    31:93
    oldest s. the newest kind of ways
    318:30
    other s. only speak; murder shrieks
    out 400:49
    result of her s. was quadruplets
    14:55
    the multitude of s.   60:11
    though yr. s. be as scarlet   48:30
Sirens: blest pair of S.   212:71
Sisera: stars ... fought against S.   39:22
Sister: a barren s. all your life   341:35
    but I kissed her little s.   225:61
Sisters: his s., and his cousins, and his
    aunts 147:25
    sphere-born harmonious s.   212:71
    two s. embrace like one brother
    287:11
Sit: can s. and look at it [work] for
    hours 171:35

Sit (*continued*)
    here I and sorrows s.   326:39
    I will s. down now, but   122:88
    If I s. on a pin   13:51
    not fit that you shd. s. here   115:90
    shall s. and drink with me   32:7
    s. every man under his vine   50:89
    s. on a cushion and sew   231–2:27
    s. upon the murdered reputations
    108:7
    so I did s. and eat   161:13
    test my bath before I s.   229:96
    there we s. in peaceful calm   169:5
    to s. in ... shade ... look upon
    verdure 23:70
    to s. upon a hill, as I do now   321:70
Sitivation at the lighthouse   121:77
Sitting: thee s. careless on ... granary
    floor 181:80
Situation excellent. I shall attack
    136:87
Six: it's just s. of one   206:87
    s. days shalt thou labour   37:86
    s. hours in sleep, in ... study s.
    104:40
    s. of one and half a dozen ... other
    277:41
Sixes and sevens: to be at s.   277:42
Sixpence: bang—went s.!!!   285:79
    buy a thing that costs even s.
    176:5
    he found a crooked s.   239:74
    I love s., jolly little s.   233:40
    nothink for nothink ... little for s.
    285:80
    sing a song of s.   238:70
Skating over thin ice   133:35
Skies: cloudless climes and starry s.
    86:96
    for s. of couple-colour   166:68
    his watch-tower in the s,   214:97
    in summer s. to mourn   181:88
    some watcher of the s.   185:41
Skill: simple truth his utmost s.   416:48
Skills: create by means of new s.
    292:66
Skin: and it punctures my s.   13:51
    by the s. of one's teeth   277:43
    can the Ethiopian change his s.?
    49:56
    her s. was white as leprosy   105:52
    I stuff my s. so full within   380:82
    saw the skull beneath the s.   131:13
    why, my s. hangs about me   314:78
Skins: all ... fancy dress ... except our
    ... s.   366:6
Skipped: the mountains s. like rams
    43:29

Skipper: the s. had taken his little
    daughter  199:9
Skipping: they all went s. about  28:59
Skull: laid her hand on his thick s.
    127:49
    saw the s. beneath the skin  131:13
Skulls: some lay in dead men's s.
    352:72
Sky: all the blue ethereal s.  9:9
    clothe the wold and meet the s.
    387:75
    I see him ... darkening the s.  288:13
    inverted bowl we call the s.  136:80
    larks ... about us in the s.  167:82
    lonely sea and the s.  207:14
    moving Moon went up the s.  105:56
    nursling of the S.  368:23
    old and true as the s.  190:6
    ring out ... to the wild s.  386:67
    since first our s. was overcast  114:76
    yon twelve-winded s.  167:83
Skye: over the sea to S. (Boulton)
    69:69
    over the sea to S. (Stevenson)  379:73
Slain: I am s. by a fair cruel maid
    359:88
Slanders: secondarily, they are s.
    344:87
Slant: there's a certain s. of light
    122:83
Slaughter: as a lamb to the s.  48:49
    his canon 'gainst self-s.  305:42
Slave: has been s. to thousands  345:6
    here I stand, your s.  329:73
    man that is not passion's s.  310:6
    what a rogue and peasant s.  308:89
Slavery: choice, to be a land of s.
    196:75
    it cannot ... be classified as s.  100:88
Slaves: as free-men not s.  141:48
    at the mill with s.  221:12
    Britons never will be s.  391:33
    necessity ... creed of s.  246:56
Slay: though he s. me yet will I trust
    41:68
Slays: moves, and mates, and s.  135:78
Sleek: so s. and erect and eyeable
    193:47
Sleep: a voice cry, S. no more  334:42
    be but to s. and feed  311:22
    by a s. ... end the heart-ache  309:95
    dusky hour friendliest to s.  219:80
    grey and full of s.  417:58
    how s. the brave  107:89
    I shall s. like a top  117:9
    I s., but my heart waketh  47:25
    in that s. of death  309:95
    life is rounded with a s.  356–7:50

Sleep (continued)
    Macbeth doth murder s.  334:42
    no s. till morn  83:60
    nor shall my sword s. in my hand
    67:38
    one hour's s. before midnight  267:5
    our birth ... a s. and a forgetting
    410:77
    peace ... s. with Turks and infidels
    305:56
    quiet s. and a sweet dream  208:16
    rude forefathers of the hamlet s.
    155:33
    six hours' s. for a man  277:40
    s. after toil ... greatly please  377:42
    s. l it is a gentle thing  105:57
    s., O gentle s., nature's soft nurse
    317:13
    s. of ... labouring man is sweet
    46:2
    s. that knits up the ravell'd sleave
    334:42
    s. the s. that knows not breaking
    295:97
    so he giveth his beloved s.  44:42
    sooner it's over ... sooner to s.
    189:87
    such as s. o' nights  324:94
    task is done, and we must s.  299:64
    this s. is sound indeed  318:28
    thy deep and dreamless s.  72:95
    to s., perchance to dream  309:95
    we shall not s., though poppies grow
    202:49
    we ... s. to wake  73:16
    what hath night to do with s.?
    212:74
    youth wd. s. out the rest  361:16
Sleeping: Capten, art tha s.?  230:11
    let s. dogs lie  269:71
Sleeps: after life's fitful fever he s. well
    334:51
    he that s. feels not the toothache
    305:32
    how sweet the moonlight s.  340:22
    s. sound as Johnny underground
    284:72
Sleeve: ace of trumps up his s.  191:23
    ash on an old man's s.  130:97
    my heart upon my s. for daws
    344:89
    one's heart on one's s.  282:17
Slept: I have not s. one wink  304:24
    s. well ... remembers not ... s. ill
    277:44
    the law ... hath s.  337:85
Slew: as he was ambitious, I s. him
    325:11

Slight: away, s. man! 326:25
  if she s. me when I woo 408:50
Slimy: a thousand thousand s. things 105:55
Slings and arrows of outrageous fortune 309:95
Slinks out of the race 223:39
Slip 'twixt the cup and the lip 280:20
Slippery: as s. as an eel 277:45
Slips: like greyhounds in the s. 319:47
Sloth: too much time in studies ... s. 26:31
Slough: name of the s. was Despond 77:58
Slow: s. and steady 197:89
  s. but sure 277:46
  come he s. or come he fast 295:9
  divine grace was never s. 260:78
  I am s. of study 341:41
  sun climbs s., how slowly 104:34
  too swift ... as tardy as too s. 354:10
  wisely and s. 354:7
Slowly: and s. answered Arthur 385:54
  mills of God grind s. 198:99
  ring out a s. dying cause 386:69
  sun climbs slow, how s. 104:34
Sluggard: go to the ant, thou s. 44:57
  voice of the s. 400:41
Slumber: I must s. again 400:41
  love itself shall s. on 370:54
  ports of s. open wide 317:27
Slumbering: poesy ... 'tis might half-s. 185:38
Slumbers: golden s. kiss your eyes 118:20
  soul is dead that s. 198:95
Slung atween the round shot 230:11
Slut: I am not a s. 302:2
Small: all things both great and s. 106:64
  microbe is so very s. 32:2
  souls of women are so s. 82:40
  when they said, 'Is it s.?' 195:65
  wind ... to fire ... extinguishes the s. 82:34
  yet they grind exceeding s. 198:99
Smarts so little as a fool 248:79
Smattering of everything 121:78
Smell: here's the s. of the blood still 335:69
  I know ... the sweet keen s. 291:53
  shine so brisk, and s. so sweet 313:52
  s. far worse than weeds 363:42
  taste ... better than the s. 279:11
  to s. a rat 277:48
Smells: it s. to heaven 311:15
Smile: and s., s., s. 22:56

Smile (continued)
  did he s. his work to see? 68:47
  fortune ... s. once more 328:63
  grandeur hear with a disdainful s. 155:34
  I dare not beg a s. 162:19
  if we do meet ... shall s. 326:28
  my wanton, s. upon my knee 156:48
  s. at us, pay us, pass us 99:75
  s. on the face of the tiger 13:52
  that s. we wd. aspire to 322–3:81
  you shd. forget and s. 290:45
Smiled: s. a kind of sickly smile 158:73
  until she s. on me 104:41
Smiles: daggers in men's s. 334:47
  life is ... sobs, sniffles, and s. 161:3
  Nods and Becks and wreathed S. 214:93
  s. awake you when you rise 118:20
Smilest: Thou s. and art still 21:44
Smiling: com'st s. from the ... snare uncaught? 299:63
  like Patience ... s. at grief 360:89
  Soldan of Byzantium is s. 99:70
Smilingly: flaw'd heart ... burst s. 330:3
Smite: if the rude caitiff s. the other 164:45
  whosoever shall s. thee 52:13
Smith: the s., a mighty man is he 199:6
Smithy: the village s. stands 199:6
Smoke: good cigar is a s. 190:94
  in yr. pipe and s. it 275:71
  no fire without some s. 273:92
  s. and blood is the mix of steel 293:80
Smokeless: bright and glittering in the s. air 412:96
Smooth: I am a s. man 36:59
  take the rough with the s. 276:5
Smote: and s. him—thus 346–7:22
  s. them hip and thigh 39:28
  the Lord s. all the firstborn 36:77
Smyler with the Knyf under the Cloke 97:44
Snaffle ... curb ... but where's the bloody horse? 87:17
Snail: a whiting to a s. 91:62
  like s. unwillingly to school 301:90
  the s.'s on the thorn 75:44
Snake: a s. in the grass 277:49
  earth doth like a s. renew 368:28
Snapper-up of unconsidered trifles 361:18
Snare: smiling from the world's great s. 299:63

Snatch: hear a voice ... s. a fearful joy 154:28

Sneer: without sneering, teach the rest to s. 248:83

Sneezed: not to be s. at 278:50

Sneezes: beat him when he s. 90:51

Sniffles: sobs, s. and smiles ... s. predominating 161:3

Snicker-snack: blade went s. 92:70

Snob: impossible ... not to be ... a S. 389:8

Snodgrass: Mr. S. 121:63

Snoring: while you here do s. lie 356:39

Snow: birds sit brooding in the s. 332:20

bore 'mid s. and ice 197:93
half-buried in the s. 198:94
I sh. be whiter than s. 42:8
like S. upon ... Desert's ... Face 135:68
like the s. falls in ... river 81:25
naked in December s. 348:37
never ... love the s. again 70:77
[sins] shall be ... white as s. 48:30
s. had fallen, s. on s. 290:43
s. in May's new-fangled shows 331:11
when the s. lay round about 229:3
where the s. lay dinted 229:5
white as driven s. 362:22
whitest s. on Scythian hills 204:73

Snowing: the more it goes on s. 210:49

Snows: where are the s. of yesteryear? 396:95

Snug: Skugg ... s. as a bug in a rug 138:13

So: if it was s. it might be 92:75
s. far, s. good 278:51

Soap: s. and education ... more deadly 393:64
used your s. two years ago 285:84

Sober: as s. as a judge 134:60
be s., be vigilant 60:12
neither ingenious, s., nor kind 13:45
tomorrow we'll be s. 16:78

Sobers: drinking largely s. us again 249:94

Sobs: with s. and tears he sorted out 93:81

Social: new stock for every s. occasion 169:2
one of the s. lies 169:8

Socialists: we are all S. now 157:62

Society: classes into which our s. is divided 21:48
no s. can surely be flourishing 374:97

Society (*continued*)
one great s. alone on earth 413:10
s. is no comfort 304:26
s. is now one polished horde 85:86
s. where none intrudes 84:65
solitude ... best s. 220:92
The Affluent S. 140:42
unfriendly to s.'s chief joys 112:53

Sodden: Midlands ... s. and unkind 32:5

Sodium: odium of having discovered s. 33:18

Sodom: in S. fifty righteous 36:55

Sofa: I sing the s. 113:68
wheel the s. round 114:73

Soft: her voice was ever s., gentle 331:5
s. falls the dew 30:84

Soften rocks, or bend ... oak 108:5

Softly: fair and s. goes far 262:45
s. she was going up 105:56
sweet Thames! run s. 377:47
Zephyrus did s. play 377:46

Softness: for s. she 219:66

Soil: fame is no plant ... on mortal s. 215:14
subject is the fattest s. to weeds 317:26

Soiled: name ... s. with all ignoble use 387:72

Solace: with s. and gladness 373:93

Sold: he s. his birthright unto Jacob 36:58
s. my Reputation for a Song 136:82

*Soldat: tout s. ... porte dans sa giberne* 228:86

Soldier: Ben Battle was a s. bold 165:57
can always tell an old s. 364:62
drinking is the s.'s pleasure 127:53
every French s. ... in his cartridge-pouch 228:86
in the s. is flat blasphemy 337:88
s., full of strange oaths 301:90
s., rest! thy warfare o'er 295:97
s.'s pole is fall'n! 299:66
statesman, s., merchant 9:6
the boastful s. 247:63
very poor s. ... a chocolate cream s. 364:63

Soldiers: like s., armed in their stings 318:39
old s. never die 18:99
old s. ... surest 400:52
onward, Christian s. 28:57

Soliciting: this supernatural s. 333:28

Solitary: be not s., be not idle 82:33
life of a s. man 173:65

Solitary (*continued*)
the s. child 411:85
took their s. way 221:3
Solitude: a state more gloomy than s.
173:66
as my S. is sublime 187:63
in s. what happiness? 220:87
O S.! where are the charms? 114:78
race ... has ... disturbed its s. 27:48
s. sometimes is best society 220:92
which is the bliss of s. 410:71
whosoever is delighted in s. 26:20
*Solitudinem faciunt, pacem appellant*
383:27
Solomon: S. Grundy, born on a
Monday 238:71
the wisdom of S. 40:54
Some: S. chicken! S. neck! 101:1
s. ... fou o' love ... s. ... o' brandy
80:10
s. glory in their birth 363:41
s. hae meat ... s. wad eat 81:24
s. talk of Alexander 18:6
Somebody: how dreary to be s. 122:81
s. bet on de bay 137:1
when every one is s. 143:78
Somer: in a s. season 193:39
Something: a man's worth s. 73:18
add s. more to this wonderful year
141:48
always doing s. for posterity 10:11
in our embers is s. that doth live
411:80
s. left to treat my friends 203:59
s. rich and strange 355:35
s. sensational to read in the train
405:14
s. ... that doesn't love a wall 139:27
s. was dead in each of us 404:95
that s. ... which prompts th' eternal
sigh 250:15
time for a little s. 212:66
'tis s., nothing 345:6
what's s. rarish 13:47
Sometime: come up and see me s.
402:74
Somewhat: more than s. 291:58
Somewhere: time was away and s. else
203:57
Son: a foolish s. ... heaviness 45:61
a virgin shall ... bear a s. 48:34
a wise s. ... a glad father 45:61
as a man chasteneth his s. 38:8
he gave his only begotten S. 55:99
Jehu ... s. of Nimshi ... driveth
40:62
marry yr s. when you will 271:49
my s., if thou come to serve 62:46

Son (*continued*)
O Absalom, my s., my s.! 40:51
O Lucifer, s. of the morning 48:38
she will ... renounce me for a s.
142:64
spareth his rod hateth his s. 45:67
unto us a s. is given 48:36
Song: a s. to sing, O! 148:45
broke into a quavering s. 401:63
fierce wars ... shall moralize my s.
377:40
give ear unto my s. 150:75
glorious the s. when God's the theme
374:94
he sings each s. twice over 74:23
let satire be my s. 85:88
not given a penny for a s. 417:51
old s. of Percy and Douglas 373:87
one grand, sweet s. 189:86
pipe a s. about a lamb 68:49
run softly till I end my S. 377:47
sang a most topical s. 13:53
sea grew civil at her s. 341:44
self-same s. that found a path 184:30
sold my Reputation for a S. 136:82
s. for yr. delight 93:87
suck melancholy out of a s. 301:84
that glorious s. of old 296:19
the Lord's s. in a strange land
44:47
this subject for heroic s. 220:90
unlike my subject ... frame my s.
98:64
we'll sing another s. 416:44
Songs: Book of S. and Sonnets here
340:28
for ever piping s. for ever new
183:19
our sweetest s. ... saddest thought
370:50
piping s. of pleasant glee 68:48
sing no sad s. for me 290:47
the s. of Apollo 332:21
their lean and flashy s. 215:16
there shall the Sussex s. be sung
32:6
where are the s. of Spring? 181:81
Sonne: when soft was the s. 193:39
Sonnet: a s. is a moment's monument
290:49
scorn not the s. 412:95
s.'s scanty plot of ground 411:90
Sonnets: onlie begetter of ... insuing s.
362:28
Sons: bears all its s. away 400:40
free as the s. of the waves 141:48
s. of Belial, flown with insolence
217:38

Sons (*continued*)
> s. of Belial had a Glorious Time 126:46
> the s. of the prophet were brave 18:7
> things are the s. of heaven 172:41

Soon: belovèd Night ... come s., s. 369:33
> day returns too s. 86:98
> it [the future] comes s. enough 129:83
> s. as she was gone ... a traveller came 67:41
> s. got, s. spent 278:55
> s. hot, s. cold 278:56
> s. ripe, s. rotten 278:57
> you have waked me too s. 400:41

Sooner it's over, the s. to sleep 189:87

Soot: black as s. 256:40

Sooth: poesy ... friend to s. the cares 185:39

Sophisters: age ... of s., economists, calculators 78:78

Sore: sight ... good for s. eyes 382:7
> sleep ... s. labour's bath 334:42
> trust in critics who themselves are s. 85:91

Sorrow: and not be in s. too 68:53
> and wear a golden s. 322:75
> any s. like unto my s. 49:59
> brief s., short-lived care 229:1
> down, thou climbing s. 328:64
> ere the s. comes with years 73:11
> from the sphere of our s. 371:56
> has brought [war] untold s. to mankind 394:76
> I feel it when I s. most 386:59
> increaseth knowledge increaseth s. 46:97
> more in s. than in anger 306:50
> no more death, neither s. 61:34
> O S., why dost borrow? 181:87
> parting is such sweet s. 354:6
> pluck from the memory a rooted s. 336:72
> pure and complete s. 392:50
> s. comes unsent for 278:58
> s. goes, and pleasure tarries 143:74
> s. will come fast enough 265:24
> the guttural s. of the refugees 203:56
> then to come, in spite of s. 214:97
> there is no greater s. 116:3
> to think is to be full of s. 184:25
> truly that hour foretold s. 86:99
> write s. on the bosom of the earth 349:53

Sorrows: a man of s. ... acquainted with grief 48:47
> here I and s. sit 326:39

Sorrows (*continued*)
> losses are restor'd and s. end 363:38
> s. come ... not single spies 311:26
> there are few s. ... in which 374:1
> when age, disease, or s. strike him 103:27

Sorry: better ... safe than s. 255:19
> dreadful s., Clementine 225:59
> truly s. man's dominion 80:17

Sort: a s. of men whose visages 338:97
> travel, in the younger s. 25:12

Sorts: all s. and conditions of men 63:81

Sought: that I s. to destroy institutions 403:79
> the prize we s. is won 403:81
> those men that s. him 323:87

Soul: a day for a man to afflict his s. 49:52
> a thing which enters ... s. 186:54
> all thy heart ... all thy s. 38:9
> and his s. sincere 155:41
> as if that s. were fled 226:62
> asleep in body ... become a living s. 415:33
> body Nature is, and God the s. 250:11
> body presseth down the s. 62:44
> breathes there the man, with s. so dead 295:5
> build ... stately mansions, O my s. 164:50
> call upon my s. within the house 359:80
> cold waters to a thirsty s. 45:82
> confession is good for the s. 258:23
> distress hath humanized my s. 409:62
> dull wd. he be of s. 412:96
> for my s., what can it do to that? 307:61
> for my unconquerable s. 160:93
> foredoom'd his father's s. to cross 248:78
> gain the ... world, and lose his own s. 54:58
> give not thy s. unto a woman 62:50
> hae mercy o' my s., Lord God 202:50
> half conceal the S. within 386:58
> harrow up thy s., freeze thy young blood 307:64
> Helen, ... give me my s. again 204:63
> her lips suck forth my s. 204:63
> hidden s. of harmony 215:5
> his s. is marching on! 157:57
> I am black ... my s. is white 68:51

Soul (*continued*)

I am the captain of my s.  160:95
I ... invite my s.  403:83
iron entered [into] his s.  43:25,
  267:19
it is the cause, my s.  346:18
joy's s. lies in the doing  358:65
King Cole was a merry old s.
  236:58
largest and most comprehensive s.
  127:58
lose his own s.  54:58
memorial from the S.'s eternity
  290:49
merit wins the s.  252:39
most offending s. alive  320:56
my prophetic s.!  My uncle!  307:67
my s. in agony  105:54
my s. into the boughs does glide
  206:1
my s., like to a ship  401:55
my s., there is a country  396:87
no coward s. is mine  71:84
our s.'s left hand  123:5
perdition catch my s.  345:5
pouring forth thy s. abroad  184:29
praise my s., the King of Heaven
  201:34
pray for my s.  386:55
prepare thy s. for temptation  62:46
rap and knock and enter in our s.
  73:17
sleepless S. that perished  413:12
s. and ... gift of articulate speech
  366:93
s. hath been alone  106:62
s. is dead that slumbers  198:95
s. is in a ferment  181:84
s. is not more than the body  403:86
s. of the Age!  179:53
s. rememb'ring my good friends
  349:44
s. was sad ... glance was glum
  148:46
the s. of Adonais, like a star  368:20
the s. that rises with us  410:77
the s. to feel the flesh  71:87
thou art a s. in bliss  330:96
thy rapt s. sitting in thine eyes
  213:84
thy s. was like a Star  413:4
to bear my s. away  10:13
was not spoken of the s.  198:95
what a dusty answer gets the s.
  209:34
what of s. was left  76:48
with all thy s. ... all thy might  38:6
yet my s. drew back  161:12

Souls: fire our s. to regale  68:45
have ye s. in heaven too?  181:83
immediate jewel of their s.  345:6
Lord, thou lover of s.  62:45
our s., whose faculties can comprehend  205:76
poor s. who dwell in Night  66:31
prosperity has damned more s.
  275:65
s. of Poets dead and gone  183:14
s. of the righteous ... in the hand of
  God  62:43
s. of women are so small  82:40
such harmony is in immortal s.
  340:22
two s. with but a single thought
  200:18
unless they've s. that grovel  87:13
we that have free s.  310:10
ye have left yr. s. on earth  181:83
Sound: full of s. and fury  336:76
hear dat mournful s.  138:3
no s. save the rush of the river  30:84
sighing s., the lights around the shore
  291:53
s. must seem an echo to the sense
  249:99
s. of a voice that is still  384:37
s. of public scorn  220:96
s. of revelry by night  83:59
s. upon the bugle-horn  387:78
the s. is forc'd, the notes are few
  68:55
the s. of his horn  154:20
to heal the blows of s.  164:44
Sounds: s. will take care of themselves
  91:58
with s. that echo still  385:45
Soup: he screamed out, 'Take the s.
  away!'  164:39
of s. and love, the first  278:59
s. of the evening, beautiful s.  91:65
Sour: how s. sweet music is  351:63
lost his taste, sweet is s.  270:7
love is ... s. in the ending  270:14
things sweet ... prove in digestion s.
  348:35
will not taste the s.  260:69
Source: true s. of human offspring
  219:71
South: beaker full of the warm S.
  184:24
he went by the s.  235:54
I ... go s. in the winter  131:11
Oh, I went down S.  18:97
yes, but not in the S.  252:46
South country: great hills of the S.
  32:5

Spermatozoa: a million million s., all
... alive 169:4
Sphere: from the s. of our sorrow
371:56
    their motion in one s. 315:90
    world's storm-troubled s. 71:84
Spheres: as the restless s. 205:76
    stand still, you ever-moving s.
    204:65
    stars shot madly from their s. 341:44
Spice: variety's the very s. of life
114:71
Spick and span 278:66
Spider: said a s. to a fly 168:86
    there came a big s. 235:51
Spies: as if we were God's s. 330:99
    sorrows ... come not single s. 311:26
Spires: City with her dreaming s. 21:46
    dim-discover'd s. 107:88
Spirit: a bold s. in a loyal breast
347:30
    a pardlike S. beautiful and swift
    367:14
    a S. still, and bright 414:18
    a S., yet a Woman too 414:17
    expense of s. in a waste 363:50
    follow your s., and upon this charge
    319:47
    give me the s. 317:20
    hail to thee, blithe s. 370:49
    have not that alacrity of s. 353:85
    history of the human s. 21:53
    how oft, in s. ... sylvan Wye 415:34
    I am thy father's s. 307:63
    life-blood of a master s. 223:38
    music ... gentlier on the s. lies
    388:85
    my s. is too deeply laden 370:55
    pipe to the s. ditties of no tone
    183:17
    present in s. 57:47
    rarely comest thou, S. of Delight
    370:52
    same s. that its author writ 249:95
    s. ... is willing ... flesh is weak
    53:50
    s. of health or goblin damn'd 307:60
    s. that will start the world along
    416:44
    s. to bathe in fiery floods 337:90
    spur that the clear s. doth raise
    215:13
    the worser s. ... a woman 364:55
    Wild S. ... moving everywhere
    369:36
Spirits: actors ... were all s. 356:50
    choice and master s. of this age
    324:7

Spirits (continued)
    comfort and despair, which like two
    s. 364:55
    her wanton s. look out 358:73
    I can call s. from the ... deep
    314:72
    pluck up thy s., man 226:67
Spit: 'Please don't s. on the floor'
14:56
    s. fire; spout rain 328:72
    s. in my face, call me horse 314:65
    s. upon my Jewish gaberdine 338:6
Spite: cursed s., that ... I was born
307:71
    cut off ... nose to s. ... face 259:46
    reckless what I do to s. the world
    334:49
    S. of cormorant devouring Time
    331:8
    s. of pride, in erring reason's s.
    250:12
    victory in s. of all terror 100:93
Splash: a scream, a s. 18:4
Spleen or Vapors 127:57
Splendid: and by the vision s. 411:78
    in ... our s. isolation 152:8
    man is ... s. in ashes 72:7
    s. tear from the passion-flower
    388:87
Splendour: the s. falls on castle walls
388:97
Split: part ... to make all s. 341:40
Spoil: come and s. the fun 92:77
    company ... hath been the s. of me
    315:79
Spoiled: had s. his nice new rattle
92:74
Spoilers of ... symmetry of shelves
192:26
Spoils: it s. the singing of the nightin-
gale 181:88
Spoke: English as she is s. 393:57
    less he s., the more he heard 285:82
    put a s. in one's wheel 278:68
Spoken: sure of being kindly s. of
23:67
Spoon: dish ran away with the s.
232:33
    have a long s. that sups with the
    devil 270:99
    silver s. in his mouth 257:58
Spoons: measured out my life with
    coffee s. 131:2
    the faster we counted our s. 132:27
Sport: detested s., that owes its pleasure
114:72
    dog laughed to see such s. 232:33
    S. that wrinkled Care derides 214:94

Sport (*continued*)
s. with Amaryllis in the shade 215:12
the chase, the s. of kings 375:23
they kill us for their s. 329:85
to s. wd. be as tedious as to work 313:50
Sported: and by him s. on the green 376:28
Sports: let us prove ... the s. of love 179:61
Spot: Out, damned s.! out, I say! 335:68
Spout: cataracts and hurricanoes s. 328:71
spit fire; s. rain 328:72
Sprang: I s. to the stirrup 74:26
Sprat: a s. to catch a mackerel (whale) 278:69
Spray: never a s. of yew 21:37
Spread: money ... like muck ... be s. 25:8
Sprightly: tossing their heads in s. dance 410:69
Spring: a linnet courting ... in the s. 70:76
absent in the s. 363:44
all the breathing s. 107:87
apparell'd like the s. 347:24
can S. be far behind? 369:38
how this s. of love resembleth 361:6
in s., when woods are getting green 93:88
in the Fire of S. 135:66
in the s. a young man's fancy 387:79
it is s., moonless night 390:23
lived light in the s. 20:31
no s. ... beauty hath such grace 123:7
sweet lovers love the s. 303:7
the year's at the s. 75:44
when the hounds of s. 382:15
where are the songs of S.? 181:81
Springs: four wanton s. end in a word 348:34
steeds to water at those s. 304:20
Sprites: [tale] ... of s. and goblins 361:13
Spur: do not s. a free horse 278:70
fame is the s. 215:13
no s. to prick the sides of my intent 333:37
on the s. of the moment 278:71
Spurns that patient merit ... takes 309:95
Spurs: let the boy win his s. 129:80
Squandering wealth was his peculiar art 126:44

Squeaking: with shrieking and s. 75:38
Squeals: if he s., let him go 232:29
Squeers, Mr Wackford 120:52
Stable: nothing s. in the world 186:53
Stables: the s. are ... centre of the household 365:72
Stabs: with bemock'd-at s. kill ... waters 356.49
Staff: I'll break my s. 357:55
my s. of faith to walk upon 286:94
Stag at eve had drunk his fill 294:94
Stage: after a well-grac'd actor leaves the s. 351:61
all the world's a s. 301:90
frets his hour upon the s. 336:76
if ... played upon a s. now 360:96
mellow glory of the Attic s. 20:35
on the s. he was natural 151:82
s. where every man must play a part 338:96
the wonder of our S. 179:53
to this great s. of fools 330:94
two hours' traffic of our s. 353:89
your daughter on the s. 112:44
Stages: wher'er his s. may have been 371:60
Stagger: they reel .., s. like a drunken man 43:27
Stain: true blue will never s. 281:58
without fault or s. on thee 70:78
Stairs: somebody stopped the moving s. 203:57
Stake: when honour's at the s. 311:24
Stamford: bullocks at S. fair? 317:17
Stamp: s. of his lowly origin 117:6
too late to save the s. 153:10
Stand: s. still, you ever-moving spheres 204:65
s. up for Jesus! 128:73
Sun, s. thou still 38:20
who will s. on either hand? 201:37
Standard: raise the scarlet s. high 109:21
Standing: Jackson s. like a stone wall 30:79
Stanley: here S. meets,—how S. scorns 76:53
on, S., on! 296:15
Stanza: pens a s. when he shd. engross 248:78
Star: and a s. or two beside 105:56
desire of the moth for the s. 371:56
dropped from the zenith, like a falling s. 217:44
eve's one s. 182:96
go and catch a falling s. 124:11
hitch yr. wagon to a s. 133:43

Star *(continued)*

Soul ... rises with us, our life's S. 410:77

s. to steer her by 207:14

there was a s. danc'd 343:67

thy soul was like a S. 413:4

twinkle, twinkle, little s. 384:36

we have seen his s. 51:2

Star Chamber matter of it 340:27

Star-crossed: a pair of s. lovers 353:88

Stare: and all the world wd. s. 113:59

time to stand and s. 117:11

Starry: cloudless climes and s. skies 89:96

Stars: a country far beyond the s. 396:87

and one [sees] the s. 193:38

branch-charmed by the earnest s. 182:98

certain s. shot madly 341:44

clad in the beauty of a thousand s. 204:64

continuous as the s. 410:68

eyes, like s., start from their spheres 307:64

make guilty ... the sun ... the s. 327:53

opposition of the s. 206:98

s. above us govern our conditions 329:87

s. hide their diminished heads 218:61

s., hide your fires 333:31

s. in their courses fought 39:22

s. threw down their spears 68:47

s. through the window-pane are my children 187:63

stone that puts the S. to Flight 134:65

the silent s. go by 72:95

till you are ... crowned with the s. 392:52

true as the s. above 16:81

two s. keep not their motion 315:90

we are ... the s.' tennis balls 400:51

yoke of inauspicious s. 354:18

you chaste s., it is the cause 346:18

Star-spangled banner 188:80

Start: get the s. of the majestic world 323:92

Startle: singing, s. the dull night 214:97

s. it or amaze it with itself 186:54

Starve: let not poor Nelly s. 96:22

State: a continual s. of inelegance 24:81

all were for the s. 201:38

beat a Venetian and traduc'd the s. 346–7:22

State *(continued)*

grant me ... a middle s. 203:59

hides from himself his s. 174:70

his s. is kingly 223:30

I am the S. 199:12

I have done the s. some service 346:22

object in the construction of the s. 247:62

other two ... like us, the s. totters 356:45

the worth of a S. ... individuals 210:43

this is the s. of man 322:80

Stately: a s. pleasure-dome decree 106:71

the s. homes of England 111:39, 160:90

Statements was interesting but tough 393:60

States: many goodly s. and kingdoms 185:40

s. unborn and accents yet unknown 324:5

Statesman: a witty s. said 89:32

chymist, fiddler, s. and buffoon 126:43

speculative s., soldier, merchant 9:6

too nice for a s. 151:79

Statesmen: when s. ... say ... be realistic 22:59

Statistics: lies, damned lies, and s. 393:63

Statues: Epp's s. are junk 14:57

Status quo: restored the s. 378:55

Stay: and here I s. 202:51

without thee here to s. 221:2

wd. not s. for an answer 24:85

Stay-at-home: sweet s. 117:12

Steadily: saw life s. and ... whole 20:35

Steady, boys, steady 141:48

Steaks: smells of s. in passageways 131:7

Steal: cut loaf to s. a shive 357–8:63

shadows ... s. across the sky 28:56

s. from the world, and not a stone 251:29

thou shalt not s. 37:90

Stealing: not hanged for s. horses 157:56

picking and s. 64:98

s. and giving odour 358–9:75

wronging ... s., fighting 361:16

Steals: s. something from the thief 344:94

who s. my purse s. trash 345:6

Steed: his s. was the best 295:10

Steeds: Phoebus 'gins arise, his s. to water 304:20

Steel: clad in complete s. 212:76
    foeman bares his s., tarantara 148:32
    smoke and blood ... mix of s. 293:80
    to thy soul with hoops of s. 306:55

Steeples: spout till you have drench'd our s. 328:71

Steer: happily to s. from grave to gay 250:18
    our ... policy to s. clear 399:32
    s. too nigh the sands 126:39

Stein: wonderful family called S. 14:57

Step: a great s. to knowledge 123:97
    became ... bad in one s. 180:68

Stephen: Feast of S. 229:3

Stepmother: take heed of a s. 278:72

Stepney: say the bells of S. 236:61

Stepping-stones: on s. of their dead selves 386:57

Steps: heavy s. of the ploughman 417:55
    in his master's s. he trod 229:5
    invites my s. and points to yonder glade 248:72
    to these dark s. 221:11
    with how sad s., O Moon 373:85
    with wandering s. and slow 221:3

Stew in one's own juice 278:73

Stick: a riband to s. in his coat 74:28
    fling dirt ... some will s. 263:73
    I am a kind of burr; I shall s. 338:93

Sticking-place: courage to the s. 333:38

Sticks and stones may break my bones 278:74

Stiff: keep a s. upper lip 94:99
    s. in opinions, ... in the wrong 126:43

Stiffnecked: a s. people 37:95

Stile: merrily hent the s.-a 361:19
    sixpence against a crooked s. 239:74

Still: how s. we see thee lie 72:95
    mighty heart is lying s. 412:97
    sound of a voice that is s. 384:37
    Thou smilest and art s. 21:44

Stillness: air a solemn s. holds 155:31
    modest s. and humility 319:45
    soft s. and the night 340:22

Stimulate the phagocytes 365:71

Sting: death, where is thy s.? 57:60
    O Death! where is thy S.? 247:71
    s. is in the tail 278:78
    s. of a reproach ... truth of it 278:79
    where is death's s.? 201:33

Stings: armed in their s. 318:39

Stir: no s. of air was there 182:97

Stirring dull roots with spring rain 131:10

Stirrup: betwixt the s. and the ground 87:16
    I sprang to the s. 74:26

Stitch: a s. in time saves nine 278:81
    s.! s.! s.! 166:64

Stockings: commended the yellow s. 360:92

Stole: fause lover s. my rose 81:28
    I s. the Prince 143:71
    s. a pig and away he run 240:83

Stolen sweets are best 102:13

Stomach: an army marches on its s. 228:87
    have the ... s. ... of a King of England 132:20
    my s. is not good 380:81

Stone: heaviest s. ... the devil can throw 159:84
    kill two birds with one s. 268:34
    leave no s. unturned 269:68
    let him first cast a s. at her 55:3
    not a s. tell where I lie 251:29
    precious s. set in the silver sea 348:41
    rolling s. gathers no moss 276:1
    s. that lieth not in yr. way 278:82
    s. which the builders refused 44:35
    virtue is like a rich s. 26:27
    water like a s. 290:43
    we raised not a s. 408:53

Stones: in glass houses ... never throw s. 264:12
    inestimable s., unvalued jewels 352:72
    labour of an age in piled s. 216:23
    o, ye are men of s. 330:4
    sermons in s. 300:75
    you blocks, you s.! 323:89

Stools: between two s. one falls 256:34

Stop: Shelley ... did he s. and speak? 74:30
    s.; look; listen 395:78
    s. me and buy one 11:31
    time ... must have a s. 315:91
    when the kissing had to s. 76:48

Stopped: he [Death] kindly s. for me 122:44
    it s. short—never to go again 416:43

Stoppeth: he s. one of three 104:42

Store: oft amid thy s. 181:80
    s. of ladies, whose bright eyes 214:2

Storied windows richly dight 213:88

Stories: s. ... not to thy credit 87:15
    tell sad s. of the death of kings 350:54

Stretched: there was things ... he s. 393:59

when I s. out my hand 379:69

Strew: shall I s. ... rose or rue or laurel? 382:17

s. on her roses, roses 21:37

Strife: agonies, the s. of human hearts 185:37

ancient forms of party s. 386:69

are God and Nature ... at s. 386:62

books ... dull and endless s. 414:26

ignoble s. 155:39

in the s. of Truth with Falsehood 200:24

poverty breeds s. 275:53

Strike: no right to s. against the public safety 110:28

s. while the iron is hot 279:85

take heed ... thou s. not awry 226:67

String: chewing little bits of s. 31:90

harp not on that s. 352:81

provided ... s. to tie them together 225:57

strangling in a s. 167:80

untune that s. 358:68

Strings: the languid s. do scarcely move 68:55

there are s. in the human heart 119:32

Stripes: whose broad s. and bright stars 188:79

Strive: four champions fierce, s. here 218:57

s. to set the crooked straight? 227:71

Striving to better, mar what's well 328:59

Strode: out to Severn s. 99:72

Stroke: tune of flutes kept s. 298–9:54

Strong: be s. and of a good courage 38:18

but wants that little s. 164:47

out of the s. ... sweetness 39:27

s.-backed and neat-bound 192:30

we know ... that the wall is s. 404:97

we then that are s. 57:45

what will it help ... once you were s.? 70:72

Strove: a little still she s. 84:67

I s. with none 192:34

Struggle: manhood a s. 123:95

say not the s. naught availeth 103:32

Struggling for life in the water 174:78

Strumpet: transform'd into a s.'s fool 298:49

Struts: that s. and frets his hour 336:76

Stubble: chin ... show'd like a s. land 313:51

Stubble (*continued*)

he lies in the s. 12:42

Studies: s. serve for delight, for ornament 26:30

too much time in s. 26:31

Study: every Jack ... must s. the knack 149:50

his s. was but litel on the bible 97:37

I am slow of s. 341:41

much s. ... weariness of the flesh 47:13

proper s. of Mankind is Man 250:13

s. what you most affect 355:20

Stuff: ambition ... made of sterner s. 325:14

listen all day to such s. 90:49

'S. and nonsense!' said Alice 91:68

s. of life to knit me 167:83

such s. as dreams are made on 356–7:50

written such volumes of s.! 194:59

Stumble: they s. that run fast 354:7

Stupidity: confirm'd in full s. 128:69

no sin except s. 404:2

*Sturm und Drang* 191:18

Stygian: in S. cave forlorn 213–14:91

s. smoke of the pit 170:19

*Style: le s. est l'homme* 76:51

Style: s. is the man himself 76:51

true definition of a s. 381:3

Subdue: it [force] may s. for a moment 78:72

Subject: every s.'s duty ... soul 320:53

load every rift of yr. s. 187:69

poetry ... startle ... with its s. 186:54

s. to the same diseases 339:13

s. we old men are to ... lying 317:21

this s. for heroic song 220:90

Subjects: my s. for a pair of carved saints 350:55

poorest s. are at this hour asleep! 317:13

*Sublime: du s. au ridicule ... un pas* 228:84

Sublime: from the s. to the ridiculous 228:84

my object all s. 146:6

one step above the s. 243:19

s. and the ridiculous are ... related 243:19

we can make our lives s. 198:97

Sublimity: a S. to welcome me home 187:63

Submit: King do now? Must he s.? 350:55

Subscribers: he for s. baits his hook 100:84

not printing any list of s. 177:33

Substance of things hoped for 59:99
Subtlety is better than force 279:86
Succeed: if at first you don't s. 163:28
   those who ne'er s. 121:80
Succeeds: nothing s. like excess 406:31
   nothing s. like success 273:11
Success: s. and miscarriage are empty
   sounds 172:43
   s. is counted sweetest 121:80
   this ecstasy, is s. in life 244:29
   to command s. 9:4
   to make a marriage a s. 293:75
   true s. is to labour 380:80
   yours [religion] is S. 28:63
Sucked: I s. the blood 105:51
Sucker: a s. born every minute 28:58
Sucks: my baby ... s. the nurse asleep
   300:71
   where the bee s., there suck I 357:56
Sudden storms are short 348:40
Suddenly: shall s. come to his temple
   51:99
Sudetenland is the last ... claim 163:31
Sue: less used to s. than to command
   294:96
   we were not born to s. 347:31
Suez: somewhere East of Suez 190:8
Suffer: but doth s. a sea-change 355:35
   not s. a witch to live 37:94
   s. for the truth's sake 64:92
   s. me to come to thee 402:70
   s. the little children to come 54:61
   than one innocent s. 66:26
   ye s. fools gladly ... yourselves are
   wise 58:64
Sufferance is the badge of all our tribe
   338:6
Suffered: Lord Hippo s. fearful loss
   32:3
   love a place the less for having s.
   23:74
Suffering: been s., nothing but s. 23:74
Sufficiency: an elegant s., content
   391:34
Sufficient: s. conclusions from insufficient premises 82:44
   s. unto the day is the evil 52:22
Sugar: I must s. my hair 91:64
   s. and spice and all that's nice 240:85
Suggests: the word Intellectual s.
   22:61
Suit: silk s. ... cost me much money
   245:41
Sultry: more common where the
   climate's s. 84:66
Summer: a wind in s. 185:34
   after s., merrily, merrily 357:56
   all on a s.'s day 237:65

Summer (continued)
   bud of love by s.'s ripening breath
   354:3
   compare thee to a s.'s day 362:32
   dry as s. dust. 409:64
   eternal s. gilds them 84:77
   haunt of flies on s. eves 184:28
   I only know that s. sang in me
   210:47
   in their s. beauty kiss'd 352:79
   last rose of s. 226:63
   live murmur of a s.'s day 21:40
   on s. eves by haunted stream 214:3
   one swallow does not make a s.
   279:89
   s. and winter ... shall not cease
   35:48
   s. by this sun of York 351:64
   s. has o'er-brimm'd ... clammy cells
   181:79
   s. has set in with ... severity 107:81
   s. is icumen in 15:71
   s.'s lease ... too short a date 362:32
   s.'s velvet buds 318:39
   thinking on fantastic s.'s heat 348:37
   thy eternal s. shall not fade 362:33
   to ... men that sought him sweet as s.
   323:87
   warmed ... by the same ... s. 339:13
   with love in s.'s wonderland
   230–1:20
Summits: snowy s. old in story 388:97
Sun (see also Sonne): all, except their
   s., is set 84:77
   and I will sing of the s. 252:48
   at the going down of the s. 65:20
   before the rising s. 399:39
   between me and the s. 122:86
   birds are faint with the hot s. 185:42
   cannot make our s. stand still 206:96
   close to the s. in lonely lands 385:47
   dominions, on which the s. never
   sets 230:18
   early-rising s. has not attained
   162:18
   eyes are nothing like the s. 364:52
   far from the s. and summer-gale
   156:44
   follow the fair s. 88:23
   furnish'd ... by Aldershot s. 34:25
   glory of the s. will be dimmed 27:48
   go out in the midday s. 112:42
   hath Britain all the s.? 304:25
   I am too much in the s. 305:39
   I gin to be aweary of the s. 336:77
   just as the s. was rising 16:80
   late eclipses in the s. and moon
   327:52

Sun (*continued*)

light ... dies with the dying s. 69:70

light ... where no s. shines 390:21

love that moves the s. 117:4

loves to live i' th' s. 301:85

make guilty ... the s. 327:53

make hay while the s. shines 271:27

Mother, give me the s. 169:10

never shall s. that morrow see 333:34

no new thing under the s. 46:96

now the s. is laid to sleep 178:50

self-same s. that shines 362:23

she grew in s. and shower 415:30

so when the s. in bed 216:22

s. breaks through the darkest clouds 355:25

s. came up upon the left 104:44

s. climbs slow, how slowly 104:34

s. go down upon your wrath 58:71

s. shines upon all alike 279:87

S., stand thou still 38:20

s. that warms you ... shine on me 348:33

s. was shining on the sea 92:76

thank heavens, the s. has gone in 374:4

the chambers of the s. 68:54

the maturing s. 180:78

the rising of the s. 16–17:87

the s. is lost, and th' earth 123:3

the s. of righteousness arise 51:1

the s. shall not smite thee 44:38

this s. of York 351:64

to have enjoy'd the s. 20:31

white founts ... in the Courts of the s. 99:70

with the setting s. dropped from the zenith 217:44

Sunday: golf may be played on S. 194:52

here of a S. morning 167:82

killing ... mouse on S. 70:74

shot through his heart on S. 379:71

S. clears away the rust 9:7

Sunk: all s. beneath the wave 113:64

Sunless: down to a s. sea 106:71

Sunny Jim: they called him S. 157:60

Sunny pleasure-dome 107:75

Sunrise: in eternity's s. 66:34

Suns: blest by s. of home 71:93

Sunset: s. and evening star 385:44

s. ran, one glorious blood-red 74:24

Sunshine: no s. but has some shadow 273:2

the s. is a glorious birth 410:74

Sup: who sipped no s. 148–9:46

Supercilious: a s. knowledge in accounts 371:70

Superfluity of good things 11:21

Superfluous: in the poorest thing s. 328:67

Superior: revolt ... that they may be s. 20:27

Superiority: one shall acquire an evident s. 175:96

Superstition is the religion of feeble minds 78:80

Superstitions: new truths ... end as s. 169:6

Supper: hope is ... a bad s. 26:38

sings for his s. 235:52

to s. with a flood of tears 119:39

Support: help the feeble ... s. him after 357:59

Sure: his mercy is for ever s. 188:78

s. way to see it lost ... last ditch 79:90

Surfeit: feast ... where no crude s. reigns 213:77

Surfeit-swelled: so s., so old 318:34

Surfeiting: give me excess ... that s. 358:75

Surfeits: the s. of our own behaviour 327:53

Surgery: honour hath no skill in s. 315:88

Surmise: with a wild s. 185:41

Surprise: poetry shd. s. by a fine excess 186:55

Surprised by joy ... I turned 411:91

Surrender: unconditional and immediate s. 153:15

we shall never s. 100–101:94

Survey: monarch of all I s. 114:77

time that takes s. 315:91

Survival: s. of the fittest 117:8, 376:34

without victory there is no s. 100:93

Survive: but one ... Noah dare hope to s. 169:4

Suspects: man s. himself a fool 418:63

Suspension: willing s. of disbelief 107:79

Suspicion: Caesar's wife ... above s. 87:10

s. ... haunts the guilty mind 322:72

Suspicions amongst thoughts ... bats amongst birds 26:23

Sussex: and the story of S. told 32:6

there shall the S. songs be sung 32:6

Swagman: jolly s. camped by a billabong 244:30

Swain: no better than a homely s. 321:70

Swains: all our s. commend her 361:8

Swallow: hope ... flies with s.'s wings 352:83
  one s. does not make a summer 279:89
Swallows: gathering s. twitter 181:82
  whitethroat builds and all the s. 74:22
Swan: Sweet S. of Avon 179:58
Swanee Ribber: 'way down upon de S. 138:5
Swans: all his geese are s. 264:4
  seven s. a-swimming 238:73
  s. sing before they die 106:70
Swap horses in mid-stream 196:80
Swat: Akond of S. 194:54
Sway: mercy is above this sceptred s. 339:15
  regions ... thy posterity shall s. 112:50
  truth ... prevailed with double s. 150:67
Swear: s. me, Kate, like a lady 314:76
  when very angry s. 394:71
Sweat: blood, toil, tears and s. 100:92
  in the s. of thy face 35:38
  none will s. but for promotion 300:79
  s. for duty not for meed 300:79
Sweating: quietly s. palm to palm 169:5
Sweats: Falstaff s. to death 313:59
Sweep on, you fat and greasy citizens 300:76
Sweet: a lady s. and kind 18:9
  and s. girl-graduates 388:95
  back to the great s. mother 383:25
  both s. things ... all s. things 69:65
  but then, how it was s.! 73:20
  by any other name wd. smell as s. 353:1
  deserves not the s. 260:69
  each op'ning s. of earliest bloom 107:87
  how sour s. music is! 351:63
  how s. and fair she seems to be 398:17
  how s. the moonlight sleeps 340:22
  how s. their memory still 113:62
  law beyond its own s. will 403:88
  little s. ... kill much bitterness 182:4
  love is s. for a day 383:23
  love is s., given or returned 369:44
  naught so s. as Melancholy 81:29
  revenge is s. 276:89
  sessions of s. silent thought 362:37
  sleep of labouring man is s. 46:2
  stolen waters are s. 45:60
  s. as love 384:30

Sweet (*continued*)
  s. breathing Zephyrus did ... play 377:46
  s. is pleasure after pain 127:53
  s. is revenge – especially to women 84:68
  s. Little Buttercup I 146–7:20
  s. singing in the choir 16–17:87
  s. Stay-at-Home, s. Well-content 117:12
  s. Thames! run softly 377:47
  s. to look into ... face of heaven 186:47
  s. to taste ... indigestion sour 348:35
  swing low, s. chariot 18:8
  the s. o' the year 361:17
  to have a s. tooth 279:91
  when you speak, s. 362:21
  you'll look s. upon the seat 116:99
Sweet and twenty: kiss me, s. 359:84
Sweet-briar: through the s. or the vine 214:97
Sweeten: children s. labours 24:95
  civet ... to s. my imagination 329:91
  perfumes of Arabia will not s. 335:69
Sweeter: anything to me is s. 164:42
  s. manners, purer laws 386:69
  s. than the berry 141:51
Sweetest: last taste of sweets is s. last 348:39
  s. li'l feller 378:58
  s. thing that ever grew 411:86
Sweethearts: old soldiers, s., are surest 400:52
Sweeting: trip no further, pretty s. 359:83
Sweetly flows that liquefaction 162:23
Sweetness: out of the strong came forth s. 39:27
  passion for s. and light 21:52
  pursuit of s. and light 21:47
  two noblest things ... s. and light 381:95
  waste its s. on the desert air 155:37
Sweets: as the last taste of s., is sweetest last 348:39
  perpetual feast of nectared s. 213:77
  stolen s. are best 102:13
  s. and a ride in the train 211:58
  s. to the sweet; farewell! 312:33
Swept: if seven maids ... s. it 92:79
Swift: Cousin S., you will never be a poet 128:67
  too s. ... as tardy as too slow 354:10
Swifter than eagles ... stronger than lions 40:48

Swim: a naughty night to s. in 329:80
but said I cd. not s. 91:67
Swine: nor yet feed the s. 231–2:27
pearls before s. 52:24
s., women and bees cannot be turned
279:92
Swing low, sweet chariot 18:8
Swoon: at twelve noon the natives s.
112:42
Swoons: wearied band s. to a waltz
169:5
Swop for my dear old Dutch 99:80
Sword: a Sigh is the s. of an angel king
66:35
believed he had a s. upstairs 417:51
his father's s. ... girded on 226:64
I with s. will open 340:30
is the s. unsway'd? 352:82
man for the s. 389:2
more cruel the pen ... than ... s.
81:30
nor shall my s. sleep 67:38
nor the deputed s. 337:84
pen is mightier than the s. 76:54
Swords: beat ... s. into plowshares
48:31
with paper hats and wooden s.
395:81
Swore: Frankie and Johnny ... s. to be
true 16:81
Swound: like noises in a s. 105:46
Syllable: last s. of recorded time
336:76
Symmetry: frame thy fearful s. 68:46
spoilers of the s. of shelves 192:26
Sympathize: the Walrus said: 'I
deeply s.' 93:81
s. with ... pains ... not ... pleasures
169:1
Sympathy: without feeling or exciting
s. 173:66
System: energies of our s. will decay
27:48
Systems: our little s. have their day
386:56

Ta-ra-ra-boom-de-ay 294:84
Table: crumbs ... from the rich man's
t. 55:86
Tables: to turn the t. 281:69
Tabor: as to the t.'s sound 410:75
Tail: better ... than the t. of a lion
255:20
he's treading on my t. 91:62
improve his shining t. 89:45
sting is in the t. 278:78
such a little t. behind 31:89
thereby hangs a t. 345:4

Tails: and bring their t. behind them
234:48
cut off their t. with a carving knife
240:80
frogs and snails and puppy-dogs' t.
240:85
stings in their t. 61:29
t. like unto scorpions 61:29
Take: t. a farthing away 279:93
t. any man's horses 318:33
t. away my good name 279:95
Taken: when t. to be well shaken
108:95
Takes: a man who shaves and t. a train
402:77
blesseth ... him that t. 339:15
Talcum: a bit of t. is always walcum
229:94
Tale: a round unvarnish'd t. 344:91
an honest t. speeds best 352:80
cd. ever hear by t. or history 341:36
every shepherd tells his t. 214:98
every t. condemns me 353:86
every tongue brings in a ... t. 353:86
had we lived, I shd. have had a t.
294:91
I cd. a t. unfold 307:64
it is a t. told by an idiot 336:76
point a moral, or adorn a t. 174:69
sad t.'s best for winter 361:13
t. which holdeth children from play
327:41
tedious as a twice-told t. 327:41
thereby hangs a t. 301:88, 355:23
with a t. forsooth he cometh 373:86
yr. t., sir, wd. cure deafness 355:50
Talent: one t. which is death to hide
223:29
t. does what it can 209:37
t. of flattering with delicacy 23:78
Talents: if you have great t. 287:6
Tales: and tell old t., and laugh
330:99
dead men tell no t. 259:57
natural fear ... increased with t.
24:86
tell t. out of school 279:4
Talk: Cabots t. only to God 69:67
I dont want to t. grammar 366:94
I want to t. like a lady 366:94
make little fishes t. ... t. like whales
152:4
some t. of Alexander 18:6
t. of censorious old men 94:3
t. of court news ... t. with them
330:99
t. of many things 93:80
t. of the devil 279:6

Tears (continued)
tired of t. and laughter  382:19
watered heaven with ... t.  68:47
wipe away all t.  61:34
with mine own t. I wash away my
balm  350–1:58
Teases: he knows it t.  90:51
Tedious: people are ... charming or t.
405:18
returning were as t. as go o'er  335:57
scandal is gossip made t.  406:20
t. as a twice-told tale  327:41
thinking his prattle to be t.  351:61
Teeth: bid them ... keep their t. clean
303:14
by the skin of one's t.  277:43
children's t. are set on edge  49:58
escaped with the skin of my t.  41:71
sparkling eyes, and t. like pearls
75:43
Teetotaller: I'm only a beer t.  365:68
Tell: I can t. you anyhow  77:69
I cannot t. what you ... think  323:91
never seek to t. thy love  67:40
our dead bodies must t. the tale
294:91
t. it not in Gath  40:47
t. me not, in mournful numbers
198:95
t. me not, sweet, I am unkind  199:16
t. me what she sings?  414:21
t. thee what thou art  95:12
to dream of, not to t.  106:66
when or how I cannot t.  291:53
Telling: not arguing ... I am t. you
402:75
Temper: I shall t. ... justice with mercy
220:95
keep me in t.; I wd. not be mad!
328:60
man of such a feeble t.  323:92
Temperance hotels: I prefer t.  399:28
Temperate: more lovely and more t.
362:32
Tempered by war, disciplined by ...
peace  188:74
Tempers: God t. the wind  379:68
Tempests: looks on t. and is never
shaken  363:47
Temple: shall suddenly come to his t.
51:99
Temples: for ... the t. of his gods
201:36
mortal t. of a king  350:54
solemn t., the great globe itself
356:50
Tempora: O t.! O mores!  102:19
t. mutantur et nos mutamur  19:21

Temporary: use of force alone is but t.
78:72
Tempt: t. me no more  117:15
to t. my Lady Poltagrue  31:96
Temptation: can resist everything except t.  405:19
lead us not into t.  52:18
maximum of t. ... of opportunity
366:89
not over-fond of resisting t.  30:77
prepare thy soul for t.  62:46
the last t. is the greatest treason
132:17
watch ... that ye enter not into t.
53:50
way to get rid of a t.  406:24
Tempted: My Lady, t. by a ... whim
31:96
one thing to be t., Escalus  337:81
to his ... annoyance t. him  31:96
Tempts: all that t. yr. wand'ring eyes
154:26
Tempus: fugit ... inreparabile t.  397:6
t. edax rerum  243:14
t. fugit  280:18
Ten: as the strength of t.  389:3
better that t. guilty ... escape  66:26
t. to make ... match to win  230:13
Tender is the night  184:26
Tenderly: take her up t.  165:56
Tenders: a shoal of fools for t.
109:10
Tenement: o'r informed the T. of clay
126:39
Tennis: we are ... the star's t. balls
400:51
Ten-sixty-six and All That  297:27
Tenterhooks: to be on t.  280:19
Tent-royal of their emperor  318:39
Terminological: some risk of t. in-
exactitude  100:88
Terms: fair t. and a villain's mind
339:7
Terrible as an army with banners
47:26
Territorial: last t. claim ... in Europe
163:31
Terror: so full of dismal t. was the
time  351–2:71
victory in spite of all t.  100:93
Test: source, and end, and t. of Art
249:92
Text: of that t. a pulled hen  96:29
Thais: lovely T. by his side  127:50
Thames: every drop of the T. is liquid
history  79:94
set the T. on fire  277:29
sweet T.! run softly  377:47

Thought: an holy and a good t. 63:65
  best that is known and t. 21:50
  every third t. ... my grave 357:58
  evil is wrought by want of T. 165:62
  green t. in a green shade 206:99
  he t. I t. he t. I slept 244:31
  I t. so little 147:27
  learning without t. ... t. without
    learning 108:4
  never t. of thinking for myself
    147:27
  oft was t., but ne'er so well express'd
    249:97
  pale cast of t. 309:95
  sessions of sweet silent t. 362:37
  sweetest songs ... tell of saddest t.
    370:50
  t. does not become a young woman
    371:65
  t. is free 280:31
  to have loved ... t. ... done 20:31
  two lads that t. ... no more behind
    361:12
  two souls with but a single t. 200:18
  use t. ... to justify ... wrong-doing
    397:10
  use ... words ... to conceal ... t.
    397:10
  whose armour ... honest t. 416:48
  wish was father ... to that t. 318:29
Thoughtless: the hour of t. youth
  415:35
Thoughts: give thy t. no tongue 306:55
  in t. more elevate 218:55
  lift the t. of man 185:39
  my t. are not yr. t. 48:51
  my t. remain below 311:16
  pansies, that's for t. 311:28
  penny for yr. t. 274:36
  second t. are best 277:21
  Sensations rather than of T.I 186:51
  speech was given ... to disguise his t.
    384:32
  suspicions among t. are like bats
    26:23
  t. of a dry brain 130:93
  t. that wander through eternity
    217:49
  t. ... too deep for tears 411:82
  thy t., when thou art gone 370:54
  turns to t. of love 387:79
  what fond and wayward t. 414:24
  when pleasant t. bring sad t. 411:83
  wording of his own highest t. 186:55
  words without t. never to heaven go
    311:16
Thousand: a race, 'tis for a t. pound
  113:57

Thousand (*continued*)
  a t. ages in thy sight 399:39
  a t. lost golf balls 131:8
  a t. t. slimy things 105:55
  a t. years as one day 60:14
  a t. years in thy sight 43:16
  after t. aves told 182:92
  difference of forty t. men 401:58
  face that launch'd a t. ships 204:63
  give me a t. kisses 94:4
  heart-ache ... t. natural shocks
    309:95
  here's twenty t. Cornish men
    158–9:74
  I heard a t. blended notes 411:83
  I, in twelve t., none 350:57
  if I had five t. a year 389:15
  laugh broke into a t. pieces 28:59
  more than sixscore t. 50:88
  my conscience hath a t. ... tongues
    353:86
  night has a t. eyes 69:70
  O that we now had ... ten t. of those
    men 320:54
  of many t. kisses the poor last
    299:65
  one day ... as a t. years 60:14
  one man ... out of ten t. 308:76
  Shallow, I owe you a t. pound
    318:35
  take a farthing ... from a t. pounds
    279:93
  ten t. saw I at a glance 410:69
  the t. creeds 71:85
  the t. years of peace 386:70
  t. fearful wrecks, a t. men 352:72
  used to sing it—fifty t. strong 416:44
  what a t. pities ... that Adam 165:63
  will you give ... t. guilders? 75:39
  Yesterday's Sev'n T. Years 135:69
Thousands: has been slave to t. 345:6
  Jesu ... the t. He hath freed 95:18
  makes countless t. mourn 80:14
  slain his t. ... his ten t. 39:44
  t. at his bidding speed 223:30
  where t. equally were meant 381:97
Threadneedle Street: the old lady of T.
  280:33
Threaten: you t. us, fellow? 75:42
Threatened men live long 280:34
Three: a t.-pipe problem 124:19
  actors are ... the usual t. 209:32
  all Gaul ... in t. parts 87:6
  Church clock at ten to t. 71:91
  going on ... for t. hundred years
    406:26
  handsome in t. hundred pounds a
    year 341:32

Time (*continued*)

bid t. return  349:51

busiest man who has t. to spare 244:25

but a short t. to live  65:13

conspiracy his t. doth take  356:39

cormorant devouring T.  331:8

creeping hours of t.  301:89

dark backward and abysm of t. 355:29

did those feet in ancient t.  67:38

dust on antique t.  303:15

fixed figure for the t. of scorn  346:13

fleet the t. carelessly  300:72

fly envious T.  223:34

fool all the people all the t.  197:82

footprints in the sands of t.  198:97

friends are thieves of t.  264:95

full of dismal terror was the t. 351-2:71

greatest part of a writer's t.  176:11

half as old as t.  77:70

happiness takes no account of t. 266:62

he hath shook hands with t.  137:92

how long a t. lies in one ... word 348:34

I had liv'd a blessed t.  334:46

in t. all haggard hawks  191:22

in t. small wedges cleave  191:22

in t. the flint is pierced  191:22

in t. the savage bull  191:22

inaudible and noiseless foot of T. 298:48

just going outside ... may be some t. 241:93

life, t.'s fool  315:91

look into the seeds of t.  333:27

many a t. and oft  338:5

never the t. and the place  74:31

new wail my dear t.'s waste  362:37

no t. like the present  280:41

no t. to stand and stare  117:11

not of an age but for all t.!  179:57

nothing is ours but t.  273:8

old in hours if he have lost no t. 26:26

old t. is still a-flying  162:24

panting t. toiled after him  173:58

patience, money and t.  274:30

remember that t. is money  138:10

repeat how T. is slipping  135:74

seen better faces in my t.  328:62

sent before my t. into this ... world 351:66

such is T. that takes in trust  286:93

that passed the t. It wd. have passed 30:75

Time (*continued*)

that t. may cease, and midnight 204:65

the Bird of T. has but a little way 135:66

the holy t. is quiet as a nun  412:92

the last syllable of recorded t.  336:76

the show and gaze o' th' t.  336:79

'the t. has come,' the Walrus said 93:80

the t. is out of joint  307:71

the t. of our Ford  168:97

the t. will come ... you will hear me 122:88

thief of t.  418:62

this bloody tyrant T.  362:31

T. ambles ... trots ... gallops  302:98

t. and chance happeneth to ... all 47:8

t. and the hour  333:29

t. and thinking tame ... grief  280:38

t. and tide wait for no man  280:39

t. enough to think of the future 366:95

t. flies  280:18

t. future contained in t. past  130:90

t. hath ... a wallet  358:71

t. is broke and no proportion kept 351:63

t. is flying  397:6

t. is on our side  149:51

t. is the greatest innovator  26:17

t., like an ever-rolling stream  400:40

t. ... man is always trying to kill 376:31

t. ... must have a stop  315:91

t. of life is short  315:89

t. of the singing of birds  47:22

t. present and t. past are both  130:90

t. spent on any item of the agenda 244:26

T., ... subtle thief of youth  223:28

t. that takes survey of all the world 315:91

t., the devourer of things  243:14

T. travels in divers paces  302:98

t. was away and somewhere else 203:57

t. will not be ours for ever  179:61

t. will run back  215:21

t., with a gift of tears  382:16

T., you old gypsy man  163:37

T.'s winged chariot  206:94

to choose t. is to save t.  26:18

too much t. in studies is sloth  26:31

want to know the t., ask a P'liceman 288:22

whips and scorns of t.  309:95

Tom (*continued*)
T. went howling down the street 240:83
Tom o' Bedlam: a sigh like T.   327:54
Tom Pearse, lend me yr. grey mare 19:12
Tomb: for such a t. wd. wish to die 216:25
monument without a t.   179:54
Tommy: it's T. this, an' T. that   190:11
little T. Stout   232:28
little T. Tucker   235:52
Tom-tit: a little t. sang 'Willow' 146:12
Tomorrow: can say, T. do thy worst 128:71
egg today ... hen t.   255:13
hour today is worth two t.   267:4
never put off till t.   273:85
same flower ... t. will be dying 162:24
such a day t. as today   361:12
think today and speak t.   280:26
t. and t. creeps in this petty pace 336:76
t. blossoms ... bears his blushing honours   322:80
t. is a new day   280:44
t. is our wedding day   113:55
t. never comes   280:43
t. we'll be sober   16:78
T.!—Why, T. I may be   135:69
unborn T. and dead Yesterday 135:74
Tomorrows: one today is worth two t. 280:42
Tone: take the t. of the company 98:57
that t. and gesture bland   294:96
Tongs: the t. and the bones   342:51
touch him with a pair of t.   280:51
Tongue: an understanding, but no t. 306:51
breast forges ... t. must vent 303–4:17
customs, politics and t.   245:32
every t. brings in a ... tale   353:86
eye, t., sword   310:1
fellows of infinite t.   321:61
give thy thoughts no t.   306:55
iron t. of midnight   342:55
keep one's t. between one's teeth 268:29
keep wel thy t. ... keep thy freend 97:49
no venom to that of the t.   282:91
one t. is enough for a woman   280:45
our English t. a gallimaufry   377:48

Tongue (*continued*)
sad words of t. or pen   403:90
sharp t. ... edged tool ... grows keener   170:17
though his t. dropped manna   217:48
t. can no man tame   60:5
t. cleave to ... roof of my mouth 44:49
t. is not steel ... it cuts   280:46
t. of idle people   280:47
t. sounds ... as a sullen bell   316:97
t. that Shakespeare spake   413:5
use of my oracular t.   372:71
virtue dwells not in the t.   282:93
Tongues: conscience ... thousand several t.   353:86
done to death by slanderous t. 344:88
finds t. in trees   300:75
lack t. to praise   363:46
silver-sweet ... lovers' t. by night 354:5
these poor t. ... shall be silent   196:76
Tonight: along the Potomac t.   30:84
t. we'll merry be   16:78
Too: this t., t. solid flesh   305:42
t. nice ... t. proud ... cool ... fond 151:79
Tool: man is a t.-making animal 139:17
sharp tongue ... edged t. ... grows keener   170:17
Tools: bad workman quarrels with his t.   255:88
give us the t. ... finish the job 101:98
t. to work ... for those who will 200:22
Tooth: a t. for a t.   52:12
Nature, red in t. and claw   386:63
sharper than a serpent's t.   328:58
t. to t., hand for hand   37:93
to have a sweet t.   279:91
thy t. is not so keen   302:91
Toothache: endure the t. patiently 344:86
Top: always room at the t.   400:46
I shall die at the t.   382:13
sleep like a t.   117:9
t. of it reached to heaven   36:61
T. People take *The Times*   11:33
Topical: sang a most t. song   13:53
Topics: high life ... other fashionable t. 152:1
Tops: mountain t. that freeze   322:77
t. were close against the sky   165:61
Topses: herring boxes without t. 225:60

Topsy: persisted T., 'never had no father' 380:84

Torch: a bright t. and a casement 185:33

t. ... passed to a new generation 188:74

Torches: doth teach the t. to burn bright 353:94

Tories own no argument but force 72:8

Torment: love in a palace ... grievous t. 183:11

there shall no t. touch them 62:43

Torments: our t. ... may ... become our elements 217:51

Torn: man all tattered and t. 239:79

Tortoise: why did you call him T.? 91:59

Torture: touch him not and t. not again 367:16

Tory ... with more propriety ... the Conservative 115:87

Tossed: you t. and gored several persons 175:97

Tossing their heads in sprightly dance 410:69

Totter: charming to t. into vogue 398:22

Totters: the state t. 356:45

Touch: men t. them and change 382:18

O for the t. of a vanish'd hand 384:37

one t. of nature 358:72

that I might t. that cheek 353:98

t. him with a pair of tongs 280:51

t. not, taste not, handle not 59:81

t. wood 280:52

unkind as the t. of sweating metal 117:14

Touching: a sight so t. in its majesty 412:96

Toujours gai archy 205:84

*Tous pour un, un pour tous* 129:74

*Tout passe, t. casse, t. lasse* 281:53

Toves: the slithy t. 91:69

Tower: fall'n ... that t. of strength 388:93

King's name is a t. of strength 353:84

to the dark t. came 329:82

yonder ivy-mantled t. 155:32

Towers: burnt the topless t. of Ilium? 204:63

cloud-capp'd t., ... gorgeous palaces 356:50

Town: a tavern in the t. 19:10

in Scarlet t., where I was born 12:36

Town (*continued*)

King sits in Dunfermline t. 12:37

lived in a pretty how t. 116:94

O little t. of Bethlehem 72:95

spring, moonless night ... small t. 390:23

t. ... is lighter than vanity 77:60

Town-crier: as lief the t. spoke 310:3

Toy: foolish thing was but a t. 360:3

I count religion ... childish t. 204:69

Toys: all is but t. 334:46

Trace: learned to t. the day's disasters 150:68

Traces: hounds of spring are on winter's t. 382:15

Trade: and now there isn't any t. 161:8

every t. save censure 85:90

half a t. and half an art 170:12

homely, slighted, shepherd's t. 215:11

no nation was ever ruined by t. 138:11

others ... venture t. abroad 318:39

where the old t.'s plying 230:12

Tradesmen: bow, ye t., bow, ye masses 143:80

lying ... becomes none but t. 362:26

Tradition: t. approves all forms of competition 103:30

youth of America ... oldest t. 406:26

Traduced: beat a Venetian and t. the state 346–7:22

Trafalgar Square fountains like Government Clerks 285:78

Traffic: the two hours' t. of our stage 353:89

Tragedies: all t. are finished by a death 84:75

there are two t. in life 365:83

Tragedy: go litel myn t. 98:52

t. is ... a certeyn storie 97:47

world ... a t. to those who feel 398:23

Tragical-historical, t.-comical-historical- 308:84

Trail: long, long t. a-winding 189:84

Train: a man who shaves and takes a t. 402:77

something ... to read in the t. 405:14

Train-band: a t. captain eke was he 112:54

Training is everything 394:69

Traitor: thou art a t. Off with his head! 352:75

Traitors: cowards flinch, and t. jeer 109–10:21

translators, t. 281:54

Tram: not even a bus, but a t. 158:68

Tranquillity: dismiss it with frigid t. 172:43

    emotion recollected in t. 416:42

    t.! thou better name 107:78

Translated: Bottom! ... thou art t. 342:49

Translators, traitors 281:54

Transport: I turned to share the t. 411:91

Trapeze: daring young man on ... t. 196:71

Trappings and the suits of woe 305:41

Trash: who steals my purse steals t. 345:6

Travel: does not t. to see Englishmen 379:65

    farther from the east must t. 411:78

    I never t. without my diary 405:14

    I t. light ... as a man can t. 140:31

    to t. hopefully is a better thing 380:80

    t. ... part of education ... of experience 25:12

Travelled: I t. among unknown men 409:66

    much have I t. 185:40

Traveller: a t., by the faithful hound 198:94

    a t. came by 67:41

    a t. from an antique land 369:39

    'anybody there?' said the T. 118:23

    from whose bourne no t. returns 309:95

Travellers: t. must be content 300:81

    t. ne'er did lie 356:48

Travelling: all t. becomes dull 291:59

Travels: fool wanders, the wise man t. 263:81

    t. far, knows much 281:55

Treachery: kings that fear ... t.? 322:71

Treacle: cloying t. to the wings of independence 187:66

Tread: fiend doth close behind him t. 106:60

Treading on my tail 91:62

Treason: during his office, t. was no crime 126:46

    gunpowder t. and plot 15:69

    if it prosper, none dare call it t. 158:70

    last temptation ... greatest t. 132:17

    love grows bitter with t. 383:23

    pay given to ... hireling for t. 172:50

    t. doth never prosper 158:70

Treasons: fit for t., stratagems and spoils 340:24

Treasure: Bacchus' Blessings are a t. 127:53

    justice, counsel, and t. 25:7

    preserve it as yr. chiefest t. 31:88

    privilege ... we t. beyond measure 143:76

    purest t. mortal times afford 347:30

    rich the t., sweet the pleasure 127:53

Treat: something left to t. my friends 203:59

Treaty: hand that signed the t. 390:20

Treble: turning again toward childish t. 301:90

Tree: and on the T. of Life ... sat 219:64

    as the twig is bent the t.'s inclined 251:22

    bark up the wrong t. 255:94

    billboard lovely as a t. 229:97

    ever-green t. of diabolical knowledge 371:68

    fool sees not the same t. 69:60

    forbidden t., whose mortal taste 216:27

    I had a little nut t. 233:39

    I shall be like that t. 382:13

    I'll never see a t. at all 229:97

    middle t. and highest three 219:64

    on a t. by a river 146:12

    only God can make a t. 189:82

    poem lovely as a t. 188:81

    round the elm-t. bole 74:21

    this t. continues to be 191:20

    t. is known by its fruit 281:57

    under the greenwood t. 300:83

Trees: all the t. were bread and cheese 15:65

    amid their tall ancestral t. 160:9

    and all the t. are green 189:88

    beside the lake, beneath the t. 410:67

    birds ... hide in cooling t. 185:42

    climbing t. ... they do best 210:51

    finds tongues in t. 300:75

    great t. ... nothing but shade 265:45

    my apple t. will never ... eat 139:26

    procreate like t. 72:5

    see the wood for the t. 277:23

    straight t. have crooked roots 279:84

    the fir t. dark and high 165:61

    t. ... bow themselves when he did sing 322:77

    t. where you sit 251:32

    with rocks, and stones, and t. 414:19

Trelawny: and shall T. die? 158:74

Tremblers: boding t. learned to trace 150:68

Trust (*continued*)

failing to t. everybody ... t. nobody 262:43

men dare t. themselves with men 357:60

never t. a woman who tells one her real age 406:29

none that put ... t. in him 63:63

put not your t. in princes 44:53

some t. in chariots 42:90

though he slay me yet will I t. 41:68

t. God: see all 75–6:46

t. not a new friend ... old enemy 281:60

under his wings shalt thou t. 43:19

Truth: a melancholy t. ... poor relations 119:35

beauty is t., t. beauty 183:20

constantly speak the t. 64:92

error ... highly heap'd for t. to o'erpeer 303:15

found t. in all but one 350:57

great is T., and mighty 61:37

greater the t., the greater the libel 265:46

habit ... all the test of t. 114:79

he is less remote from the t. 171:32

his t. at all times firmly stood 188:78

however improbable ... the t. 125:25

it is a t. universally acknowledged 23:75

love swears that she is made of t. 364:54

mainly he told the t. 393:59

mathematics possesses not only t. 292:67

my way of joking ... tell the t. 365:75

nowadays t. ... greatest news 273:14

one t. is clear 250:12

patiently suffer for the t.'s sake 64:92

Pilate saith ... What is t.? 56:12

Plato is dear ... dearer still is t. 20:28

simple t. his utmost skill 416:48

single hast maintained ... the cause of t. 219:82

so few enthusiasts ... speak the t. 27:49

speaking nothing but the t. 405:16

strife of T. with Falsehood 200:24

takes two to speak the t. 391:39

tell the t. and shame the devil 279:16

the t. is rarely pure 405:5

the unclouded face of t. 294:88

T. beareth away the victory 61:36

t. comes out in wine 247:65

Truth (*continued*)

t. fears no colours 281:61

t. from his lips prevailed 150:67

t. has such a face 127:61

t. in every shepherd's tongue 286:96

t. in masquerade 85:82

t. is always strange 85:87

t. is stranger than fiction 281:62

t. is the daughter of God 281:63

t. never grows old 281:64

t. of Imagination 186:50

t. sits upon the lips of dying men 21:45

t. ... told with bad intent 66:29

what is t.? said jesting Pilate 24:85

who ever knew T. put to the worse 224:45

whole t. and nothing but the t. 281:65

wine in, t. out 283:37

Tulip: not number the streaks of the t. 173:63

Tune: all the t. that he cd. play 240:82

Cassio kill'd! ... murder's out of t. 346:20

Heaven tries earth if it be in t. 200:25

pays the piper ... call the t. 274:33

sweetly played in t. 81:21

to the t. of flutes kept stroke 298–9:54

Tunes: devil shd. have all the good t. 163:29

weight of Cathedral t. 122:83

Tupman: Mr T. 121:65

Turbulent: free me of this t. priest? 160:99

Sagacious, Bold, and T. of wit 126:38

Turk: a malignant and a turban'd T. 346–7:22

French, or T., or Proosian 147:30

Turks: peace shall go sleep with T. 350:56

Turn: fortune ... t. thy wheel 328:63

let not each gay t. ... move 249:1

one good t. deserves another 265:36

person t. in his grave 281:67

tread on a worm ... will t. 281:56

t. an honest penny 281:66

t. over a new leaf 281:68

t. the tables 281:69

t. to God to praise and pray 74:25

t. up one's nose 281:70

t. up trumps 281:71

Turned: having once t. round walks on 106:60

'in case anything t. up' 119:39

Turnips: if the man who t. cries 172:56

Unburied: bodies of u. men 400:54

Uncertain: u., coy, and hard to please 296:14

u. glory of an April day 361:6

Uncharitableness: envy, hatred, ... and all u. 63:77

Uncle: my prophetic soul! My u.! 307:67

u. me no u. 349:45

Uncle Toby: our armies swore ... cried my U. 379:70

Uncle Tom Cobbleigh and all 19:12

Unclubbable: a very u. man 175:93

Uncomely: all things u. and broken 417:55

Uncomfortable: thinks he is moral ... is only u. 365:82

we u. feel 148:32

Uncommon: the thing that's most u. 251:31

Unconfined: let joy be u. 83:60

Unconscionable time dying 96:20

Uncover, dogs, and lap 357:61

Under-belly: the soft u. of the Axis 101:4

Underlings: fault ... in ourselves that we are u. 323–4:93

Underneath are the everlasting arms 38:17

Underpaying: better than the u. instinct 364:67

Underrate ... the duty of being happy 379:79

Understand: a man will ne'er quite u. 245:32

I u. thy kisses, and thou mine 314:75

no one can u. Ein 14:57

one half ... world cannot u. 23:65

Understanding: brute beasts that have no u. 64:4

Donne's verses ... pass all u. 170:20

give it an u., but no tongue 306:51

light a candle of u. 61:38

peace of God, which passeth all u. 58:78

Undeserver may sleep 317:12

Undeserving: Im one of the u. poor 366:96

Undo: pray you u. this button 331:6

Undone: u. those things which we ought to have done 63:67

what's done cannot be u. 335:70

wish th' estate of th' world were now u. 336:77

Uneasy: this swift business I must u. make 356:36

u. lies the head that wears a crown 317:14

Uneatable: in full pursuit of the u. 406:27

Unexpected: moment foreseen may be u. 132:18

the u. ... always happens 282:87

Unfaithful: faith u. ... falsely true 385:50

Unfit: worse man ... u. for the married state 177:18

Unfold: O clouds, u.! 67:38

Unfortunate: one more U., weary of breath 165:56

Unfriendly to society's chief joys 112:53

Unhanged: not three good men u. 314:64

Unhappy: had been very u. in marriage 176:1

instinct for being u. highly developed 292:69

no one till his death ... called u. 73:9

u. family is u. in its own way 392:49

Unheard: heard melodies are sweet, but those u. 183:17

Unholy: refrain from the u. pleasure 31:88

shrieks, and sights u.! 213–14:91

Unicorn: lion and the u. were fighting 234:47

Unintelligible: weary weight of ... this u. world 415:32

Union: broken Nature's social u. 80:17

Liberty and U., now ... for ever ... inseparable 400:44

O U., strong and great! 197:92

Unite: workers of the world, u. 207:9

United Nations: we the peoples of the U. 394:76

Unity: brethren ... swell together in u. 44:43

u. is strength 282:88

Universally acknowledged ... a single man 23:75

Universe: born for the U. [Burke] 151:78

wide vessel of the u. 320:50

Universities: state of both his u. 393:54

University: don't think one 'comes down' from Jimmy's u. 242:10

true U. ... is a collection of books 89:37

we are the U. 378:54

Unjust steals the just's umbrella 70:71

Unkind: Midlands ... sodden and u. 32:5

Vain: hour when you too learn that all is v. 290:50
  labour and the wounds are v. 103:32
  mock on, 'tis all in v. 67:39
  name of the Lord thy God in v. 37:85
  no great man lives in v. 89:36
  they labour in v. that build 44:41
  use not v. repetitions 52:17
  v. are the thousand creeds 71:85
  v. for you to rise up early 44:42
  Why, all delights are v. 331:9
  youth is v. 106:67
*Vaincre sans péril ... triomphe sans gloire* 110:32
Vainly: tired waves, v. breaking 103:33
Valet: no man is a hero to his v. 111:35
  to his very v. ... a hero 83:54
Valiant: as he was v., I honour him 325:11
  he who would v. be 77:64
  the v. man and free 387:71
  v. ... taste of death but once 324:1
Valley: all in the v. of Death 385:40
  in the v. of decision 50:81
  maid singing in the v. 16:18
  v. of the shadow of death 42:93
Valleys: piping down the v. wild 68:48
Valour: better part of v. is discretion 315:93
  discretion ... better part of v. 260:76
  for contemplation he and v. 219:66
Value: price of everything ... v. of nothing 406:21
  then we rack the v. 343:81
Valued: never v. till they make a noise 114:82
Van Dycks have to go 111:40
Vanish: ah, wd. the scandal v. 349:42
Vanished: dream that v. with the morn 71:86
  the touch of a v. hand 384:37
Vanity: it beareth the name of V. Fair 77:60
  that v. in years 314:68
  two passions, v. and love 98:62
  v. of vanities, saith the Preacher 46:93
Vanquished: woe to the v. 197:85
Variable: Woman ... v. as the shade 296:14
Variation: each slight v., if useful 117:7
Variety: great source of pleasure is v. 178:42
  nor custom stale her infinite v. 299:55

Variety (*continued*)
  v. is pleasing 282:89
  v. is the mother of enjoyment 123:99
  v. is the soul of pleasure 30:86
  v.'s the very spice of life 114:71
Various: as you are woman ... so be v. 154:22
  so v., that he seem'd ... Epitome 126:43
*Varium et mutabile ... femina* 397:1
Vase: 'twas on a lofty v.'s side 154:23
Vassals and serfs at my side 76:55
Vasty fields of France 318:37
Vault: that heaven's v. should crack 330:4
Vaults: been in these here v. 12:41
Vegetable: my v. love shd. grow 206:93
  v., animal, and mineral 147:31
Vegetate: one does but v. 79:92
Veil: this that was the v. of thee 382:17
  V. past which I cd. not see 135:73
Veils: peace ... dropping from the v. of the morning 417:53
Vein: not in the giving v. today 352:78
Veins: jigging v. of rhyming mother-wits 204:72
Venetian: Turk beat a V. 346-7:22
Vengeance: noblest v. is to forgive 282:90
  rarer action ... virtue than in v. 357:53
  v. is mine ... saith the Lord 57:40
*Veni, vidi, vici* 87:8
Venice: here with us in V. 338:3
  in V., on the Bridge of Sighs 84:62
Venom: no v. to that of the tongue 282:91
*Vent: ce qu'est au feu le v.* 82:34
Vent: what his breast forges, that his tongue must v. 303-4:17
Venture: nothing v., nothing win 273:13
Ventures: take the current ... or lose our v. 326:27
'Verboojuice': 'Sesquippledan v.' 401:64
*Verbum sapienti sat est* 282:92
Verdict: Sentence first—v. afterwards 91:68
Verdure: content to see no other v. 185:43
  different shades in the v. 173:63
Verge: on the very v. of her confine 328:65
Verified: they have v. unjust things 344:87
Verify: always v. yr. references 291:56

**Villain** (*continued*)
fair terms and a v.'s mind 339:7
hungry, lean-fac'd v. 303:12
O v. ... condemned into ... redemption 344:84
**Villainous:** foreheads v. low 357:52
**Villains:** God shd. go before such v. 344:82
**Villainy:** thus I clothe my naked v. 351:70
**Vinci:** they spell it V. 394:66
**Vindicate** the ways of God to Man 250:8
**Vine:** Daughter of the V. 135:76
every man under his v. 50:89
**Vines:** bless with fruit the v. 180:78
our v. have tender grapes 47:23
**Vineyard:** thou shalt not glean thy v. 37:98
**Violence:** to offer it the show of v. 305:35
**Violent:** laid v. hands upon themselves 65:12
nothing ... v. is permanent 273:12
so over v. or over civil 126:44
**Violet:** the nodding v. grows 341:46
the v. smells to him as ... to me 320:52
throw a perfume on the v. 327:43
**Violets:** breathes upon a bank of v. 358–9:75
daisies pied and v. blue 332:19
from her ... flesh may v. spring 312:32
odours, when sweet v. sicken 370:54
**Vipers:** generation of v. 51:6
**Virgin:** a v. shall conceive, and bear 48:34
**Virtue:** a fugitive and cloistered v. 223:39
admire v. ... follow not her lore 221:4
assume a v. if you have it not 311:19
enterprises ... of v. or mischief 24:96
every v. ... founded on compromise 78:74
forbearance ceases to be a v. 78:77
if V. feeble were 213:81
. lilies and languors of v. 382:18
love V., she alone is free 213:81
much v. in If 303:10
O infinite v., com'st thou smiling? 299:63
only reward of v. is v. 132:30
power ... extirpates ... gentle v. 78:89
rarer ... in v. than in vengeance 357:53

**Virtue** (*continued*)
saw v. in her shape how lovely 219:73
some rise by sin, and some by v. fall 337:82
there is no v. like necessity 348:36
useful life, progressive v. 391:34
v. dwells not in the tongue 282:93
v. is ... best plain set 26:27
v. is its own reward 282:94
v. never grows old 282:95
v. of necessity 282:96
v. that possession wd. not show 343:81
wars that makes ambition v. 345:10
**Virtues:** be to her v. very kind 253:50
lady ... of wondrous v. 338:99
their v. we write in water 323:86
world to hide v. in? 359:77
**Virtuous:** be in general v., and ... happy 138:12
think, because thou art v. 359:87
**Visages:** whose v. do cream and mantle 338:97
**Vision:** a v. or a waking dream? 184:32
baseless fabric of this v. 356:50
by the v. splendid ... attended 411:78
not disobedient unto ... heavenly v. 56:27
saw the V. of the world 387:80
where ... no v., the people perish 46:89
write the v., ... make it plain 51:93
**Visionary:** whither is fled the v. gleam? 410:76
**Visions:** young men shall see v. 50:80
**Visit:** let us never v. together 109:17
v. us with thy salvation 402:72
**Visiting** the iniquity of the fathers 37:84
**Vital:** I cannot give it v. growth again 346:19
**Vitality:** extreme busyness ... deficient v. 379:78
**Vive:** Napoleon's armies ... shouting 'V. l'intérieur' 297:33
**Vocabulary:** the v. of Bradshaw is nervous 125:28
**Vocation:** no sin ... to labour in his v. 312:47
'tis my v., Hal 312:47
**Vogue:** charming to totter into v. 398:22
**Voice:** a certain what-is-it in his v. 408:51

Voice (continued)

a distant v. in the darkness   198:4
a still small v.   40:58
a v. cry, Sleep no more   334:42
bird, or but a wandering v.?   415:37
every man thy ear, but few thy v.
    306:56
harmonious sisters, V. and Verse
    212:71
hear a v. in every wind   154:28
heart and soul and v.   229:2
her v., and her hair, and eyes   207:11
her v. was ever soft   331:5
his big manly v.   301:90
I sing with mortal v.   219:83
its familiar v. wearies not ever
    369:44
lost my v. most irrecoverably   401:56
my v. ... lost it with hallooing
    316:99
no v.; but oh! the silence sank
    106:61
no v. but the v. of complaining
    227:72
no v. I'll be quit of the singing   12:43
sing to the Lord with cheerful v.
    188:77
so charming left his v.   220:85
sound of a v. that is still   384:37
still raise ... the supplicating v.
    174:71
the v. is Jacob's v.   36:60
the v. of all the gods   331:15
the watchdog's v. that bayed   150:65
'tis the v. of the Lobster   91:64
'tis the v. of the sluggard   400:41
v. ... crying in the wilderness   51:5
v. I hear this passing night   184:30
v. of the people ... of God   10:15
v. of the turtle is heard   47:22
v. ... run from hedge to hedge
    185:42
v. whose sound was like the sea
    413:4
warm, thrilling v. cry out   242:8
Voices: ancestral v. prophesying war
    107:74
I hear the gentle v. calling   138:8
music, when soft v. die   370:54
two v. are there   412:1
two v. are there ... of ... deep ... of
    sheep   378:62
v. of children ... on the green   68:52
v. telling me what to do   366:2
Void: have left an aching v.   113:62
without form, and v.   34:26
Volscians: flutter'd yr. V. in Corioli
    304:19

Voltaire: mock on, V., Rousseau
    67:39
Volume: desideratum of a v.   192:30
foretells ... a tragic v.   316:96
Volumes: borrowers ... creators of odd
    v.   192:26
written such v. of stuff!   194:59
Vomit: dog is turned to his ... v.
    60:13
dog returneth to ... v., ... fool ... to
    ... folly   46:84
Vorpal blade went snicker-snack   92:70
Vote: v. ... as ... leaders tell 'em to
    144:88
Voted at my party's call   147:27
Votes: anyone who v. Labour   225:58
Vow: I v. to thee, my country   377:53
Vows made in storms are forgotten
    282:97
Vox populi, vox dei   10:15
Voyage: about to take my last v.
    163:35
Voyager: lands the v. at last   132:23
Vulgar: familiar, but by no means v.
    306:55
think with the wise, but talk with
    the v.   280:28

Wabe: gimble in the w.   91:69
Wacht am Rhein   294:87
Wade: shd. I w. no more   335:57
Wages: be content with your w.   54:71
home art gone, and ta'en thy w.
    304–5:29
w. of sin is death   56:32
Wagon: hitch yr. w. to a star   133:43
Wail: with old woes new w. ... time's
    waste   362:37
Wailing for her demon lover   106:72
Wait: learn to labour and to w.   198:98
make 'em laugh ... cry ... w.   287:2
time and tide w. for no man   280:39
w. and see   22:57, 282:98
who only stand and w.   223:30
Waiter: dam' good head w.   157:54
w. roars it through the hall   192:37
Waiting for the long-promised invasion
    101:97
Waiting-gentlewoman: talk so like a w.
    313:52
Waits: everything comes to him who
    w.   262:32
the dinner w., and we are tired
    113:58
Wake: do I w. or sleep?   184:32
held we ... sleep to w.   73:16
w. up, America   141:46
w. up, England   142:62

**Wake** (*continued*)
　you must w. and call me early
　　388:89
**Waked:** you have w. me too soon
　400:41
**Wakes:** and whoever w. in England
　74:21
**Walcum:** a bit of talcum is always w.
　229:94
**Walk:** can two w. together? 50:82
　doth w. in fear and dread 106:60
　w. humbly with thy God 51:91
　w. upon England's mountains green
　　67:38
　we w. by faith, not by sight 58:62
　wher'er you w., cool gales 251:32
　will you w. a little faster? 91:62
　will you w. into my parlour? 168:86
　within a w. of the sea 32:7
**Walked:** as I w. through the wilderness
　76:57
　when she has w. before 150:73
**Walking:** I nauseate w. 109:16
　life's but a w. shadow 336:76
**Walks:** having once turned round w.
　on 106:62
　I wish I liked the way it w. 286:97
　she w. in beauty, like the night
　　86:96
　w. the night in her silver shoon
　　118:27
**Wall:** green hill ... without a city w.
　11:20
　Jackson standing like a stone w.
　　30:79
　know ... the w. is strong 404:97
　little pin bores through his castle w.
　　350:54
　serves it in the office of a w. 348:41
　something ... that doesn't love a w.
　　139:27
　washes its w. on the southern side
　　75:36
　weakest goes to the w. 282:15
**Wallet:** his w. lay ... in his lappe 97:43
　time hath ... a w. at his back 358:71
**Wallow** naked in December snow
　348:37
**Wallowing:** sow ... to her w. in the
　mire 60:13
**Walls:** banners on the outward w.
　336:74
　stone w. do not a prison make
　　199:15
　w. have ears 282:99
　watches from his mountain w.
　　385:47
**Walrus and the Carpenter** 92-3:78-82

**Waltzing:** you'll come a-w., Matilda
　244:30
**Wander:** whither shall I w.? 232:32
　you shall w. hand in hand 230-31:20
**Wandered:** I w. lonely as a cloud
　410:67
　when we have w. all our ways
　　286:93
**Wandering:** a w. minstrel I 145:95
　w. between two worlds 20:36
　w. Dong through the forest goes!
　　194:56
**Want:** Adam ... did not w. the apple
　394:68
　all we w. is a limousine 203:54
　freedom from w. ... everywhere
　　289:32
　I shall not w. 42:91
　if you w. to get somewhere else
　　92:72
　not good to w. and to have 265:35
　the w. of money is so [the root of all
　　evil] 82:41
　w. it [advice] most ... like it least
　　98:58
　w. of a thing is perplexing 395:83
　w. of Thought ... w. of Heart
　　165:62
　waste not, w. not 282:8
　worth ... best known by w. 284:60
　you w. the best seats 11:35
**Wanted:** every man is w., ... no man
　is w. much 133:34
　map ... not be w. these ten years
　　247:58
**Wanting:** robb'd, not w. what is stol'n
　345:9
　weighed ... and art found w. 49:69
**Wanton:** w. love corrupteth 25:99
　weep not, my w. 156:48
**Wantonness:** kindles in clothes a w.
　162:16
**Wants:** but w. that little strong ·164:47
　man w. but little here below 150:72
　w. money, means, and content
　　302:93
**War:** advise none to ... go to w. 254:61
　all is fair in love and w. 254:65
　Americans ... tempered by w.
　　188:74
　ancestral voices prophesying w.
　　107:74
　desires peace, prepare for w. 396:88
　Don John of Austria is going to the
　　w. 99:71
　ease after w., death after life 377:42
　he that first invented w. 205:74
　I know the disciplines of w. 320:49

War (*continued*)
    image of w. without its guilt 375:23
    in w. ... no winners, ... all are losers
        95:15
    in W.: Resolution. In Defeat:
        Defiance 102:10
    infection and the hand of w. 348:41
    let slip the dogs of w. 324:9
    looks on w. as all glory 372:81
    love ... is exactly like w. 379:71
    magnificent, but ... not w. 69:66
    marching as to w. 28:57
    my sentence is for open w. 217:46
    neither shall they learn w. 48:31
    never was a good w. 138:15
    pride, pomp, and circumstance of ...
        w. 345–6:10
    so dauntless in w. 296:11
    some ... depos'd, some slain in w.
        350:54
    stupid crime ... devil's madness—W.
        297:36
    succeeding generations from ...
        scourge of w. 394:76
    the arts of w. and peace 84:77
    w. and the pity of w. 243:18
    The W. between Men and Women
        392:45
    to w. and arms I fly 199:16
    w. ... endless w. still breed? 223:33
    w. is done and youth stone dead
        293:82
    w. is ... national industry of Prussia
        224:47
    W. is Peace, Freedom is Slavery
        242:2
    w. makes rattling good history
        158:64
    w. ... too serious ... to be left to
        military 384:34
    w. upon this bloody tyrant, Time
        362:31
    when I speak, they are for w.
        44:36
    when the blast of w. blows 319:45
    when there was w., he went 22:62
    when w. begins, hell opens 282:3
    wither'd is the garland of the w.
        299:66
    Women ... and Power and W.
        189:93
Warble his native wood-notes wild
    214:4
Ward: thou knowest my old w. 314:65
Ware: I shd. dine at W. 113:59
Warm: let the w. Love in 185:33
    this sensible w. motion to become
        337:90

Warmed: w. and cooled ... winter and
    summer 339:13
    w. both hands ... fire of life 192:34
Warn: to w., to comfort, and command
    414:18
Warned: be w. by me that breakfast
    31:92
Warring within our breasts 205:76
Wars: end to the beginnings of all w.
    289:34
    fierce w. and faithful loves 377:40
    let w. give way to peace 102:17
    more ... fears than w. or women
        322–3:81
    still w. and lechery! 358:74
    the thousand w. of old 386:70
    w. and rumours of w. 53:45
    w. bring scars 282:4
    w. that makes ambition virtue
        345:10
Wars of the Roses: leave Moses out of
    the W. 34:21
Warts: roughnesses, pimples, and w.
    115:91
Wash: bid them w. their faces 303:14
    I w. away my balm 350–51:58
    tears ... w. out a word of it 136:79
    w. dirty linen in public 282:6
    w. me ... whiter than snow 42:8
    w. the balm ... from ... anointed
        king 349:50
    w. ... yr. feet seldom ... head never
        282:7
    will all great Neptune's ocean w. this
        blood 334:43
Washed the dishes with his wife 226:70
Washes: river Weser ... w. its wall
    75:36
Washing: no cooking, or w., or sewing
    12:43
    painting a face ... not w. it 140:37
    w. ... clean linen in public 405:7
Waste: barrel of meal shall not w.
    40:55
    in a w. of shame 363:50
    wail my dear time's w. 362:37
    w. not, want not 282:8
Wasted: some nine moons w. 344:90
Wasteful and ridiculous excess 327:43
Wastes: tell her that w. her time and
    me 398:17
Watch: has a w. and chain, of course
    288:22
    keeping w. over ... flock by night
        54:68
    one to w., and one to pray 10:13
    our w. ... have indeed comprehended
        343:79

Watch (*continued*)
   secret whispers of each other's w. 320:50
   take ye heed, w. and pray  54:64
   w. and pray, that ye enter not  53:50
   W. on the Rhine  294:87
   w. that ends the night  399:39
   w. to babble and to talk  343:75
Watchdog: the w.'s voice that bayed 150:65
Watched: he w. the ads and not the road  228:91
   o'er the ramparts we w.  188:79
   w. pot never boils  282:9
Watcher of the skies  185:41
Watches: a heart that w. and receives 415:29
   he w. from his mountain walls 385:47
   with our judgments as our w.  249:91
Watching: Big Brother is w. you  242:1
Watchman, what of the night?  48:39
Watch-tower: from his w. in the skies 214:97
Water: as w. unto wine  387:83
   blood is thicker than w.  256:49
   by w. and the Word  380:83
   carry w. in a sieve  282:10
   deepest w. ... best fishing  260:67
   Eeyore ... looked at himself in the w. 212:64
   give him w. to drink  45:81
   I came like W.  135:72
   I don't care where the w. goes  99:77
   like w. off a duck's back  282:11
   may lead a horse to the w.  269:62
   more w. glideth by the mill  357–8:63
   name was writ in w.  187:70
   never know the worth of w.  268:44
   not all the w. in the rough rude sea 349:50
   smooth ... w. where the brook is deep  321:65
   unstable as w. ... shalt not excel 36:66
   virtues we write in w.  323:86
   w. is best  246:53
   w. out of a stone  282:12
   w., w. every where  105:50
Watered heaven with ... tears  68:47
Waterfall: from the w. he named her 198:2
(A)-Watering the last year's crop 130:85
Waterloo: battle of W. was won ... Eton  401:61
   bodies high at Austerlitz and W. 293:78

Waterloo (*continued*)
   every man meets his W. at last 246:52
   Marathon to W.  147:31
Water-mill: noise like that of a w. 381:98
Water-rugs: shoughs, w., and demi-wolves  334:48
Waters: a fen of stagnant w.  413:3
   beside the still w.  42:92
   cast thy bread upon the w.  47:9
   cold w. to a thirsty soul  45:82
   dreadful noise of w. in my ears 352:72
   fades o'er the w. blue  83:57
   kill the still-closing w.  356:49
   many w. cannot quench love  47:28
   still w. run deep  278:77
   stolen w. are sweet  45:60
   w. of the heart push in their tides 390:21
Watson: you know my methods, W. 124:20
Wave: all sunk beneath the w.  113:64
   chin upon an orient w.  216:22
   glassy, cool, translucent w.  213:80
   lift me as a w., a leaf  369:37
   walk o'er the western w.  368:32
Waved: long has it w. on high  164:46
Waves: sons of the w.  141:48
   the tired w., vainly breaking  103:33
   w. make towards the pebbled shore 363:40
   when ... w. went high ... sought ... storms  126:39
Wax-works: if you think we're w. 92:73
Way: a damned long, dark ... w. 151:84
   all taking the easiest w. out  401–2:69
   catch the nearest w.  333:32
   every day, in every w. ... better 111:37
   go by the king's high w.  38:3
   gull's w. and the whale's w.  208:16
   keep his distant w. [Milton]  156:45
   long is the w. and hard  218:54
   love will find a w.  271:22
   perilous w. from a tree's summit 185:35
   plods his weary w.  155:30
   primrose w. to the ... bonfire  334:44
   roses, roses all the w.  74:35
   set out ... in a relative w.  76:52
   steep and thorny w. to heaven 306:54
   the w. of all flesh  400:53
   the w. to dusty death  336:76

Way (continued)
travel on life's common w.   413:4
w. of an eagle ... serpent   46:91
w. was long, the wind was cold 295:99
where there's a will ... a w.   283:33
which w. shall I fly?   218:62
Ways: among the untrodden w.   413:15
gave once ... her w. to roam   71:93
he had his little w.   211:52
her w. are w. of pleasantness   44:56
let all her w. be unconfined   253:50
Mr Facing-both-w.   77:61
neither are yr. w. my w.   48:51
oldest sins the newest ... w.   318:30
when ... w. be foul   332:20
We: put it down a w., my lord   121:75
Weak: bear the infirmities of the w. 57:45
concessions of the w.   77:71
idleness ... refuge of w. minds   98:61
surely the w. shall perish   297:35
to be w. is miserable   216:31
w. and therefore pacifistic   22:59
Weakest goes to the wall   282:15
Weakness: show no more w. than is natural   392:41
silence ... all else is w.   396:94
w. is thy excuse   222:20
Wealth: as their w. increaseth, so inclose   204:70
bear w.   255:98
consume w. without producing it 364:66
he that marries for w.   271:42
health is better than w.   266:76
let w. and commerce ... die   292:68
love rememb'red such w. brings 362:36
neither wit nor w.   16:85
squandering w. ... his ... art   126:44
there is no w. but life   292:64
w. accumulates and men decay 150:62
w. is contentment with a little 282:16
w. is not without its advantages 141:43
w. maketh many friends   45:74
where w. and freedom reign   151:92
Weapons: hurt with the same w. 339:13
in this war ... books are w.   289:33
women's w., water-drops   328:68
Wear: better to w. out than ... rust out 115:92
better w. out shoes than sheets 256:32

Wear (continued)
if the cap fits, w. it   257:83
our souls ... will us to w. ourselves 205:76
to w. the breeches   282:18
w. him in my heart's core   310:6
Wearied: wherein have I w. thee? 50:90
Weariest: even the w. river ... safe to sea   383:20
Weariness: much study ... a w. of the flesh   47:13
Wearing: everything is the worse for w. 262:34
Weary: age shall not w. them   65:20
how my heart grows w.   138:6
how w., stale ... uses of this world 305:42
long w. day have end   377:39
sae w., fu' o' care   81:26
Unfortunate, w. of breath   165:56
Weasel: as a w. sucks eggs   301:84
pop goes the w.!   203:60
Weather: I like the w.   83:55
if it prove fair w.   380:86
need to pray for fair w.   25:7
no enemy but winter and rough w. 300:83
the w. the cuckoo likes   158:67
two Englishmen ... talk is of the w. 172:51
what dreadful hot w.!   24:81
who's there, besides foul w.?   328:70
you won't hold up the w.   203:55
Weave: tangled web we w.   296:13
w. a circle round him thrice   107:76
Weaving: I work at the w. trade   17:95
Web: w. of our life ... mingled yarn 298:46
what a tangled w. we weave   296:13
Webster was ... possessed by death 131:13
Wed: with this ring I thee w.   65:9
Wedding: has bought her w. clothes 9:10
Wedding-day: brightly dawns our w. 145:4
said John, 'It is my w.'   113:59
tomorrow is our w.   113:55
wager ... w. ... is ... fixed on   134:59
Wedding-gown: I chose my wife, as she ... her w.   152:97
Wedding-guest: O W.! this soul hath been   106:62
Wedge: thin end of the w.   280:23
Wedges: in time small w. cleave   191:22
w. of gold, great anchors   352:72
Wedlock is a padlock   282:19

Wednesday: he that died o' W.   315:88
  married on W.   238:71
  W.'s child is full of woe   235:56
Wee, sleekit, cow'rin' ... beastie   80:16
Wee-wee-wee: little pig cried w.   239:78
Weed: O thou w. who art so lovely
  346:14
  pernicious w. whose scent ... annoys
  112:53
Weeds: her winter w. outworn   368:28
  lilies ... smell far worse than w.
  363:42
  subject is the fattest soil to w.   317:26
  worthless as wither'd w.   71:85
Week: in his beak enough food for a
  w.   209:38
  murdered reputations of the w.
  108:7
  no admittance till the w. after next
  94:97
  rust of the whole w.   9:7
  takes me as much as a w.   393:65
Weeks: love alters not with ... w.
  363:48
Weep: I w. for Adonais – he is dead!
  367:9
  I w. for joy to stand   349:49
  'I w. for you,' the Walrus said   93:81
  men that laugh and w.   382:19
  no, I'll not w.   328:69
  or ere I'll w. ... I shall go mad
  328:69
  such ... tricks ... the angels w.
  337:87
  that he shd. w. for her?   308:90
  'tis that I may not w.   85:79
  w., and you w. alone   404:91
  w. no more, my lady   138:4
  w. not for little Leonie   153:12
  w. not, my wanton, smile   156:48
  w. with them that w.   57:38
  who wd. not w., if Atticus were he?
  248:84
Weeping: all de darkies am a w.   138:3
  dwell a w. hermit there   107–8:90
  I have full cause of w.   328:69
  Rachel w. for her children   51:3
  the children w., O my brothers   73:11
  w. may endure for a night   42:95
Weeps: our country sinks ... it w., it
  bleeds   335:65
Weighed: thou art w. in the balances
  49:69
Weight: able and willing to pull his w.
  289:36
  he carries w.! he rides a race   113:57
  heavy ... weary w. ... of ... world
  415:32

Weight (*continued*)
  heavy w. from off my head   350:58
  w of Cathedral tunes   122:83
*Wein, Weib und Gesang: wer nicht
  liebt* W.   200:28
Welcome: advice is seldom w.   98:58
  constant guest is never w.   258:24
  eat and w., fast, and heartily w.
  261:10
  he that plays the king shall be w.
  308:82
  so let us w. peaceful evening   114:73
  thrice w., darling of the Spring
  415:38
  warmest w. at an inn   371:60
  w. is the best cheer   282:20
  w. to yr. gory bed   81:22
Welcomes: and w. little fishes in
  89–90:45
Well: all is not w.   306:52
  all is w. that ends w.   254:68
  Chaucer, w. of English undefiled
  377:44
  deep w. of unconscious cerebration
  170:22
  did nothing ... did it very w.   144:90
  he preaches w. that lives w.   275:59
  lov'd not wisely, but too w.   346:22
  not feeling very w. myself!   285:85
  prayeth w. who loveth w.   106:63
  Pussy's in the w.   232:28
  worth doing is worth doing w.
  283:24
*Well-a-way*: made every youth cry *W.*!
  12:36
Wellbred: as w. as if ... not married
  109:17
  moral, sensible, and w. man   112:52
  very strange and w.   109:17
  w. Captain of the *Pinafore*   147:24
Well-content: sweet W.   117:12
Weller: Mr W.'s knowledge of London
  121:66
Well-favoured: to be a w. man is the
  gift of fortune   343:73
*Weltgeschichte: die W. ... Weltgericht*
  294:86
Wen: fate of the great w. [London]
  104:36
Wenceslas: good King W.   229:3
Wench: beside the w. is dead   204:71
Wenches: getting w. with child   361:16
Went: and she w., and came, and
  gleaned   39:35
  when there was war, he w.   22:62
Wept: my mother groan'd, my father
  w.   67:44
  they w. like anything to see   92:78

West: East is East, and W. is W.
189:92
  go W., young man  156:47, 376:24
  Lochinvar is come out of the w.
  295:10
West port: open the W., and let me
  gang free  294:92
*Westen: im W. nichts Neues*  287:4
Western: All Quiet on the W. Front
  287:4
  wind of the W. Sea  388:96
Westminster Abbey or victory  229:6
Westward: but w., look, the land is
  bright  104:34
Wet: out of ... w. clothes and into a
  dry Martini  409:57
  to w. one's whistle  283:22
  w. and dirty from hunting  381:92
Wetting: saved his friend from a w.
  212:70
Whale: gull's way ... w.'s way  208:16
  sprat to catch a w.  278:69
  very like a w.  310:12
Whales: they wd. talk like w.  152:4
What-is-it: a certain w. in his voice
  408:51
Wheat: orient and immortal w.  392:53
Wheel: a w. ... in the midst of a w.
  49:63
  fortune ... turn thy w.  328:63
  put a spoke in one's w.  278:68
  put yr. shoulder to the w.  275:72
  upon a w. of fire  330:96
  w. is come full circle  330:2
Wheelbarrow: as she wheeled her w.
  17:89
Wheels: all the w. of Being slow
  386:60
  w. within w.  283:26
Where: leads – God knows w.  85:80
  w. are the snows of yesteryear?
  396:95
  w. ish dat barty now?  195:68
Wherefore: for every why he had a w.
  82:36
  never mind the why and w.  147:28
  w. stopp'st thou me?  104:42
Whiff: a w. of grapeshot  89:34
Whig: first W. was the Devil  177:28
Whigs: caught the W. bathing  122:89
  W. ... no force but argument  72–3:8
Whim: tempted by a private w.  31:96
  the strangest w. has seized me  98:66
Whimper: not with a bang but a w.
  130:96
  'twixt a smile and a w.  369:42
Whipped: she w. them all soundly
  239:76

Whipping: who shall 'scape w.?
  308:88
Whips and scorns of time  309:95
Whirligig of time brings ... revenges
  360:2
Whiskers: runcible cat with crimson w.
  195:63
Whisky: freedom and W. ... thegither
  79:2
Whisper: hush! hush! w. who dares!
  211:61
Whispering: where there is w. ... lying
  283:29
  w. of fields unsown  243:17
Whispers: blood of Jesus w. peace
  65:19
  secret w. of each other's watch
  320:50
Whist: loved a good game of w.  192:27
Whistle: as clean as a w.  258:8
  hir joly w. wel y-wet  97:46
  to wet one's w.  283:22
Whistles o'er the furrowed land  214:98
White: a moment w., then melts  81:25
  as w. as leprosy  105:52
  fleece was w. as snow  157:55
  I shall wear w. flannel trousers  131:4
  in winter, when the fields are w.
  93:87
  my soul is w.  68:51
  one w., and two khaki  14:55
  [sins] shall be ... w. as snow  48:30
  some gave them w. bread  234:47
  the w. foam flew  105:48
  the W. Man's Burden  190:12
  two blacks do not make a w.  281:74
  w. radiance of Eternity  367:19
  yr. hair has become very w.  90:48
Whiten: w. the green plains under
  368:22
  willows w., aspens quiver  387:76
Whiter: I shall be w. than snow  42:8
Whites: don't fire ... see the w. of their
  eyes  253:49
Whitethroat builds, and all the swallows  74:22
Whither: one knows not w. nor why
  208:17
  soul ... driven ... I know not w.
  401:55
  w. goest thou?  56:11
  w. is fled the visionary gleam?
  410:76
Whiting: said a w. to a snail  91:62
Who: w. killed Cock Robin?  241:88
  w. kill'd John Keats?  86:94
  w., or why, or which  194:54
  w. was then the gentleman?  27:50

Will (*continued*)

where there's a w. there's a way 283:33

where there's a w., there's trouble 283:34

w. in us is over-rul'd by fate 205:80

William: you are old, Father W. 90:48

Williamanmary ... ruled by an Orange 297:32

Willow: a w. cabin at yr. gate 359:80

a w. grows aslant the brook 311:30

w., titwillow 146:12

w. w. waly 146:17

Willows: our harps upon the w. 44:45

w. whiten, aspens quiver 387:76

Wills: choose executors and talk of w. 349:53

the w. above be done 355:28

women must have their w. 283:52

Wilson: the 14th Mr W. 165:53

Win: heads I w., tails you lose 115:86, 266:75

hope from outward forms to w. 106:69

nothing ... foul to those that w. 315:85

Wind: a roaring in the w. all night 413:11

absence is to love what w. is to fire 82:34

all aloud the w. doth blow 332:20

and the w. shall say 131:8

bayed the whispering w. 150:65

blow, blow, thou winter w. 302:91

blow w., come wrack 336:77

fair stood the w. for France 125:31

frosty w. made moan 290:43

gentle w. does move 67:40

God tempers the w. ... shorn lamb 265:26

hey, ho, the w. and the rain 360:3

hope constancy in w. 85:91

how the w. doth ramm! 252:47

ill w. that blows nobody good 267:15

impatient as the W. 411:91

know which way the w. blows 268:45

like W. I go 135:72

likewise a w. on the heath 69:65

man in the w. 390:17

more gentle than a w. in summer 185:34

O Wild West W. 369:35

only argument ... with an east w. 200:27

readers ... sway in the w. 130:89

Wind (*continued*)

reed shaken with the w. 52:29

roaring of the w. is my wife 187:63

sail near the w. 276:10

shorter in w., as in memory long 70:72

streams ... *against* the w. 84:63

swoln with w. and the rank mist 215:16

tempers the w. ... to the shorn lamb 379:68

the w. of change is blowing 203:53

they have sown the w. 50:76

when the w. is southerly 308:83

where the w. comes from ... goes 211:53

w. bloweth where it listeth 55:98

w. blows it back again 67:39

w. blows, the cradle will rock 233:38

w. of the Western Sea 388:96

w. out of one's sails 279:2

w. that follows fast 116:96

w.'s like a whetted knife 208:16

words but w. 82:37

Window: at my w. bid good morrow 214:97

love comes in at the w. 270:12

the little w. where the sun 165:60

what light through yonder w.? 353:97

Windowed: loop'd and w. raggedness 329:78

Window-panes: fog ... rubs its back upon the w. 131:1

Windows: cleaned the w., ... swept the floor 147:26

not by eastern w. only 104:34

storied w. richly dight 213:88

Winds: blow, w., and crack yr. cheeks 328:71

courted by all the w. 222:18

four-square to all the w. 388:93

rough w. do shake the darling buds 362:32

so perfumed that the w. were love-sick 298:54

the w. will blow the profit 203:55

w. somewhere safe to sea 383:20

wound the loud w. 356:49

young w. fed it with ... dew 370:46

Windy: keep o' th' w. side of the law 360:98

Wine: a little w. for thy stomach's sake 59:90

as water unto w. 387:83

bring me flesh ... wine 229:4

cedarwood, and sweet white w. 207:12

Witty: a w. statesman ... prove anything 89:32

it shall be w. and it shan't be long 98:64

not only w. in myself 316:98

Wive: hard to w. and thrive ... in a year 283:43

Wives: a man with seven w. 231:22

married three w. at one time 224–5:52

profane and old w.' fables 59:88

sky changes when they are w. 302:4

some poison'd by their w. 350:54

w. are young men's mistresses 24:97

w. must be had ... good or bad 283:44

Wiving: hanging and w. goes by destiny 339:11

Wobbly: my spelling is w. 212:67

Woe: a thurghfare ful of w. 97:45

all our w., with loss of Eden 216:27

bitter groan of a martyr's w. 66–7:35

can I see another's w.? 68:53

cry w., destruction, ruin 349:52

life protracted is protracted w. 174:70

man was made for joy and w. 66:30

the w.'s to come 351:59

trappings and the suits of w. 305:41

Wednesday's child is full of w. 235:56

w. to the vanquished 197:85

w. to them ... at ease in Zion 50:84

w. unto them that call ... good evil 48:33

Woes: with old w. new wail 362:37

Wold: fields ... that clothe the w. 387:75

Wolf: keep the w. from the door 283:45

to cry 'W.' 259:40

w. ... shall dwell with the lamb 48:37

Wolf's-bane, tight-rooted 183:21

Wolves: inwardly ... ravening w. 52:27

Woman: a fair w. ... without discretion 45:64

a perfect W., nobly planned 414:18

a Spirit, yet a W. too 414:17

a virtuous w. is a crown 45:65

a w. is a foreign land 245:32

a w. is only a w. 190:94

A W. Killed with Kindness 163:27

a w. mov'd ... a fountain troubled 355:26

a w. sat, in unwomanly rags 166:64

a w. seldom asks advice 9:10

a w.'s face ... hast thou 362:35

Woman (continued)

a w.'s preaching is like 175:90

a w.'s whole history 170:16

a w., therefore to be won 321:64

a w. who tells her ... age 406:29

a w. with fair opportunities 389:12

a w. yet think him an angel 389:10

a worthy w. al hir lyve 97:39

a young w. called Starkie 14:55

a uncommon pretty young w. 129:84

as you are w., so be lovely 154:22

believe a w. or an epitaph 85:91

but what is w.? 112:48

but w. has her way 164:48

constant ... but yet a w. 313:61

die because a w.'s fair 408:49

do you not know I am a w.? 302:96

dumb jewels ... move a w.'s mind 361:7

every w. false like thee 222:19

every w. is at heart a rake 251:23

every w. is ... to be gained by ... flattery 98:63

every w. shd. marry – and no man 123:96

fat white w. whom nobody loves 111:34

frailty, thy name is w. 306:45

give not thy soul unto a w. 62:50

God made the w. for the man 385:48

great glory in a w. 392:41

had a w. ever less? 80:12

her voice ... soft – an excellent thing in w. 331:5

I could be a good w. if 389:15

I know a reasonable w. 251:31

if a w. have long hair 57:52

in a post-chaise with a pretty w. 177:23

in argument with men a w. 222:22

in her first passion w. 84:73

lays his hand upon a w. 392:48

love and good company improves a w. 134:56

man that is born of a w. 41:69, 65:13

never yet fair w. but 329:74

no other but a w.'s reason 361:5

no other purgatory but a w. 29:73

no w. shd. ... be quite accurate 405:15

no w. shd. have a memory 406:32

none of w. born shall harm Macbeth 335:62

nor hell a fury like a w. scorned 108:6

Woman (*continued*)

O W.! in our hours of ease 296:14
of every ill, a w. is the worst 153:17
old w. lived under a hill 239:75
old w. who lived in a shoe 239:76
one tongue is enough for a w. 280:45
poor w. who was always tired 12:43
seven [hours' sleep] for a w. 277:40
she is a w., ... may be woo'd ... won 357–8:63
teaches such beauty as a w.'s eye 331:14
the rib ... made he a w. 35:33
the worser spirit a w. colour'd ill 364:55
there's a broken-hearted w. 159:76
this w. to thy wedded wife 64:6
thought does not become a young w. 371:65
'tis w.'s whole existence 84:70
to show a w. when he loves 74:34
wavers ... in a word, she is a w. 285:92
when lovely w. stoops to folly 131:12, 152:2
who can find a virtuous w.? 46:92
wickedness of a w. 62:55
wit no more ... sincere than a w. constant 109:9
without the ... w. I love 129:81
w. as old as she looks 107:86
w. ... at the bottom of [mischief] 273:94
w. conceals what she knows not 283:46
w. ... fickle and changing 397:1
w. for the hearth 389:2
w. ... if she have the misfortune 23:73
w. in this humour woo'd ... won? 351:69
w. is his game 388:1
w. is the lesser man 387:83
w.'s at best a contradiction 251:26
w.'s happiest knowledge 219:70
w. that deliberates is lost 9:5
w. to obey 389:2
w. wailing for her demon-lover 106:72
w. will be the last thing civilized 209:35
w. with the heart 389:2
w.'s work is never done 283:47
worse occupations ... than feeling a w.'s pulse 379:67
yield to one of w. born 336:78

Womb: from his mother's w. untimely ripp'd 336:78

Womb (*continued*)

this teeming w. of royal kings 348–9:41
through the foul w. of night 320:50

Women: a bevy of fair w. 221:99
alas! the love of w. 84:72
an experience of w. which extends 125:24
Bah! I have sung w. 252:48
by bad w. been deceived 222:15
dally not with money or w. 259:50
discreet w. ... neither eyes nor ears 260:75
England ... a paradise for w. 81:31
England is the paradise of w. 136:86, 261:20
fair w. and brave men 83:59
for w. to keep counsel 324:2
from w.'s eyes this doctrine I derive 331:16
goes with w., and champagne 31:95
happiest w. ... have no history 130:86
how w. pass the time when ... alone 161:4
I speak ... Italian to w. 96:24
Italy ... hell for w. 81:31
let your w. keep silence in ... churches 57:56
loved Esther above all the w. 40:64
Monstrous Regiment of W. 191:19
most w. are not so young as ... painted 30:81
music and w. I ... give way to 245:43
other w. cloy the appetites 299:55
passing the love of w. 40:49
souls of w. are so small 82:40
sweet is revenge – especially to w. 84:68
the more w. look in ... glass 283:51
the third wrote, W. are strongest 61:36
three w. ... goose make a market 280:36
tide in the affairs of w. 85:80
where there are w. and geese 283:48
W. and Horses and Power 189:93
w. and music shd. never be dated 151:88
w. are always in extremes 283:49
w. are angels, wooing 358:65
w. are glad to have been asked 243:12
w. are necessary evils 283:50
w. become like their mothers 406:30
w. ... care ... more for a marriage 27:44
w. in London who flirt 405:7

Women (*continued*)
 w. ... more like each other than men
  98:62
 w. must have the last word 283:53
 w. must have their wills 283:52
 w. must weep 189:87
 w. never look so well as when 381:92
 w. require both 83:51
 w. sit or move to and fro 403:78
 w.'s letters ... pith is in the postscript
  159:77
 w.'s weapons, water-drops 328:68
 w. ... talking of Michelangelo
  131:99
 w., worst and best 385:52
Won: a woman, therefore to be w.
  321:64
 marks – not that you w. or lost
  287:9
 melancholy as a battle w. 401:57
 prize we sought is w. 403:81
 things w. are done 358:65
 woman, therefore may be w. 357:63
 w. on the playing fields of Eton
  401:61
Wonder: all the w. that wd. be 387:80
 and still the w. grew 150:69
 how I w. what you are! 384:36
 how I w. what you're at 90:53
 the common w. of all men 72:3
 we ... have eyes to w. 363:46
Wonderful: all things wise and w.
  10:17
 how w. is Death! 368:24
 O w., w. ... out of all whooping
  302:95
 W., Counsellor, The Mighty God
  48:36
Wonderment: I'm always moved to w.
  229:96
Wonders: His w. to perform 113:63
 w. will never cease 283:54
Won't: will you, w. you, will you, w.
  you? 91:63
Woo: was to w. a fair young maid
  17:95
Wood: my house in the high w. 32:7
 old w. burn brightest 400:52
 one impulse from a vernal w. 414:28
 see the w. for the trees 277:23
 springeth the w. new 15:71
 through w. and dale the sacred river
  106:73
Woodbine: over-canopied with luscious
  w. 341:46
Woodman, spare the beechen tree
  88:18
Wood-notes: his native w. wild 214:4

Woods: a pleasure in the pathless w.
  84:65
 and the w. have no voice 227:72
 in spring, when w. are getting green
  93:88
 senators of mighty w. 182:98
 the w. shall to me answer 376:38
 though he build his house in the w.
  133:48
 tomorrow to fresh w. 215:18
 we'll to the w. no more 167:79
 w. or steepy mountain yields 205:82
Woodshed: something nasty in the w.
  142:68
Wooed: beautiful, and therefore to be
  w. 321:64
 woman in this humour w. 351:69
 woman, therefore may be w. 357:63
Wooing: a frog he wd. a-w. go 232:30
 women are angels, w. 358:65
Wool: have you any w.? 231:23
 pull the w. over a person's eyes
  284:55
Word: a character dead at every w.
  372:76
 a tale unfold whose lightest w.
  307:64
 at every w. a reputation dies 251:36
 by water and the W. 380:83
 every w. stabs 342:63
 every w. that proceedeth 38:7
 fairer than that w. 338:99
 four ... winters ... springs end in a
  w. 348:34
 Greeks had a w. for it 10:14
 his w. was still 'Fie, foh, and fum'
  329:82
 in the captain's but a choleric w.
  337:88
 in w. mightier 219:82
 Latin w. for three farthings 331:12
 let the w. go forth 188:74
 many a true w. ... in jest 281:59
 Mum's the w. 108:94
 nor all thy tears wash out a w. of it
  136:79
 some with a flattering w. 404:94
 suit ... the w. to the action 310:5
 that I kept my w., he said 118:24
 the W., and the W. was with God
  55:92
 the W. was made flesh 55:95
 there wd. have been a time for such
  a w. 336:76
 what is honour? A w. 315:88
 'when I use a w.,' Humpty Dumpty
  said 93:86
 whose w. no man relies on 288:21

Word (*continued*)

women must have the last w.  283:53
w. for w. without book  359:76
w. is as good as his bond  267:92
w. ... teems with hidden meaning  148:41
yawning at every other w.  94:94
yesterday the w. of Caesar  325:15
Words: actions speak louder than w.  254:58
all sad w. of tongue or pen  403:90
as many w. into the last line  13–14:54
best w. in the best order  107:82
comprehending much in few w.  62:56
dumb jewels ... more than quick w. do move  361:7
eat one's w.  261:11
few w. are best  262:58
her last w. on earth  12:43
in two w.: im-possible  152:5
let the w. of my mouth ... be acceptable  42:89
let thy w. be few  46:1
like a whore, unpack my heart with w.  309:93
long w. Bother me  212:63
men of few w. ... best men  320:48
much matter decorated into few w.  140:38
my w. fly up, my thoughts remain  311:16
neither wit, nor w., nor worth  325:21
noun ... verb ... abominable w.  321:68
oaths are but w. ..., w. but wind  82:37
on the pedestal these w. appear  369:40
proper w. in proper places  381:3
report thy w. by adding fuel  222:25
scatter ... my w. among mankind  369:38
the w. of Mercury are harsh  332:21
use ... w. only to conceal ... thoughts  397:10
what do you read ...? W., w., w.  308:77
when you let proud w. go  293:79
w. are the daughters of earth  172:41
w., like Nature, half reveal  386:58
w. may be false  297:38
w. ... so nimble ... full of ... flame  29:70
w. that frightened the birds  13:53
w. will never hurt me  278:74

Words (*continued*)

w. without thoughts never to heaven go  311:16
Wore enough for modesty  76:50
Work: a w. that aspires to ... art  110:25
all in the day's w.  254:64
all things w. together for good  56:34
all w. and no play  284:56
because he can't w. any faster  237:68
day is short ... w. is long  259:52
doing more w. than I shd. do  171:35
I have left no immortal w.  187:68
I have protracted my w.  172:43
I like w.; it fascinates me  171:35
I w. at the weaving trade  17:95
if any wd. not w., neither shd. he eat  59:86
men must w. and women must weep  189:87
my w. is left behind  32:5
night ... when no man can w.  55:5
no more hard w. for poor old Ned  138:9
nothing to do but w.  189:83
old Kaspar's w. was done  376:27
smile his w. to see  68:47
so w. the honey bees  318:39
sport wd. be as tedious as to w.  313:50
strive on to finish the w.  196:81
the way to spread a w.  176:5
there is always w. and tools to w.  200:22
to w. is to pray  268:50
whose w. is not born with him  200:22
woman's w. is never done  283:47
w. ... curse of the drinking classes  406:35
w. expands so as to fill the time  244:25
w. like madness in the brain  106:67
w. yr. hands from day to day  203:55
Workers of the world, unite  207:9
Workhouse: Christmas Day in the W.  373:89
Working: another for w.-days  343:65
fiery Soul, which w. out its way  126:39
Workman: a bad w. quarrels ... tools  255:88
Workmen: good w. are seldom rich  265:40
Works: devil and all his w.  64:95
faith without w. is dead  60:4

Works (*continued*)

its [sea's] w. ... are wrapped in mystery 110:26

Saturday's child w. hard for his living 235–6:56

World: a balm upon the w.  182:94

a citizen ... of the w.  375:20

a man if he shall gain the whole w. 54:58

a w. in a grain of sand  66:27

a w. of happy days  351–2:71

a w. too wide for his shrunk shank 301:90

a w. where nothing is had for nothing 103:25

aching void the w. can never fill 113:62

all de w. am sad  138:6

all sorts to make a w.  254:70

all's right with the w.  75:44

all the uses of this w.l  305:42

all the w. and his wife  284:57

all the w. as my parish  402:73

all the w. is queer  243:15

all the w.'s a stage  301:90

all this sad w. needs  404:93

all this the w. well knows  363:51

and all the w. would stare  113:59

another W., the happy seat  218:53

any author in the w.  331:14

any portion of the foreign w.  399:32

any way to perpetuate the w.  72:5

as good be out of the w.  102:12

as they did in the golden w.  300:72

banish ... Jack and banish all the w. 314:69

before my time into this breathing w. 351:66

body is aweary of this great w.  338:1

brave new w. ... such people in't 357:57

Britain is a w. by itself  304:21

called from the w.  13:46

cankers of a calm w.  315:83

Clearing-house of the w.  95:13

commodity, the bias of the w. 326:37

compare this prison ... unto the w. 351:62

consider the w. as made for me 375:16

constant service of the antique w. 300:79

contain and nourish all the w. 331:16

deceits of the w., the flesh, and the devil  63:78

enthusiasm moves the w.  27:49

World (*continued*)

ever shall be: w. without end  63:68

fast, and the w. goes by  404:92

flash in this w. of trouble  12:42

funniest joke in the w.  365:75

gave me ... a w. of sighs  344:92

get the start of the majestic w.  323:92

gone into the w. of light  396:85

greatest thing in the w.  225:54

had we but w. enough, and time 206:92

he doth bestride the narrow w. 323:93

he is a citizen of the w.  25:5

hold the w. but as the w.  338:96

hope before you blacken their w. 395:79

how the w. its veterans rewards 251:24

how this w. is given to lyingl  315:94

I called the New W. into existence 88:26

if all the w. were paper  15:65

in this harsh w. draw thy breath in pain  312:38

into the dangerous w. I leapt  67:44

justice ... though the w. perish 134:58

knaves and fools divide the w. 268:40

laugh, and the w. laughs with you 404:91

leaves the w. to darkness and to me 155:30

light of the bright w. dies  69:70

love is enough though the w.  227:72

love makes the w. go round  270:17

mad w.l mad kingsl  326:36

more ... wrought by prayer than this w. dreams  386:55

nature is too noble for the w.  303:17

never enjoy the w. aright  392:52

no enjoying the w. without [health] 179:60

not loved the w., nor the w. me 83:61

nothing stable in the w.  186:53

official ... undercuts the problematical w.  140:33

on ... shore of the wide w.  186:49

one half ... w. cannot understand 23:65

reckless what I do to spite the w. 334:49

ring'd with the azure w. he stands 385:47

same the whole w. over  18:5

Saviour of the w.  83:52

World (*continued*)
saw the Vision of the w. 387:80
so shines a good deed in a naughty w. 340:25
some say the w. will end in fire 139:25
the correction of the w. 224:49
the excellent foppery of the w. 327:53
the Federation of the W. 387:81
the ... increase of the w. 385:48
the light of the w. 55:4
the rack of this tough w. 331:7
the workers ... have a w. to gain 207:9
the wilderness of this w. 76:57
the w. forgetting, by the w. forgot 248:76
the w. is too much with us 412:93
the w. must be peopled 343:70
the w. shd. listen then 370:51
the w.'s great age begins anew 368:28
the w.'s grown honest 308:79
the w.'s mine oyster 340:30
the w. was all before them 221:3
this dark w. and wide 223:29
the dark w. of sin 65:19
this happy breed ... this little w. 348:41
this is the way the w. ends 130:96
this w. ... a thurghfare ful of wo 97:45
thro' the w. we safely go 66:30
to save your w. you asked 22:58
two soul-sides, one to face the w. 74:34
up above the w. so high 384:36
vanity of this wicked w. 64:96
vile blows and buffets of the w. 334:49
weight of ... unintelligible w. 415:32
when all the w. is young 189:88
when Rome falls—the W. 84:64
where in all this small-talking w. 140:34
whole w.'s in a state o' chassis 241:94
wondrous architecture of the w. 205:76
word of Caesar ... against the w. 325:15
w. grew pale 174:69
w. history is the w.'s judgment 294:86
w. is a comedy ... a tragedy 398:23
w. is charged with the grandeur 166:67

World (*continued*)
w. must be made safe for democracy 408:47
w. of doubts and fancies 186:53
w. of vile, ill-favour'd faults 341:32
w.'s great snare uncaught 299:63
w.'s storm-troubled sphere 71:84
w. to hide virtues in 359:77
w. wd. be wiser than ever 409:59
w. wd. go round ... faster 90:50
you shut out the w. 401:68
Worldly: name ... was Mr W. Wiseman 77:59
with all my w. goods 65:9
Worlds: best of possible w. 397:7
exhausted w., and then imagin'd new 173:58
the little less, ... what w. away 73:19
wandering between two w. 20:36
Worm: concealment, like a w. i' th' bud 360:89
early bird catches the w. 261:4
tread on a w. and it will turn 281:56
who ... sets foot upon a w. 114:75
wish you joy o' th' w. 299:69
Worms: have made w.' meat of me 354:11
I was one of the w. 110:23
talk of graves, of w. and epitaphs 349:53
w. have eaten them 302:3
you have tasted two whole w. 377:50
Wormwood and the gall 49:60
Worried: poem ... not ... w. into being 139:29
w. the cat that killed the rat 239:79
Worry: no one to w. ... to hurry us 112:41
Worse: as Heaven made him, and ... w. 95:9
goes by the w., whatever be her cause 222:22
make the w. appear the better 217:48
really w. than interrupting 131:15
remedy is w. than the disease 25:9
sell w. kinds of liquor 399:28
there is no w. heresy 9:1
w. than being talked about 406:23
Worship: are come to w. him 51:2
with my body I thee w. 65:9
Worshipper: Nature mourns her w. 295:3
Worst: do your w., blow your pipe 75:42
hope ... best and prepare for the w. 267:98

Worst (*continued*)

so long as we can say 'This is the w.' 329:84

so much good in the w. of us 163:36

things at the w. will mend 280:25

things present, w. 316:4

whose puppets, best and w. 75:45

women, w. and best 385:52

Worth: doings without charity are nothing w. 64:87

none was w. my strife 192:34

slow rises w., by poverty depressed 172:55

w. a guinea a box 11:34

w. ... best known by the want 284:60

w. doing ... w. doing well 98:55, 283:24

w. of a State ... w. of ... individuals 210:43

w. reading ... w. buying 291:60

w. seeing ... not w. going to see 177:32

Worthington: daughter on the stage, Mrs W. 112:44

Worthless as wither'd weeds 71:85

Worthy: labourer is w. of his hire 54:75

Worts: went to W. 252:41

Wound: did help to w. itself 327:47

jests at scars that never felt a w. 353:97

take away the grief of a w. 315:88

what w. did ever heal? 345:3

w. the loud winds 356:49

Wounds: bind up the nation's w. 196:81

faithful ... the w. of a friend 46:87

gash is added to her w. 335:65

labour and the w. are vain 103:32

talk ... of guns ... and w. 313:52

these w. in thine hands 51:97

Wrangle: men will w. for religion 108:96

Wrapped up in a five-pound note 195:60

Wrath: day of w., that dreadful day 295:7

infinite w. and infinite despair 218:62

sun go down upon your w. 58:71

the w. to come 51:6

Wreck: decay of that colossal w. 369:40

Wrecks: like w. of a dissolving dream 368:28

Wren: four Larks and a W. 195:66

robin redbreast and the w. 400:54

Wren (*continued*)

Sir Christopher W. said 33:16

the w. goes to't 329:90

Wrestle: we w. not against flesh 58:74

Wretch: excellent w.! 345:5

needy, hollow-ey'd ... w. 303:12

*patron.* – commonly a w. 172:49

w., concentred all in self 295:6

Wretched: scrannel pipes of w. straw 215:16

the only w. are the wise 253:52

the w. child expires 31:92

w. matter and lame metre 216:26

Wretchedness: the w. of being rich 374:2

Wretches: poor naked w., wheresoe'er you are 329:78

to feel what w. feel 329:79

Wrinkled: the w. sea beneath him 385:47

w. with age ... Old Nod 118:25

Writ: if this be error ... I never w. 363:48

over that same door was ... w. 377:43

Write: as much as a man ought to w. 393:56

contrive to w. so even 23:77

firm restraint with which they w. 87:17

hope to w. well hereafter 223:36

I never read books – I w. them 285:83

look in thy heart and w. 373:84

to w. and read comes by nature 343:73

when I want ... novel I w. one 123:2

why did I w.? 248:80

w. God first 344:82

w. me down an ass 344:85

Writers of small histories, dictionaries 172:45

Writes: the moving finger w. 136:79

Writing: in w. or in judging ill 249:90

true ease in w. comes from art 249:99

w. [maketh] an exact man 26:33

Written: what I have w. I have w. 56:13

w. such volumes of stuff 194:59

Wrong: and if you w. us, shall we not revenge? 339:13

but he done her w. 16:81

fifty million Frenchmen can't be w. 156:53

for telling a man he was w. 104:37

house of Tarquin ... suffer w. no more 201:35

Wrong (*continued*)
I always feel I must be w.   404:1
King can do no w.   66:25, 268:35
losers are always in the w.   270:5
never dreamed ... w. wd. triumph 73:16
only thing that I ever did w.   17:95
or whether laws be w.   404:97
our country, right or w.   118:16
physical effect is good ... action ... w.   175:84
right divine of kings to govern w. 247:70
something ... w., however slightly 252:44
something w. with ... ships   29:69
stiff in opinions, always in the w. 126:43
to do a great right do a little w. 339:16
we do it w., being so majestical 305:35
w. never comes right   284:61
Wrong number: if I called the w., why ... answer?   392:44
Wrote: no man ... ever w. except for money   177:21
who w. like an angel   141:49
Wroth: to be w. with one we love 106:67
Wrought: being w., perplexed in the extreme   346-7:22
first he w., ... afterwards he taughte 97:40
more things are w. by prayer   386:55
Wye: turned to thee, O sylvan W. 415:34

Xanadu: in X. did Kubla Khan   106:71

Yankee Doodle came to town   241:90
Yarn: all I ask is a merry y.   208:16
web of our life ... a mingled y. 298:46
Year: about two hundred pounds a y. 82:38
add ... to this wonderful y.   141:48
any book ... not a y. old   133:42
before the mellowing y.   215:8
each day is like a y.   404:97
grief returns with the revolving y. 367:10
how many days will finish ... y. 321:70
I like two months of ... y.   83:55
if ... y. were playing holidays   313:50
in the season of the y.   18:98
measure of the y.   185:45

Year (*continued*)
pleasure of the fleeting y.   363:43
proper opinions for ... time of y. 22:62
say no ill of the y.   277:15
stolen ... my three-and-twentieth y. 223:28
sweet o' the y.   361:17
the y. is going, let him go   386:68
the y.'s at the spring   75:44
twentieth y. is well-nigh past   114:76
wive and thrive both in a y.   283:43
Yearning: man of y. ... aspiration 291:52
Yearnings for equal division   132:25
Years: a thousand y. as one day 60:14
age ... not weary ... nor the y. condemn   65:20
alas, Postumus, the fleeting y. 167:76
all the hopes of future y.   197:92
before the beginning of y.   382:16
come to the y. of discretion   64:2
cuts off twenty y. of life   324:4
eight y. with a strange man   169:7
evil days come not ... y. draw nigh 47:11
forty y. on   70:72
fourteen hundred y. ago were nail'd 312:43
hasn't been kissed for forty y. 291:57
if the British Empire ... last for a thousand y.   101:95
Myself with Yesterday's Sev'n Thousand Y.   135:69
O for ten y.   185:36
our hope for y. to come   399:38
parted ... to sever for y.   86:99
sorrow comes with y.   73:11
tell me where all past y. are   124:11
the thousand y. of peace   386:70
three y. she grew in sun and shower 415:30
time-lag of fifty y.   401:66
together now for forty y.   99:80
y. a mortal man may live   321:70
y. that the locust hath eaten   50:79
young in y. ... old in hours   26:26
Yellow: come unto these y. sands 355:44
commended thy y. stockings   360:92
green and y. melancholy   360:89
her locks were y. as gold   105:52
the sear, the y. leaf   336:71
y., and black ... and hectic red 369:35

Yellow (*continued*)

y. god forever gazes down  159:76

Yeomanry ... people with whom  23:64

Yeovil: our H.Q. at Station Road, Y. 252:45

Yes, and back again  233:36

Yesterday: children dear, was it y.? 20:33

dead Y., why fret?  135:74

not born y.  257:60

O, call back y., bid time return 349:51

Yesterdays: all our y. have lighted fools 336:76

Yet: young man shd. not marry y. 284:62

Yew: my shroud ... stuck all with y. 359–60:88

never a spray of y.  21:37

Yield: courage never to submit or y. 216:30

to get rid of temptation ... y.  406:24

Yo-ho-ho and a bottle of rum  379:74

Yoke: our country sinks beneath the y. 335:65

savage bull sustains the y.  191:22

shake the y. of inauspicious stars 354:18

that he bear the y. in his youth 49:62

who best bear his mild y.  223:30

Yonghy-Bonghy-Bò: lived the Y. 194:55

Yorick: a Cock and a Bull, said Y. 379:72

alas, poor Y.!  311:31

York: glorious summer by this sun of Y.  351:64

You: Daddy, what did y. do?  11:25

for y. but not for me  16:76

I am I, and y. are y.  74:27

room with a view – and y.  112:41

sight of y. is good for sore eyes  382:7

y. too, Brutus?  87:9

Young: America ... country of y. men 133:46

compliment him about looking y. 170:15

crime of being a y. man  246:54

happy while we are y.  19:20

I have been y., and now am old  42:3

if ... world and love were y.  286:96

my heart was y. and gay  138:7

no y. man believes he shall ... die 159:80

not so y. as they are painted  30:81

old are more beautiful than the y. 403:78

Young (*continued*)

our clever y. poets  107:82

so y. and so untender? So y. ... and true  327:50

the embarrassing y.  141:50

to be seventy years y.  164:52

to be y. was very Heaven!  413:9

when all the world is y.  189:88

y., and so fair!  165:56

y. blood must have its course  189:89

y. ones ... pistols: ... old ones grub 364:62

Yours: as I y. for ever  154:22

what's mine is y., ... y. is mine 338:95

what's y. is mine  283:25

y. [religion] is Success  28:63

y. is the Earth  190:5

Yourself: *do it y.*  27:51

Youth: a y. of frolics, an old age of cards  251:24

a y. to fortune and to fame unknown 155:40

age ... perform the promises of y. 173:61

crabbed age and y.  364:56

good ... that he bear the yoke in ... y.  49:62

home-keeping y. have ... homely wits 360:4

I wd. ... that y. would sleep  361:16

if only y. knew  133:50

let age approve of y.  76:47

let no man despise thy y.  59:89

loves the meat in his y.  343:69

made every y. cry *Well-a-way!*  12:36

mewing her mighty y.  224:43

must be right ... done it from my y. 114:79

noble y. did dress themselves  316:8

our y., our joys, our all  286:93

rejoice ... in thy y.  47:10

remember ... thy Creator in ... y. 47:11

riband in the cap of y.  311:29

rule y. well  276:7

spirit of y. in every thing  363:44

the hour of thoughtless y.  415:35

the rose of y. upon him  299:60

the y. ... still is Nature's priest 411:78

Time, the subtle thief of y.  223:28

war is done and y. stone dead 293:82

when Y. and Pleasure meet  83:60

y. and age will never agree  284:66

y. grows pale and spectre-thin 184:25

Youth (*continued*)

    y., I do adore thee  364:57

    y. is a blunder  123:95

    y. is full of pleasance  364:56

    y. like summer morn  364:56

    y. of America ... oldest tradition 406:26

    y. of England are on fire  319:40

    y. of labour ... age of ease  150:64

    y. shows but half  75–6:46

    y. who bore 'mid snow and ice 197:93

    y. will be served  284:67

    y. will have its course (fling)  284:68

    y.'s a stuff will not endure  359:84

Yukon: this is the law of the Y.  297:35

Zeal: holy, mistaken z. in politics 180:67

    not too much z.  384:33

Zeal (*continued*)

    serv'd my God with half the z. 323:84

    z. is ... found mostly in fools  284:69

    z., when ... a virtue  284:70

    z. without knowledge  284:71

Zeal-of-the-Land Busy  178:48

Zed: whoreson z.! ... unnecessary letter!  328:61

Zenith: dropped from the z., like a ... star  217:44

Zenocrate: fair Z.!—divine Z.!  205:77

    Z., lovelier than the love of Jove 204:73

Zephyr: roses by the z. blown apart 182:3

Zion: at ease in Z.  50:84

    one of the songs of Z.  44:46

    wept, when we remembered Z.  44:44

Zuleika on a desert island  30:82

# Notes

# Notes

# Notes

# Notes

# Notes

# Notes

# Notes

Jonathon Green
**The Pan Dictionary of
Contemporary Quotations** £6.99

'Words are all we have' – Samuel Beckett; wise words, witty words, weird
words, all from the mouths of the famous and fashionable of the last four
decades – seven thousand quotations from prophets and punks, movie
scripts and millionaires, just about everyone from Wittgenstein to Ernie Wise.

edited by
Laurence Urdang and Martin Manser
**The Pan Dictionary of Synonyms
and Antonyms** £3.99

An alphabetically organised 'thesaurus' for quick and easy use, an
invaluable modern reference work for anyone working with words, this
dictionary provides easy access to words which can be used as alternatives
to improve and add variety to speech or writing, or to provide the
expression for exact meaning. The entries listed are those words in most
common use, for which synonyms are most often needed; different
meanings are numbered and examples of usage given; antonyms –
words with a meaning opposite to that of the entry – are given; and
cross-references are included where another word provides a more
suitable synonym.

Compiled by Martin H. Manser
# The Pan/Chambers Book of Business Quotations £6.99

Who said:

'A bank is a place that will lend you money if you can prove you don't need it.'

'We're overpaying him but he's worth it.'

'Behind every successful man there stands an amazed woman.'

'The meek shall inherit the earth, but not the mineral rights.'

'The two most beautiful words in the English language are "Cheque Enclosed".'?

You'll find the answers in *The Pan/Chambers Book of Business Quotations*, an informative, entertaining selection of 2000 sayings from the world of commerce.

Clearly presented with a comprehensive index, this is the ideal reference book whether you're looking for a quotation to enhance a report, an article, a speech or merely a point of view.

'Invaluable . . . there is something here for everyone'
INTERNATIONAL MANAGEMENT

## The Pan/Macmillan Encyclopedia £8.99

*The Pan/Macmillan Encyclopedia* contains the best of the most comprehensive one-volume encyclopedia on the market. Lively, accessible and completely up to date – here is all the information you need, in a format that needs no explanation.

There are over 10,000 entries, covering science, technology and commerce, the arts, politics and sports, alongside numerous biographies, with the emphasis on 20th century celebrities. The text is illustrated with diagrams and line drawings throughout.

With more facts about more people, more places and more things in one portable volume, *The Pan/Macmillan Encyclopedia* is suitable for school and college students, for the family and its leisure activities, or for the office and the professional worker.

Erika Langmuir
**The Pan Art Dictionary**
Volume One: 1300–1800 £6.99

*The Pan Art Dictionary*, a major reference work in two volumes, provides a full treatment of artists, and especially concepts of art. Comprehensive and up to date, it is an authoritative companion to the work of all major Western artists.

Clearly presented and arranged alphabetically, with extensive cross referencing between entries, it gives explanations of technical terms, schools of art, styles, genres, movements and groups, making *The Pan Art Dictionary* invaluable to gallery visitors and travellers as well as to students and general readers.

In the first volume Professor Erika Langmuir, Head of Education at the National Gallery, London, covers the period from 1300 to 1800. *The Pan Art Dictionary Volume Two* by Professor Norbert Lynton covers the period from 1800 to the present day.

All Pan books are available at your local bookshop or newsagent, or can be ordered direct from the publisher. Indicate the number of copies required and fill in the form below.

Send to: **CS Department, Pan Books Ltd., P.O. Box 40, Basingstoke, Hants. RG21 2YT.**

or phone: 0256 469551 (Ansaphone), quoting title, author and Credit Card number.

Please enclose a remittance* to the value of the cover price plus: 60p for the first book plus 30p per copy for each additional book ordered to a maximum charge of £2.40 to cover postage and packing.

*Payment may be made in sterling by UK personal cheque, postal order, sterling draft or international money order, made payable to Pan Books Ltd.

Alternatively by Barclaycard/Access:

Card No.

Signature:

Applicable only in the UK and Republic of Ireland.

*While every effort is made to keep prices low, it is sometimes necessary to increase prices at short notice. Pan Books reserve the right to show on covers and charge new retail prices which may differ from those advertised in the text or elsewhere.*

NAME AND ADDRESS IN BLOCK LETTERS PLEASE:

..........................................................................................................................

Name————————————————————————————

Address————————————————————————————

————————————————————————————

————————————————————————————

————————————————————————————